PRINCIPLES

OF

CONSTITUTIONAL

LAW

Second Edition

By

John E. Nowak
David C. Baum Professor of Law Emeritus
University of Illinois

Ronald D. Rotunda
George Mason University Foundation Professor of Law
George Mason University School of Law

CONCISE HORNBOOK SERIES®

THOMSON
™
WEST

Mat #40438499

Concise Hornbook Series, WESTLAW and West Group are
registered trademarks used herein under license.

© West, a Thomson business, 2004
© 2005 West, a Thomson business
       610 Opperman Drive
       P.O. Box 64526
       St. Paul, MN 55164–0526
       1–800–328–9352

ISBN–13: 978–0–314–16690–6
ISBN–10: 0–314–16690–4

 TEXT IS PRINTED ON 10% POST
CONSUMER RECYCLED PAPER

To Gabriela & Julia,
Happy 1st & 3rd Birthdays!

Grandpa John

To Irene & Victor

R.D.R.

*

Preface to Second Edition

The first edition of our Concise Hornbook followed seven editions of our one volume treatise, NOWAK & ROTUNDA, CONSTITUTIONAL LAW (7th ed., 2004, Thomson-West, Hornbook Series), and three editions of our five-volume treatise, ROTUNDA & NOWAK, TREATISE ON CONSTITUTIONAL LAW: SUBSTANCE AND PROCEDURE (3rd ed., Thomson-West, 1999, with annual supplements)]. Our one volume treatise is intended to provide students with an in-depth analysis of all the subjects that might come up in law school constitutional law courses, and to offer assistance for those persons beginning their research into most constitutional issues. The mulitvolume treatise, we are pleased to say, has become a standard reference work for attorneys, judges, and scholars seeking an extensive analysis of most constitutional law issues, including those topics rarely studied in law school. It has been cited several thousand times by state courts, federal courts, and commentators in the law reviews.

We hope that the second edition of the Concise Hornbook will provide both students and non-students with an understanding of the most fundamental principles of constitutional law commonly studied in the basic constitutional law courses offered in U.S. law schools. This text is designed to explain and analyze those principles, and to provide a guide as to how judges and practitioners use them in the world outside the classroom, and how professors use them in the classroom and on examinations. Students who want further analysis of the case law and a discussion of additional cases on any subject should stop by their law library and consult one of our more complete works.

The cut-off date for cases included in this text was July 1, 2005. Because this volume deals with basic principles, we trust that students will have little, if any, difficulty in using it to analyze cases that the Supreme Court will be deciding in the years ahead. The Court's future cases are based on the principles discussed here. They are the foundation used to develop new precedents, for the Justices do not own the law; they are its guardians, taking it from the prior generation, nurturing it, and then passing it on to the next.

We owe a special debt of gratitude to the late Professor J. Nelson Young, who was our coauthor on the early editions of our single volume and multivolume treatises from which we derived this concise book. We cannot overstate Nelson's contribution to our growth as teachers and scholars. We express our thanks, as well, to all those students and staff who have assisted us with the preparation of all of the editions of our coauthored works. Professor Nowak would like to acknowledge the invaluable help provided by his faculty assistant, Mrs. Sally Cook, who has caught, and corrected, as many of his grammatical errors as was humanly possible. Professor Rotunda would like to express his thanks for the invaluable substantive and grammatical advise that Kyndra Rotunda provided.

Finally, we need to express our thanks to Ms. Roxanne Birkel of West Group. The help that she provided us was essential to the production of this text.

J.E.N.
R.D.R.

October, 2005

Summary of Contents

Table of Contents

CHAPTER 15. CONGRESSIONAL ENFORCEMENT OF CIVIL RIGHTS

CHAPTER 17. FREEDOM OF RELIGION

PRINCIPLES
OF
CONSTITUTIONAL
LAW

Second Edition

*

Chapter 1

THE ORIGINS OF JUDICIAL REVIEW

Table of Sections

§ 1.1 *Marbury v. Madison*—The Setting of the Case

The last years of the eighteenth century were a time of intense political rivalry for the new nation. The Federalist Party controlled the national government and did not hesitate to use its powers for partisan purposes, exemplified by the Sedition Act, which punished those who spoke out against President Adams or the Federalist Congress. The opposition responded with animosity towards the Federalists and the Federalist judges who enforced the Sedition Act against competing political parties.

In 1800, the Federalists lost power for a variety of reasons, including popular reaction against their use of the Sedition Act and the growing tensions with Great Britain. Jefferson won the popular vote for the presidency but there was a tie vote between Jefferson and Aaron Burr in the electoral college. Jefferson was to be chosen President by the new House of Representatives.

Although the Federalists were facing the end of their era of power (the Federalists would never again win the White House), Adams remained President until the end of his term on March 4, 1801. In December 1800, Oliver Ellsworth, third Chief Justice of the United States, resigned his position on the Supreme Court. President Adams first sought to reappoint former Chief Justice John Jay to the Court, but Jay refused the appointment. Then Adams nominated John Marshall, his Secretary of State and a leading figure in the Federalist Party. On January 27, 1801, the lame duck Senate confirmed Marshall's nomination, and he became

Chief Justice on February 4, 1801, only a month before Jefferson would take office. At President Adams' request, Marshall continued to serve as Secretary of State for the remainder of Adams' term.

On February 27, 1801, the holdover Federalist Congress authorized the appointment of 42 Justices of the Peace to serve five-year terms in the District of Columbia and Alexandria. President Adams appointed Federalists to these positions, and the Senate confirmed them on March 3, the day before the Republicans were to take office. The formal appointments were made by delivery of sealed commissions by the Secretary of State. John Marshall, as Secretary of State, executed and sought to deliver these commissions but, even though he had some assistance, there remained a few undelivered commissions that night.

Jefferson's Secretary of State, James Madison, refused to deliver the remaining commissions for the Justices of the Peace. William Marbury was one of the Justices of the peace whom Adams had appointed, but who had failed to receive his commission. Marbury sued the new Secretary of State, James Madison, for delivery of his commission. He filed an original action in the Supreme Court seeking an order of mandamus to compel Madison to deliver the commission. He asserted jurisdiction under § 13 of the Judiciary Act of 1789, one of the first acts of that the new Congress, created by the new Constitution, had enacted.

§ 1.2   *Marbury v. Madison*—The Opinion of the Court

Chief Justice Marshall delivered the opinion of the Court in *Marbury v. Madison* (1803), holding that Marbury had a right to his judicial commission, but that the Court would not enforce this right because the jurisdictional law under which he was suing was unconstitutional. In so doing, the Court found that the executive was subject to Constitutional restraints that could be enforced by the judiciary. The Court also held that it could not grant a remedy because this original action was not within the jurisdiction that Article III fixed for the Court. Marshall interpreted a section of the Judiciary Act of 1789 as placing this action within its original jurisdiction, but then found that this law conflicted with the Constitution and thus was invalid.

Marshall began his opinion by framing the case in terms of three issues. First, does Marbury have a right to the commission? Second, do the laws of the country establish a remedy for the deprivation of the right? Third, can a mandamus be issued in an original action before the Supreme Court?

Marshall first ruled that Marbury had a right to the commission once it was signed by the President and sealed by the Secretary of State. Based on the act of Congress authorizing the appointment of Justices of the Peace for the District of Columbia, the opinion ruled that the commission was a "vested legal right."

The Court might have held that the right did not vest until delivery of the commission, thus avoiding the constitutional issues, but the Court instead stated that an irrevocable right accrued to the individual after the execution of the commission. The Court thus criticized the new administration and President Jefferson, who was Marshall's political adversary.

On the second issue, the opinion found that the "essence of civil liberty" required a legal remedy for a legal wrong. Because the government of the United States is one "of laws and not of men" it must grant a remedy for violation of vested legal rights. Marshall did note that there would not be a judicial remedy for a wrong if the subject matter was political in nature or otherwise committed to the discretion of the executive. In such instances the individual's remedy would have to be left to the political process. But, where individual rights depend on a duty established by law, there was a remedy that must be judicially enforced to protect the injured individual. This argument laid the basis for his conclusions in the next section concerning the scope of judicial review.

The crucial issue in the case thus became whether Marbury was entitled to the remedy for which he had applied to the Supreme Court. Marshall subdivided this issue into two further questions concerning the nature of the writ of mandamus and the power of the Court.

In examining the nature of the writ, the opinion asserted a judicial power to review the acts of the executive branch. Because the writ of mandamus is an order to an officer to take a specific action, Marshall inquired as to whether it could be used against officers of the executive branch. Marshall found two classes of executive acts that were not subject to judicial review. Where the action by the President or executive officers was in its nature "political" the matter was not one for judicial intervention. Similarly, where the Constitution or federal law placed a subject matter within the sole discretion of the executive, it could not be reviewed by the Court. However, Marshall found that it was not the nature of the executive branch that limited judicial review but only the nature of the act.

If the Constitution or federal law imposed some duty on the executive branch, the judiciary can enforce that duty. In such a case there is no intrusion into the power granted to the President, but only an inquiry into the charge of a specific illegality.

This analysis left the question whether the mandamus against the executive should issue in this particular case. On this question, Marshall found a conflict between the Court's statutory jurisdiction and that fixed by Article III of the Constitution. Although he could have interpreted Section 13 of the Judiciary Act of 1789 in a different manner, he ruled that it authorized original actions in the Supreme Court for writs of mandamus to officers of the United States. Because the statute, as construed, provided for original actions, such as Marbury's action in this case, it violated Article III, which Marshall interpreted as limiting the original jurisdiction of the Supreme Court.

The opinion concluded that Congress might have the power to alter the appellate jurisdiction of the Court, but Article III intended to fix the original jurisdiction. Thus, there was a clear conflict between the jurisdictional statute and the Constitution, leading Marshall to the essential question: whether a law that was in conflict with the Constitution is valid and whether the Supreme Court has the power to invalidate or, at least, disregard such a law.

Marshall claimed that the question of whether a federal statute contrary to constitutional provisions could be the law of the land was "not of an intricacy proportioned to its interest." Marshall believed that the people of the nation had the right to establish binding, enforceable principles for the governing of society. While the people might have ratified a Constitution that created a government of general powers, they chose instead a Constitution that created one of defined and limited powers.

There could be, in Marshall's view, no middle ground between these types of government. That left the Court the choice either to declare the Constitution to be the superior and binding law, or to allow the legislature to be an entity of unlimited powers. The fact that the people chose a *written* Constitution with fundamental principles to bind the government in the future was evidence that the Constitution should be the superior and binding law. If the Constitution was the superior law, then an act repugnant to it must be invalid.

There remained the question of whether the courts were obliged to follow the act of the legislature despite judges' view as to the statute's incompatibility with the Constitution. Marshall's argument for judicial review—the power of the courts to invalidate laws as unconstitutional—is deceptively simple. The essence of the argument is his first point, that "it is emphatically the province and duty of the judicial department to say what the law is." Having previously recognized the Constitution as being the superior "law" in the nation, Marshall, with this statement, lays claim to the judiciary's final authority on matters of constitutional interpretation. It is this concept of the Constitution as law, and the judiciary as the institution with the *final* responsibility to interpret that law, that is the cornerstone of judicial review today.

Marshall advanced several other points in support of the judicial power to invalidate laws found to be in violation of the Constitution. Because the Court would be required to follow either the statute or the Constitution in a given case, an inability of the Court to reject the statute in favor of the Constitution would subvert "the very foundation" of a written Constitution. The Constitutional text provided further support, for it extended the judicial power to "all cases arising under the Constitution." Marshall reasoned that this jurisdictional power inevitably leads to the conclusion that the framers of that provision must have been willing to allow the judiciary to use and interpret the Constitution in the cases arising under it.

Marshall cited several provisions that imposed specific limitations on the acts of government, such as the export tax clause, the Bill of Attainder and *ex post facto* prohibitions, and the establishment of requirements for proof of treason. In cases that involve these provisions, Marshall argued, the framers of the Constitution must have contemplated that the courts would follow its terms rather than any contrary act of the legislature. He drew further support for this conclusion from the oath for the judges, which required them to support the Constitution. To Marshall this required the judges to follow the Constitution rather than any subordinate law.

Marshall's argument closed as it began, with the concept of the Constitution as the superior law. He focused on the Supremacy Clause of Article VI the Constitution. That clause explicitly states that the Constitution is the supreme law of the land, and that the statutes and laws of the United States that are granted recognition are "those only which shall be made in *pursuance* of the Constitution." Judges should only follow laws that are "in pursuance of the Constitution." Thus, he reasoned, the supreme law of the land must be the Constitution, and the Justices must follow it rather than any provisions of federal legislation that are inconsistent with the Constitution.

Accordingly, the Court denied Marbury his commission, because the Court held that it could not entertain an original action for mandamus inconsistent with its jurisdiction under Article III. To the extent that Section 13 of the Judiciary Act included a contrary provision, it was unconstitutional and void.

§ 1.3   Notes on the *Marbury* Decision

Marbury v. Madison has been the subject of continuing analysis and historical inquiry. Although the doctrine of judicial review is now firmly established, a recapitulation of the commentary concerning *Marbury* and its historical antecedents has more than historical interest. Theories concerning the proper scope of judicial actions under the Constitution often focus upon the legitimacy of the judiciary's claim to authority: commentators often argue that, to the extent that the authority for judicial review is weak, it should be exercised most sparingly.

The criticisms of John Marshall's opinion in *Marbury v. Madison* fall into two general areas. First, there is disapproval of the way in which Marshall strove to reach the conclusion concerning the constitutional authority of the Court over the other branches of government. Second, there is criticism of Marshall's arguments supporting judicial authority as merely bare assertions of authority rather than reasons justifying that authority.

It is certainly true that Marshall was eager to use this decision to establish a claim to the power of judicial review. The very fact that he heard the case (rather than disqualifying himself) demonstrated his view of its importance and his desire to use the decision on behalf of the judicial branch.

Marshall clearly had opportunities to avoid the constitutional questions concerning both the executive and legislative acts. A ruling that Marbury lacked a right to the commission until delivery, or that the political process governed the remedy for refusals to honor appointments, would have avoided these issues. Or, Marshall could have interpreted the section of the Judiciary Act governing mandamus as establishing only a remedy, not jurisdiction. A construction that the Judiciary Act authorized mandamus only when jurisdiction was otherwise properly invoked would have avoided the ruling on the constitutionality of the statute.

Marshall's effort to reach the constitutional question is open to criticism under today's generally accepted principle that the Court should avoid ruling on a constitutional issue when a case can be decided on a narrower ground. However, this principle is the modern rule, only a general guide for Court action, and not an ironclad precept that has bound the Court at all times in its history. Even is modern times, when Justices believe that a constitutional decision is important for the protection of certain values, they have always felt free to decide the issue rather than to avoid it—provided the Court has jurisdiction.

Admittedly, Marshall's arguments concerning the relationship between the actions of the other branches of the federal government and the Constitution can be subdivided into a series of assertions, none of which inexorably leads to the conclusion that Marshall draws from them. His discussion of judicial control of the powers of the executive is especially troublesome for its vagueness as to standards for the exercise of judicial power.

While Marshall makes it clear that the President is subject to specific legal restraints established either by statute or the Constitution, he does not further define the nature of the duties that are subject to judicial review. Instead, Marshall asserts an open-ended power to review executive actions based upon the principle that the executive can have no right to disregard a specific duty assigned to him by law. This general assertion of authority to review executive acts that gave rise to the greatest dispute at the time of *Marbury*. Over the years, several Presidents have, to varying degrees, disputed this judicial claim. However, it was also this general principle that provided the Supreme Court, over one hundred and seventy years later, with a basis for holding that not even the President could disregard judicial subpoenas for evidence in ongoing criminal cases. *United States v. Nixon* (1974).

Marshall's discussion of the constitutionality of legislative acts falls into two parts. First, Marshall found that a law that was not in conformity with constitutional principles could not be the law of the land. This proposition established the Constitution as a binding law superior to any other federal action.

Second, having found that the Constitution was to be a form of law superior to legislation, Marshall went on to consider whether the judiciary must follow a law that was in conflict with the Constitution. He argued that the Constitution is "law," and it is the institutional responsibility of the judiciary to interpret law and apply the law that is superior in any conflict between the Constitution and legislation. However, this principle does not establish that the judiciary is the proper body to make the *final* determination of whether the statute is in fact so inconsistent with the provisions of the superior document that it is invalid.

The supremacy clause of Article VI does not solve the problem, for it states only that federal laws are superior to state laws and state constitutions; it says nothing concerning the relationship between the Federal Judiciary and the other branches of the Government: the Executive and Legislative Branches. Marshall's argument, that only laws made in pursuance of the Constitution are the supreme law of the land, assumes the point in dispute: who determines which statutes are not in pursuance of the Constitution? We are still left with the question of whether the judiciary, or Congress, or the President has the final determination of when a law is made in pursuance of the Constitution.

Although we can divide and attack, Marshall's decision, it still stands as an impressive argument when taken as a whole. The Chief Justice, in this case, asserts that the Constitution is a superior form of law established by the direct will of society, and that judges must follow the law, including this higher law, in the course of deciding issues before them. This concept of judicial review and the role that courts must play is a unique American contribution to jurisprudence.

The concept of judicial review really rests upon three separate bases: (1) that the Constitution binds all parts of the federal government, (2) that it is enforceable by the Court in actions before it, and (3) that the judiciary is charged with interpreting the Constitution in a unique manner so that its rulings are binding on all other departments of the government. *Marbury* seeks to establish the first two of these principles and only implies the existence of the third. The first two principles are, in fact, both historically and logically easier to prove than the third.

In *McCulloch v. Maryland* (1819), Marshall laid claim to the judicial authority to bind all branches of government by constitutional interpretation. *McCulloch* treated the Constitution as a law capable of interpretation and of definition by the normal legal process. It also looks at the Constitution as a document of enduring principles requiring an independent judiciary to interpret and apply it throughout changing historical periods.

Marshall also explored and explained the concept of judicial supremacy and matters of constitutional interpretation in other decisions. In his opinions concerning the reviewability of actions of state government under the contract clause and the commerce clause, Marshall emphasized that the Constitution is a law that the judiciary has to interpret and enforce in order to maintain its supremacy. Throughout his thirty-four year tenure as Chief Justice of the United States, Marshall established the theoretical basis of judicial review with arguments both on and off the Court. That Marshall did not accomplish this goal with a single opinion is hardly an indictment of his ability or contribution to the shaping of our legal history.

§ 1.4 Review of State Laws: The Early Cases

There are three decisions of particular importance that established federal judicial power over state laws. The first, *Fletcher v. Peck* (1810), is important because it was the earliest exercise of the Court's authority after it suffered a period of intense attack, 1803 and 1810. After surviving these attacks, the Court, for the first time, invalidated a state law under the U.S. Constitution.

Fletcher involved a Georgia statute that sought to annul earlier conveyances of land to private persons. An earlier, corrupt state legislature had authorized these conveyances, and the state now wished to cancel what seemed to be fraudulent acts. However, the land had since passed to a private good faith purchaser who sought the enforcement of his contract and ownership rights.

The Supreme Court construed the term "contract" to include an executed state contract or grant. The Court then held that the annulment was an impairment of the obligation of contract within the meaning of Article I. The repealing statute was, therefore, unconstitutional. It was immaterial that the state was the grantor, for the Court found no distinction between the obligation of contracts where the contract was between two individuals and where the contract was between the state and an individual.

The second major early decision concerning federal judicial power is *Martin v. Hunter's Lessee* (1816). This case involved conflicting claims to land in the northern portion of Virginia. Lord Fairfax was a former British national who had become a citizen of Virginia prior to his death. In 1781 he willed the extensive land he held in Virginia to his nephew in England, Denny Martin. Virginia later passed acts to confiscate the lands of those who had been British citizens or loyalists during the Revolutionary War. Virginia then granted a portion of Lord Fairfax's land to David Hunter. The stage was set for the litigation between the representatives of Martin and Hunter. The litigation spanned two decades and was complicated by a series of related actions.

Before he became Chief Justice, John Marshall, acting on behalf of the British representatives, had negotiated a compromise and personally purchased a large share of the land. His personal involvement and financial interests led him to recuse himself from deciding these cases when they came to the Court.

In connection with Marshall's compromise, the Virginia legislature adopted the 1796 Act of Compromise, but the U.S. Supreme Court did not mention this act in its original decision on the ownership of the land. The existence of that compromise, and the complicated transactions, make it unclear whether the "right" persons ever did receive the benefits of the property pursuant to the Supreme Court's mandate. What is important today is that the Court enforced its decision on the constitutionality of state acts over the objections and contrary opinions of the state officials and judges.

Martin's representatives based their claim to the land on the anti-confiscation clauses of treaties between the United States and Great Britain. Hunter, and the State of Virginia, claimed that title had vested in Virginia prior to these treaties so that they were not applicable to his title. The highest court of Virginia, the Court of Appeals, had ruled for Hunter and the state, but in 1813 the Supreme Court of the United States found that the treaties secured title in Martin.

Because state law is subordinate to federal treaties under the supremacy clause, the case was returned to the Virginia courts for the entry of a judgment in favor of Martin's representatives and successors. The Virginia Court of Appeals refused to follow this order because it claimed that the case should have been decided differently on the basis of the compromise under state law.

The state court also stated that the U.S. Supreme Court could not constitutionally exercise jurisdiction over a state supreme court. The Virginia state court held section 25 of the Judiciary Act, which extended the appellate jurisdiction of the U.S. Supreme Court to state courts, was unconstitutional. This state court decision was a direct challenge to the authority of the national government in general, and the Supreme Court in particular.

Martin v. Hunter's Lessee ruled that the Supreme Court had the jurisdiction and authority to review all state acts under the Constitution, laws and treaties of the United States. Writing for the Court, Justice Story found that the Judiciary Act properly recognized the existence of appellate jurisdiction in the Supreme Court over actions in state courts. Story explained that the supremacy clause of Article VI plainly indicates that the framers realized that federal issues might arise in state cases. The grant of jurisdiction to the Supreme Court in Article III over *all* cases within the judicial power of the United States was intended to include such decisions.

Virginia argued that it was a sovereign and that the U.S. Supreme Court could not restrict its judicial rulings. Story countered by noting that the people of the nation had chosen to limit state sovereignty when they established a Constitution that specifically restricted state acts in a variety of ways, such as the limitations included in Article I. There was no reason to exempt actions of the state judiciary from these restrictions. Moreover, the lack of any exemption did not unduly impair the functions of the state judiciary because the supremacy clause already required state judges to follow federal law.

Story concluded by asserting the Supreme Court's right and duty to be the single, final interpreter of federal law and the Constitution. A national government, whose parts are subject to a single Constitution, must include an entity to give a final interpretation to its laws. Moreover, state courts had to be subject to the rulings of the Supreme Court in federal issues so that the meaning and application of the laws, treaties and Constitution of the United States would have a uniform interpretation and application throughout the country.

Although the Court, in effect, rejected Virginia's claims of sovereignty, it did not consider the propriety of issuing a mandamus order against state judges. The Court merely held that the judgment of the Virginia Court of Appeals had to be reversed.

Marshall had an opportunity to speak for the Court in asserting jurisdiction over state acts in another third case, *Cohens v. Virginia* (1821). This case upheld the state prosecution of interstate sellers of lottery tickets, but in so doing established its authority to review state criminal proceedings. The decision came at a time when there were severe challenges to the Court from southern states fearing the growing national power.

In *Cohens,* Virginia had prosecuted persons who sold lottery tickets in the state in violation of state law. The appellants claimed that the sales were permitted by a federal statute authorizing a lottery in the District of Columbia. Marshall held that the federal act did not protect these persons, but in the course of so deciding, he asserted federal authority to review state acts and criminal proceedings.

The Court ruled that the Eleventh Amendment was inapplicable in cases like this one (a criminal case) when state itself instituted suit. Most importantly, Marshall used *Cohens* to expound on the nature of the Constitution's control of state acts. Marshall explained that the Constitution was an original act of the people, which was apart from, and superior to, any concept of state sovereignty. To the extent that the people created a national power, the federal judiciary shared in it with the other branches of the federal government. Because the Constitution was created to be a paramount and enduring law, it would often require enforcement against outside challenges. In Marshall's opinion the federal courts were a proper institution for this purpose.

§ 1.5 State Court Review of State Laws

State courts may be called upon to review the constitutionality of either state or federal laws in the course of deciding issues in cases before them. When reviewing federal laws these courts must enforce federal laws over inconsistent state acts. If the state courts refuse to follow U.S. Supreme Court rulings, the Supreme Court can reverse. However, more difficult problems arise when state courts review state laws.

State courts are the final interpreters of state law even though their actions are reviewable under the federal constitution, treaties, or laws. The supreme court of a state is truly the highest court in terms of this body of law; it is not a "lower court," even in relation to the Supreme Court of the United States. It must follow the Supreme Court's rulings on the meaning of the Constitution of the United States or federal law, but it is free to interpret state laws or the state constitution in any way that does not violate principles of federal law.

This power is an extremely important one, for it means that the state courts are always free to grant individuals more rights than those guaranteed by the Constitution, provided it does so on the basis of state law. The federal Constitution establishes minimum guarantees of rights. Granting additional liberties does not violate its provisions. Thus, if a state court rules that the death penalty is absolutely barred by the Eighth Amendment, the U.S. Supreme Court can overturn its ruling as contrary to Court interpretation of federal law. But, if the state court based its decision on the state constitution, it cannot be overturned, for the Eighth Amendment only allows the states to execute people under certain circumstances—it does not require it. Thus, individual state courts, relying on their state constitutions, have taken actions that are not required by the Supreme Court, such as declaring sex classifications to be "suspect", requiring equal financing of state schools, or actively reviewing economic classifications.

All of the federal principles we discuss in this treatise apply with full force to the ruling of state courts, because they are required to follow the Supreme Court's interpretation of the Constitution of the United States. Nevertheless, state courts are supreme in the interpretation of their own statutes and the state's own constitution, so they may interpret state law to grant more rights federal law guarantees (as long as they do not violate a valid federal law or treaty, or the U.S. Constitution).

The state courts are in an appellate relationship to the U.S. Supreme Court but not in an appellate relationship to any lower federal courts. Because the state courts are not "lower courts," they are not required to follow the interpretation of lower federal courts, such as the Court of Appeals with jurisdiction over their state, even on matters relating to federal law. The federal court orders are *res judicata* and binding to the particular parties before the court, but when a similar issue appears in a new state case, the state supreme court need only follow the rulings and interpretations of the Supreme Court of the United States.

If a state court issues rulings contrary to the lower federal court, it may be engaging in a futile action, because the federal court may be able to enforce its interpretation of federal law by the use of habeas corpus, or by the imposition of a state-wide injunction against state officials. However, if the state supreme court believes that the lower federal court is in error as to the meaning of the Constitution, it may legitimately continue to hold an opposite interpretation so long as it does not interfere with a ruling of the federal court in a specific case. When such inconsistent rulings arise, it is common for the Supreme Court of the United States to exercise its appellate jurisdiction over a case involving the issue so that the matter can be finally resolved.

Chapter 2

FEDERAL JURISDICTION

Table of Sections

§ 2.1 An Introduction to the Jurisdictional Framework of the Supreme Court

Article III Courts. The Supreme Court is the only federal court that the Constitution created directly. Article III mandates that the judicial power be vested in "one Supreme Court." As to the inferior courts, the Constitution vests the judicial power only as Congress "may from time to time ordain and establish" lower courts.

The lower courts that Congress creates pursuant to its Article III powers are called Article III courts. The judges of Article III courts have the Constitution's guarantee of lifetime tenure, with no diminution of salary.

Article III of the Constitution sets out the jurisdiction of all federal courts, which is limited in nature. Congress cannot expand federal jurisdiction beyond the contours set out in Article III. Federal courts can hear cases only because of the nature of the question, or the nature of the parties.

In other words, federal courts can hear cases "arising under" the Constitution, laws, and treaties of the United States (including admiralty cases). They can also hear cases because of the nature of the parties, that is, cases affecting ambassadors, other public ministers, and consuls, controversies to which the United States is a party, controversies between two or more states, between a state and citizens of another state, between citizens of different states, between citizens of the same state claiming lands under grants of different states, and between a state or its citizens and foreign states, citizens, or subjects.

Article I Courts. In addition to creating these Article III courts, Congress also has the power, within certain limits, to create what are called *legislative courts* or Article I tribunals. These courts are tribunals that are inferior to the Supreme Court, but they are neither limited by, nor protected by, Article III.

Article I tribunals are really akin to administrative agencies. The "judges" of Article I courts do not have any constitutionally guaranteed lifetime tenure and protection from salary diminution; they are not governed by the case or controversy limitation of Article III and thus may render advisory opinions. To some extent these courts (e.g., territorial courts) may receive business that Congress could have sent to an Article III court, but chose not to do so. Congress must have an appropriate reason to create Article I courts. It may not simply give any and all Article III business to an Article I court, or otherwise the very concept of a court protected and limited by Article III would have no meaning.

Supreme Court Jurisdiction. When the Supreme Court considers a case under its original jurisdiction, it is the trial court (the court that originally takes jurisdiction). The Supreme Court has original jurisdiction, under Article III, of all cases affecting ambassadors, other public ministers and consuls, and cases in which a state is a party. Congress cannot constitutionally expand this original jurisdiction. Article III also gives the Court appellate jurisdiction of all the other cases within the limited jurisdiction of Article III, but this appellate jurisdiction is given "with such Exceptions, and under such Regulations as the Congress shall make."

The Jurisdictional Framework. At the present time Congress has created thirteen judicial circuits, numbered one through eleven, plus the District of Columbia Circuit, plus the Court of Appeals for the Federal Circuit. The Federal Circuit Court hears appeals from a final decision of the United States Claims Court, similar appeals from the federal district courts, the Court of International Trade, the Board of Patent Interferences, patent appeals from the federal district courts, and similar miscellaneous matters. Cases heard in the federal court system normally are heard in district courts in one of these circuits.

From the district courts, the parties may appeal to the court of appeals for that circuit (or the Federal Circuit). The circuit normally sits in panels of three.

From there the parties may seek review in the Supreme Court, normally by way of certiorari (discretionary review); by way of appeal (obligatory review, at least in theory); or by certified questions. In 1988 Congress finally eliminated most of the Supreme Court's mandatory appellate jurisdiction, giving that Court a great deal of control over its own docket. The 1988 legislation converts almost all Supreme Court review to a discretionary, certiorari approach.

In addition to this basic federal court system, Congress has sometimes established more specialized Article III courts. For example, it set up a special railroad court, composed of already sitting federal judges designated for part-time sitting on this court.

Federal jurisdiction often raises not only statutory questions— when is a state decision "final"; is the review by appeal or certiorari; and so on—but also constitutional questions. These constitutional questions occur because Article III allows Congress to grant federal courts only limited jurisdiction. For example, is the claim brought before the federal court a "case or controversy" within the meaning of Article III? If the case is brought on diversity grounds, are the parties really citizens of diverse states? In a diversity case, is the amount in controversy requirement of the diversity statute met by the plaintiff?

In addition to the statutory and constitutional questions that must be resolved prior to the court hearing the case on the merits, the Supreme Court has developed many rules of self restraint to avoid exercising its power to strike laws violative of the Constitution. In the remainder of this Chapter we shall consider these questions of constitutional jurisdiction, statutory jurisdiction, and self-imposed rules of restraint. We will also examine how the Court uses various doctrines, such as standing and ripeness, as tools to avoid reaching the merits. But first, let us turn to the long historical development that has led to the present jurisdictional framework of the Supreme Court.

§ 2.2 Jurisdiction of the Supreme Court

The basic statutes governing Supreme Court jurisdiction are found in title 28 of the U.S. Code. Section 1251 governs original jurisdiction and provides, in general, that the high court has original *and* exclusive jurisdiction of controversies between two or more states. The Supreme Court must hear these cases.

The Supreme Court also has original, but not exclusive, jurisdiction of cases in which ambassadors or other public ministers or counsels or vice counsels of foreign states are parties; cases between the United States and a state; and cases brought by a state against citizens of another state or aliens. Because federal district courts may hear these cases as well, the Supreme Court rarely accepts original jurisdiction. Typically the Supreme Court refers cases within the original jurisdiction to a special master, who will receive evidence and prepare a record. Original jurisdiction in practice accounts for but a small percentage of the Supreme Court caseload.

Although Congress, by statute, has always provided for the original jurisdiction of the Supreme Court, the Court has often stated in dictum that "the original jurisdiction of the Supreme Court is conferred not by Congress but by the Constitution itself. This jurisdiction is self-executing and needs no legislative implementation."

Appellate Jurisdiction. Under "direct appeal" the appellant can bypass the courts of appeal and have the Supreme Court directly hear the case. If review is by "appeal" the appellant will receive Supreme Court review, in theory, as of right. Under "certiorari," review for the petitioner is discretionary.

Direct Appeal. Congress limited direct appeals in 1988, as part of its reform to give the Supreme Court much greater control over its own docket. The federal jurisdictional statute now gives litigants the right of direct appeal from decisions of three-judge courts. But modern federal statutes severely limit the use of three-judge courts, so the number of such direct appeals is correspondingly reduced.

Certiorari and Appeal. After the 1988 statutory revisions, sections 1254 and 1257 grant the Supreme Court effective control of its docket. The basic principle behind the 1988 reforms is that the Court itself, "in the light of the discretionary standards it has developed and is constantly refining and applying to new types of situations" is the—

best judge of what cases, out of the thousands put forward each year, are from the national standpoint the most deserving of a hearing on the merits.

As a result, virtually all review to the Supreme Court now occurs when the Supreme Court, in its discretion, decides to accept a case. The Court has almost complete control of its docket, with review by discretion, by certiorari.

Certiorari. Under the Supreme Court's rules, a review on writ of certiorari is not a matter of right, but of sound judicial discretion, and the Court will grant it only where there are special and important reasons to do so. Consequently, the Court need not explain its refusal to accept certiorari and one cannot deduce any decision on the merits or other precedential value from such denials. The Court grants certiorari for the interest of the public, not merely for the interest of the parties. Thus, the Court will not ordinarily grant certiorari merely to achieve justice in a particular case.

The denial of certiorari technically means that fewer than four members of the Court, as a matter of their sound discretion, have voted to review a decision of the lower court. Nonetheless, some members of the Court have frequently written lengthy dissents to denials of certiorari. Individual Justices have used their dissents to denial of certiorari to express their concern about the facts of the particular case, to reemphasize their earlier dissents, to urge reconsideration of a settled point, or to comment on the Court's workload.

Other Justices have objected to these written dissents as "totally unnecessary," "the purest form of dicta," and "potentially misleading." Yet, "it is just one of the facts of life that today every lower court does attach importance to denials and to presence or absence of dissents from denials, as judicial opinions and lawyers' arguments show."

Appeal. When a party seeks review by appeal, the litigant, under the relevant statute, is invoking review as of right. The Supreme Court rules require the appellant to file a jurisdictional statement, which is similar to the petition for certiorari. The appellee may, on the basis of these papers, file a motion to dismiss or affirm. If there is a technical deficiency the Court may dismiss the appeal summarily on this procedural issue.

It may also dismiss an appeal on the merits for *want of a substantial federal question*. "Substantiality" is considered jurisdictional:

> [A]lthough the validity of a law was formally drawn in question, it is our duty to decline jurisdiction whenever it appears that the constitutional question presented is not, and was not at the time of granting the writ, substantial in character.

Thus, unlike certiorari, decisions to affirm summarily, and to dismiss for want of a substantial federal question are votes on the merits of a case binding as precedent on the lower courts. But, interestingly enough, this precedent is not as binding on the Supreme Court as would be one of its own more considered opinions.

Affirmance by an Equally Divided Court. Sometimes when the Court reviews a decision, it affirms by an equally divided Court. This type of affirmance is not entitled to precedential weight. The decision only records the fact that the Supreme Court was equally divided and that the lower court decision stands. There is no reversal, for the Court issues no order.

§ 2.3 "Court Packing" and the Number of Justices on the Supreme Court

Article III does not mention how many Justices compose the Supreme Court. The first Judiciary Act provided for a chief Justice and five associate Justices. A few years later, the Act of 1801 provided that "after the next vacancy ... [the Supreme Court] shall consist of five Justices only; that is to say, of one Chief Justice, and four associate Justices," but Congress repealed this entire act in 1802. The Act of 1807 then increased the number of Associate Justices to six; in 1837 the number of Associate Justices increased once again to eight, and in 1864, to nine.

President Roosevelt and Efforts to Pack the Court. While the total number of Justices has remained at nine (including the Chief Justice), in 1937 President Franklin D. Roosevelt proposed to increase that number, also amid charges of court-packing. The President proposed to appoint an additional Justice for each Justice on the Court who had served at least ten years and had failed to retire within six months of reaching his 70th birthday. The maximum number of Justices on the Supreme Court would be set at 15. The proposal included new retirement privileges for Supreme Court Justices. Roosevelt argued that new blood was needed on the Court and that the older Justices were less efficient. In reality, Roosevelt was reacting to the fact that a bare majority of unsympathetic Justices were often invalidating his legislative programs dealing with the economic depression.

The great majority of the Congress, led by members of Roosevelt's own party, defeated the plan. The Congress did provide retirement benefits for Supreme Court Justices in a Judiciary Act passed in 1937, which caused conservative Justice Van Devanter to resign in May of 1937. Also during the fight over the proposal, the Supreme Court appeared to change its position and upheld the validity of several important items of New Deal and state economic legislation.

§ 2.4 Tenure and Salary Protections for Judges of Article III Courts

All of the federal judges appointed pursuant to Article III have lifetime tenure, and a constitutional guarantee that their salary "shall not be diminished during their Continuance in Office." This clause is a specific means of ensuring the independence of the judiciary.

Congress is not required to keep judicial salaries growing with inflation rates; Congress may, in its discretion, increase the salaries of federal judges or refuse to increase them, so long as it does not reduce the nominal compensation of the judges. Congress can also nullify previously authorized increases in judicial salaries *if* the Congressional nullification becomes law *before* the beginning of the fiscal year in which the previously authorized increase was to take effect. Congress cannot repeal an increase in judicial salaries that takes effect under a formula previously set forth by statute, if the repealing act becomes law *after* the beginning of the fiscal year in which the increase took place.

Article III judges also have lifetime tenure. They can be removed only by impeachment. The purpose of this guarantee is to insulate "the individual judge from improper influences not only by other branches but by colleagues as well," in order to promote "judicial individualism."

§ 2.5 *Ex Parte McCardle* and the Power of Congress to Limit the Jurisdiction of Federal Courts

Some commentators and courts often rely on the Supreme Court's post Civil War decision of *Ex parte McCardle* (1868) as supporting a broad power of Congress to limit the jurisdiction of the lower federal courts and the Supreme Court. The case is a significant one and it is worth analyzing in detail.

Under the authority of the Reconstruction Acts, the military government had imprisoned McCardle, who then brought a habeas corpus action alleging that the Reconstruction legislation was unconstitutional. The lower court upheld the Act, and McCardle appealed under authority of the recently passed Act of February 5, 1867, providing appeal to the Supreme Court from the circuit courts.

After the Court had acknowledged jurisdiction in the case, but before it issued any decision on the merits, Congress withdrew the statutory right of appeal, seeking to avoid a Supreme Court determination that the Reconstruction legislation was unconstitutional. The Court complied with the withdrawal, dismissed the case for want of jurisdiction, and remarked that while the appellate jurisdiction of the Supreme Court "is, strictly speaking, conferred by the Constitution . . . it is conferred 'with such exceptions and under such regulations as Congress shall make' " according to Article III, section 2, clause 2.

People have used *McCardle* to support unsuccessful efforts to assert extensive congressional power over the jurisdiction of the courts in order to control substantive results of court decisions in a variety of cases, for example, reapportionment, subversive activities, and school busing.

This broad interpretation is troubling. If Congress can, in effect, overrule a constitutional decision by using its power over jurisdiction to control the substantive results of a case, to decision, then *Marbury v. Madison* is a lot less significant than most people think. For several reasons, it is not necessary to interpret *McCardle* in a way that gives *carte blanche* power to Congress.

First, it is noteworthy that *McCardle* explicitly recognized the limited nature of the statutory withdrawal that was involved in that case:

> Counsel seems to have supposed, if effect be given to the repealing act in question, that the whole appellate power of the court, in cases of habeas corpus, is denied. But this is an error. The act of 1868 does not except from the jurisdiction any cases but appeals from Circuit Courts under the act of 1867. It does not affect the jurisdiction which was previously exercised.

The Court clarified the meaning of this statement several months later, in *Ex parte Yerger* (1868), where it held the repealing act at issue in *McCardle* did not affect its certiorari jurisdiction. The Court concluded that writs of habeas corpus and certiorari could revise the decision of the circuit court and free the prisoner from unlawful restraint.

Yerger is important because it indicates that the limitation of the appellate jurisdiction in *McCardle,* while important to Mr. McCardle, had little practical effect on similar cases because an alternative review was available. In the actual facts of *McCardle*, Congress was not withdrawing all jurisdiction from the lower federal courts and the Supreme Court. Rather, it was only withdrawing one avenue of appeal to the Supreme Court.

If Congress were to remove all appellate avenues to the Supreme Court, that would not give Congress the ability to use the power over jurisdiction to control the outcome of a case. It would only make the lower federal courts the final decision-makers; it would not oust the federal courts from their essential role in the constitutional plan of exercising judicial review. In other words, even a wholesale removal of the Supreme Court's appellate jurisdiction—a fact situation much broader than that presented in *McCardle*—does not imply a congressional power to prevent all federal courts from exercising judicial review; it only implies a power to make lower federal courts the final decision makers.

The jurisdictional limitation in *McCardle* was neutral. The denial of appeal to the Supreme Court applied to both the Government and a private party. If the Government had lost the habeas action below (as it might lose it in a future case), the Government would, like Mr. McCardle, be denied an appellate remedy. The neutrality of a jurisdictional limitation helps to assure that congressional withdrawal will not be an attempt to alter the results of specific cases.

Some commentators have argued that the historical evidence surrounding the exceptions clause of Article III, granting Congress power to regulate the Supreme Court's appellate jurisdiction, supports the view that the clause be read in light of the contemporary state practice to confine regulation basically to housekeeping matters and to certain proceedings where neither error nor certiorari traditionally had been available. This proposition is controversial and historically inaccurate, for Congress has used its power over jurisdiction to effectuate results that are more significant than "housekeeping." For example, the Judiciary Act of 1789 did not provide for any general federal question in the federal courts, nor did it give federal courts direct appeals of criminal cases.

Whatever the merits of this "housekeeping" argument, there is no evidence that the framers intended that the exceptions clause authorize Congress to control the results of particular cases. Analogously then, Congress may not use the power to restrict the federal courts' jurisdiction in order to control the results of particular cases and achieve the result forbidden by a proper interpretation of the exceptions clause.

A principle implied in Article III (and not refuted by *McCardle)* is that the guarantee of an independent federal judiciary limits the legislature in the exercise of its power to regulate federal court jurisdiction. A post-*McCardle* decision, *United States v. Klein* (1871), directly supports this principle. *Klein* holds that Congress may not enact legislation to eliminate an area of jurisdiction in order to control the results in a particular case.

An 1863 statute allowed the recovery of land captured or abandoned during the Civil War if the claimant could prove that he had not aided the rebellion. Klein, relying on this statute, sued in the Court of Claims to get his property back. Relying on an earlier Supreme Court decision that a presidential pardon proved conclusively that he had not assisted the rebellion, Klein won his case in the Court of Claims. The government appealed his to the Supreme Court, and while that appeal was pending, Congress, perhaps emboldened by recent victory in *McCardle,* passed a statute to reverse this result.

This new law, written in the guise of a jurisdictional statute, provided, first, that a presidential pardon would not support a claim for captured property. Second, acceptance without disclaimer of a pardon for participation in the rebellion was conclusive evidence that the claimant had aided the enemy. And, third, if the Court of Claims based its judgment in favor of the claimant of such a pardon, then the Supreme Court lacked jurisdiction on appeal.

The Supreme Court declared this restriction of its jurisdiction unconstitutional. The Court agreed that Congress had the power under Article III to confer or withhold the right of appeal from Court of Claims decisions but held that Article III also requires that the judicial branch be independent of the legislative and executive branches, and that requirement restricts Congressional power. The Court found that the withdrawal of jurisdiction was only a means to deny to presidential pardons the effect that the Court previously had held them to have. Such a denial of jurisdiction prescribes for the Court a rule for the decision of its cases. Thus, Congress had exceeded its power to regulate appellate jurisdiction and had passed the limit separating the legislative from the judicial branch.

Klein strongly supports the contention that Congress must exercise its power to limit jurisdiction in a manner consistent with constitutional limitations and with the independence of the judiciary. Any jurisdictional limitation must be neutral; that is, Congress may not decide the merits of a case under the guise of limiting jurisdiction. Congress' power under the exceptions clause is subject, like any other congressional power, to the limitations that the Constitution imposes, including the restrictions of the Bill of Rights. Let us now consider, in more detail, the nature of these restrictions on Congress' power to restrict the jurisdiction of the federal courts.

Article III grants Congress the power to affect the jurisdiction of the lower federal courts, but we should not be surprised that other parts of the Constitution limit that power. All other federal powers are subject to Constitutional limitations. For example, Congress has the right to define and punish piracy, but it cannot do so in a way that violates the Bill or Rights. The power over federal court jurisdiction should be treated no differently. Congress, in short, should not be able to exercise its power to create exceptions to federal jurisdiction that would violate the due process clause of the Fifth Amendment, or other Constitutional limits.

For example, a law providing that federal courts have no jurisdiction in diversity cases where Catholics are plaintiffs should violate the First Amendment's free exercise clause. No one would seriously contend that a federal law that discriminated on religious belief should be exempt from the First Amendment simply because the law is found in title 28 of the United States Code (dealing with the jurisdiction of federal courts) rather than in another title.

Similarly, a law preventing federal courts from exercising jurisdiction in cases where the plaintiff alleges racial discrimination should violate the equal protection component of due process.

§ 2.6   The Eleventh Amendment

(a) Introduction and Historical Note

The Eleventh Amendment provides:

> The Judicial power of the United States shall not be construed to extend to any suit in law or equity, commenced or prosecuted against one of the United States by Citizens of another State, or by Citizens or Subjects of any Foreign State.

The Eleventh Amendment raises extremely important and complex issues. Court interpretations of the Amendment have involved both expansions and restrictions of the literal application of its wording. This provision acts to bar suits brought against state governments in the federal courts. It does not grant the states true immunity, for it does not exempt them from the restrictions of federal law.

Congress proposed, and the states ratified, the Eleventh Amendment as a reaction to the Supreme Court's decision in *Chisholm v. Georgia* (1793). Alexander Chisholm brought an original action against Georgia in the Supreme Court. Chisholm was the executor of the estate of a South Carolina decedent, Robert Farquar. During the revolutionary period, Farquar had delivered supplies to Georgia under a contract that remained unpaid at his death. Georgia never contested the debt but, instead, refused to appear on the grounds that the federal court had no jurisdiction over such a suit.

By a vote of four to one the Supreme Court decided that it had jurisdiction in the case and entered a judgment by default against Georgia. The Court had not yet begun the tradition of majority opinion for the Court (Chief Justice Marshall started that practice), so the Justices delivered individual opinions *seriatim*.

None of the Justices relied on a congressional grant of jurisdiction. The four voting together rested their decisions on a belief of a general power under Article III, and the view that states had only limited sovereignty in a national democracy. The one dissenting Justice refused to find any federal court jurisdiction over state governments absent specific congressional authorization. We know that the history of Article III simply does not resolve the issue of federal jurisdiction over debt actions against states.

Congress proposed the Eleventh Amendment immediately after the *Chisholm* decision and the states ratified it in less than five years. The reasons for this reaction may have included popular opinion about the meaning of Article III; theoretical problems concerning the available judicial procedures against a sovereign, if subordinate, unit in the federal system; and a general fear of suits by Tory creditors. The provision passed with such little debate that its history is silent on a great many issues.

Chief Justice Marshall gave us the earliest interpretation of the Eleventh Amendment. In *Cohens v. Virginia* (1821), Marshall indicated that the Amendment had no part in suits other than debt actions, and he held it inapplicable to suits that the state brought against a private individual, such as criminal proceedings. Later, in *Osborn v. Bank of the United States* (1824), Marshall stated that the Amendment was inapplicable whenever the state was not a party of record. These interpretations were to be narrowed in future years. Nevertheless, Marshall's opinions are the only judicial exposition of the meaning of the Amendment at a time close to its adoption.

(b) An Outline of the Current Rules

The Eleventh Amendment acts as a bar to federal jurisdiction over state governments, as such, when they are sued by anyone other than the federal government or another state. The bar applies to all types of suits for damages or retroactive relief for past wrongs, but it is not an effective barrier that exempts the state from prospectively complying with federal law. The Eleventh Amendment did not repeal the supremacy clause.

As we shall see, if the Eleventh Amendment applies, the suit may be heard in federal court *if* the state consents. In spite of the Eleventh Amendment, Congress may create federal causes of action against states without their consent if such causes of action are necessary to enforce Constitutional rights, such as those in the Fourteenth Amendment. Now, let us consider this points in more detail.

In resolving issues under the Eleventh Amendment one should ask five basic questions:

- (1) is the plaintiff one to whom the Amendment applies?

- (2) is the suit truly against the state?

- (3) is the suit seeking relief in a manner that is barred by the Amendment?

- (4) has the state waived its immunity?

- (5) is there a valid federal statute in the area that overrides the immunity?

Is the Plaintiff Within the Amendment?

First, one must determine if the plaintiff is subject to the jurisdictional bar. By its own terms the Amendment bars suits by citizens of other states or foreign nationals. The Court held in *Hans v. Louisiana* (1890) that the Amendment, by implication, also bars suits by citizens of a state suing their own state. Thus all private plaintiffs are subject to the Amendment.

However, if the state brings an action against the private person, that suit does not come under the restrictions. Similarly, a state may sue another state, or the United States. And the United States may sue a state, even if the purpose of the suit is to protect private individuals. Thus the Secretary of Labor of the United States may bring a federal suit against a state government to establish the rights of individual employees whose personal suit would be barred.

The Eleventh Amendment also does not bar an award of money damages when one *state* sues another state in an original action brought before the U.S. Supreme Court. That Amendment applies, by its own terms, to suits by citizens against a state.

The "State" for Purposes of the Eleventh Amendment.

The second major issue concerns whether a "state" is being sued. Suit is barred only when the state government is the defendant. Agencies of the state come under this heading, but its political subdivisions do not. Thus suits in federal court against municipal corporations, counties and school boards raise no Eleventh Amendment issue. An entity that is merely the instrumentality of state government shares its immunity, but an entity that is a politically independent unit enjoys no Eleventh Amendment protection.

The fact that the federal government has agreed to indemnify a state instrumentality against the costs of litigation (including adverse judgments) does not divest that state agency of Eleventh Amendment immunity. The issue that is relevant in determining the Eleventh Amendment immunity is the entity's potential legal liability for judgments, not its ability to require a third party to reimburse it.

The Eleventh Amendment was designed to prevent federal courts from issuing judgments that must be paid out of the state treasury. Thus, in determining whether an agency is entitled to share in the state's Eleventh Amendment immunity, the court should determine if the state is obligated to pay any of the agency's indebtedness. If the state has no legal obligation to bear the debts of the enterprise, then the Eleventh Amendment is not implicated.

Similarly, state officers may be sued in their personal capacity for damages in a federal action, because the amendment grants them no immunity from federal action even where they are acting in their official capacity. However, if the suit actually requests that the officer be ordered to pay funds from the state treasury for wrongful acts of the state, or return property in the state's possession, the suit will be barred because the state is the real party in interest.

In other words, if the plaintiff sued a state official in his or her "official capacity," that really is simply another way of pleading an action against the state, and is thus within the Eleventh Amendment. However, a "personal capacity" suit seeks to impose individual, personal liability on the government officer for actions taken under color of state law, with the badge of state authority. The Eleventh Amendment does not bar suits against state officers sued in their "individual capacity."

There is no longer any requirement that the state be a named party of record. Thus, if a suit requests that the head of a state department of welfare be ordered to personally pay damages the suit is permissible, but if it requests an order requiring him to pay past due amounts from the state treasury it is barred. The one exception to the real party in interest rules arises in connection with the issue as to the nature of the relief sought, discussed next.

The Nature of the Relief Sought.

The third issue concerns the nature of relief sought in the federal action. Where the action is one for damages, past debts or retroactive relief of any type, it is barred whether it is brought in law, equity, or admiralty. Thus federal suits at law for return of improperly collected state taxes are barred. Similarly, when the Court of Appeals for the Seventh Circuit attempted to order the payment of illegally withheld welfare payments under an "equitable-restitution" theory, the Supreme Court reversed.

The one exception to the amendment based on the form of action is that a private person may bring an equitable action to force state officers to comply with federal law in the future even though they will be required to spend state funds to so comply. The distinction had its genesis in *Ex parte Young* (1908), where the Court held that a state officer could be forbidden in a federal suit from enforcing state law. This holding was based on the legal fiction that the officer could not be given authority to violate federal law so that the suit was not against the state authority itself. Today the fiction is maintained to the extent that a state officer must be the named defendant in such a suit. Federal courts can issue prospective relief against state officials in order to enforce federal law, even if the relief may involve the official using state funds.

Although the state is the real party in interest, the Eleventh Amendment was never intended to grant states the ability to subvert the supremacy clause by granting immunity to the states or their officials from judicial orders to comply with federal law. Thus, in *Edleman v. Jordan* (1974) the Court struck the lower federal court's order to the state officer to pay past due welfare checks, but the Supreme Court upheld the lower court order that forced him prospectively to disburse state payments in conformity with federal laws.

Similarly the Supreme Court unanimously held that state officers could be subject to a federal cause of action, and ordered by a federal court, to force them to disburse state funds to institute educational programs in connection with a suit to desegregate public schools. If state officials do not comply in good faith with the federal court order of prospective relief, the federal courts may impose monetary penalties upon either the particular state officers or the state itself.

If a plaintiff seeks a federal court order to state government officials to transfer to the plaintiff specifically identified pieces of property there will be an issue in the case regarding the applicability of the Eleventh Amendment. If the action is brought against the state government itself or if the plaintiff is merely seeking compensation from the state treasury based on a claim that the state has improperly taken funds from him or refused to pay money to him, the suit will be barred by the amendment. However, if the plaintiff brings suit against the state officials and claims that the officials are acting unconstitutionally and beyond the scope of their authority by having in their possession specific pieces of property owned by the plaintiff, a federal court may be able to attach the property and adjudicate all parties' rights to the property in an *in rem* proceeding.

This exception to the amendment's bar to federal court jurisdiction over state governments, allowing federal courts to order state officers to comply with federal law, does not open federal courts to all those who seek judgments against state governments that might be described as something other than "retroactive" relief. Federal courts are not allowed to adjudicate claims against state governments unless the cause of action falls into a specific category of actions which the Supreme Court has held not to be barred by the amendment. Thus, the executor of an estate could not use the Federal Interpleader Act, 28 U.S.C.A. § 1335, as a jurisdictional basis for forcing officials of two state governments to litigate in federal court the states' inconsistent claims of jurisdiction to tax the estate represented by the executor.

This last point is important and occasionally overlooked: the Eleventh Amendment does not permit any suits in federal court against states and those agencies that are "arms of the State," regardless of the relief sought. The Eleventh Amendment is a bar to such suits, whether the relief sought is equitable or legal, prospective or retroactive, declaratory or injunctive. The exception in *Ex Parte Young* does not violate this basic principle because it only applies where the injunctive suit is against state *officials* and the action to be restrained is without authority of state law or contravenes the statutes or Constitution of the United States.

The Supreme Court views the Eleventh Amendment as a bar to federal suits against state officials when the state is the real, substantial party in interest regardless of whether the suit seeks retroactive or injunctive relief. The *Ex parte Young* exception to this principle allows federal courts to hear suits against state officials if the suit seeks to force them to conform their conduct to *federal law*. That exception does not apply to suits that would seek to have federal judges order state officials to conform their conduct to *state* law. The Eleventh Amendment bars federal jurisdiction over suits that seek relief, whether prospective or retroactive, against state officials on the basis of state law and, similarly, bars jurisdiction over such claims that are brought as pendent claims in suits alleging federal causes of action.

The Eleventh Amendment does not prevent a federal court from issuing an order requiring state officials to comply with a consent decree that they had entered into and that required the official to take steps to comply with a federal statute. *Frew v. Hawkins* (2004).

A bankruptcy proceeding initiated by a former student to discharge a loan debt to a corporation administered by a state for student assistance is not a suit against the state for the purposes of the Eleventh Amendment. *Tennessee Student Assistance Corp. v. Hood* (2004).

Waiver of Immunity.

Express Waiver. The fourth issue is whether the state has waived its Eleventh Amendment immunity for purposes of the particular suit. The Eleventh Amendment bar is not absolute and the state may consent to the suit in federal court. Although it is customary to refer to the Eleventh Amendment as a "jurisdictional bar," it is not jurisdictional in the same sense that Article III diversity jurisdiction is jurisdictional. Parties cannot waive the requirement of being citizens from diverse states, but a state can waive its Eleventh Amendment immunity. The purpose of the Eleventh Amendment is to protect the state, and the state can waive that protection. The purpose of the jurisdictional limitations in Article III is to limit the federal courts, so parties cannot confer jurisdiction on a federal court by simply agreeing the submit to the court.

A waiver is typically defined as the voluntary relinquishment of a known right. Thus, in order for the state to waive its rights, its consent should be express. To constitute an express waiver the state must do more than merely allow suits to be brought in courts already having jurisdiction.

Implied Waivers. If a state does not wish to waive its immunity expressly, the Court will not imply a waiver merely because the state appeared in federal court. The state's failure to plead immunity at the trial level also does not constitute a waiver, because the Court allows the State to raise the Eleventh Amendment as a bar on appeal.

The Supreme Court initially embraced a doctrine of implied waiver of a state's sovereign immunity, but it no longer does so. In *College Savings Bank v. Florida Pre–Paid Postsecondary Education Expense Board* (1999), the State of Florida was charged with violating federal patent and trademark laws. The Supreme Court, in a majority opinion by Chief Justice Rehnquist, found that Congress could not remove a state's Eleventh Amendment immunity from suit through one of its Article I powers, be it the commerce power or the patent power. The Supreme Court in this case also overruled an earlier decision and held that it would not find implied or constructive waiver of Eleventh Amendment immunity by a state government. Thus, the state of Florida would only be subject to suit in federal court for monetary damages, based on a violation of the federal trademark laws, if Florida had consented to the suit. The Supreme Court majority ruled that the judiciary could not find a waiver of a state's Eleventh Amendment rights unless the State's waiver was explicit. The majority concluded that Florida's activities in interstate commerce in general did not constitute an express waiver of Florida's immunity from suit and it dismissed the claim against the State of Florida.

Federal Statutes that Abrogate a State's Eleventh Amendment Immunity.

The fifth issue is whether federal statutes that grant specific jurisdiction to federal courts can abrogate the Eleventh Amendment immunity of state governments. Here we must separate congressional powers granted by the Constitution of 1787, and the first ten Amendments, from congressional powers granted by Amendments after the Eleventh Amendment.

By the start of the twenty-first century, the Supreme Court had taken the position that the Eleventh Amendment prohibits Congress from using its powers under the original Constitution of 1787 to make a state government liable to monetary suit in a federal court. In other words, if a private person plaintiff alleged in a federal court law suit that a state government had hurt the plaintiff in a manner that violated a federal statute that was passed pursuant to one of Congress's Article I powers, (such as the commerce clause or the patent clause), the plaintiff could not receive monetary damages from a federal court. In the 1980s, in *Pennsylvania v. Union Gas Co.*, the Supreme Court without majority opinion indicated that Congress might be able to make states liable for money damages if they violated federal statutes that could only be justified by the commerce clause power of Congress. In 1996, in *Seminole Tribe of Florida v. Florida*, the Supreme Court overruled an earlier case and held that Congress could not use the commerce clause to create private rights of action against state governments for monetary damages that could be litigated in the federal courts.

It is important to remember that the Eleventh Amendment only protects state government from suits under federal statutes that are brought by private persons for the purpose of seeking some type of retroactive relief, such as monetary damages. A ruling that the state is protected from a federal court lawsuit by the Eleventh Amendment does not free the state from the requirement of following a valid federal law passed under the commerce power. As we will see in Chapter 4 of this text, states have not been given exemptions from federal commercial regulations that apply to both public sector and private sector persons. Thus, the Court held in *EEOC v. Wyoming* (1983) that state and local governments could not fire employees in violation of the Age Discrimination in Employment Act. In *Kimel v. Florida Board of Regents* (2000) the Supreme Court ruled that the Age Discrimination in Employment Act was merely a commerce power act, and not a statute that came within Congress's power to enforce the Fourteenth Amendment. For that reason, persons who allegedly were fired from their jobs by the state of Florida in violation of the Age Discrimination Act could get some type of prospective or injunctive relief, but they could not receive money damages. Florida was not subject to a money damages claim due to the State's Eleventh Amendment immunity. Under the supremacy clause of Article VI the State of Florida is still required to follow the valid federal commercial statute banning certain types of age discrimination in employment, because the federal statute is within Congress's Article I commerce power.

The Court has held that federal statutes based upon the congressional power to enforce the Fourteenth Amendment are not subject to Eleventh Amendment jurisdictional rules. This position is clearly supported by history. Whatever power was given to Congress to enact legislation by section 5 of the Fourteenth Amendment limited the earlier enacted Eleventh Amendment immunity for state governments. The Supreme Court will not find that a state is subject to suit under a statute passed under Congress's Fourteenth Amendment powers unless it finds both that Congress clearly made the state subject to such a suit and, second, that the congressional statute was truly justifiable under section 5 of the Fourteenth Amendment. The Court in 1976, in *Fitzpatrick v. Bitzer,* found that Congress had explicitly made states subject to Title VII of the Civil Rights Act, which prohibits race and gender discrimination in employment matters. Because the Court found that the protection against sex discrimination and race discrimination in employment by state governments could come within the Fourteenth Amendment power of Congress, persons who had allegedly had their jobs terminated in violation of Title VII could bring suit against their state government employer in a federal court.

Some civil rights acts, by their own terms, will not apply to state governments. In *Monell v. Dept. of Social Services* (1978), the Supreme Court ruled that cities and other local government units were "persons" who could be sued for violating an individual's civil rights or other federal rights under 42 U.S.C.A. § 1983. Cities and local governments enjoy no immunity under the Eleventh Amendment and so the Court did not have to address any question as to whether the city or local government was entitled to immunity from a federal court action for money damages if a plaintiff successfully showed that the city or local government had violated the plaintiff's federal rights.

In *Quern v. Jordan* (1979), the Supreme Court ruled that as a matter of statutory interpretation state governments were not "persons" who could be sued under 42 U.S.C.A. § 1983. The majority opinion in *Quern* distinguished earlier cases concerning Title VII and the Civil Rights Attorney's Fees Award Act on the basis that Congress had clearly intended to override state's Eleventh Amendment immunity when it extended Title VII to the states and when it passed the Civil Rights Attorneys Fees Act.

In Chapter 15 of this text, we will examine the ways in which the Court determines whether a specific statute passed by Congress comes within the power granted to Congress by section 5 of the Fourteenth Amendment. The student must remember that only those statutes that the Supreme Court finds come within power granted to Congress by an Amendment after the Eleventh Amendment (such as the Thirteenth, Fourteenth or Fifteenth Amendments) could override a state's Eleventh Amendment immunity.

Limits on Federal Power to Subject States to Suits in State Court.

The Eleventh Amendment, by its own terms, limits, the "Judicial power of the United States." It speaks to federal courts and says nothing about states being sued in their own state courts. In *Alden v. Maine* (1999) the Court acknowledged that fact but, nonetheless, held that the sovereign immunity principles, which are derived from the structure of the Constitution, mean that Congressional powers under Article I do not include the power to subject nonconsenting States to private suits for damages in state courts. Just as Congress cannot force a state to be sued in federal court, Congress cannot force a state to be sued in its own court system. However, a state may explicitly consent to waive its sovereign immunity.

In *Alden*, state probation offices sued the State of Maine for violation of the overtime provisions of the Fair Labor Standards Act in federal district court. After the Supreme Court held that Congress could not use its commerce clause powers to take away a state's Eleventh Amendment sovereign immunity, the federal district court dismissed the probation officers' suit, and they then filed the same action in state court in Maine. The Fair Labor Standards Act authorized such a suit in state court, but the state trial court dismissed on sovereign immunity grounds, because Maine had not consented to suit. The Maine Supreme Judicial Court affirmed. The U.S. Supreme Court, five to four, affirmed.

The majority readily acknowledged that the text of the Eleventh Amendment did not control this case. Instead, the Court held that "the powers delegated to Congress under Article I do not include the power to subject nonconsenting States to private suits for damages in state courts." Later the Court reemphasized this point: "[W]e hold that the States retain immunity from private suit in their own courts, an immunity beyond the congressional power to abrogate by Article I legislation."

Alden was decided by a 5 to 4 vote of the Justices. The Justices in the majority and the Justices who dissented in *Alden* had a truly irreconcilable disagreement. The dissenters in *Alden* found that there was no evidence that existed that the drafters or ratifiers of Article III of the Constitution, or the Eleventh Amendment, meant to give the states immunity from suits in state courts if the state had violated a statute that had been validly passed by Congress under the powers granted to it by the Constitution of 1787. However, a majority of the Justices in *Alden* found that evidence surrounding the ratification of the Constitution of 1787 demonstrated that the states retained immunity from suits by private persons in their own courts unless they had expressly consented to suit. The Eleventh Amendment did not grant this immunity according to the majority. Rather, the states simply had retained immunity from suit in their own courts when the Constitution was drafted and ratified. The *Alden* majority concluded that the Eleventh Amendment was designed "not to change", but to restore the original constitutional design, and that state therefore retained "immunity of a sovereign in its own courts."

One must be careful not to read too much into *Alden*. *Alden* made clear that the state's constitutional privilege to assert its sovereign immunity in its own courts does not give a state the right to disregard the Constitution or a valid federal law. Plaintiffs can continue to seek relief against state officers under *Ex parte Young*, for injunctive or declaratory relief or for money damages when sued in their individual capacities.

A state's sovereign immunity does not prevent the Federal Government itself from suing the state to enforce federal law. Congress could enact a federal criminal statute that would apply to state actors, such as state prosecutors, state marshals, and so forth, that would impose severe criminal penalties for any state officials who violate federal statutes.

Nothing in *Alden* alters the scope of federal power under the Civil War Amendments. As *Alden* specifically stated: "Congress may authorize private suits against nonconsenting States pursuant to its § 5 enforcement power" in order to protect those rights that arise from section 1 of the Fourteenth Amendment.

§ 2.7　Case or Controversy and Related Doctrines

(a) Introduction

Article III, section 2 of the Constitution confines federal court jurisdiction to "cases" and "controversies." In addition to its constitutional meaning, this requirement has also prompted a nonconstitutional doctrine of judicial self-restraint, which is a significant, self-imposed limitation on judicial review. To rule on either federal constitutional or statutory issues, an Article III court must have a "case or controversy".

Although the analogy may at first seem foolish, the Supreme Court of the United States has defined the case or controversy requirement of Article III in a manner that makes the role of any Article III judge quite similar to the role of a referee at a boxing match. The referee at the boxing match is not paid to give general interpretations of the rules of boxing. The referee's job really begins when there are at least two fighters in the ring, and the fight has begun. The job of the referee is over when the final bell ends the fight. Article III courts require adversary parties, just as a referee's job require at least two adversaries; Article III judges cannot issue advisory opinions. Article III courts only have a job when there is a live controversy (a fight in progress). The job of the Article III judge does not begin unless there is a case that is ripe (the fight has started) and the issue is not moot (the fight has not ended).

Just like referees at boxing matches, Article III judges can only answer questions from persons who are part of the fight, rather than members of the audience. Using the concept of "standing", the Supreme Court will separate those persons who have a sufficient injury or controversy that justifies an Article III court ruling on their claims from disgruntled citizens (who will not be able to invoke federal court jurisdiction).

Not surprisingly, determining whether there is an adversary proceeding, a ripe but not moot issue, or whether a person has standing is more difficult in the legal world than in the boxing arena.

The Supreme Court has found that the Article III case or controversy requirement establishes a minimum amount of adversariness, and a requirement of minimal injury to a party who wishes to raise an issue in a federal lawsuit. The Article III threshold requirements for adversariness and injury may be fairly low.

In addition to the constitutionally required attributes of adversariness and injury, the Supreme Court has found that Article III court should not rule on federal claims unless there is a very clear adversary proceeding and the person making the claim clearly has an injury that is different from the injury that was suffered by the general public. Article III sets a minimum hurdle for parties wishing to raise a federal issue in an Article III court. The Court requires more than the Article III minimums (based on so-called "prudential concerns") because the judiciary should not rule on open constitutional or federal statuary questions unless there is clear need for the judiciary to resolve a real controversy.

(b) Advisory Opinions

The problem of advisory opinions and the case or controversy requirement formed the theoretical framework for *Muskrat v. United States* (1911). In 1902 Congress enacted a statute providing, as of a certain date, for a transfer of Cherokee property from tribal ownership to individual ownership by citizens of the Cherokee Nation. The statute also imposed certain restrictions on alienation of this land. Two later acts increased the number of Cherokees permitted to enroll, and increased the restrictions on alienation. Plaintiffs sued to have these subsequent statutes declared unconstitutional because they increased the number of Indians entitled to share in the final distribution of property. Other plaintiffs also sued to have the restraints on alienation removed. Plaintiffs claimed that the restrictions on alienation and the increase in the number of enrollees constituted a taking of property without just compensation.

A special act of Congress authorized plaintiffs to institute suit in the Court of Claims to determine the validity of these acts "in so far as said acts ... attempt to increase or extend the restrictions upon alienation, encumbrance, or the right to lease the allotments of lands ... or to increase the number of persons entitled to share in the final distribution of lands and funds...." The state gave jurisdiction to the Court of Claims with a right of appeal in the Supreme Court. The United States, under the statutory scheme, was the party defendant, and if the plaintiffs were successful the statute authorized the government to pay the attorneys fees of the plaintiffs.

The Supreme Court reversed the Court of Claims and directed it to dismiss for want of jurisdiction. The government purported to be the defendant, but it had no interest in the outcome of this litigation. Plaintiffs do not "assert a property right as against the Government, or ... demand compensation for alleged wrongs because of action upon its part." The Court concluded that the jurisdictional act was merely an attempt to provide for a test in the Supreme Court of the validity of an act of Congress, without regard to the requirement of a case or controversy. That attempt was unconstitutional.

The power to declare a law unconstitutional exists only because the Court finds the law that one of the parties has relied on to be in conflict with "the fundamental law." In such a case, the Court rules the act unconstitutional because, in the course of deciding the actual controversy, it must choose the fundamental law over the statute. There is otherwise no general power to revise actions of Congress.

Part of the law in question in the *Muskrat* case—the restriction on alienation—was self-executing. If a Native American were to sell his land to a private party in violation of the alienation provisions, the case of the Native American versus the private person would create an appropriate case testing the constitutionality of the alienation provisions. The court might have to decide, for example, the claim of the Native American that the land should be returned if the sale was not valid. The private party could also seek a declaratory judgment that his title was valid, if a declaratory judgment procedure existed.

Declaratory Relief. Coercive relief is not an essential element of the case or controversy requirement. That is, if there is an actual case or controversy, the court may issue only declaratory relief. Thus the constitutionality of a declaratory judgment statute is now accepted. A federal court may even issue prospective rulings, but, if it does, the relief must at least apply to the parties before it, so that the opinion will not be merely advisory.

The Court of Claims, at the time of the *Muskrat* decision, was an Article I Court, not a Court created pursuant to Article III. Article III does not bind Article I courts, so they may give advisory opinions. In fact, until the statute was changed and the Supreme Court held that the Court of Claims had become an Article III Court, the Court of Claims routinely fulfilled a congressional reference jurisdiction by rendering advisory opinions to Congress.

The Supreme Court did not explain why it did not uphold the part of the *Muskrat* jurisdictional statute giving, in effect, the Court of Claims (at that time, an Article I court) the power to render an advisory opinion. The Justices must have thought that the jurisdictional statute was not severable, that is, Congress did not want only the Court of Claims opinion as to the constitutionality of the statute; it wanted the Supreme Court's final judgment.

Extrajudicial Duties by Federal Judges and the United States Sentencing Commission.

Rulemaking. In *Wayman v. Southard* (1825), Chief Justice Marshall wrote an opinion for the Court finding that Congress could confer rulemaking power on judges. In later years, the Court would find that Congress acted properly when it allowed the Court to establish rules of conduct for its own business, and rules for court procedures.

Sentencing Commission. In 1984 Congress enacted the Sentencing Reform Act, in response to serious disparities among prison sentences by different judges operating in an indeterminate sentencing system. The Sentencing Reform Act created the United States Sentencing Commission, with seven voting members, at least three of whom must be Article III federal judges chosen from a list of six judges recommended by the Judicial Conference of the United States. Congress authorized the Sentencing Commission to issue binding Sentencing Guidelines establishing a range of determinate sentences for all categories of federal offenses and for defendants according to various specific and detailed factors.

The Act, in effect, consolidated the power that had been exercised jointly by the sentencing judge and the Parole Commission to decide what punishment the convicted defendant should suffer. The Act stated that it rejected imprisonment as a means to promote rehabilitation. However, it acknowledged that punishment should serve retributive, educational, deterrent, and incapacitative goals.

The Act made all sentences determinative. The Sentencing Commission's "guidelines" are, in fact, binding on the courts. Although the trial judge has discretion to depart from the guidelines, the trial judge must find aggravating or mitigating factors, and give "the specific reason" for departing from the guidelines. There is limited appellate review of the sentence.

Mistretta v. United States (1989) rejected multiple challenges to the constitutionality of the United States Sentencing Commission. Congress provided that at least three federal judges should serve on the Commission and share their commission authority with non-Article III judges.

In upholding the constitutionality of the Sentencing Commission, the Court said that the Constitution does not prevent Congress from some non-Article III duties to Article III judges. The constitutional question is whether the particular extrajudicial assignment "undermines the integrity of the Judicial Branch."

(c) Mootness and Collusiveness

Article III Courts may not decide moot questions, only actual cases or controversies.

A case or issue is moot when the judgment of the Court would not affect the parties to the case in the real world. The issue in a controversy may resolve itself. Parties may die; settlements may be reached concerning controversies before a court's final ruling. If an issue has already been resolved by the parties, so that the court's ruling would not affect the parties to the case, any court ruling on the question presented in the case would be academic in nature.

While the Supreme Court has sometimes stated that mootness is a constitutional limitation, it has at other times been willing to relax the mootness rule so that the requirement will not be so "rigid" as to prevent the review of important constitutional issues. Mootness should therefore properly be regarded as rooted in part in the constitutional limitation of the judicial power to cases and controversies, and in part rooted in a rule of self-restraint, a rule that the Court relax at times. In deciding mootness issues, the Court is not always clear when it is deciding based on self-restraint, or deciding based on the command of Article III.

A case may become moot for several reasons. The controversy must normally exist at every stage of the proceeding, including the appellate stages. Thus, a case that was not initially moot may become moot because the law has changed; or, because defendant has paid moneys owed and no longer wishes to appeal, notwithstanding plaintiff's desire to obtain a higher court ruling. A case may also become moot because allegedly wrongful behavior has passed, and could not reasonably be expected to recur; or, because a challenged statute no longer can affect the litigant.

For example, a law regulating rights of minors becomes moot when the complaining party, through lapse of time, is no longer within the age brackets governed by the statute; or the party has died.

Voluntary Cessation of Challenged Practice. To prevent either party from creating a technical mootness as a sham to deprive the Court of jurisdiction, the Court has created various exceptions to the doctrine. Thus, if a party voluntarily stops allegedly illegal conduct, that change does not make the case moot, if the defendant would be free to return to his old ways.

Vacating Lower Court Judgements When They Become Moot on Appeal. If a case is brought in the *federal* system and then becomes moot on appeal, the Supreme Court practice is to vacate the appellate court judgment and remand to the lower court with instructions to dismiss the complaint. The case then has no binding effect on the parties.

However, if the case had been brought in the *state* system and is now before the U.S. Supreme Court, the situation is different, because Article III and federal rules of self restraint do not bind state courts and because the Supreme Court has no supervisory power over state courts. The state constitution may give its courts the power to issue advisory opinions. If a case, originally brought in state court, becomes moot on appeal, the Supreme Court held, in *Doremus v. Board of Education* (1952), that it cannot decide the case; it must normally dismiss the appeal, but it will not require the state court to vacate the judgement or dismiss the complaint.

However, the U.S. Supreme Court will not treat the case from the state court as moot in the situation where state judgement causes real harm to the parties who petition for review, assuming that otherwise the requisites of a case or controversy are met. Even though the plaintiffs would not have had standing if they had brought their case in federal court, they brought their case in state court. The state court ruled in their favor and adverse to the defendants. That judgement, in effect, supplies the requisite injury (and injury to the defendants), which prevents the case from being premature or moot for federal purposes. Thus, we have a paradox: *Doremus* remains good law for plaintiffs who lack standing and lose in state court on the merits of their claim, but *Doremus* is not good law for plaintiffs who lack standing and prevail in the state courts on the merits of their federal claim.

Actions Capable of Repetition Yet Evading Review. Another exception to the general mootness rule concerns those cases that are "capable of repetition, yet evading review." A mere "physical or theoretical possibility" is not enough to meet the test of "capable of repetition, yet evading review," otherwise any matter of short duration would be reviewable. There must be a "reasonable expectation" or a "demonstrable probability" that "the same controversy will recur involving the *same* complaining party."

Such cases may be divided into two main categories. In one, the challenged order is so short that it will normally expire before review may be had. Such cases include short sentences in criminal cases, short term orders of agencies that usually will come up again, short term injunctions that may be repeated, and similar circumstances.

In the second category, the challenged order is not short term, but the factual circumstances appear to make the order moot by the time of appeal. Election cases illustrate this problem. To beat the election clock, the Court may issue its decision as soon as possible prior to the election, with the opinion coming later. Or, the Court may decide the issue after the election, if the issue is otherwise capable of repetition yet evading review.

Collateral Consequences. Collateral consequences may prevent a case from being moot, even though some of the original relief requested may be moot. A case is not moot as to the party defendant if another party paid the joint judgment rendered against them and then demanded a contribution from the other party. Then, the party "is still subject to a suit because of the original judgment as to its liability."

In *Powell v. McCormack* (1969), Congressman Powell's claim of improper exclusion from the House of Representatives was not mooted by his later seating, because there was a collateral consequence that a ruling would decide, the issue of his back pay remained.

Even though the primary dispute has settled through the passage of time, if there are collateral consequences to one of the parties—even if they are quite minor—the controversy is not moot.

Criminal Cases and Collateral Consequences. In criminal cases, the collateral consequences of a conviction serve to prevent mootness. Serving the sentence does not necessarily mean the case is moot. A criminal case is moot only if there is no possibility that any collateral consequences will be imposed because of the challenged conviction.

A corollary to this principle is that the state may seek Supreme Court review of a lower court reversal of a criminal defendant's conviction, even if the defendant has already served his sentence. The case is not moot. If the conviction is allowed to stand, the state could impose collateral legal consequences on the defendant.

Mootness and Class Actions. A class action will not become moot so long as a member of the class has an injury and a claim that is not moot. In *Sosna v. Iowa* (1975), decided the year after *DeFunis*, the Court explicitly held that, while there must be a live controversy at the time of Supreme Court review, the "controversy may exist, however, between a named defendant and a member of the class represented by the named plaintiff, even though the claim of the named plaintiff has become moot."

Similarly, if the lower court erroneously denies class action certification, the mootness of the named plaintiff's personal claim does not moot the controversy because class certification, if granted by the appellate court, may be treated as related back to the original erroneous denial. Thus, in a class action the mootness of the named plaintiff's personal claim does not render the controversy moot if the class is certified either before or after the individual's personal claim is mooted.

Feigned and Collusive cases. A federal court will not rule on a case if the parties have agreed to a statement of facts that is not in accordance with the actual facts concerning the issue they wish to place before the court. In other words, parties may deceive a court into ruling on an issue by entering into a feigned or collusive pact that misleads the court as to the facts. If the parties have a common interest in receiving a ruling and both favor the same type of ruling, there is no adversary proceeding and there is no case or controversy upon which an Article III federal court can rule. Thus, if both sides in a case agree that a law is constitutional or unconstitutional, a federal court should not take their case, because there is no real controversy between the parties.

To be distinguished from collusive suits are cases where there is a default judgment, or where the Solicitor General confesses error, or a state's attorney confesses error, or a party seeks naturalization and no one opposes the petition. In all of these cases there is a real, not a feigned, dispute. The Court does not have to accept the Solicitor General's confession. In all these instances, there is no collusion, and the results of the court action has real and direct consequences operating on the parties before the court.

(d) Ripeness, Prematurity, and Abstractness

Just as a case can be brought too late, and thereby be moot, it can be brought too early, and not yet be ripe for adjudication.

Ripeness is an important enough requirement that federal courts may consider it on their own motion and dismiss a case as not yet ripe, even if it is the Court's prudential self-restraint rather the Article III requirement of a case or controversy that is the reason to find lack of ripeness.

The purpose of the ripeness requirement is to avoid premature adjudication. Ripeness is designed to prevent the courts from entangling themselves in abstract disagreements over administrative policies that may never need to be decided. The ripeness rule also protects the agencies from judicial interference until an administrative decision has been formalized and its effects felt in a concrete way by the challenging parties.

While this general ripeness principle is not disputed, its application by the Supreme Court has resulted in a line of cases with seemingly inconsistent rulings. The longer versions of this text include descriptions of a wide variety of these rulings.

(e) Standing

(1) Taxpayer and Citizen Standing

No individual has a right to go into court to get a ruling concerning an interpretation of a statute or the resolution of a constitutional question unless that individual has an injury that he can redress by a claim against an adversary party. In the boxing match referee hypothetical that we used at the start of this section, we mentioned that referees can only answer questions from the boxers (the persons in the fight) and not from people who are in the audience. The concept of standing mirrors that simple fact about boxing matches. An individual may see a government official, or another person, violate the Constitution or a federal law. The individual who witnessed this event may be outraged and willing to spend great amounts of time and money to obtain a ruling that the government official, or the private person, has violated a federal law or the Constitution. However, the individual will not have his claim heard by an Article III court unless the allegedly aggrieved individual can show that he has suffered some injury from the complained about action that is different from the harm the action caused to all members of the public.

Standing is a personalization of the ripeness requirement. The Court will not rule on an issue unless the challenged action has created some harm or threat of imminent harm to some individual. In order to have standing, an individual must show that he or she has suffered some harm from the challenged action that is different from the harm to the public generally. Thus, the Court has ruled that individuals do not simply have standing as a citizen to challenge a government action that they believe is unconstitutional. It is for that reason that the person challenging the government action must demonstrate that the government act caused some harm to her or him that is different from the harm that it caused to the public generally.

Before raising the subject of taxpayer standing, we should note that taxpayer standing and citizen standing problems are intertwined. The very label of "taxpayer standing" has mislead many lawyers and students. Let us assume that Susan Smith has reported a taxable income of $100,000 to the Internal Revenue Service, following her computations of deductions from her gross income. Let us also assume that the Internal Revenue Service believes that Susan's taxable income is $200,000 and that she owes twice the amount of income tax that she had paid to the federal government for that year. Susan has standing to contest the Internal Revenue Service claim that she owes twice as much tax as she paid during the taxable year. The injury that the Internal Revenue Service will impose on her is unique to her; if she wins her claim the court will be able to redress her grievance by stopping the Internal Revenue Service from seizing her assets. Specific federal statutes may make it very difficult for Susan to actually have her claim litigated, when she disputes the computation done by the Internal Revenue Service. Nevertheless, there is no doubt that Susan would have standing, in the Article III case or controversy sense, to challenge the IRS's claim for her money. It must be remembered that a taxpayer, in defense of a prosecution by the government, will be able to allege that the government tax itself violates the provisions to the Constitution or an amendment to the Constitution. Thus, a taxpayer may claim that the tax is a penalty on a constitutionally protected activity or that the method for reporting amount of taxable income or property violates the self-incrimination clause of the Fifth Amendment.

Sometimes an individual who is not directly harmed by a statute wishes to challenge the statute on the basis that it violates the Constitution. The person would not have standing simply by being a citizen with a constitutional complaint against the government. Recognizing that fact, the aggrieved citizen claims that he has an injury because the government is misusing his tax money by enforcing an unconstitutional law or operating some type of government program that violates the Constitution. The person who claims taxpayer standing is asserting that he has a harm that is different than to the public generally, because some members of the public do not pay taxes. In other words, the taxpayer standing case is one in which a citizen is trying to use their taxpayer status to get around the principle that citizens do not generally have standing to challenge a government action that they believe is unconstitutional. It is to that subject of taxpayer standing that we now turn.

In *Frothingham v. Mellon* (1923), Mrs. Frothingham challenged the constitutionality of a federal Maternity Act, which provided appropriations to the states if they would comply with its provisions. The intent of the Act was to reduce maternal and infant mortality. Plaintiff alleged that she was a taxpayer and in that capacity she was therefore injured because "the effect of the appropriations complained of will be to increase the burden of future taxation and thereby take her property without due process of law."

The Court found this alleged injury unpersuasive. The Supreme Court, *Frothingham*, was concerned that granting standing to a federal taxpayer *qua* taxpayer would allow virtually anyone to challenge any federal act if its administration requires the outlay of money. And virtually every piece of federal legislation requires the outlay of money. If the statute is administered, the administrators must be paid. It even costs money to publish the statute.

A taxpayer, if successful on the merits in declaring an expenditure unconstitutional, would not have her taxation burden reduced, even minutely. Prohibiting an expenditure does not prohibit the taxation, for the two are not normally tied together. The federal government normally levies taxes without any limitation of purpose. An individual pays her income tax, for example, and the money collected becomes part of the government's general funds. These taxes are not earmarked for special expenditures, so prohibiting one particular expenditure, or many expenditures, does not affect the tax.

Earmarked Taxes. Taxpayers can challenge earmarked taxes in a variety of ways. A taxpayer may contest paying the earmarked tax because the purposes for which it is earmarked are alleged to be unconstitutional. In that case, if the expenditure is invalid, a court may enjoin collection of the special tax earmarked for an invalid expenditure. The Court may not agree with the merits of the litigant's claim, but the litigant has standing to raise that claim, even under *Frothingham*.

Flast v. Cohen and its Progeny. *Flast v. Cohen* (1968) undertook a fresh examination of the limitations on standing to sue in a federal court and the application of those limitations to taxpayer suits. In *Flast*, federal taxpayers challenged, under the establishment clause, the expenditure of federal funds under the Elementary and Secondary Education Act of 1965 to finance teaching of reading, arithmetic, and other subjects in, and purchase of textbooks for use in, religious schools.

Flast first held that the rule of *Frothingham* was based on judicial self-restraint. It was not required by the Constitution, for "we find no absolute bar in Article III to suits by federal taxpayers challenging allegedly unconstitutional federal taxing and spending programs." The Court, however, did not overrule *Frothingham.* Rather it established an important exception to its application:

> [I]n ruling on standing, it is both appropriate and necessary to look to the substantive issues ... to determine whether there is a *logical nexus* between the status asserted and the claim sought to be adjudicated....

The nexus demanded of federal taxpayers has two aspects to it. *First* the taxpayer must establish a logical link between that status and the type of legislative enactment attacked. Thus, a taxpayer will be a proper party to allege the unconstitutionality *only of exercises of congressional power under the taxing and spending clause* of Art. I, § 8, of the Constitution. It will not be sufficient to allege an incidental expenditure of tax funds in the administration of an essentially regulatory statute.... *Secondly*, the taxpayer must establish a nexus between that status and the precise nature of the constitutional infringement alleged. Under this requirement, the taxpayer must show that the challenged enactment *exceeds specific constitutional limitations imposed upon the exercise of the congressional taxing and spending power* and not simply that the enactment is generally beyond the powers delegated to Congress by Art. I, § 8. When both nexuses are established, the litigant will have shown a taxpayer's stake in the outcome of the controversy and will be a proper and appropriate party to invoke a federal court's jurisdiction.

The Court went on to explain that the *Flast* plaintiffs established both nexuses but Mrs. Frothingham had only met the first nexus. First, both the plaintiffs in *Flast* and in *Frothingham* complained of the exercise of the spending power under Article I, section 8. And, in both cases, the challenged program involved a substantial expenditure of funds, *not an incidental expenditure* of tax funds in the administration of an essentially regulatory statute.

However, only the *Flast* taxpayer fulfilled the second requirement, that there must be a nexus between the status as a taxpayer and the precise nature of the constitutional infringement alleged. The Court reached this conclusion after it examined the history behind the establishment clause of the First Amendment and concluded that one of the "specific evils feared" was that the taxing and spending power would be used to favor one religion over another. Thus, the challenged statute allegedly exceeded a specific constitutional limitation imposed on the taxing and spending power.

The basis of the challenge in *Flast*, unlike the *Frothingham* case, was not simply that the taxing and spending was generally beyond Congress' powers. The plaintiffs in *Frothingham* relied on the Tenth Amendment. Under the *Flast* analysis, the Tenth Amendment is not a specific limit on the taxing and spending powers.

The *Flast* majority found that the establishment clause was a specific limitation to Congress' taxing and spending power. It offered no examples of what other types of constitutional provisions are specific limitations that grant standing to any taxpayer under the second nexus of the *Flast* test. Neither have later cases.

As of 2004, the United States Supreme Court had never found that an individual's status as a taxpayer, in itself, gave the individual the right to challenge any government program other than by raising an establishment clause issue regarding certain types of subsidies to individuals or organizations. In The *Flast* standards appeared to be analytically neutral. Nevertheless, the Court's rulings appear to be totally result oriented, in that the Court will allow taxpayers, simply by being taxpayers, to challenge most, but not all, government programs under the establishment clause of the First Amendment; the Supreme Court has not allowed taxpayers to have standing, simply by being taxpayers, to raise other constitutional issues.

For example in *Schlesinger v. Reservists Committee to Stop the War* (1974), the Court held that plaintiffs had no standing, either as taxpayers or as citizens generally, to challenge the membership of Members of Congress in the military reserve as being in violation of Article 1, section 6, clause 2.

The narrowness with which the Court has interpreted *Flast* is well illustrated by *Valley Forge Christian College v. Americans United for Separation of Church and State, Inc.* (1982). The Secretary of Health, Education, and Welfare (now called the Secretary of Education) disposed of surplus federal property—in this instance, a 77 acre tract of real property—by giving it to the Valley Forge Christian College, which would use it to train "men and women for Christian service as either ministers or laymen." The Secretary acted pursuant to a federal regulation, which implemented and helped effectuate a federal statute, which in turn was authorized by Article IV, section 3, clause 2 of the Constitution, which vests in Congress the power to "dispose of" and make "all needful Rules" regarding federal property.

Justice Rehnquist for the Court held, surprisingly, that the plaintiffs had failed the first prong of the *Flast* test. First, they "do not challenge the constitutionality of the Federal Property Administrative Services Act itself, but rather a particular Executive branch action arguably authorized by the Act;" thus the "source of their complaint is not a congressional action, but a decision by HEW to transfer a parcel of federal property." Second, said Rehnquist, "and perhaps redundantly," the property transfer was not pursuant to the taxing and spending clause but rather the property clause of Article IV, section 3.

These arguments are unusual, because the source of the federal regulation was a federal statute. In addition, before the government could dispose of the property, it had to acquire and improve it, which required it to use it taxing and spending power.

The *Valley Forge* majority did not purport to overrule any prior cases, but the juxtaposition of that case with prior cases leads to surprising results. No one has standing to sue—that is, no one could be a plaintiff—to challenge the decision of the federal government to give a 77–acre plot of federal land to a Christian College with the self-described mission of training "leaders for church related ministries."

Yet the *Valley Forge* majority agreed that taxpayers would have standing to challenge federal financial aid to religious schools. The *Valley Forge* plaintiffs had no standing to sue because they were objecting to transfer of property pursuant to Article IV, section 3, cl. 2. Thus, Congress cannot give *money* to religious schools to aid their religious mission, but (because no one has standing), Congress can give away *property*.

Property can include personal property; it cannot be limited to real property; after all, Article IV refers to "Territory or other Property." The result then is that Congress cannot give money to religious schools to purchase educational tools, but it can buy the tools directly and give them to the religious schools. Congress cannot give money to religious schools to buy buildings, but Congress can give these schools the buildings themselves.

Perhaps the Chief Justice, in *Valley Forge*, was simply stating that *Flast* would be limited precisely to its facts.

(2) Personal Standing, Nontaxpayer Suits and the Requirement of Injury in Fact

In nontaxpayer actions, the determination of whether plaintiff has suffered something deemed to be an "injury" for purposes of the standing requirement has been the subject of much litigation and changing trends in the Supreme Court. For personal standing, the plaintiff must establish, at a minimum, a "personal stake" in the outcome. This stake requires a two-fold showing: first, a "distinct and palpable injury" to the plaintiff, and second, a " 'fairly traceable' causal connection" between the claimed injury and the conduct that plaintiff challenges. Plaintiff can meet the second prong of this requirement by showing that there is a "substantial likelihood" that the relief requested of the court will redress the claimed injury.

The Role of Congress in Creating Standing. In general if the plaintiff is protesting a claimed invasion of a generalized constitutional injury, the Court appears to be more reluctant to find standing—and thus create the need to dispose of a constitutional claim—than in cases where the plaintiff is arguably within the zone of interests protected by a federal statute, or a statute appears to grant standing in the case. In other words, if Congress speaks, either explicitly or implicitly, the Court will accept Congress' decision to confer standing to litigate constitutional or statutory claims.

When Congress has acted, the requirements of Article III remain: "the plaintiff still must allege a distinct and palpable injury to himself, even if it is an injury shared by a large class of other possible litigants." The injury-in-fact requirement is not satisfied by an "abstract, self-contained, noninstrumental 'right' to have the Executive observe the procedures required by law." If plaintiff has only a generally available grievance about government and seeks relief that provides him no more benefit than the public at large, there is no injury in fact. On the other hand, Congress can often create standing by conferring a cash bounty on the victorious plaintiff. That would assure that plaintiff's relief gives him or her tangible benefit not available to the public at large.

If Congress has not spoken, the plaintiff alleging a constitutional injury must not only overcome the Article III standing requirements but also the judiciary's use of standing as a tool of judicial self-restraint.

Standing and Nonconstitutional Cases. In *Association of Data Processing v. Camp* (1970) the Court, through Justice Douglas, held that the petitioners, who sold data processing services to businesses, had standing to challenge a ruling, by the Comptroller of the Currency, that allowed national banks to make data processing services available to other banks and bank customers. The petitioners claimed that this ruling was contrary to statutory prohibitions restricting the activities of national banks. Unlike *Flast*, the petitioners sued not as taxpayers but as competitors. To determine if these petitioners have standing, Douglas fashioned a two-part test.

First, the plaintiffs must allege that the challenged action has caused them "injury in fact, economic or otherwise." Petitioners met this first test because, as competitors with banks, the ruling by the Comptroller threatened them with loss of future profits. Second, a court must determine "whether the interest sought to be protected by the complainant is arguably within the zone of interests to be protected or regulated by the statute or constitutional guarantee in question."

The Zone of Interests Test. This zone of interests test is not supposed to be a trap for the unwary. Cases following *Association of Data Process* have treated the test as creating no particularly high burden; rather, the question is whether the entire statutory scheme (not merely the statute under which plaintiffs have sued) evidences an intent to *preclude* judicial review at the plaintiff's request.

This zone of "interests" is not limited to economic interests any more than the "injury in fact" requirement includes only economic injury. The requisite injury may be aesthetic, conservational and recreational, economic, or reflect First Amendment values of free exercise and establishment. One who is financially injured "may be a reliable private attorney general to litigate the issues of the public interest in the present case." Presumably one suffering a noneconomic loss will also be a reliable private attorney general.

A case that probably represents "an all-time high in Supreme Court liberality on the subject of standing," is *United States v. Students Challenging Regulatory Agency Procedures (SCRAP)* (1973). SCRAP was an unincorporated association representing five law students who sought to enhance the quality of the environment. SCRAP protested the failure of the Interstate Commerce Commission to suspend a 2.5% surcharge on nearly all freight rates. SCRAP claimed standing because each of its members suffered economic, recreational, and aesthetic harm caused by the adverse environmental impact of the freight structure. Each of SCRAP's members, it was alleged, had to pay more for finished products because of this freight structure. The SCRAP members alleged that the increased freight rates adversely affected their use of the forests, rivers, streams, and so on. Moreover, they alleged, this modified rate structure made the air that the SCRAP members breathed more polluted. And, SCRAP alleged, each of its members has been forced to pay increased taxes because of the sums that must be expended to dispose of otherwise reusable waste materials. The surcharge, SCRAP argued, was unlawful because the I.C.C. had failed to file a detailed environmental impact statement. SCRAP claimed that the 2.5% surcharge allegedly had an adverse impact on recycling and thus was a major federal action significantly affecting the environment.

The Court admitted that "all persons who utilize the scenic resources of the country, and indeed all who breath its air, could claim harm similar to that alleged by the environmental groups here." But, said the Court, "standing is not to be denied simply because many people suffer the same injury." The majority thus found standing: "We cannot say on these pleadings that the appellees could not prove their allegations which, if proved, would place them squarely among those persons injured in fact by the Commission's action, and entitled under the clear impact of *Sierra Club* to seek review." The Court specifically refused to limit standing to those "significantly" affected by agency action.

In *SCRAP* the majority was convinced that Congress wanted citizens to be able to enforce its regulation. For that reason, the Court reduced the injury requirement to the Article III minimum. However, Congress cannot give standing to persons who have no injury. That point was made in *Lujan v. Defenders of Wildlife* (1992), which ruled that in plaintiffs who objected to the Secretary of Interior's interpretation of the Endangered Species Act did not have standing to bring suit against the Secretary. The interpretation applied the Act only to actions that federal agencies take within the United States or on the high seas. The plaintiffs wanted the law to apply to actions that federal agencies fund in foreign nations. The Court rejected as "beyond all reason" plaintiffs' argument that anyone who sees Asian elephants in the Bronx Zoo can challenge a development project in Sri Lanka that a federal agency funds in part.

Standing and Constitutional Cases. While *SCRAP* shows that the Article III threshold of case or controversy is very low indeed, it does not follow that the Court will always allow standing to plaintiffs who satisfy this minimum threshold and who seek to litigate constitutional claims.

Elk Grove Unified School District v. Newdow (2004) ruled that the father of a child, who had divorced her mother and who was not the legal custodian of his daughter, did not have standing to challenge the use of the phrase "under God" in the Pledge of Allegiance recited in the public school his daughter attended. The child and her mother did not object to the Pledge. The father was in no better a position to sue the school district than any taxpayer.

The requirement that an individual be able to show an injury resulting from the governmental action in order to bring a constitutional challenge formed the basis for the Court's decision in *Allen v. Wright* (1984). The Court held that parents of minority race children attending public schools in districts undergoing desegregation did not have standing to require judicial review of the sufficiency of Internal Revenue Service standards that would deny tax exempt status to racially discriminatory private schools.

The diminution of the children's ability to receive an education in an integrated school was a "judicially cognizable injury," but standing was lacking because the injury was not "fairly traceable" to the challenged Internal Revenue Service conduct. The parents could not show that the IRS's allegedly illegal conduct caused their children's diminished ability to receive an education in a racially integrated school. The Court insisted that the parents must show that the Internal Revenue Service, by adopting stricter standards to withdraw tax exemptions from discriminatory schools, would make "an appreciable difference" in public school integration.

Related to these cases are those instances where plaintiffs allege that threatened governmental action will injure them in the near future. The Court is not entirely consistent when it finds that a threat is sufficient to confer standing and when it finds the threat insufficient.

O'Shea v. Littleton (1974) found no Article III standing by plaintiffs (residents of Cairo, Illinois) who had brought a civil rights action against the State's Attorney, his investigator, the Police Commissioner, the county magistrate and an associate judge. Plaintiffs alleged that defendants, under color of law, engaged in a continuing violation of constitutional rights in administering the criminal justice system by setting illegal bonds, imposing higher sentences on nonwhites, and requiring members of plaintiffs' class to pay for trial by jury. The majority found insufficient allegations of actual continuing injury.

Yet *Doe v. Bolton* (1973) held that physicians, whom pregnant women consulted, had standing to contest the constitutionality of the state's abortion law—

> despite the fact that the record does not disclose that any one of them has been prosecuted, or threatened with prosecution, for violation of the State's abortion statutes. The physician is one against whom these criminal statutes directly operate in the event he procures an abortion that does not meet the statutory exceptions and conditions. The physician-appellants, therefore, assert a sufficiently direct threat of personal detriment. They should not be required to await and undergo a criminal prosecution as the sole means of seeking relief.

What distinguishes *Doe* from *O'Shea* is not so much the reality of the threat—which was not dissimilar in all these cases—but the concreteness of the factual allegations, which were more precise in *Doe*. Also relevant is the nature of the relief sought, which required less judicial supervision and exertion of continual judicial power in *Doe* than in *O'Shea*.

(3) Third Party Standing

The general rules is that if the application of a statute to a litigant is constitutional, he will not be heard to attack the statute on the ground that impliedly it might also be taken as applying to other persons or other situations in which its application might be unconstitutional. The basis for this rule of self restraint lies in prudential concerns. The Court desires to avoid constitutional questions and to assure that the most effective and concerned advocate attacking the statute is before the Court. The Court is normally not interested in hearing how the statute, if creatively interpreted, could be applied in a way that makes that particular, and hypothetical, application unconstitutional. However, this basic rule has several important exceptions that give third-parties standing to assert the rights of others not before the Court. In general, the Court will allow litigants to assert the rights of third parties after weighing the importance of the relationship between the litigant and the third party, the ability of the third party to vindicate his or her own rights, and the risk that the rights of third parties will be diluted if third party standing is not allowed.

The Court may find that the sellers of products that the government banned have standing to raise the rights of potential buyers when they defend themselves from government lawsuits. In most cases, the seller and buyer will have an identity of interests. In many instances potential buyers would not be able to intervene in prosecutions of sellers or otherwise to protect the right of access to a product.

In cases concerning the right to purchase contraception, the Supreme Court allowed sellers of contraceptives to raise and assert the rights of the users of contraceptives when the government attempted to prosecute them for selling these products. The would-be purchasers of contraceptives would have difficulty in protecting their rights, because it would be difficult for them to intervene in a case where the government was prosecuting the seller of contraceptives. The seller and purchaser of contraceptives had such an identity of interest that the Court could have faith that the seller would adequately defend the constitutional claims of prospective purchasers.

In *Craig v. Boren* (1976), bar owners and bartenders were prosecuted for selling beer to men at the age of 18, even though they could have sold beer legally under the statute to women who were under the age of 18. The Court allowed the sellers of beer to raise the equal protection claims of young men between the ages of 18 and 21 and found that the classification allowing sales of beer to women at those ages, but not men, violated equal protection. Once again, the seller of the product and the potential purchasers had an identity of interest; it would have been difficult for the potential purchasers of beer who were young men between the ages of 18 and 21 to intervene in prosecutions of bar owners or otherwise protect their right to be free from sexual discrimination.

Of course, the seller of a product stands in no better stead than does the buyer of the product. Thus, persons who wish to sell obscene materials do not have a right to do so because while potential buyers may have a right to possess obscene materials in their home, they have no right to purchase the materials outside of their home or bring them to their home. The Supreme Court's obscenity rulings are examined in the Free Speech Chapter of this text.

Third Party Standing and the First Amendment. Before considering specific case applications of these exceptions, keep in mind that litigants also may challenge a statute as overbroad and violative of free speech. In overbreadth cases, the litigant challenges a statute on its face because, it is argued, the challenged statute is overbroad and appears to include activity that is constitutionally protected. The actual litigant before the Court in such cases is injured because the Court finds he or she has a right to be prosecuted only under a statute that is narrowly drawn.

(4) Standing by State Governments, Associations, and Congressmen

State Governments. A state may sue on behalf of its citizens as *parens patriae*, "to protect the general comfort, health, or property rights of its inhabitants threatened by the proposed or continued action of another State, by prayer for injunction...." But when a state joins the Union, it loses the power as a sovereign to present and enforce individual claims of its citizens as their trustee against a sister state. Individual citizens, of course, can enforce their own claims against a state.

The state may also sue individuals, business, or other states as *parens patriae* to protect its citizens. But a state cannot sue the federal government as representative of its citizens. In other words, a state may not be *parens patriae* as against the federal government.

If a state is suing because it has suffered loss as a state, then it is suing on its own behalf and not under a *parens patriae* theory. Thus *Wyoming v. Oklahoma* (1992) held that Wyoming had standing to challenge Oklahoma legislation that required all Oklahoma coal-fired electric generating plants (including privately owned ones) producing power for sale in Oklahoma to burn at least 10% Oklahoma-mined coal. That law resulted in less mining of Wyoming coal, thus reducing the severance taxes that Wyoming received. The state did not claim merely a loss in *general* tax revenues. It lost specific tax revenues that "fairly can be traced" to the Oklahoma law. The Court found standing and then invalidated the law under the dormant commerce clause.

States do not have standing to sue the federal government or a federal agency merely because the state alleges that federal action injured the state's economy, thereby causing a decline in general tax revenues. If that kind of general allegation were enough for standing, states could convert federal courts into a virtual "Council of Revision," reviewing any federal action that had economic consequences.

Associations. Associations of individuals have standing to invoke judicial protection of the association *qua* association.

Associations may also establish standing (even if they have no injury to themselves) as representative of the injury to their members, but the association must still allege the kind of injury that would satisfy the standing requirement had the individual members themselves brought suit. As long as the nature of the claim and of the relief sought does not make the individual participation of each injured party indispensable to proper resolution of the cause, the association may be an appropriate representative of its members, entitled to invoke the court's jurisdiction.

The standing of an association to sue on behalf of its members and assert their rights depends on the nature of the relief sought. It is easier for such an association to secure injunctive, declaratory, or some other form of prospective relief because then, if the remedy is granted, it will benefit those members of the association who are actually injured. This assurance does not exist if the remedy sought is money damages and if the association has not suffered damages *qua* association. If the damage claims are not common to the entire membership, nor shared by all in equal degree, an association does not have standing to sue for its members' damage claims. In these cases, any alleged injury will have been suffered by the individuals, and both the fact of injury and its degree require individualized proof.

Standing of Legislators. *Raines v. Byrd,* (1997) denied standing to members of Congress as such. Various member of Congress brought an action challenging the constitutionality of the Line Item Veto, which Congress had enacted in 1996. The law in question authorized "Any Member of Congress" or any person adversely affected to sue to invalidate the law as unconstitutional, with an expedited appeal direct to the Supreme Court. *Raines* held that the individual members of Congress who were the plaintiffs (and voted against the line item veto law) did not have a sufficient personal stake in the dispute and did not allege a sufficient concrete injury to establish the minimum standing required under Article III. The plaintiffs were not singled out for unfavorable or discriminatory treatment compared to other members of the House and Senate. While they claim that the line item veto law lessened congressional power, that is not a loss to which they are personally entitled (unlike a case where Congress refused to seat a Representative who was personally entitled to his seat).

In *Raines*, all the votes that plaintiffs had cast in Congress were counted and given effect. This case is not like *Coleman v. Miller* (1939). In *Coleman*, Kansas state legislators claimed that their votes (opposing ratification of the Child Labor Amendment to the U.S. Constitution) were nullified because the Kansas Lieutenant Governor broke a deadlock and voted, when he allegedly was not eligible to do so. *Coleman* only stands for the proposition that legislators whose votes would have been sufficient to defeat or enact a specific legislative action have standing to sue if that legislative action goes into effect (or is defeated) on the grounds that their votes were completely nullified. But the plaintiffs in *Raines* voted on the specific bill and their votes were counted and given full effect. The Line Item Veto Act passed notwithstanding their opposition. The institutional injury that plaintiffs alleged in *Raines* is not personal to the plaintiffs, is widely dispersed among all the legislators (unlike *Coleman*), and is wholly abstract.

§ 2.8 Adequate State Grounds and Federal Questions

As a general rule, when the Supreme Court reviews a decision of a state court, it only reviews the federal questions, not the state law questions. Hence, it is the general principle that the Court does not review state court judgments that rest on what are called *adequate and independent state grounds*.

A state court may rule that a state law is repugnant to the state constitution, and also find, as an independent, alternative holding, that the state law violates the U.S. Constitution. In this case, there is no federal question for the Supreme Court to review. If the Supreme Court agrees with the state court interpretation of the U.S. Constitution, then it will affirm the state decision. And if the Supreme Court disagrees with the state court interpretation of the U.S. Constitution, it will still affirm the decision, because the U.S. Supreme Court cannot reverse the state court as to a decision resting on an interpretation of the state constitution.

Similarly, there should be no federal review if the state court, though presented with a federal ground of decision, does not have to reach it, and chooses to base its decision only on the nonfederal ground. For example, in the above hypothetical, assume that the state court holds that the state law violates the state constitution. The state court could have reached the federal ground but chose not to do so. Again, the general rule is that there should be no U.S. Supreme Court review. The state court is the final arbiter of what its own state constitution means. If the U.S. Supreme Court reaches out and decides the federal ground, that would not change the result in the case, because—whether the U.S. Supreme Court holds that the state law violates, or does not violate, the U.S. Constitution—the state court already invalidated the state law on state constitutional grounds.

If the state court holds the state law valid under both state and federal constitutional provisions, then the Supreme Court may review. In that case, if it disagreed with the state court's view of the federal constitution (or of the federal statute or of the treaty), the state decision would be reversed, regardless of the interpretation of the state law.

If the state court in fact decided the case on a federal ground, there can be Supreme Court review even though the state court ruling might have been decided on an adequate nonfederal ground. For example, if a litigant claims that a state law violates the state and U.S. Constitution, the state court may hold that it violates the U.S. Constitution, and not bother to reach the state law ground. The U.S. Supreme Court can review, because, if it disagrees with the state court on the federal ground, the case will be reversed and remanded. The state court then will decide the state issue.

The Problem of Ambiguity. Sometimes the state ground of decision is unclear. For example, the state court may strike a statute but the state court opinion may be ambiguous as to its basis. The decision may cite federal cases, reflect federal reasoning, or otherwise indicate its reliance on federal law.

When it is unclear whether the state court has relied only on state grounds, *Michigan v. Long*, developed the following rule:

> [If] a state court decision fairly appears to rest primarily on federal law, or to be interwoven with the federal law, and when the adequacy and independence of any possible state law ground is not clear from the face of the opinion, we will accept as the most reasonable explanation that the state court decided the case the way it did because it believed that federal law required it to do so. If a state court chooses merely to rely on federal precedents as it would on the precedents of all other jurisdictions, then it need only make clear by a plain statement in its judgment or opinion that the federal cases are being used only for the purpose of guidance, and do not themselves compel the result that the court has reached.... If the state court decision indicates clearly and expressly that it is alternatively based on bona fide separate, adequate, and independent grounds, we, of course, will not undertake to review the decision.

A state court has the right to go further in creating constitutional rights (based on the *state* Constitution) than a federal court would have gone (based on the U.S. Constitution). If state courts are going to create and expand rights, they must take the responsibility for doing so and unambiguously decide the case on state law grounds. Otherwise, state courts could, in effect, blame the federal Constitution for imposing what are really phantom constitutional restrictions on state government. In order to unleash the states from these phantom federal restrictions, the Supreme Court takes review of cases where state courts have created constitutional rights purportedly (or ambiguously) relying on the U.S. Constitution.

§ 2.9 The Abstention Doctrine

Exercising federal jurisdiction can raise unnecessary constitutional problems when a plaintiff sues in federal court protesting state action and a decision as to the applicable interpretation of state law is relevant to the federal constitutional issue. Where state law is unclear, the federal court is faced with several unpleasant alternatives. The court can proceed and decide the state law question in such a way as to avoid the constitutional issue, but a state court may later disagree with the federal court's interpretation. Or, the federal court can apply the state law in such a way as to require a decision on constitutional grounds, but this alternative is not favored if there are nonconstitutional grounds for decision. Under either alternative, the federal rule as to the constitutionality of the state law is binding on state courts, but the state courts are still free to interpret the state law differently in a later case (except in the atypical case where the Supreme Court rules that no interpretation of the state law can save its unconstitutionality).

This situation has led to the creation of the "abstention doctrine". Cases relating to the abstention doctrine are examined in the longer versions of this text.

Related to the abstention doctrine and yet representing a distinct line of cases, is the question of when a federal court may grant a declaratory injunction or declaratory relief that relates to a threatened or pending state criminal prosecution. Such federal court intrusion into state proceedings is not favored because of what has been termed "Our Federalism." In the "Our Federalism" cases, the state authorities have begun, or are about to begin, state proceeding, and the state wants the whole case to be litigated in that proceeding.

These principles of "Our Federalism" apply to state civil proceedings if "the State is a party to the ... proceeding, and the proceeding is both in aid of and closely related to criminal statutes," as in a state civil action to abate the showing of an allegedly obscene movie as a nuisance, or a state contempt process. These principles also apply in federal suits seeking to enjoin executive branches of "an agency of state or local governments...." However, federal courts give no deference based on "Our Federalism" to a state administrative board if it is incompetent by reason of bias to adjudicate the issues before it.

§ 2.10 Political Questions

(a) Introduction

The political question doctrine states that certain matters are really political in nature and best resolved by the body politic rather than suitable for judicial review. In a sense, it is a misnomer. It should more properly be called the doctrine of nonjusticiability, that is, a holding that the subject matter is inappropriate for judicial consideration.

An important consequence of the political question doctrine is that it renders the government conduct immune from judicial review. Unlike other restrictions on judicial review—doctrines such as case or controversy requirements, standing, ripeness and prematurity—all of which may be cured by different factual circumstances, a holding of nonjusticiability is absolute in its foreclosure of judicial scrutiny.

(b) The Leading Cases

An early and leading case developing the political question doctrine was *Luther v. Borden*, an 1849 opinion by Chief Justice Taney. The case, in theory, was a simple action of trespass. Martin Luther sued Luther M. Borden and others, for breaking and entering plaintiff's house. The facts, however, made this case much more significant.

The defendants justified their actions on the grounds that they were agents of the state of Rhode Island and pursuant to military orders, broke into the house to search for and arrest plaintiff, who was engaging in insurrection against that state. The plaintiff retorted that this justification was invalid, because "before the acts complained of were committed, that government had been displaced and annulled by the people of Rhode Island, and that the plaintiff was engaged in supporting the lawful authority of the State, and the defendants themselves were in arms against it." Thus, out of a simple trespass action, the Supreme Court was called on to determine which group represented the legitimate government of Rhode Island.

Chief Justice Taney found that Article IV, section 4 of the United States Constitution, the guaranty clause presented a question that could not be answered by the judiciary. He ruled: that Congress and the President had the sole authority to enforce that clause; the question as to who represented the lawful government of Rhode Island was nonjusticiable; and the guaranty clause is nonjusticiable.

Baker v. Carr (1962) upheld the justiciability of legislative reapportionment. The case is considered in more detail below, in connection with other reapportionment decisions. Here it is important to outline the general theories and tests of political questions that *Baker* developed.

Baker reviewed in considerable detail the political question cases and concluded that it is the relationship between the judiciary and the coordinate branches of the Federal Government, and not the federal judiciary's relationship to the states, that gives rise to the "political question." To determine if, given that coordinate relationship, the doctrine should be invoked, the Court fashioned the following test:

> Prominent on the surface of any case held to involve a political question is found a textually demonstrable constitutional commitment of the issue to a coordinate political department; or a lack of judicially discoverable and manageable standards for resolving it; or the impossibility of deciding without an initial policy determination of a kind clearly for nonjudicial discretion; or the impossibility of a court's undertaking independent resolution without expressing lack of the respect due coordinate branches of government or an unusual need for unquestioning adherence to a political decision already made; or the potentiality of embarrassment from multifarious pronouncements by various departments on one question.

The Court found that the guaranty clause cases involve the elements of a political question and, thus, are nonjusticiable. But those reasons for nonjusticiability have "nothing to do with their touching on matters of state governmental organization." A reapportionment case is not foreclosed from judicial review if it is based on the equal protection clause rather than on the guaranty clause.

Another leading case clarifying the political question standard is *Powell v. McCormack* (1969). After Congressman Adam Clayton Powell was elected to Congress in November of 1966, the 90th Congress refused to seat him. Powell sued to be seated, to receive back pay, and for a declaratory judgment that his exclusion was unconstitutional.

Before reaching the issue of justiciability, Chief Justice Warren, for the majority, held that the case not to be moot nor precluded by the legislative immunity granted by the speech or debate clause. Then the Court found that Powell was "excluded" from the 90th Congress rather than "expelled".

This last point is complex, but crucial to understanding the case. Article I, section 5, clause 2 governs expulsions and provides that each House "with the Concurrence of two-thirds" may expel a member. The respondents argued that the House could expel a member for any reason whatsoever. The Court did not have to decide this argument, for it ruled that Powell would only be subject to expulsion if he had been allowed to take his seat and *then* required to surrender it. Powell, the Court ruled, was "excluded." That is, the House did not permit him to take his seat and his oath of office.

Only a majority of the House is required for exclusion. Although two-thirds voted against Powell, the Court did not find that it should judge the legality of his exclusion by the expulsion standard. The difference between calling the vote an exclusion rather than an expulsion was one of substance and not form for several reasons: (1) the House treated the vote as one of exclusion and not expulsion; (2) while the law is unclear, the historical evidence and the belief of the House members was that expulsion cannot be applied for actions taken during a prior Congress, which was Powell's case; and (3) some Congressmen expressed the view that they would have not voted to "expel" Powell though they did vote to "exclude" him.

Then, applying *Baker v. Carr*, the Court decided that, while the vote to expel Powell might not have been justiciable, the vote to exclude Powell was justiciable and was not a political question. Exclusion is governed by Art. I, § 5, cl. 1, which provides that each House is "the Judge of the Elections, Returns and Qualifications of its own Members. . . ." To determine if the Constitution provided a textual commitment to a coordinate branch of the federal government the Court said it had to interpret this clause. After examining the relevant historical materials the Court, in considering the House's power to discipline its members, ruled that the Constitution does not authorize the House "to *exclude* any person, duly elected by his constituents, who meets all the requirements for membership expressly prescribed in the Constitution." The power to exclude, governed by a majority vote, is narrower than the power to expel, governed by a two-thirds requirement. The Court concluded that the House was without power to discipline Powell by excluding him, because it was clear that he met the requirements of age, residence, and citizenship.

Because the petitions only sought declaratory relief it was unnecessary for the Court to express an opinion as to the appropriateness of coercive relief. The Court thought it was an "inadmissible suggestion" that the House might disregard the Court's ruling.

Another particularly significant political question case is *United States v. Nixon* (1974). The Supreme Court affirmed the District Court decision ordering *in camera* examination of certain material including certain taped conversations, that the Watergate Special Prosecutor subpoenaed from President Nixon. The unanimous opinion rejected the argument that a claim of executive privilege is a political question.

(c) A Few Decided Areas

(1) Foreign Affairs and the War Making Power

Baker explicitly rejected the dictum, found in some earlier cases, that anything touching foreign affairs is immune from judicial review. The fact that a matter relates to foreign policy or international affairs is certainly relevant, because of the need to avoid conflicting public postures or because of the nonjudicial discretion that lies with the executive or legislative branches. Thus a court will not usually decide if a treaty has been terminated, because on that issue, "governmental action ... must be regarded as of controlling importance," but if there has been no conclusive "governmental action" then a court can interpret the treaty and may find that it provides the answer.

In connection with the Vietnam War the lower courts generally ruled that the issue of its legality was nonjusticiable, but the Supreme Court either denied certiorari or summarily affirmed, over the objection of several Justices who wanted full oral argument. Given the sensitive problems of holding a war to be illegal, most issues relating to the constitutionality of a war may well be nonjusticiable. The effect of such a holding would be that, while only Congress can declare war, the President can make war, and Congress can authorize an undeclared war. That is, the decision whether or not war should formally be declared may be a political question.

(2) Amendments to the Constitution

The leading case in this area is *Coleman v. Miller* (1939), where plaintiffs included members of the Kansas Senate whose votes against ratification of a Constitutional Amendment had been overridden. They sued in state court to compel the Secretary of State to erase an endorsement on a resolution ratifying the proposed Child Labor Amendment and indicate instead that it "was not passed." They also asked the court to restrain the officers of the Senate and House from signing the resolution and the Kansas Secretary of State from authenticating it and delivering it to the Governor. The petitioners had three claims: (1) that the Lieutenant Governor could not cast the deciding vote in the Senate because he was not part of the "Legislature" within the meaning of Article V of the U.S. Constitution; (2) that Kansas could not ratify the Amendment because it had previously rejected it; and (3) that the Amendment could not be ratified because it was no longer viable, not having been ratified within a reasonable time.

Chief Justice Hughes' opinion for the Court held that the complaining senators had standing, with Justices Frankfurter, Roberts, Black, and Douglas dissenting on this point. The Court was equally divided on the issue of whether the Lieutenant Governor could cast the deciding vote on ratification, with the same four Justices arguing that this issue was nonjusticiable.

Petitioners also argued that either a ratification or rejection of a proposed Amendment cannot later be changed. The Court held that the "question of the efficacy of ratifications by state legislatures, in the light of previous rejection or attempted withdrawal, should be regarded as a political question pertaining to the political departments, with the ultimate authority in the Congress in the exercise of its control over the promulgation of the adoption of the Amendment." Congress, the Court said, could have enacted a statute relating to ratification after rejections (and rejections after ratification) but had not done so then.

Finally the petitioners argued that the proposed Amendment was no longer viable, and could not be ratified because of the length of time—thirteen years—between its proposal and the Kansas ratification. Previously the Supreme Court had held that Congress may fix a reasonable time for ratification. But Congress had not— and still has not—enacted any general statutory provisions governing the length of time. In the past, various proposed Amendments provided that they must be ratified within seven years. But the proposed Child Labor Amendment did not include a time limit. At the time of *Coleman*, the average time to ratify an Amendment, excluding the first ten, had been three years, six months, and 25 days.

The Court acknowledged that, to the extent that economic, political, and social conditions relate to a proposed Amendment, make it nonviable, those factors change. Weighing those factors to determine viability was inappropriate for the judiciary. Thus, it concluded that the issue of a reasonable time "lies within congressional province." And that question should be "regarded as an open one for the consideration of the Congress when, in the presence of certified ratifications by three-fourths of the States, the time arrives for the promulgation of the adoption of the Amendment. Th[at] decision by the Congress ... of the question whether the Amendment had been adopted within a reasonable time would not be subject to review by the courts."

Justice Butler dissented and would have held that more than a reasonable time had elapsed.

The separate opinion of Justice Black joined by Frankfurter, Roberts, and Douglas stated: "Congress, possessing exclusive power over the amending process, cannot be bound by and is under no duty to accept the pronouncements upon that exclusive power by this Court or by the Kansas courts. Neither state nor federal courts can review that power."

The Court is not entirely excluded from the Amendment process. The Court has upheld the power of Congress to fix a reasonable time for ratification and it has determined, where statutes required, when an Amendment has gone into effect. But if statutes do not provide for a judicial role and if the power of Congress to enact such statutes is not the matter in dispute, it may be the rule that all Amendment questions relating to the constitutionality of acts of Congress affecting the Amendment procedure should be regarded as political.

(3) Impeachment

The Supreme Court, in *Nixon v. United States* (1993), considered the impeachment and removal from office of Judge Walter L. Nixon, the former Chief Judge of the District Court for the Southern District of Mississippi. He argued that the vote of the full Senate removing him from office (after he had been impeached by the House of Representatives) was unconstitutional, because the Senate used a *committee of Senators* to hear evidence against him and to report that evidence to the full Senate. Senate Rule XI authorized this use of an impeachment committee. Chief Justice Rehnquist, for the Court, held that Nixon's claim was not justiciable.

A federal jury convicted Nixon of two counts of making false statements before a federal grand jury, which was investigating reports that Nixon had accepted a gratuity from a local Mississippi businessman in exchange for asking a local district attorney to halt the prosecution of the businessman's son. The Court of Appeals affirmed the conviction, but Nixon refused to resign, so that he continued to collect his salary while serving his prison term. He, in fact, collected his salary until the Senate voted to remove him from office.

The full trial did not occur on the Senate floor. Instead, the Senate's Rule XI Committee held four days of hearings and heard 10 witnesses, including Judge Nixon. This Committee presented the full Senate with a transcript of the proceeding, a report of the uncontested facts, and a report summarizing the evidence of the contested facts. Nixon was permitted to address the full Senate, which he did. Several Senators asked him questions and he responded. Any Senator could have attended the Rule XI hearing, or could watch videotapes of it. After the Senate voted to impeach by more than the necessary two-thirds majority, he sued for a declaratory judgment that his impeachment was void on the grounds that using the Rule XI Committee violated the Constitutional command of Article I, § 3, clause 6 that the Senate "try" all impeachments.

The Supreme Court held that this claim was nonjusticiable. The Court examined the history, policy, and the language of the Constitution, the difficulty of fashioning relief, and the delay caused by judicial intervention. It Court concluded that the framers intended that the judiciary, and the Supreme Court in particular, should have no role in impeachments.

(4) Political Gerrymandering

Nearly a quarter of a century after *Baker v. Carr* upheld the justiciability of lawsuits attacking malapportioned legislative districts, the Court in *Davis v. Bandemer* (six to three) held that political gerrymandering cases are also justiciable under the equal protection clause. But the Court had no majority opinion on any other issue.

Even if *Bandemer* is never overruled, it seems unlikely that anyone will be able to prove the existence of unconstitutional political gerrymandering. In *Vieth v. Jubelirer* (2004) the Court, without a majority opinion, affirmed a district court ruling that considered political gerrymandering to be a justiciable question, but that rejected a claim of unconstitutional political gerrymandering. Four justices, in plurality opinion written by Justice Scalia, found that all political gerrymandering claims should be deemed nonjusticiable political questions. Justice Kennedy joined only in the ruling affirming the district court's rejection of the claim of unconstitutional gerrymandering in this case; he refused to join any portion of the plurality opinion. Nevertheless, Kennedy indicated that it would be extremely difficult for the the Court, in the future, to find that a legislative districting map involved unconstitutional political gerrymandering. The four dissenting Justices in *Vieth* would have ruled that gerrymandering was not a political question and that the district court should reconsider the plaintiff's claim in this case.

(5) Apportionment of Congressional Districts Among the States

The Constitution provides that each state shall have at least one representative and that the number of representatives shall not exceed one for every 30,000 persons. In addition, implicit in the Constitution, and the continuous historical practice is the requirement that congressional districts not cross state lines. So, apportionment of districts often results in *fractional remainders:* the fractional portion of the number that results when the state's total population is divided by the population of the ideal district must either be ignored or rounded to one whole Representative, because states are only represented by a whole number of legislators.

Over the years, Congress has tried various plans to deal with this problem. In 1941, Congress enacted a law that used the "equal portions" method. Montana objected because the use of this method, after the 1990 census, resulted in reducing its House delegation from two representatives to one. A unanimous Court held that Montana's claim were justiciable. Montana's victory was short-lived, however, because the Court then turned to the merits, rejected Montana's claim, and held that Congress had broad discretion to enact the "equal portions" method.

In *Department of Commerce v. United States House of Representatives* (1999), various U.S. residents sued federal agencies and officials objecting to their planned use of a statistical sampling during the next decennial census. Proponents of "sampling" (as opposed to an actual "counting" of people) claimed that it would address a problem of undercounting some groups of individuals. O'Connor, for a fragmented Court, held that several state residents had Article III standing because they showed that the use of statistical sampling would result in a loss of U.S. representatives from their state. In addition, there was intrastate vote dilution because states use the population numbers generated by the federal decennial census for redistricting state legislative districts. This vote dilution is injury in fact. Moreover, this injury is "fairly traceable" to the use of statistical sampling, and the requested relief—a permanent injunction against such sampling—will redress the alleged injury. The Court went on to hold that the Census Act prohibited the use of statistical sampling, either as a supplement or substitute to the traditional enumeration method for calculating the population for apportionment purposes.

(6) The Origination Clause

The Origination Clause requires that all bills for raising revenue "shall originate" in the House of Representatives. In *United States v. Munoz–Flores* (1990), defendants claimed that a federal law that required courts to impose a monetary "special assessment" on a person convicted of a federal misdemeanor was unconstitutional because the law raised revenue, but it did not originate in the House. In this case the defendants claimed that the Senate was the first chamber to pass the assessment.

The Court held that the case was justiciable because none of the characteristics of *Baker v. Carr* applied. The Origination Clause is not a textually demonstrable commitment of the issue to Congress. A holding that the assessment statute violated the clause entails no more disrespect for Congress than the invalidation of any other law that Congress enacts. The Court, in short, should be able to engage in the prosaic judgment of creating judicially manageable standards to determine where a bill "originates" or if it is for "raising revenue." On the merits, the Court ruled against the defendants.

Chapter 3

SOURCES OF NATIONAL AUTHORITY

Table of Sections

----

§ 3.1 Introduction

In order to determine whether any action of the federal government complies with the U.S. Constitution, a court must ascertain if the federal action meets two criteria. First, because the federal government is one of enumerated rather than inherent powers, the court must decide if the action is pursuant to one of the powers that the Constitution grants to the federal government. The central government can act only to effectuate the powers granted to it (expressly, or by implication) rather than acting for the general welfare of the populace. Second, the court must determine whether the action violates some specific check on federal power, such as those contained in the Bill of Rights. These specific constitutional limitations restrict the federal government even if it is acting pursuant to one of its enumerated powers.

This two step method of review should be contrasted with the way that federal courts review state laws. Because *state* constitutions, not the U.S. Constitution, are the source of state powers, it is not for federal courts to determine whether state acts are authorized by *state* law. Federal courts test only whether a state act violates some specific check on state power contained in the U.S. Constitution or the Amendments to the U.S. Constitution. For the purposes of federal law, state governments (or their instrumentalities) are not creatures of limited powers. They have a general "police power"—the power to protect the health, safety, welfare or morals of persons within their jurisdiction.

§ 3.2   *McCulloch v. Maryland* and the Basis of Federal Power

In *McCulloch v. Maryland* (1819) the Supreme Court interpreted the necessary and proper clause as the Justices considered the ability of the federal government to charter the second Bank of the United States.

Following the War of 1812, the states seemed incapable of dealing with the problems of a disrupted economy. Despite his Antifederalist heritage, President Madison approved the establishment of the second Bank of the United States in 1816. Unfortunately, the Bank did not provide an answer to many of the economic ills. A very serious economic depression took place and people blamed the Bank's monetary practices for aggravating the situation. Also, it appeared that many of the branches were engaged in corrupt practices. Many of the states responded with attempts to limit the powers of the branches of the Bank located within their boundaries. It was a state action of this type that gave rise to *McCulloch*.

Maryland enacted a tax on the issuance of bank notes that was, in effect, a discriminatory tax on the national bank. The law required any bank that was not chartered by the state to pay a $15,000 per year state tax, or use certain "stamped" paper for its notes, which resulted in a 2% tax on those notes. Branches of the Bank of the United States continued to operate and issue bank notes in Maryland, but refused to comply with the statute. The state then brought an action for taxes and penalties against the cashier of the Bank, McCulloch. The Supreme Court, speaking through Chief Justice Marshall, held the tax invalid.

In order to determine the validity of the Maryland tax, the Court had to determine the constitutionality of the national bank legislation. If Congress could not establish such a bank, the Maryland statute did not interfere with any legitimate federal authority. Maryland argued that the states did not surrender to the national government their ability to regulate banks because the Constitution gave the federal government only a limited amount of power; the states retained important sovereignty rights. Marshall and the Court rejected this "states' rights" argument and, in so doing, established the basis for federal supremacy.

Chief Justice Marshall, in *McCulloch v. Maryland,* dealt with three distinct aspects of federal power. First, he established the principle that the federal government draws its authority directly from the people. Second, he interpreted the Article necessary and proper clause to allow Congress a wide scope of authority to implement the enumerated powers. Third, he concluded that state legislation (including state taxation) that might interfere with the exercise of these federal powers is invalid.

Marshall began by examining the general basis of authority for the federal government and the Constitution. The states had claimed that the Constitution emanated from their independent sovereignties and that the exercise of the federal power could not predominate over the states' claims to power. Marshall rejected this theory by stating that the federal government emanates directly from the people and not from the states. Marshall implied the existence of wide ranging powers for the federal government in general, and the judiciary in particular, when he stated that "we must never forget that it is a *constitution* we are expounding."

The second major part of the *McCulloch* opinion deals with the breadth of the powers that the federal government can exercise. Flexibility being essential, Marshall defined the broad standards within which federal laws must fall. He interpreted the grant of powers to Congress as allowing for the full effectuation of national goals. The necessary and proper clause, when combined with the specific grants of powers, evidenced the granting of broad powers to Congress.

Marshall adopted what has become the classic test for the existence of federal power:

Let the end be legitimate, let it be within the scope of the constitution, and all means which are appropriate, which are plainly adapted to that end, which are not prohibited, but consist with the letter and spirit of the constitution, are constitutional.

Under this test, federal laws are valid so long as they bear a reasonable relationship to an enumerated power of the government. Hence, Congress can create the second Bank of the United States because there is a reasonable connection between it and the enumerated Congressional powers to 'lay and collect taxes; to borrow money; to regulate commerce; to declare and conduct a war; and to raise and support armies and navies.'

Marshall derived implied federal powers from the principle that every legislature must have the appropriate means to carry out its powers. Because the framers intended the nation to endure, the federal government had to have the normal discretionary powers of a sovereign so that Congress could choose how to best effectuate national goals.

Marshall also relied on the structure of the Constitution. The necessary and proper clause followed the enumerated powers: the framers of the Constitution thus treated the necessary and proper clause as an additional power, another enumerated power. The placement of the clause indicated that the necessary and proper clause, rather than a limitation on the enumerated powers, was an express recognition of the need to provide additional law-making powers for the execution the other enumerated powers.

Marshall explained that the language of the necessary and power clause does not require Congress to use only means that were "absolutely" necessary to pursue an enumerated federal power. It would be illogical to establish a nation with only very restricted powers. *McCulloch* ruled that the necessary and proper clause authorizes the federal government to select any reasonable means to effectuate the exercise of the enumerated powers.

Whether a law met the test of reasonableness is a question of degree that Marshall said Congress was better suited than the judiciary to answer. Thus, the Court would not void the law unless it were clear that it was designed for "the accomplishment of objects not intrusted to the government."

In the third major portion of the opinion, Marshall held that the Maryland tax had to be stricken because it interfered with the exercise of a valid federal action. In all cases of conflict between federal and state laws, the Constitution established the supremacy of federal law. States cannot possess incompatible powers that might be hostile to the federal actions.

§ 3.3 Sources of Federal Power—Overview

The *McCulloch* analysis applies to the judicial examination of the scope of any congressional power. The necessary and proper clause of Article I, by its own terms, relates to every source of congressional power regardless of whether the power is listed in Article I. The judiciary should be engaging in the same form of analysis, and with the same degree of deference to Congress, when it interprets the necessary and proper scope of Congressional authority to implement any federal power.

The great bulk of the constitutional cases dealing with Congress' power to enact laws focus on only a few clauses in the Constitution, particularly the commerce clause and section 5 of the Fourteenth Amendment. For that reason, this concise hornbook examines only those sources of federal power. Our hornbook, and our multi-volume Treatise have expanded treatment of the topics covered here as well as other topics such as, the admiralty power (both the ability of Congress to create substantive rules of admiralty and to create federal court jurisdiction regarding admiralty cases); the admission of states to the Union (including the "equal footing" doctrine regarding the equality of the states); the bankruptcy power; the federal power over copyrights and patents; the power to control the currency; federal "common law"; litigation between the states; the postal power; and the property power (including the Article I property power, the status of the District of Columbia, and the Article IV property power).

§ 3.4   The Separation of Powers Principle

The phrase "separation of powers" does not appear in the Constitution. The fact that the powers of the legislative executive and judicial branches of the federal government are set out in separate articles of the Constitution gives rise to the expectation that there must be some limit on the powers of each branch. The structure of the Constitution is the basis for a judicially implied separation of powers principle that prevents any one, or two, of the branches of the federal government from impairing the ability of another branch of government to perform its constitutionally assigned duties. While the Constitution created separate executive, legislative, and judicial departments, it established no air tight compartmentalization of the branches. Instead, the drafters of the Constitution sought to establish a system of checks and balances to ensure the political independence of each branch and to prevent the accumulation of power in a single department.

Because there is no clear rule or test that governs decisions relating to separation of powers, this text will not analyze "separation of powers cases" as a unit. Instead we have placed the cases that might arguably fall into such a category in the sections concerning the central issue in each of those cases. Thus, the sections dealing with such issues as political questions, congressional vetoes, presidential powers, and executive privilege all refer to the separation of powers principle.

§ 3.5   Term Limits on Federal Legislators

Term limits on executive branch officials are quite common on the state level. On the federal level, the U.S. Constitution, since 1951, has limited the President to two terms of office. In the early 1990s, voters throughout the United States voted on proposals to extend these term limits to a broader assortment of officials. Term limit proponents in some states were successful in passing referenda that limited state officials, both legislative and executive, and federal legislators (both Senate and House members).

The Supreme Court rejected the constitutionality of term limits on federal legislators in *U.S. Term Limits, Inc. v. Thornton* (1995). The Court held (5 to 4) that it is unconstitutional for states to impose term limits on federal legislators. Justice Stevens spoke for the majority (which included Kennedy, Souter, Ginsburg, and Breyer) and Justice Thomas spoke for the dissent (which included Rehnquist, O'Connor, and Scalia).

Justice Stevens examined the history behind the qualifications clauses and broadly held that there can be no additional qualifications added to those already provided for in Article I, dealing with age, citizenship, and residency. The framers intended, said Stevens, for the Constitution to be the exclusive source of qualifications of Members of Congress, and intended to divest the states of any power to impose additional qualifications.

After *Thornton*, supporters of term limits unsuccessfully lobbied for a constitutional amendment while also seeking to secure pledges by candidates that they will vote for and/or abide by term limits. The Supreme Court dealt with one manifestation of this reaction in *Cook v. Gralike* (2001). In that case, Missouri voters adopted an amendment to their State Constitution designed to bring about a "Congressional Term Limits Amendment" to the U.S. Constitution. Among other things, Article VIII "instruct[s]" Missouri's Members of Congress to use all their powers to pass the federal amendment; prescribes that "DISREGARDED VOTERS' INSTRUCTION ON TERM LIMITS" be printed on ballots by the names of Members failing to take certain legislative acts in support of the proposed amendment; provides that "DECLINED TO PLEDGE TO SUPPORT TERM LIMITS" be printed by the names of nonincumbent candidates refusing to take a "Term Limit" pledge to perform those acts if elected; and directs the Missouri Secretary of State to determine and declare whether either statement should be printed by candidates' names. A nonincumbent House candidate sued to enjoin petitioner from implementing Article VIII on the ground it violated the Federal Constitution.

Stevens, J., for the Court, held that the state constitutional amendment was unconstitutional because it was not a permissible exercise of the state's power to procedurally regulate the time, place, and manner of holding state elections for federal offices.

Chapter 4

THE FEDERAL COMMERCE POWER

Table of Sections

§ 4.1 Introduction: The Commerce Clause—Its Origins and Development

Article I, Section 8 of the Constitution provides in part that Congress shall have the power "To regulate Commerce with foreign Nations, and among the several States, and with the Indian Tribes." The brevity of this clause belies the fact that its interpretation has played a significant role in shaping the concepts of federalism and the permissible uses of national power throughout our history.

This chapter first places in historical perspective the Court's interpretations of the commerce power. The early cases defining the commerce power demonstrate both the justices' historical and theoretical uncertainty in defining the scope of powers for the new national government. Next, we will examine the Court's attempt (from the 1880s to 1937) to restrict the commerce power, primarily to protect the role of the states in the federal system rather than to hold the federal government to an original limited grant of power.

The concluding sections of this chapter, examine how the Supreme Court has developed what we will term modern commerce clause standards. In those sections we will find that the Supreme Court has made a distinction between the scope of Congress's power to control private sector activities and the scope of Congress's power to regulate state and local governments.

Commerce With Foreign Nations. The Court has always recognized a plenary power in Congress to deal with matters touching upon foreign relations or foreign trade.

The history of the commerce clause and the shaping of the Constitution itself also endorse the finding of a broad Federal power in this area. As noted in the next section, one of the prime areas of commercial problems meant to be solved by the Constitution was the imposition of restrictions on imports and exports by the states. The Constitution specifically prohibits state government from imposing such duties without the consent of the national government. The Article I section 10 listing of activities that are prohibited to the states primarily focuses upon matters touching upon foreign trade or relations with foreign countries. Thus it can be safely asserted that there was no constitutional recognition of any "reserved powers" of the states to act in these areas.

The primary concern over congressional power in the international area came from the Southern states who feared that a broad power might be used to restrict the importation of slaves following the ratification of the Constitution. This possible use of Federal power was restricted by Article I Section 9, which prohibited Congress from banning the importation of slaves until 1808.

There were similar fears that certain states might be favored in matters of foreign trade. Thus Section 9 of Article I insures that Congress will not tax exports or give preference to certain ports in matters of foreign trade.

§ 4.2 Judicial Interpretations of the Commerce Power Prior to 1888

In *Gibbons v. Ogden* (1824) Chief Justice Marshall examined the scope of both federal and state powers under the commerce clause. The opinion today ranks as one of the most important in history. In it Marshall laid the basis for later Justices to uphold a federal power to deal with national economic and social problems. But before that time would come, the Court would go through periods disregarding the basis of Marshall's ruling.

Gibbons concerned the granting of a steamboat monopoly to a private company. New York had granted the exclusive right to engage in steamboat navigation in the waters of New York to a partnership that had transferred the monopoly to Ogden. Gibbons began a competing service between New York and New Jersey. When Ogden sued Gibbons for encroachment on the monopoly, he defended by asserting that the state granted monopoly violated the commerce clause.

Instead of giving a definitive ruling on the scope of state powers under that clause, the Court found the monopoly invalid because it conflicted with a valid federal statute. Marshall's opinion held that the federal statute governing the licensing of ships granted those ships the right to engage in coastal trade and that the federal statute governed the issue because it was the supreme law of the land. Because the state law conflicted with a valid federal law, the state law violated the supremacy clause of Article VI.

In the course of the opinion, Marshall gave a broad reading to the powers of Congress under the commerce clause. Marshall defined commerce as "intercourse" and recognized that it extended into each state. Congress had the power to regulate "that commerce which concerns more states than one." The federal power extended to commerce wherever it was present, and thus, "the power of Congress may be exercised within a state."

The commerce power, in Marshall's opinion, was not to be restricted by the judiciary. His opinion for the majority of the Court found that the commerce power, "like all others vested in Congress, is complete in itself, may be exercised to its utmost extent, and acknowledges no limitations other than are prescribed in the Constitution."

Marshall did state that some "internal" commerce of a state would be beyond the power of Congress to regulate. According to Marshall's opinion for the Court, the only commercial activities that were immune from federal power, and reserved for state or local regulation, were those "which are completely within a State, which do not affect other States, and with which it is not necessary to interfere, for the purpose of executing some of the general powers of the government." Marshall thus described the "internal commerce of a state" as beyond the reach of federal power but simultaneously created a standard under which few commercial activities could be found to meet the definition of internal commerce.

Cooley v. Board of Wardens (1851) established the concept of "selective exclusiveness" whereby commercial subjects requiring uniform national regulation could be regulated only by Congress, while subjects of local concern might be regulated to some extent by the states. The opinion did not attempt to define the scope of federal power, but its division between "national" and "local" subjects would one day be used by Justices who sought to restrict federal power.

In the late nineteenth century, the Supreme Court began to assert its authority to control the actions of the other branches of the federal government.

§ 4.3   1888 to 1933

Two early cases from Iowa concerning the manufacture and sale of alcoholic beverages strengthened the distinction between intrastate activities and interstate commerce, although neither decision concerned the scope of federal power. In *Kidd v. Pearson* (1888) the Supreme Court upheld an Iowa statute prohibiting the manufacture of intoxicating beverages within the state. The basis for this ruling was the Court's view that this activity could be regulated by the state because it was "manufacturing" and not "commerce." Thus, in *Leisy v. Hardin* (1890) the Supreme Court held that an Iowa ban on the importation of intoxicating beverages violated the commerce clause because it regulated an item of commerce before it became part of the general property within the state.

These cases might still have led to a recognition of wide federal powers. Congress disagreed with the effect of the *Leisy* decision. A federal statute was enacted the same year that subjected liquors transported in interstate commerce to the laws of the state into which they were shipped. In *Wilkerson v. Raher* (1891) the Supreme Court upheld this statute against the claim that it delegated federal powers to the states. The opinion recognized that Congress had simply enacted a national commerce law with a rule of localized control. The statute did not allow any state to control another state's laws.

In *United States v. E. C. Knight Co.* (1895) the majority held that the Sherman Antitrust Act could not be applied to a monopoly acquisition of sugar refineries. The majority found that regulation of "manufacture" was reserved to the states by the Tenth Amendment and, hence, beyond the commerce power. Nor could use of the statute be justified in this case under the theory that the monopoly might adversely affect interstate commerce because this market effect was only "indirect." The act was not struck but it was interpreted to exclude application to such manufacturing enterprises in order to avoid constitutional infirmities.

The Supreme Court quickly eased its most restrictive interpretations of the antitrust acts. The Court held that the acts could be applied to agreements to fix prices by iron pipe manufacturing companies and that joint control of competing parallel railways could be broken up. The majority agreed that these practices had a sufficient connection to commerce. It should be noted that Justice Holmes dissented in the later case because he did not see how the

Court could stop short of allowing Congress to regulate every individual activity under these theories.

In the first few years of the twentieth century, the Court sustained the exercise of federal regulation or prohibition of items under the commerce and taxing powers. In *"The Lottery Case" (Champion v. Ames),* (1903) the Court upheld the Federal Lottery Act, which prohibited the interstate shipment of lottery tickets. The majority opinion, by the elder Justice Harlan, held that Congress had the power to prohibit as well as regulate interstate movement or transportation. But it was clear that the majority agreed that lottery tickets were an "evil." The Justices did not hold that Congress could exercise its regulatory power with a totally free hand.

In 1905 Holmes created the "current" (or "stream" or "flow") of commerce metaphor. He wrote the opinion for a unanimous Court in *Swift & Co. v. United States* upholding the application of the Sherman Act to an agreement of meat dealers concerning their bidding practices at the stockyards that would fix the price of meat. Although the stockyard activity took place within a single state, it was but a temporary stop in the interstate sale of cattle. It was, in Holmes' words, only an interruption in "a current of commerce among the States, and the purchase of the cattle is a part and incident of such commerce."

After 1911, the Court sustained almost all congressional actions that regulated the nature of items that could be shipped in interstate commerce. The Court upheld prohibition of impure or adulterated food and drugs as well as retail labeling requirements for items that traveled through interstate commerce. The Court reversed an earlier decision and held that Congress could restrict the sale of intoxicating beverages to Indians. Additionally, the Court upheld the Mann Act, which prohibited the transportation of women across state lines for immoral purposes. In 1918, however, the Court would restrict federal labor regulation.

In *Hammer v. Dagenhart (The Child Labor Case)* (1918) the Court, by a five to four vote, invalidated a federal statute that prohibited the interstate shipment of goods coming from a mining or manufacturing establishment that employed children under certain ages. The majority found the act to exceed the commerce power because it regulated the conditions of production. This subject matter was reserved for state regulation by the Tenth Amendment.

The government justified the law as necessary to eliminate unfair competition against products from states that prohibited child labor. The majority of the Supreme Court found that Congress had no power to equalize market conditions that were not a part of interstate commerce. The majority attempted to distinguish the earlier cases that allowed Congress to prohibit or set the terms of interstate transportation of products. The majority opinion stated that the earlier prohibitions had all related to the elimination of a harmful item or commercial evil, but in the majority's view, there was nothing harmful about products made by children.

Writing for the dissenters in *The Child Labor Case*, Holmes expounded an embargo theory of congressional power over the interstate transportation of people or products. Holmes stated that the child labor regulation was clearly the regulation of commerce among the states and that the Court was wrong to invalidate it because of its effect or economic basis. He would not interpret the power of Congress in terms of its effect on the states. Thus, Congress could set any terms for the transport of items between the states.

In evaluating Holmes' theory, one must remember that he was not addressing a situation where the congressional prohibition of transport infringed a more specific guarantee of the Bill of Rights, such as the First Amendment. There is no indication that Holmes would have exempted the commerce power from more specific constitutional restraints. Rather, Holmes simply did not recognize the Tenth Amendment as a general limitation on the exercise of congressional control of commerce.

Congress sought to circumvent the *Child Labor* decision by levying an excise tax on anyone who employed child labor under the terms proscribed in the earlier regulation. The only difference between the two statutes was that this tax applied to businesses whether or not they shipped the goods in interstate commerce. In *The Child Labor Tax Case* (1922), the Court held that this tax was not a true tax but only a "penalty" for violation of a commercial regulation. As such, it was invalid under the prior decision because it exceeded the power of Congress and invaded the areas reserved for control by the states. The Court distinguished earlier cases that had allowed prohibitory taxes. "Incidental" regulatory motives could be tolerated, but there was some point "in the extension of the penalizing features of the so-called tax when it loses its character as such and becomes a mere penalty, with the characteristics of legislation and punishment."

The Court, in this era, upheld many new federal commercial regulations. In *Stafford v. Wallace* (1922) the Court found that Congress could subject meat stockyard dealers and commission men to regulation by the Secretary of Agriculture. The opinion by Chief Justice Taft was notable because it not only resurrected Holmes' "current" or "stream of interstate commerce" theory but also implied that activities that had an economic effect on commerce could be regulated. But the Court did not follow up on this concept until 1937.

As we turn to the period of the New Deal, we can see several distinct lines of decisions regarding the commerce power. Under the *Shreveport Rate Case* (1914), Congress could regulate activities that had an economic effect on commerce among the states. The Court, however, did not apply this theory beyond the railroad regulation cases. The Court had also allowed the regulation of single-state activities that were a part of the stream or current of commerce, but this theory required a tangible connection of the activity to interstate commerce. The Court would allow other regulation of commerce only if the subject matter had a direct effect on interstate commercial transactions.

§ 4.4   1933–36: The New Deal Crisis

The election of 1932 created a public mandate for a new approach to ending the economic depression that beset the country. Franklin D. Roosevelt had been elected president on the promise of a "new deal" and of immediate action. Congress cooperated by passing a wide variety of laws to alter economic conditions. However, the decisions of the Supreme Court over the previous fifty years indicated that the third branch of government might not acquiesce in the new federal approaches to economic problems. From 1933 to 1937 the Court vacillated in the degree to which it controlled state economic regulations.

In the first decision on New Deal legislation, the Court for the first time in history struck down a statute as an excessive delegation of legislative power to the executive branch. The National Industrial Recovery Act of 1933 [NIRA] had been designed to regulate competitive practices in hopes of increasing prices and improving the conditions of labor. The president was authorized by the Act to establish and enforce "codes of fair competition" for trades or industries. These codes were to be approved by industrial organizations or trade associations in each industry before the president adopted them. The Act also contained a specific provision allowing the president to prohibit the transportation of petroleum products produced in violation of state statutes, so-called "hot" oil.

In *Panama Refining Co. v. Ryan* (1935), the Supreme Court held that the Act was an excessive delegation of the legislative power to the executive because it did not set any standards for when the president should exercise his discretionary power to prohibit shipment of these products. The Court did not reach the validity of the basic portion of the Act, the trade codes, at this time. But while the particular defect in this statute was easily remedied by legislative prohibition of all interstate shipments of "hot" oil, the majority's use of the new anti-delegation concept indicated that much New Deal legislation might meet with constitutional disapproval.

In *Railroad Retirement Board v. Alton R. Co.* (1935), the Court, by a five to four vote, held that the Railroad Retirement Act of 1934 exceeded the commerce power. The Act required and regulated pension systems for railroad employees. The majority opinion distinguished earlier cases upholding the regulations of railroad employment conditions because those regulations related to safety or efficiency aspects of interstate commerce. Here the majority found the Act to be designed only to help "the social welfare of the worker, and therefore remote from any regulation of commerce." The dissenting Justices would have accepted the congressional decision that there was a relationship between the financial well-being and morale of railroad employees and commerce, but this relationship was not a sufficiently direct one in the view of the majority.

The NIRA was next declared to be invalid, this time by a unanimous vote. Pursuant to the code provisions already mentioned, a code of competition set for poultry dealers in and near New York City regulated the conditions and price of labor. In the "sick chicken cases," *A.L.A. Schechter Poultry Corp. v. United States* (1935), the Court invalidated the Act for two reasons: first, allowing the President to approve and adopt the trade codes constituted an excessive and unconstitutional delegation of power; and second, the act exceeded the scope of the federal commerce power.

The opinion was troublesome more for what it said than for what it did. The NIRA had proved to be an administrative disaster and the executive branch had already decided to allow the Act to expire without seeking its renewal. The striking of the statute on a delegation theory also proved to be little problem because promulgating some standards could easily be done in legislation. Indeed the delegation concept died out after these cases and the Court has never again invalidated congressional actions on this ground.

However, the majority's discussion of the commerce power, in *Schechter Poultry*, showed the Court ready to strike down federal attempts to deal with the national problems of the 1930's. The majority opinion by Chief Justice Hughes found that the employment practices of a poultry business did not have a sufficiently "direct" connection to interstate commerce. The wages that employees engaged in "internal commerce" were paid or the hours they were required to work were subjects reserved for regulation by the States.

The most important decision of this period came in *Carter v. Carter Coal Co.* (1936) when the Court struck down the Bituminous

Coal Conservation Act of 1935. Under the Act, all coal producers were required to follow the maximum hour labor terms negotiated between miners and the producers of more than two-thirds of the annual national tonnage production for the preceding calendar year. The minimum wages of employees were fixed in a similar manner, and there was a tax on the coal producers who did not comply with these restrictions. The Act also regulated coal prices, but the majority found it unnecessary to discuss this provision because it found the provision inseparable from the wage and hour requirements that it held invalid.

The majority held that the setting of requirements by private producers was an unconstitutional delegation of legislative power to private persons. This Act went beyond the earlier acts that had been stricken as improper delegations because it allowed competitors to set the regulations for other members of the industry. However, the Court treated the delegation point and instead focused on the national commerce power.

The majority opinion found that federal regulation of the wages and hours of employees involved in mining and production was outside the commerce power. The majority followed now typical Tenth Amendment analysis by holding that the relationships between employers and employees in all production occupations "is a purely local activity." As such, the subject matter was reserved for the exclusive jurisdiction of the states unless it had a "direct" effect on interstate commerce. The majority believed that employment relationships had only an indirect effect on interstate commerce. The majority was simply unconvinced that labor relations had such a close relationship to interstate commerce that they should be removed from those subject matters reserved for the exercise of state power.

The *Carter* opinion showed that the Court was going to actively enforce its view of the Tenth Amendment against the national attempts to deal with the economic depression. The federal government would be precluded from controlling employer-employee relationships unless the Court changed its position.

Regulations of Some Local Activities Upheld. Even during this period the Court did not restrict federal power when there was no legitimate *state* interest at stake. Thus, the Court upheld federal legislation abrogating the gold clauses in contracts as a reasonable measure to regulate the national currency. The states had no Tenth Amendment interest in the regulation of the monetary system, so the Court had little problem in upholding this legislation. Similarly, the Court upheld the establishment of a federal dam and the sale of hydroelectric power from that facility. The Court was not going to prevent the Federal Government from competing with private businesses: the majority found no Tenth Amendment violation by the establishment of such a federal facility. Furthermore, the Court upheld a tax on firearms that was clearly designed to be a regulation of transactions in such items. But the majority here found no constitutionally significant interest of either state governments or private persons in the absence of federal taxes or regulations concerning firearms and, therefore, the majority had no problem upholding this "tax." And in January of 1937, the Court upheld a congressional statute prohibiting the transportation of articles made by convict labor into states that had prohibited the sale of such goods. In so doing, the Court recognized a broad power of Congress to set the terms of interstate transactions if it did not transgress any reserved powers of the states.

The Court Packing Plan. In February of 1937 President Roosevelt unveiled his now famous "Court Packing Plan." The President asked for legislative authority to appoint an additional federal judge for each judge who was 70 years of age and had served on a court for at least ten years. There would be a maximum of 50 judges who might be appointed under the proposed legislation, with a total maximum of fifteen members on the Supreme Court of the United States. Had this plan been approved, there would actually have been fifteen Justices on the Court because six Justices were over 70 years of age in 1937.

The plan was eventually defeated, perhaps in part because the Justices reformed themselves. Beginning in the spring of 1937 the Court began to defer to the other branches of government in matters of economics and social welfare. While the full impact of the majority's change of position could not be appreciated for several years, it was immediately apparent that the Court would no longer threaten economic reforms.

§ 4.5   1937 to Present: Summary

The Supreme Court today interprets the commerce clause as a broad grant of power. The Court now will defer to the legislature's choice of economic policy; the possible economic impact of an activity on commerce among the states will bring it within this power. Thus the old concepts of physical connection to commerce and the "current of commerce" theories have been discarded as inappropriate judicial restrictions on the commerce power.

Commerce Power Tests: 1937–1995. There are three ways that an item, person, or activity may come under the federal commerce power. First, Congress can set the regulations, conditions, or prohibitions regarding the permissibility of interstate travel or shipments if the law does not contravene a specific constitutional guarantee. Second, the federal government may also regulate any activity, including "single state" activities, if the activity has a close and substantial relationship to, or effect on, commerce. This relationship or effect may be based on economic relationships or economic impact. The activity may be subject to congressional power where it is one of a generic type of activities that have a cumulative effect on commerce. Third, Congress may regulate single-state activities that otherwise have no effect on commerce if the regulation is "necessary and proper" to regulating commerce or effectuating regulations relating to commerce.

Adjustment of Standards in 1995. For a half-century the Court described the scope of the federal commerce power in terms of the standards set forth in the previous paragraph. Then, in 1995, the Supreme Court defined the scope of federal commerce clause power in a slightly different manner. In *United States v. Lopez* (1995), the Justices, by a five to four vote, invalidated a federal law that prohibited any person from carrying a firearm near any school by ruling that this law did not fall within the federal commerce power. Chief Justice Rehnquist, writing for the majority, described the scope of federal commerce powers as follows:

> "We have identified three broad categories of activity that Congress may regulate under its commerce power ... First, Congress may regulate the use of the channels of interstate commerce ... Second, Congress is empowered to regulate and protect the instrumentalities of interstate commerce, or persons or things in interstate commerce, even though the threat may come only from intrastate activities ... Finally, Congress' commerce authority includes the power to regulate those activities having a substantial relation to interstate commerce ... i.e., those activities that substantially affect interstate commerce."

The *Lopez* majority opinion divided the traditional first commerce clause standard (allowing Congress to regulate anything or anyone that crosses a state line) into two standards. Under the first standard, Congress can regulate the channels of interstate commerce. Under the second standard, Congress can regulate the instrumentalities of commerce or people or products that travel in interstate commerce.

The third commerce clause standard set forth in *Lopez* (regarding the regulation of single state activities that have a substantial effect on interstate commerce) is similar to the language of prior cases concerning the regulation of intrastate activities that have a close and substantial relationship to, or effect on, commerce.

Lopez modified the standard for determining the scope of the federal commerce power to regulate intrastate activity in two ways that may, or may not, prove to be important in the future. First, the majority ruled that Congress can regulate only single state activities that as a class have a *substantial* effect on interstate commerce. Prior to *Lopez,* the opinions of the Supreme Court between 1937 and 1994 could have been read to allow Congress to regulate a class of intrastate activities that had only an insignificant, or trivial, effect on interstate commerce. Second, the *Lopez* majority found that the federal judiciary would give less deference to the congressional decision to regulate single state activity if the activity was not commercial or economic in nature. After *Lopez,* the judiciary should independently review the factual basis for determining the regulated single state activity had a substantial effect on interstate commerce, if the regulated activity is not commercial in nature.

The majority opinion in *Lopez* did not overturn any prior case. In fact, it cited with approval *Perez v. United States* (1971), where the Court upheld, under the commerce clause, a federal crime of extortionate credit transactions, that is, "loan sharking," even though the crime in this case did not cross any state lines and was "intrastate" activity. Yet that was a *commercial* crime, and the Court is willing to aggregate data to show that it *affects* interstate commerce when the date aggregated is commercial in nature.

While one should not read too much into *Lopez,* one also should also not read too little into *Lopez,* for it was the first post–1937 case that found that an activity—possessing a gun near a school—did not "affect" interstate commerce. The majority explained, as discussed more fully below, that the non-commercial, the non-economic criminal nature of the conduct at issue was central to its decision.

The Court in *United States v. Morrison* (2000) invalidated a federal law that created a tort for the victims of "gender-motivated violence." The act was titled, "The Violence Against Women Act." Congress made numerous findings that gender-motivated violence imposes a serious impact on victims and their families, but the majority (5 to 4) concluded that those finding were irrelevant. The Court will not aggregate intra-state non-commercial activities (such as the gender-motivated violence, or violence in general) to determine if intra-state actions *affect* interstate commerce. But, the Court will aggregate inter-state commercial activities (such as loan-sharking or wheat grown to compete with wheat transported in interstate commerce) to determine that the intra-state commercial activities affect inter-state commerce.

The modern Court easily finds an activity is subject to federal regulation under the commerce clause if the activity crosses a state line. In *United States v. Robertson* (1995), the Court said that if goods or people cross state lines, there is no need to apply the "affects" test, which only is necessary to define Congressional power over "purely intrastate commercial activities that have a substantial interstate effect".

When state or local governments engage in activities that are governed by federal statutes or regulations they may claim that either federalism principles or the Tenth Amendment exempt them from such federal laws. In the closing section of this chapter, we will examine the Supreme Court decisions that have prohibited the federal government from directly ordering state or local governments to take legislative or regulatory actions and that have indicated that state and local governments have some immunity from federal commerce power regulations when Congress subjects states to laws that are not "generally applicable."

The Modern Delegation of Power Doctrine—Delegations to States or the Executive Branch. Today, there is no significant anti-delegation principle that restricts the exercise of the commerce power. Congress may pass laws that allow states to independently regulate interstate commerce; such laws involve a federal adoption of varying structures for commerce rather than any unconstitutional delegation of the commerce power to the states. The Supreme Court will allow Congress to share its legislative power with the executive branch by delegating aspects of that power to executive agencies. Such legislative delegations will be upheld unless Congress abdicates one of its powers to the executive agency or fails to give legislative definition of the scope of the agency's power.

§ 4.6   Development of New Standards

The 1937 Decisions. In April of 1937, the Supreme Court, by a five to four vote, adopted an approach to defining the commerce power that was quite different from that of the previous period. The Court upheld the National Labor Relations Act and the labor board's orders against an employer's unfair interference with union activities in *NLRB v. Jones & Laughlin Steel Corp.* (1937). The majority opinion found no fault in the Act, which by its terms regulated labor practices "affecting commerce." The Act defined commerce in terms of transactions among states and "affecting commerce" as those practices or labor disputes that might burden or obstruct commerce. The case involved orders against practices in steel and iron works, but the Court rejected the production versus commerce distinction. This was most important for it meant that the Court would no longer define the commerce power in terms of Tenth Amendment reserved power concepts.

The steel company was a vertically integrated enterprise that operated in many states. Labor disruptions in its manufacturing component could affect commerce in several states. The majority opinion, however, did not rest on a "stream of commerce" theory; it dismissed this phrase as only a metaphor to describe some valid exercises of the commerce power. The majority opinion stated that intrastate activities could be regulated if they had "a close and substantial relation to interstate commerce." The opinion did not completely disregard the direct-indirect distinction; the case involved a large multistate corporation.

Redefining the Role of the Court in Commerce Clause Cases. In 1941 the Justices gave a more definite sign that economic impact was a basis for exercise of the commerce power. The Fair Labor Standards Act of 1936 prescribed the minimum wage and maximum hours for employees "engaged in [interstate] commerce or the production of goods for [interstate] commerce." The Act prohibited the interstate shipment of goods made in violation of these regulations and also imposed direct penalties on employers who violated the requirements.

The Supreme Court in *United States v. Darby* (1941) unanimously upheld both the terms of prohibition and direct regulation of wages and hours. The opinion, by Justice Stone, first recognized Congress' plenary power to set the terms for interstate transportation. It made no difference that Congress was attempting to regulate production in this way because the "motive and purpose of a regulation of interstate commerce are matters for the legislative judgment upon the exercise of which the Constitution places no restriction and over which the Courts are given no control." So long as Congress did not violate a specific check on its power such as the provisions of the Bill of Rights, it could set any terms for interstate transportation. The only impediment to this interpretation was *Hammer v. Dagenhart,* which the Court overruled in *Darby*.

The *Darby* Court upheld the direct regulation of the hours and wages of employees engaged in the production of goods for interstate shipment. The opinion found that Congress could regulate intrastate activities that "so affect interstate commerce or the exercise of the power of Congress over it." The Court discarded the production-commerce distinction as well as the directness test. Congress was free to set the terms of intrastate activities to protect or regulate interstate commerce. Congress could choose to protect commerce from competition by goods made under substandard labor conditions. Because competition was a sufficient economic tie to interstate commerce, it made no difference how small the individual producer's share of shipments in commerce might be.

In *Darby*, the Court also upheld the requirement that employers who sold items for interstate commerce keep records of the hours and wages of all employees. Even if some employees worked solely on an intrastate product not directly affecting commerce, these regulations were necessary to full enforcement of the provision relating to employees who worked in production for interstate commerce.

In *Wickard v. Filburn* (1942) the Supreme Court held that a marketing quota legitimately could be applied to a farmer who grew a small amount of wheat, although the wheat was primarily to be consumed on his own farm with some to be sold locally.

The Court had no difficulty in upholding regulation of this farmer even though it would be difficult, if not impossible, for him to affect interstate transactions. Total supply of wheat clearly affects market price, just as does current demand for the product. The marketing quotas were designed to control the price of wheat. If many farmers raised wheat for home consumption, they would affect both the supply for interstate commerce and the demand for the product. The possibility of such an effect by a class of hypothetical actors (farmers) justified regulation of the individual farmer.

The Court deferred to the legislative judgment concerning relationships between local activities and interstate commerce. It was not for the judiciary to restrict congressional power either by limiting the subject matter of the power or independently reviewing the "directness" of connections to commerce. The opinion explicitly returned to Chief Justice Marshall's broad definition of commerce in *Gibbons v. Ogden*. The Court had come full circle and returned to the broad view of the commerce power that had existed for most of our history. Commerce was once again considered to be intercourse that affected more states than one.

Between 1942 Wickard decision and 1995, the tests for proper exercise of the commerce power were settled. First, Congress could set the terms for the interstate transportation of persons, products, or services, even if this constituted prohibition or indirect regulation of single state activities. Second, Congress could regulate intrastate activities that had a close and substantial relationship to interstate commerce; this relationship could be established by congressional views of the economic effect of this type of activity. Third, Congress could regulate—under a combined commerce clause-necessary and proper clause analysis—intrastate activities in order to effectuate its regulation of interstate commerce.

The Court, in an unbroken line of cases from 1937 to 2004 has found that Congress can restrict the use of items following their transportation in interstate commerce. Thus, the Court has upheld the provision of the Food, Drug, and Cosmetic Act that required precise labeling for the retail sale of items that have been a part of interstate commerce. The Court has rejected any possible "original package" limit on the commerce power and held that Congress could set the labeling requirements after shipment to assure that later sale did not undermine Congressional policies.

During the period from 1937 to 1995, the Supreme Court majority gave great deference to Congressional decisions a single state activity could be regulated on the basis that the regulated activity had a substantial effect on multi-state economic concerns and interstate commerce. However, during those years, the Court was only examining the regulation of single state activities that were arguably commercial, or economic, in nature.

1995–2004. In 1995, the Court examined the extent of congressional power to regulate single state non-commercial activities. In *United States v. Lopez,* (1995) the Court (five to four) invalidated a federal statute that prohibited simply carrying firearms near any school in the United States. The statute was not within the scope of Congress's commerce clause power.

Chief Justice Rehnquist's majority opinion in *Lopez* ruled that there were three basis upon which Congress could regulate persons, things, or activities under its Article I power to regulate interstate commerce: "First, Congress may regulate the use of channels of interstate commerce ... Second, Congress is empowered to regulate and protect the instrumentalities of interstate commerce, or persons or things in interstate commerce, even though the threat may come only from intrastate activities ... Finally, Congress's commerce authority includes the power to regulate, those activities having a substantial relation to interstate commerce ... i.e., those activities that substantially affect interstate commerce."

Lopez constitutes a complete endorsement of Congress's power to regulate all activities, persons, or products that cross state boundaries. So long as a federal regulation relates to interstate transactions or interstate transportation, the federal regulation would be justified under the first two branches of the *Lopez* description of the federal interstate commerce power.

The Chief Justice's opinion in *Lopez* indicated that the federal judiciary would continue to give great deference to a congressional determination that a class of single state commercial activities had a substantial effect on interstate commerce. The Chief Justice found that the judiciary should not give similar deference to a congressional determination that intrastate activities that were not commercial in nature had a substantial effect on interstate commerce. The *Lopez* majority considered the distinction between commercial and noncommercial single state activities to be a necessary one, even though Chief Justice Rehnquist's majority opinion recognized that a determination of whether an intrastate activity is commercial or noncommercial may in some cases result in legal uncertainty.

Lopez did not change the basis upon which the federal government could regulate single state activities. As was true in all of the cases since 1937, the Court held that Congress could regulate single state activities that had a substantial effect on commerce. However, in *Lopez*, the Court created a distinction regarding the degree of deference that the judiciary would give to Congress when determining whether a class of regulated single state activities had a substantial effect on interstate commerce. If the regulated single state activity is commercial, or economic in character, the Court will continue to give great deference to Congress. Federal regulations of single state economic activities will enjoy a presumption of constitutionality, so that they will be upheld as being within the commerce power so long as there is any rational basis on which Congress could have concluded that the activities have a substantial affect on interstate commerce. Federal regulation of single state activities that are not commercial (not economic) in character will not be upheld unless the federal government can demonstrate that there is a real factual basis (rather than a mere theoretical argument) for the conclusion that the single state activities, as a class, have a substantial effect on interstate commerce.

Lopez provided no specific guidance regarding the principles that the judiciary should use when determining whether a single state activity that was subject to federal regulation in fact was commercial or economic in character.

The Chief Justice's opinion in *Lopez* also did not examine in detail the relationship of the necessary and proper clause to the commerce clause. The necessary and proper clause allows Congress to employ all means that are reasonably related to carrying out any federal power, including the commerce power.

In *Reno v. Condon* (2000), the Court ruled that the federal driver's Privacy Protection Act was within the scope of Congress's commerce power, and that it did not violate the Tenth Amendment. The Act prohibited *state governments* from disclosing information they receive from an individual who applies for a driver's license unless the individual driver consents to the disclosure or the disclosure falls within some specific exemptions from the ban, such as disclosures for law enforcement purposes. The Act also prohibited *private parties* who have received information concerning a driver from a state (pursuant to one of the exemptions in the Act) from disclosing the information about the driver except under certain circumstances.

Chief Justice Rehnquist, speaking for a unanimous Court in *Condon*, found that the information that the state received from drivers, which it would be turning over to private persons subject to the regulations in the Act, was obviously an item in interstate commerce. Thus, the Federal Act fell within the first two branches of the *Lopez* definition of the scope of the commerce power. Congress was regulating the channels of interstate commerce, and something in interstate commerce. It was unnecessary for the Court to consider whether the disclosure of drivers license information would have a substantial effect on interstate commerce.

Condon also unanimously ruled that the application of the Act to state agencies did not violate any Tenth Amendment principles because the states were being regulated with an otherwise valid commerce power law that applied to both private sector actors and public entities. The fact that states would have to spend money to comply with the federal Act, by setting up administrative systems for regulating disclosure of drivers license information, did not interfere with any aspect of state sovereignty that was protected by the Tenth Amendment.

Condon did not represent a rejection of the *Lopez* standards. In *United States v. Morrison* (2000), the Court ruled that the commerce clause did not justify a federal statute that created a remedy for sex-motivated assaults. *Morrison* is examined § 4.7(b), below.

In the period from 1937 to 1995, it was common to state that Congress's commerce power included the power to regulate: (1) persons, things, or transactions that crossed state boundaries; (2) single-state activities, persons, things, or transactions that had a substantial affect on, or a substantial relationship to, interstate commerce; and (3) anything that was necessary and proper to regulate in order to fully effectuate its regulation of interstate commerce. The third category involved necessary and proper clause analysis. Article I, § 8, which, by its own terms, applies to all federal powers, including Congress's commerce power.

After *Lopez*, Congress, using only its commerce clause power, can regulate: (1) the channels of interstate commerce; (2) the instrumentalities of interstate commerce or persons or things (including activities and transactions) that cross state lines, whether or not they are commercial; and (3) single-state activities that have a substantial effect on, or a substantial relationship to, interstate commerce. *Lopez* clarified the commerce clause standards by subdividing the first part of the older standards into two parts [the first and second parts of the *Lopez* standards]; and making the second part of the older standards the third commerce clause standard. The majority in *Lopez*, did not explicitly refer to the necessary and proper clause, unlike Justice Thomas, concurring, and Justice Souter, dissenting. The *Lopez* majority would not have changed it mind based on the necessary and proper clause, for the Justices concluded that simply holding a gun near a school was not a commercial act and could not affect a commercial act in any realistic sense.

However, it is still important to bear in mind the necessary and proper clause. The next section analyzes *United States v. Morrison* (2000) and *Gonzales v. Raich* (2005). Those cases clarify *Lopez* and show the interplay between the commerce clause and the necessary and proper clause.

§ 4.7   Refinement and Application of the New Standards

There are decisions in three subject areas—civil rights legislation, federal criminal laws concerning traditionally local crimes, and the regulation of activities of state governmental entities—that further refine general commerce clause principles. One must be aware of the approaches that the Court has taken in the review of the federal legislation in these areas in order to have a complete picture of current commerce clause analysis.

(a) Civil Rights Legislation

In 1964, the Supreme Court upheld the constitutionality of Title II of the Civil Rights Act. This provision imposed penalties on anyone who deprived another person of equal enjoyment of places of public accommodation on the basis of the individual's race, color, religion, or national origin. The Act covered all but the smallest rooming houses or hotels, restaurants, entertainment centers, or other retail establishments that made use of products that had moved in interstate commerce or that had otherwise affected commerce.

The Court upheld the application of the restrictions to hotels in *Heart of Atlanta Motel Inc. v. United States* (1964). There were no congressional findings connected to the bill regarding the relationship between discriminatory practices in hotels and interstate commerce. However, the opinion found that there was no need for formalized congressional findings to support commerce power legislation because the Court does not treat Congress like it treats an administrative agency. Congress can properly collect information from outside the record of a congressional hearing; it can listen to the views of its constituents; it can respond to letters from voters. And, as a logical matter, the decision of motels to not serve blacks or other minorities, like the decision of restaurants not to serve blacks or other racial minorities, makes it much more difficult for these people to travel from state to state.

The Court stated that commerce power legislation would be upheld if there were any arguable connection between the regulation and commerce that touched more states than one. Congress' motive did not have to be commercial because the interstate commerce power was plenary. The opinion dictated the deference due Congress under the commerce power.

It stated the proper questions for judicial review:

> The only questions are: (1) whether Congress had a *rational basis* for finding that racial discrimination by motels affected commerce, and (2) if it had such a basis, whether the means it selected to eliminate that evil are reasonable and appropriate.

The records of the congressional consideration of these bills was "replete with evidence" of the ways in which racial discrimination affected interstate travel by black persons. The Court recognized, as it had done in the time of Chief Justice Marshall, that interstate transactions and transportation fell under the commerce power. Crossing state lines is classically treated as interstate commerce, at least since the *Lottery Act Cases.* Congress can forbid the crossing of the state lines when it does not involve a commercial transaction—such as federal prohibition, found in the White Slave Traffic Act, of crossing state lines for debauchery and immoral purposes (noncommercial vice), as the Court held in the early part of the Twentieth Century.

In *Katzenbach v. McClung* (1964) the Court upheld the application of Title II of the Civil Rights Act to the now famous "Ollie's Barbeque," a family-owned restaurant in Birmingham, Alabama, located over a mile away from an interstate highway or major method of transportation. The Act by its terms applied to any restaurant that either served interstate travelers or that served to intrastate patrons products of which a substantial portion had moved in interstate commerce.

No interstate travelers were served at the restaurant. However, Ollie's had purchased almost $70,000 worth of meat the previous year from a supplier who received it from out-of-state sources. This purchase both brought the restaurant under the terms of the Act and sustained a constitutional exercise of the commerce power over it. As a logical matter, if the restaurant would not serve interstate travelers, that also would *affect* interstate transportation because it would make it harder for all interstate travelers (whether or not members of a racial minority) to travel from state to state, because some restaurants would not serve interstate travelers.

Katzenbach v. McClung recognized that no direct congressional testimony clearly established a relationship between discrimination in such establishments and interstate commerce. However, a search for such detailed evidence would have been based on an erroneous view of the role of the Court in reviewing commerce power legislation. There could be no argument with the rationality of the theory that restricting the availability of food and public accommodations services to members of minority races had a restrictive effect upon their interstate travel. It made no difference that Ollie's Barbeque was quite small, for the *Wickard* principle already established that Congress could regulate what seemed to be trivial activities if, added together, they had, as an aggregate, a non-trivial affect on commerce. There were additional bases for regulating the practices of Ollie's Barbeque based upon the affect of the discrimination on commerce and the regulations of goods that had passed across state lines.

(b) Federal Criminal Laws

Another area in which the Supreme Court has given increased deference to the legislature is its use of the commerce power to establish jurisdiction for federal criminal laws. Congress has the inherent power to establish criminal penalties for actions that interfere with any federal interest. Thus, Congress may establish crimes related to any action taken on federal lands under its property power, activities relating to interstate communications under the postal power, the evasion of tax statutes under the taxation power, or the violation of federal civil rights under the powers granted by certain Amendments to the Constitution. The federal government may also place conditions on the use of federal money or activities taken with, or against, persons who have received federal grants.

The commerce power also offers an independent basis for the enactment of federal criminal laws. The tests here are identical to those used to analyze the validity of any federal regulation under the commerce power. To be a proper subject for a commerce-based criminal statute, an activity must either relate to interstate transactions, have an effect on interstate commerce, or be an activity that is necessary and proper to regulate in order to effectuate the commerce power.

Perhaps the most far-reaching federal criminal statutes have related to the prohibition of interstate transportation incident to some other crime. These include such well known statutes as the Mann Act, which outlaws the transportation of women for immoral purposes, the Dyer Act, which punishes the interstate transportation of stolen vehicles, and the Lindbergh Law, which punishes kidnapings that are related to interstate transportation or commerce.

Congress, when establishing criminal statutes, may also make use of its power to regulate items that have passed in interstate commerce. Thus, Congress has made it a crime for a person who is convicted of a felony to receive or possess a firearm that was transported at any time in interstate commerce. The Supreme

Court has not only upheld this statute but has applied it to a person who was not convicted of a felony until after he had received the firearm and long after it had been the subject of interstate commerce.

The Supreme Court has given great, but not total, deference to Congress when reviewing criminal statutes enacted under the commerce power. In *Perez v. United States.* (1971) the Court upheld Title II of the Consumer Credit Protection Act, which makes a federal crime of extortionate credit transactions, an activity otherwise known as "loan sharking." The statute made it a crime to charge excessive rates of interest, or to use violence or the threat of violence to collect debts.

The defendant Perez had been found guilty of engaging in an extortionate credit transaction in his loans to a person in New York. All of the activities took place in the State of New York and there was no evidence that Perez was connected to organized crime or that he had ever used the instrumentalities of commerce in connection with his loan sharking business. The Court, nonetheless, upheld his conviction under the commerce power. Justice Douglas, for the majority, found that it was rational for Congress to conclude that even intrastate loan sharking (a commercial activity) affected interstate commerce by altering property ownership on a massive scale and by financing criminal organizations that might operate in several states.

Only Justice Stewart dissented in the *Perez* decision. He stated that there were simply no facts upon which he could make a rational distinction between loan sharking and other local crimes. Because he could find no clear connection between intrastate loan sharking activities and interstate commercial problems, he would have held that the regulation of this local, intrastate crime was "reserved to the states under the Ninth and Tenth Amendments." But no other Justice was of the opinion that the Constitution required that the states be given primary jurisdiction over any subject matter—even traditional forms of local commercial crime.

Almost a quarter of a century after the *Perez* decision, the Supreme Court, without overruling *Perez,* limited the scope of Congress' power to make a single state activity a federal crime. In *United States v. Lopez* (1995), the Supreme Court, by a five to four vote, invalidated a federal statute that imposed criminal penalties on persons who "possessed" a firearm within one thousand feet of any school building. Writing for the majority in *Lopez,* Chief Justice Rehnquist ruled that the law exceeded the scope of congressional authority under the commerce clause.

Less than a week after *Lopez*, the Court decided *United States v. Robertson* (1995). The Government secured a conviction of Juan

Robertson for various narcotics offenses and for violating a provision of the Racketeer Influenced and Corrupt Organizations Act (RICO) by investing proceeds of his unlawful activities in an enterprise "engaged in, or the activities of which affect, interstate or foreign commerce." Robertson invested in a gold mine in Alaska. The Ninth Circuit reversed the RICO count because the Government had failed to introduce sufficient evidence that the gold mine was "engaged in or affect[ed] interstate commerce." A unanimous Supreme Court reversed. It was unnecessary to consider whether the activities of the gold mine affected interstate commerce because the effects test is necessary only to "define the extent of Congress' power over purely intrastate commercial activities that nonetheless have substantial interstate effects." In this case, there was proof of *inter*state activity: money, workers, and goods crossed state lines.

Congress can regulate crossing a state line, even if there is not "commercial" act, because of its power over interstate transportation. If there was no United States but only individual states, any of the states would have had the power to forbid importation or transportation of goods or services into its borders, even if the transportation was not a commercial act. With the formation of the union and the delegation of the commerce power to Congress, the Federal Government now has the power to forbid importation or transportation of goods or services across state lines, even if the transportation was not a commercial act.

The theoretical argument that widespread intra-state crimes (which do not involve commercial or economic activity) somehow affect commerce will not justify federal regulation under the commerce clause.

In *United States v. Morrison* (2000) the majority would not allow Congress to aggregate the effects of a non-commercial, intra-state act (a sexual assault). The *Morrison* majority specifically approved of lower courts that accepted other parts of the same statute that prohibited interstate activity, such as punishing a person who "travels across a State line or enters or leaves Indian country with the intent to injure, harass, or intimidate that person's spouse or intimate partner."

The majority opinion in *Morrison* invalidated parts of the "Violence Against Women Act" on the grounds that sex-based assaults wholly within one state are not "commerce" under the interstate commerce clause. The Court was concerned that we would no longer have a government limited to enumerated powers (either express or implied) if non-commercial acts wholly within one state like violence (even violence based on animus towards one's sex) are enough to justify any federal action under the commerce clause. While the Court, after *Lopez,* will give great deference to

Congress' regulation of single state activities that are commercial in nature (like the money lending activities regulated in *Perez*), that deference does not apply if a regulated single state activity is noncommercial in nature.

Justice Souter's dissent in *Morrison* (joined by Stevens, Ginsburg, and Breyer) argued that it was "the Founders' considered judgment that politics, not judicial review, should mediate between state and national interests as the strength and legislative jurisdiction of the National Government inevitably increased through the expected growth of the national economy."

The majority's distinction between commercial or economic matters (where it will aggregate intra-state activity) and noncommercial or non-economic matters (where it will not apply the aggregation theory) is important. Future cases may raise questions as to exactly what is "commercial" or "economic". For example, a simple mugging is "economic" in the sense that money changes hands, which is the intent of the mugger. Nevertheless, one would be surprised to see the five Justices who voted to strike the law in *Morrison* vote to uphold a federal law regarding a local crime that was not connected to business activity.

Morrison showed that the if an activity is noncommercial (*i.e.*, holding a gun or engaging in an assault) and if it does not cross state lines, Congress cannot regulate it under the commerce clause unless the Federal Government can prove that the activity in fact has a substantial effect on interstate commerce. That burden may be impossible for the Federal Government to meet. *Gonzales v. Raich* (2005), however, held that Congress can regulate growing marijuana for personal use because "production," said Justice Stevens for the majority, is part of commerce. California's Compassionate Use Act authorized limited marijuana use for medicinal purposes. The plaintiffs were California residents who used doctor-recommended marijuana for serious medical conditions, but the Federal Controlled Substances Act [CSA] banned all marijuana, whether or not it crossed a state line. The Court (6 to 3) upheld the CSA: unlike "*Lopez* and *Morrison*, the activities regulated by the CSA are quintessentially economic." Citing Webster's dictionary, the Court said: " 'Economics' refers to 'the production, distribution, and consumption of commodities.' "

Gonzales demonstrates the interplay between the commerce clause and the necessary and proper clause. *Raich* upheld the federal law on its face, and as applied to persons who grew and used marijuana within a single state as authorized by state law for medical purposes. It was irrelevant that state law permitted such use of marijuana, because a valid federal statute overrides a contrary state law pursuant to the Article VI supremacy clause. Thus, the only issue in *Raich* was whether the federal government's prohibition of the marijuana use was a regulation of interstate commerce.

Five Justices in *Raich* believed that the federal law was valid under the third *Lopez* standard. Because the regulated activity (the market for marijuana) was economic in nature, the majority ruled that Congress did not have to make a specific finding, or produce evidence, that single-state possession of marijuana for medical purposes had a substantial effect on commerce. Rather, Congress only needed a rational basis for concluding that intrastate transactions might substantially affect the interstate market. Relying on *Wickard v. Filburn*, the Court in *Raich* found that the fact that an individual's use of a product might not in itself have an effect on commerce was irrelevant, because Congress could rationally conclude that class of activities (the single-state use of marijuana by many people) would have an effect on the interstate market for marijuana (which Congress sought to strictly regulate).

The majority cited both the commerce clause and the necessary and proper clause, but Justice Scalia, concurring in the judgment, was the only one who focused on the combination of the two clauses to give what he called a "more nuanced" view. He relied on the importance of the necessary and proper clause to provide a rationale for upholding federal laws that prohibit intrastate activities so that the Government can control interstate activities. Scalia found that these two clauses justify Congress' total prohibition of, or strict regulation of, marijuana (including marijuana grown within a single state for personal medicinal use).

All nine Justices agreed that Congress could regulate or prohibit marijuana that crossed state lines, whether or not there was any commercial transaction. Justice Scalia believed that federal authorities, in order to control effectively the interstate market for marijuana, had to have the power to also disallow marijuana possessed for medical reasons. Otherwise, federal law enforcement officers might face greater difficulty to obtain search warrants for illegal marijuana, or arrest persons who possessed marijuana, if the agents also needed probable cause to believe that the marijuana growing in someone's back yard, or found in someone's car, was headed for interstate transactions rather than for local, medicinal use.

Justice Scalia's opinion concurring in the judgment in *Raich* demonstrates the importance of the necessary and proper clause and provides a rationale for upholding federal laws that prohibit intrastate activities that, if allowed, would impair the federal government's ability to control interstate activities.

Justice Scalia's analysis may allow the Court to invalidate a federal law that prohibited street corner robberies without overturning *Raich*. The Court could rule that street corner crime is non-economic (even though money changes hands in robberies), and that federal government did not need to control local robberies in order to protect a national market that came under Congress's commerce clause power. On the other hand, the Court allowed Congress to control extortionate loan transactions in *Perez*, because, as the Court explained in *Lopez*, loans are commercial, so it may well be the case that Congress could prohibit street corner robberies.

Chief Justice Rehnquist and Justices O'Connor and Thomas dissented in *Raich*. O'Connor's dissent attacked the majority's decision to categorize the personal use of marijuana as a commercial activity. Justice Thomas, in a separate dissent, attacked both the majority's reasoning, which he believed would allow the regulation of virtually any single-state activity, and Justice Scalia's necessary and proper clause analysis.

(c) Regulation of State and Local Government Entities

(1) Federal Orders to State and Local Governments

In the 1990's the Supreme Court ruled that the federal government could not use its power over interstate commerce to require (or commandeer) state or local governments to take legislative acts, or certain executive actions.

The federalism principle that prevents the federal government from ordering state or local government to take certain governmental actions does not grant state and local government immunity from federal regulation of commercial activity. Thus, a federal labor law regulating the wages paid to employees could apply to state and local governments just as it would apply to private sector entities. Similarly, a federal law regulating the disposal of waste products that affect interstate commerce (such as atomic waste or chemically hazardous waste), can be applied to state or local governments that dispose of such waste in the same way as they apply to private persons or corporations.

In *New York v. United States* (1992) the Justices held that federal legislation could not order states to adopt state legislation that would set state standards for the disposal of low level radioactive waste nor could federal legislation order the states to take ownership of privately owned radioactive waste in their states.

In an attempt to deal with the multistate problems inherent in the creation and disposal of low level radioactive waste, Congress had taken three distinct steps, two of which *New York v. United States* upheld unanimously.

First, Congress allowed states that had adopted regulations regarding the storage and disposal of radioactive waste (or that had joined multistate compacts adopting such standards) to impose a charge on the disposal of such waste. This charge would provide funds for a federal grant program that, in turn, would provide assistance money to states that had storage sites for radioactive waste that complied with federal guidelines. Justice O'Connor wrote for a unanimous Court in upholding this grant program, because Congress' powers under the spending clause allowed it to condition grants to states that were fulfilling federal goals. Such grants did not violate any form of sovereignty protected by the Tenth Amendment or other federalism principles.

Second, the federal legislation gave states that adopted radioactive waste storage and disposal guidelines, or that entered multistate compacts for the disposal of radioactive waste consistent with federal guidelines, the authority to impose a discriminatory tax against, or to completely bar, the importation of radioactive waste from states that had not adopted storage and disposal programs or compacts consistent with federal guidelines. Absent federal authorization, a state law banning the importation of out-of-state garbage or waste for disposal in local landfills would violate the commerce clause if the out-of-state waste did not represent a unique health hazard to the people of the state that enacted the tariff or trade barrier. A unanimous court found that Congress could authorize the states to create such trade barriers. This exercise of Congress' commerce power would make the state law immune from any commerce power challenge. The effect of these federal legislative provisions on states that had failed to adopt federal guidelines (and whose citizens and businesses, therefore, could not easily export their waste to other states) did not intrude on any element of sovereignty that was protected by federalism principles or the Tenth Amendment.

Third, Congress offered the states the "option" of either enacting state laws (through legislation or through joining a regional compact of states) that regulated the storage and disposal of radioactive waste in conformity with federal guidelines or, in the alternative, taking possession and ownership of all radioactive waste in the state (including all radioactive waste that had been produced by private persons or corporations in the state). The only part of the federal program designed to guard against the hazards of low level radioactive waste that the Supreme Court in *New York v. United States* invalidated was the so-called "take title provision" of the federal legislation.

New York v. United States invalidated the "take title" provision. Justice O'Connor, for the majority, found that federal judges had a proper role in defining the limit of federal power over state and local governments due to the structure of the federal system established by our Constitution and the Tenth Amendment. The

Tenth Amendment, she said, is a tautology. The real question is whether the commerce power, an enumerated power, authorizes the federal government to conscript the states to enact legislation that Congress orders the states to enact. The majority concluded that the power of Congress to order a state to enact a law is a power the Constitution did not confer on Congress through the commerce clause.

Justice O'Connor's opinion recognized a wide scope of congressional power to regulate commerce. Congress could have directly regulated the disposal of radioactive waste. However, Congress did not have the power "to regulate state governments' regulation of interstate commerce" because Congress could not simply "direct the States to provide for the disposal of radioactive waste." Requiring the state to take possession and ownership of the radioactive waste was the same as requiring the state to use its legislative and executive powers. Thus, the portion of the take title provision that ordered noncomplying states to take ownership of radioactive waste was invalid.

If Congress wishes to regulate radioactive waste in a particular way, after *New York v. United States*, it can (1) regulate the activity directly (and take political accountability if members of the populace dislike the federal regulations); (2) reward states with monetary grants conditioned on achieving federal standards for the disposal of radioactive waste; and (3) strengthen the commerce powers of states that meet federal guidelines by allowing them to prohibit the importation of radioactive waste from states that do not meet federal safety guidelines.

In 1993, Congress passed, and the President signed, the "Brady Handgun Violence Prevention Act" [the Brady Act], which modified the Gun Control Act of 1968. A key provision of the Brady Act required a background check, under certain circumstances, for persons attempting to purchase firearms. The Act required the Attorney General of the United States, by 1998, to set up a national system that would check the background of persons attempting to purchase a gun. However, for the period prior to the establishment of the national background check system, the Brady Act required the chief law enforcement officer (CLEO) in the jurisdiction in which the would-be purchaser of the gun resided, under most circumstances, to review a form filled out by the gun purchaser and determine whether the purchaser was within a group of persons who were prohibited by federal law from purchasing guns. Congress did not want to spend the money to pay for these background checks during this interim period (either by offering money to the states or hiring federal workers directly). Congress, instead, imposed what amounted to an unfunded mandate on state executive branch officials.

In *Printz v. United States* (1997) the Court (by a 5 to 4 vote) ruled that the provision of the Brady Act violated the principles of federalism and the Tenth Amendment because it imposed administrative duties on state and local law enforcement officials to administer federal law. Justice Scalia's majority opinion rested *Printz's* ruling on three principles that the majority found to exist. First, the history of the Constitution, and its Amendments, provided no evidence that Congress had been given authority to control the activities of state legislatures or executive legislative officials. Second, the federal system that the Constitution of 1787 created did not give the federal government the power to control state or local legislative or executive officers merely for the purpose of implementing federal law. Third, earlier decisions of the Court, including *New York v. United States*, "have made clear that the federal government may not compel the states to implement by legislation or executive action, federal regulatory programs."

Justice O'Connor concurred, noting that *Printz* involved only an application of the principles of *New York v. United States*. In addition, she noted the Court had left open important questions. For example, she believed that the decision did not preclude Congress from establishing "purely ministerial reporting requirements."

Justices Stevens, Souter, Ginsburg, and Breyer dissented in *Printz*. They rejected the majority's historical evidence related to the drafting or ratification of the Constitution and the subsequent history.

The federal government may subject states to commerce power regulations that are applied to both private sector businesses and public sector entities engaged in similar types of activities that are involved in interstate commerce. In some instances compliance with those laws will require a state to change its administrative systems. Compliance with such laws will not violate the principles established by the *New York* and *Printz* cases.

In *Reno v. Condon* (2001) the Court unanimously upheld the Federal Drivers Privacy Protection Act, which prohibited state governments from disclosing information they received in drivers license applications except under limited circumstances. The Act *also limited* the use of such information by private persons who received the information through one of the exemptions established in the Act. Chief Justice Rehnquist easily found that the drivers license information is an article in commerce, and that the Federal Act came within the scope of Congress's Article I commerce power. The state alleged that the Act violated the Tenth Amendment by requiring the state to adjust its administrative systems to deal with the disclosure of drivers license information in conformity with the

Federal Act. The Chief Justice responded that this Federal Act "does not require the states in their sovereign capacity to regulate their own citizens. [The Act] regulates the states as owners of databases. It does not require the South Carolina legislature to enact any laws or regulations, and it does not require state officials to assist in the enforcement of federal statutes regulating private individuals." The law applied to private parties as well as the state: neither could buy or sell the information if certain circumstances applied.

(2) State and Local Government Immunity from Federal Commerce Regulations

(i) Introduction and Summary

The previous subsection examined the Court's decisions that established a limited, but significant, principle that prohibits the federal government from using the Commerce Clause to order the executive or legislative branches of state or local governments to take legislative, regulatory, or executive actions. We will now turn to the question of whether the Tenth Amendment or other federalism principles create doctrines that would provide states with a broader immunity from federal regulatory laws. We will first look at the brief flirtation the Court had with the idea of creating a principle and then concentrate on the Court's current position, which denies state and local governments a broad constitutional immunity from most, if not all, federal legislation.

The general principle now is that Congress can impose commercial regulations that also apply to states and their instrumentalities. Congress may impose generally applicable commercial rules on private entities and states or it, as a matter of policy, may exempt states from the normal rules that, for example, apply to overtime work, minimum wage, and so on.

Between 1976 and 1985, the Court attempted to limit the power of the federal government to subject state or local governments to federal commercial regulations. Even during this period, the Court did not restrict federal power to regulate private sector commercial activities merely because activities intrastate but affected interstate commerce. A majority of the Justices between 1976 and 1985, however, eventually developed this test to determine if state and local governments had immunity from the application of a federal commercial regulation to them; they were immune if the particular federal regulation: (1) addressed the "states as states;" (2) regulated attributes of state or local sovereignty; (3) directly impaired the ability of state or local governments to structure operations in areas of traditional functions; and (4) was not related to an overriding federal interest.

The problem, of course, is that this test is quite vague. What are, for example, "attributed of state sovereignty"? When does a regulation "directly impair" state functions and which functions are "traditional"?

Finally, in 1985, in *Garcia v. San Antonio Metropolitan Transit Authority*, the Court overruled prior caselaw and held that neither the Tenth Amendment nor the structure of the federal system justified restriction of Congress' power to apply otherwise valid commercial regulations to state or local governments. The law in question was generally applicable: the state faced "nothing more than the same minimum-wage and overtime obligations that hundreds of thousands of other employers, public as well as private, have to meet."

Garcia held open the possibility that the Justices would defend state governments against congressional actions that would eliminate the sovereignty that states must possess to be a member of the federal system. However, it is unlikely that the Court, so long as it remains true to the view of the judicial power set forth in *Garcia*, would invalidate any federal regulation of state or local governments that did not directly impair the territorial integrity of the state or constitute a direct command from the federal government to alter basic local government policies. After *Garcia*, state or local governments must persuade Congress rather than the Court that they should not be subject to general commerce power regulations when compliance with those regulations would impair their ability to structure and operate their governmental departments and carry out their governmental functions. Laws that apply to both public and private sector commercial activity are to be reviewed now only under the general test regarding the scope of the federal commerce power that was set forth previously in this chapter.

(ii) The Wirtz and National League of Cities Decisions

In 1968, the Supreme Court considered the application of the federal minimum wage requirements to employees of state and local government institutions such as hospitals and schools. *Maryland v. Wirtz* (1968), upheld such an application of the statute with only two Justices dissenting.

In *Maryland v. Wirtz* there was no question that the regulation of the hours, conditions, and wages of laborers in enterprises affecting interstate commerce fell within the power of Congress. The sole issue was whether the Constitution carved out an exemption for the employment practices of state and local governments. The Court said no; the federal government could act to achieve the proper goals of its enumerated powers in a manner that might override important state interests. The majority opinion indicated that Congress could not engage in "the utter destruction of the state as a sovereign political entity" but otherwise set no specific limits on the commerce power. Only Justices Douglas and Stewart, in dissent, would have held that the Tenth Amendment prohibited federal regulations that constituted an undue interference with the performance of sovereign or governmental functions of the state.

Wirtz was temporarily overruled by *National League of Cities v. Usery* (which the Court overruled in 1985). In *National League of Cities* the Justices held (five to four) that it was unconstitutional to apply the minimum wage and overtime pay provisions of the Fair Labor Standards Act to the employees of the state governments, even though they were in or affecting interstate commerce. The Court agreed with the Appellants' essential contention "that the 1974 amendments to the Act, while undoubtedly within the scope of the Commerce Clause," cannot constitutionally "be applied directly to the States and subdivisions of States as employers." In so doing, the Court dismissed as "wrong" statements in earlier opinions that the states were not entitled to special exemptions from the exercise of the federal commerce power. But the Court did not otherwise disturb basic commerce clause analysis.

It is important to recognize that the Court did not hold that the wages and hours of state employees were not commerce nor that they did not affect commerce. The opinion did not disturb the modern tests for finding relationships between intrastate activities and the commerce power.

The majority concluded that the Tenth Amendment guaranteed that Congress would not abrogate a state's plenary authority over matters "essential" to the state's separate and independent existence. This test is vague, and its application uncertain. Is it really "essential" for a state to pay its state employees less than the federal minimum wage? If the commerce clause does not allow the Federal Government to force states to pay their employees the minimum wage, does that mean that Congress similarly lacks power to prevent states from using child labor?

In *National League of Cities v. Usery*, Justice Rehnquist, for the majority, found that a local government or state's ability to determine its employees' wages was an "attribute" of state sovereignty that the Federal Government could not federalize. The federal wage regulation, Rehnquist said, could not apply to state or local governments because it impaired essential governmental activities by restricting the freedom of choice of local governments as to how to allocate local resources in carrying out traditional state and local governmental functions.

The majority opinion established no clear test for determining when a federal law so impaired the sovereignty of a state or local government that it could not be applied to those governmental units. Justice Blackmun provided the crucial fifth vote in the *National League of Cities* decision, filing a concurring opinion. However, Justice Blackmun saw the decision as establishing only a "balancing test," which required the judiciary to determine whether a federal interest in commercial regulation was "demonstrably greater" than the state's claim for an exemption whenever a state alleged that the application of federal commercial regulations to it constituted an impairment of its sovereignty. He did not explain how to calibrate the scales or weigh the ingredients. How, for example, does a Court decide that minimum wages are not important enough to the federal government but environmental decisions are important enough? How does one weigh or compare apples to electricity?

The dissenters in *National League of Cities* argued that the majority had gone beyond the proper role of the judiciary in our constitutional system. They believed that the scope of federal power to regulate state governments should be decided by the democratic process, rather than by the courts. They claimed that neither constitutional text nor history supported the Court's ruling. Because the majority had failed to ground its ruling on a clear constitutional principle or objective test, the dissenters asserted that future rulings would be based on Justices' personal views of the proper balance of federal and state power rather than on legal standards.

The dissenters would be vindicated in 1985, when the Court overruled the *National League of Cities* decision.

(iii) 1976–1985: The Aftermath of National League of Cities

Following *National League of Cities*, the Court embarked upon a period in which the Justices attempted to establish formal tests for the determination of when a federal law could or could not be applied to state and local governments consistently with the autonomy assured the states by the Tenth Amendment. In a series of cases, the Court established that a federal law would only be held to be an undue extension of the commerce power and inapplicable to state and local governments consistently with the Tenth Amendment if the federal law: (1) regulated "the states as states"; (2) addressed matters that were "indisputably attributes of state sovereignty"; (3) required state compliance with the federal law in a manner that directly impaired a state's ability to "structure integral operations in areas of traditional functions." The Court also appeared to add a balancing test to this three-part test for the validity of a federal law. The Court several times mentioned that even if the application of a federal law to state and local governments met all three parts of the previously described test, the Court would uphold the law when the federal interests were sufficiently important to justify the impairment of state or local government autonomy. It was unclear during this period whether the three-part test was a prelude to a judicial balancing of state and federal interests or whether the three-part test itself was a form of structuring a judicial balancing of national and local interests.

The *Hodel* Decision. *Hodel v. Virginia Surface Mining and Reclamation Association, Inc.* (1981), upheld a federal statute controlling surface mining and replacing state control over the amount and conditions of such mining. In so doing the Court attempted to clarify the standard for the protection of state sovereignty previously established in *National League of Cities v. Usery*.

The federal act at issue in *Hodel* empowered the Department of Interior to set standards for surface coal mining on "steep slopes" and the preservation of land or topsoil affected by such mining within each state. While a state could participate in the establishment of standards for mining within its jurisdiction, states were not required to act as enforcement agents for the federal government. However, once permanent standards were established, states could assume control over mining operations only if they adopted regulations approved by the Secretary of Interior. This federal action, in a sense, removed an element of state sovereignty by taking over the regulation of an activity that otherwise would have been within these states' jurisdiction, but the Supreme Court found that the Tenth Amendment did not invalidate this federal law. The federal law created a regulatory program that a state could adopt (if that program met federal minimum standards) or there would be a federal program for any state that chooses not to submit a program. Enforcement of the permanent programs rests either with the States (if they chose to participate) or with the Secretary of Energy as to nonparticipating States.

The majority opinion stated: "When Congress has determined that an activity affects interstate commerce, the courts need inquire only whether the finding is rational." *Hodel* contrasted the regulation of "States as States," which required judicial scrutiny under the Tenth Amendment, to federal regulation of private individuals and businesses. Legislation merely regulating nongovernmental enterprises, the Court concluded, does not raise Tenth Amendment problems but is only tested under the rational basis test. The Tenth Amendment does not limit "congressional power to pre-empt or displace state regulation of *private* activities affecting interstate Commerce."

The *F.E.R.C.* Decision. In *Federal Energy Regulatory Commission v. Mississippi* (1982), the Justices (five to four) upheld the constitutionality of Titles I and III and Section 210 of Title II of the

Public Utility Regulatory Policies Act of 1978, referred to by the Court as "PURPA" or, simply, "the Act."

PURPA had three features to which state governments objected. First, the Act required each state agency with authority over public utilities to consider specific approaches for structuring utility rates and specific standards relating to the terms and conditions of public utility operations. Consideration of the federal standards was a condition for state regulation of public utilities: if the state failed to consider the federal standard, the Federal Government would impose its standards, occupy the field, and force the state to abandon regulation in this field. Second, the Act prescribed specific procedures to be followed by the state regulatory authorities or nonregulated utilities when considering the proposed standards. Third, the Act required the Federal Energy Regulatory Commission, FERC, after consultation with state regulatory authorities, to prescribe rules exempting certain cogeneration and small power facilities from state laws governing electric utilities and to issue such rules as necessary to "encourage cogeneration and small power production" and to require each state regulatory authority to implement the FERC rules regarding cogeneration and small power production facilities.

All of the Justices in *FERC v. Mississippi* found that the regulation of public utilities, even a public utility that operated in a single state, was within the scope of congressional power under the commerce clause. The issue in *FERC v. Mississippi*, which created the division among the Justices related to the meaning and enforceability of the Tenth Amendment. Five Justices found that there was no violation of that Amendment in this case because Congress, in this instance, was only setting the conditions for the sharing of federal power with the states rather than interfering with the sovereignty of the states or traditional local government functions.

Justice Powell wrote a brief dissent objecting to the majority upholding the provision of the Act that prescribed exact procedures that state agencies must follow in considering the proposed federal standards. Justice O'Connor, joined by Chief Justice Burger and Justice Rehnquist, filed a dissent arguing that Titles I and III of the Act were unconstitutional because they interfered with attributes of state sovereignty and the ability of states to structure integral operations in areas of traditional government functions.

1983: *E.E.O.C. v. Wyoming.* The Supreme Court upheld the application of the Age Discrimination in Employment Act to state and local governments in *Equal Employment Opportunity Commission (EEOC) v. Wyoming* (1983). Justice Brennan wrote the majority opinion and found that this ruling was technically consistent with the *National League of Cities, Hodel,* and *FERC* decisions.

Wyoming objected to being prohibited from discharging state park and game commission employees at age 55; the Act prohibited discrimination based on age against employees or potential employees between the ages of 40 and 70. In denying Wyoming's Tenth Amendment challenge, Brennan said that the Age Discrimination Act did not meet the third prong of the *Hodel* test: it did not " 'directly impair' the State's ability to 'structure integral operations in areas of traditional governmental functions.' "

Chief Justice Burger,, joined by Justices Powell, Rehnquist, and O'Connor dissented in *EEOC v. Wyoming*, because they believed the decision undercut the *National League of Cities* decision.

The Court did not explicitly overrule *National League of Cities* until 1985. It is to that decision we now turn.

(iv) The Overruling of National League of Cities: The Garcia Decision

In 1985, Justice Blackmun, who had joined the majority in *National League of Cities* now changed his mind and wrote the majority opinion in *Garcia v. San Antonio Metropolitan Transit Authority,* which overruled the *National League of Cities* decision. The five person majority in this case was made up of the four dissenters in *National League of Cities* and Justice Blackmun, who had been voting with those four persons to uphold federal laws since 1976.

Garcia involved the application of the federal minimum wage and overtime provisions of the Fair Labor Standards Act (which the Court had found could not be applied to local police and highway departments in *National League of Cities*) to a municipally owned and operated mass transit system. The case was first argued on the issue of whether the operation of the buses and trains in a mass transit district should be considered a "traditional" government function and, therefore, exempt from wage regulation under *National League of Cities*, or like state-operated railroads, and not exempt. Rather than deciding whether the operation of mass transit districts was—unlike the operation of a railroad—a traditional governmental function, the majority rejected the basic premise of *National League of Cities* and found that there was no principled role for the judiciary in granting to state and local governments an area of immunity from otherwise valid federal commerce power legislation that similarly governs private parties.

Justice Blackmun began his majority opinion in *Garcia* by noting the difficulty that both the Supreme Court and lower courts had faced when trying to implement *National League of Cities*. Neither historical nor functional approaches had been able to provide a clear and principled basis for judicial determination of the scope of state powers that were immune from federal regulations.

Justice Blackmun found that workings of the federal political process created restraints on undue federal interference with state and local governments. The states have a meaningful role in the creation of federal legislation. Although state legislatures no longer appoint senators, the states have a significant voice in congressional deliberations and influence upon the executive. Most importantly, voters in a state are not likely to return to office federal legislators whose actions they find to be destroying the ability of their state and local governments to provide them with basic governmental services.

Ultimately the question was whether the decisions of the country, obtained through the political process, regarding the relative scope of federal and state powers should be rejected when a majority of Justices believed that it contravenes their view of the proper balance of state and federal powers. Justice Blackmun, writing for the majority in *Garcia,* concluded that there is no principled basis for the rejection of the decisions of the democratic process in this situation. Thus, the Court overruled *National League of Cities v. Usery.*

Garcia left open the possibility that there was some role for the judiciary in protecting state governments from federal actions that truly eliminated their sovereignty. For example, *Garcia* noted that Article IV of the Constitution protects state governments from having their territory altered by the federal government; Article IV and the Tenth Amendment limit the scope of congressional power to order states to make certain basic governmental decisions, such as where each state may locate its capital.

Four Justices, in three separate opinions, dissented in *Garcia*. They attacked the majority's view of the role of the judiciary in the federal system and its overruling a Supreme Court decision rendered only nine years earlier. Justice Powell's dissent argued that the Court's overruling of *National League of Cities*, and its reaffirmation of *Maryland v. Wirtz*, was improper because it rejected both the history that underlaying the formation of the Constitution, and the historic role of the states in our federal system. The dissenters did not believe that the Court's acknowledgement that states might retain some area of sovereign power under the Constitution was meaningful since the majority opinion "does not identify even a single aspect of state authority that would remain when the Commerce Clause is invoked to justify federal regulation."

The Court may interpret some federal statutes narrowly to avoid other questions as to the limits on federal power to regulate states. For example, *Gregory v. Ashcroft,* (1991) ruled that the federal Age Discrimination in Employment Act [ADEA] did not apply to state laws that require state judges to retire at a specified age. Justice O'Connor found that the ADEA should be interpreted narrowly in order to avoid serious constitutional questions concerning the scope of congressional power over the state governments. Justice O'Connor's opinion raised some of the concerns that underlie *National League of Cities.* The majority stated that a federal statute that regulated a state's ability to control its judiciary would raise significant constitutional questions.

Gregory did not establish any constitutional restrictions on the scope of federal power. The majority opinion simply established a "plain statement rule" as a principle of statutory construction. Under the *plain statement rule,* the Court will not interpret a federal statute in a manner that will interfere with essential state or local government functions unless Congress plainly states its intention to do so in the statute itself. The plain statement rules, as a canon of statutory construction, does not undercut *Garcia.*

Commandeering State or Local Governments. In 1992, a majority of Justices created a very limited federalism restriction on congressional power over state and local governments. In *New York v. United States* (1992), and *Printz v. United States* (1997), five Justices found that Federalism principles that prevented the federal government from requiring state and local governments to enact legislation, and also prohibited the federal government from requiring state or local executive officers to implement federal law. *New York v. United States* and *Printz* do not grant states immunity from regulations of commercial activities engaged in by both private sector businesses and public sector entities. Thus, in *Reno v. Condon* the Court unanimously upheld the application of the Federal Drivers Privacy Protection Act to state governments. These decisions were examined at the start of § 4.7(c)(1).

Chapter 5

FEDERAL POWER TO
TAX AND SPEND

Table of Sections

---

§ 5.1   The Taxing Power

Section 2 (clause 3) and section 8 (clause 1) of Article I, and the Sixteenth Amendment, give Congress a broad power to tax. Section 9 (clauses 4 and 5) of Article I sets three restrictions on the taxing power of Congress. These restrictions are: (1) direct taxes and capitation taxes must be allocated among the states in proportion to population; (2) all customs, duties and excise taxes must be uniform throughout the United States; and (3) no duty can be levied on exports from any state.

The Sixteenth Amendment, which permits imposition of a federal income tax without apportionment among the states, was necessitated by the Court's rather odd decision in *Pollock v. Farmers' Loan and Trust Co.* (1895). Prior to the decision in *Pollock*, the term "direct" tax employed in the Constitution was generally believed to relate only to taxes on land (real property) and poll (voting) or per capita taxes. By a 5 to 4 vote of the Justices, *Pollock* held that the income tax of 1894 was a direct tax insofar as it imposed a tax on income from real estate and personal property without apportionment among the states. However, in its decision on rehearing, the *Pollock* Court noted that a federal tax on income from business activities would not be considered a direct tax, and that business income could be subject to federal income taxation without apportionment on the basis of population.

The *Pollock* decision was rejected by the country before it could be rejected by later Justices. The Sixteenth Amendment, giving the federal government broad power to tax all sources of income, was ratified in 1913. The entire reasoning of *Pollock* was later rejected by the Court in *New York ex rel. Cohn v. Graves* (1937), which rendered the Sixteenth Amendment a redundant statement of a broad federal power to tax income.

The dichotomy between direct and indirect taxes is no longer a real problem. Thus, the Supreme Court has held that taxes such as the following are indirect taxes, and, thus, do not require apportionment by population: the federal tobacco tax; a special tax on refining sugar; a federal estate tax; a federal gift tax; and a federal tax on the purchase and registration of aircraft.

§ 5.2   Federal Taxes as Regulatory Measures

The motives of Congress, and the President, in enacting a tax law (through the Article I section 7 process) are irrelevant to determining the validity of a federal tax. Congress sometimes uses taxes for the purpose of raising revenue, and sometimes uses taxes to affect the conduct of individuals or businesses. For example, Congress may tax a certain activity or product so heavily that individuals will not engage in the activity. If there is a theoretical possibility that the federal statute might produce some income for the federal government, the Court should find the statute to be within the federal taxing power.

In *McCray v. United States* (1904) the Court sustained what was then a very heavy federal excise tax (10 cents per pound) on the sale of colored oleomargarine that had been transported across a state line. Margarine of that type, without color in it, looks very much like Vaseline. The Court in *McCray* said that it would be improper for the judicial branch to inquire into the underlying motives of Congress. Thus, whether Congress's motive was to raise any money through the tax, or to help dairy farmers avoid competition from the new margarine substance, was irrelevant.

A tax statute deemed to be a penalty would violate the Constitution only if the Court found that the statutory penalty was designed to regulate a form of activity that the Court had held to be beyond the regulatory powers of the federal government.

Hammer v. Dagenhart (1918) [*the Child Labor Case*] held that the commerce power did not justify a federal law that would restrict the transportation of goods across state lines that were made by child labor. A few years later, in *Bailey v. Drexel Furniture Co.* (1922) [*the Child Labor Tax Case*] the Court invalidated a federal statute that imposed a tax on goods made through child labor that was so high that it would effectively prohibit the types of child labor that Congress had attempted to end with its original child labor statute. Because the Supreme Court took the position that the Tenth Amendment meant that child labor could only be regulated by states, and not the federal government, it also took the position that Congress could not use its taxing power to end child labor. After 1937, a federal tax on income produced for employers by child laborers would be upheld on two bases: (1) the law would be seen as within the tax power of Congress because it might produce some revenue for the government; and (2) if the tax were deemed a "penalty," it would be upheld as a regulatory law that was within the federal power to regulate commerce.

Today, if the Court were to find that a specific federal tax was a "penalty," rather than a tax, the Court would uphold the federal statute so long as it found that Congress had the power to regulate the activity that was being subject to taxation by the statute. For example, Congress could impose an extremely high tax on any type of drug that crossed state lines and defend the law as being either a tax (in that the law might raise some income for the federal government), or, alternatively, as a penalty that was justified by Congress's power to regulate or prohibit items from crossing state lines.

Federal tax laws are not exempted from specific constitutional limitations on the federal power, such as those contained in Article I, section 9, or the Bill of Rights. Thus, for example, a federal tax imposed only on the income of persons who were members of the Roman Catholic faith would violate the free exercise clause of the First Amendment.

§ 5.3 The Power to Spend

The constitutional power to spend is coupled with the federal power to tax in the first clause of Article I, section 8. Congress has the power to spend for the general welfare. Congress cannot justify general regulations of private conduct simply by stating that it is passing the regulations to promote the general welfare of people in the United States. However, Congress is given the power to tax and spend for the general welfare; Congress can tax and spend for purposes that are not set forth in the Constitution.

United States v. Butler (1936) adopted a very broad view of the federal spending power. The majority opinion in *Butler* stated: " ... the power of Congress to authorize expenditure of public moneys for public purposes is not limited by the direct grants of legislative power found in the Constitution." Although *Butler* provided a strong broad construction of the Article I spending power, the majority in *Butler* invalidated part of the Agricultural Adjustment Act of 1933 because the majority found the conditional grants to farmers created by the Act (which were designed to reduce crop production) violated the Tenth Amendment. The majority in *Butler* believed that the power to regulate farm practices had been reserved for states by the Tenth Amendment. In 1937, the United

States Supreme Court specifically rejected this Tenth Amendment limit on the spending power.

The *Butler* decision is good law, so to speak, only insofar as it defined a broad power of the federal government to spend for the general welfare. *Butler* is not good law insofar as it found the Tenth Amendment to be a restriction on the federal spending power. Today, federal spending programs will not be invalidated merely because they invade the so-called "police power" of the states, or influence state or local government activities. A federal spending law will be upheld so long as it arguably might help the welfare of the country (a congressional judgment that the Court will not second guess), and the federal spending law does not violate a specific check on the federal power.

A modern example of these principles is *Buckley v. Valeo* (1976), wherein the Court upheld the establishment of the Presidential Election Campaign Fund. The Court would not second guess Congress's decision that providing public funding for presidential candidates might help the public or general welfare. Because the grant of public funds for presidential candidates did not violate any specific check on the federal power, the Presidential Campaign Fund was upheld.

Similarly, *Oklahoma v. United States Civil Service Commission* (1947) upheld the congressional power to withhold federal highway funds from a state unless the state removed a state official who engaged in certain political activities that were prohibited by the federal law known as the Hatch Act. The Court in that case stated: "while the United States is not concerned with, and has no power to regulate, local political activities as such of state officials, it does have the power to fix the terms on which its money allotments to states shall be disbursed." See also, *Sabri v. United States* (2004) (the necessary and proper clause and the spending clause justify a federal law making it a crime to bribe any agent of a state or local government receives $10,000 in federal funds).

The modern four-part test to measure the validity of a federal spending law.

South Dakota v. Dole (1987) upheld the power of Congress to use conditional spending to withhold federal highway funds from states that allowed the purchase or possession of alcoholic beverages by persons under the age of 21. The Court rejected South Dakota's argument that it should be able to keep the entirety of federal highway funds, and disregard the condition, on the basis that the Twenty–First Amendment gave the states complete power over the conditions of the sale or importation of liquor within a states' boundaries. The Court held that the Twenty–First Amendment, like the Tenth Amendment, was not a restriction on the federal government's power to impose conditions on federal spending programs. The most important aspect of the *Dole* case was not its limited ruling concerning the Twenty–First Amendment, but, rather, the Court's creation of a four-part test for the review of all federal spending programs.

Chief Justice Rehnquist, writing for the majority in *Dole*, found that there was a four-part test for reviewing federal spending power laws. First, the spending power should be used for the general welfare. The Chief Justice, relying on earlier cases, indicated that the Court would not second guess a congressional judgment as to whether a disbursement of federal money might help the welfare of the people in the United States. Second, if Congress wants to place conditions on the granting of money to a state or local government Congress must do so unambiguously, so that those governmental entities could make a knowing choice in deciding whether to accept the conditional grant. Third, the Chief Justice stated: "Our cases have suggested (without significant elaboration) that conditions on federal grants might be illegitimate if they are unrelated to the interest in particular national projects or programs." Fourth, a federal spending program would be invalid if the statute (or any conditions placed on the persons who received the money from the spending program) violated an "independent bar" to the spending power that was set forth in the Constitution or the Amendments to the Constitution.

In *Dole,* the majority had no problem in finding that the four conditions were met in the federal program at issue in that case. First, it is reasonably arguable that granting money for building and maintaining highways promotes the general welfare. Second, Congress had explicitly stated that states would sacrifice part of their grants if they did not establish a 21 year old drinking age. Third, the condition established by the law at issue (that a state have a 21 year old drinking age to receive a complete highway program grant) was arguably related to the purpose for which the federal government funded highways (the purpose of having safe roads for travel). Finally, there was no independent bar to this use of the spending power, because the majority ruled that the Tenth Amendment was not a limit on the exercise of the federal spending power.

In an important portion of the *Dole* opinion, the Chief Justice explained what the Court meant by an independent constitutional bar: "The independent constitutional bar limitation on the spending power is not [as South Dakota argued] a prohibition on the indirect achievement of objects which Congress is not empowered to achieve directly. Instead ... the power may not be used to induce the states to engage in activities that would themselves be unconstitutional. Thus, for example, a grant of federal funds conditioned on invidiously discriminatory state action or the infliction of cruel and unusual punishment would be an illegitimate exercise of the Congress's broad spending power."

The Chief Justices's opinion in *Dole* also reaffirmed a long-standing principle that a condition on a federal grant that might induce a state or local government to take certain actions is not an unconstitutional coercion of state or local government autonomy. The Chief Justice stated that any other conclusion would "plunge the law in endless difficulties."

Students must beware of the phrase "the doctrine of unconstitutional conditions." The doctrine of unconstitutional conditions (believe it or not) means no more than a governmental entity cannot use conditions that would violate the Constitution or its Amendments. No kidding, that is all the doctrine entails. There is no requirement that Congress refrain from using conditions in its grants. In other words, there is no constitutional requirement that the Congress act like grandparents, rather than like parents, when giving money to state or local governments (or to anyone else). Your grandparent gives you money with no strings attached (i.e., no conditions) just because your grandparent likes to see you smile. On the other hand, your parents may condition your receiving your allowance on doing tasks such as mowing the lawn or shoveling snow.

The federal government may place a condition on the grant of money to persons or governmental entities, so long as the condition does not violate a specific constitutional restriction on the actions of the federal government. The Court in *Dole* ruled that the Tenth Amendment was not a prohibition on the conditional spending of the federal government. On that basis, in *New York v. United States* (1992), the Supreme Court upheld a reduction in the amount of federal grants to states that did not adopt specific legislation dealing with environmentally dangerous waste, even though the Court, in the same case, ruled that Congress could not simply order state governments to enact such legislation.

Congress could not require an individual to become a Roman Catholic as a condition of receiving a federal grant, because that condition would violate both the establishment and free exercise clauses of the First Amendment. Congress could not condition a grant of federal law enforcement money to states or cities on the basis that the state or city had to authorize police to engage in searches of houses that would violate the Fourth Amendment. The First and Fourth Amendments are independent constitutional restrictions on federal actions that would invalidate the conditions in those hypothetical federal spending laws.

Chapter 6

INTERNATIONAL AFFAIRS

Table of Sections

§ 6.1 Introduction—The Executive

The United States, in its capacity as a sovereign nation, must interact with other countries in the international realm, for the ability of a nation to conduct foreign relations is inherent in the concept of sovereignty. Because specific constitutional references to foreign relations are sparse, much of the foreign affairs power has evolved from constitutionally implied powers and, perhaps, from extra-constitutional sources.

Traditionally the President is responsible for conducting the foreign affairs of the United States. Justice Sutherland, speaking for a unanimous Court, acknowledged this principle in the leading case of *United States v. Curtiss–Wright Export Corp.* (1936).

> [T]he President alone has the power to speak or listen as a representative of the nation.... As Marshall said in his great argument of March 7, 1800, in the House of Representatives, "The President is the sole organ of the nation in its external relations, and its sole representative with foreign nations."

Interestingly, one cannot find such plenary executive power explicitly mentioned anywhere in the text of the Constitution. Nor will any examination of the affirmative grants of foreign affairs power in the Constitution reveal that the President is the "sole organ" of foreign relations.

116

Article II of the Constitution specifically enumerates the executive's foreign affairs. The President is empowered to make treaties, with a concurrence of two-thirds of the Senate, and to appoint ambassadors, public ministers and consuls with the Senate's advice and consent. The Constitution also authorizes the chief executive, as the representative of the United States, to receive ambassadors and public ministers. The Commander–in–Chief power, constitutionally delegated to the President, also profoundly affects United States' international relations. Although these provisions attest to the fact that the President has an active role in foreign affairs, the executive, over time, has gone far beyond these express grants in conducting international relations.

Theories Based on the President's Role as "Commander–in–Chief" and His Duty to "Take Care" that "The Laws Be Faithfully Executed." One may extrapolate implied foreign affairs powers from the Commander–in–Chief clause and the Constitutional provision that the executive shall "take care" that "the laws be faithfully executed." Presidents have authorized forceful intervention in foreign conflicts under the auspices of "take care" clause, contending that the duty to see all laws are faithfully executed also encompasses international law. These assertions have, however, often been thought to be unpersuasive because it is generally understood that this clause applies to international law only to the extent it has been incorporated into the law of the United States in situations occurring either in situations within the United States or affecting American citizens or the government.

The _Curtiss–Wright_ Case. The Court acknowledged the unique role of the executive in _United States v. Curtiss–Wright Export Corp._ (1936). The case involved a controversy surrounding a Presidential Embargo Proclamation of May 28, 1934, prohibiting the sale of arms to countries involved in the Chaco conflict in South America. Authorization for this declaration was granted in a joint congressional resolution passed earlier on the same day empowering the President to issue a proclamation limiting arms and ammunition sales to those involved in the conflict. Congress revoked the proclamation in November of 1935. At a time when the Court was hostile to delegations of power in the domestic sphere, the Court had no trouble upholding the resolution, finding the proclamation valid. Justice Sutherland, writing for the majority, addressed the special role of the President in international relations.

Although Sutherland depicts presidential predominance in foreign affairs, it should not be forgotten that, in that case, the President was acting _in accord with_ congressional policy. Sutherland's broad language should be read in light of the facts with which he was faced. As Justice Jackson, in his concurrence in _Youngstown Sheet & Tube Co. v. Sawyer_ (1952) noted, _Curtiss–_

Wright was dealing with situations arising when the presidential actions are in harmony with an act of Congress, not when the President acts contrary to Congress.

Based on dicta in Supreme Court rulings, practical experience, and Congressional acquiescence, the executive has usually predominated the foreign affairs sphere. The President's expansive international relations power is not plenary, nor may it be exercised contrary to restrictions in the Constitution such as the Bill of Rights. Compare, *Ex Parte Quirin* (1942) (approving the use of court martial proceedings to try persons—including one who claimed U.S. citizenship—who allegedly entered the country illegally for the purpose of sabotage), and *Rumsfeld v. Padilla* (2004) (on jurisdictional grounds, the Court avoids ruling on the extent of the President's power to keep a U.S. citizen in military custody as an enemy combatant), with *Hamdi v. Rumsfeld* (2004) (without a majority opinion, the Court requires the government to give a U.S. citizen held in the United States to be given some type of hearing at which he could contest the facts on which the government based a decision to treat him as an enemy combatant), and *Rasul v. Bush* (2004) (ruling that federal courts had jurisdiction to consider habeas corpus petitions from foreign nationals captured in another country and held in detention at the U.S. military base at Guantanamo Bay, Cuba).

§ 6.2 Congress

There is a continual controversy between Congress and the executive as to the extent of each branch's foreign affairs power. The dispute centers on whether Congress and the President act as constitutional equals in this sphere or whether the executive initiates foreign policy, while Congress acts merely to implement the President's policy.

There are specific Constitutional provisions granting Congress authority in foreign affairs matters. Article I, § 8 defines these powers broadly: "Congress shall have Power to provide for the common Defence," to regulate foreign commerce, and to "define and punish Piracies and Felonies committed on the high Seas, and Offences against the law of Nations," to declare war, to make rules of war, grant letters of marque and reprisal, and to raise, support and regulate an army and a navy. Two-thirds of the Senate must consent to treaties before they are ratified. The Senate also is authorized to advise the President on the contents of the treaty.

The President relies on congressional legislation and appropriations to implement foreign affairs policy. Congress can stymie implementation of executive international policy by refusing to appropriate necessary funds. Foreign aid programs depend on Congressional authorization as provided for in the spending power clause. Indeed, if the Senate ratifies a treaty that calls for money to be spent, the House and Senate must pass a law to enact the necessary spending. The treaty itself cannot provide for the appropriation because the Constitution provides that all bills for raising revenue must originate in the House.

§ 6.3   The Judiciary

Although the executive and legislative branches of the federal government dominate United States foreign affairs, Supreme Court decisions also influence foreign policy. Specific constitutional provisions in Article III, § 2 indicate that the Court is in a position to wield substantial power in international affairs. Historically, however, the Court frequently defers to the judgment of Congress and the Executive when a conflict arises that may have an impact on foreign relations.

The Court's Jurisdiction. The Article III grant of judicial power to the federal courts includes: cases involving foreign nations, suits by United States citizens against aliens or foreign diplomats, and suits to interpret and enforce treaty terms. Federal courts also consider cases arising under the "Laws of the United States," which include all laws made in pursuance of the Constitution.

Congress is constitutionally authorized to define and punish international law violations, thereby incorporating international law into United States law. The Constitution thus grants Federal court jurisdiction over cases involving international law. Consequently, the Court will occasionally address issues involving international law and will make pronouncements that affect both the structure of United States foreign policy and international law.

The Political Question Doctrine and Foreign Affairs. The Court hesitates to exercise any authority in the area of foreign affairs that would exceed the scope of these express constitutional grants. Although the Supreme Court is empowered to review acts of the legislature and executive to insure conformance with constitutional provisions, the political question doctrine is an important exception to this judicial review, and demonstrates the Court's reluctance to take an active role in formulating foreign policy. As *Baker v. Carr* (1962), explained:

> The conduct of the foreign relations of our Government is committed by the Constitution to the Executive and Legislative—"the political"—Departments of the Government, and the propriety of what may be done in the exercise of this political power is not subject to judicial inquiry or decision.

Baker indicated that there are some instances when the political question doctrine will not exempt foreign affairs issues from judicial review, but these exceptions are primarily limited to situations where the judiciary is acting in the absence of any conclusive action by the executive or Congress.

In practice the Supreme Court employs the political question rationale to abstain from foreign affairs cases only infrequently. Typically, in order to maintain judicial independence and integrity, the Court refrains from reviewing executive and legislative action relating to foreign affairs by deciding that the political branches are acting within the scope of their constitutional authority.

The Supreme Court exercises considerable influence over foreign affairs legislation. The federal judiciary interprets laws, international law, executive agreements and treaties.

§ 6.4 The Treaty Power

Constitutional provisions confer the treaty making power specifically on the President and the Senate. The Constitution empowers the President " ... by and with the Advice and Consent of the Senate, to make treaties provided two thirds of the Senators present concur." Other language expressly prohibits states from entering, in their own right, into treaties or alliances. Treaties are proclaimed to be the supreme law of the land and binding upon states. Federal judicial power, in addition, is constitutionally extended to encompass cases involving treaties made under the authority of the federal government. Another constitutional directive relevant to the treaty power is the necessary and proper clause, which enables Congress to enact all law needed to implement and enforce treaties.

As Justice Field stated, in often quoted dictum in *De Geofroy v. Riggs* (1890), the treaty power, like all other powers that the Constitution grants, is subject to constitutional limitations.

Justice Black's opinion in *Reid v. Covert* (1957) made what is often considered the definitive pronouncement on this issue:

[N]o agreement with a foreign nation can confer power on the Congress, or on any other branch of Government, which is free from the restraints of the Constitution.

Black concluded that Constitutional provisions limit the acts of the President, the joint actions of the President and the Senate, and consequently they limit the treaty power. Given these limitations on the scope of the treaty making power, unless treaties are contrary to the Constitution, they are equal in status to congressional legislation, and, as expressly provided in the Supremacy Clause of Article VI, the supreme law of the land.

Treaties and the Tenth Amendment. The states have sometimes argued that the Tenth Amendment imposes additional limitations upon the treaty power. They claim that, under the Constitution, they retain control over certain matters, and the federal government cannot alter these reserved powers through treaties. The Court confronted this issue in *Hauenstein v. Lynham* (1879).

Hauenstein was a suit by the heirs of a Swiss citizen who died intestate owning property in Virginia. The plaintiffs sought to recover the proceeds from the sale of the property by the local escheator. The heirs, invoking provisions of a treaty between the United States and Switzerland, prevailed over local law, which prevented such aliens from taking property by descent or inheritance. The Court held that, under the supremacy clause of Article VI, treaties (like federal statutes) are the supreme law of the land and superior to the laws and constitutions of the individual states. Treatise, like federal statutes and the U.S. Constitution, "are as much a part of the law of every State as its own local laws and Constitution."

Missouri v. Holland (1920) rejected any Tenth Amendment limitation on the federal treaty power. Initially, Congress enacted a statute to protect migratory birds in danger of extinction. Lower courts invalidated this Act because they found that no specific constitutional provision empowered Congress to regulate matters of this nature. (This was a time when the Court interpreted the interstate commerce clause narrowly.) Later, the United States concluded a treaty with Great Britain involving the same issues that the statute had covered. New statutes were passed to implement the treaty. In *Missouri v. Holland* the state brought a bill in equity to prevent the federal game warden from enforcing the Migratory Bird Treaty and the regulations made pursuant to it.

Missouri claimed that the treaty and new statutes interfered with its Tenth Amendment reserved rights. Justice Holmes, writing for the Court, concluded that the Tenth Amendment does not limit the treaty power. *Before* the Treaty existed, the migratory bird act (assuming the correctness of the earlier decisions) did not implement any federal power. *After* the Treaty the migratory bird act did implement a federal power, the treaty power. The provisions of the Treaty, and the statute implementing the Treaty, did not contravene the Bill of Rights or any other constitutional provisions limiting congressional powers. Therefore, Holmes concluded, any limitation upon the treaty would have to be based upon the general terms of the Tenth Amendment. But the treaty power is specifically delegated to the federal governments and the Tenth Amendment only purports to apply to nondelegated powers. Thus the Tenth Amendment does not limit the treaty power.

The President's Power to Terminate Treaties. For a time, efforts to limit the treaty power focused on the President's authority to terminate treaties. In *Goldwater v. Carter* (1979) several Senators and others sued for declaratory and injunctive relief against President Carter after he announced that he planned to terminate the mutual defense treaty with Taiwan, the Republic of China. The President gave the one year notice that the termination clause of the treaty required. He also recognized the Peoples Republic of China (the Peking Government) rather than the Nationalist Government of Taiwan as the Government of China.

The Court, without opinion, granted certiorari and ordered the district court to dismiss the complaint. Justice Marshall, without issuing a separate opinion, concurred in the dismissal. Justices Blackmun and White voted to set the case for argument.

Justice Rehnquist, joined by Chief Justice Burger and Justices Stevens and Stewart, concurred in the judgment and filed a statement concluding that the "basic question presented by the petitioners in this case is political and therefore nonjusticiable because it involves the authority of the President in the conduct of our country's foreign relations and the extent to which the Senate or the Congress is authorized to negate the action of the President."

Justice Brennan rejected the majority's view of the political question doctrine. However, he would have held that President Carter's action was justified by Article II, which, in Brennan's view, gave the president the exclusive power to recognize foreign governments. The President abrogated the treaty with Taiwan because he recognized the Peking Government.

Only Justice Powell's concurrence argued that there were judicially discoverable and manageable standards because decision in this case "only" required the Court to interpret the Constitution. He did not tell us what these standards are. Nonetheless he concurred in the dismissal of the case because he thought that the issue was not yet "ripe" and would not be until Congress chose to "confront the President," and reached a "constitutional impasse."

§ 6.5 Executory and Self–Executing Treaties

Although no provisions in the Constitution discuss the nature of a treaty, the Court has recognized that two types of treaties exist. Treaties may be either executory, [a ratified treaty that requires implementing legislation before it takes effect as domestic law]; or self-executory [a ratified treaty that takes effect as domestic law immediately upon ratification]. *Foster v. Neilson* (1829) held that state and federal courts should regard treaties as equivalent to an act of Congress whenever the treaty operates by itself without the aid of any federal statute to implement it [in other words, whenever the treaty is self-executory in nature]. The *Foster* opinion stated:

> But when the terms of the stipulation import a contract, when either of the parties engages to perform a particular act, the treaty addresses itself to the political, not the judicial department; and the legislature must execute the contract before it can become a rule for the Court.

Whitney v. Robertson (1888) acknowledged that executory treaties have no effect until the necessary legislation is enacted.

Thus, treaties are the "supreme law of the land," so a self-executing treaty, just like a statute, serves to override or preempt contrary state law. But if a treaty is not self-executing, there must be implementing legislation before an American court can enforce the treaty as domestic law.

An international agreement of the United States is not "self-executing" if either: (1) the agreement itself states or indicates that it will require the enactment of implementing legislation; or (2), the Senate, when ratifying the treaty, or Congress, by resolution, requires implementing legislation; or (3), if the Constitution itself requires implementing legislation. As for requirement (3)—when the Constitution itself requires implementing legislation—it is generally thought that a treaty alone (one that the President has signed and the Senate has ratified) cannot appropriate money or impose a new tax or impose a new tariff (because the Constitution has a special clause providing that all revenue bills shall originate in the House of Representatives). On the other hand, it is not uncommon for a treaty regulating foreign commerce to affect tariffs by including clauses that give "most-favored-nation" status to the signatories. But those treaties do *not* impose any new tariffs.

§ 6.6 Conflicts Between Treaties and Acts of Congress

While treaties as well as federal statutes are the supreme law of the land, the Constitution provides no explicit solution when a self-executing treaty conflicts with acts of Congress. *Whitney v. Robertson* (1888) addressed this issue. The case involved a dispute arising between the United States and the Dominican Republic over the terms of a sugar trade treaty to which the two nations were parties.

Whitney stated that treaties and legislative acts are equal, both being the supreme law of the land. When the treaty and statute:

> relate to the same subject, the courts will always endeavor to construe them so as to give effect to both, if that can be done

without violating the language of either; but if the two are inconsistent, the one last in date will control the other....

Acts of Congress passed after the date of the treaty, the Court held, control over the treaty terms. Similarly, a self-executing treaty is valid as domestic law and takes precedence over a federal law enacted earlier. In short, the last expression of the sovereign will controls.

Chae Chan Ping v. United States (1889) [the *Chinese Exclusion Case*] held that an act excluding Chinese laborers from the United States was a constitutional exercise of legislative power even though it conflicted with an existing treaty. Because treaties are equivalent to acts of the legislature, they can, like statutes, be repealed or amended. The last expression of the sovereign will was the statute, which conflicted with the earlier enacted treaty.

However, as a rule of interpretation, the Court will not deem a treaty to be abrogated or modified by a later statute unless the Congressional purpose was clearly expressed. The courts will not find that ambiguous congressional action has implicitly repealed a treaty. A *fortiori*, legislative silence is insufficient to repeal a treaty.

§ 6.7 Executive Agreements and Acts of Congress

International Agreements by Statute and Executive Agreement. The Constitution expressly provides that the President, "shall have Power, by and with the Advice and Consent of the Senate to make Treaties, provided that two thirds of the Senators present concur...." This clause does not explicitly provide that it is the exclusive method of making international agreements, and neither historical practice nor the Supreme Court has interpreted the clause in this manner.

It is not unusual for both Houses of Congress to enact (by simple majority) a statute or joint resolution that approves of an international agreement in lieu of ratification by two-thirds of the Senate. While this conclusion may be initially surprising, historical tradition strongly supports it, and the commentators treat the question as no longer controversial.

Presidents have also used Executive Agreements to make accords with foreign countries, without Senatorial approval. These agreements, while they cannot be termed treaties because they lack the constitutional requirement of consent by the Senate, frequently cover the same subject matter as treaties.

The Types of Executive Agreements. There are basically four types of executive agreements. FIRST, the President may conclude an executive agreement based on exclusive presidential powers, such as the power as commander-in-chief of the armed forces pursuant to which he conducts military operations with our allies, or his power to receive foreign ambassadors and recognize foreign governments. SECOND, the President may conclude an executive agreement in pursuance of an authorization contained in a prior treaty. THIRD, the President may derive power to conclude an executive agreement from prior Congressional authorization. That is, the House and Senate together may delegate certain powers to the President, which he exercises together with his independent powers in the areas of foreign affairs. FOURTH, the President may obtain Congressional confirmation by both Houses of an agreement that the President has negotiated.

The *Pink* Case. The Supreme Court discussed the status of an executive agreement in *United States v. Pink* (1942). That case involved a dispute over the title to the New York assets of a Russian insurance company. Russia had nationalized all her insurance companies in 1918 and 1919 by decrees intended to include the foreign assets of all Russian insurance businesses. In 1933, President Roosevelt and the Soviet Government concluded the Litvinov Assignment, an executive agreement whereby the United States agreed to recognize the Soviet Government. In return, the Soviet Union assigned (to the United States Government) its interests in the assets of the Russian insurance company located in New York. This agreement was the first type of executive agreement discussed above: it was entered into pursuant to the President's constitutional authority to recognize foreign governments.

Under the terms of the executive agreement, the United States became entitled to the property; the rights of the United States were to be superior to the claims of the corporation and foreign creditors. The Supreme Court found that the New York state court's policy not to recognize the Soviet government and the state's refusal to enforce the Litvinov Assignment ran counter to the executive agreement made by President Roosevelt in connection with his recognition of the Government of the U.S.S.R. Thus, the state's refusal was invalid, because it conflicted with the executive agreement.

Justice Douglas, for the Court, noted that the Litvinov Assignment was an international compact, an executive agreement, which did not require Senate approval. The majority opinion stated:

> A treaty is a "Law of the Land" under the supremacy clause ... of the Constitution. Such international compacts and agreements as the Litvinov Assignment have a similar dignity.

Just as state law yields to treaties, so must provisions of the executive agreement prevail over state policy. The Court found that the provisions of the Litvinov Assignment passing the vested Soviet right in the property to the United States must be recognized as valid by New York.

The Executive Agreement in *Pink* explicitly preempted the inconsistent state law. Just like statutes, constitutionally Executive Agreements can preempt inconsistent state law even if the preemption is implicit.

If property had been taken, nothing in *Pink* suggests that just compensation was unavailable. *Pink* merely reaffirmed the President's ability to enter into agreements that would override state law, provided the agreement itself did not violate any provision of the Bill of Rights or other provision of the Constitution.

The Iranian Assets Litigation. *Dames & Moore v. Regan* (1981) illustrates the broad presidential power to settle foreign claims by use of executive agreements. Iranians seized the American Embassy in Tehran on November 4, 1980, and held the occupants hostage. President Carter, acting pursuant to his powers under the International Emergency Economic Powers Act, eventually issued a blocking order that froze all the Iranian Government assets subject to the jurisdiction of the United States. Eventually, Iran released the American hostages, after the United States and Iran signed an agreement concerning the settlement of claims.

That agreement required the United States to terminate all suits brought in the U.S. courts against Iran and to "nullify all attachments and judgments obtained therein, to prohibit all further litigation based on such claims, and to bring about the termination of such claims through binding arbitration" before an Iran–United States Claims Tribunal. President Carter, and later President Reagan, signed a series of executive orders to implement this agreement. These orders purported to nullify all attachments, liens, or other non-Iranian interests in Iranian assets subject to President Carter's November 14, 1979 freeze of Iranian assets.

Petitioner sued for declaratory and injunctive relief against the enforcement of the Executive Orders and the Treasury Department's implementing regulations. They claimed that enforcement was unconstitutional to the extent that it adversely affected petitioner's final judgment on a contract claim against the Government of Iran and the Atomic Energy Organization of Iran, its execution of that judgment in the state of Washington, its prejudgment attachments, and its ability to continue to litigate against the Iranian banks.

The Court, per Justice Rehnquist, upheld the constitutionality of the Executive Orders, relying in large part on Justice Jackson's seminal analysis in *Youngstown Sheet & Tube Co. v. Sawyer* (1952). The Court's opinion in *Dames & Moore* was narrowly drafted and attentive to the civil liberties implications. It held that, if the

President's freeze amounted to a taking of property, the Government must provide just compensation. This opinion provides no support for the proposition that the President has inherent authority to sign an Executive Agreement that is inconsistent with any of the other provisions of the Bill of Rights. On the contrary, the decision reaffirms the supremacy of the Bill of Rights.

The Court first concluded that Congress, by statute, had explicitly authorized the President to nullify the post-freeze attachments and to direct that the blocked Iranian assets be transferred to the New York Federal Reserve Bank and later to Iran. The purpose of this statute is to permit the President to maintain the foreign assets at his disposal for use as a "bargaining chip" when negotiating with a hostile nation.

In addition to the attachments of the Iranian assets there were also underlying claims against Iran. The Court was unable to find any explicit authority to suspend the claims pending in the U.S. Courts. However, while there was no evidence of contrary congressional intent, there was evidence of legislative intent to invite broad presidential action. There was also a long history of congressional acquiescence of similar presidential conduct. "Crucial to our decision today is the conclusion that Congress has implicitly approved the practice of claim settlement by executive agreement."

The exercise of presidential power in this case did not unconstitutionally divest the federal courts of jurisdiction, any more than a finding of sovereign immunity divests the courts of jurisdiction. Rather the President has directed the federal courts to apply a different rule of substantive law.

Petitioner also charged that the suspension of its claims constituted a taking of their property without just compensation. The Court found this question was not ripe for review. However the majority did find ripe the question whether petitioner would have a remedy at law in the Court of Claims if in fact there was a taking. And the Court held that, if there were a taking, the Court of Claims would have jurisdiction to provide compensation.

When Executive Agreements Conflict with Federal Statutes. Questions still remain as to what extent an executive agreement is equivalent to a treaty. To what extent does an executive agreement override an earlier enacted federal statute? And when does a federal statute override an executive agreement promulgated earlier?

If the President has authority under the Constitution or otherwise to promulgate an executive order, and if that order is consistent with previously enacted federal law, then that executive agreement is also the supreme law of the land and must prevail over contrary state law; such an executive agreement should also prevail over earlier Congressional enactments *if* the President is, in fact, entering into an agreement pursuant to his exclusive presidential authority in the field of foreign relations. If the President's authority to promulgate an executive agreement does not derive from his exclusive presidential powers—if, for example, it does not derive from his power to recognize foreign governments or his power as commander-in-chief—then the executive agreement should not be able to override an earlier enacted federal statute.

§ 6.8   The Historical Development of the War Power

Constitutional language suggests that the President and Congress share the war power. The nature of the executive and congressional war powers is the subject of a long debate—a debate that was initiated when the Constitution was written and continues to the present day.

In the *Prize Cases* (1862), which arose during the Civil War, the Supreme Court found President Lincoln had the right to blockade southern states without a congressional declaration of war. Writing for a five to four majority, Justice Grier stated that the President has the power to determine if hostilities are sufficiently serious to compel him to act to suppress the belligerency or take defensive measures:

> [The President] has no power to initiate or declare a war either against a foreign nation or a domestic State. But by the Acts of Congress of February 28, 1795, and 3d of March, 1807, he is authorized to call out the military and naval forces of the United States in case of invasion by foreign nations, and to suppress insurrection against the government of a State or of the United States.
>
> If a war be made by invasion of a foreign nation, the President is not only authorized but bound to resist force by force. He does not initiate the war, but is bound to accept the challenge without waiting for any special legislative authority. And whether the hostile party be a foreign invader, or States organized in rebellion, it is none the less a war, although the declaration of it be "unilateral."

The executive, the Court indicated, was also authorized to determine what degree of force should be used to respond to the conflict.

In recent decades the trend has been for the President to secure general Congressional authorization to fall back upon in case the executive's power to authorize military intervention in foreign conflicts is later attacked.

§ 6.9   Economic Regulations and the War Power

The power of the President and Congress to impose economic regulations in times of war provides insight into the nature and scope of the war power. In *Woods v. Cloyd W. Miller Co.* (1948) the Supreme Court reversed the District Court, which had held that Congress' authority to regulate rent by virtue of the war power ended with the Presidential Proclamation terminating World War II hostilities. The Supreme Court found that the war power sustained Title II of the Housing and Rent Act of 1947.

The Steel Seizure Case. *Youngstown Sheet & Tube Co. v. Sawyer* (1952) discussed the President's power to impose economic regulations under the Commander–in–Chief clause and other constitutional provisions. Apprehensive that an impending steel worker's strike would endanger national security, President Truman issued an executive order instructing Secretary of Commerce Sawyer to seize and operate many of the nation's steel mills. Truman justified the executive order as valid under the constitutional and statutory power vested in him as President and Commander–in–Chief.

Pursuant to the President's order, the Secretary of Commerce seized the steel mills. Sawyer directed the presidents of the mills to operate their facilities in compliance with regulations that the Department of Commerce issued. Truman immediately informed Congress of these events, but the legislature failed to take any action. Congress had previously enacted legislation for handling situations of this nature but, had expressly refused to authorize governmental seizure of property.

The steel companies filed suit against Secretary of Commerce Sawyer in the district court praying for declaratory judgment and injunctive relief. The district court granted the plaintiffs a preliminary injunction, which the appellate court stayed. The Supreme Court, in an expedited proceeding, affirmed the district court's order in a six to three decision finding the executive's seizure order invalid.

Justice Black wrote the opinion for the Court, which was joined by Justices Frankfurter, Douglas, Jackson and Burton. Justice Clark concurred in the judgment of the Court. Three Justices dissented.

Justice Black's majority opinion found that no express or implied statutory provision authorized the President's seizure order. The Court rejected the argument that the order should be upheld as a valid exercise of the President's Commander–in–Chief power. Black concluded that the executive power vested in the President by the Constitution, particularly his duty to see that the laws are faithfully executed, refuted the idea that the chief executive can make laws. Congress has "exclusive constitutional authority to make laws necessary and proper to carry out the powers vested by the Constitution" in the federal government. The "necessary and proper" clause applies to Congress, not to the executive branch.

In his concurring opinion Justice Frankfurter indicated he was not drawing conclusions as to what powers the President would have had in the absence of legislation applicable to the seizure. What was at issue was the President's authorization of the steel seizure after Congress had expressly refused to support this course of action. Prior incidents of industrial seizures, Frankfurter concluded, did not indicate a past history of Congressional acquiescence of executive authority in this area.

Justice Jackson's Three–Part Analysis. Justice Jackson, in his separate concurrence in the *Steel Seizure Case*, argued that the President's powers "are not fixed but fluctuate, depending upon their disjunction or conjunction with those of Congress." The scope of the President's war powers, Jackson believed, depended upon a three part analysis.

First, the President's authority is at its maximum, if he acts pursuant to an express authorization of Congress. If the President had seized the steel mills pursuant to Congressional grant of authority, the constitutional validity of his action would probably have been upheld.

Second, if the President acted:

in the absence of either a congressional grant or denial of authority, he can only rely upon his own independent powers, but there is a zone of twilight in which he and Congress may have concurrent authority, or in which its distribution is uncertain. Therefore, congressional inertia ... may sometimes ... enable, if not invite, measures on independent presidential responsibility.

Third, if, the President acts contrary to the express or implied will of Congress then the executive power falls to an extremely low level. The President can then rely only upon his own constitutional powers minus any constitutional powers of Congress over the matter. Courts can sustain exclusive presidential control in such a case only by disabling the Congress from acting upon the subject. Presidential claim to a power at once so conclusive and preclusive must be scrutinized with caution.

Jackson concluded that the steel seizure order was contrary to the will of Congress and, as a consequence, could only be upheld if such seizures were found to be within the power of the executive and beyond the scope of congressional authority. Jackson, like

Justice Black, believed that the President's actions were not of that type.

§ 6.10 The War Powers Resolution

The ability of the executive to deploy the military to foreign nations to fight in informal wars created a growing discontent with what many have regarded as the President's assumption of congressional war power during the Viet Nam conflict. To restore what has been argued to be the balance intended by the framers, Congress passed the War Powers Resolution over a presidential veto on November 7, 1973.

The War Powers Resolution restricts the executive's authority to involve the United States in foreign controversies without Congressional approval. Specific provisions of the Resolution, however, allow the President to send the military into combat without requesting authorization from Congress if the United States or one of its territories is attacked.

The War Powers Resolution raises many interesting and unresolved questions. Is the Resolution binding? If it is, who has standing to sue claiming a violation of the provisions? No specific language in the Resolution resolves the standing issue.

If standing is found to exist, it may well be that judicial review of cases under this law is foreclosed by the doctrine of political questions. The impact on foreign affairs of a judicial decision contrary to the President's military actions already underway may suggest that questions regarding provisions of the War Powers Resolution should be considered nonjusticiable and immune from judicial review as political questions.

Even if this War Powers Resolution were reviewable in litigation, its constitutionality may be subject to a presidential claim that the resolution improperly seeks to subtract from her or his inherent powers. However, in that case, the War Powers Resolution should still be relevant, for under Justice Jackson's analysis in the *Steel Seizure case*, the President's war powers should be at their lowest ebb: if she would act contrary to the War Powers Resolution, she would then have only her own powers minus any Constitutional powers of Congress.

Legislative Veto. Even without raising the specter of inherent presidential powers, some commentators have concluded that section 5(c) of the War Powers Resolution is an unconstitutional legislative veto and therefore invalid in the wake of *Immigration and Naturalization Service v. Chadha* (1983). Section 5(c) purports to allow Congress to force the President to withdraw U.S. armed forces engaged in hostilities outside the territorial United States. *Chadha* requires that action having "the purpose and effect of altering the legal rights, duties and relations of persons, including . . . Executive Branch officials,'' must be subjected to the possibility of presidential veto. But section 5(c) is not subject to a presidential veto. Adoption of a concurrent resolution under section 5(c) has the purpose and effect of altering the rights and duties of the President. Thus, *Chadha* should invalidate the legislative veto provision in the War Powers Resolution.

Chapter 7

THE PRESIDENT AND CONGRESS: SELECTED ISSUES

Table of Sections

§ 7.1   Executive Privilege

Beginning with *Marbury v. Madison* (1803), the Court has always asserted power to determine and enforce constitutional and other legal obligations of executive branch officials. The longer versions of this text include additional analysis of these issues.

(a) Executive Privilege: *United States v. Nixon*

In *United States v. Nixon* (1974), President Nixon claimed that the secret tape recordings (which were subject to subpoena) were directly under his control and solely in his custody.

A grand jury sitting in the District of Columbia had indicted seven of President Nixon's presidential aides and campaign staff for conspiracy to defraud the United States and to obstruct Justice. The grand jury named the President as an unindicted coconspirator. Based on the notion of the Special Prosecutor the District Court issued a subpoena *duces tecum* requiring the President to produce certain memoranda, papers, and tapes that related to specific meetings between the President and others.

In *United States v. Nixon*, Chief Justice Burger wrote for a unanimous Court. The Court summarily rejected the President's first line of argument, that the separation of powers doctrine precludes judicial review of a presidential claim of privilege.

President Nixon's second argument was that, as a matter of constitutional law, executive privilege prevails over the subpoena *duces tecum*. The Court agreed that the President has a prima facie privilege to maintain the confidentiality of internal executive communications. Although the Court recognized the need for executive privilege, the Court made it clear that such a privilege is not absolute and unqualified. The prima facie privilege must yield to the higher claims of judicial process in any criminal case where either the prosecution or defense has demonstrated a need for the evidence subpoenaed, and the evidence would otherwise be admissible at trial.

The Court stated that it would upset the constitutional balance to accept a generalized claim of confidentiality by the President in "nonmilitary and nondiplomatic discussions...." Finally, the Court made it clear that it is for the judicial branch to decide the extent of the duty of the President and other executive officials to produce evidence.

The President's generalized claim could not prevail over the "demonstrated, specific need for evidence in a pending criminal trial." Nevertheless, the Supreme Court ruled that the trial court, in conducting its *in camera* examination, must excise all material not relevant and admissible.

Noncriminal Litigation. The *Nixon* decision leaves open how the Court would weigh a generalized interest in confidentiality with the need for relevant evidence, in *civil litigation* or in a *congressional hearing*.

The Court also did not consider the President's interest in preserving military or diplomatic secrets. The Court will view itself as the arbiter of all inter-branch disputes over this issue and balance its view of the interest in confidentiality against its view of the need of the other branch of government to obtain evidence to effectuate its functions.

(b) The Presidential Recordings and Materials Preservation Act

Nixon v. Administrator of General Services Administration (1997), focused on a special federal statute dealing with executive privilege. After President Nixon resigned, Congress enacted the

Presidential Recordings and Materials Preservation Act. Title I of this Act directed the Administrator of the General Services Administration to take custody of former President Nixon's presidential papers and tape recordings; provide for their orderly processing and screening; return to the former President those items that were personal in nature; and establish the terms on which public might eventually have access for the remainder of the materials.

The Supreme Court upheld the Act and decided some important questions of separation of powers and executive privilege.

The Court held that a former President could assert executive privilege. Although one need not be an incumbent to claim the benefit of the privilege, the Court found it significant that neither of the incumbent Presidents after President Nixon supported his claim. The fact that later Presidents disagreed with Nixon detracted from his claim that the Act intrudes into the executive function.

The fact that the Act provided for the screening of materials persuaded the Court that there would be adequate safeguards to protect executive privilege. It is true that someone will be doing the screening and thus will be seeing the materials, but that intrusion is limited to personnel already in the executive branch and sensitive to executive concerns. Moreover, this limited intrusion has adequate justification: "the American people's ability to reconstruct and come to terms with their history [should not] be truncated by an analysis of Presidential privilege that focuses only on the needs of the present."

§ 7.2   Absolute Versus Qualified Immunity From Civil Damage Claims Brought Against the President and Other Executive Officials

Clinton v. Jones (1997) held that a private citizen could sue President Clinton for alleged illegal acts that were not part of his official duties and were allegedly committed in his personal capacity prior to the time he became the President of the United States.

The Justices unanimously ruled that the doctrine of separation of powers does not require a federal court to stay all private actions against a sitting President until he leaves office. Finally, *Clinton v. Jones* held that the District Court had abused its discretion in this case in deferring the trial until after the President left office.

Two important cases involving civil liability of the President and presidential aides were decided the same day in 1982: *Nixon v. Fitzgerald*, and *Harlow v. Fitzgerald*.

Fitzgerald was a management analyst for the Department of the Air Force; he was dismissed from his job after having "blown the whistle" in congressional hearings regarding cost overruns of the C–5A transport plane. The Air Force claimed that it terminated him as part of a reduction in force and not in retaliation for his embarrassing testimony. Claiming that he had been punished for his testimony, Fitzgerald sued President Nixon and various of his aides. The defendants claimed presidential immunity, and in *Fitzgerald*, the Court, speaking through Justice Powell, dealt with this question.

Nixon v. Fitzgerald held that "a former President of the United States is entitled to absolute immunity from damages liability predicated on his official acts. We consider this immunity a functionally mandated incident of the President's unique office, rooted in the constitutional tradition of the separation of powers and supported by our history." This immunity from money damages is absolute, but it is limited to claims "predicated on his official acts." The Court emphasized that this absolute civil damage immunity exists only in those cases where Congress has taken no "express legislative action to subject the President to civil liability for his official acts."

The President has absolute immunity from money damage claims based on acts within the *outer perimeter* of his official responsibility. The reason that this immunity is broader than the absolute immunity of prosecutors and similar government agents (who have immunity limited to the performance of particular functions) is that the President is a different type of agent. The President, as the head of the Executive Branch, has a unique role in the constitutional system.

The Qualified Immunity of Other Executive Officials. In *Harlow v. Fitzgerald*—the companion case to *Nixon v. Fitzgerald*—the Court ruled that the scope of immunity for senior presidential aides and advisers was only qualified, not absolute. "For executive officials in general," said the Court, "qualified immunity represents the norm."

Harlow fashioned a new, more objective rule that would allow for summary judgment in appropriate cases:

> Reliance on the *objective reasonableness* of an official's conduct, as measured by reference to clearly established law, should avoid excessive disruption of government and permit the resolution of many insubstantial claims on summary judgment. . . . We therefore hold that government officials performing discretionary functions generally are shielded from liability for civil damages insofar as their conduct does not violate clearly established statutory or constitutional rights of which a reasonable person would have known.

§ 7.3   The Pardoning Power

English common law vested the monarch, absolutely and exclusively, with the power to pardon those accused or convicted of crime. According to Lord Chief Justice Coke, the English King had great discretion and leeway in the exercise of this power; this pardon could be "either absolute, or under condition, exception, or qualification...."

The idea of executive pardoning power was so firmly established in the common law that delegates to the Constitutional Convention adopted, with little debate, a clause granting the President the power of executive pardon. Article II § 2 of the Constitution gives the President "... Power to grant Reprieves and Pardons for Offences against the United States, except in Cases of Impeachment." Case law has now developed the extent of the power to pardon far beyond that recognized at common law.

American courts early accepted the notion of broad discretion in the use of the presidential. In *United States v. Wilson* (1833), Chief Justice Marshall recognized that a pardon was an act of mercy, "an act of grace, proceeding from the power entrusted with the execution of the laws...." For almost a full century after *Wilson* most courts adhered to this view of a pardon as the executive's personal act of mercy toward an individual. Common law remained the basis for resolving questions concerning the reach of this "merciful" power.

Moving Beyond the Common Law. The Supreme Court ultimately abandoned the historical "act of grace" approach in *Biddle v. Perovich* (1927), which enunciated, for the first time, a theory of presidential pardon that went beyond simple adherence to common law precepts. The Court upheld a presidential commutation of sentence from death to life imprisonment even though the prisoner did not consent to the change in his sentence.

It is easy to appreciate the significance of *Biddle* by comparing it with an earlier case, *Burdick v. United States* (1915), which had held that acceptance of the pardon was essential and that a witness in a grand jury proceeding could refuse to accept a pardon and instead assert his privilege against self-incrimination. *Burdick* recognized that in some instances the stigma of a pardon would not be wanted and that one could therefore reject the "merciful" act. In *Biddle*, however, Justice Holmes' opinion for the Court made it clear that a pardon is an act for the public welfare, "not a private act of grace from an individual happening to possess power." The Court recognized presidential power to impose "less severe" punishments for the public welfare and ruled that consent was not necessary in such a situation, because the prisoner "on no sound principle ought to have any voice in what the law should do for the welfare of the whole.''

In addition to changing the theoretical focus of the pardon power from a private act to one for the general welfare, *Biddle,* for the first time, refused to sanction a technical distinction between the power to pardon and the power to commute a sentence. Courts had previously viewed commutation as completely different forms of clemency. The Court recognized that the President's power extends to imposition of less severe punishments; where the substituted sentence is one generally recognized as being less hard, the President need not grant full pardon. The Court expanded the scope of the pardoning power to include commutation without the prisoner's consent, but it did not go so far as to hold that the President has unlimited freedom in substituting punishment.

Ex parte Garland (1866) considered the effect of President Andrew Johnson's pardon of Garland for all offenses committed by him arising from his participation in the Civil War. Prior to the pardon, Congress had enacted a law providing that any individual who wished to practice law in the federal courts had to take an oath stating that he had never voluntarily borne arms against the United States or given aid to its enemies. Finding the Act to be unconstitutional as a bill of attainder, the Court held that the presidential pardon had relieved Garland from all penalties and disabilities, including the oath, for the named acts.

In speaking of the scope of the President's Constitutional pardoning power, the Court noted that ''[i]t extends to every offence known to the law, and may be exercised at any time after its commission, either before legal proceedings are taken, or during their pendency, or after conviction and judgment.'' A full pardon erases the act and its legal consequences so that ''in the eye of the law the offender is as innocent as if he had never committed the offense'' and restores the offender to ''all his civil rights.''

Ex parte Grossman (1925), held that the President's power extended not only to indictable crimes but also to contempt of court. Other early decisions have made it clear that the pardoning power encompasses the capacity to remit fines and forfeitures; to commute sentences; to grant amnesty to specified classes or groups; and to pardon conditionally as well as absolutely.

The pardon power of Article II, § 2 does have some limitations. *Knote v. United States* (1877) explained that a pardon could not compensate the offender for personal injuries suffered by imprisonment, nor can a pardon affect any rights that have vested in others due to the judgment against the offender. *Knote* went on to point out:

However large ... may be the power of pardon possessed by the President, and however extended may be its application, there is this limit to it, as there is to all his powers—it cannot touch moneys in the Treasury of the United States, except expressly authorized by act of Congress. The Constitution places this restriction upon the pardoning power.

Schick v. Reed (1974) affirmed the power of the President to attach conditions to grants of clemency. A divided Court upheld the presidential commutation of a death sentence to life imprisonment conditioned on permanent ineligibility for parole, even where no statute provided for such a commuted sentence. *Schick* emphasized that the only limits that can be imposed on the presidential pardon power are those in the Constitution itself. To require the executive to substitute a punishment only if a statute already permitted it would place unauthorized congressional restrictions on the pardoning power. *Schick* continued the historical trend of the Supreme Court of extending the pardoning power beyond the scope of its English common-law counterpart, although *Schick* recognized that the President may not aggravate punishment.

§ 7.4   The Speech or Debate Clause: An Introduction

Article I, section 6 of the Constitution, known as the speech or debate clause, recognizes the need for protection of legislative independence in a governmental system of separation of powers, a theme long found in English law. The Supreme Court has written only a handful of decisions involving the construction, scope and interpretation of the speech or debate clause.

Kilbourn v. Thompson (1881) expressly adhered to a broad, liberal interpretation of the speech or debate clause. *Kilbourn* noted that the privilege should extend "to things generally done in a session of the House by one of its members in relation to the business before it."

Kilbourn dealt with the question whether the House possessed a general contempt power, and it also examined the scope of the Congressional power to investigate. The scope of the speech or debate clause was a secondary issue. In this case, the House was attempting to investigate the history and character of what was termed "the real estate pool" of the District of Columbia. The Jay Cooke Co. held a large portion of the pool when it went bankrupt, with the United States as one of its creditors. In the course of the House investigation, the committee investigating the scandal summoned (by a subpoena duces tecum) Hallett Kilbourn, a member of the Cooke Firm, to appear. Kilbourn appeared and answered some questions of the committee, but refused to answer others. He also refused to produce subpoenaed books or papers. As a result, a vote of the entire House cited him for contempt. Kilbourn sued for false imprisonment.

Later expansion of Congress' legitimate investigative role have made many of *Kilbourn's* responses to the investigative issues questionable. However, Justices on all sides of the speech or debate controversy still cite the opinion with approval. *Kilbourn* held that, even though the investigation was outside the legitimate powers of Congress, the speech or debate clause protected the Congressmen who voted for the contempt from a civil suit for false imprisonment. However, the Sergeant–at–Arms, who had taken Kilbourn into custody pursuant to the congressional order, was not within the ambit of the clause and was therefore liable for damages.

The Speech or Debate Clause in the 1960's. Several significant constructions of the clause, usually in the form of dicta, are in three cases that dealt with the speech and debate clause during the 1960's—*United States v. Johnson* (1966), *Dombrowski v. Eastland* (1967), and *Powell v. McCormack* (1969).

In *Dombrowski*, plaintiffs alleged that the Chairman of a Senate subcommittee and that subcommittee's counsel conspired with Louisiana officials to violate the plaintiffs' Fourth Amendment rights. The Court found sufficient evidence against the counsel of the subcommittee to allow plaintiffs to go to trial. But the Court dismissed the complaint against Senator Eastland on grounds of the speech and debate clause.

In *Powell* the Court decided Congressman Powell's charge that the House unlawfully excluded him from taking his seat in the House of Representatives. The Court dismissed the action against House Speaker McCormack and other Congressmen on speech or debate grounds, but then held that the speech or debate clause was not a bar to Powell's action against the House *employees*, who were acting under House orders. On the merits, the Court ruled for Powell.

Johnson held that the speech or debate clause covered a speech delivered by a Senator on the floor of Congress and the Senator's motivation for delivering it. Thus, the speech could not form the basis of a criminal charge of conspiracy to defraud the government. However, the Court went on to hold that the prosecution could still proceed with the conspiracy charge on the condition that the speech itself could not constitute an overt act. This limitation, the *Johnson* Court assumed, would purge the prosecution of all elements offensive to the speech or debate clause.

In these cases, liberal rationales combined with narrow, restrictive holdings make the precise scope of legislative privilege under the speech or debate clause unclear. None of these opinions, alone or in tandem, defined with any particularity the nature of legislative activity that would be protected by the clause.

§ 7.5 Modern Speech and Debate Synthesis

The speech and debate clause has two basic aspects. First, it provides a testimonial privilege. The person whom the clause protects has a right not to be questioned about matters within the protection of the clause. The clause, after all, specifically states that the member "shall not be questioned in any other Place." Second, the clause provides an immunity from liability. If a court, or the legislature, or the executive imposes liability, that certainly "questions" the speech or debate. The clause immunizes the person from liability (either civilly or criminally) for matters within its protection.

In order to develop a test that explains the boundaries of the clause's protection, the Court has focused on a legislative-political distinction.

The Legislative–Political Distinction. The Court has bypassed the broad dicta of earlier cases to take a narrow view of the activities of Congress protected by Article I, section 6. *United States v. Brewster* (1972) held that the government could try Senator Daniel Brewster on a criminal charge of general application so long as the criminal case did not rest on legislative acts or the motives of the Senator in performing those acts. The Court distinguished between legislative acts that are "clearly a part of the legislative process—the *due* functioning of the process" and activities that, while legitimate, are unprotected because they are essentially "political in nature." The Court held that the speech or debate clause "does not prohibit inquiry into activities that are casually or incidentally related to legislative affairs but not a part of the legislative process itself."

Gravel v. United States (1972) further developed the legislative-political distinction of *Brewster* by pointing out that acts do not become "legislative in nature" simply because members of Congress "generally perform [them] in their official capacity." *Gravel* expressly held that, for purposes of the speech or debate clause, a member of Congress and his assistant are treated as one in the performance of their legislative functions. Any act that is protected by the clause if performed personally by a member of Congress is thus equally protected if performed by a legislative aide or assistant.

Applying these principles, the *Gravel* Court held a Senator and his aide were immune from questioning by a grand jury concerning their investigatory acts in preparation for a subcommittee hearing, except insofar as those acts were criminal or related to third-party crime. This position did not reject the distinctions between employees and Congresspersons found in the earlier cases, for the *Gravel* Court carefully distinguished the previous holdings.

Gravel interpreted *Kilbourn* as a case where the House resolution authorizing legislative arrest was immune from judicial review. "But the resolution was subject to judicial review insofar as its execution impinged on a citizen's rights as it did there. That the House could with impunity order an unconstitutional arrest afforded no protection for those who made the arrest." Presumably if a congressman actually made the arrest in *Kilbourn,* he would not be protected for that action, though he would be protected for voting for the arrest.

Gravel distinguished *Dombrowski* as a case where the "record contained no evidence of the Senator's involvement in any activity that could result in liability ... whereas the committee counsel was charged with conspiring with state officials to carry out an illegal seizure of records...."

And *Gravel* interpreted *Powell* as a case where the Court could afford relief against House aides seeking to implement invalid resolutions. As in *Kilbourn*, the *Powell* Court had noted that it did not reach the issue of the Congressmen's liability if they themselves would implement the resolution and no other remedy was available.

Republication of Materials Not Protected. *Gravel* made clear that the speech and debate clause did not protect any private *re*publication of materials that Congressmen or their aides had introduced and made public at a committee hearing. This ruling was a significant narrowing of the clause because it excluded from protection the informative function of Congress in publishing information for the benefit of constituents.

Helstoski and the Legislative–Political Distinction. *United States v. Helstoski* (1979) clarified the legislative act-political act distinction. The government charged that a former congressman had, while a Member of Congress, accepted money in return for promising to introduce, and in fact introducing, private bills to suspend the application of the immigration laws. The government indicted Helstoski for violating a law that makes it a crime for a public official to corruptly ask for, or accept, anything of value in return for being influenced in the performance of official duties.

The majority in *Helstoski* held that the speech or debate clause precludes any inquiry into acts that occur in the regular course of the legislative process and into the motivation for those acts. While such exclusion will make prosecution more difficult, "references to past legislative acts of a member cannot be admitted without undermining the values protected by the Clause." However, the Court held that "[p]romises by a Member to perform an act *in the future* are not legislative acts." Thus the government may prosecute a Congressman for promising to vote a particular way on a bill, but it may not introduce the vote itself.

Individual Waiver. The Fifth Amendment is subject to implied waivers. Thus, the government argued that Helstoski had impliedly waived the speech or debate clause privilege. The majority held that, assuming that it is possible for a congressman to waive the speech or debate privilege, such a waiver can only be found after explicit and unequivocal renunciation of the privilege.

The Speech and Debate Clause, Civil Cases, and the Legislative–Political Distinction. The cases discussed above all deal with the scope of legislative immunity as applied to criminal cases. *Doe v. McMillan* (1973) applied the speech or debate clause to civil litigation, and continued the distinction drawn in the earlier criminal cases between legislative and political acts.

In *McMillan*, parents of District of Columbia school children sued members of the House Committee on the District of Columbia, federal legislative employees of the Government Printing Office, and district school officials and employees seeking damages and declaratory and injunctive relief for alleged invasion of privacy resulting from public dissemination of a Committee report on the District of Columbia school system. This report identified, by name, students in highly derogatory contexts. The Court held that the scope of the speech or debate clause immunized members of Congress from liability for all of the acts on which the civil suit was based. The Court granted similar immunity to the committee staff, the consultant and investigator introducing material at the committee hearings.

The Court went on to hold that, in private suits, the speech or debate clause affords no immunity to those who, at the direction of Congress, distribute actionable material to the general public. Thus, *Doe* upheld a cause of action against the public printer and superintendent of documents to the extent that they had printed excess copies of the report, that is, copies of the report for use other than internally by Congress.

No Injunctions of Congressional Subpoenas. *Eastland v. United States Servicemen's Fund* (1975) held that the federal courts may not enjoin the issuance of a subpoena by a congressional committee directing a bank to produce the bank records of an anti-war group, the USSF, which the committee was investigating. Because the subpoena was directed to the bank and not to the USSF, the USSF was not in a position to assert its alleged constitutional claim by refusing to comply with the subpoena and then defending itself in a statutory contempt action.

The Court applied the immunity privilege despite allegations that the contribution lists subpoenaed were the equivalent of the membership lists of the anti-war group. The USSF argued that revealing these contribution lists would put First and Fifth Amendment rights in danger of irreparable harm. Chief Justice Burger's majority opinion simply accepted the government's argument of absolute congressional immunity and found that the Court had no power to review the subpoena.

Defamatory Statements Outside the Legislative Chambers. *Hutchinson v. Proxmire* (1979) elaborated on the legislative-political distinction and held that the speech or debate clause provides no absolute privilege from liability to civil plaintiffs for defamatory statements made outside the legislative chamber. Even though these statements would be "wholly immune" if made on the Senate floor, or in a committee hearing (even if the hearing were held outside the chambers), even though the statements would be immune if published in a committee report, their republication in a newsletter is not privileged.

The Court conceded that the privilege applies when Congress informs itself by committee hearings and speeches on the floor; however, a congressman's individual transmittal of such information in order to inform the public "is not a part of the legislative function or the deliberations that make up the legislative process." Thus newsletters and press releases are not within the speech or debate privilege. Also, a congressman's "libelous remarks in ... follow up telephone calls to executive agencies and in radio and television interviews are not protected."

§ 7.6 The Appointment Process

Article II, section 2, clause 2 of the Constitution provides in part:

> "[The President] shall nominate, and by and with the Advice and Consent of the Senate, shall appoint Ambassadors, other public Ministers and Consuls, Judges of the Supreme Court, and all other Officers of the United States, whose Appointments are not herein otherwise provided for, and which shall be established by Law: but the Congress may by Law vest the Appointment of such inferior Officers, as they think proper, in the President alone, in the Courts of Law, or in the Heads of Departments."

This appointment process is a practical working out of the doctrine of separation of powers, with Congress establishing the federal offices and the President (subject to Senate confirmation) choosing the officers. The framers believed such a separation necessary because "the same persons should not both legislate and administer the laws." The Constitutional Convention's consideration of the appointment clause sparked several debates and the final draft was probably a compromise, part of the framers' larger effort to balance power among the three branches of government.

Primary Officers Versus Inferior Officers. The full appointment process, including Senate confirmation, does not apply to all appointments of federal officers. The Constitution itself differentiates between two classes of officers. Primary officers must be nominated by the President and confirmed by the Senate. Congress has a choice, however, with respect to inferior officers, and can vest their appointment in the President, the courts of law, or in the heads of departments.

In addition to these two classes, a third category of government appointees, "employees," is outside the constitutional appointment process altogether. As a pragmatic concession to the needs of the government bureaucracy, employees are "lesser functionaries subordinate to officers of the United States." The appointment of an employee is not subject to constitutional rules regarding the appointment process.

An "Officer of the United States." Any appointee who exercises significant authority pursuant to the laws of the United States is an "officer of the United States," and must, therefore, be appointed in the manner proscribed by Article 2, § 2, clause 2.

Thus, for example, special trial judges of the tax court are "officers of the United States." Similarly, the President must appoint, and the Senate must confirm, all commissioned offices of the Armed Forces. Every time the President appoints a commissioner officer to a higher rank, he or she receives another Presidential appointment and Senate confirmation.

Buckley v. Valeo (1976) held that Congress had violated Article II in providing that the President *pro tempore* of the Senate and the Speaker of the House could appoint a majority of the voting members of the Federal Election Commission. *Buckley* involved a suit seeking a declaratory judgment that this portion of the Federal Election Campaign Act was unconstitutional and asking for an injunction against its enforcement.

The Court held that Congress had violated the appointments clause because neither of the legislative officers purportedly given the appointment power came within the terms "courts of law" or "heads of departments" as required by Article II.

While Congress may not appoint those who execute the laws, it may lay down qualifications of age, experience, and so on. Sometimes these qualifications significantly narrow the field of choice.

However, any Congressionally imposed qualifications must have a reasonable relation to the office.

§ 7.7 Appointment Powers of the "Courts of Law"

The Constitution allows Congress the power to vest the appointment of inferior officers of the United States, "in the President alone, in the Courts of Law, or in the Heads of Departments."

In 1879, *Ex parte Siebold* held that Congress could authorize the Circuit Courts to appoint election supervisors. *Siebold* read the Article II, section 2, clause 2 broadly, holding:

> [T]he duty [of the court] to appoint inferior officers, when required thereto by law, is a constitutional duty of the courts; and in the present case there is no such *incongruity* in the duty required as to excuse the courts from its performance, or to render their acts void.

There are very few cases interpreting the *Siebold* requirement that the judicial appointment of inferior officers not be incongruous with the judicial function. The cases that have discussed the question do not interpret the "no incongruity" power so broadly that it places severe limits on the federal judicial appointment power. Thus, in *Rice v. Ames* (1901) the Supreme Court has upheld the power of Congress to authorize the lower courts to appoint commissioners to handle extradition matters.

Independent Counsel and the Ethics in Government Act.

In *Morrison v. Olson* (1988) the Supreme Court upheld the Independent Counsel provisions of the Ethics in Government Act. The provisions—set up a procedure pursuant to which Congress could require the Attorney General to ask a panel of judges (called the "Special Division" by the Act) to appoint an "Independent Counsel" to investigate and, if appropriate, prosecute certain high-ranking officials for alleged violations of the federal criminal laws.

The *Olson* case involves the naming of an Independent Counsel to investigate actions of Theodore B. Olson.

The operation of the law involved in *Olson* is complex, and Chief Justice Rehnquist's opinion for the Court discusses it in great detail. *Morrison v. Olson* decided, first, that the Act does not violate the Appointments Clause. The Independent Counsel is an "inferior office" within the meaning of that clause. The Independent Counsel is not the "Head of a Department," for she is subject to removal by a higher Executive Branch official. The Independent Counsel has power to perform only certain, limited duties; and her office is limited in jurisdiction.

The Court also rejected the argument that the Appointments Clause does not allow Congress to place the power to appoint an Independent Counsel outside the Executive Branch. The language, historical background and original intent behind the appointments clause did not support the argument of the appellees. In the past, the Court noted that federal courts have engaged in interim appointments of the U.S. Attorney, and routinely appoint defense counsel.

Restrictions on Supervisory Authority by Article III Judges. The appellees in *Morrison v. Olson* also argued that the Independent Counsel law violated the Article III "case" or "controversy" requirement. However, given that the appointments clause of Article II specifically authorizes the courts to exercise an appointment power, there can be no "case" or "controversy" problem.

Nor is there any violation of Article III because the Special Division has some discretion to define the nature and scope of the Independent Counsel's authority. Particularly when the office is temporary, it is "necessary and proper" for Congress to give power to the appointing authority to define the scope of the office as an incident to the appointments clause.

However, in *Morrison v. Olson*, the Court warned that Congress may not "give to the [Special] Division *unlimited* discretion to determine the Independent Counsel's jurisdiction." The Special Divisions' power to define the Independent Counsel's jurisdiction must be "demonstrably related to the factual circumstances that gave rise to the Attorney General's investigation and request for the appointment of the Independent Counsel in the particular case." The Special Division's power to define the Independent Counsel's jurisdiction is "incidental."

The Act also vested in the Special Division other powers that are not incident to the appointment power. Most of these powers are either passive (the power to receive the Independent Counsel's reports) or "essentially ministerial." Even when the Act authorizes the Special Division to exercise some judgment (the Special Division must determine whether the Attorney General has shown "good cause" to request an extension of the time period normally allowed for the preliminary investigation) the powers are still "essentially ministerial." Judges perform analogous functions all the time, such as the decision whether to extend a grand jury investigation, or whether to allow disclosure of matters occurring before a grand jury. The important conclusion is that the "Act simply does not give the [Special] Division the power to 'supervise' the Independent Counsel in the exercise of her investigative or prosecutorial authority." It would violate the Constitution for Article III courts to exercise such executive supervision over prosecutors.

The Court specifically noted (and did not approve of) lower court cases involving Independent Counsel where the Special Division has given advisory opinions (e.g., purporting to exempt Independent Counsel from conflict of interest laws) or issued orders not directly authorized by the Act (e.g., ordering Independent Counsel to postpone an investigation until the completion of related state proceedings). The Court warned: not only does the Act not authorize such actions, but "the division's exercise of unauthorized powers risk the transgression of the constitutional limitations of Article III that we have just discussed."

The Court appeared to be particularly troubled by the fact that the Act authorized the Special Division to terminate the office of Independent Counsel. This provision, on its face, does not authorize the Special Division to control the pace and depth of the Independent Counsel's investigation, but the Court acknowledged that this section of the law has not yet been tested in practice. In order to save the statute from constitutional infirmities, the Court said that it had to interpret this provision narrowly. "The termination provisions of the Act do not give the Special Division anything approaching the power *to remove* the counsel while an investigation or court proceeding is still underway—this power is vested solely in the Attorney General." Basically, the "termination" power must be construed to be only the power to terminate when the Independent Counsel's job is "truly 'completed' " or so substantially completed that there is no further need for any continuing action by the Independent Counsel. The Special Division, in short, should not use the termination power to supervise the Independent Counsel.

Limitations on the Attorney General's Removal Powers. *Morrison v. Olson* concluded that the Act did not violate the principle of separation of powers. First, Congress has given itself no role in the removal process.

Second, the Court upheld the Act's provisions limiting the powers of the Attorney General (or the President) to remove the Independent Counsel. After canvassing the case law, the Court acknowledged that earlier cases had spoken of legislative restrictions over the removal of executive branch officials. Some officials, the Court said, are so "purely executive" that the President must be able to remove them at will "if he is able to accomplish his constitutional role." In this case, the Court said—

> we simply do not see how the President's need to control the exercise of [the independent counsel's] discretion is so central to the functioning of the Executive Branch as to require as a

matter of constitutional law that the counsel be terminable at will by the President.

The Act did not "completely strip" the President of the power to remove the Independent Counsel. There could be removal if there was "cause;" hence, the removal restrictions did not prevent the President from engaging in the "faithful execution" of the laws.

Finally, the Court concluded that the Act, taken as a whole, did not violate the separation of powers.

Morrison v. Olson, in upholding the constitutionality of the Independent Counsel law, concluded that when the lower court (called the "Special Division") exercised power under the law and appointed an Independent Counsel at the request of the Attorney General, there was no threat that the federal judiciary would not remain impartial and independent, because "the Special Division has no power to review any of the actions of the independent counsel or any of the actions of the Attorney General with respect to the counsel."

In 1992 Congress allowed the independent counsel law to expire.

The cases on the appointment power establish several general principles. The President has the power to appoint officers of the United States. Congress may not exercise the power to appoint those who execute the laws, but, as to "inferior officers," the federal courts share with the President the power of appointment. When the court appoints, the office may be unrelated to judicial administration but it should not be "incongruous" with the judicial function.

§ 7.8   The Removal Power

There is no express Constitutional clause dealing with a removal power over executive branch officials (other than Congress' removal power in connection with impeachments). However, such a power has long been assumed to arise from Article II. Presidential control over purely executive functions would be seriously undermined by any efforts to limit this removal power.

The *Marbury* Dictum. Early judicial dictum on the removal power is found in *Marbury v. Madison* (1803).

Chief Justice Marshall offered a narrow view of the executive's power of removal:

> [W]hen the officer is not removable at the will of the executive, the appointment is not revocable, and cannot be annulled: it has conferred legal rights which cannot be resumed. . . .

[A]s the law creating the office, gave the officer a right to hold for five years, independent of the executive, the appointment was not revocable, but vested in the officers legal rights, which are protected by the laws of his country.

The holding of the case—that the Supreme Court lacked original jurisdiction in mandamus—was not dependent on the removal power; thus, Marshall's assertion that the President had no power to remove *Marbury* within the five year term of appointment was mere dictum. Indeed, subsequent decisions of the Court did not follow Marshall's statement. On its facts, *Marbury* is distinguished from the majority of cases involving presidential removal because it did not involve an executive office but a judicial office, in the local courts of Washington, D.C.

Removal by Heads of Departments. *United States v. Perkins* (1886), established that where Congress vests the power of appointment in some official other than the President, it has the ability to regulate and restrict the manner of removing that appointee. *Perkins* involved a suit in the Court of Claims for lost wages by a naval cadet-engineer whom the Secretary of the Navy had discharged because his services were not required. Congress had provided that no officer could be dismissed from the armed services except by court-martial.

Invalidating Perkins' dismissal, the Court made it clear that "when Congress, by law, vests the appointment of inferior officers in the heads of Departments it may limit and restrict the power of removal as it deems best for the public interest." Because *Perkins* was limited to removal by heads of Departments it did not reach the issue of whether Congress could place restrictions on the removal power of the President once it had vested him with a power of appointment over inferior officers.

***Myers* and the Removal of Executive Officials.** *Myers v. United States* (1926) reached the key issue of Congressional restriction of the President's removal power. The Postmaster General, in an order issued by and sanctioned by the President, discharged Myers, a postmaster at Portland, Oregon. However, Congress had provided that the President could remove postmasters only "with the advice and consent of the Senate," and that, until so removed, they would hold office for four years. President Wilson removed Myers without any attempt to secure Senate concurrence. The Court of Claims dismissed Myers' suit for lost pay because he had waited too long to sue. The Supreme Court affirmed on different grounds.

Chief Justice (and former President) William Howard Taft wrote the opinion for the Court, holding that "[t]he power to remove . . . is an incident of the power to appoint" and the Tenure of Office Act was unconstitutional insofar as it restricted the power of the President to remove officers he had appointed. Only three Justices dissented from *Myers'* holding of an absolute power of the President to remove.

The Court in *Humphrey's Executor v. United States* (1935) limited broad language of *Meyers*. *Humphrey's Executor* held that the President cannot remove a member of an independent regulatory agency in violation of restrictions in the statutory framework. The Federal Trade Commission Act provided that the President could remove any commissioner from office only for "inefficiency, neglect of duty, or malfeasance in office." President Roosevelt removed Humphrey from his position as a member of the Commission. Roosevelt candidly admitted that the removal was for policy reasons rather than for one of the causes enumerated in the statute. Humphrey's executor brought suit to cover his lost wages.

The *Humphrey* Court looked to the nature and function of the Federal Trade Commission and concluded that "its duties are neither political nor executive, but predominantly quasi-judicial and quasi-legislative." Recognizing that the independence of the regulatory agencies could be severely curtailed by a presidential power to remove members at will, the Court held that, while *Myers* applied to all purely executive officers, the Constitution does not grant the President unlimited removal power as to quasi-legislative or quasi-judicial officers, even where such hold office through presidential appointment.

Wiener v. United States (1958) further clarified the distinction between purely executive officers and those whose duties extend to non-executive functions. *Wiener* held invalid President Eisenhower's dismissal of a Truman appointee to the War Claims Commission, even though there was the absence of an express congressional restriction on the President's power of removal. The Court built on *Humphrey's Executor,* which had held that the validity of statutory limitations on presidential removal powers turns on the question of whether the involved agencies included functions either partially legislative or judicial. *Wiener* emphasized the "sharp differentiation" setting apart "those who are part of the Executive establishment and those whose tasks require absolute freedom from Executive interference."

While these cases limit the President's power to remove quasi-judicial and quasi-legislative officers, they still allowed the President the power to remove "purely executive" officers, who must be removable by the President at will if he, or she, is to be able to accomplish role set out for the President by the Constitution. However, when the Court upheld, in *Morrison v. Olson* (1988), the constitutionality of special legislation creating an "Independent

Counsel" and providing that the Independent Counsel can be removed only for cause, the Court modified the prior law and allowed greater Congressional power to limit the removal of Executive Branch officials.

Limitations on Executive Removal Powers. *Morrison v. Olson* (1988), in upholding the law providing for a special prosecutor or "Independent Counsel" to investigate and prosecute in certain cases involving officials within the Executive Branch, concluded that the Act did not violate the principle of separation of powers. The Independent Counsel Act provided that the Attorney General could only remove for cause. If the Attorney General does remove the Independent Counsel, the Attorney General must report the reasons to the Judiciary Committees of the House and Senate. In addition, the Attorney General must report the reasons to the panel of Article III judges who had appointed the Independent Counsel at the request of the Attorney General. This special panel is called the "Special Division" by the Act. The Independent Counsel can seek reinstatement by filing an action in the district court for the District of Columbia, but if she does, no judge who is on the Special Division can set on that case.

Though Congress placed limited on the power of the Attorney General to remove the Independent Counsel, Congress gave itself no role in the removal process. Because Congress could remove the Independent Counsel only through the impeachment process, it could not use the threat of removal as a way of trying to supervise the investigatory and prosecutorial (that is, executive) functions of the Independent Counsel.

The provisions limiting the Executive's powers to remove the Independent Counsel are constitutional. Although the Court acknowledged that earlier cases had spoken of legislative restrictions over the removal of executive branch officials in terms of "quasi-legislative" or "quasi-judicial"—

> [T]he real question is whether the removal restrictions are of such a nature that they impede the President's ability to perform his constitutional duty, and the functions of the officials in question must be analyzed in that light.

While some officials, are so "purely executive" that the President must be able to remove them at will "if he is able to accomplish his constitutional role." But the Independent's Counsel is not in that category. In addition, the Act did not completely strip the President of the power to remove the Independent Counsel, for there could be removal if there was "cause."

Removal of Executive Officials by Congress: The Gramm–Rudman–Hollings Act. In *Bowsher v. Synar* (1986) the Court held that powers vested in the Comptroller General under the Balanced Budget and Emergency Deficit Control Act (the Gramm–Rudman–Hollings Act) violated the rule that Congress can play no direct role in the execution of the laws. The Court emphasized that Congress cannot reserve for itself the power of removal (except by impeachment) of an officer charged with the execution of the laws. The purpose of this law was to reduce the federal deficit, by requiring, in various circumstances, reductions in federal expenditures.

The statutory scheme at issue in *Bowsher,* provided that Congress could remove the Comptroller General not only by impeachment but also by Joint Resolution. The Gramm–Rudman–Hollings Act also gave the Comptroller various executive functions. His duties, the Court concluded, were not merely ministerial. When the Comptroller interpreted a federal law enacted to implement the legislative mandate to reduce the budget deficit, that is the very essence of "execution" of the law. Congress cannot grant to the Comptroller, an officer under its control, executive power, which is power that Congress does not possess.

Removal of Article III Judges from Non–Article III Positions. *Mistretta v. United States* (1989) upheld the constitutionality of the United States Sentencing Commission, a group that promulgated sentencing guidelines in criminal cases. The law provided that the Commission was "an independent commission in the judicial branch of the United States." The Court concluded that it was appropriate for Congress to delegate to this commission nonadjudicatory functions that do not intrude on the prerogatives of another branch and that are appropriate to the central mission of the judiciary.

The President must appoint at least three of the members of the Commission from a list of six Article III judges whom the Judicial Conference of the United States recommends. Judges who are appointed to the Commission wear, in effect, two hats (an Article III judicial hat and an administrative hat), but not two hats at the same time. That is, those judges who are members of the Commission are members because the President appointed them. As members of the Commission they wield certain power, but that power is not Article III judicial power but administrative power derived from the enabling legislation.

The President can remove members of this Commission, including the judicial members, only for "good cause" such as neglect of duty or malfeasance in office. The Court concluded that this power to remove federal judges from the Commission does not violate the Constitution. The President's removal power over the members of the Commission, including those members who are also Article III judges, does not authorize or diminish the status of

Article III judges as judges. The President cannot affect either the tenure or compensation of Article III judges, even those who are also on the Commission. Even if an Article III judge is removed from the Commission, he remains an Article III judge. The Sentencing Commission Act does not prevent the Judicial Branch from performing its constitutionally assigned function of fairly adjudicating cases and controversies.

A fractured opinion in *United States v. Booker* (2005), invalidated (5 to 4) the 17–year old Federal Sentencing Guidelines. Justice Stevens, joined by Scalia, Thomas, Souter & Ginsburg, JJ., based the ruling on the Sixth Amendment requirement that the jury, not the judge, find the facts relevant to sentencing departures. Thus, in both federal and state courts the jury must find, beyond a reasonable doubt, all facts that legally determine a defendant's sentence. As to the question of remedy, it was Justice Breyer (not Stevens) who wrote the Court 's opinion (joined by the other three dissenters and Ginsburg, J., to make a 5 to 4 majority). He held that the correct remedy was to sever the part of the statute that made the guidelines mandatory, so that the Court created the equivalent of a wholly advisory Guidelines system.

Conclusion. The removal power cases establish several general principles. First, purely executive officers appointed by the President are subject to a presidential removal power that may not constitutionally be limited by Congress, unless Congress has a good reason to so limit the removal power. This test is admittedly vague, but that is the result of the holding of *Morrison v. Olson*. Second, Congress may similarly limit and regulate removal where it has vested the appointment power in some official other than the President. Third, after *Morrison v. Olson* Congress may limit the power of the President (or his delegate) to remove certain executive branch officials only for cause; the test is not whether the official is "quasi-legislative" or "quasi-judicial" but rather whether it is reasonable for Congress to restrict the Executive Branch's removal power.

The real question in each case will be whether the removal restrictions are of such a nature that they impede the President's ability to perform his constitutional duty, or whether the President's need to control the exercise of the discretion of the official in question is so central to the functioning of the Executive Branch that the official in question should be terminable at will by the President. Finally, where an executive department has established administrative regulations having the force and effect of law to govern employee dismissal, it may not remove any employee in a manner inconsistent with those regulations. The Government should abide by the rules and restrictions that it places on itself.

§ 7.9 Legislative Veto of Executive Branch Regulations and Actions

Congress, in an attempt to maintain more control over the President and over regulations promulgated by agencies of the federal government's executive branch, has in the past incorporated into legislation a provision known as the "legislative veto" or the "congressional veto." Congress sought by statute to give itself what the Constitution gives to the President. Congress typically utilized such provisions when granting the President or an executive agency the power to promulgate regulations with the force of law. These provisions required the President or an agency official to present the proposed regulations to Congress, which retained a "right" to approve or disapprove any regulations before they take effect.

Legislative veto provisions typically provided that a proposed regulation will become law after the expiration of a certain period of time, only if Congress does not affirmatively disapprove of the regulation in the meantime. Less frequently, the statute provided that a proposed regulation could become law only if Congress affirmatively approved it. Both types of provisions established what congressional action is necessary. Sometimes the required action was action by both houses, or only one house, or perhaps just the action of one committee of one chamber.

Since the early 1970's, Congress, with increasing frequency, retained veto rights when delegating powers to the executive and had utilized or attempted to utilize the congressional veto to reject agency regulations of public interest and controversy. Commentators and litigants began challenging the use of the legislative veto as unconstitutional on several grounds: (1) that one-house veto provisions violate the sections of Article I of the Constitution requiring legislation to pass both chambers of Congress; (2) that legislative veto provisions violate the presentment clause of Article I requiring the presentment of legislation to the President for approval or veto; and (3) that legislative veto provisions generally contravene the separation of powers doctrine implicit in Articles I, II and III.

In *Immigration and Naturalization Service v. Chadha* (1983) the Court held that the legislative veto provision contained in the Immigration and Nationality Act was unconstitutional. The *Chadha* holding requires that any "legislative veto" be passed as legislation by both chambers of Congress and presented to the President for approval or veto. This ruling was based on the legislature process provisions set out in Article I.

Chadha was an alien in the United States on a nonimmigrant student visa. He overstayed his visa and was ordered to show cause why he should not be deported. Pursuant to section 244(a)(1) of the

Immigration and Nationality Act, an immigration judge found that Chadha met the statutory requirements to have his deportation suspended. This suspension order, however, had to be submitted to Congress under section 244(c)(1), and either chamber of Congress was given an opportunity to pass a resolution to overrule the executive branch and order that the alien be deported. The House of Representatives chose to exercise its section 244(c)(2) legislative veto power in Chadha's case and vetoed his suspension of deportation. This resolution was not treated as "legislation" and thus was not sent to the Senate or the President for approval.

The Supreme Court held (7 to 2) that the one-house veto provision of section 244(c)(2) violated the presentment clauses contained in clauses 2 and 3 of Article I, Section 7 of the Constitution, the bicameral requirement of Article I, Section 1 and Section 7, clause 2, and the implied separation of powers structure of Articles I, II and III. The Court found that the House's resolution ordering Chadha's deportation, although not legislative in form, supplanted congressional action through legislation and was legislative in character, purpose, and effect.

Because the majority concluded that the legislative veto was really an act of legislation, *Chadha* ruled that it had to conform with the constitutional mandates of bicameral passage followed by presentment to the President.

Severability. Though the congressional veto contained in section 244(c)(2) was unconstitutional, the Court held that it was severable from the remainder of the section. Thus, the Attorney General still had the authority to suspend Chadha's deportation under section 244(a)(1) and to report this action to Congress under section 244(c)(1). A presumption of severability arose from section 406 of the Act, which provided if any provision of the Act was held invalid, the remainder of the Act was not to be affected.

Additionally, the Court concluded that the provision was severable because, even after the Court severed the offending section, the Act was fully operative as a law. Without the one-house veto provision, Burger stated, the section would operate as a "report and wait" provision. The deportation suspension order would then be reported to Congress, which could pass legislation barring its effectiveness if it found it objectionable. This legislation would have to pass both houses and be subject to presidential veto. The Court had previously upheld such report and wait provisions in *Sibbach v. Wilson & Co.*

Chadha appears to require a case-by-case examination of whether an invalid legislative veto provision veto can be severed from the rest of the act in which it is contained.

§ 7.10   Line Item Veto

At the time of the Constitutional Convention, the term "line-item" veto did not exist because the problem of unrelated bills and riders did not then exist. Shortly before the Civil War, Congress first began the practice of attaching appropriations riders to bills.

In response to this development, Presidents, for many years, have proposed creating a line-item veto—that is, a power to veto a particular item (or line) in a federal appropriations bill without having to veto the entire bill. Legislators often seek to amend essential legislation with their favorite projects, knowing that it will be difficult, if not impossible, for the President to veto the entire bill. Opponents of these techniques have urged the creation of a line-item veto, often in an effort to reduce pork barrel spending by giving the President more control over the appropriation process.

Congress could, of course, give the President a line-item veto by proposing a constitutional amendment subject to ratification by the states. The real issue was whether Congress could give the President a line-item veto by mere legislation, just as it now could authorize (or limit) presidential impoundment. When the Court finally decided the question, a majority held that Congress could not, by statute, grant the President a line-item veto.

Unconstitutionality of the Line Item Veto. In 1996, Congress enacted a statute granting the President line item veto. President Clinton exercised the line item veto a number of times, and it was eventually tested in the Court. A divided Supreme Court invalidated the law in *Clinton v. City of New York* (1998).

The City of New York and others sued President Clinton, and others claiming that they had been injured by his decision to "cancel" a portion of a federal statute that waived the federal government's right to recoup certain funds from New York. Separately, owners of certain food refiners and processors sued, claiming that they had been injured by President Clinton's "cancellation" of a provision of a law that allowed them to defer recognition of capital gains. Justice Stevens, for the Court, then held that the Line Item Veto Act violated the presentment clause.

Justice Stevens argued that the law's cancellation provisions amounted to the President amending "two Acts of Congress by repealing a portion of each," but his partial repeals did not conform to the requirements of the presentment clause. Stevens said that when the President exercises his veto of the whole bill, he returns it to Congress "*before* the bill becomes law." But, under the statute at issue, the "statutory cancellation occurs *after* the bill becomes law." The constitutional silence on the issue of a line item veto, Stevens contended, should be treated as equivalent to an express constitutional prohibition.

When Congress passed the Rules Enabling Act, it provided that the Supreme Court's enactment of the Rules of Procedure for the lower federal courts had the effect of overriding (cancelling?) prior Acts of Congress. The relevant language provided that "All laws in conflict with such rules shall be of no further force or effect after such rules have taken effect." The Court rule resulted in "repeal" of the inconsistent statute, a practice the Supreme Court upheld in 1941. The Court has also upheld statutes where Congress delegates to the President the power to suspend (cancel?) statutes allowing importation of certain goods without paying import duties.

But Justice Stevens was unpersuaded by these examples. He argued, for example, that when the President suspended an exemption under the the Tariff Act, "he was executing the policy that Congress embodied in the statute". In contrast, whenever the President cancels an item of new direct spending or a limited tax benefit he is rejecting the policy judgment made by Congress and relying on his own policy judgment. The sharply divided Court held that Congress cannot give the President a line item veto by statute.

Congress could always decide to send to the President bills containing only individual items. However, if Congress were to decide to enact many small bills instead of a few large ones, it would lose the political leverage it now has in bargaining with the President. Individual Representatives and Senators would also lose a lot of the power they now have to bring home projects to help their constituents.

Chapter 8

THE COMMERCE CLAUSE AND RESTRICTIONS ON STATE REGULATORY POWERS

Table of Sections

§ 8.1 State Regulation Affecting Interstate Commerce—Introduction

The focus of this Chapter is on the question of what, if any, limitations the commerce clause places on state or local laws that relate to items or activities that have not been the subject of federal regulation. When the Supreme Court examines the compatibility of a state or local law with the commerce clause (on a matter over which Congress has not spoken) the Court may refer to its action as involving either "dormant commerce clause" principles or "negative commerce clause" principles. Sometimes the cases speak of the "negative implications" of the commerce clause. All these phrases embody the concept that the mere grant of a commerce power to Congress in Article I, § 8, by implication, places limits upon state or local laws regulating commerce. The Commerce Clause, on its own, serves to preempt some state laws.

The commerce clause of Article I, § 8 contains an affirmative grant of power to Congress; it does not explicitly impose any limitations on state or local laws that affect interstate commerce. However, since the early Nineteenth Century, the Court has held that the Article I grant of power to Congress, by implication, placed a limitation on state or local laws related to interstate commerce.

The Court might have interpreted the commerce clause to be an exclusive grant of power to Congress, so that states would not be able to enact any legislation that affected interstate commerce until Congress had given states such authority. Alternatively, the Supreme Court might have adopted a theory under which the commerce clause placed no limitations on state or local legislation. The Supreme Court took a middle course, between these two extremes, though the path to reach this conclusion was not a straight one. The Court decided that the judiciary should interpret the dormant commerce clause to invalidate types of state or local legislation that, in general, discriminate against interstate commerce in purpose or effect, but that Congress has the power to approve state laws that otherwise would violate dormant commerce clause principles. In other words, Congress can authorize what would otherwise be a violation of the dormant commerce clause.

Chapter 9, not this chapter, analyzes state or local legislation that directly conflicts with federal law. A state law regulating commerce that conflicts with a valid federal law regulating commerce is invalid under the terms of the supremacy clause of Article VI of the Constitution. Thus, *Gibbons v. Ogden* (1824) invalidated a state law as being in conflict with a federal statute, although Chief Justice Marshall's opinion, *in dicta*, stated that the commerce clause (*i.e.* the dormant commerce clause) itself would restrict some state control of commercial matters.

If the state law violates the *dormant* commerce clause, Congress may enact a law that expressly adopts or approves of that state law. The Court will accept that Congressional judgment because Congress has the ultimate power over interstate commerce. Congress can regulate commerce for good or ill; it can ban or restrict interstate commerce, or discriminate against or in favor of interstate commerce. In other words, if Congress has enacted no legislation on the subject, the Court interprets Congressional silence and, in effect, assumes, in general, that Congress intends that we operate under a common market, with no state being able to enact laws that discriminate against commerce because of its interstate origins or destination. However, once Congress enacts a law, the Court's only role is to see if it regulates interstate commerce; if it does that and if it does not violate any other part of the Constitution (*e.g.*, it does not restrict free speech), then the law is valid, even if it authorizes what a state law could not do.

In short, federal legislation validates what would otherwise violate the dormant commerce clause. Thus, *Pennsylvania v. Wheel-*

ing and Belmont Bridge Co. (1855) (*Wheeling II*) upheld an Act of Congress declaring the Wheeling Bridge to be a lawful structure even though, in *Wheeling I* (1852), the Court had previously found that the bridge obstructed commerce. In the first case, the Court was interpreting Congressional silence and found that the state law—in the absence of federal legislation—obstructed interstate commerce. In the second case the Court was simply applying the federal law, which regulated interstate commerce. When Congress regulates commerce, it can regulate for good or ill. See also, *Wilkerson v. Rahrer* (1891), where the Court upheld a federal law that authorized states to regulate traffic in liquor that would otherwise be barred by the commerce clause; this case was obviously decided prior to the enactment of the Twenty–First Amendment, which specifically authorizes the states to ban liquor.

When the Court reviews federal legislation that allows states to regulate certain types of commerce, the Court is not reviewing the state law but, rather, the federal legislation. The federal legislation, in our example, clearly would fall within the commerce power of Congress because it involves the regulation of interstate commercial transactions. There is no requirement that the federal law help the national economy or interstate commerce. Approval of state laws that in any way affect, or even harm, interstate commerce are within the power that Article I, § 8 grants to Congress.

Several reasons support the precedent holding that there is a negative aspect of the commerce clause that limits state authority.

When the Court interprets the "dormant" commerce clause, it is really interpreting Congressional silence (that is, it is interpreting Congress' decision *not* to exercise its commerce power). One of the ways to think about this situation is as follows: assume that Congress enacted a law that said that Congress preempts the field of interstate commerce in the sense that states may not enact legislation that discriminates against interstate commerce because of its interstate origins or destination, or disproportionately burdens interstate commerce, unless Congress specifically approves of such state legislation. If that were the law on the books, one could explain almost all of the Court's present-day jurisprudence involving the dormant commerce clause. The Court interprets that clause, in general (yes, we often have to add that fudge word in explaining any large body of case law) as if Congress has enacted such a statute.

§ 8.2   The Primary Rationales Justifying Present Commerce Clause Jurisprudence

One of the key factors that led political leaders in the states to call for a meeting to revise the Articles of Confederation, which led to the eventual drafting of our Constitution, was economic competition between the states. Under the Articles of Confederation, the federal government could not resolve economic disputes between states; states were free to create trade barriers against economic competition from other states. The inability of the states to resolve commercial conflicts under the Articles of Confederation provided the impetus for calling the convention that we now refer to as the Constitutional Convention.

The Constitution of 1787 placed some specific limitations on state powers regarding commerce, primarily in Article I, § 10 and Article IV. Surprisingly, no text in the Constitution of 1787 specifically outlaws the type of tariffs and trade barriers that states had used during the Articles of Confederation era. Nevertheless, if the drafters of the Constitution intended that the affirmative grant of power to Congress was intended to deny states the power to create tariffs and trade barriers the result would be more competition, like a free trade zone—about two centuries before the creation of the European Common Market. It seems difficult to believe that the members of the Constitutional Convention, which was called, in part, to resolve interstate economic conflicts, had not intended to place some limitation on state actions that had been the source of interstate tension. Thus, judicial invalidation of state tariffs and trade barriers, pending consideration of such laws by Congress, carries forth the original purpose of the Constitutional Convention.

Judicial invalidation of state laws under the commerce clause does not reject or interfere with democratic processes in the same way as does judicial invalidation of state laws under most of the other provisions of the Constitution. When the Court invalidates state legislation as violating due process, the Court is holding that the state lacks that power unless the people approve a Constitutional amendment. On the other hand, a constitutional amendment is not needed to revise a state law that was held to violate the dormant commerce clause. When the Court holds that a state law violates the dormant commerce clause, the Court is really interpreting the silence of Congress so Congress can effectively reverse that ruling by enacting federal legislation that approves that type of state law.

For example, *Philadelphia v. New Jersey* (1978) held that a state law barring importation into the state of garbage from other states (for disposal in privately owned landfills in the state) violated the dormant commerce clause. However, Congress could enact a federal law that authorized states to discriminate against the commerce entering from other states. *New York v. United States* (1992). One state cannot make the decision to discriminate against the imports or exports from other states, but Congress (in which the people of all states are represented) can decide that the national interest is best-served if it authorizes some discrimination. Thus, Court actions invalidating state laws negative commerce clause principles are not truly incompatible with the democratic process. Rather, they simply force consideration of multistate commercial problems by the national legislature, which should have fewer parochial interests than the legislature of any given state.

Court actions enforcing dormant commerce clause principles also recognize the realities of the democratic system. When state laws relate only to domestic (in-state) economic matters, and do not shift the initial costs to out-of-state persons, all of the affected economic interests are represented in the state democratic system. When a state protects its local economic interests by creating tariffs or trade barriers against out-of-state competition, it is attempting to enrich the local populace (who has a voice in the local democratic system) at the expense of out-of-state persons (who are not represented in the local democratic system).

This aspect of the Court's dormant commerce clause rulings is sometimes said to reflect an "inner political check" theory. The phrase "inner political check" refers to the fact that all local persons affected by local legislation have the opportunity to participate in the democratic process that produces such legislation. Conversely, there is no political process designed to consider the interests of the out-of-state persons before the creation of state laws that shift costs to out-of-state persons through the establishment of tariffs and trade barriers.

Economists tell us that tariff barriers (or other laws discriminating against interstate commerce), which make out-of-state goods more expensive, not only benefit the in-state producers but also hurt in-state consumers, who are deprived of the opportunity to buy the imported good at a lower price, *i.e.*, what would be the market price but for the tariff. However, the average consumer typically thinks (perhaps because of economic illiteracy) that the burden (or, at least, the *initial* burden) is imposed on the out-of-state manufacturers, for they are the ones who must pay the tariff. These out-of-state interests have no right to vote for the laws that impose the tariffs (or other laws discriminating against interstate commerce).

§ 8.3   A Summary of Present Commerce Clause Jurisprudence

To say that the Supreme Court has consistently upheld a judicial role in the examination of state laws under the dormant (or negative) commerce clause is not to say that the Court's jurisprudence has been consistently clear, or has the rigorous logic of Euclidian geometry. Until the mid twentieth century, the Supreme

Court was opaque regarding the test it would use to determine relationship between the commerce clause's affirmative grant of power to Congress in the commerce clause and the implied negative restrictions on states.

The Court, throughout its history, has been confronted with two different types of state or local laws that affect commerce: (1) state laws that operate as discrimination in the nature of a tariff for trade barrier against out-of-state competition; and (2) state laws affecting interstate commerce that operate (or appear to operate) in an even-handed manner but that impose some burdens (often called "incidental" burdens) on interstate commerce. Of course, all these state laws must affect interstate commerce in some way or there would be no negative commerce clause issue; in other words, if the state law did not regulate commerce at all, or did not affect interstate commerce (or, what Chief Justice Marshall called that "commerce that affects more states than one") then there are no dormant commerce clause issue.

The Court has almost always invalidated laws that constitute discrimination against interstate commerce (in the sense that the state law operated as a tariff for trade barrier against out-of-state competitors or out-of-state consumers). Regardless of whether a state seeks to advantage local merchants or local consumers, barriers against interstate competition are normally invalid.

There may legislation affecting commercial matters that discriminates on a basis that does not involve in-state versus out-of-state distinctions. Two hypothetical laws about barbershops may illustrate this point. Assume that State A's law prohibits the ownership of barbershops in the state by any corporation; the law allows only individuals to own barbershops. This barbershop law would involve discrimination against corporations, but it would not discrimination against out-of-state commerce because of its out-of-state origins A commerce clause challenge to the law would fail because both in-state and out-of-state corporations would be barred from owning a barbershop. A corporation that wanted to own a barbershop would have to challenge the discrimination under another clause, such as the equal protection clause of the Fourteenth Amendment. Thus *Exxon Corp. v. Governor of Maryland* (1978) rejected the commerce clause challenge to a somewhat similar law. This case also rejected the equal protection challenge.

Assume that State B has a law that prohibits the ownership of barbershops by corporations that are domiciled outside of the state, but allows corporations that are domiciled in the state to own owner barbershops. State B's law discriminates against commerce because of its interstate origins. The Court has long recognized that the purpose of the commerce clause was to eradicate interstate trade barriers, and to prohibit the economic Balkanization of the Union. In commercial matters, the dormant commerce clause tells the states that we all sink or swim together.

The Court has not been completely clear concerning the standard that is used to judge a state law that is deemed to be discrimination in the nature of a tariff or trade barrier. In several cases the Court has made statements similar to the following: "As we use the term here, 'discrimination' simply means differential treatment of in-state and out-of state economic interests that benefits the former and burdens the latter. If a restriction on commerce is discriminatory, it is virtually *per se* invalid ... [under that standard, such a statute] must be invalidated unless [the government] can show that it advances a legitimate local purpose that cannot be adequately served by reasonable nondiscriminatory alternatives." *Oregon Waste Systems v. Department of Environmental Quality* (1994). Sometime the Court says that such laws are subject to "rigorous scrutiny," *C & A Carbone, Inc. v. Town of Clarkstown* (1994), although the Court has not compared that form of judicial review to the compelling interest test used in judging racial classifications under the equal protection clause.

The Court's decisions concerning state laws that discriminate against out-of-state economic interests uniformly place the burden of proof on the state to justify the discrimination as truly necessary to achieve a legitimate interest apart from the enrichment of local economic interests. It might be easiest to summarize the Supreme Court cases by stating that: (1) any state or local law that involves discrimination against out-of-state economic interests will only be upheld if the state can prove that the discrimination in the law is necessary to promote a significant or important interest; but (2) the economic enrichment of the local persons does not constitute any legitimate state interest. Indeed, enrichment of local persons through the use of a discriminatory trade barrier is an illegitimate state goal.

It is a rare state law that discriminates against interstate commerce and is still valid. The leading example is *Maine v. Taylor* (1986), which upheld a state statute that prohibited the importation into the state of live baitfish from out of state. In that case, the state demonstrated that there were certain types of parasites prevalent in out-of-state baitfish that were not common to the wild fish in Maine, *and* that there was no reasonably efficient way of screening live baitfish for these parasites that might harm the local live fish population. In contrast, *Hughes v. Oklahoma* (1979) invalidated a state law that prohibited transporting for sale out-of-the state minnows that had been caught within the state. Oklahoma argued it was "conserving" minnows, but the Court rejected the rationale given the way the law was drafted. The state neither limited on the numbers of minnows that can be taken by licensed minnow dealers, nor limited in any way how these minnows may be disposed of within the State. "Yet it forbids the transportation of any commercially significant number of natural minnows out of the State for sale."

It is not enough for the state merely to claim that it wants to protect the health of its people or the environment or some other worthy purpose. Thus, the Court invalidated state laws that prohibited the importation of privately owned, out-of-state garbage for disposal in privately owned landfills within the state. *E.g., Philadelphia v. New Jersey* (1978). Preserving the state's environment through restricting the growth of landfills would be a legitimate and, indeed, significant interest. However, out-of-state garbage is identical to in-state garbage, in terms of filling in-state landfills. Therefore, discrimination against out-of-state garbage is *not the least restrictive* means of promoting a significant and legitimate state interest. If the state really wanted to limit landfill, it could tax it (taxing a good or service always reduces the demand for it), if that tax is imposed on in-state dumping regardless of the origins of the garbage.

A few Justices have taken the position that courts are only rarely justified in striking down state laws under the dormant commerce clause, such as when the state law at issue is an overt tariff or trade barrier against out-of-state competition. However, the Court takes the position that the dormant commerce clause requires invalidation of state laws that impose subtle as well as overt discrimination, either in purpose or in effect, against interstate commerce. Sometimes the justices talk of "balancing" the interests, but if they do not calibrate the scales and tell us how much to weigh apples and electricity, they are not providing us with a test, only a conclusion.

Consider *Bendix Autolite Corp. v. Midwesco Enterprises, Inc.* (1988), which invalidated (8 to 1) a state statute of limitations that favored domestic corporations. Justice Kennedy, for the Court, endorsed the anti-discrimination principle, but, nevertheless, also argued that the Court would apply a balancing test in this case: "The Ohio statute before us might have been held to be a discrimination that invalidates without extended inquiry. We choose, however, to assess the interests of the State, to demonstrate that its legitimate sphere of regulation is not much advanced by the statute while interstate commerce is subject to substantial restraints." Justice Scalia concurred in the judgment because the statute discriminated against interstate corporations. He objected to using an *ad hoc* balancing test.

In the modern era, the Court no longer focuses on whether the state law "directly" affects interstate commerce or "indirectly" affects it, since those vague labels offered no real test. In general, the Court now says that a state or local law that regulates economic activities in a neutral manner (in the sense that it does *not* discriminate against out-of-state interests by creating a tariff or trade barrier) will be invalidated only if: (1) persons attacking the law can demonstrate that the state has no legitimate interest, or, perhaps, only a minuscule interest in creating the burden on interstate commerce; or (2) the state's interest can be achieved by less restrictive alternatives, by regulations that placed a lesser burden on interstate commerce. In other words, the Court adopts a type of balancing test that favors the government for the review of nondiscriminatory laws under the dormant commerce clause.

Perhaps the best summary of the Court's approach to the examination of nondiscriminatory laws under the commerce clause was given in *Pike v. Bruce Church, Inc.*, (1970):

> Although the criteria for determining the validity of statutes affecting interstate commerce have been variously stated, the general rule that emerges can be phrased as follows: where the statute regulates even handedly to effectuate a legitimate local public interest, and its effects on interstate commerce are only incidental, it will be upheld unless the burden imposed on such commerce is clearly excessive in relation to the putative local benefits. If a legitimate local purpose is found, then the question becomes one of degree. And the extent of the burden that will be tolerated will of course depend on the nature of the local interest involved, and on whether it could be promoted as well with a lesser impact on interstate activities. Occasionally the court has undertaken a balancing approach in resolving these issues, but more frequently it has spoken in terms of "direct" and "indirect" benefits and burdens.

Pike, and the cases in its wake, adopt a type of balancing test for the examination of nondiscriminatory laws that create incidental burdens on interstate commerce. Any balancing test necessarily involves *ad hoc* decision making. The Court will evaluate the importance of the interests promoted by the state legislation, and the degree to which that interest is in fact promoted by the legislation. It will then evaluate the qualitative and quantitative effects of the state regulation on interstate commerce. Finally, it will compare the degree of burden on interstate commerce to the degree of local benefit produced by the legislation.

If the Court did not give deference to state and local governments when applying this balancing test, it would be merely second guessing the decisions of state and local rule makers concerning how legitimate local interests should be promoted. But the balancing test used in modern commerce clause cases does not give the Court free reign in making its own cost-benefit decisions as to whether promoting a legitimate local interest is worth the cost on interstate commerce. The balancing test used in dormant commerce clause cases favors the government, as *Pike* indicates.

The commerce clause balancing test gives deference to the government in two ways. First, it places the burden of proof on persons who challenge nondiscriminatory state laws under negative commerce clause principles. Second, the law must place a clearly excessive burden on interstate commerce. The state is not required to prove that the social good produced by its law is worth the incidental cost it places on interstate commerce. Rather, the person attacking the law must demonstrate the public good produced by the law is so slight that the burden on interstate commerce should be considered truly excessive.

For example, *Minnesota v. Clover Leaf Creamery Co.* (1981) upheld a Minnesota law that prohibited the sale of milk in plastic, non-refillable containers. This Minnesota law was nondiscriminatory, because it prohibited the sale of milk in plastic containers regardless of whether those containers, or the milk in them, were produced within Minnesota or elsewhere. The Minnesota law placed a real burden on the interstate milk industry, because bottlers of milk in states where plastic non-refillable were permissible could not ship milk in plastic bottles into Minnesota, but this burden was not a discriminatory burden. Although the Minnesota law burdened the interstate milk and milk packaging industries, the Minnesota law helped to protect the environment in Minnesota. There were many ways for Minnesota to protect its environment, and its landfills, other than prohibiting plastic non-refillable containers for the sale of milk. However, there was no other way for Minnesota to achieve the precise goal of reducing the amount of disposed plastic material in the state except by a prohibition of some plastic products, such as non-refillable plastic milk bottles.

A state law may discriminate (and thus be invalid) even if it does not contain discriminatory language on its face. *Hunt v. Washington State Apple Advertising Commission* (1977) invalidated a North Carolina law that required apples sold into the state to be marked only with the U.S. Department of Agriculture grade or marked as "not graded." However, under this law, apples sold in North Carolina could not be marked as having met grading standards by an individual state, such as the State of Washington. The North Carolina law constituted discrimination because it removed a trade advantage of out-of-state apples. Washington apple growers, over time, had created a consumer preference for apples that received the Washington's highest grade. "Washington State Apples" are a term about as well known as "Intel Inside." North Carolina's seemingly even handed regulation actually constituted a trade barrier by taking away the trade advantage gained by Washington State apples and prohibiting the truthful designation.

North Carolina asserted that its law was designed to avoid consumer deception that might occur with conflicting types of grading standards used by different states. However, there was virtually no evidence in this litigation that consumers would be misled as to the quality of apples by the labeling of apples with Washington State grading standards in addition to the standards used by the United States Department of Agriculture. In contrast with the slight benefit to state consumers, the burden on interstate commerce created by the law was considerable. And, discriminatory. The law removed the ability of producers of high quality apples of other states to identify to consumers in North Carolina that the apples they offered for sale were superior to those grown in North Carolina. The Court found that the North Carolina law was a discriminatory trade barrier.

In evaluating state laws, the Court requires the state to show that the burden it places on interest commerce is the *least restrictive burden* that is necessary to achieve the state's legitimate interests. For example, *Dean Milk Company v. City of Madison* (1951) invalidated a Madison, Wisconsin law prohibiting the sale in Madison of any milk that had not been packaged within the county in which Madison was located. Madison asserted that the law was needed so that local inspectors could insure that locally sold milk was bottled safely. However, there were a variety of alternatives that would have imposed lesser burdens on commerce that would have guaranteed equally safe milk for consumers in Madison. Requiring the milk to be bottled near the city effectively prohibited milk supply businesses from creating bottling facilities outside of the State of Wisconsin, if these businesses wanted to have access to the Madison retail market.

Bibb v. Navajo Freight Lines, Inc. (1959), may best be understood as using the balancing test in finding that a state law violated the dormant commerce clause. In *Bibb* an Illinois law required a certain type of contour mud flap for trucks using the roads of Illinois. There was no safety advantage to the contour mudguards; evidence at trial showed that the types of mudguards used in other states actually might reduce traffic accidents. Other states did not require the type of mudguard that Illinois required. Justice Black, who normally opposed the use of a balancing test, wrote for the Court in invalidating the Illinois law on the basis of the balancing test. He found that the Illinois law produced no real safety benefit and imposed a clearly excessive burden on interstate commerce, by requiring trucks of all other states, most of which required other types of mud flaps, from entering the state without switching to the type of mudguard required by the Illinois law. Because Black used the balancing test, the majority did not have to inquire into whether the true purpose of the Illinois legislature was to create a barrier to competition. The Court's opinion did not mention the fact that one of the few contoured mudguard flap factories in the world was located in Illinois. The Court did not have to rule that Illinois legislators had attempted to discriminate against out-of-state truck parts in Illinois trucking markets.

States as "Market Participants" Instead of "Market Regulators"

Perhaps the most confusing terminology in dormant commerce clause cases is the phrase "market participant." This phrase did not appear in the Supreme Court opinions before the 1970s. The principle reflected in the "market participant" test is simply that a state may limit its own direct subsidy to persons or businesses that are domiciled in the state.

Many people may call a state subsidy a welfare benefit. We often think of welfare payments going to poor people, but the state may choose to give a subsidy to a favored class of persons or businesses. This direct subsidy may consist of money, products, or services that go directly from the government to an individual person or individual business. Money given by the government to farmers or businesses located in the state also constitutes a direct subsidy.

There has never been a time in our history when the Supreme Court has held state that gives a direct subsidy to in-state persons must give a similar subsidy to persons who reside in other states. A state may decide to give food to its poor people (or to all of its citizens), but that does not require a state to give an equal amount of food to people from all states who might come into the state merely to receive the free food and then return to their home state. A state might decide to give free tuition (or no tuition) to its residents but not to residents of other states. In the chapter on Equal Protection, we learn that there are restrictions on when a state can impose a *durational* residency requirement. In other words, if a state decides to give food benefits to its poor citizens, it cannot discriminate against them because some of its residents are only *recent* residents. But, the state, in general, can limit its welfare to its residents.

The Court created the market participant theory to describe why a state giving economic subsidies to businesses domiciled in the state does not violate the commerce clause. The term separates the state when it acts as one who provide a subsidy as distinguished from the state when it acts to regulate the market. It would have been simpler if the Court had merely stated that a state can limit direct subsidies to persons or entities who are domiciled in the state. In other words, when the state passes laws to regulate the market, the dormant commerce clause restricts state power. When the state enters the market to buy and sell goods and services, it can spend its money as it sees fit, and thus it can decide to spend its money to favor its own citizens, such as deciding to burn in its state house furnaces only coal produced within the state rather than buying the coal for a cheaper price from a out-of-state coal producer.

The fact that a state is dispensing subsidies to in-state persons or in-state businesses will not allow it to place conditions on the use of those subsidies that discriminates against interstate commerce, such as imposing a tariff or trade barrier. For example, a state can require that all professors who work at a state university live within the state's boundaries. However, the state cannot require university professors to spend their salaries only on in-state products. When the state does that, it is regulating the market, and the dormant commerce clause applies.

Thus, *South–Central Timber Development, Inc. v. Wunnicke* (1984) invalidated a state law requiring purchasers of state-owned timber to have the timber partially processed within the state before they could ship it out of the state. There was no majority opinion in this case, but most of the Justices agreed that a state did not have any right to impose "conditions downstream" in restricting how the recipient of state-owned timber (which was a direct subsidy) would be used *after* the private individual received the timber. *Wunnicke* establishes that once the state gives a subsidy to a private person it may not prohibit that private person from taking the subsidy outside of the state or using it outside the state.

Because the state cannot impose downstream conditions, there are limits to the state's largess. For example, if a state decided to give millions of dollars to each of its dairy farmers, those farmers could sell their dairy products at incredibly low costs and capture the dairy product market from out-of-state farmers who were not receiving subsidies. On the other hand, that would mean that in-state taxpayers would be subsidizing out-of-state consumers when they purchased milk At some point, one would think that the in-state taxpayers are going to wonder why they are so keen on subsidizing milk purchases in other states.

The Court's position that direct subsidies may be limited to in-state persons reflects the inner political check theory. Although interstate commerce is burdened when the state's subsidy creates market inefficiency, the primary people who bear the burden are the people of the state that is giving the subsidy. In our example, the money given to dairy farmers is money that could have been used for schools, roads, or other local interests. When a state is giving subsidies to in-state persons it is doing so at the cost to other persons who are in the state. The local political process is best suited to make a determination as to whether the subsidy is justified in terms of the promotion of legitimate local interests.

We have come a long way since *Cooley v. Board of Wardens* (1851) established the rule that states could not regulate those subject areas that, in the words of that case, require national regulation. The *Cooley* rule may appear to be irrelevant to commerce clause analysis in the twenty-first century. In the twenty-first century, it is hard to believe that there is any area of economic activity that would require uniform national regulation that has not already been subject to federal regulation of some type. On the other hand, *Cooley* may well have meant that there are some areas that states cannot regulate. If the area demands national regulation, and Congress has not imposed a rule, that must mean that Congress intends that the free market govern that area, so that state laws are preempted by the dormant commerce clause and the result is regulation only by the free market.

The following sections of this Chapter consider in a little more detail specific problem under negative commerce clause principles. The Court has not adopted separate constitutional standards for the different types of problems but these problem areas demonstrate how the Court has applied the principles to different fact situations.

§ 8.4   The *Cooley* Rule of Selective Exclusiveness

Cooley v. Board of Wardens (1851) represents the culmination of the formative period in the early days of the Court in search for an adequate standard for judicial review of state regulation of commerce in the absence of a federal law. This decision set the direction for commerce clause adjudication for almost the next 100 years. In *Cooley* the Court, speaking through Justice Benjamin Curtis—who resigned after the *Dred Scott* decision and later was counsel to President Andrew Johnson in his impeachment proceedings—upheld a Pennsylvania law requiring ships entering or leaving the Philadelphia port to engage a local pilot.

At the time, some Justices thought that the federal commerce power was exclusive, like the clause giving Congress the power to declare war, so that no state could exercise such a power. Others thought that the commerce power was like the taxing power—the fact that a clause gives Congress the power to enact certain taxes does not deprive the states to enact similar taxes unless a federal law specifically preempts the field. *Cooley* was the case in which a majority of the Court agreed on a middle ground: sometimes the commerce clause is exclusive and sometimes it is not exclusive.

In this case, Pennsylvania enacted a law that required every ship entering or leaving the port of Philadelphia to engage a local pilot. Cooley challenged the law as an impermissible state regulation of interstate commerce. The Court specifically rejected both extreme interpretations of the commerce clause; *i.e.*, either that congressional power was exclusive or that state regulation in the absence of congressional action could go unbridled.

The *Cooley* doctrine looks to the nature of the subject of the challenged regulation as the crucial factor in determining its validity. The doctrine of selective exclusiveness states that, if the item is such that national uniformity is necessitated, then Congressional power is exclusive. If, on the other hand, the item is matter of a peculiarly local concern (even though within the reach of the Congressional commerce clause power such as the Pennsylvania pilotage laws), allowing a diversity of treatment, then states may regulate the area, in the absence of congressional preemption.

While the *Cooley* Rule of Selective Exclusiveness is a major advance from the metaphysical origin-of-powers question, which *Gibbons v. Odgen* (1824) had appeared to embrace, there were pitfalls in the *Cooley* doctrine as well. First, the decision supplies no litmus test to determine when a subject is appropriate for national, as opposed to local regulation. In *Cooley,* a federal statute indicated that Congress thought the matter did not mandate a nationally uniform regulation, but such statutes will not always exist.

Even if a matter is appropriate for diverse treatment, does that mean that all state laws are constitutional, even if they discriminate against the commerce from other states? Although a state might be regulating a local subject matter, the legislation could still be discriminatory in purpose or effect, thereby favoring residents over non-residents.

An important element of *Cooley* was that the Pennsylvania laws were in fact nondiscriminatory, falling with equal weight on Pennsylvania residents, although the Court did not focus on this issue. We shall see, in later cases, that the Court is more willing to sustain state regulations that equally burden local residents. When there is no discrimination against out-of-state citizens or residents, an inner political check operating within the state assures that the effects of the law will not be too harsh, for it will operate equally on the state citizens who enacted it.

§ 8.5   Federal Incorporation by Reference of State Laws

Cooley noted that the Congressional Act of 1789 specifically endorsed the continuation of state regulation until Congress enacted other regulations. Interestingly, *Cooley* did not appear to hold the Act of 1789 binding, and decided the case as if there were no federal law on the scene that settled the issue by authorizing state pilotage laws, or at least authorizing nondiscriminatory state pilotage laws. Instead, the Court treated the federal law merely as evidence that Congress thought that the matter was appropriate for diverse treatment.

Justice Curtis raised the question of whether Congress could enact legislation adopting *future* state laws by incorporation, but he indicated that such action was not constitutional. Justice Curtis, we now know, was in error in equating Congressional adoption of future laws by incorporation as indistinguishable from Congress redelegating, back to the states, the power over interstate commerce.

We can best understand this point by looking at a few examples. Congress cannot delegate to Illinois the power to legislate federal pollution standards for the whole country. Then Congress would be abdicating interstate commerce control to one state to legislate for the nation. However, Congress can enact legislation prescribing that the federal pollution standard in each state shall be the same as the state standard. Then, Congress is not abdicating its authority but merely incorporating by reference future legislation. This type of "delegation" is appropriate because those having input into the political process creating the rule are also bound by it, assuring an inner political check. *United States v. Sharpnack* (1958). Congress is incorporating state laws as they are now or are in the future

Thus, Congress may reverse the Court's opinion of the need for uniformity by authorizing the state legislation. Thus, *Leisy v. Hardin* (1890) invalidated, as a violation of the dormant commerce clause, an Iowa statute prohibiting the sale of intoxicating liquor in Iowa. Applying *Cooley,* the Court held that "transportation, purchase, sale and exchange of commodities is national in its character," and so "must be governed by a uniform system;" the absence of federal law indicates the congressional "will that such commerce shall be free and untrammeled."

Congress reacted by enacting the Wilson Act, subjecting interstate liquor traffic to the laws of the state into which the liquor was imported. A unanimous Court upheld the Wilson Act in *Wilkerson v. Rahrer* (1891). The subsequent legislation did not represent Congressional delegation to the states of the federal power to regulate commerce, but rather a legitimate use of Congressional power under the commerce clause to authorize an acceptable form of state regulation.

Conclusion. Since the time of Chief Justice Marshall, the Court has recognized that the commerce clause has a negative implication that restricts state laws that burden interstate commerce. When the Court strikes down a state or local regulatory act as inconsistent with the dormant commerce clause, it is interpreting the silence of Congress to hold that, in the absence of federal legislation, a state or local law may not create a trade barrier or imposes a discriminatory burden on interstate commerce.

Because the commerce clause is a grant of power to Congress, it is Congress (not the Court) that has the final authority for determining the way in which interstate commerce is regulated. When Congress passes a statute that allows states to have a commercial regulation that the Court had previously found to be inconsistent with the dormant commerce clause, Congress is not really reversing the Court's rule, for it is not stating that the state law was consistent with the dormant commerce clause. Rather Congress has now made the decision that the federal government should allow the states to enact laws that regulate and discriminate against interstate commerce. There is no longer any need for the Court to interpret the dormant commerce clause—the silence of Congress—for Congress has now spoken.

The Court must uphold the federal statute so long as the activity that Congress has chosen to regulate (or to leave open for state regulation) is related to, or has an effect on, interstate commerce. There is no Constitutional requirement that Congress regulates commerce in a way that promotes efficient rather than inefficient markets.

Nevertheless, Congressional approval of state or local laws that create trade barriers or otherwise regulate commerce in a manner that would not be permissible under dormant commerce clause principles creates inefficient markets and causes economic hardship to persons in some states through the shifting of economic burdens by states that seek to promote local interests. For this reason, the Court will not find that Congress has removed state or local regulations from the limits of dormant commerce clause principles unless Congress has spoken clearly, or unless congressional intent to allow discriminatory state regulations of commerce is "unmistakably clear." *South–Central Timber Dev., Inc. v. Wunnicke* (1984). Because all segments of the country are represented in Congress, there is an inner political check, that is, less danger that one state will be in a position to exploit the others.

§ 8.6   State Regulation Affecting Interstate Commerce: The *Di Santo* Case

In the post-*Cooley* world, the Court recognized the states' concurrent power to regulate commerce in appropriate circumstances. While *Cooley* resolved the question of the exclusiveness of the commerce power, the Court still had to determine the extent of permissible, concurrent state power. Successive Courts invoked various verbal touchstones in an attempt to formulate a test to distinguish between permitted and invalid state exercise of regulatory power, but the absence of an adequate standard is evidenced by the plethora of cases that one cannot reconcile merely by applying the *Cooley* doctrine.

In these decisions the Court finds that one factor is crucial: a legitimate state regulation must not burden interstate commerce, in either purpose or effect, unless the extent of that burden is outweighed by a legitimate state objective that cannot be achieved in a less burdensome manner. The Court looks to the effect of the law and not merely its stated purpose in order to prevent states from easily avoiding the dormant commerce clause.

While the post-*Cooley* Court acknowledged discrimination against interstate commerce as one emerging test, the Court focuses on what where the supposed "direct" or "indirect" effect of the law. Thus, the Court had continuing difficulty with the practical application of the *Cooley* doctrine. It never could develop a test to determine if the state law had a "direct" effect on interstate commerce. The supposed test really described a conclusion, not a rule to determine a conclusion.

Di Santo v. Pennsylvania (1927) was a typical case that neatly illustrates the problem. A Pennsylvania regulation required sellers of steamboat tickets to apply for and be granted a license. In addition, the law charged the licensees an annual fee and subjected them to license revocation. The state claimed that the law protected local citizens from fraudulent acts.

The Court struck down the regulation as an unnecessary, burdensome interference with interstate commerce. It said that the law was not an "indirect" burden on commerce but a "direct" one, which the state could not justify as an exercise of the police power to prevent possible fraud. The Court said that, under *Cooley,* Congress has exclusive authority to regulate this commerce because the subject demands uniform treatment. Therefore, this state legislation is necessarily repugnant to the Congressional power.

In his now famous dissent, Justice Stone departed from the majority's position and implored the Court to adopt a more appropriate standard for adjusting the conflicting claims of the federal government and the states. Stone advocated a more realistic test, abandoning reliance on conclusory labels such as "direct" or "indirect." He shifted the focus from a metaphysical concern with "direct" burdens to a focus on burdens that discriminated against commerce from other states. Instead of rigid verbal formulae, the Court should use a more pragmatic test:

[I]t seems clear that those interferences not deemed forbidden are to be sustained, not because the effect on commerce is nominally indirect, but because a consideration of all the facts and circumstances, such as the nature of the regulation, its function, the character of the business involved and the actual effect on the flow of commerce, lead to the conclusion that the regulation concerns interests peculiarly local and does not infringe the national interest in maintaining the freedom of commerce across state lines.

The congressional will controls. If the Court sustains the state action as not discriminating or constituting an unreasonable burden on interstate commerce, and Congress concurs, no subsequent congressional action is required. If Congress concludes that the state action is undesirable, it retains the power to terminate its dormant state, and assert its will pursuant to its commerce clause power. Similarly, if the Court invalidates the state regulation, Congress can consequently resurrect the state law by expressing its consent to such state action.

The demise of formalistic tests and metaphysical attempts to interpret congressional silence has led to an era of more understandable rules.

§ 8.7   State Powers Over Transportation

A majority of the Court adopted the approach that Justice Stone had advocated in his *Di Santo* dissent in the early landmark case of *Southern Pacific Co. v. Arizona* (1945). Arizona charged Southern Pacific with violating a state law prohibiting trains with more than 14 passenger cars or 70 freight cars from operating within the state. Ostensibly, the state regulation was a safety measure. Nonetheless, its practical effect was to impose a disproportionate burden on shippers who engaged in long hauls, as opposed to short hauls, and these long haul shippers were more likely to be using interstate as opposed to intrastate rail lines.

Stone, now Chief Justice, wrote the majority opinion. The trial court had found that the operation of long trains is standard practice through the United States; that approximately 93% of the Arizona freight traffic and 95% of the passenger traffic is interstate; that the train limit law required the Southern Pacific to haul over 30% more trains in Arizona. To comply with the Arizona train limit laws, trains must either be broken up as they enter the border or conform to the lowest train limit restriction of all the states they travel through, thus allowing a state's train length regulations to have a substantial extraterritorial effect. Given the interstate nature of the train lines, "the Arizona law often controls the length of passenger trains all the way from Los Angeles to El Paso."

In addition, the safety data presented at the trial was ambivalent at best. It turned out that the increased safety resulting from shorter trains was more than overcome by the added risks inherent in increasing the number of trains operating within the state. "The decisive question," the Court said, is whether in the these circumstances "the total effect of the law as a safety measure in reducing accidents and casualties is so slight or problematical as not to outweigh the national interest in keeping interstate commerce free from interferences which seriously impede it and subject it to local regulation which does not have a uniform effect on the interstate train journey which it interrupts."

The majority agreed with the trial court that the Arizona law had no reasonable relation to safety, and found that the burdens on interstate commerce outweighed the state's equivocal evidence of safety. The majority weighed and evaluated the evidence. It did not accept the state's factual assertions of safety because the interests in interstate commerce are "not to be avoided by 'simply invoking the convenient apologetics of the police power.'" The Court indicated by its language and actions that the test of "reasonableness" under the interstate commerce clause cases is much stricter than the modern test of "reasonableness" when the Court evaluates state or federal economic regulations challenged under the due process and equal protection cases.

The Court decided *Southern Pacific* in the wake of *South Carolina State Highway Department v. Barnwell Brothers, Inc* (1938). In that case a unanimous Court had sustained a South Carolina weight and width limitation for trucks operated within the state. Again Stone, then a Justice, wrote the opinion.

Barnwell upheld a South Carolina highway statute that prohibited trucks over 90 inches in width and with a loaded weight in excess of 20,000 pounds. All other states permitted the standard width of 96 inches and only four other states prescribed a gross weight as low as 20,000 pounds. Justice Stone emphasized that a state "may not, under the guise of regulation, discriminate against interstate commerce." "[S]o long as the state action does not discriminate, the burden is one which the Constitution permits...."

But other language seems inconsistent with Chief Justice Stone's language in *Southern Pacific*. In *Barnwell*, Stone argued that "[C]ourts do not sit as legislatures...." The adoption "of one weight or width regulation, rather than another, is a legislative not a judicial choice," and "courts are not any the more entitled, because interstate commerce is affected, to substitute their own for the legislative judgment."

While it is difficult to reconcile all of the language of these two cases, they are consistent in their results. In *Barnwell*, the evidence of the relationship between the state law and safety requirements was much stronger than the *Southern Pacific* case. In spite of the *Barnwell* language quoted above, the Court did in fact summarize and analyze the evidence of safety. For example, 100 miles of South Carolina roads at the time were only 16 feet wide, too narrow for two 96 inch wide trucks. The Court also emphasized the local nature of the state highway system. While this reference to the local nature of state highways is not valid in modern times, it was convincing when *Barnwell* was decided in 1938.

Summary. Commentators on the various problems and court tests in this area abound, but perhaps the best summary of the law in this area is the Supreme Court's in *Pike v. Bruce Church,* Inc. (1970):

> Although the criteria for determining the validity of state statutes affecting interstate commerce have been variously stated, the general rule that emerges can be phrased as follows: Where the statute regulates even-handedly to effectuate a legitimate local public interest, and its effects on interstate commerce are only incidental, it will be upheld unless the burden imposed on such commerce is clearly excessive in relation to the putative local benefits. If a legitimate local purpose is found, then the question becomes one of degree. And the extent of the burden that will be tolerated will of course depend on the nature of the local interest involved, and on whether it could be promoted as well with a lesser impact on interstate activities. Occasionally the Court has candidly undertaken a balancing approach in resolving these issues, but more frequently it has spoken in terms of "direct" and "indirect" benefits and burdens.

§ 8.8   Incoming Commerce

The Court no longer uses the so-called "original package" doctrine as the definitive test to evaluate state regulatory power over products imported from out of state. The real question is whether the state legislation discriminates against interstate commerce, that is, whether the state law involves economic protectionism. If the statutory purpose or effect is to protect state producers from competitive interstate commerce, the parochial legislation is invalid. State laws affecting the national market, even justified under the guise of local health and safety concerns, are also invalid under the dormant commerce clause if there is a less burdensome, nondiscriminatory alternative.

The seminal case invalidating a state regulatory scheme that involved economic protectionism is *Baldwin v. G. A. F. Seelig, Inc.* (1935). Justice Cardozo, writing for a unanimous court, rejected New York's efforts to rely on the original package doctrine or any direct/indirect burden distinction to justify its restriction of the sale of Vermont milk within New York's borders.

New York established minimum milk prices that dealers had to pay to producers. The Supreme Court had no problem with New York's minimum price laws as applied to products originating within the state. But New York milk dealers, in order to avoid paying the high milk prices in-state, preferred to buy their milk out-of-state. To keep the system unimpaired by competition from afar, the Act tried to extend its the protective prices to that part of the supply (about 30%) that came from other states. In other words, a New York milk dealer could not sell his milk within the state unless she had paid the milk producer (wherever the latter is located) whatever the dealer, what she would have had to pay the New York producer. When Seelig bought its milk from a Vermont creamery at less than the New York set price, the New York Commission refused to license it to do business in New York. The New York procedure, in effect though not in name, imposed a tariff on the out of state milk. Even though the state collected no money, it artificially raised the price of out-of-state milk so that out-of-state purchasers could not underprice the local product.

No state has any power to project its legislation into another state by regulating the price to be paid in that other state for goods purchased there. Such a power, if allowed, violates one of the reasons for our Constitution. As *Seelig* said—

> [A] chief occasion of the commerce clauses was "the mutual jealousies and aggressions of the States, taking form in customs barriers and other economic retaliation." . . . If New York, in order to promote the economic welfare of her farmers, may guard them against competition with the cheaper prices of Vermont, the door has been opened to rivalries and reprisals that were meant to be averted by subjecting commerce between the states to the power of the nation.

The Court rejected the argument that the purpose of the New York law was to maintain an adequate supply of pure milk, the supply being put in jeopardy when the farmers of the state are unable to earn a living income. This argument proves too much, for it would allow virtually all state trade barriers against other states. "The Constitution was framed under the dominion of a political philosophy less parochial in range. It was framed on the theory that the people of the several states must sink or swim together, and that in the long run prosperity and salvation are in union and not division.''

Baldwin invalidated a New York milk regulatory scheme that was an attempt to aid local milk producers by making more expensive the importation of milk from a sister state. In effect, the state imposed a wealth transfer to local producers directly financed by the out-of-state producers. There was no inner political check working within New York state to assure that the people of New York directly paid for this wealth transfer.

Tax Subsidies. The Court would have upheld the transfer of direct cash payments or tax subsidies (e.g., lower property tax assessments of dairy land) to New York milk producers (financed by the New York general taxpayer). An inner political check would assure that the people within the state, who directly paid for the subsidy, would weigh the costs and benefits. But when there is an attempt to shift the direct costs to out-of-state persons, this inner political check is not working as well and so there is a broader role for judicial review.

On the other hand, the Court will not uphold crude tax subsidies. For example, the state may not enact a crude tax subsidy scheme that taxes a given business and then subsidizes the in-state competitors with the money collected from the out of state competitors. There is no inner political check because those who pay the tax are out of state residents or companies with no real input into the taxing state's political processes. Any in-state taxpayers are won over to the tax because they more than recoup their losses by a subsidy in the form of a rebate of the tax. *West Lynn Creamery, Inc. v. Healy* (1994).

In *West Lynn Creamery*, Justice Scalia wrote an opinion that sounded much like Professor Scalia explaining the problem to his students, during his days on law school faculties. He stated:

> There are at least four possible devices that would enable a state to produce the economic effect [the subsidy to local milk farmers] that Massachusetts has produced here: (1) a discriminatory tax upon the industry, imposing a higher liability on out-of state members than on their in-state competitors; (2) a tax upon the industry that is non-discriminatory in its assessment, but that has an exemption or credit for in-state members; (3) a non-discriminatory tax upon the industry, the revenues from which are placed into a segregated fund, which fund is disbursed as rebates or subsidies to in-state members of the industry (the situation at issue in this case); and, (4) with or without non-discriminatory taxation of the industry, a subsidy for the in-state members of the industry, funded from the state's general revenues. It is long settled that the first of these

methodologies is unconstitutional ... the second of them, exemption or credit against a neutral tax, is no different in principle from the first, and has likewise been held invalid ... the fourth methodology, application of a state subsidy from general revenues, is so far removed from what we have hitherto held to be unconstitutional, that prohibiting it must be regarded as an extension of our negative-commerce clause jurisprudence, and, therefore, to me, unacceptable ... the issue before us in the present case is whether the third of these methodologies must fall. Although the question is close, I conclude it would not be a principled point at which to disembark from a negative-commerce-clause train. The only difference between methodology (2) (discriminatory exemption from nondiscriminatory tax) and methodology (3) (discriminatory refund of a nondiscriminatory tax) is that the money is taken and returned rather than simply left with the favored in-state taxpayer in the first place. The difference between (3) and (4), on the other hand, is the difference between assisting in-state industry through non-discriminatory taxation and assisting in-state industry by other means. I would therefore allow a state to subsidize its domestic industry as long as it does so from non-discriminatory taxes that go to the state's general revenue fund. [(Scalia, J., joined by Thomas, J., concurring in the judgment) (internal quotation marks, internal citations, and internal paragraph divisions omitted).]

There are some important economic differences between tax subsidies and tariffs, even though both are economically inefficient and both negatively affect free trade and the free flow of goods and services. Although *West Lynn Creamery* does not make the point explicitly, it was implicit in the Court's acknowledgment that one could not rely on the "state's political processes" to prevent "legislative abuse" in the situation that existed in *West Lynn Creamery*. Pure subsidies are usually more transparent to voters than tariffs; their economic affects are more obvious. In the case of tariffs the voter who is less economically sophisticated thinks that the party who is out-of-state is paying the tariff, while voters do know that it is they who must pay the taxes to raise the money that is given to the favored recipient in a tax subsidy situation.

Compensating Use Taxes. *Baldwin* does not forbid a state from using its tax laws to subject interstate goods sold in its state to the same tax levied on intrastate goods sold in its state, i.e., a "compensatory use" tax. The tax laws in such a case are nondiscriminatory and are not used to compensate for natural competitive advantages of another state. Unlike the *Baldwin* situation, a "compensating use" tax does not smother competition but removes the artificial competitive disadvantage that the state's own tax laws would otherwise impose on products produced in the state; the state tax simply subjects imported goods to the same nondiscriminatory tax that in-state goods already have to pay. *Henneford v. Silas Mason Co.* (1937).

The Least Restrictive Means Test. In order to discriminate against interstate commerce, some states drafted complex schemes that have more than a perfunctory reference to local health and safety interests but are really trade barriers. To deal with these situations the Court has developed a strict, active judicial review to assure that the legitimate safety measures can be accomplished by means imposing the least restrictive effects on interstate commerce.

This principle is well illustrated by *Dean Milk Co. v. City of Madison* (1951). A Madison, Wisconsin ordinance made it illegal to sell pasteurized milk unless it had been processed and bottled at an approved pasteurization plant within a radius of five miles from the central square of Madison. The state court approved the five mile radius on the grounds that it promoted convenient, economical, and efficient plant inspection.

The Court invalidated the state law. First, it was unimpressed that Madison's law also excluded Wisconsin milk from outside the Madison area (i.e., some in-state milk) as well as interstate milk. The Court did not elaborate, but its principle should be clear. If a locality could avoid the requirements of the dormant commerce clause by also discriminating against some in-state area, then it would be fairly easy to engage in economic discrimination. For example, each town in a state could discriminate against all interstate commerce and the commerce from other portions of the state. Or each half of the state could discriminate against all out-of-state goods and goods from the other half of the state. Under the theory of the city of Madison, the state as a whole would be accepting no out-of-state goods, but it would be able to avoid dormant commerce clause scrutiny merely because portions of the state would also be discriminating against other portions of the state.

Similarly the Court did not accept Madison's health rationale, for there were "reasonable nondiscriminatory alternatives, adequate to conserve legitimate local interests" that were available. For example, if the city insisted that it was necessary for its own officials inspect distant milk sources, it could do so, and charge the actual and reasonable cost of such inspection to the importing producers and processors.

When regulating to protect the health or welfare of its people, a state or local government only has to use the means with the least burden on commerce if the party challenging the state or local law can demonstrate that the state or local government could achieve exactly equal benefits through a law that would not place a great burden on commerce.

The State Reciprocity Requirements. The Court has looked with suspicion on state reciprocity agreements. Consider, for example, *Great Atlantic & Pacific Tea Co. v. Cottrell* (1976). A Mississippi law admitted interstate milk for sale only if the producing state had agreed to a reciprocal inspection standards agreement. The Mississippi law was not really designed to promote health and safety, for it permitted Louisiana milk to be admitted to Mississippi *if* Louisiana entered into a reciprocity agreement with Mississippi, even though Louisiana's standards were lower than Mississippi's. "The reciprocity clause thus disserves rather than promotes any higher Mississippi milk quality standards." If a state may insist that a sister state either sign a reciprocal agreement or be foreclosed from exporting its products to Mississippi, then such a rule would invite a multiplication of preferential and retaliatory trade barriers that are contrary to the purpose of the Commerce Clause. Although Mississippi, ostensibly, sought to guarantee safe milk, its law was not carefully designed to do that.

If Mississippi imposed the reciprocal trade barrier in an effort to persuade other states to eliminate their restrictions on the importation of Mississippi milk, that still did not justify the Mississippi rule. If other states had improper trade barriers, Mississippi's remedy is to sue in court to invalidate those barriers, not institute its own trade barrier.

The Commerce Clause and Privacy. When the alleged local benefit outweighs the degree of the state-imposed burden, states are not necessarily barred from restraining incoming interstate commerce. In *Breard v. Alexandria* (1951) the Court upheld a municipal ordinance forbidding uninvited door-to-door solicitation. The Court said that the local homeowner's right to privacy outweighed the economic burden even though "interstate commerce itself knocks on the local door."

The Court gave greater deference to legislation designed to protect the privacy interests of the community than it would give local regulatory schemes revealing an attempt to preserve local prosperity at the expense of nonresidents. Our federalist system recognizes state power to reasonably regulate incoming commerce pursuant to legitimate local health and safety objectives, *but only* to the extent that the nondiscriminatory burden imposed on the national market place does not exceed the alleged local benefits.

Prohibition of Harmful Products. The Court's emphasis on nondiscrimination is important, because even products that are concededly harmful are still "commerce" and therefore subjected to standard commerce clause analysis. For example, if an article's worth in interstate commerce is "far outweighed" by the dangers in its movement—such as items that spread pestilence—then the state could prohibit its transportation across state lines.

In contrast, a state cannot prohibit the out-of-state importation of solid or liquid wastes in order to extend the life of landfill within the state and protect its environment. Such wastes are in commerce and protected by the commerce clause. The garbage dump owner is selling space, and the waste hauler is buying that space. *Philadelphia v. New Jersey* (1978). The state discriminated against out-of-state waste because it allowed *non-imported* wastes to be transported and buried within the state. A state cannot distinguish between in-state and out of state wastes by allowing the former but not the latter to be disposed of in landfill sites within the state, because a state cannot slow down or prohibit the flow of commerce in order to conserve for those within its borders privately-owned land fill. Whatever health or safety concerns might exist did not vary with the point of origin of the waste. What is really purchased in such cases is not the waste, but rather it is the landfill. States cannot prevent private landfill owners from selling portions of their landfill to out of state landfill users, any more than Wisconsin could prevent its dairy farmers from selling their cheese to out-of-state consumers.

If a state can demonstrate that it needs to keep a product out of the state in order to protect significant local interests, other than the economic well being of in-state persons or businesses, it may exclude the out-of-state products. For example, *Maine v. Taylor* (1986) upheld a Maine statute that prohibited the importation of live bait fish into the State of Maine. At trial, the state had shown that there was no economically reasonable way for the state to screen live bait fish for parasites that might be foreign to the State of Maine. It was not possible for the state to screen all live bait fish for possible parasites. Therefore, the law survived the difficult standard imposed on states for demonstrating the legitimacy of a tariff or a trade barrier.

Commerce and the Twenty–First Amendment. To be distinguished from state power to regulate commerce in general is the state power to regulate commerce over *liquor*. Liquor is no longer treated like other products because of the Twenty–First Amendment, section two, which provides: "The transportation or importation into any State, Territory, or possession of the United States for delivery or use therein of intoxicating liquors, in violation of the laws thereof, is hereby prohibited."

The Twenty–First Amendment does not repeal the commerce clause as to state regulation of the importation or transportation of liquor, but it certainly affects it, and serves to give the state wide latitude. Thus a state may exact a license fee for the privilege of importing into that state liquor from another state, although in the absence of the Twenty–First Amendment the dormant commerce clause would have forbade such an import fee. *State Board of Equalization v. Young's Market Co.* (1936).

Nonetheless, there are limits to the state's power. For example, a state cannot tax liquor imported into that state from a foreign country, in violation of the export import clause. Even though the Twenty–First Amendment does impose some limits on the commerce clause, it does not impose those limits on the export import clause because there are foreign policy concerns that are present as to imports from abroad. *Department of Revenue v. James B. Beam Distilling Co.* (1964).

The state power over liquor does not insulate state regulations from the limitations of the Fourteenth Amendment. *Craig v. Boren* (1976). It was not a purpose of the Twenty–First Amendment to limit the Bill of Rights. Congress also has the commerce clause power to prohibit resale price maintenance in violation of the Sherman Act. *California Retail Liquor Dealers Ass'n v. Midcal Aluminum, Inc.* (1980).

Even as to the commerce clause, the Twenty–First Amendment does not completely insulate state power for all judicial review. For example, New York may not constitutionally require every liquor distiller who sells liquor to wholesalers within that state to sell at a price that is no higher than the lowest price that the liquor distiller charged to wholesalers anywhere in the United States. This state law regulated out of state transactions in violation of the commerce clause. *Brown–Forman Distillers Corp. v. New York State Liquor Authority* (1986). The New York rule made it illegal for a distiller to reduce its price in other states during the period it is posted in New York, thus directly regulating commerce in other states. New York cannot constitutionally require that distillers surrender whatever competitive advantages they may possess in other states, and New York may not regulate the out of state transactions of distillers who sell in-state.

The Court, in each case challenged under the commerce clause, must carefully scrutinize the competing state and federal interests. The Court must determine whether a state law relating to the transportation, sale, or use of alcoholic beverages that would otherwise violate the commerce clause is so related to the central purpose of section two of the Twenty–First Amendment that it should be upheld despite its adverse effect on commerce or inconsistency with federal regulations.

The Court has used the dormant commerce clause to invalidate laws that constitute tariffs or trade barriers to competition from out-of-state producers of alcohol. For example, in *Granholm v. Heald* (2005) the Court (5 to 4), invalidated state laws that prohibited out-of-state wineries from shipping wine directly to in-state consumers, but that allowed in-state wineries to direct shipments to in-state consumers. *Granholm* ruled that the law constituted discrimination in the nature of a tariff or trade barrier, which it would uphold only if the state demonstrated that there was no other means to protect a significant state interest. Preventing the sale of alcohol to minors, or reducing alcoholism among a state's populace, are significant interests, but the state's discriminatory law (allowing in-state but not out-of-state wineries to ship wine) were not the least restrictive means of promoting those interests. For example, the state could require the delivery person to require proof of age before turning over the wine.

The *Granholm* dissenters believed that both the Twenty–First Amendment and federal statutes justified the states ability to restrict out-of-state shipment of alcoholic beverages, but the majority rejected both arguments. The purpose of the Twenty–First Amendment is to allow the states to promote abstinence, not to discriminate against out-of-state alcohol producers. See also, *Bacchus Imports, Ltd. v. Dias* (1984), holding (6 to 3) that Hawaii's exemption of locally-produced alcoholic beverages from a 20% excise tax imposed on wholesale liquor sales violated the commerce clause.

Summary. In general, if the state law does not discriminate on its face or as applied, the Court tends to sustain the state action unless there is clear interference with commerce and the local interest is not very substantial. If there is discrimination, then it must appear that there is no other reasonable method of safeguarding a legitimate local interest. If a state law has no other purpose than to favor local industry, this balancing of interest approach should not be used, because the purpose of the state regulation would be illegitimate.

§ 8.9   Outgoing Commerce

The dormant commerce clause restricts states that seek to prevent home products from being exported into the national market. State statutes burdening the marketing of local products out-of-state are the equivalent of embargoes. Although embargoes *per se* are repugnant to a national common market, the Court recognizes that some state laws that affect the export of goods are legitimate when they represent the least burdensome alternative for achieving legitimate state goals and do not interfere with any federal law.

Parker v. Brown (1943) upheld a California marketing scheme involving raisins and concluded that a State may fix prices without violating either the dormant commerce clause or the federal anti-trust laws.

A California law required each raisin producer to deliver over two-thirds of his crop to a marketing control committee that, in effect, engaged in price fixing. The purpose of the state law was to eradicate "injurious" price competition and stabilize raisin market. Between 90 and 95 percent of the raisins grown in California ultimately entered interstate or foreign commerce.

Justice Stone, at first, applied a mechanical test: did the state impose its regulation *before* or *after* the raisins entered interstate commerce? Under this approach, the measure was within state power, because the regulation occurred *before* interstate commerce operation, but he acknowledged that courts should not be bound by such mechanical formulas. After all, the raisin regulations *affected* interstate commerce, and Congress could have preempted the state law. Stone said that the real question was whether the local interests to be served outweighed the competing national interests.

The California law did not violate the Sherman Antitrust Act because the Court interpreted that law as not applying to a state. If all the raisin producers got together to set the price, that would be a violation of the antitrust laws. But here the producers were obeying a state law. The producers did not "conspire" with the state. Instead, the producers were merely obeying state law.

The Court found that the state law did not violate the dormant commerce clause either. Stone noted the significance of the raisin industry in the California economy, where almost all of this nation's raisins are produced. He concluded that, on balance, the regulation should be sustained as a legitimate state attempt to deal with a peculiarly local problem that Congress did not specifically address. The California law restricted the flow of goods in interstate commerce, because the state law required price fixing. If there were no state price fixing, the prices would be lower, and more raisins would go to market. But Stone's evaluation of federal law showed that Congress, itself, had recognized the distressed conditions of the agricultural production of the United States; the California program in fact supported (did not interfere with) this Congressional policy. Therefore, the state could legitimately fix the prices of goods within the state even though those commodities affected interstate commerce.

Embargoes to Promote Local Economic Objectives. The states may not burden the exportation of local products in order to enhance the reputation of local products, *Pike v. Bruce Church, Inc.* (1970), retain domestic resources for local consumption, *H. P. Hood & Sons v. Du Mond* (1949), insure local employment, *Foster–*

Fountain Packing Co. v. Haydel (1928), or keep a particular market open only to their own residents, *Toomer v. Witsell*, (1948).

A state also violates the dormant commerce clause if it requires an in-state industry to use a certain amount of the locally produced good. The state is simply using its regulatory power to favor a local industry and discriminate against interstate competition. Thus, *Wyoming v. Oklahoma* (1992) invalidated an Oklahoma law that required privately owned coal-fired electric generating plants to use at least 10% of Oklahoma-mined coal.

Embargoes of Natural Resources and Wild Game and Fish. In 1896, *Geer v.* Connecticut (1896) upheld a state law that prohibited the export of game birds, even though hunters had lawfully killed the game birds within the state. Oddly enough, even the early cases prohibited a state from placing an embargo on natural gas. *West v. Kansas Natural Gas Co.* (1911). It was not until 1979 that *Hughes v. Oklahoma* (1979) finally overruled *Geer v. Connecticut*, and explicitly rejected the legal fiction that interstate commerce is not involved on the theory that the state "owns" all the wild animals within the state. The state can regulate fishing, but it does not "own" the fish anymore than a wishful fisherman. Once the fisherman catches the minnows and reduces them to possession, he owns them, not the state. And when the state regulates, it must do so in a way that does not discriminate against interstate commerce.

Hughes invalidated an Oklahoma statute that provided that no natural minnows seined or procured within the state could be shipped outside of the state for sale. The statute on its face discriminated against interstate commerce of natural minnows by overtly blocking their export for sale. The law did not restrict what the modest fisherman could do with his catch as long as he did not sell them out of state. The Oklahoma law also did not limit the number of minnow that licensed minnow dealers could capture. If one sought to justify such a law for conservation reasons, but then, the law would not discriminate based on where the minnows went after they had been caught.

Once reduced to possession, the state allowed minnow dealers to process the fish for commercial purposes, so long *as the processing was within the state*. But, no one could take the fish out of state *for sale* to an out of state processor. The real purpose of the Oklahoma law was to favor in-state processing of minnows, in violation of the dormant commerce clause.

While the state can conserve natural resources it must do so in a nondiscriminatory fashion that recognizes that the relevant economic unit is the nation. Thus a state cannot prohibit the exportation of hydroelectric power that *private* facilities within the state produce, nor can it reserve for its own citizens the "economic benefit" of that hydroelectric energy. *New England Power Co. v. New Hampshire* (1982).

Privately owned water is also an article of commerce. Thus, if a state allows individuals to own groundwater (water taken from subland surface by means of piping) or water from lakes and streams, the government will have difficulty in keeping the private owner from sending that water out of the state. *Sporhase v. Nebraska ex rel. Douglas* (1982) invalidated a state law that prohibited anyone from taking groundwater with a well or pit and sending it to another state unless they had a permit. The permit would only be issued if the amount of water taken was reasonable, did not hurt the ecology or the people of the state, and if the water was being sent to another state that allowed private owners of water to send their water to Nebraska.

Sporhase found that the restrictions concerning the withdrawal of only a reasonable amount of water protected the health and welfare of citizens, but the barrier against exporting water constituted discrimination that violated the dormant commerce clause. The state law that required that water be sent only to states that had a reciprocal water transfer provision was simply a discriminatory means of allowing local residents to purchase water more cheaply than they could through a free national market: "there is no evidence that this restriction [limiting water to states that would allow sales back to Nebraska] is narrowly tailored to the conservation and preservation rationale [advanced by the state] ... if it could be shown that the state as a whole suffers a water shortage, that the intrastate transportation of water from areas of abundance to areas of shortage is feasible regardless of distance, and that the importation of water from adjoining states would roughly compensate for any exportation to those states, then the conservation and preservation purpose might be credibly advanced for the reciprocity provision. A demonstrably arid state conceivably might be able to marshal evidence to establish a close means-end relationship between even a total ban on the exportation of water and a purpose to conserve and preserve water."

The State as a Market Participant. When the state itself enters the market as a purchaser or seller of interstate commerce, nothing in the dormant commerce clause forbids it from restricting its own purchases or limiting its sales to its own citizens. Such self-imposed restrictions are typically not economically efficient, but the state is not acting as a market regulator; it is a market participant. The state is not using its sovereign powers to regulate; rather, it is using the powers that any private person has over what it owns.

For example, a state may follow a policy of confining the sale of cement produced at a *state owned* cement plant solely to state residents. *Reeves, Inc. v. Stake* (1980). What is really important is not that cement is the end-product of a complex process but that the state really owned the cement factory. However, a state may not compel *privately owned* cement plants within the state to sell their products solely to state residents. *New England Power Co. v. New Hampshire* (1982). The state does not own the privately owned coal mine, and so, it cannot use its regulatory power to discriminate against out of state commerce.

When a state actually *owns* a business and favors its own citizens it is not violating the commerce clause because it is not using its regulatory powers. What the state is really doing is using its power of the purse to give money to some people within the state. In the state-owned cement plant, for example, what the state is doing when it limits the sale of its cement to its own residents is the economic equivalent of giving money to some of its citizens, those who buy cement. *McCarthy v. Philadelphia Civil Service Commission* (1976) (state can require residence within a specific area as a requirement for *public* employment).

The mere fact that a state owns a resource does not give it *carte blanche*, or total power, to allocate that resource in a way that discriminates against competition from out-of-state persons in local economic interests. Antitrust laws, for example, impose some limits in how the private owner of a resource can use or restrict that resource. The Constitution imposes somewhat analogous restrictions on what a state can do. For example, in our cement case, the state could not forbid the in-state purchasers of cement from the state-owned cement plant from reselling that cement to out of state residents. Cf. *South–Central Timber Development, Inc. v. Wunnicke* (1984)(Court invalidates similar restrictions on state-owned timber once it sells the timber).

Some restrictions on the ability of out-of-state persons to engage in commercial activities may constitute a deprivation of the privileges of state citizenship that violates Article IV. Even if the Article IV privileges and immunities clause is inapplicable, the mere fact that the state is "participating" in the marketplace through the use of its financial or natural resources does not completely immunize its actions from review under the commerce clause.

When the state places regulations on the use of materials sold or distributed by the state, the courts must determine: (1), whether the regulation is one that results in the residents of the state bearing the cost for providing benefits to various persons within the state's jurisdiction or, (2), whether the regulation is an unconstitutional shifting of the cost for local benefits to out of state persons or interests by improper restrictions on competition.

The state may sell its *state-owned* resources to local residents at a lower price that the state charges to out-of-state interests because the state is acting as a "market participant"—that is, the residents of the state are bearing the cost of providing a welfare benefit to some persons within the jurisdiction. When the state is bearing the cost of providing economic benefits, there is little reason for the Supreme Court to intervene because the political process within the state should serve as an inner political check on the state's decisions to participate in the marketplace.

Thus, if a state offers a company a cash bonus or tax exemption in exchange for the company locating a factory in the state, its action can be upheld because the state is bearing the cost of producing some economic benefits for people in the state. However, if the state seeks, by law, to force a company (not owned by the state) to keep its factory in the state or to force such a company to give employment preference to local residents, then the state law violates the commerce clause because it attempts to shift to out-of-state interests the cost of producing local economic benefits.

Summary. If the state regulation, even under the guise of a legitimate goal, attempts to afford residents an economic advantage at the expense of a free-flowing national market, the countervailing national interest will override. Local economic measures are more likely to be upheld if there is no discriminatory purpose or effect. As Justice Stewart, in *Pike v. Bruce Church, Inc.* (1970) explained:

> Where the state regulates even handedly to effectuate a legitimate local public interest, and its effects on interstate commerce are only incidental, it will be upheld unless the burden imposed on such commerce is clearly excessive in relation to the putative local benefits. If a legitimate local purpose is found, then the question becomes one of degree. And the extent of the burden that will be tolerated will of course depend on the nature of the local interest involved, and on whether it could be promoted as well with a lesser impact with interstate activities.

§ 8.10 Personal Mobility

Because the definition of commerce includes the movement of persons, the Court has invoked the commerce clause to invalidate state regulations impairing the free mobility of citizens. The Court, however, has other arrows in its quiver, and it has also used these other constitutional provisions to protect the free movement of persons within our national common market. Indeed, the concept of personal mobility is part of the warp and woof of our constitutional system.

Crandall v. Nevada (1867) made this important point as it struck down a state law imposing a capitation tax of one dollar on "every person leaving the state by any railroad, stage coach, or other vehicle engaged or employed in the business of transporting passengers for hire." Justice Miller discussed the applicability of the commerce clause to the resolution of the question, but then held that it was unnecessary to resolve the issue on that ground because the right of the citizenry to enjoy unrestricted travel is inherent in the very fiber of a federal form of government.

Justice Clifford agreed with the result, but argued that the Nevada Act should have been invalidated as inconsistent with congressional power under the commerce clause. Later, the Court adopted this reasoning in striking a California law making it a misdemeanor for any person knowingly to bring a non-resident indigent into the state. *Edwards v. California* (1941) held that the state's attempt to bar the entry of indigent citizens was analogous to the economic barrier burdening the importation of milk products, invalidated in *Baldwin v. G. A. F. Seelig, Inc.* (1935).

Edwards relied on the national common market theory of *Baldwin* to support the principle that, just as a state cannot shut its gates to the influx of competitive commodities, it also is prohibited from thwarting the influx of indigents. The majority rejected the contention that such state legislation could be justified as a valid exercise of the police power, noting that the statute's sole purpose was to burden interstate commerce by impeding the movement of people across state lines. The absence of an inner political check was an additional weakness inherent in the California statute: persons burdened by the state regulation, non-resident indigents, had no voice in the political process responsible for the enactment of the legislation.

Justice Douglas, concurring separately in *Edwards*, warned that relying on the commerce clause could dilute the right of personal mobility. Congress, after all, could authorize what would otherwise be a violation of the dormant commerce clause. Douglas argued that the right of persons to move from state to state is a fundamental right implicit in national citizenship. Therefore, in his view, it is incorporated in the privileges or immunities clause of the Fourteenth Amendment. Moreover, argued Douglas, the right to travel is akin to the right to privacy; it is a "penumbra right" existing prior to, and independent of, the Fourteenth Amendment, emanating from the body of the Constitution itself and inuring to the benefit of all citizens.

Subsequent personal mobility decisions have incorporated both the majority's reluctance to enlarge the scope of the privileges and immunities doctrine and Justice Douglas' concern about relegating the protection of the right to travel solely to the commerce clause. Consequently, the Court has increasingly turned to equal protection as a preferential ground for challenging state legislation that impinges the right to travel. See *Shapiro v. Thompson* (1969).

The Article IV Privileges and Immunities Clause. The privileges and immunities clause of Article IV, section 2, protecting the privileges of state citizenship and assuring that states do not discriminate against the citizens of other states, sometimes provides an appropriate basis for voiding restrictive state regulations. Historically, the Court has resisted acknowledging that provision as a broad source of individual rights. It has interpreted the clause narrowly as a prohibition of local legislation that discriminates against non-residents.

The Court relied on this Article IV clause to invalidate a discriminatory licensing fee in *Toomer v. Witsel* (1948). South Carolina imposed a $2500 licensing fee on out-of-state shrimpers but only a $25 charge for resident shrimpers. Ostensibly, the prohibitive charge was necessary to discourage excessive trawling, and thereby enhance the preservation of the state's shrimp supply. Although that goal was a legitimate state purpose, the Court rejected the means as unreasonable. South Carolina directed its restriction only at nonresidents. Because trawlers follow migrating shrimp, and marginal sea fishing occurs off the coast of several Southern states, the statute inevitably invited retaliatory measures by neighboring jurisdictions. This was the exact situation that the framers of the Constitution intended the privileges and immunities clause to prevent.

If a state or local law uses a residency or citizenship classification to allocate the ability to engage in an activity sufficiently fundamental to the preservation of interstate harmony to be protected by the clause (*e.g.,* employment on city projects, where the employees are working for the city), the Court must determine whether there is a substantial, legitimate reason for the difference in treatment between local residents and out-of-state persons. The commerce clause does not forbid this state discrimination because the state is acting as a market participant, but the Privileges and Immunities Clause might.

The market participant theory does not automatically excuse the need for an inquiry under the Privileges and Immunities Clause of Article IV. In *United Building and Construction Trades Council v. Mayor and Council of Camden* (1984), the Court concluded that state and local governments are not absolutely prohibited from using local citizenship or residency classifications for purposes of hiring workers on city or state public works projects, *if* nonresidents in fact are shown to cause a particular harm to state or local interest. Then, the state may treat them differently from local residents. However, the state must demonstrate, by making a factual record at the trial, that there is a "substantial reason" for the difference in treatment between the local residents or citizen and nonresident. Unfortunately, the Court did explain what that meant; it just remanded the case. It is an understatement to say that the standard of review in these cases is not clear.

Chapter 9

ARTICLE VI & IV ISSUES: PREEMPTION & COMITY

Table of Sections

---

§ 9.1   Introduction

When you read the Constitution [following your professor's suggestion] you may have noticed that Article IV and Article VI deal with some very important interests of the states. In this text, we will only look at the privileges and immunities clause of Article IV, section 2 and the nature of federal preemption in constitutional analysis, which is related to the supremacy clause of Article VI. In the longer versions of this text, we deal at greater length with the provisions of Article IV and Article VI.

§ 9.2   The Article VI Supremacy Clause

The supremacy clause, contained in Article VI of the Constitution, establishes the primacy of federal law over state or local law. Of course, the Constitution of the United States, and its Amendments, govern state and local governmental actions. Due to the supremacy clause, if a state or local law (be it an ordinance, local or state statute, state court ruling, or a state constitution) comes into conflict with a law of the United States (which include regulations made by federal agencies acting within the scope of authority delegated to them by Congress and the President) or a treaty (which includes executive agreements) the state or local law will be invalid to the extent that it conflicts with the federal law or treaty.

When a court discusses federal preemption, it is simply discussing the issue of whether a federal statute excludes, and, thereby, invalidates any and all state or local laws regarding the subject that is governed by the federal statute. The decision as to whether a federal law was meant to preempt state or local laws is not a decision that is based on the Constitution. Rather, a decision as to whether a federal law preempts state or local law is based on statutory interpretation. If the United States Supreme Court determines that Congress, through the statute being considered in a case, intended to exclude state or local legislation, the Court will rule that state or local legislation is preempted. On the other hand, if the Court interprets the federal law so that it does not exclude the possibility of state or local law regulating the same subject matter, the Court will rule that the federal law does not preempt state or local law.

When you, as a student, see a problem wherein a federal law and a state law relate to the same subject matter, you must consider the preemption issue. You also must anticipate both types of possible preemption rulings : the possibility that a court will find that the federal law preempts the state law; and the possibility that the court will rule that the state law was not preempted by the federal law.

If a court decides that a federal law preempts a state law, then the state law will be invalid, unless the federal law itself violates the Constitution. Let us use a rather absurd, but easy to understand example. The State of Illinois has its capitol in the City of Springfield, Illinois. Let us assume that persons from Chicago influence the Congress of the United States to pass a law ordering the State of Illinois to switch its capitol from Springfield, Illinois to the most populous city in the state, which is Chicago, and that the President signs this federal law. The federal law would preempt the state law regarding the location of the Illinois capitol so long as the federal law was itself valid. However, the federal statute ordering the state to locate its capitol in a certain place would be unconstitutional for at least two reasons. First, the Court, in *Coyle v. Smith* (1911), ruled that Congress was not given the power to treat new states in any different manner than he could have treated the original states that formed the Union. [The *Coyle* ruling was based on the "equal-footing" doctrine, which requires that any new state have the same rights in the United States as would one of the original thirteen states.] Second, the Tenth Amendment, and the concept of federalism and Tenth Amendment principles, as explained in modern cases such as *New York v. United States* (1992) prohibit federal legislation that orders a state to take legislative action [which a state would have to do if it were to change the location of the state capital]. The state law regarding the location of the state capital would remain in force, despite the conflict with the federal statute. A state statute that is preempted by federal law will be invalid under the supremacy clause if, but only if, the federal law [which preempts the state law] does not violate any limit on the federal power.

If federal law does not preempt a state law, the state law may still be invalid. Let us assume that no federal statute or federal agency regulation establishes any standards for the type of mud guards that can be used by trucks throughout the United States. A state law that regulates truck mud guards would not be preempted under such circumstances. Nevertheless, such a truck mud guard law would be invalid if it imposed a tariff or trade barrier or if it imposed a clearly excessive burden on commerce. Indeed the State of Illinois once had a truck mud guard law that was not preempted but that the Court held was a violation of the commerce clause. See, *Bibb v. Navajo Freight Lines, Inc.* (1959).

Professors who focus on statutory interpretation issues may describe many types of preemption. There are two basic forms of preemption.

First, Congress might expressly preempt a state or local law. Thus, if Congress were to pass a law regulating atomic energy plants with a section in the law that said "all state or local law regarding atomic energy is hereby preempted," any state or local law on the subject would be invalid under the supremacy clause of Article VI because any such law would conflict with the federal statute. This situation is usually referred to as one involving expressed preemption.

Second, if Congress does not specifically preempt the possibility of state or local regulation of a subject matter, then the interpretation of the federal statute (on the preemption issue) a court must ask: did Congress implicitly mean to exclude the possibility of state or local legislation or regulation on the subject matter that is addressed in the federal law? Administrative law and statutory interpretation scholars may use a variety of terms to describe court approaches to the second type of problem. A student must pay very careful attention to how her professor discusses the factors that a court will consider in deciding whether a federal statute was meant to implicitly preempt state or local regulation. In this Chapter, we will mention only a few of the cases that have addressed this problem.

In *Hines v. Davidowitz* (1941) the Court held that the Federal Alien Registration Act of 1940 precluded enforcement of Pennsylvania's Alien Registration Act of 1939. The Court noted the supremacy of national power in the field of foreign policy, and the sensitivity of the relationship between the regulation of aliens and the conduct of foreign affairs. It concluded that Congressional enactment of uniform national immigration laws "occupied" the field so as to preempt state regulations requiring the registration of aliens.

Justice Black, speaking for the majority, acknowledged that no rigid verbal formulae are *a fortiori* determinative of displacement of concurrent state regulation. The test is whether, under the circumstances of a particular case, the state law "stands as an obstacle to the accomplishment and execution of the full purposes and objectives of Congress."

Pennsylvania v. Nelson (1956) elaborated the *Hines* rationale. Chief Justice Warren enunciated a three-pronged inquiry to ascertain preemption: 1. pervasiveness of the federal regulatory scheme; 2. federal occupation of the field as necessitated by the need for national uniformity; 3. the danger of conflict between state laws and the administration of the federal program.

Applying this three-part standard in *Nelson*, the Supreme Court held that federal anti-communist legislation superseded the state's Sedition Act. Enforcing the state sedition laws might lead to conflicts with federal laws because the sporadic local prosecutions might obstruct federal undercover operations. Under the state law, even private individuals could initiate a prosecution, thus increasing the chance of interference with federal enforcement plans and undercover operations. The Court stressed that the need for national predominance mandated the conclusion that Congress intended to occupy the field. Federal regulation of seditious conduct preempted the state statute prohibiting seditious acts.

In modern decisions the Supreme Court has refused to assume that a federal law preempts state and local laws. The Court has stated that it requires that Congress "manifest its intention clearly...." However, Congress need not manifest its intention by explicitly providing that the federal statute preempts the state law. Rather the Court seeks to find the intent of Congress.

If Congressional intent is not clear from the language of the statute—that is, if Congress did not explicitly provide that federal law does, or does not, preempt state law—then Congress' intention may be clear from the pervasiveness of the federal scheme, the need for uniformity, or the danger of conflict between the enforcement of state laws and the administration of federal programs, of the state law "stands as an obstacle to the accomplishment of the full purposes and objectives of Congress." Absent persuasive reasons evidencing Congressional intent favoring preemption, the Court will not presume the invalidity of state regulations.

The Supreme Court presumes that Congress does not intend to preempt state legislation unless there is an appropriate indication from the language or purposes of the federal action or regulation. Nonetheless, the Court may find part, or all, of a state law or other state action preempted because of the Court's interpretation of the intent or purpose of federal law.

In *Pacific Gas & Electric Co. v. State Energy Resources Conservation & Dev. Commn.* (1983) the Court summarized basic preemption guidelines as follows:

> Absent explicit preemptive language, Congress' intent to supersede state law altogether may be found from a scheme of federal regulation so pervasive as to make reasonable the inference that Congress left no room [for the states] to supplement it, because the Act of Congress may touch a field in which the federal interest is so dominant that the federal system will be assumed to preclude enforcement of state laws on the same subject, or because the object sought to be obtained by federal law and the character of obligations imposed by it may reveal the same purpose.... Even where Congress has not entirely displaced state regulation in a specific area, state law is preempted to the extent that it actually conflicts with federal law. Such a conflict arises when compliance with both federal and state regulations is a physical impossibility, ... or where state law stands as an obstacle to the accomplishment and execution of the full purposes and objectives of Congress.

Foreign Affairs. The fact that a state law touches foreign affairs does not automatically require preemption. Yet, that fact is hardly irrelevant. For example, in *Crosby v. National Foreign Trade Council* (2000), Justice Souter, for the Court, invalidated a Massachusetts law that barred state entities from buying goods or services from companies doing business with Burma. Three months later after the state enacted this law, Congress passed a law imposing various mandatory and conditional sanctions on Burma. The federal law authorized the President to remove or modify sanctions if he certified Burma had made progress in civil rights, to impose new sanctions if he found repression, and to suspend sanctions in the interest of national security.

The federal law preempted state law and violated the Supremacy Clause because it frustrated federal statutory objectives. It was "implausible" that Congress would have gone to such lengths to empower the President if "it had been willing to compromise his effectiveness by deference to every provision of state statute or local ordinance that might, if enforced, blunt the consequences of discretionary Presidential action." The federal law has no explicit preemption provision, but this failure "may reflect nothing more than the settled character of implied preemption doctrine."

In *American Insurance Association v. Garamendi* (2003), it was an Executive Agreement instead of a federal statute that preempted state law. Various insurance companies and a trade association of insurance companies sought to enjoin the California Insurance Commissioner from enforcing a California statute requiring disclosure of information about Holocaust-era insurance policies. Again, Justice Souter, for the Court, held that California's Holocaust Victim Insurance Relief Act (HVIRA), and in particular a provision of the HVIRA requiring any insurer that did business in California and that sold insurance policies in Europe which were in effect during Holocaust-era to disclose certain information about those policies to the California Insurance Commissioner or risk losing its license, impermissibly interfered with the President's conduct of foreign affairs, and was therefore preempted. Souter conceded that the executive agreements at issue did not include any preemption clause, but there is a "sufficiently clear conflict to require finding preemption" based on the intent of the executive agreements and statements of high-level Executive Branch officials. HVIRA compromises " 'the very capacity of the President to speak for the Nation with one voice in dealing with other governments' to resolve claims against European companies arising out of World War II."

§ 9.3　Interstate Comity: The Article IV Privileges and Immunities Clause

Various sections of the Constitution, particularly sections 1 and 2 of Article IV, serve to insure comity among the states. As the Court stated in *Toomer v. Witsell* (1948), the primary purpose of Article IV "to help fuse into one Nation a collection of independent, sovereign states."

Article IV section 2, clause 1, [known as the comity clause or the privileges and immunities clause of Article IV] states: "The Citizens of each State shall be entitled to all Privileges and Immunities of Citizens in the several States."

The comity clause protects only United States citizens. Corporations may not advance a privileges and immunities clause claim: although a corporation as a legal entity may be considered a person, it is not a citizen for purposes of this clause.

This clause does not protect alien residents of the United States because they are not United States citizens. However, a lawful resident alien may receive very similar protection against unjust residency requirements or citizenship requirements from the equal protection clause. Durational residency requirements may also be challenged as violating the right to travel under either due process or equal protection clause guarantees, or, in some cases, as violating the commerce clause.

While the Article IV privileges and immunities clause is written in terms of state citizenship guarantees, it applies to the citizenship or residency restrictions set up by local governments as well as those found in state law. The Court will evaluate a municipal ordinance that establishes a city citizenship or residence requirement in the same manner as a state law, even though the municipal ordinance has the effect of burdening in-state as well as out-of-state residents. Otherwise it would be too easy for a state government or its instrumentalities to escape the requirement of Article IV. Each city of a state could impose residency requirements for private sector employment which would result in excluding all out-of-state residents but only a fraction of in-state residence. And, taken as a whole, the cities would be excluding all out-of-state residents and no in-state residences. Also, in-state residents have the option of seeking redress at the polls, while out-of-state residents have no input into the political processes of other states. Thus, if a municipal ordinance creates a city residency requirement for the exercise of basic rights, a nonresident of the state may attack the clause under Article IV.

The Judicial Test. If a state law establishes a state citizenship or state residency classification, the Court uses a two-step methodology for determining the compatibility of the law with the privileges and immunities clause of Article IV. First, the Court determines whether the benefit or activity constitutes one of the "privileges and immunities" protected by the clause. Second, the Court will determine if there is a substantial state interest in the differing treatment of nonresidents. Reciting this test is easier than applying it.

Not all forms of benefits or activities fall within the protection of the clause. The Supreme Court often quotes an early nineteenth century opinion by Justice Washington for the proposition that the clause protects only "those privileges and immunities which are, in their nature, fundamental; which belong, of right, to the citizens of all free government; and which have, at all times, been enjoyed by the citizens of the several states which compose this Union. . . ."

The modern Court's determination that a right is sufficiently "fundamental" to be protected by privileges and immunities clause of Article IV should not be confused with a determination of whether an activity constitutes a fundamental right so as to require strict judicial scrutiny under the due process and equal protection clauses. For example, the regulation of conditions of employment is not considered a limitation of a fundamental right for due process and equal protection analysis, but the ability to engage in a private sector activity or employment is a fundamental right protected by the privileges and immunities clause.

Article IV case law states that the Court determines whether the restriction of a certain type of activity has a "bearing upon the vitality of the nation as a single entity" in determining whether the activity is one of the privileges and immunities protected by the clause. Because *private* sector employment, like many other forms of commercial activity, is essential to the economic vitality of the nation, it is a fundamental right for Article IV analysis. In contrast, the states may create residency or citizenship requirements in relation to recreational activities, such as recreational hunting or fishing, because those activities are not deemed sufficiently fundamental to be considered Article IV privileges or immunities.

True welfare benefits—giving goods or services directly to a group of recipients who have no inherent constitutional claim to them—may be restricted to state or city residents. Nevertheless, the state may not impose a *durational* residency requirement, which requires persons to maintain residency for a certain period of time before receipt of any welfare benefits: that would be a violation of the right to travel, which we will examine in Chapter 16.

A city requirement that city employees must be residents of the city does not violate the right to travel or the equal protection clause. When the state or city requires that a certain percentage of all jobs on construction projects funded in whole or in part by city funds be filled by bona fide city residents there is no dormant commerce clause violation because the state or city is acting as a market participant. On the other hand, the Court will evaluate, under Article IV, a state or city effort to bias *private* employment decisions by pressuring or requiring city contractors to favor the employment of state or city residents when the private contractors engage in public works projects funded in whole or in part by the city or state.

All rights directly protected by the Constitution, such as First Amendment rights, or other constitutional rights that the Court has been found to be fundamental for the purposes of due process and equal protection analysis, constitute privileges and immunities of citizenship. Thus, state or municipal laws that make local residency a requirement for the exercise of such rights are subject to the restraints of Article IV.

The Court has made clear that state or local residency classifications that relate to private sector commercial activity or civil liberties (other than voting), are subject to Article IV limits. However, the Court has been less clear in explaining how to determine such a residency requirement is invalid under Article IV.

In *United Building and Construction Trades Council v. Mayor and Council of Camden* (1984) the Court adopted a two-step methodology to judge a state or local law that imposes a residency or citizenship classification in order to allocate construction jobs on city projects. The majority opinion concluded that the Court first must decide if the discrimination against out of state residents is on a "matter of fundamental concern." *Camden* quickly concluded that the ability to seek employment with private construction companies working on projects funded with state or city dollars meets that test. However, the fact that "Camden is merely setting conditions on its expenditures for goods and services in the marketplace does not preclude the possibility that those conditions violate the Privileges and Immunities Clause."

Second, if the law fits part one of the standard, a court must determine if the government can justify the residency requirement. The Court explained that state and local governments are not absolutely prohibited from using local citizenship or residency classifications. Nonresidents may be treated differently from local residents when they in fact are shown to cause a particular harm to state or local interest—"to constitute a peculiar source of the evil at which the state statute is aimed." In *United Building and Construction Trade Council*, the Court remanded the case for further proceedings; the standard of review is not clear. The Court did say that the state must demonstrate that there is a "substantial reason" for the difference in treatment between the local residents or citizen and nonresident. In reviewing the state's attempt to justify the discrimination, the Court must continue to bear in mind the purpose of the Article IV privileges and immunities clause to insure harmony between the residents of various states and the vitality of the nation as a single Union.

Commercial Activity v. Recreational Activity. The modern cases interpreting the privileges and immunity clause of Article IV fall into several main groups.

The first group deals with commercial rights and is illustrated by the leading case of *Toomer v. Witsell* (1948). Several South Carolina statutes regulated commercial shrimp fishing within three miles of the coast of that state. No federal regulations governed any of the shrimp fishing extending from North Carolina to Florida. The regulations of the various states involved often aimed against non-resident fishing "have now irritated retaliation to the point that the fishery is effectively partitioned at the state lines...." One of the challenged South Carolina laws required payment of a license fee of $25 for each shrimp boat owned by a resident and $2500 for each boat owned by a non-resident. That law was successfully challenged under the privileges and immunities clause of Article IV.

Chief Justice Vinson in *Toomer* explained that the test to determine a violation of the Article IV privileges and immunities clause is whether there are valid reasons for a state to make distinctions based on one's state citizenship and whether the degree of discrimination bears a "close relation" to these reasons. This clause outlaws "classifications based on the fact of non-citizenship unless there is something to indicate that non-citizens constitute a peculiar source of the evil at which the statute is aimed."

Vinson then noted that the South Carolina statute frankly and plainly discriminates against non-residents, that it serves to virtually exclude non-residents from South Carolina fishing waters, and that, even though the South Carolina statute is written in terms of residence rather than citizenship, it is still within the privileges and immunities clause.

Next, Vinson rejected the state's arguments based on need to conserve natural resources by carefully and actively scrutinizing the means used to achieve such an objective.

Hicklin v. Orbeck (1978) invalidated the Alaska Hire Act under the Article IV privileges and immunities clause. The Court was unanimous. This Alaska law gave employment preference to Alaska residents over nonresidents for all oil and gas leases and other such agreements to which the state was a party. Alaska justified its action on the grounds that the state *owned* the oil and gas, and the Alaska Hire Act sought to leverage the state's power over its oil and gas.

The Court noted, first, that prior cases have held that such state discrimination against nonresidents seeking to pursue a trade, occupation, or common calling within the state violates this clause. Second, even if a state could seek to alleviate its unemployment problem by requiring such hiring preferences, the state's law could not withstand scrutiny under this clause because it was not sufficiently tailored to aid its intended beneficiaries. Finally, and most importantly, while Alaska's actual ownership of the oil and gas resources are a factor to be considered in judging the law, that ownership was insufficient to justify the pervasive discrimination. The "extensive reach" of the state law covered and extended to employers who had no connection "whatsoever" with the state's oil and gas. The law covered not only contractors and subcontractors but also suppliers of subcontractors. It sought to reach suppliers who had no direct dealings with the state's oil or gas and never even set foot on state land. The Court rejected Alaska's efforts to leverage its oil and gas ownership to impose an "economic ripple effect" on all those who dealt, even indirectly or tangentially, with Alaskan oil and gas.

The privileges and immunities clause protects nonresidents of a state who engage in commerce involving, for example, wild animals (or fish); in contrast, that clause inapplicable to non-residents who hunt wild animals as *recreational* sport. *Baldwin v. Montana Fish and Game Commission* (1978) created this distinction. A six to three majority upheld a Montana hunting license system—under which nonresidents were charged 7½ times more than residents for a hunting license entitling one to hunt elk and other game—against challenges that the system violated the privileges and immunities clause of Article IV and the equal protection clause of the Fourteenth Amendment.

Justice Blackmun for the majority stated that, while the "contours" of the privileges and immunities clause of Article IV "are not well developed", it was nevertheless the law that States must treat its citizens and nonresidents equally only "with respect to those 'privileges' and 'immunities' bearing upon the vitality of the Nation as a single entity." He concluded that it would be improper to link the right to hunt for sport with such things as the right to travel and the right to pursue a calling. He distinguished *Toomer v. Witsell* and other such cases as involving "commercial" licensing, but elk hunting "in Montana is a recreation and a sport."

However, the Court did not consider the fact that, while elk hunters may be involved in a sport, the people who support them (such as guides, hunting lodges, equipment rental stores, etc.) are involved in a livelihood. These support services are in businesses that affects interstate commerce. These businesses are disproportionately in-state enterprises. Thus, to the extent that state hunting regulations hurt these businesses, the state is really hurting its own residents (more than the out-of-state hunters), and these residents have input into the state's political process, and can change these regulations if they wish.

Private Employment on Public Works Projects. As we explained earlier in this section, the two step methodology used in reviewing Article IV privileges and immunities clause claims is exemplified by the Court's decision in *United Building and Construction Trades Council v. Mayor and Council of Camden* (1984). In this case the Court held that a city ordinance requiring that at least forty percent of the employees of contractors and subcontractors working on city construction projects be city residents was subject to the restriction of the privileges and immunities clause. Justice Rehnquist, writing for eight members of the Court, found that employment on public works projects was "sufficiently fundamental to the promotion of interstate harmony so as to fall within the purview" of Article IV.

Justice Rehnquist distinguished private sector employment funded through governmental contracts from full time employment in the public sector. Although the Court did not rule that the privileges and immunities clause was totally inapplicable to full time public employment, the Court's reference to other cases upholding restrictions on public employment against equal protection and commerce clause attacks indicates that the Court is unlikely to invalidate city or state residency requirements for public sector employment under the privileges and immunities clause. In contrast, restrictions on private sector commercial activity, even though the activity is undertaken on the basis of state contracts, must be subject to judicial review under Article IV to avoid the undercutting of the harmonious economic relationships between states.

Justice Rehnquist, for the majority, admitted that the commerce clause did not restrain the state acting as a market participant when it spent its own money to employ people. However, he said that the values protected by the privileges and immunities clause are different, and they required courts to examine the factual basis for discrimination against nonresidents in these settings. The Court said that it could not complete the second step of the analysis because there was an insufficient factual record to determine whether there was a substantial, legitimate reason for guaranteeing that a minimum percentage of persons (whom the private contractors employed on governmentally funded projects) were residents of the funding governmental unit. The Court said that the government's ability to use its funds to help a state's residents and its local economy might be an important or even determinative factor in ruling on the permissibility of the law, but there still must be an independent judicial review of the need for cities and states to use its spending power to protect its local residents.

The Practice of Law. In order for the Court to determine whether states may limit the ability to be a member of the bar to the residents of the state, the Court does not merely rely on its general statements that an attorney allowed to practice in one state has no inherent right to practice in another state's bar without meeting its entrance qualifications. Instead, the Court first determines whether the ability to be a lawyer is a type of public sector commercial activity protected by the privileges and immunities clause, and then determines whether the state has a substantial interest in restricting admission to its bar to persons who are residents of the state.

The Court engaged in this more careful analysis in *Supreme Court of New Hampshire v. Piper* (1985), which held that the State Supreme Court rule limiting bar admission to state residents violated the privileges and immunities clause. Kathryn Piper was a resident of Vermont, living about 400 yards from the New Hampshire border. She could not be admitted to the bar in New Hampshire because she was not a resident of that state. She was otherwise qualified. So she sued the State Supreme Court, its five Justices and its Clerk, alleging that State Supreme Court Rule 42, which excluded nonresidents from the bar, violated the privileges and immunities clause of Article IV. *Piper* began its analysis by reasoning that the privileges and immunities clause "was intended to create a national economic union," and that one of the privileges it protected was the privilege of a citizen of State *A* doing business in State *B* on terms of substantial equality with the citizens of State *B*. While the state could provide for residency requirements that relate to it as a separate political community (like "the right to vote and the right to hold elective office") a lawyer is not an "officer" of the State in any political sense. Thus the practice of law is a "privilege" that Article IV protects.

Then the Court turned to the question of whether the State could nonetheless justify the discrimination against nonresidents because (i) there is a substantial reason for the difference in treatment; and (ii) the discrimination practiced against nonresidents bears a substantial relationship to the State's objective; and (iii) this discrimination could not be met by less restrictive means. The State asserted that nonresident members of the bar would be less likely: "(i) to become, and remain, familiar with local rules and procedures; (ii) to behave ethically; (iii) to be available for court proceedings [sometimes on short notice]; and (iv) to do pro bono and other work in the State." The Court found that none of the reasons met the test of "substantiality" and that the means chosen did not bear the necessary relationship to the State's objectives. Ms. Piper got her license.

Chapter 10

INDIVIDUAL LIBERTIES—
AN OVERVIEW

Table of Sections

§ 10.1 Guarantees in the Original Text (Body) of the Constitution

The text of the Constitution contains three specific guarantees of individual rights that are rarely the subject of intensive constitutional study or litigation. Although they are examined elsewhere in this book one should note at the outset that these guarantees exist and that they may apply differently to different governmental entities.

Article I, section 10 specifically prohibits a *state* from impairing the obligation of contracts, but the Court has interpreted the due process clause of the Fifth Amendment to also bar any federal legislation that retroactively impaired the obligations of contract in a similar manner.

The ex post facto clauses (U.S. Constitution, article I, § 9 & article I, § 10) effectively prohibit either the federal or state governments from punishing persons criminally for actions that were not illegal when performed.

Another prohibited form of retroactive legislation is a law that imposes punishment on particular individuals whom the legislation names. Such a law is known as a bill of attainder. Whether or not a legislature enacts a bill of attainder on the basis of a person's prior acts or on the basis of his political beliefs, the measure still is a legislative punishment that denies that person recourse to the courts. Consequently, the Constitution abolished bills of attainder. The federal government is prohibited from enacting such bills by Article I, section 9, clause 3 bars the federal government, and a similar provision bars states in Article I, section 10, clause 1.

§ 10.2 The Bill of Rights Provisions and Their Incorporation in the Fourteenth Amendment

The first ten Amendments to the Constitution are often called the Bill of Rights. These Amendments were submitted to the States by the first Congress in response to expressions of concern for guarantees of individual liberty that had been raised during the debates on the ratification of the Constitution. The Ninth and Tenth Amendments, however, usually are often not considered as specific guarantees of individual liberties, so sometimes only the first eight Amendments are called the Bill of Rights.

In an early decision the Supreme Court ruled that these Amendments to the Constitution did not apply to the states. *Barron v. Mayor and City Council of Baltimore* (1833). This holding was correct historically because the drafters of the Bill of Rights designed the Amendments as a check on the new national government.

The Fourteenth Amendment changed all that, for it imposed important limitations on the states. Some people argued that this Amendment, through both its privileges and immunities clause and its due process clause, made the guarantees of the first ten Amendments applicable to the states. The Supreme Court, however, continually rejected this theory of total incorporation of the Bill of Rights into the Fourteenth Amendment. The Court, instead, adopted a theory of selective incorporation.

Selective Incorporation. Only those provisions of the Bill of Rights that the Court considers fundamental to the American system of law are applied to the states through the due process clause of the Fourteenth Amendment. Therefore, the states cannot violate the first ten Amendments directly. They violate those Amendments insofar as those provisions are incorporated into the Fourteenth Amendment and applied to the states. Thus, if a state were to abridge the freedom of speech, it would be abridging the First Amendment as applied to it through the Fourteenth Amendment. However, courts and commentators constantly use short hand phrases such as, the state law violated the First Amendment.

Knowing which of the Bill of Rights the Supreme Court has applied to the state governments is important when determining what specific constitutional limitations may be placed on a state. Under their own terms the Ninth and Tenth Amendments seem inapplicable to the states.

Of the first eight Amendments the Supreme Court has held explicitly that only three of the individual guarantees are inapplicable to the states. The three unincorporated guarantees are: (1) the Second Amendment guarantee of the right to bear arms; (2) the Fifth Amendment clause guaranteeing criminal prosecution only on a grand jury indictment; and (3) the Seventh Amendment guarantee of a jury trial in a civil case.

Two provisions of the Bill of Rights have not been the subject of litigation that would establish their application to the states. Third Amendment, which prohibits the quartering of soldiers in private houses, has not been the subject of U.S. Supreme Court interpretation. The Court also has not determined whether the "excessive fine" provision of the Eighth Amendment is applicable to the states. However, because the provision seems logically intertwined with the other provisions of that Amendment, it may already have been impliedly made applicable to the states.

The Eighth Amendment's prohibition of the imposition of excessive bail presents a different problem. No specific case exists in which the Court has ruled that this provision is applicable to the states. In a number of state cases, however, the Court has assumed that the clause is applicable. E.g., *Schilb v. Kuebel* (1971). Consequently, the provision for all practical purposes should be treated as incorporated into the Fourteenth Amendment.

Another specialized problem relates to the just compensation clause of the Fifth Amendment. The wording of the Amendment specifically requires the government to give just compensation for property taken for public use. The due process clause of the Fourteenth Amendment, however, fails to contain this specific language, though it does prohibit the state governments from taking property without due process of law.

The Fifth Amendment guarantee of just compensation technically has not been incorporated into the Fourteenth Amendment. Nevertheless, the Court has held that the Fourteenth Amendment due process guarantee provides the same safeguard against a state's taking of property without just compensation. Thus, the rules that govern when a government may take property for public use and when it must pay just compensation to private individuals when exercising its regulatory or eminent domain powers are identical under the two clauses.

The Court has not yet used the Ninth Amendment to define a set of rights protected from government regulation and, therefore, it cannot be said with certainty that it to the states.

§ 10.3 The Privileges and/or Immunities Clauses

Two clauses of the Constitution guarantee certain privileges to citizens against infringement by the state government. Article IV, section 2 requires that the citizens of each state receive all the "privileges *and* immunities" of citizens of other states. Section 1 of the Fourteenth Amendment prohibits the states from making laws which would abridge "the privileges *or* immunities of citizens of the United States." Despite the similar wording of the two provisions they have widely differing applications.

The Article IV Privileges and Immunities Clause. This Article IV provision often is referred to as the comity clause. It prohibits any distinctions in law between citizens of a state and citizens of other states if those distinctions are unreasonable. The clause is a specialized type of equal protection provision that guarantees that all classifications that burden persons because they are not citizens of the state must reasonably relate to legitimate state or local purposes.

The Fourteenth Amendment Privileges or Immunities Clause. In contrast, the Court has seldom used the privileges or immunities clause of the Fourteenth Amendment to protect rights. The Court held that this clause neither incorporated any of the Bill of Rights nor protected all rights of individual citizens. *Slaughter–House Cases* (1873).

The Court, instead, decided that the provision only protected those rights peculiar to being a citizen of the federal government; it does not protect those rights that relate only to state citizenship. The Court said that the clause only protects uniquely federal rights such as the right to petition Congress, the right to vote in federal elections, the right to interstate travel or commerce, the right to enter federal lands, or the rights of a citizen while in the custody of federal officers.

The rights protected by the privileges or immunities clause of the Fourteenth Amendment cannot be terminated by a state or local government. However, that clause only protects uniquely federal rights, such as those referred to in *The Slaughter–House Cases*. One of those uniquely federal rights is the right of a U.S. citizen who establishes residency in a state to be treated in a similar manner as long-time residents of the state. *Saenz v. Roe* (1999) held that the privileges or immunities clause protected "the right of the newly arrived citizen to the same privileges and immunities enjoyed by other citizens of the same State." For that reason, the *Saenz* Court held that California could not give reduced welfare benefits to a newly arrived person who was a bona fide citizen of the State of California during the first year in which the person resided in California.

The Supreme Court has not invalidated any restriction of civil liberties under the privileges or immunities clause, except for the

Court's ruling in the *Saenz* case. In one case during the 1930's the Supreme Court found that a classification related to economic activity violated the privileges or immunities clause, but it reversed that decision five years later. *Colgate v. Harvey* (1935), overruled in *Madden v. Kentucky* (1940).

§ 10.4 Which Individuals Are Protected by the Constitutional Guarantees?

The wording and interpretation of several constitutional provisions limit the application of their specific guarantees to certain types of persons or entities. For example, the term "citizen" in Article III ("between Citizens of different States") includes corporations. The Court has held that suits involving corporations involve "citizens" for federal jurisdictional purposes. *Louisville, C. & C.R. Co. v. Letson* (1844).

The term "citizen", however, does not include corporations in the definition of "citizen" in the Fourteenth Amendment. That language refers to persons "born or naturalized in the United States" and corporations fall into neither group. Hence, neither corporations nor aliens receive the protection of the privileges or immunities clause of the Fourteenth Amendment or the comity clause of Article IV, because those clauses protect only citizens.

Under the Fifth Amendment's prohibition of compulsory self-incrimination, "person" fails to include corporations or other business entities. Aliens within the United States, however, are "persons' and thus receive protection from self-incrimination under this provision. Both aliens and corporations are "persons" for the purposes of the due process clauses of the Fifth and Fourteenth Amendments and the equal protection clause of the Fourteenth Amendment. Similarly, aliens and corporations are included within the protection of the Fourth Amendment, which guarantees the right of the people to be free from unwarranted searches and seizures.

The equal protection clause of the Fourteenth Amendment only requires that a state not practice discrimination against persons "within the jurisdiction" of the state. Nevertheless, even persons not physically present in the state are protected by the clause because this provision guarantees equal treatment under the law to all people who are subject to the law of a state.

§ 10.5 Procedural Due Process versus Substantive Review

(a) Introduction—Overview

When the Court reviews a law to determine its procedural fairness, it reviews the system of decision-making to determine whether or not a government entity has taken an individual's life, liberty, or property without the fair procedure or "due process" required by the Fifth and Fourteenth Amendments. This type of review is easily justified because it involves no more than a judicial assessment of a decision-making process that has determined that a specific individual should suffer some burden. It may involve the review of the general fairness of a procedure authorized by legislation or merely the review of the fairness of a decision in an individual case.

Procedural Review. Procedural review is much more limited in scope than review of the substance of legislation. Procedural due process guarantees only that there is a fair decision-making process before the government takes some action directly impairing a person's life, liberty or property. This aspect of due process does not protect against the use of arbitrary rules of law that are the basis of those proceedings. It is only necessary that a fair decision-making process be used.

For example, if a state legislature enacted a law that imposed the death penalty upon any person who had been found guilty of double parking an automobile after a determination of guilt through trial by jury and appellate review, the law would comport with the *procedural* restrictions of due process. The law might violate the substantive guarantees of the Eighth Amendment, as applied to the states by the Fourteenth Amendment. Indeed the law might also violate the substantive guarantee of the due process clause of the Fourteenth Amendment insofar as it was an irrational and arbitrary abuse of the government's power to protect against traffic hazards. However, so long as the decision-making process by which the burden of the death penalty was handed out was a fair one the law would not be stricken on the basis of procedural due process.

Substantive Review. By "substantive review" we mean the judicial determination that the substance of a law or governmental action is compatible with the Constitution. The Court is concerned with the constitutionality of the underlying rule rather than with the fairness of the process by which the government applies the rule to an individual. Every form of review other than procedural due process is a form of substantive review. For example, if the Court were to strike a law restricting the freedom of the press because it violated the First Amendment, the case would involve a form of substantive review by the Court. The Court would have determined that the substance or rule of the legislation was incompatible with the language of the Amendment.

Because the Constitution gives an indication through specific language that certain types of legislation or executive action are beyond the power of government, the ability of the judiciary to overrule state or federal law on the basis of specific textual provisions has not been challenged widely in the past century. The Court's ability to determine the constitutionality of state or federal laws or executive actions under more vague standards, such as the requirement that no state shall deprive any person of life, liberty or property "without due process of law" is subject to greater criticism.

The Supreme Court used the substantive due process test to control a wide variety of economic legislation during the period from 1885 to 1937. During this period the Court concluded that interference with certain types of economic liberty was unconstitutional and that the Court was free to determine what types of legislation rationally promoted legitimate economic goals. This role gave the Court the power of a super legislature. If the Justices disagreed with any law, they could declare the measure unconstitutional because it failed to comport with their sense of the legitimate economic role of American government.

After 1937, a dramatic shift took place in the Court's manner of reviewing legislation under the due process clauses. The Court realized that nothing either in the language of the Constitution or in the basic judicial function gave federal judges a claim to superiority in determining the rationality of economic legislation. The Court, therefore, abandoned the role of an independent reviewer of economic and social welfare legislation under the due process clause. If the law can arguably be said to rationally relate to a legitimate goal of government, the Court will uphold the law even though it might disagree with its wisdom.

The Supreme Court continues to make an independent determination of the legitimacy of laws that affect the "fundamental rights," which we discuss in Chapter 11.

(b) The Mixing of Procedural & Substantive Issues in Administrative Cases

The rational relationship standard, referred to in the previous subsection, is easy to apply in cases involving a challenge to a legislative rule that governs all persons and that gives no discretion to an administrator or administrative agency to interpret the rule in individual cases. For example, assume a school board establishes a rule that every public high school teacher must complete one college level course each academic year in order to retain his or her job in the public high school. If a teacher who does not wish to take such a course in order to retain his job challenges the requirement, the judiciary should defer to the school board and uphold the regulation because it has an arguably rational relationship to a legitimate interest of the state. A court should not substitute its judgment for that of the school board by independently determining whether a person is a better teacher if he takes a college level course each year.

If the school informed the teacher that it was firing him for failing to take the required college course, and he asserts that he had completed the course requirement, this factual dispute raises a procedural due process issue. The school board might be required to give him a hearing to determine whether or not he had taken the course that was the condition of retaining his employment. Chapter 13, on procedural due process, discusses these issues.

Consider, for example, *Regents of the University of Michigan v. Ewing* (1985), which upheld the decision of medical school faculty and administrators to dismiss a student from a combined undergraduate degree and medical degree program. To qualify for the final two years of the program, the rules required the students to pass a standardized examination. The student in the case earned the lowest score on the examination that had been recorded in the history of the combined degree program. Even though all other persons who previously had failed this examination had been given a chance to retake the examination, the school dismissed this student from the program without the opportunity to retake the examination.

The unanimous Court held that there was no significant procedural issue in this case because the student's dismissal had been reviewed in accordance with established school policies. The issue in the case was substantive: whether the basis for the faculty decision was a violation of the due process clause. Justice Stevens, for the Court, stated: "When judges are asked to review the substance of a genuinely academic decision, such as this one, they should show great respect for the faculty's professional judgment. Plainly, they may not override it unless it is such a substantial departure from accepted academic norms as to demonstrate that the person or committee responsible did not actually exercise professional judgment."

Procedural due process requires the government to give an individual a fair process if it deprives the person of a life, liberty or property interest, and if the individual whose interests are at stake has a factual dispute with the government. The due process clause does not give an individual a right to a hearing if the person admits that the law applies to him. The individual, however, may make a substantive claim against the law by challenging the rule of law created by the statute or regulation. E.g., *Dixon v. Love* (1977), held that a driver has is no right to a hearing concerning suspension of his license when the state bases his suspension on violations of traffic laws that had been previously established in separate court proceeding. The driver already had his procedural rights when the government proved, in earlier proceeding, (or the driver admitted in earlier proceedings) that the driver had driven recklessly, or in excess of the speed limit. There is no need to determine that three violations amount to three violations when the driver admits that he had three violations.

(c) Mixing Procedural Due Process, Substantive Due Process, and Equal Protection Issues in Police Protection Cases

In two cases with facts that the majority and dissenting opinions correctly describe as tragic, the Court held that there was no due process right to police protection for individuals who are not in custody of the government.

DeShaney v. Winnebago County Department of Social Services (1989) involved a child whose father beat him until he was severely disabled. The plaintiff did not sue his father, who was not a state actor. Rather, he sued the county department of social services, which the state court charged with monitoring the child's well-being of the child. The divorce court gave the father custody of the child. The civil rights lawsuit, brought on behalf of the child, claimed that the government's failure to protect the child, after the social service caseworker had seen evidence that someone in the household was abusing the child, violated the Fourteenth Amendment due process clause.

Chief Justice Rehnquist, writing for the majority, rejected the child's substantive due process claim. He noted that the child was not claiming that he had been denied fair process to prevent or remedy his injury. Rather, the child claimed a substantive due process right to state protection; and that the state's failure to protect him violated due process. *DeShaney* found that government would have a duty to provide some level of protection for a child's well-being only if the government had taken custody of the child. But the state did not have custody of the child. Justices Brennan, Marshall, and Blackmun dissented.

Castle Rock v. Gonzales (2005) (7 to 2) followed *DeShaney*. A woman repeatedly asked the police to enforce a court's restraining order against her former husband in order to protect her children, but the police refused. In the early hours of the next day, the ex-husband arrived at a police station with his three murdered daughters, and fired on the police, who then killed him. Justice Scalia, held that Colorado law did not give plaintiff a property interest in police enforcement of the restraining order. Therefore: "In light of today's decision and that in *DeShaney*, the benefit that a third party [the person who might be harmed, such as the injured or murdered children or their mothers in these cases] may receive from having someone else [the fathers in these cases] arrested for a crime generally does not trigger protections under the due process clause, neither in its procedural nor its substantive manifestations." Justices Stevens and Ginsburg dissented.

In spite of these cases, the police may be violating the equal protection guarantee if they refuse to grant police protection to a class of persons. *DeShaney* noted that plaintiff did not allege that the police denied him protection because he was part of a disfavored minority. In § 14.4 we will discuss the problem of attempting to show that the government acted with a "discriminatory purpose" when no specific classification is set forth in a statute or in administrative policies.

§ 10.6 The Equal Protection Clause

Analysis under the equal protection clause of the Fourteenth Amendment is identical to due process analysis. The only equal protection clause appears in the Fourteenth Amendment and it only applies to the states. The Court, however, has interpreted the due process clause of the Fifth Amendment to test federal classifications under the same standard of review. In other words, an aspect of due process is equal protection. *Bolling v. Sharpe* (1954).

Review under equal protection is always substantive in nature. The equal protection guarantees require the government to treat similarly situated individuals in a similar manner. They do not govern the process employed in decision-making but they do regulate the ability of the government to classify individuals as different in type, either for the purposes of dispensing governmental benefits or punishments.

Under the due process clause the Court asks whether the legislation rationally relates to a legitimate end of government. The identical test exists under the equal protection clauses except that legislation reviewed under these guarantees always involves a classification. If a law burdens all persons equally when they exercise a specific right, then the courts will test the law under the due process clause. If, however, the law distinguishes between who may and who may not exercise a right, then judicial review of the law falls under the equal protection guarantee because the issue now is whether the distinction between these persons is legitimate. The classification employed is the "means" used to achieve some end. Thus, the Court reviews the issue of whether the classification rationally relates to a legitimate end under the equal protection guarantees. With respect to suspect classes, or fundamental rights, or other classifications, the Court uses a more active review. Chapter 14 discusses these issues.

Chapter 11

SUBSTANTIVE DUE PROCESS

Table of Sections

§ 11.1   Judicial Control of Legislation Prior to the Civil War

Almost since the beginning of the nation, various Justices of the Supreme Court have suggested that they had an inherent right to review the substance of legislation that either the Congress or state legislatures had enacted. Seventeenth and eighteenth century political theory had built on an earlier philosophical base in espousing the position that certain natural rights prevailed for all men and that the government cannot limit or impair these rights. In short, these rights existed in every society whether they arose from a social compact or from divine right. From this seventeenth and eighteenth century political thought grew the concept that a higher or natural law limited the restrictions on liberty that a temporal government could impose on an individual.

In the case of *Calder v. Bull* (1798), the Justices for the first time engaged in a debate on their ability to overrule legislation on the basis of natural law. *Calder* held that the Connecticut legislature had not violated the Constitution when it set aside a probate

219

decree. The case, however, is important for the opposing opinions of Justices Iredell and Chase, rather than for the precise issue or result of the litigation.

Justice Chase believed that the drafters of the constitutions of the federal and state governments intended to create governments of limited powers and that natural law, as well as the specific provisions of written constitutions, restricted and regulated governmental power. Therefore, Chase decided that the proper role of the Supreme Court was to invalidate legislation if it interfered with rights that the natural law had vested in the people.

Justice Iredell, on the other hand, made a plea for what is now known as judicial restraint. He contended that—even if natural law ought to prevail—no valid legal theory authorized the courts to enforce the natural law over the will of the people as that will was reflected by the other (more democratic) branches of government. The people had limited the acts of Congress and the states with specific constitutional checks; if those specific checks were violated, the Court only would be enforcing democratic principles by declaring the legislation void. However, if the Court relied upon natural law to overturn legislative acts, it would assume powers not granted them under the Constitution and would disparage the democratic process. Iredell believed that the courts had no role in enforcing natural law principles because enforcement of such principles would result in the subservience of the people to the individual views of the Justices.

In form, the Court has adopted the views of Justice Iredell and ruled that it only may invalidate acts of the legislative and executive branches of the federal and state governments on the basis of specific provisions of the Constitution. In substance, however, the beliefs of Justice Chase have prevailed as the Court has expanded its basis for reviewing the acts of other branches of government.

During the early years of the republic the Court refrained from overturning acts of the federal government. Indeed, the Court only held two major acts of the federal government unconstitutional during the period from the Court's formation to the Civil War: the first was when *Marbury v. Madison* (1803) invalidated a section of the Judiciary Act of 1789; the second was when *Dred Scott* (1856) held the Missouri Compromise unconstitutional. In a third, little-know decision, *Hodgson v. Bowerbank* (1809), Chief Justice Marshall appeared to invalidate section 11 of the Judiciary Act of 1789.

The Bill of Rights might have provided specific provisions for controlling the activities of state governments. The history of the Bill of Rights, however, clearly showed that the authors of the Amendments intended that they only apply to the federal government. *Barron v. Mayor and City Council of Baltimore* (1833) confronted the question of whether or not the Fifth Amendment prohibition on taking private property for a public use without just compensation applied to state governments. Chief Justice Marshall answered that none of the first ten Amendments could apply to the state governments because the history of the Bill of Rights supported their application only to the activities of the newly formed central government.

The original text of the Constitution contains few specific checks on the powers of state government. Article 1, section 10 limits the ability of state governments to take certain specific actions (grant Letters of Marque, emit Bills of Credit) absolutely and it limits the states' ability to take other actions without the consent of Congress. The prohibitions against bills of attainder or *ex post facto* laws eliminated the ability of state governments to imprison people by legislative act, but these prohibitions had little to do with general police power legislation. Indeed, only the provision prohibiting the states from "impairing the obligation of contracts" offered any hope for controlling legislation that eliminated vested property rights.

The Contract Clause. The Court used the contract clause in its attempt to gain some control over the substance of general police power legislation during the years prior to the Civil War. Chief Justice Marshall wrote the unanimous opinion in *Fletcher v. Peck* (1810), which held that a state legislature cannot rescind grants of land to original purchasers. So long as the original purchasers transferred the land to innocent third parties, the contract clause protected the original grant (even though, in this case, the original purchaser had bribed the members of the legislature to acquire the property initially).

Fletcher was a rather adventuresome interpretation of the contract clause because the Court had to find that the clause applied to contracts made by the state as well as to state invalidation of private contracts. Furthermore, the Court also had to hold that grants of property rights by the state could be construed as contracts. Nevertheless, once he laid the groundwork for these positions in *Fletcher*, Marshall enlarged upon these rulings so that they could become a basis for the control of state legislation.

In *Trustees of Dartmouth College v. Woodward* (1819), the Court confronted the question of whether a state legislature could control a college established by grant of the British Crown to publicly appointed trustees. Chief Justice Marshall held that the corporate charter was a contract within the meaning of the contract clause and that the state could not alter the charter materially without violating the prohibition of Article I.

Dartmouth College could have established a basis for controlling many forms of state legislation. But the Court was unwilling to extend the *Dartmouth* opinion this far. For example, in 1827, the Supreme Court upheld state bankruptcy laws that provided for the discharge of debts and held that the contract clause did not control *prospective* state interference with the use of property. *Ogden v. Saunders* (1827).

The Doctrines of Vested Rights and the Police Power. Proponents of natural law and the contract clause favored what is often called "the doctrine of vested rights." Professor Corwin, in his classic work, Liberty Against Government (1948), explained that the general theme of vested rights "was that the effect of legislation on existing property rights was a primary test of its validity; for if these were essentially impaired then some clear constitutional justification must be found for the legislation or it must succumb to judicial condemnation."

Yet the Court also recognized what it often called "the police power" of the state to deal with health, safety, and morals. The "police power" does not relate to any specialized power of government. Instead, it encompasses the right of state and local governments to enact legislation protecting the health, safety, morals or general welfare of the people within their jurisdiction.

States derive their powers from state constitutions, not from the "police power," but the police power was the Court's way of recognizing that state and local governments exist to protect the health, safety, welfare or morals of their people and that the reasonable exercise of the police power did not violate the contract clause. Thus, in *Proprietors of Charles River Bridge v. Proprietors of Warren Bridge* (1837) the owners of a state-chartered toll bridge contended that the legislature could not authorize any competing bridges. The owners argued that any authorization of competing bridges would diminish the worth of their chartered monopoly. The Court held that, although it would construe the charter as a contract that bound the state, it would interpret the contract narrowly in favor of the state. The Court recognized the need of the legislature to act to provide for the welfare of its citizens. Consequently, it held that, whenever possible, it would interpret public grants and business charters so as to allow reasonable police power regulation. Thus, the contract clause was limited as a tool for controlling the substance of the state legislation. The clause would not become a major consideration, because after the Civil War new means would exist to control the states through the Civil War Amendments.

The Supremacy Clause and the Commerce Power. The commerce clause provided the Court a method to control state legislation and, thus, to protect private property rights prior to the

Civil War. The Court held that the commerce clause prohibited state legislation that would interfere unreasonably with the free flow of commerce between the states.

Substantive Due Process. Both the English concept of due process of law and the early American legal theorists' idea of due process focused on the procedural feature of the concept. With the rise of natural rights philosophy, however, some theorists intimated that due process also should have a substantive content.

Under this theory, if a legislature passed any law that restricted vested rights or violated natural law, it exceeded all bounds of the social compact in restricting the freedom of some individuals. Therefore, some authorities reasoned that the legislature had denied due process of law to those individuals whose rights or liberties were limited by such legislation because the legislature had denied those deprived persons the guarantees of the basic social compact.

The federal decision invalidating a law as totally beyond the legislative power came in the case of *Dred Scott v. Sandford* (1856). Dred Scott had been taken as a slave into the state of Illinois and the northern part of the Louisiana Purchase territory. Illinois forbade slavery, and the Missouri Compromise had declared the territory into which Scott's "owner" had taken him to be free territory. Dred Scott sued his present owner and argued that, having been taken into free areas, he had been made a free man. A bitterly divided Court ruled against Dred Scott.

The eight separate opinions filed in the case make the basis of the holding and the exact principle of the case unclear. Three reasons, however, do appear for the ruling. First, the majority simply announced that black slaves were not citizens of the United States and can never be citizens. Second, the majority said it must respect the Missouri law declaring Scott a slave notwithstanding his previous entry into area that banned slavery. Third, and most important for the growth of the concept of due process, the majority said that the Missouri Compromise exceeded Congress' power. On this last rationale Chief Justice Taney suggested that the original Constitution had not given Congress any power to interfere with an "owner's" vested rights in his slaves. Thus, the Missouri Compromise deprived the owners of their vested property rights (the right to have slaves) without due process. The dissent objected that the majority's theory was not grounded in precedent, historical understanding, or logic.

§ 11.2 The Growth of the Substantive Due Process Concept—1865 to 1900

The end of the Civil War prompted a great flurry of Congressional activity. Although the states ratified the Thirteenth Amendment forbidding involuntary servitude in 1865, the former slaves were unable to enjoy their new freedom. The southern states enacted "Black Codes" and other repressive measures to restrict the ability of blacks to enjoy and exercise their rights. To counteract these repressive measures Congress passed the Civil Rights Act of 1866. The Act made all people born in the country citizens of the United States and gave to such citizens the same rights and "equal benefits of all laws and proceedings for the security of person and property, as is enjoyed by white citizens...."

Unlike Congress during the Civil War and the Reconstruction years, the Supreme Court at this time largely was inactive, exercising its power of judicial review infrequently, perhaps because of its reluctance to entangle itself in the passions and emotions that its decision in *Dred Scott* had aroused in the nation.

The Supreme Court's reluctance to give an expansive reading to the Constitution was exemplified dramatically in The *Slaughter-House Cases* (1872), which concerned a Louisiana law that prohibited livestock yards and slaughterhouses within New Orleans and the immediate area surrounding the city except for the Crescent City Company, to which the law granted a monopoly. Butchers and others adversely affected brought an action to have the measure declared void, but the Louisiana state courts sustained the statute. The butchers contended that the Louisiana law violated the Thirteenth Amendment and the Fourteenth Amendment's privileges and immunities clause, and its due process and equal protection clauses. The Court, however, rejected not only the Thirteenth Amendment argument, but also all three Fourteenth Amendment contentions. The Court argued that the sole purpose behind the Thirteenth Amendment was to abolish slavery, and, therefore, the Amendment had no application to this case. The Court's reasons for rejecting the Fourteenth Amendment contentions, however, were more complex.

The majority opinion by Justice Miller focused on the first sentence of the Fourteenth Amendment, which declared that "[A]ll persons born ... in the United States ... are citizens of the United States and of the state wherein they reside." The majority read this language to create two types of citizenship: state citizenship and national citizenship. The second sentence of the Amendment, therefore, only prohibited states from making and enforcing laws that infringed on the privileges and immunities of *national* citizenship.

The Court listed some of the rights that it considered to be the privileges and immunities of United States citizenship. These rights included a group, some of which were not exactly earth-shaking: the privilege to come to the seat of government to assert a claim; the right of free access to the country's seaports; the right to travel to the government's subtreasuries, land offices, and courts; the right to use the nation's navigable water, and rights secured for citizens by national treaties. The Louisiana statute creating the monopoly did not impair any of the privileges and immunities of the national citizenship. Thus, the Court held that the butchers had no cause of action under the privileges and immunities clause of the Fourteenth Amendment.

The Court also decided that the due process provision only guaranteed that states would enact laws that followed *procedural* due process. The Court rejected the butchers' equal protection argument because it believed that the drafters of the Fourteenth Amendment only intended to protect blacks from discriminatory actions by a state, a prophesy that has not been a good one.

Justices Field, Justice Bradley and Swayne dissented. They contended that the majority's reading of the Fourteenth Amendment's privileges and immunities clause rendered that clause useless. The dissenters argued that the Fourteenth Amendment did guarantee equal protection of the laws to all persons in all the states. They believed that the drafters of the Fourteenth Amendment did not intend to limit the equal protection clause to black citizens. Moreover, they believed that the Fourteenth Amendment protected the natural and inalienable rights of all citizens. In their view, the Amendment prevented states from enacting arbitrary laws that limited these natural rights.

The great industrial revolution the country experienced during the latter half of the nineteenth century led many states to attempt to regulate these industries. As the states attempted to control industry, representatives of the regulated businesses would seek to have the state or federal declare these state regulatory schemes unconstitutional.

Initially, the Supreme Court's reaction to these attempts was restrained. The Court recognized that the states had a legitimate authority under their police powers to control business activity within their borders. The Court, between 1874 and 1896, invalidated state regulatory measures only if the law violated a specific prohibition contained in the Constitution or if the law interfered with interstate commerce.

At the same time that the legal representatives of large businesses were pressing the Court to take a bold and affirmative stance to protect rapidly growing industries from government regulations, contemporary legal thought began actively to advocate a substantive interpretation of the due process clauses. Although the Court continued to defer to legislative judgments when it reviewed the constitutionality of state and federal laws, it began to suggest that certain limits existed that would control the legislative power.

Munn v. Illinois (1876) dealt with Illinois laws regulating the rates of grain elevators. The grain elevator operators argued that the Illinois statutes violated the due process clause of the Fourteenth Amendment. The Court rejected the due process argument but noted that a state could exercise its police power to control the use of property when it is necessary for the public good. The regulation of private property in this case was particularly appropriate because the operation of grain elevators was "affected with a public interest." The Court, however, qualified its approval of a state's use of its police power when it stated that "[u]ndoubtedly, in mere private contracts, relating to matters in which the public has no interest, what is reasonable must be judicially ascertained . . . this is because the legislature has no control over such a contract."

Mugler v. Kansas (1887) explicitly stated that the Court would use substantive due process to determine the constitutionality of governmental regulatory measures. However, *Mugler* upheld a statute that prohibited the sale of alcoholic beverages. The legislature could exercise its police powers once it determined what laws were needed to protect the public health, morals, and safety. At the same time, however, *Mugler* said that limits existed beyond which the legislature could not go. *Mugler* decided that the judiciary must look to the substance of the laws to see if the legislature had surpassed its authority.

Mugler gave notice that a statute had to have a substantial relation to the protection of the public health, morals, or safety before the Court would sustain the measure as a valid exercise of the state's police power.

In *Santa Clara County v. Southern Pacific R. Co.* (1886), the Court held, without discussion, that corporations are "persons" for purposes of the Fourteenth Amendment. Therefore, any protection of fundamental or natural rights that the Fourteenth Amendment offered applies to incorporated business entities as well as to people.

Allgeyer v. Louisiana (1897) used substantive due process to invalidate a state statute. A Louisiana statute prohibited anyone from giving effect to marine insurance on Louisiana property if the insurance company that issued the policy had not complied in all respects with Louisiana law. The state had convicted Allgeyer for violating the statute when he mailed a letter advising a New York insurance company about the shipment of some insured goods. The New York insurer was not registered to do business in Louisiana. The Supreme Court reversed the conviction and held that the statute violated the Fourteenth Amendment because it deprived the defendant of his liberty without due process of law.

Allgeyer reasoned that Louisiana had no jurisdiction over contracts made outside of the state with a foreign corporation. Although the Court primarily relied on this jurisdictional reasoning to void the law, it extensively discussed the liberty of contract and the Fourteenth Amendment's protection of liberty interests. *Allgeyer* argued that the "liberty" that the Fourteenth Amendment protected was a more extensive liberty than merely the right of a person to be free of physical restraints. The Fourteenth Amendment's due process clause also guaranteed that a person would be free to enjoy "all his faculties; to be free to use them in all lawful ways...." To insure that a person could enjoy "all his faculties," the *Allgeyer* Court's dicta said that the Fourteenth Amendment authorized a person to seek any type of employment or to pursue any type of avocation. To facilitate this liberty, that Amendment protected the freedom of contract. The Louisiana statute deprived *Allgeyer* of his liberty to contract "which the state legislature had no right to prevent...."

§ 11.3 Substantive Due Process From 1900 to 1936

The broad dicta of *Allgeyer v. Louisiana* revealed the Court's willingness to use the substantive due process doctrine to void any economic or social legislation that the Court believed unreasonably infringed on the liberty to contract.

The substantive due process can be summarized as follows: the government must employ means (legislation) that bear some reasonable relation to a legitimate end. If the courts conclude that the law does not relate to a legitimate end, then the courts may invalidate the law because the government had no power to enact this limitation of liberty. Similarly, no matter how temperate the legislation might seem to others, it is void if the Justices think it relates to some end that they considered beyond the proper role of government. Freedom in the marketplace and freedom to contract are viewed as liberties that the due process clause protects.

Thus, the Court would invalidate a law if it concluded that it restricts economic liberty in a way that was not reasonably related to a legitimate end. Because the Court did not view labor regulation, price control, or other economic measures as legitimate ends in themselves, only a limited amount of business regulation could pass this test. Only when the Justices were convinced that the regulation actually promoted public health, safety, or some other important "public interest" would they uphold the law. Independent judicial review of such legislation made the constitutionality of these laws dependent on the Justices' individual views. While many laws were invalidated on this basis, we will examine only a few during this period.

Holden v. Hardy (1898) upheld a Utah statute that limited the hours men could work in mines and smelters, because the Court was convinced that the extremely unsafe and unhealthy working conditions of mines made the regulation reasonable.

In contrast, the Court invalidated a New York law that limited the number of hours a baker could work to only 60 hours a week or 10 hours a day. In *Lochner v. New York* (1905) the Court held the law unconstitutional because it was an arbitrary and unnecessary interference with the liberty to contract between an employer and employee—a liberty protected by the Fourteenth Amendment. New York had infringed unreasonably on "the freedom of master and employee to contract with each other in relation to their employment." The job of baker is not as dangerous as the job of miner.

While the *Lochner* majority stated that it would not "substitut[e] the judgment of the court for that of the legislature," it also stated, in a more candid passage, that "[w]e do not believe in the soundness of the views which uphold this law." The law, in the Court's view, was purely a piece of labor legislation and as such was an improper exercise of the state's police power.

Justice Holmes and Justice Harlan wrote dissents in *Lochner*. Holmes believed that the majority was imposing its own theory of a proper economic policy on the state of New York by invalidating this law. His remark that "[t]he Fourteenth Amendment does not enact Mr. Herbert Spencer's Social Statics" has become one of the most famous in constitutional history. Holmes believed the founding fathers created a Constitution "for people of fundamentally differing views," and the Court should not void a law simply because it implements an economic policy that the Justices do not embrace. Holmes stated that the Court should invalidate a law only when "a rational and fair man necessarily would admit that the statute proposed would infringe fundamental principles as they have been understood by the traditions of our people and our law."

Justice Harlan's dissent was willing to accept the New York statute as a valid health measure. He cited the evidence that supported the contention that limiting the number of hours bakers could work would protect the welfare of these workers whose health standard was below the national average. Harlan believed that as long as the statute arguably was a health measure the Court should sustain the law.

The majority and dissenting opinions in *Lochner* reveal the problem the Supreme Court experienced between 1900 and 1937. The state legislatures and the national government were enacting an ever-increasing amount of legislation that regulated the economic and social life of Americans. Many of the Justices believed they had an obligation to protect the free enterprise system as embodied in the concept of laissez faire. These Justices, as exemplified by the *Lochner* majority opinion, were willing to use not only the substantive due process concept, but also the commerce clause, the contract clause, and the equal protection clause to void those laws that they believed unreasonably infringed on free enterprise. At the same time, however, the Court had a tradition of judicial forbearance. Because this tension existed, the Court of the early twentieth century failed to follow a systematic and uniform approach to the legislation it reviewed.

Three years after *Lochner* the Court sustained state legislation that limited the number of hours that women could work. In *Muller v. Oregon* (1908), then-attorney Louis D. Brandeis presented the Court with the now-famous "Brandeis brief," a brief that contained massive documentation—not only to legal precedent but also references to laws of other states and foreign countries; reports of European and American committees, inspectors of factories, commissioners of hygiene, and studies of statistical bureaus—to justify the regulation of the work hours for women. Brandeis presented to the Justices the kind of information that a legislative committee would hear in determining whether to favor a law. The need for that type of brief suggests that arguing before the *Lochner* Court was almost like taking just another step in the legislative process.

Bunting v. Oregon (1917), without mentioning *Lochner*, sustained statutes that limited the work hours for men in certain industries. But *Bunting* did not abandon substantive due process; in *Bunting*, unlike *Lochner*, the state had presented sufficient evidence to convince the Court that the legislation was a proper exercise of the state's police power. If the states failed to justify adequately a particular labor regulation as an appropriate police power measure, the Supreme Court would invalidate the statute as violative of substantive economic due process.

During this period, sometimes the Court also relied on the equal protection clause. but the due process clause was its favorite tool.

Beginning in 1923 the Court began to use the negative implications of the public interest concept to void legislative regulation. The Court decided a series of cases where it held various regulatory devices violative of the Fourteenth Amendment because the regulated businesses were not affected with a public interest. As the law developed, unless the business (1) resulted from a public grant or franchise, (2) was subject traditionally to regulation, or (3) "which though not public at their inception may be said to have risen to be such and have become subject in consequence to some government regulation," the state could not regulate the business.

The Court's guidelines to determine whether a state properly could regulate a business were of little help to the states. Those businesses that fell within the first two categories always had been subject to state supervision. The third category was the critical class of businesses, and the Court retained the power to determine, with a very subjective test, the parameters of that class of businesses.

Nebbia v. New York (1934) reversed the public interest line of cases. New York had established a regulatory board that had the authority to set minimum prices for the retail sale of milk. The Court sustained the legislation as a legitimate exercise of the state's police power. The petitioner contended that the milk industry was not a business affected with a public interest, and consequently, the state could not control the retail price of milk. The Court rejected that contention because "there is no closed class or category of businesses affected with a public interest. . . ." *Nebbia* said that the Court's function "is to determine in each case whether circumstances vindicate the challenged regulation as a reasonable exertion of governmental authority or condemn it as arbitrary or discriminatory."

The opinion contained language that suggested that the use of the substantive due process doctrine to invalidate economic or welfare legislation was at an end. The Court stated that "a state is free to adopt whatever economic policy may reasonably be deemed to promote public welfare and to enforce that policy by legislation adapted to its purpose." Moreover, *Nebbia* observed, the courts did not have the authority either to establish an economic policy or to overrule the legislative choice of an appropriate policy.

Immediately after his election to his first term in office, President Roosevelt marshaled his support in Congress and persuaded Congress to enact his New Deal legislation designed to help the nation recover from the Great Depression. The issue of the constitutionality of some of this legislation came before the Supreme Court between 1934 and 1936. With a remarkable series of decisions the Court invalidated many of the New Deal acts. The New Deal legislation presented to a majority of the Justices the greatest threat to their concept of free enterprise that they could imagine. Therefore, the Court used a narrow interpretation of the commerce clause to declare New Deal provisions unconstitutional.

The Court also refused to follow *Nebbia's* formulation of the Court's proper role when reviewing economic legislation under the due process clause. The Court declared unconstitutional another New York statute that had established a minimum wage for women in *Morehead v. New York ex rel. Tipaldo* (1936). Only the dissent cited *Nebbia*. The majority argued that the minimum wage law violated the Fourteenth Amendment because it impaired the liberty to contract. The Court decided this case shortly after it invalidated much of President Roosevelt's New Deal legislation. Hence, the *Morehead* decision announced to the states, as the Court's decision on the New Deal legislation had announced to Congress, that the Court would continue to construe strictly the powers the government had to control business.

FDR's Court Packing Proposal. The Court's refusal to sustain much of the New Deal-type legislation of the early 1930's precipitated a constitutional crisis. The voters re-elected Franklin Roosevelt to a second presidential term by an overwhelming margin in 1936. The President interpreted his landslide margin of victory as a mandate from the people to do whatever was necessary to end the Depression. Before he could implement that mandate, however, he had to eliminate the Supreme Court as an obstacle to his programs. Therefore, Roosevelt proposed a plan whereby the President could appoint a new Justice if an incumbent Justice failed to retire when he reached seventy. Roosevelt wanted the opportunity to appoint Justices who would interpret the Constitution in a way that would allow the New Deal legislation to stand.

The President's plan confronted the Court with the most serious threat to its constitutional authority since the Court's inception. The President was proposing to "pack" the Court with his appointees largely because he disapproved of the Court's invalidation of his legislation. This plan threatened to destroy the concept of the Court as a neutral arbiter of constitutional issues. Congress debated the merits of the plan for almost six months. Ultimately Congress, controlled by members of the President's party, voted against the President's plan. At this time the Court reversed its position and began to sustain much of the economic and labor legislation enacted by Congress and the states. The Court began to abandon its substantive due process review of economic and welfare legislation as well as broadening its interpretation of the federal commerce power.

For example, *West Coast Hotel Co. v. Parrish* (1937) upheld a Washington State minimum wage law. In the course of the majority opinion, the Court said: "What is this freedom? The Constitution does not speak of freedom of contract. It speaks of liberty and prohibits the deprivation of liberty without due process of law."

Civil Rights and *Lochner* Era Court. The Court during the first third of the twentieth century also started to apply the doctrine to the area of civil rights. Although the number of civil liberty cases the Court decided was small, the number increased as the years passed. The Supreme Court cases principally involved state statutes and the due process clause of the Fourteenth Amendment.

For example, *Buchanan v. Warley* (1917) voided a Louisville city ordinance that precluded blacks from moving into areas where the residents were primarily white. The ordinance violated the due process clause because it was an unwarranted interference with property rights.

Later, in *Meyer v. Nebraska* (1923) the Court declared unconstitutional a Nebraska statute that prohibited teaching in any language other than English. The Court held that this state law improperly infringed upon the liberty to make educational decisions.

In a series of cases during this period, the Court also held that the states could not deny an individual a right to counsel nor could the state use forced confessions in criminal prosecutions. Under the theory of due process, the Court began to incorporate into the Fourteenth Amendment some of the liberty guarantees of the first eight Amendments.

§ 11.4 Substantive Due Process After 1937

Introduction. Since 1937 the Court has focused on equal protection, rather than substantive due process, in most cases involving challenges to governmental regulations in the area commonly referred to as "economic and social welfare" legislation. The reason for this fact is quite simple: most laws do not regulate all persons evenhandedly but, instead, involve classifications of persons. Regardless of whether a court is employing substantive due process or equal protection analysis, it uses the same standards of review. If a law regulating all persons involves only matters of economics or social welfare, a court should defer to the legislature and uphold the law so long as it is rationally related to a legitimate interest of government. If a law involves a classification that relates only to matters of economics or social welfare, a court similarly should uphold the law so long as the classification is rationally related to a legitimate interest of government.

If a law regulates the exercise of a "fundamental right" such as voting, or free speech, or affects a suspect class, the courts should give less deference to the legislature and independently scrutinize the law or classification to determine if it complies with equal protection.

Most fundamental rights cases since 1937 have involved Supreme Court rulings based upon equal protection rather than due process principles. First, the experience from *Lochner* to the 1937 Court-packing plan has made substantive due process not a preferred ground for decision. Second, virtually all government laws regulating fundamental rights involve classifications. Laws, by their nature, classify, and equal protection is the clause that the Court uses most frequently to judge laws that classify. The equal protection clause is the topic of chapter 14.

Footnote 4 of *Carolene Products*. The most important part of *United States v. Carolene Products Co.* (1938) is not the holding but its footnote 4. Congress had passed legislation that prohibited the interstate shipment of "filled" milk. The appellee contended that the legislation violated the Fifth Amendment's due process provision. The Court rejected that invitation to resurrect substantive economic due process.

Justice Stone, speaking for the Court, said that "where the legislative judgment is drawn in question, [the inquiry] must be restricted to the issue whether any state of facts either known or which could reasonably be assumed, affords support for [the legislation]." The Court found sufficient facts in *Carolene Products* to support the finding of a rational basis for the measure. The legislative findings that filled milk was injurious to the public health revealed the congressional rationale behind the act.

Justice Stone, however, emphasized that even absent these legislative findings the Court would sustain the legislation because "the existence of facts supporting the legislative judgment is to be presumed, for regulatory legislation affecting ordinary commercial transactions is not to be pronounced unconstitutional unless ... it is of such a character as to preclude the assumption that it rests on some rational basis...." In the now famous footnote 4, which he added at the end of this sentence, he gave reasons for the continued independent judicial review of some governmental actions:

4. There may be narrower scope for operation of the presumption of constitutionality when legislation appears on its face to be within a specific prohibition of the Constitution, such as those of the first ten Amendments, which are deemed equally specific when held to be embraced within the Fourteenth....

It is unnecessary to consider now whether legislation which restricts those political processes which can ordinarily be expected to bring about repeal of undesirable legislation, is to be subjected to more exacting judicial scrutiny under the general prohibitions of the Fourteenth Amendment than are most other types of legislation....

Nor need we enquire ... whether prejudice against discrete and insular minorities may be a special condition, which tends seriously to curtail the operation of those political processes ordinarily to be relied upon to protect minorities, and which may call for a correspondingly more searching judicial inquiry. . . .

Post–1937 Decisions and the Blending of Substantive Due Process and Equal Protection. Since 1937, the Supreme Court has required the judiciary to give great deference to federal, state and local law makers when reviewing economic and social welfare legislation under either due process or equal protection principles. An economic or social welfare law will be subject to more rigorous standards of review under equal protection if the law employs a classification that receives special constitutional protection (such as sex or illegitimacy classifications or the suspect classifications of race, national origin, and alienage. These cases are examined in Chapter 14.

If a law impairs a fundamental constitutional right it will be subject to independent judicial review. If the law limits the ability of all persons to exercise a fundamental right it will be tested under due process. If the law restricts the ability of a class of persons to exercise a fundamental right, it will be tested under equal protection.

Post–1937 Decisions Regarding Economic and Social Welfare Legislation. The exact dimension of the Court's deference to legislative economic judgments remained unclear after *Carolene Products*. The Court had suggested that it may consider the validity of the proffered rational basis for economic legislation. Subsequent Court decisions, however, indicate that judicial deference to the legislature's economic regulations is virtually complete.

Williamson v. Lee Optical of Oklahoma, Inc. (1955), for example, rejected the due process and equal protection arguments made against an Oklahoma statute that restricted the ability of opticians to fit or duplicate eyeglasses. The Court was unable to find a specific constitutional prohibition that the Oklahoma measure violated, and it was willing to conceive of possible reasons for the enactment that would furnish a rational basis for the law. The Court, for example, speculated that the legislature may have concluded that it should regulate eyeglass frames in order to regulate eye glass lenses effectively.

Williamson indicates that the Court will not only presume that a legislature had a reasonable basis for enacting a particular economic measure, but also will hypothesize reasons for the law's enactment if the legislature fails to state explicitly the reasons behind its judgment. Consequently, anyone attempting to argue for the invalidation of a legislative economic enactment will have to discredit the Court's conceived reasons for the legislature's actions as well as the arguments of those who support the measure.

Ferguson v. Skrupa (1963) provides an appropriate epilogue for the demise of economic substantive due process. In sustaining a Kansas law that prohibited anyone from conducting the business of debt adjusting unless incident to the practice of law, the Court, speaking through Justice Black, stated: "[W]e refuse to sit as a 'superlegislature to weigh the wisdom of legislation'.... Whether the legislature takes for its textbook Adam Smith, Herbert Spencer, Lord Keynes or some other is no concern of ours." Justice Holmes's *Lochner* dissent had become the Court's standard.

From time to time, a few Justices have indicated a desire to review the reasonableness of some economic or social welfare legislation but, thus far, a majority of Justices continue to use the rational basis test to approve laws allocating welfare benefits, restricting the use of property, or regulating business or personal activity that does not involve a fundamental right. There are individual justices who argue against complete abdication, from time to time, but they do not constitute a majority of the Court, at least not yet.

§ 11.5   Incorporation of the Bill of Rights

Prior to the Civil War, the Court had held that the provisions of the Bill of Rights were not applicable to the activities of state and local governments. However, not long after the passage of the Fourteenth Amendment, litigants claimed that the guarantees of individual rights contained in those Amendments were made applicable to the states by the Fourteenth Amendment. The Supreme Court, initially, did not embrace these arguments.

First, the Court gave a restrictive meaning to the privileges and immunities clause of the Fourteenth Amendment in one of its first decisions on the meaning of that Amendment. *The Slaughter–House Cases* (1872). This decision had the effect of eliminating the provision that was both historically and logically the one most likely intended to include within its protections the guarantees of the Bill of Rights. At the close of the twentieth century, the Supreme Court would find that the privileges or immunities clause of the Fourteenth Amendment protected one aspect of the "right to travel." *Saenz v. Roe* (1999). The Court, however, has not used that clause as the basis for protecting civil liberties generally, or for applying the Bill of Rights to the states.

There was also little need for the Court to analyze the incorporation issue because of the its expansive reading of the due process clause. The Court could protect any form of individual freedom or natural law rights it desired without the need to resort to a specific textual basis in the Constitution.

Thus when the Court, under the general concept of due process, invalidated a state law that prohibited private religious schools, there was no need to resort to the religion clauses of the First Amendment. *Pierce v. Society of Sisters* (1925). Similarly, the Court struck down a state law prohibiting the teaching of foreign languages in private as well as public schools by relying on due process, not on the First Amendment. *Meyer v. Nebraska* (1923). Because of this approach, there was no clear focusing on whether specific provisions of the Bill of Rights were "incorporated" into the due process clause of the Fourteenth Amendment.

In 1897 the Court decided that the Constitution required state and local governments to pay just compensation when they exercised their powers of eminent domain and took an individual's property for public use. *Chicago, B. & Q.R. Co. v. City of Chicago* (1897). But the first Justice Harlan's opinion of the Court did not state that the just compensation clause of the Fifth Amendment applied to the states through the due process clause of the Fourteenth Amendment. Rather it only held that the due process clause protected individuals against having their property taken without just compensation. It was unnecessary to reflect upon the issue of "incorporation," for the Justices felt quite secure in their ability to control all forms of state activities through the due process clause.

As the Court left the era of substantive due process, it focused more of its attention on whether the due process clause of the Fourteenth Amendment made some or all of the specific guarantees of the Bill of Rights directly applicable to the states. Thus, in 1925 the Court assumed that the free speech clause of the First Amendment applied to the states by the due process clause. *Gitlow v. New York* (1925). In 1932 when the Court intervened to grant the criminal defendants some protection in the now famous "Scottsboro Boys" case, it found that the Fourteenth Amendment made at least some elements of the right to counsel under the Sixth Amendment applicable to state and local governments. *Powell v. Alabama* (1932).

However, the Court did not develop any consistent approach towards the concept of incorporation until after its denouncement of substantive due process. As late as 1934, the Supreme Court could reject the claims of religious conscientious objectors to attending state colleges with mandatory military training requirements by concentrating on whether the meaning of liberty included the right to entertain religious beliefs, rather than focusing on the First Amendment religion clauses. *Hamilton v. Regents of the University of California* (1934).

The Court did not require the exclusion of a coerced confession by a defendant in a state criminal proceeding under the Fourteenth Amendment until 1936. *Brown v. Mississippi* (1936). And it did not incorporate the self-incrimination clause until 1964. *Malloy v. Hogan* (1964). However, even federal defendants did not, at this time, receive significant protections in the criminal process. Until 1938 the Sixth Amendment right to counsel in federal courts meant only that a defendant would be able to have an attorney to represent him at certain points in the proceeding if he could afford to retain one. *Johnson v. Zerbst* (1938).

Eventually, the Court focused its attention on incorporation. The issue became one of identifying what rights or values are of such a nature that they should be judicially enforced against the other branches of government. Today we phrase the issue as whether the provisions of the Bill of Rights are "incorporated" into the meaning of the word "liberty" so as to be protected by the due process clause of the Fourteenth Amendment and applied to the states.

Following 1936 the Supreme Court decided that some, but not all, of the Bill of Rights guarantees were applicable to the states. A few Justices, most notably Justice Black, argued that the history of the Fourteenth Amendment indicated that all of the Bill of Rights were to be made directly applicable to the states. *Adamson v. California* (1947) (Black, J., dissenting, joined by Douglas, J.) Other Justices, most notably Justice Frankfurter, argued that the concept of "liberty" must a judicially defined meaning that is not dependent upon the incorporation of specific guarantees of the Bill of Rights. *Adamson v. California* (1947) (Frankfurter, J. concurring).

The Supreme Court had not followed an approach based on the historical view. Instead, it settled on the concept of "selective incorporation." The Court will make a provision of the Bill of Rights applicable to the states if the Court concludes that it was meant to protect a "fundamental" aspect of liberty. In the early cases the Court asked whether the specific Amendment is so fundamental that it could be said to be "implicit in the concept of ordered liberty," and "so rooted in the traditions and conscience of our people as to be as fundamental." *Palko v. Connecticut* (1937).

Eventually the Court altered the test, so that the determination of whether the right to jury trial guaranteed by the Sixth Amendment is incorporated into the fourteenth depended on whether that guarantee is "fundamental to the American scheme of justice." *Duncan v. Louisiana* (1968). This new language means that the Court is willing to enforce values that it sees as having a special importance in the development of individual liberty in

American society, whether or not the value was one that was theoretically necessary in any system of democratic government.

The Provisions of the Bill of Rights That Are Incorporated. Today virtually all the provisions of the Bill of Rights have been incorporated into the Fourteenth Amendment and made applicable to the states. Since 1934 there has been a steady process of judicial inclusion of provisions of the Bill of Rights into the Fourteenth Amendment. All of the provisions of the first Amendment concerning freedoms of religion, speech, press, assembly and petition have been held applicable to the states. The Court has not held that the Second Amendment concerning the right to bear arms is applicable to the states. The Third Amendment, which prohibits the quartering of soldiers in private homes, has not been the subject of any constitutional litigation in the Supreme Court.

The Fourth Amendment's regulation of searches and seizures is applicable to the states. Of the guarantees of the Fifth Amendment, the Court has only held that the grand jury clause is not applicable to the states. The Court has specifically incorporated both the double jeopardy and self-incrimination provisions of that Amendment. The Fifth Amendment just compensation clause applies to the states, although it is unclear whether it is incorporated into the Fourteenth Amendment or whether the Fourteenth Amendment's due process clause merely has an identical meaning to that provision. The Court has held that each of several guarantees of the Sixth Amendment concerning rights in the criminal process are applicable to the states through the due process clause. The Seventh Amendment right to jury trial in civil cases is not applicable to the states.

The cruel and unusual punishment clause of the Eighth Amendment is applicable to the states and the excessive bail provision is applicable by implication. There are no cases concerning the applicability of the "excessive fine" provision of the Eighth Amendment to the states. It would seem to be applicable because it is intertwined with the other two and the Court has already regulated the imposition of fines on indigents through the equal protection clause of the Fourteenth Amendment. The Ninth Amendment has not been the source of specific rights or rulings although some Justices would give it greater impact. The Tenth Amendment, by its own terms, has no application to the states.

Some Justices have argued that, even if the Bill of Rights are applicable to the states, the Court should not hold state laws to the same standards as it holds the federal government. However, the Court has rejected this concept and have held that when a provision of the Bill of Rights is applicable to the states, it applies to state and local acts in the same manner as it does to federal actions.

Thus, rulings on the meaning of any incorporated provision of the Bill of Rights are of equal meaning for both federal and state laws.

This concept is sometimes known as the "bag and baggage" theory for it holds that when a provision of the Bill of Rights is made applicable to the states it is applied with all of its previous federal interpretation—it comes to the states, complete with its "bag and baggage." When the Supreme Court holds a provision of the Bill of Rights applicable to the states, it does so because the Justices are of the opinion that it is a right which can be deemed "fundamental" to the American system of government. Accordingly, the Court will not tolerate either federal or state activities that impair the right.

§ 11.6 Fundamental Rights

Today the Court will apply strict forms of review under the due process clauses and the equal protection clause to any governmental actions which limit the exercise of "fundamental" constitutional rights. These are rights that the Court recognizes as having a value so essential to individual liberty in our society that they justify the Court reviewing the acts of other branches of government in a manner quite similar to the substantive due process approach of the pre–1937 period. Little more can be said to accurately describe the nature of a fundamental right, because fundamental rights analysis is simply no more than the modern recognition of the natural law concepts first espoused by Justice Chase in *Calder v. Bull* (1798).

It was not long after the 1937 Court Packing Plan, in *United States v. Carolene Products Co* (1938), the Court indicated, footnote 4, that it might not follow the rejection of substantive due process in areas which touched upon specific constitutional guarantees or disadvantaged certain minority groups. A few years later, the Court struck down a statute authorizing sterilization of some convicts because it arbitrarily classified persons in terms of a fundamental right. *Skinner v. Oklahoma*, (1942).

The Justices often do not agree from where these rights derive. *Griswold v. Connecticut* (1965) struck down a law that prohibited the use of contraceptives by married persons. The majority opinion by Justice Douglas found a fundamental "right to privacy" that the state law infringed. He found this right in the "penumbras" of several guarantees of the Bill of Rights. He gave no indication of how to search the shadows, or penumbras, of the Bill of Rights to find other fundamental guarantees.

Justice Goldberg, concurring, said that the right of privacy should be recognized without reliance on any specific guarantees of the Bill of Rights. He argued that the Ninth Amendment gave textual recognition to the fact that there are other values of equal importance to the specific provisions to the Bill of Rights even though the first Eight Amendments do not mention them. While the Ninth Amendment did not directly create those rights, Goldberg argued that it authorized the Court to identify them and protect them against the acts of the other branches of government. He attempted to give some guidelines to the search for these values by stating that the Court should rely on "the traditions and conscience" of the nation in determining what values were to be so protected.

Only Justice Harlan was able to give a very clear basis for why he was recognizing the right to privacy as worthy of constitutional protection. He was, frankly, willing to protect the right to privacy based on a natural law approach. Harlan stood quite ready to defend the judicial function as selecting values that had a historical and philosophical right to be called fundamental and enforcing them against even the will of the majority. He did not advocate a return to the pre–1937 period, for there were very few rights that he would define as truly fundamental; Harlan did not advocate overturning laws merely because they offended his individual sense of reasonableness.

Justice Black, who objected to this natural law approach to the definition of due process, dissented in *Griswold* because he found no clear basis for this right in the text of the Bill of Rights.

The concept of fundamental rights remains vague today. All that can be said with certainty is that the Justices have selected a group of individual rights that do not have a specific textual basis in the original Constitution or its Amendments and deemed them to be "fundamental." There can be no doubt that this judicial value selection must be based on the Court's decision to enforce some natural law rights against the acts of organized society.

In 2003, in *Lawrence v. Texas* (2003) overruled *Bowers v. Hardwick* (1968) and ruled that a Texas law that prohibited sodomy between persons of the same sex violated the Fourteenth Amendment due process clause. The majority opinion in *Lawrence*, written by Justice Kennedy, did not find that sexual activity between unmarried persons was a fundamental right. Nevertheless, Justice Kennedy invalidated any possible restrictions on private sexual activity between two consenting adults in private that did not cause physical or mental harm to either party. Justice Kennedy argued that there was no legitimate interest of government that would support a restriction on this type of activity.

Justice O'Connor voted to invalidate the homosexual sodomy law on the basis that it was designed to harm a politically unpopular group. The dissenting Justices in *Lawrence* believed that the ruling in that case constituted a return to *Lochner*-era substantive due process adjudication. Only time will tell whether the *Lawrence* decision was a limited ruling concerning a fundamental aspect of liberty or an indication that the Court will become more active in other areas as well.

§ 11.7 The Contract Clause

(a) Introduction

The framers drafted the contract clause to prevent the states from enacting debtor relief laws. Under the leadership of Chief Justice John Marshall, however, the clause received an expansive reading. During the Marshall years the Court used the provision to invalidate statutes that retrospectively impaired almost any contractual obligation of private parties. The Court never used the clause to void laws that *prospectively* modified contractual obligations. Nevertheless, until the late nineteenth century the contract clause was the principal provision the Court used to void legislation that infringed on private property rights. Within the last 100 years, however, the Court rarely has relied on the clause as a reason to invalidate state legislation which retroactively affected contractual rights or obligations.

The Supreme Court has used the contract clause to restrict the ability of states to modify or alter public charters and contracts as well as private contracts. If a state is to retain the ability to modify a charter or public contract, it must explicitly so provide in the charter or in the enabling legislation. Moreover, if third parties' rights have accrued under the charter or public contract, the state may be unable to alter the contract even if it has made a general reservation to modify the contract. On the other hand, the contract clause will not prevent a state from altering its own contractual obligations that involve its inherent police powers. The Court has recognized that a state cannot bargain away its police power. If, however, the state commits itself to a financial obligation, the Court will review both the reasonableness and the necessity of any legislation that impairs that obligation. If the Court finds that the state law at issue is unnecessary and unreasonable in the way it alters the state's financial commitment, it may void the measure as violative of the contract clause.

(b) The Case Law

The contract clause of the Constitution (art. I, § 10) prohibits the states from enacting any law that will impair "the Obligation of Contracts." This prohibition, in general, prevents the states from passing any legislation that would alleviate the commitments of one party to a contract or make enforcement of the contract unreasonably difficult.

The primary intent behind the drafting of the clause was to prohibit states from adopting laws that would interfere with the contractual arrangements between private citizens. Specifically, the drafters intended to inhibit the ability of state legislatures to enact debtor relief laws. Those who attended the Constitutional Convention recognized that banks and financiers required some assurance that their credit arrangements would not be abrogated by state legislatures. The drafters also realized that the country's economic growth depended in large measure on providing a stable environment for those who had money to invest or loan. Therefore, as a means to help provide a stable economic environment, the draftsmen not only reserved in Congress the power to establish uniform bankruptcy laws but also adopted the contract clause to restrict the power of the states to annul or void valid credit arrangements.

The Contract Clause and Chief Justice Marshall. Although the framers of the Constitution believed the contract clause would have limited application, John Marshall, as Chief Justice, saw the provision as a valuable weapon to protect property interests from unwarranted state regulation. *Fletcher v. Peck* (1810) was Marshall's vehicle.

In 1794 the Georgia legislature granted thirty-five million acres of land to speculators for a purchase price of $500,000. When, however, the public learned of the widespread fraud and bribery that influenced the legislation, it demanded repeal of the statutory grant, and the Georgia legislature rescinded the legislation a year later.

Peck had purchased some of the Georgia land from one of the original grantees and had resold the land to Fletcher. When Fletcher learned of the statutory repeal of the grant, he demanded rescission of the contract and his money back because of Peck's inability to convey good title. Peck, however, responded with the argument that he was a purchaser in due course and the rescinding act could not affect his title to the land.

Although Marshall's opinion in *Fletcher v. Peck* declared the rescinding statute unconstitutional, the constitutional basis for the opinion is somewhat uncertain. Some language in the decision implies that the Georgia statute violated the contract clause because the grant was in the nature of a contract. Other language in the opinion, however, reflects Marshall's uncertainty on whether he could rest the entire decision on that clause. He stated that the rescinding legislation violated not only general principles of society and government but also the concept of natural law.

After *Fletcher v. Peck* the Court decided *New Jersey v. Wilson* (1812) and *Dartmouth College v. Woodward* (1819). These cases removed any doubt that the contract clause would prohibit a state from abrogating agreements to which it was a party. In the *Wilson* case the New Jersey legislature enacted a statute that repealed a tax exemption which the colonial legislature had granted certain lands fifty years earlier. The Supreme Court invalidated the repealing measure as violative of the contract clause.

In *Dartmouth College* the Court applied the clause to a statute that attempted to change the provisions of a charter issued to Dartmouth College. The Court stated without reservation or qualification that the clause applied to a state's obligation in a contract, that a charter was a contract, and that the covenants in the charter were not voidable even though the holders of the charter, the college trustees, had no beneficial interest in the instrument. Although *Dartmouth College* involved a charitable and educational institution, the Court readily expanded the principles announced in the opinion to corporate charters issued for business purposes. Consequently, the decision protected industrial and financial corporations from much government regulation.

Modification of Contracts Between Private Parties. The Supreme Court did not apply the clause to invalidate a debtor relief law until *Sturges v. Crowninshield* (1819). This case declared unconstitutional a New York insolvency law that discharged the obligations of debtors once they had surrendered their property. The principal constitutional defect of the law was its retroactive effect: the act released debtors from obligations assumed before the act's passage. *Sturges*, therefore, implied that the Court would sustain debtor relief legislation that had a prospective effect.

Ogden v. Saunders (1827) expressly adopted the implication of *Sturges* and held a debtor relief law with prospective impact to be constitutional. Marshall contended that the contract clause prohibited states from enacting *prospective* debtor legislation, but the majority of the Court disagreed.

Modification of State Contracts—The Taney Court and Modification of Remedies. In *Bronson v. Kinzie* (1843), the Taney Court attempted to give added definition to the remedy-obligation distinction enunciated in *Sturges*. *Sturges* had conceded that although the contract clause precluded a state from adopting laws that impaired the obligation of contracts, the state may enact legislation that modifies the available remedies for the breach of a contract. *Bronson* stated that the scope of allowable modifications of remedies under the clause depended on the reasonableness of those modifications and whether the modifying legislation affected substantial rights of the parties. This distinction was, frankly obscure. Nevertheless, highlighting the difference between the two concepts gave the Court and state legislatures some flexibility in approving debtor relief statutes.

The Contract Clause From 1874 to the Turn of the Century. The Supreme Court from 1874 to 1898 used the clause in thirty-nine cases to invalidate state legislation. At the same time, however, the Court had reached the end of the period of the expansive reading of the clause. During the latter part of the nineteenth century the provision lost its importance as the principal constitutional clause available to protect vested rights. Several developments help explain the diminished value of the contract clause as a defense for property interests.

First, the states were reserving the right to amend or alter the charters they granted. If a state reserved the right to modify the terms of a charter either by a provision in the charter or by a general statutory scheme, a state could subsequently modify a granted charter without violating the contract clause. Therefore, states took advantage of this concession by passing the appropriate legislation or including the necessary charter provision.

Additionally, the rule that the Court would construe strictly the terms of any public grant prompted the states to write their grants carefully. Consequently, the states rarely would enact a statutory grant that would fail to give the state the necessary flexibility to pass legislation that may modify the previously issued public grant.

Finally, the Court began to rely on the doctrine of substantive due process to void legislation that would infringe on property or business interests. More often than not, any state legislation that impaired the obligation of contract would not only violate the contract clause but also would violate the Court's notions of economic substantive due process. The substantive due process doctrine gave the Court more discretion and flexibility than the contract clause in passing on the constitutionality of state legislation. Hence, if the Court had a choice, it would use substantive due process analysis rather than contract clause analysis to void state legislation during this period.

Twentieth Century Rulings—The *Blaisdell* Decision. During the Court's substantive due process era the contract clause faded in importance. When, however, the Great Depression came and states began to enact debtor relief legislation, the Court began to hear numerous cases where the opponents of the debtor relief measures relied on the clause to attack the constitutionality of the legislation. Earlier Supreme Courts had invalidated many of these laws if they had a retroactive effect. Nevertheless, in *Home Build-*

ing & Loan Association v. Blaisdell (1934) the Court sustained a debtor relief law despite its retrospective impact.

In 1933, Minnesota enacted a law that gave the state courts the authority to *extend* the redemption period after a foreclosure sale. The law did not wipe out the debt; it only authorized the court to postpone the sale of the property and extend the time during which the owner could redeem it. Before a court could approve an extension of the redemption period, it had to order the mortgagor to pay toward a reasonable rental value of the property. The mortgagee in *Blaisdell* contended that the law violated the contract clause, but the Court rejected the contention.

The Court recognized the economy emergency that the country faced when Minnesota passed the Mortgage Moratorium Law of 1933. Relying on the principle first announced in *West River Bridge Co. v. Dix* (1848) and clarified in later cases, the Court stated that a state always retained a power to react to emergency situations and to protect the security of its people. Minnesota's adoption of this "Mortgage Moratorium" provision fell within this reserved power and, thus, did not violate the Constitution. The Court noted that the authority the mortgage law conferred was of limited duration and would not outlast the emergency it was designed to meet. These considerations underscored the reasonableness of the measure.

When the Court examined "emergency" debtor relief legislation that totally exempted major assets of debtors from creditors' claims or eliminated remedies for claims without protecting the creditors' rights, it found that such actions violated the contract clause. E.g., *W. B. Worthen Co. v. Thomas* (1934). Under *Blaisdell* the state could alter remedies for debts if the legislation reasonably related to a public purpose and protected the basic value of creditor claims; the states were not permitted to significantly impair the basis of creditors' accrued rights in order to improve the economic position of debtors.

Although the Court did void a few state enactments as violative of the contract clause after the *Blaisdell* decision, it did sustain the great majority of state laws against attacks to their constitutionality under the contract clause. Perhaps the best example of the Court's reluctance to use the clause to invalidate state legislation is *El Paso v. Simmons* (1965).

In *El Paso*, Texas had sold land under contract for a small down payment. The purchaser could forfeit his right to the property by failing to make interest payments on the land, but could reinstate his claim to the land by paying in full the overdue interest as long as rights of third parties had not intervened. The reinstatement right had no time limit to its exercise. Some thirty years after the initial sale of the land Texas amended the statute governing the reinstatement right and placed a five-year limit on its exercise.

Simmons contended that the amending legislation violated the contract clause. The Court disagreed. The unlimited reinstatement period had generated a lot of land speculation and also much uncertainty over land titles. In addition, the "promise of reinstatement, whether deemed remedial or substantive, was not the central undertaking of the seller nor the primary consideration for the buyer's undertaking." Laws that "restrict a party to those gains reasonably to be expected from the contract are not subject to attack under the Contract Clause, notwithstanding that they technically alter an obligation of a contract." Therefore, although the law had modified a state's own contractual obligation, the Court sustained the measure as constitutional under the contract clause.

The *United States Trust Co.* Decision—Modification of Government Contracts. In *United States Trust Co. v. New Jersey* (1977) the Court revived declared a New Jersey statute unconstitutional because the law impaired the state's contractual obligation to the bondholders of The Port Authority of New York and New Jersey.

In 1962 the New York and New Jersey legislature decided that the Port Authority should take over and subsidize a bankrupt passenger railroad line that serviced the New York City metropolitan area. To reassure the Port Authority bondholders that the Authority would not be asked in the future to take over mass transit deficit operations beyond the Authority's financial reserves, the two states agreed to limit the number of such operations the Authority would absorb. However, in 1974 New Jersey repealed the legislation that implemented the limitation agreement. The bondholders sought a declaratory judgment that the repealing legislation violated the contract clause because it reduced the financial security of their bonds. The state responded that removing the limitation was necessary to permit the Port Authority to subsidize mass transportation programs for the New York City metropolitan area. The state highlighted the need for the repealing measure by relating it to the energy crisis of 1973 and to the air pollution problems faced by northern New Jersey.

The state was asking the Court to sustain a law that relieved the state of its *own* contractual obligation. Consequently, the Court's customary deference to the legislative judgment was not in order. The state cannot refuse "to meet its legitimate financial obligation simply because it would prefer to spend the money to promote the public good rather than the private welfare of its creditors." Because alternative means were available to promote these goals, the Court reasoned that the repealing measure was both unreasonable and unnecessary. Hence, the Court declared the New Jersey statute unconstitutional because it impaired the state's own obligation of contract without promoting an overriding police power interest.

The *Allied Structural Steel* Decision—Modification of Private Contracts. *Allied Structural Steel Co. v. Spannaus* (1978) invalidated economic legislation that altered *private* contracts. A Minnesota law effectively increased the monetary obligations of companies that had a pre-existing pension plan for employees and that either terminated the plan or closed their business facility in Minnesota. The law required employers to give to employees who had worked for such a company in excess of ten years benefits upon termination or the closing of a plant regardless of the provisions of the employer's pension plan.

Spannaus violated the contract clause because of the following factors: (1) the impairment of contract caused by the law was "substantial;" (2) the plaintiff company had "relied heavily, and reasonably" on actuarial calculations as to the amount of funding necessary to sustain the projected payouts from the pension fund only to incur unexpected additional obligations as a result of the new law; (3) the law was not necessary to remedy an "important and general social problem," but rather focused on a limited number of employers who "had in the past been sufficiently enlightened as voluntarily to agree to establish pension plans;" (4) the law was not a temporary measure to deal with an emergency situation; and (5) the law regulated a field that the state had not previously sought to regulate.

Although *Spannaus* appears to be a limited holding hedged by a number of qualifying factors and tied closely to the facts before the Court, the dissent objected that the case enlarged the scope of the contract clause. The majority, however, refused to give total deference to state legislative decisions concerning the need to alter contractual obligations or to rule that the clause did not apply to alteration of contract terms that merely increased contractual obligations. The Court only held that a state was not free to severely alter contractual obligations or impair contractual rights unless the state could demonstrate that its legislation was a reasonable and narrow means of promoting important societal interests.

Later, *Energy Reserves Group, Inc. v. Kansas Power & Light Co.* (1983) upheld a state law placing a statutory ceiling on price increases that a natural gas supplier could charge a public utility under the escalator clause of a pre-existing contract. To the extent that the law substantially impaired contract rights it was a narrowly tailored means of promoting the important state interest in protecting consumers from imbalance in market prices caused by federal deregulation. Thus, the *Allied Structural Steel Co. v. Spannaus* decision represents only a refusal to abdicate the judicial role in the enforcement of the contract clause, not a return to the pre–1937 model of judicial protection of economic interests.

If legislation affects contracts but it does not substantially impair contract rights in a retroactive manner, there is no significant contracts clause question. If the legislation constitutes a substantial impairment of contracts, then the courts must determine whether the legislation is reasonably tailored to promote a significant and legitimate public purpose that justifies the impairment.

For example, *Keystone Bituminous Coal Association v. DeBenedictis* (1987) upheld a state statute that required that 50 percent of the coal beneath certain structures be kept in place for surface support. The law prohibited types of coal mining would cause subsidence damage to a variety of publicly and privately owned properties. The statute was valid even though it prohibited the extraction of a fixed percentage of the coal owned by persons or corporations who held the "mineral estate" to the underground coal deposits and even though owners of the "surface estate" over these coal deposits had entered contracts with the coal owners waiving any claim for damages that might result from the removal of the coal. The statute did not constitute a taking of property because it allowed owners of the mineral rights to engage in the profitable mining of coal.

The percentage of coal that must to be left in the ground to support the surface estate did not unjustly reduce the investment-backed expectations of the owners of the mineral rights. The owners of the mineral estates alleged that the statute violated the contract clause insofar as it overrode the contractual waiver of liability for surface damage. The Court responded: "it is well settled that the prohibition against impairing the obligation of contracts is not to be read literally."

The Supreme Court upheld legislation that required mine owners to leave sufficient coal in the ground to avoid damage to surface property (or to repair or provide funds for the repair of any surface damage caused by the mine). The new legislatively imposed obligation changed contract rights, but this change did not constitute a violation of the contract clause because the legislature could determine that requiring coal companies to avoid or repair damage to surface property was reasonably tailored to deterring or repairing environmental damage caused by the activities of the miners. This legitimate societal interest justified adjustment of the rights and responsibilities of the parties to the mining contracts.

§ 11.8   Other Forms of Restrictions on Retroactive Legislation

(a) Due Process Limitations

A statute or law that establishes or changes the legal significance of transactions that have occurred *before* its enactment is called "retroactive legislation." The courts traditionally have opposed retroactive legislation because it tends to create instability and also because the legislature can benefit or harm disfavored classes of citizens more easily with retrospective laws than it can with prospective laws. The Constitution reflects this bias against retroactive statutes by prohibiting both the Congress and the states from enacting any ex post facto laws (Article I, § 9, cl. 3, § 10, cl. 1.). The contract clause of the Constitution, discussed in the previous section, also prevents states from passing any legislation that impairs the obligations of contracts.

Besides the explicit constitutional provisions against retroactive laws, the Supreme Court has also used the due process clauses of the Fifth and Fourteenth Amendments to void certain legislation that has a retrospective impact. The federal government may have more latitude to create retroactive legislation under the due process clause than states, which are also regulated by the contract clause.

The framers of the Fifth and Fourteenth Amendment due process clauses, however, did not specifically design those provisions to cover retroactive legislation. Therefore, unlike the contract or ex post facto clauses, the history of the due process clauses fails to provide the Court with any special criteria to determine when retroactive legislation violates constitutional principles. Nevertheless, the cases where retroactive legislation is an issue fall into four main categories and the Court appears to treat each category differently.

The four categories of cases involving retroactive legislation under the due process clause are: (1) cases that involve emergency retroactive legislation; (2) cases that challenge the constitutionality of curative statutes; (3) cases that involve the constitutional merits of retroactive taxing legislation; and (4) cases that contest the constitutionality of retroactive general legislation. Although the constitutional criteria for determining when retroactive legislation will violate due process is unsettled, an analysis of each of these issues help to predict when a certain piece of legislation will infringe on the right to due process of law.

The Tests of The Due Process and Contract Clauses Compared. Although state legislation is subject to due process restrictions against retroactive legislation, any state legislation that violates the contract clause will also violate the Fourteenth Amendment due process clause. For this reason most of the due process cases regarding retroactive legislation are federal cases because the federal government is not subject to the restrictions of the contract clause.

Pension Benefit Guaranty Corp. v. R. A. Gray and Co. (1984) offered the only general principles that the Court has given us regarding the constitutionality of retroactive legislation under due process principles:

> ... the strong deference accorded legislation in the field of national economic policy is no less applicable when that legislation is applied retroactively. Provided that the retroactive application of a statute is supported by a legitimate legislative purpose furthered by rational means, judgments about the wisdom of such legislation remain within the exclusive province of the legislative and executive branches. . . . [R]etroactive legislation does have to meet a burden not faced by legislation that has only future effects. . . . But that burden is met simply by showing that the retroactive application of the legislation is itself justified by a rational legislative purpose.

Retroactive Emergency Legislation. If the constitutionality of retroactive emergency legislation is challenged, the Court usually will sustain the measure and defer to the emergency measures. Consider *Lichter v. United States* (1948). Petitioner contested the constitutionality of the Renegotiation Act of 1942. This wartime measure allowed the War Department to renegotiate any contract it had with private citizens to prevent those citizens from realizing excessive profits from the government contract. The Act applied not only to contracts that arose after the law's enactment but it also applied to uncompleted contracts that the government entered into before the Act's passage. The petitioners challenged the retrospective impact of the measure under the Fifth Amendment.

In sustaining the Renegotiation Act the Court emphasized the history of the Act as a part of the nation's wartime posture. The Court suggested that Congress could have appropriated private enterprise and placed it into a governmental unit for wartime production. Congress, however, by enacting this law did less and preserved private enterprise. Therefore, because Congress unquestionably had the power to act substantively in this area, the Court deferred to the legislative judgment on what was the best approach to restrain private enterprise in an emergency.

The Supreme Court will not always sustain emergency retroactive legislation. *Louisville Joint Stock Land Bank v. Radford* (1935) invalidated an emergency depression measure because it substantially reduced the value of existing mortgages. Although the Court recognized the public interest of saving existing farms from mortgage foreclosure, the retrospective impact of the legislation deprived the mortgagees of the value of their mortgages without due process of law. Two years later the Court upheld a federal statute modified in light of the *Radford* decision: the new statute gave the farmer normally a three-year stay of foreclosure rather than an absolute one; the property, though possessed by the debtor-farmer, was under the custody, supervision, and control of the court. If the debtor failed to pay the reasonable rental, or failed to comply with court orders, or it became evident that he could not reasonably rehabilitate himself financially within the three-year period, or if the emergency ceased to exist, the court could terminate the stay and order a sale. *Wright v. Vinton Branch of the Mountain Trust Bank* (1937).

Curative Statutes. The Court almost always sustains retroactive curative statutes. Curative statutes either ratify prior official conduct or make a remedial adjustment in an administrative scheme.

The issues of *FHA v. The Darlington, Inc.* (1958) began when Congress authorized the Federal Housing Administration to insure mortgages on residential housing for veterans of World War II. The FHA established a policy that housing mortgaged under the FHA program must be residential housing exclusively and not housing for transients. In 1954 Congress ratified that policy by amending the Veterans Emergency Housing Act of 1946 with a provision that codified the FHA policy. The appellee had constructed an apartment building under the FHA program that contained some rentals for transients. When Congress adopted the 1954 Amendment, the appellee sought a declaratory judgment that the Amendment was unconstitutional if it applied to his building. He contended that a retrospective reading of the Amendment would violate his right to due process of law. The Court rejected his argument.

Darlington noted that the appellee was not penalized for anything done in the past. On the contrary, the Court found that the Act had only a prospective effect: "federal regulation of future action based upon rights previously acquired by the person regulated is not prohibited by the Constitution. So long as the Constitution authorizes the subsequently enacted legislation, the fact that its provisions limit or interfere with previously acquired rights does not condemn it."

Several reasons help explain the Court's willingness to sustain curative or remedial legislation. First, curative statutes often are the result of previous court decisions that overrule certain administrative conduct. The curative legislation is simply correcting the statutory flaw. Second, the courts recognize that the smooth functioning of the government is an important public interest. Remedial statutes remove unintended flaws in existing legislation and help give full effect to the legislative intent behind the original legislation.

Retroactive Tax Legislation. Retroactive legislation may violate the ex post facto clauses or the contracts clause under limited circumstances. The due process clauses of the Fifth Amendment and Fourteenth Amendments do not place significant restrictions on retroactive legislation. The Court has adopted the principle that retroactive legislation will violate due process only if the legislation does not have a rational relationship to a legitimate government interest.

Since the Court Packing Plan of 1937, the Court has been very deferential to Congress in upholding retroactive changes in tax laws. In *Welch v. Henry* (1938), for example, the Court upheld a state tax law that was applied to corporate dividends received two years before the law was enacted. A taxpayer subjected to a modified income tax simply received income that became subject to a higher tax rate than the taxpayer anticipated.

The Supreme Court has little difficulty in upholding amendments to income tax laws because of its view that individuals should be on notice that all income may be subject to federal or state taxation at some future time. Congress often increases taxes in order to meet revenue goals. Congress typically considers changes in the Internal Revenue Code for several months prior to their enactment. Statutes modifying the Internal Revenue Code often have a retroactive application of a year or less. The Court concludes that application of such tax changes to a prior tax year is rationally related to the legitimate government interest in raising revenue in accordance with current government economic policies.

United States v. Hemme (1986) upheld a statutory change to gift and estate tax deductions and credit provisions. The new tax law had the effect of retroactively denying a portion of an earlier gift tax exemption to persons who died after a certain date. This law involved a transition from separate estate and gift taxes to a unified tax. The change in the tax law was alleged to result in "double taxation" of some gratuitous transfers of wealth. However, the statute in reality only represented an increase in the tax rate on certain types of economic transactions. *Hemme* held that the due process clause did not bar the application of the higher tax rate, or the so-called double taxation, for the estates of persons dying after a certain date. The tax at issue in *Hemme* did not involve a congressional attempt to create and apply a higher tax rate to the estate of persons who had long since died. In other words, Congress had not created a new tax that would be applied to the estates of persons who had died in earlier calendar years.

United States v. Carlton (1994) involved that issue. The Court unanimously upheld the retroactive application of a 1987 federal estate tax amendment to a person who had died in 1985. The Court ruled that all retroactive tax legislation should be subjected only to the rational relationship test regardless of whether the legislation involved estate, gift, or income taxes. The dispute in *Carlton* involved an estate tax deduction for the sale of stock to an employee stock ownership plan. In the Tax Reform Act of 1986, Congress created a special estate tax deduction for half of the proceeds of the sale to an employees' stock ownership plan of the securities of the business entity that employed the members of the plan. The decedent had died in 1985 but her estate tax return was not filed until the close of 1986, and Congress enacted the amendment in 1987.

In December of 1986, the executor had purchased shares of a large corporation and sold those shares to the corporation's employee stock ownership plan in order to make use of the 1986 deduction. In December of 1987, the estate tax statute was modified so that the deduction would be granted only to the estates of taxpayers who, before their death, owned the securities that were later sold to the employee stock ownership plan. The Internal Revenue Service then disallowed the deduction for the 1986 transactions of the executor, which had been taken on behalf of the taxpayer who had died in 1985.

Although the Court did not emphasize this point, the *Carlton* case did not involve the retroactive application of a wholly new tax to the estate of an individual who had died before the tax statute was enacted. The decedent taxpayer could not have altered her economic plans based upon the section of the estate tax at issue in *Carlton* because both the creation and modification of the estate tax deduction came after the time of her death.

The Court ruled that retroactive tax legislation should be upheld so long as the legislation did not violate the "prohibition against arbitrary and irrational legislation that applies generally to enactments in this sphere of economic policy." (Internal quotation marks and citations omitted.) The retroactive effect of the 1987 Amendment, which extended for only a little more than one year, was rationally related to Congress' attempt to modify the estate tax so that revenues would not be lessened by granting a deduction to those who had made "purely tax-motivated stock transfers."

If a legislature creates a completely new tax, and retroactively applies that tax to economic transactions that occurred many years before the tax was enacted, the retroactive application of the new tax might violate due process.

Retroactive General Legislation. The concepts of reasonable notice and reasonable expectations are important considerations for the Court when it considers the constitutional validity of general retroactive legislation. If the measure affects a remedy, the Court reasons that no one reasonably can expect a remedy to remain immune from legislative controls, and, consequently, it will sustain the retroactive legislation. However, there is no rigid distinction between "rights" and "remedies." Although modification of a remedy normally does not violate due process, if a governmental change to a contract remedy substantially impairs the value of a person's property it may fall under due process principles.

The distinction between a right and a remedy can become hazy. The Court may base the distinction on some type of expectational interest. In cases involving the alteration of statute of limitations, the Court reasons that any reliance on a belief that the legislature will not alter a legislatively created procedural bar to a remedy is unreasonable and cannot rise to the status of a property right. Therefore, the Court will sustain legislation that modifies procedural rules because the expectational interest involved is minimal. The Court generally defers to the legislative judgment on procedural rules with retrospective effects.

Usery v. Turner Elkhorn Mining Co. (1976) showed a great deference to Congress even in cases not involving procedural remedies. Congress enacted legislation that provided benefits to mine workers who had contracted "black lung" disease. Congress placed some of the financial responsibility for the legislation on the coal mine operators. The operators contended that the law violated their right to due process of law because it required them to pay benefits to miners who had left mine employment *before* the effective date of the Act. The operators argued that the Act charged them with a liability that was completely unexpected.

The Court acknowledged that the operators may have been unaware of the danger of the disease. Moreover, the operators may have relied on the current state of the law that had failed to impose any liability on them. Therefore, the Court would not justify the legislation on any theory of deterrence or blameworthiness. Nevertheless, the Court believed the Act met due process. Justice Marshall, writing for the Court, first noted that retroactive legislation is not unconstitutional simply "because it upsets otherwise settled expectations." This measure was justified as a rational method to spread the costs of the mine workers' disabilities to those who have benefitted from their labor. He was unwilling to weigh competing interests to assess the constitutionality of the legislation, and refused "to assess the wisdom of Congress' chosen scheme."

Turner Elkhorn Mining suggests that the legislature generally may overcome the traditional bias against retroactive civil statutes as long as it rationally relates the legislation to a legitimate governmental purpose.

When federal economic legislation restricts private contractual rights a court must determine whether the federal legislation in fact is altering substantive contractual rights in more than a minimal fashion, just as it would if the court was examining the alteration of contractual rights by state legislation under the contracts clause. Recall that the contracts clause only applies to state legislation. The Supreme Court has stated the principle to be applied as follows:

> "When the contract is a private one, and when the impairing statute is a federal one, the next inquiry [after determining that there is a substantial impairment of contractual obligations] is especially limited, and the judicial scrutiny quite minimal. The party asserting a Fifth Amendment due process violation must overcome a presumption of constitutionality and establish that the legislature has acted in an arbitrary and irrational way." *National Railroad Passenger Corp. v. Atchison, Topeka & Santa Fe Railway Co.* (1985).

When the Government Modifies its Own Contractual Obligations. The Court uses a higher level of review of legislation that modifies the government's own contractual obligations than it does to federal legislation that alters or regulates private contracts. The rationale is simple: the government's own self-interest is at stake when it enacts legislation that modifies its own contracts and lessens its obligations.

In *Lynch v. United States* (1934) the plaintiffs were beneficiaries of government insurance issued under the War Risk Insurance Act. The plaintiffs sought to recover amounts allegedly due under the insurance contract but the government resisted because Congress had repealed the law creating the insurance. The plaintiffs contended that the repealing measure violated their right to due process. The Supreme Court agreed. The insurable events occurred while the policy was in force. The insured had paid the premiums. The Fifth Amendment protects rights against the United States arising out of a valid contract. Therefore, Congress cannot annul these rights unless the action taken to void these rights "falls within the federal police power or some other paramount power."

(b) The Ex Post Facto Clauses

The Constitution contains two *ex post facto* clauses: one that applies to the states (Art. I, § 10, cl. 1) and one that applies to the federal government (Art. I, § 9, cl. 3). The clauses limit Congress and state legislatures when enacting *penal* laws that have a retrospective effect. An *ex post facto* law is a statute that imposes criminal liability on past transactions. Early in its history the Supreme Court determined that the *ex post facto* clauses only prohibited the states and the federal government from passing *criminal or penal* measures that had a retroactive effect.

Justice Chase's opinion in *Calder v. Bull* (1798) described four types of laws that would clearly violate the *ex post facto* clauses:

"1st. Every law that makes an action done before the passing of the law and which was innocent when done, criminal; and punishes such action. 2d. Every law that aggravates a crime, or makes it greater than it was, when committed. 3d. Every law that changes the punishment and inflicts a greater punishment, than the law annexed to the crime, when committed. 4th. Every law that alters the legal rules of evidence, and receives less, or different testimony, than the law required at the time of the commission of the offence, in order to convict the offender." (emphasis deleted).

A law that imposes a harsher penalty or a potentially harsher penalty for unlawful conduct than existed before the passage of the law will violate the *ex post facto* prohibition. Even a statute altering penal provisions "accorded by the grace of the legislature" violates the *ex post facto* clause if the statute is both retrospective and harsher than the law in effect at the time of the offense. For example, *Weaver v. Graham* (1981) held that a Florida law which retrospectively reduced the good time credits available to a prisoner violated the *ex post facto* clause.

An *ex post facto* clause violation involves both a change to substantive law and the application of the changed law to a particular defendant. There are three types of *ex post facto* violations. First, the application of a statute to a defendant that would impose a criminal punishment on him for taking an act that was innocent (not punishable under the criminal law) when he took the act would violate the clause. Second, application to a defendant of a statute that increased the punishment for the crime the defendant committed (from the punishment that existed under the substantive law applicable to the defendant's crime at the time that he committed it) would violate the clause. Third, applying, to a defendant's case, a law that removed a defense to the crime that was available under the substantive law at the time that the defendant committed the crime would be an *ex post facto* clause violation.

A mere change in the type of penalty, however, will not violate the provisions. If, for example, a state properly had imposed the death penalty on an individual, altering the form of capital punishment from death by hanging to death by electrocution would not violate the constitutional prohibition on *ex post facto* laws. *Malloy v. South Carolina* (1915). Moreover, the *ex post facto* clauses do not prevent the state legislatures or Congress from *reducing* either the harshness of a penalty or the scope of an existing penal statute. Finally, a legislature can impose a penalty on a person for continuing once lawful conduct that the legislature has subsequently declared illegal.

When Is a Law Penal for Ex Post Facto Purposes? An issue that often arises when a law is challenged under an *ex post facto* clause is whether the legislature has actually imposed a penalty for past conduct. The Supreme Court labeled as punitive a post-Civil War law that required attorneys to take an oath before they could practice law in federal court. *Ex parte Garland* (1866). The attorneys had to swear that they had not participated in the rebellion against the Union. The law was punitive because no lawyer who had participated in the war on the side of the Confederacy would take the oath. Congress was punishing these people although the taking of the oath (and the prior participation) had no relationship to the professional duties of attorneys. Hence, the Court held that the law was penal in nature, applied to past conduct, and violated the *ex post facto* clause.

On the other hand, the Court has held that laws that require deportation for past conduct that did not merit deportation before the deportation law was passed are not penal and hence do not violate the ex post facto rule. *Marcello v. Bonds* (1955). Similarly, the Court has ruled that statutes that deny future privileges to convicted offenders because of their previous criminal activities, are not penal.

Kansas v. Hendricks (1997) held that a statute designed to require the commitment of a person as a "sexually violent predator" is civil in nature, and hence could be applied to a prison inmate who was scheduled for release when the statute was enacted. The purpose of the statute is not "punitive" (to punish the sexual predator for past acts) but forward-looking (to protect the public from future acts).

Procedural Changes. Laws that alter rules of criminal procedure but do not affect the substantive rights of the defendant are not violative of the *ex post facto* clause even though the legislature makes the change during the process of the trial. Laws that change the number of appellate judges or enlarge the potential class of competent witnesses do not affect substantive rights and are constitutional. Such laws do not impose an increased penalty for past conduct.

A law that changed the procedures for imposition of the death penalty could be applied to a person whose crime predated the change. *Dobbert v. Florida* (1977) involved a defendant sentenced to death for murder in Florida. When the defendant committed the murder, Florida had a statute imposing the death sentence for that crime. However the state supreme court invalidated the procedures for imposing this sentence. Then, the state legislature passed a new statute for imposing the penalty that met current constitutional standards. The defendant was sentenced under this statute and the U.S. Supreme Court upheld this sentence. This new statute was only a change in procedure because the old statute had declared that murder was a capital offense, thus giving the defendant fair notice. Because the new statute made imposition of the penalty more difficult, the majority saw it as "ameliorative."

When a legislature changes procedures that apply to the sentencing of a convicted criminal between the date of the crime and the date of a defendant's sentencing, the courts must determine whether the statutory changes are truly procedural or whether they effectively increase the nature of the penalty for the previously committed crime. If the sentencing procedures change the nature of the punishment for the crime they cannot be applied to a defendant who committed the crime before the date when the statutory changes became effective.

Laws That Aggravate Crimes. Another category of legislative actions that constitute an *ex post facto* law are any "law that aggravates a crime or makes it greater than it was, when committed." Until the twenty-first century, it was unclear whether the extension of a statute of limitations for prosecution of a crime would constitute an increased punishment that would be invalid under Justice Chase's description of prohibited *ex post facto* clause legislation.

Stogner v. California (2003) held that a law enacted *after* a previously applicable statute of limitations period had run for a criminal activity violated the *ex post facto* clause when the law applied to a previously time-barred prosecution. *Stogner* involved a 1998 criminal statute that allowed for prosecution of sex-related crimes to children within one year of a victim's report to the police, even if the crime had been committed at a time when there was a specific statute of limitations that would have barred prosecution for the offense. Because of the new California law, which was enacted in 1998, the defendant was indicted for sex-related child abuse activities committed prior to 1974. At the time that the alleged crimes had been committed by the defendant, California had had a three year statute of limitations regarding the sex abuse crimes. The Court held that defendant could not be prosecuted for the crimes for which the statute of limitations had previously been expired without a violation of the *ex post facto* clause. *Stogner* did not rule on whether extensions of unexpired statutes of limitations would violate the *ex post facto* clause. Justice Breyer stated the Court's conclusion narrowly: "We conclude that a law enacted after expiration of a previously applicable limitations period violates the *ex post facto* clause when it is applied to revive a previously time-barred prosecution."

Laws That Alter the Rules of Evidence. Another category of *ex post facto* law are laws that alter the rules of evidence so that less or different testimony can be used to convict the defendant than what was required at the time that the defendant committed the crime. Laws that merely change evidentiary rules, such as laws that increase the types of people who are competent to be witnesses at a trial, do not constitute an *ex post facto* law because the law would neither increase the defendant's punishment nor lower the type or amount of evidence that could be used to establish the defendant's criminality. It is sometimes difficult to determine whether a law that nominally changes only evidentiary rules actually is a law that changed the quantum of proof necessary to convict a defendant.

Carmell v. Texas (2000) examined a case where a man had been convicted of twenty criminal charges relating to his sexual assault and sexual abuse of his stepdaughter when she was between the ages of 12 to 16 years old. Prior to the defendant's trial, state law did not allow a person to be convicted of an alleged sexual offense against another person based on the uncorroborated testimony of the victim, unless the victim was younger than 14 years of age at the time of the offense. Before a defendant's trial, the legislature changed the state law to allow convictions for such crimes based solely on the uncorroborated statement of a victim who was under 18 years of age at the time that the alleged offense occurred. In *Carmell* the defendant was convicted on four counts of sexually abusing the victim for acts that occurred when the child was 14 years of age or older, which was when the state evidentiary law would not have allowed conviction on those offenses based solely on the uncorroborated testimony of an alleged victim over 14 years of age. The Court ruled (5 to 4) that the defendant's conviction on those four counts of alleged sexual abuse, based solely on the uncorroborated testimony of the victim, violated the ex-post facto clause. The statutory change reduced the "minimum quantum of evidence necessary to sustain a conviction." For that reason, the law could not be applied retroactively to an offense that had been committed when a higher quantum of evidence was required for conviction. The four dissenting Justices believed that the law did not act so as to change the quantum of evidence necessary but, rather, merely allowed the testimony of a person between the ages of 14 and 18 to be considered credible.

(c) Bills of Attainder

Traditionally, bills of attainder were legislative acts that imposed the death penalty without the usual judicial proceedings on persons allegedly guilty of serious crimes. If the legislature imposed a lesser punishment than the death penalty, the measure was called, historically, a bill of pains and penalties. The Constitution contains two bills of attainder clauses—one that applies to the states (Art. I, § 10, cl. 1) and one that applies to the federal government (Art. I, § 9, cl. 3). The Court has held that these provisions prohibit both bills of attainder and bills of pains and penalties.

The bill of attainder provisions prohibit the state or federal legislatures from assuming judicial functions and conducting trials. Consequently, the clauses proscribe any legislative act "no matter what [its] form, that appl[ies] either to named individuals or to easily ascertainable members of a group in such a way as to inflict *punishment* on them without a judicial trial." This clause only protects individuals, not entities such as states.

Because any legislative act that employs a classification might be said to burden or punish the class of persons who do not receive the benefits established by the legislation or who are disadvantaged by the classification, the Court has developed various tests to determine when the law inflicts prohibited punishment: the mere fact that a law imposes burdensome consequences does not mean that there is the forbidden "punishment." Rather the courts must determine first whether the law imposes a punishment "traditionally judged to be prohibited by the Bill of Attainder Clause." Such historical punishments include "imprisonment, banishment, and the punitive confiscation of property by the sovereign, [and] a legislative enactment barring designated individuals or groups from participation in specified employments or vocations, a mode of punishment commonly employed against those legislatively banded as disloyal." *Nixon v. Administrator of General Services* (1977).

Second, in addition to this historical test, the Court has developed a functional test: can the law reasonably be said to further nonpunitive goals, given the type and severity of the burdens imposed? For example, a law is a bill of attainder if its purpose is to "purge the governing boards of labor unions of those whom Congress regards as guilty of subversive acts...." *United States v. Brown* (1965).

Third, the Court looks to the legislative motivation: does the legislative record evidence a congressional intent to punish? For purpose of this test the Court looks to the legislative record, floor debates, and so on. It also examines the features of the law to see if it demonstrates any punitive interpretation.

Fourth, the Court finds it "often useful to inquire into the existence of less burdensome alternatives by which [the] legislature could have achieved its legitimate nonpunitive objectives." The Court determines whether the legislative judgment is "rational and fair-minded." *United States v. Brown* (1965).

The bill of attainder clauses do not replace equal protection analysis and should be used only to invalidate legislative punishments.

A bill of attainder is a legislatively declared punishment (often with a legislative finding of guilt regarding some crime or activity) for certain specific individuals. A bill of attainder may name the individuals or it may describe a class of persons subject to punishment because of specific conduct when in effect the description of that conduct operates to designate particular persons. If legislation denies a benefit or imposes a burden upon persons who have engaged in particular conduct, the law will be invalid as a bill of attainder if the law imposes "punishment" on those persons. The law will be upheld if it denies a benefit to individuals whose past conduct might reasonably be said to make them ineligible for the benefit. The legislature, in defining eligibility by conduct, may further a nonpunitive governmental interest.

For example, if the legislature enacted a law stating that all doctors who had worked at a specific hospital would thereafter be ineligible to practice medicine, the law will likely be a bill of attainder. The conduct used to define the group relates merely to identifying persons for punishment rather than identifying any reasonable trait which would make someone unfit to practice medicine. However, if the legislature prohibited persons previously convicted of committing medical malpractice from continuing to practice medicine the legislation likely will be upheld as establishing nonpunitive licensing criteria. Thus, if the litigant claims that legislation constitutes a bill of attainder, the Court must determine whether the designation of persons based on past conduct simply names individuals for punishment or whether the designation promotes a *nonpunitive* goal based on reasonable criteria over which the individual has some control.

The Court has used the prohibition against bills of attainder to void a congressional measure that prevented the payment of salaries to three named federal employees because the House of Representatives believed the three were subversives. *United States v. Lovett* (1946). Similarly, the Court invalidated a law that declared unlawful the employment of a member of the Communist Party in a labor union. *United States v. Brown* (1965). The Court reasoned that the law impermissibly designated a class of persons (members of the Communist Party) for punishment.

The Court upheld a municipal ordinance that required municipal employees to take an oath that they were never members of the Communist Party or any similar organization that advocated the violent overthrow of the government. *Garner v. Board of Public Works of Los Angeles* (1951). The Court believed that the ordinance only established eligibility for employment.

Nixon v. Administrator of General Services (1977) sustained the Presidential Recordings and Materials Preservation Act, which former President Nixon challenged on the ground that it constituted a bill of attainder because it provided for governmental custody of only his presidential papers. The Court ruled that the statute was not a bill of attainder because the law did not inflict punishment and was nonpunitive. The Act merely set the policy that historical materials should be preserved. Furthermore, the Act did not become a bill of attainder merely because it applied only to President Nixon, who was a "legitimate class of one" because the papers of all other past Presidents were already safely housed in libraries.

Selective Service System v. Minnesota Public Interest Research Group (1984) upheld a federal statute that denied federal higher education financial assistance to male students who had failed to register for the draft. The Court, as a matter of statutory interpretation, held that the statute allows male students to receive these federal benefits even though they registered more than thirty days after their eighteenth birthday, in violation of federal law requiring registration within that period. Because the statute allowed late registration, the Court had little problem holding that the statute was not a bill of attainder. The statute denied benefits to persons based on past conduct but the conduct did not merely define persons the legislature wished to punish, because the group disqualified for benefits was not defined "by irreversible acts committed by them." Moreover, even if the statute defined a specific group for denial of a benefit, the statute, in the Court's view, still did not constitute a bill of attainder because it was not punitive in nature. Although the denial of federal educational benefits might be quite serious, "the severity of a sanction is not determinative of its character as punishment."

This opinion summarized the test to determine whether denial of a benefit to a discreet group of individuals constitutes a punishment and attainder:

"In deciding whether a statute inflicts forbidden punishment, we have recognized three necessary inquiries: (1) whether the challenged statute falls within the historical meaning of legislative punishment; (2) whether the statute, viewed in terms of the type and severity of burdens imposed, reasonably can be said to further nonpunitive legislative purposes; and (3) whether the legislative record evinces a congressional intent to punish."

The Court concluded that the legislation reasonably furthered nonpunitive goals in limiting federal aid to those persons who "meet their responsibilities to the United States by registering with the Selective Service." Also, "the legislative history provides convincing support" that Congress sought by this law to "promote compliance with the draft registration requirement and fairness in the allocation of scarce federal resources" rather than to inflict punishment.

§ 11.9 The Taking of Property Interests: Introduction

One of the powers of sovereign governments is the ability to take privately owned property by paying adequate compensation. This authority is called the power of eminent domain. Both the federal government and the individual state governments possess the power of eminent domain. Scholars and judges generally classify eminent domain as an incidental power and a means of fulfilling other governmental responsibilities.

The term "police power" is often used to define the panoply of governmental power, including the power of government to take acts that promote the public health, safety, welfare or morals. But in the area of eminent domain cases and analysis, "police power" is used more narrowly to designate only the power of government to regulate the use of land and property *without* paying compensation. Commentators of the law of eminent domain view that power as distinct from such powers as the general police power and the power to tax.

§ 11.10 Limitations on the Exercise of Eminent Domain

The term "eminent domain" is said to have originated with Grotius, the seventeenth century legal scholar. Grotius believed that the state possessed the power to take or destroy property for the benefit of the social unit, but he believed that when the state so acted, it was obligated to compensate the injured property owner for his losses.

Blackstone, too, believed that society had no general power to take the private property of landowners, except on the payment of a reasonable price. The just compensation clause of the Fifth Amendment to the Constitution was built upon this concept of a moral obligation to pay for governmental interference with private property.

The natural law philosophy that so greatly affected the development of American political and legal thought also had an impact on the law of eminent domain. Early state court cases held that limitations on eminent domain existed independently of written constitutions. The eminent domain clause of the Fifth Amendment was not seen as creating a new legal restriction on the exercise of the power but rather as recognizing the existence of a principle of natural justice. In the first half of the nineteenth century state courts applied this theory of natural law to protect private property interests from state appropriations.

State governments, as political sovereigns, also possess the power of eminent domain. State constitutions now almost universally require that landowners be compensated when their property is taken by the state for a public use. Only two of the original state constitutions adopted between 1776 and 1780, however, required states to pay compensation when private property was taken for a public use. Nevertheless, state courts applied doctrines of natural justice to require that such takings be made only for public uses and only upon the payment of just compensation.

In two 1896 cases, the Supreme Court finally held that the due process clause required that land taken by the state be used for a public purpose. It was not until a year later, that *Chicago, Burlington & Quincy R.R. Co. v. Chicago* (1897), held that the due process clause of the Fourteenth Amendment not only required the statute to follow a prescribed procedure, but also required that the state take the property for a public purpose and compensate the property owner for his loss.

Although some cases and commentators have viewed these Supreme Court decisions as incorporating the compensation clause into the Fourteenth Amendment, this view does not appear strictly correct. Rather the Court appears to have found independent public use and just compensation requirements inherent in the definition of due process. Today, the Supreme Court itself cites the *Chicago, Burlington & Quincy R.R. Co. v. Chicago* decision as incorporating the compensation clause into the Fourteenth Amendment.

§ 11.11   The "Taking" Issue

(a) Introduction

The Fifth Amendment provides that the Federal Government may not "take" private property without just compensation. The central issue in many eminent domain cases is whether the governmental interference amounts to a "taking". Although the concept of a taking may originally have contemplated only physical appropriation, it is plain today that non-acquisitive governmental action may amount to a taking in a constitutional sense, as discussed in the next subsection.

The takings clause of the Fifth Amendment has been incorporated into the due process clause of the Fourteenth Amendment. Therefore, state and local governments may not "take" property for "public use" without payment of "just compensation. "

The issue whether a government action is a "taking" is distinct from the issue of whether a government action, in itself, is unconstitutional. For example, if a factory owner attacks a state law regulating the amount of pollution that goes into the air from a certain type of factory, there are separate due process and takings clause issues. The factory owner may assert that the government does not have the power to regulate his business activity simply to improve the environment. That claim would involve a substantive due process challenge to the law. As we have seen, a court will uphold the law so long as the government has a rational basis for concluding that regulating smoke promoted some legitimate end of government (such as protecting the environment). After the court determined, as it surely would, that the government had the power to regulate air pollution, it will address the question whether the regulation so interfered with property rights of the factory owner as to amount to a "taking." If there is a taking, the court then determines what compensation is due. In assessing whether the government regulation is a taking, a court will not ask whether the government action in fact promotes a legitimate interest of government; the court decided that question when it held that there was no substantive due process violation.

In *Lingle v. Chevron U.S.A. Inc.* (2005) the Supreme Court Justices unanimously disavowed dicta in earlier cases that would have led lower courts to question whether a government action promoted a legitimate government interest when making a determination of whether that government action constituted a taking of property. In other words, a court must not inquire whether a government action in fact promotes a legitimate interest, when the court determines whether the government action should be deemed a "taking," so as to require that just compensation be paid to a property owner.

We examine the categories of takings in § 11.11. All taking of property occurs in one of the following ways:

- The government "takes" property (and hence must pay compensation) if it physically occupies it, unless emergency conditions justify the government action.

- A taking occurs if the government transfers the right to occupy property from a property owner to another person. Thus, if the government decrees that a property owner must give a right of access to his or her property to the public, the government will owe the property owner just compensation for the fair market value of the property easement it has taken from the owner. However, no taking occurs when the government prohibits the owner of business property from excluding persons based on personal traits such as race, religion, or sex. Business property already is substantially regulated, and the property, such as the department store, restaurant, etc., is already open to the general public.

• If the government intentionally harms the property of an individual, it will owe just compensation for the value of the property damage, unless the government action is justified by emergency circumstances.

• If the government requires the owner of land to transfer an easement (a right of access to the property) to the public in exchange for the right to develop the land, the action will constitute a taking unless the value of the easement taken from the property owner is "roughly proportional" to the cost imposed on society by the type of land development that the property owner will undertake.

• If the government creates zoning or land use regulations that permanently reduce the value of real property (land) to zero value, the government will owe just compensation to the owner of the real property.

• Some property use regulations may result in such an unfair and unjust shifting of social costs to a limited group of property owners that the regulation will be deemed a taking, so that compensation must be paid to those property owners.

In regulatory takings cases, the court will balance the nature of the costs imposed on the individual against the benefits to society from the regulation. Only rarely will a court find that government regulation of property use constituted a taking of property. Nevertheless, when the property owner challenges a regulatory act as being a taking of property, a court will have to consider: the economic impact of the regulation; the extent to which the regulation interferes with the property owner's investment-backed expectations; and the character of the government action.

Connolly v. Pension Benefit Guaranty Corporation (1986) upheld federal legislation that required an employer who was withdrawing from a multiemployer pension plan to pay a share of the plan's unfunded vested benefits even though the original pension plan trust agreement did not establish liability. The Court held that this was not a taking of property but only a reasonable economic regulation, even though the law required the employer to pay money to a pension benefit system in order to help specific workers. Many types of economic regulations result in economic costs being imposed on one class of persons or businesses and economic benefits being awarded to another group. However, these laws normally will not constitute a taking of property because they are really economic regulations in the public interest.

In determining whether this regulation of property is a taking of property, the Court said that three factors were of particular importance:

> "(1) 'the economic impact of the regulation on the claimant [the person who was required to pay money or whose property suffered a diminution in value]'; (2) 'the extent to which the regulation has interfered with distinct investment-backed expectations'; (3) 'the character of the governmental action.'"

Because the imposition of liability on employers withdrawing from the pension plans was not a direct government use of property but only the establishment of a program that "adjusted the benefits and burdens of economic life to promote the common good," it was not a direct interference with property rights. The economic obligation imposed on a withdrawing employer was not necessarily "out of proportion to its experience with the plan." The employers who participated in the pension plans should have been aware that pension plans would be subject to government regulation to protect employees. Thus, the pension plan regulation was not a taking of property. After *Connolly*, the three listed factors should apply in all cases where judges must determine whether an economic regulation constitutes a taking of property.

There is uncertainty regarding the nature of interests that the takings clause protects, as illustrated in *Eastern Enterprises v. Apfel* (1998). In this case five justices, but without a majority opinion, concluded that Industry Retiree Health Benefit Act (Coal Act) was unconstitutional in requiring a former operator to fund health benefits for retired miners who had worked for the operator before it left the coal industry. However, there was not a majority who could agree on which clause of the Fifth Amendment was violated. Justice O'Connor, writing a plurality opinion for four members of the Court, found that the assessment against Eastern Enterprises violated the takings clause of the Fifth Amendment. Justice Kennedy concurred in the judgment of the Court in *Eastern Enterprises*, but dissented from the plurality's takings clause analysis. He believed that the monetary assessment against Eastern Enterprises was the type of retroactive governmental action that violated the due process clause, even though it did not, in his view, involve a taking of property.

The four dissenting Justices in *Eastern Enterprises* believed both that there was no basis for using the takings clause to determine the constitutionality of the assessment against Eastern Enterprises and that the Court should defer to Congress concerning economic and social welfare legislation.

(b) Property Use Regulations

The Early Cases. In *Pennsylvania Coal Co. v. Mahon* (1922) a state statute prohibited the mining of coal in such a way as to cause the subsidence (the sinking down) of certain types of improved property. The issue before the Court was whether, through the exercise of its police power, the state could destroy the coal company's mining rights without compensation. The Court, per Justice Holmes, held the state must pay compensation.

Although the opinion noted that values incident to property could be reduced by non-compensable use regulation, Holmes stated that, "when [regulation] reaches a certain magnitude, in most if not in all cases, there must be an exercise of eminent domain and compensation to sustain the act." Under this view, the police power and eminent domain exist in a continuum. Once regulation went so far, there was a "taking" and the state has to pay compensation to the injured land owner. Here the extent of the regulation was so great as to constitute a taking: "To make it commercially impracticable to mine certain coal has nearly the same effect for constitutional purposes as appropriating or destroying it."

Contrast *Euclid v. Ambler Realty Co.* (1926), which upheld, for the first time the constitutionality of a comprehensive land use regulatory ordinance. In 1922 the Village Council of Euclid adopted a comprehensive zoning ordinance. The statute restricted the location of trades, industries, apartment houses, two-family houses, single-family houses and other land uses. The plan also regulated aspects of property use such as the size of lots and the size and heights of buildings.

The plaintiffs complained that the zoning ordinance deprived the property owner of liberty and property without due process of law, and that the use classifications deprived him of equal protection of law. The issue was whether the owner was unconstitutionally deprived of property "by attempted regulations under the guise of the police power, which are unreasonable and confiscatory." The Court rejected the claims and concluded that the statute was a valid police power regulation because there was a sufficient public interest in the segregation of incompatible land uses to justify the diminution of property values. Since *Euclid*, the Court, with few exceptions, has rejected due process and equal protection challenges to the zoning power.

In two cases, considered shortly after *Euclid*, the Court invalidated land use regulation as a violation of due process. *Washington ex rel. Seattle Title Trust Co. v. Roberge* (1928) struck down an ordinance that allowed for the issuance of use variances upon the two-thirds consent of surrounding landowners. The Court said the variance provision violated due process because the surrounding landowners would be free to withhold consent for arbitrary and capricious reasons. However, the Court later said there is no due process violation when a general referendum can grant exemptions from zoning requirements.

Nectow v. Cambridge (1928), a confusing case, struck down a zoning ordinance on the ground that it deprived the plaintiff landowner of property without due process of law. The Court held that a zoning restriction "cannot be imposed if it does not bear a substantial relation to the public health, safety, morals or general welfare." The Court said that regulation of the plaintiff's land was not necessary to promote the general welfare of the city's inhabitants. *Nectow* did not dispute the legitimate nature of the zoning power; it only found that an individual landowner was denied due process when his land was arbitrarily classified.

Federal Judicial Review of Zoning Laws and Property Use Regulations as Takings of Property. After these early zoning cases the Supreme Court withdrew from the area for an extended period and allowed the state courts to develop rules governing the permissible scope of zoning regulation. However, in *Goldblatt v. Town of Hempstead* (1962), the Court reexamined the constitutionality of zoning regulation and upheld an expansive power of local government to regulate land use. The landowner held a thirty-eight acre tract within the town of Hempstead. He used the land as a sand and gravel quarry continuously since 1927. The town, having grown around the quarry, attempted to restrict the quarry's operation. In 1958, the town amended its zoning ordinance to prohibit any excavation below the water-line, which effectively prohibited continuance of the use to which the property had been devoted.

Emphasizing that there was a presumption that the statute was constitutional, the Court upheld the ordinance, finding "no indication that the prohibitory effect of the [ordinance was] sufficient to render it an unconstitutional taking...." The Court adopted a two-part test to determine validity. First it must appear that "the interests of the public ... require such interference; and, second, that the means are reasonably necessary for the accomplishment of the purpose, and not unduly oppressive upon individuals." After evaluating the nature of the menace caused by the quarry, the availability of less drastic steps, and the loss suffered by the landowner, the Court found the statute constitutional.

Hence, only the most unusual and totally arbitrary zoning ordinance or property use regulation will require the granting of compensation to a property owner. So long as the zoning ordinance reasonably advances some arguable "police power" interest and does not literally transfer an existing property interest of the owner to the government or other parties, it is unlikely that the zoning of property will require compensation.

Eliminating the entire value of land—a per se taking. *Lucas v. South Carolina Coastal Council* (1992) ruled that "when the owner of real property has been called to sacrifice *all* economically beneficial uses in the name of the common good, that is, to leave his property economically idle, he has suffered a taking." If the value of real property is completely eliminated by governmental actions (regardless of whether those actions were called regulatory by the government), the government can only defend its action (as being something other than a taking) by showing that the owner had acquired title to the property subject to regulations that eliminated all of the economically beneficial uses for the property.

Lucas involved a property owner who had purchased two residential lots in what was eventually deemed a coastal zone; government actions taken after the owner purchased the lots prohibited the construction of any building that could be occupied, and eliminated any development of the property. The lower courts found that the property was rendered completely "valueless," a finding not challenged on appeal.

The state supreme court had argued that the total deprivation of value in the coastal land was not a taking of property because it believed that the act promoted an important societal interest (in protecting the coast line) and prevented the owner from using this land in a harmful manner (by altering the beauty and nature of the coast line). The Supreme Court found that irrelevant to the question of whether the state owed compensation for a taking.

Lucas is an important, but limited, ruling. Three points, in particular, must be kept in mind. First, *Lucas* establishes a per se rule that will require a finding of a taking of property when governmental actions result in the total loss of all economically beneficial use of real property. Second, *Lucas* does not apply to the governmental regulations of personal property. *Lucas* stated that the state's "traditionally high degree of economic control over commercial dealings" left open the possibility that some regulations that prohibited sale or manufacture for sale of personal property might be upheld even if those regulations made the personal property totally valueless. Third, *Lucas* reinforces the judicial role in examining the question of when regulatory actions of government constitute a taking of property.

The per se rule established by the *Lucas* decision applies only when a government action results in the permanent loss of virtually all economically beneficial use of real property. If the government temporarily bans development of a parcel of land, whether by a statutory moratorium on development pending the revision of land use ordinances or a delay in the granting of a building permit, the government action does not constitute a total loss in the economic value of the land, and, therefore, that government action is not to be deemed a per se taking of property under *Lucas*. A temporary prohibition of land development should be examined under the multi-factor balancing test adopted by the Supreme Court in other land use regulation cases. When using the multi-factor balancing test, courts must consider the economic impact of the regulation, the diminution in investment-backed expectations of the property owner, and the nature of the government interest as well as the reasonableness of the regulation.

Tahoe–Sierra Preservation Council, Inc. v. Tahoe Regional Planning Agency (2002) reviewed government actions that prohibited the development of parcels of land near Lake Tahoe for over thirty months. The landowners in the case wanted to develop property that was subject to the control of the Tahoe Regional Planning Council, which had been established by a multi-state compact. The two moratoria adopted by the agency resulted in a period of 32 months during which there could be no development of the land. Following that 32 month time period, litigation that California (one of the parties to the compact) started further delayed land development.

Tahoe–Sierra considered only whether the 32 month ban on the development of the landowners' property constituted a per se taking. Justice Stevens, for the Court, held that temporary bans on development did not constitute a *per se* taking of property requiring compensation. *Tahoe–Sierra*, found that an independent analysis of the history and purposes of the takings clause did not justify creation of a new *per se* rule that would require the government to pay compensation whenever there was a temporary ban on property use. In the view of the majority, property owners must expect that a variety of government actions will result in their having to wait to develop property. Stevens described the ability to build on property within a certain time period as merely one aspect of a parcel or bundle of rights that the owner had in the property.

Justice Stevens emphasized that the Court was not ruling that temporary delays in the ability of a property owner to develop the property would never constitute a taking. Instead, *Tahoe–Sierra* only ruled that the courts should evaluate temporary restrictions on property development by looking at all of the relevant facts and circumstances in the particular case to determine whether "fairness and justice" required a judicial finding that the government action causing the delay constituted a taking of property for which compensation is required under the Fifth Amendment takings clause. When a court examines a challenge to a temporary ban on property development, that court should consider the economic impact of the ban on the investment-backed expectations of the property owners, the nature of the government's interest, and the relationship of the temporary ban to the promotion of legitimate government interests.

General Property Use Regulations. In *Agins v. Tiburon* (1980), Justice Powell, for a unanimous Court, stated that the determination of whether property has been taken by a zoning ordinance requires a judicial weighing of private and public interest. *Agins* involved an "open space" zoning ordinance that required the owners of a five acre tract of land to build no more than five single-family residences on their property. Prior to the zoning the property owners might have been able to subdivide their land into smaller parcels and allow for the development of more single-family dwellings. However, the government's interest in "assuring careful and orderly development of residential property with provision for open space areas" outweighed the property owner's interest in avoiding any diminution in the market value of their land. The Court engaged in a balancing of the public and private interest and concluded that: "It cannot be said that the impact of general land use regulations has denied the appellants the 'justice and fairness' guaranteed by the Fifth and Fourteenth Amendments."

Some lower federal judges misinterpreted dicta in *Agins* to authorize a judicial inquiry into whether a government action in fact promoted a legitimate governmental interest. *Lingle v. Chevron U.S.A. Inc.* (2005) made clear that *Agins* used the balancing test of earlier cases, such as *Penn Central. Agins* does not authorize judges to make an independent determination of whether the government action in fact promoted a legitimate government interest.

A zoning ordinance, or other property use regulation, will constitute a taking of property for which compensation is due, if the regulation unjustifiably shifts social costs to an individual property owner or a group of property owners. When a court upholds a zoning or property use statute "on its face," it is only holding that the statute does not constitute a per se taking of property from all persons whose property is regulated by the statute. A particular government statute regulating property use may not constitute a taking on its face but may still constitute a taking for which just compensation is due if the statute, as applied to an individual item of property or property owner, deprives a property owner of the value of the property.

Keystone Bituminous Coal Association v. DeBenedictis (1987) held that a state statute and administrative regulatory system that required the owners of subsurface mineral rights to leave 50% of the coal in the ground below certain types of structures and surfaces was not a taking of property for which just compensation was due. The purpose of this rule was to protect a wide variety of public and private uses of surface property. The statute was not merely a wealth transfer from the coal owners to the private owners of surface property rights. The mining restriction was not declared a taking on its face because it did not make the mining of coal impractical or in any sense unprofitable. Regardless of statutory restrictions, the technological state of the mining industry already required that the mining interests leave a significant percentage of coal in the ground. The statute imposed, in the majority's view, only a slight and reasonable diminution in the value and investment-backed expectations of coal company operations. The Court was unwilling to find that a statute requiring a percentage of coal to be left in the ground was a physical appropriation of that coal. The "test for regulatory takings requires us to compare the value that has been taken from the property with the value that remains in the property ...". Because the statute promoted a significant public interest, and resulted in only a slight diminution in value of mining operations, no taking was found.

However, *Keystone* did not eliminate the possibility that an individual owner of subsurface coal rights might have his property taken. If an individual property owner could show that the application of the mining restriction to his property eliminated any economically viable use of the subsurface coal rights for that particular area, the Court might find that the property owner was owed just compensation by the government.

Landmark Zoning—The *Penn Central* Case. *Penn Central Transportation Co. v. New York* (1978) held that the New York City Landmarks Preservation Law, consistently with due process, could limit building rights in the vicinity of the historic Grand Central Station. The limitation imposed by New York's Landmarks Preservation Commission did not constitute a "taking" or otherwise require exercise of the eminent domain power.

Under the New York law, the Landmark Preservation Commission could designate property as a "landmark," and "landmark site," or a "historic district." This designation was then approved by higher administrative authority in light of New York's overall zoning plan, and was ultimately subject to judicial review. Designation carried with it certain restrictions on the use of designated property, among which were that the owner must keep the property in "good repair," and that the commission had to approve alterations of the external appearance of the property. There was judicial review for denial of approval. New York law also provided, however, for certain benefits to owners of property designated by the commission. Chief among these was the right of the owner to transfer unused development rights from restricted property to nearby property that had not been restricted by the commission. The effect of this allowance was to permit owners of both non-historic property and property designated as historic to exceed existing zoning regulations on the development of their non-historic property to the extent that development had been curtailed by the Landmark Law on their nearby historic property. This allowance was intended to mitigate much of the economic deprivation that would inevitably result from development restrictions on historic property.

In *Penn Central*, the Landmark Preservation Commission had denied Penn Central permission to build a multi-story office building above Grand Central Station. The Commission concluded that "to balance a 55–story office tower above a flamboyant Beaux–Arts facade seems nothing more than an aesthetic joke...." Rather than refrain from the endeavor and transfer its unused building rights to its other adjacent property, however, Penn Central sought review of the commission's decision.

Penn Central ruled that there had been no "taking" of property, and the regulations were a reasonable means of promoting important general welfare interests in environmental control and historic preservation. The Court did, however, specifically note that the fact that the law created transferred development rights mitigated the loss to owners of historic property, and was thus a factor both in the finding that the law itself was a reasonable exercise of the police powers and in the finding that the magnitude of Penn Central's loss did not rise to the level of a "taking."

The *Penn Central* case involved a type of "spot zoning," a term often used to describe a government regulation that is applicable only to one specific parcel of land. In *Penn Central*, the government regulated a unique parcel of land in order to promote the public interest in the protection of a historic landmark. Because the owners of Grand Central Station, following the spot zoning, still received a reasonable return on their investment by developing and managing the property within the regulatory limits, *Penn Central* found that the spot zoning regulation did not constitute a taking of property.

The *Palazzolo* Case. Let us assume that in 1970 Mr. Able, who was then 35 years old, purchased a 100 acre tract of land to fulfill his lifelong dream of owning his own farm. He used 80 of the acres of this land for his residence, farm buildings and crops that he grew and sold, but 20 acres of the property was not usable for farming, because it was covered with water throughout much of the year. We will refer to the 20 acres that were not usable as "wetland."

We will also assume that, in 1980 the state government enacted a law that prohibits any development of wetland that is used as a habitat by certain types of birds. This legislation allows a government established land use board to grant an owner of wetland permission to develop the wetland if the Board determines that the intended use of the land, for which the waiver is sought, would serve an overriding need.

In 1990, Mr. Able applied to the land use board [the Board] for a permit to farm the final 20 acres of his land, which had been designated as a wetland area. Mr. Able waited until 1990 to apply for the permit, because that was the first time when it would be economically practical to drain the land and use it for farming. The Board turned down Mr. Able's application in 1990. A lawyer advised Mr. Able that he might be able to have the land use statute or the denial of his permit be declared an invalid taking of property without just compensation. Nevertheless, Mr. Able decided not to appeal from, or otherwise challenge, the ruling of the government board.

In the year 2000, Mr. Able decided to retire from farming and to sell his land. He sold the entire 100 acre tract to Ms. Baker, an entrepreneur who previously had successfully established several industrial parks and residential developments. Mr. Able sold the property to Ms. Baker for $800,000. Indeed, the fair market value of the land, subject to the wetlands restrictions and assuming the 20 wetland acres could not be developed, was exactly $800,000. However, if the wetlands legislation were repealed, or if the Board would allow development of the 20 acres, the fair market value of the land would be $1,000,000.

In 2001, after purchasing the land for $800,000, Ms. Baker submitted a plan to the Board for development of the entire 100 acre tract of land as a business center. She asked for permission to fill in the 20 acres and to make the entire 100 acres a place where a variety of high technology (non-polluting) businesses might locate offices and research facilities. The types of uses that Ms. Baker planned for the land were entirely consistent with all state and local zoning laws, except for her intended use of the 20 acres of wetlands. In other words, Mrs. Baker could have developed an 80 acre business center without securing a waiver. The Board turned down Ms. Baker's development plan by refusing to grant her a waiver for the development of the wetlands area. Ms. Baker chose not to submit a new plan for the use of the land. Instead, she brought suit against the government for taking her property by denying her the ability to fully develop the 100 acres.

Our Able–Baker hypothetical would present three questions that should be fairly easy to analyze. First, should Ms. Baker be able to challenge the denial of her plan as being an unconstitutional taking of property based on the permit denial alone? Second, if Ms. Baker can challenge the denial of the permit can she assert that the wetlands regulation (which applied to the land *before* she purchased it) took her property without just compensation or, in the alternative, did Mr. Able waive any such claim relating to the land (in the sense that he was the only person whose property was taken by the government action)? Third, if Ms. Baker can assert that the wetlands regulation, and the denial of permit to her, constitute a taking of property, should the courts treat the government wetlands law as a law that eliminates the entire use of real property (the 20 acres) which would be a *per se* taking under *Lucas* or, in the alternative, should a court analyze the issue in terms of the extent to which the regulation had diminished the value of the entire 100 acre tract of land?

These hypothetical questions were presented in *Palazzolo v. Rhode Island* (2001). In 1959, Mr. Palazzolo and some associates formed a corporation that purchased land. Eventually, Mr. Palazzolo became the sole shareholder in the corporation. Most of the real property owned by the corporation was a salt marsh, which was subject to flooding at certain times of the year. Several times Mr. Palazzolo, and his corporation, attempted to develop the property, but the development plans were always turned down by government agencies prior to the time when the State of Rhode Island sought to protect certain coastal properties and wetlands. In the early 1970's Rhode Island created a government council with the responsibility of protecting certain coastal properties; that government council enacted regulations preventing the development of coastal wetlands, except under very limited circumstances.

In the late 1970's, Mr. Palazzolo's corporation's charter was revoked due to his failure to pay corporate taxes. When the corporate title was revoked, title to the marshland property passed to Mr. Palazzolo as an individual. In 1983 and in 1985 he applied for permission to fill 11 of the property's 18 wetland acres to build a private beach club. When his last permit application was denied, he brought suit in the state courts alleging that his property had been taken through the denial of his request to use the land. The Rhode Island State Supreme Court affirmed a lower court ruling against Mr. Palazzolo by finding that: his claim was not ripe; he had no right to challenge regulations that were enacted prior to 1978 when he took legal ownership of the property as an individual; and he could not assert a takings claim based on denial of 100% of the value of the wetlands acre because the regulation simply lowered the value of the entire tract of property.

The key difference between our hypothetical and the *Palazzolo* case is that the facts of the hypothetical are clear. In our hypothetical, we had two very distinct owners, Mr. Able and Ms. Baker. In the *Palazzolo* case there were two technically distinct owners, the corporation with one shareholder and the individual shareholder who took title to the property when the corporation ceased to exist. Nevertheless, in the *Palazzolo* case only the interests of one person, Mr. Palazzolo were at stake, both prior to and after the government regulations were enacted. For reasons known only to the Justices, the Court chose to decide the case as if there were two distinct owners: one that owned the land at the time the property regulation took effect (the corporation, which would be the equivalent of our Mr. Able); and one owner who purchased the land that had already been subject to the regulations and the refusal to allow usage of the wetlands area (Mr. Palazzolo in his personal capacity, who would be the equivalent of our Ms. Baker).

Justice Kennedy spoke for the Court in *Palazzolo*. Justice Stevens concurred with the part of the Kennedy opinion regarding the ripeness issue [what we described as the first question in our hypothetical], although he dissented on the merits of the case. Only the Chief Justice and Justice Thomas joined the Kennedy opinion without further comment. Justice O'Connor and Justice Scalia concurred in the majority opinion while offering separate views of how taking of property issues should be dealt with in the future.

Palazzolo ruled that the taking of property issues were "ripe" for adjudication. The ripeness issue centered on the fact that the property owner had not put forth a specific alternative use for the land, following the denial of his petition to develop the case. Six Justices, however, found that once Mr. Palazzolo's request for a permit to fill in the wetlands was denied by the government council, there was a distinct harm to the individual property owner who could then litigate the takings issue. Justice Ginsburg wrote a dissenting opinion that addressed only the ripeness issue. She argued that the owner could only show a specific harm if he had had a more specific plan for development of the property.

The Court assumed that the corporation was sufficiently distinct from Mr. Palazzolo that it had to address the question of whether he could challenge the government regulation as a taking even though the regulation had occurred when the land was technically owned by the corporation. If the Court had simply found that the corporation and individual landowner should be treated as one and the same, there would have been no issue concerning whether he could now raise the takings issue.

Justice Kennedy, for the Court, concluded that the person who purchased land that was subject to prior property use regulations could challenge those regulations under the takings clause. The language in *Lucas* indicating that the government could defend against a takings claim by showing that the property owner purchased the property after it had been subjected to certain government regulations did *not* prohibit a new property owner from challenging these regulations.

Justice Stevens dissented because he believed that the harm that occurred to the property at the time of the taking was personal to the individual (whether the individual was an actual human being or a legal entity such as a corporation) that owned the land at the time of the alleged regulatory taking. In other words, in our hypothetical example, Stevens would have found that Mr. Able could sue for the alleged taking of his property. Ms. Baker could not have an injury from a government regulation, because she only purchased property that was 80% usable at the time she bought it, so she paid the fair market value for the property as subject to the regulation.

The separate opinions in *Palazzolo* appear to conclude that between six and eight of the Justices would agree in that our hypothetical Ms. Baker could pay fair market value for land subject to regulation and then challenge the regulation as an improper taking of property. If Ms. Baker won that claim, one might argue that she would have received a bargain, because she purchased the land at a lower value than it would have been worth if Mr. Able had himself sued the government under the takings clause. On the other hand, one could view her as only buying a lawsuit—the opportunity to sue to invalidate the rules that made the property less valuable.

Justice Stevens was the only Justice who argued that a property owner should be completely barred from alleging that any property use regulations that had applied to the land prior to the time of his purchase constituted a taking of his property. Ginsburg's dissent, joined by Souter and Breyer, focused only on the ripeness issue.

Justice O'Connor joined the majority opinion in *Palazzolo*. Nevertheless, she wrote separately to explain her belief that the fact that land was subject to regulation at the time of purchase was only one factor to consider when assessing a regulatory takings claim. Justice Breyer dissented because he believed that the takings issue was not ripe for adjudication. He also stated that he "would agree with Justice O'Connor that the simple fact that a piece of property has changed hands (for example, by inheritance) does not always and automatically bar a takings claim."

Justice Scalia also joined the majority opinion in *Palazzolo*. In a separate opinion he stated that when a purchaser of land that is subject to property regulations decides to challenge those regulations as a taking of property, a court should give absolutely no weight to the fact that the land had been subject to the regulation at the time he bought it. In such a situation, Scalia argued that the courts must allow the second owner [Ms. Baker in our hypothetical, and Mr. Palazzolo, in his personal capacity, in the real case] to receive the benefit *if* the second owner is able to show that the regulation had constituted a taking of property when it was first applied to the land.

In Scalia's view, the "investment-backed expectations" of a current property owner include the assumed invalidity of a restriction that deprives the property of so much of its value as to be unconstitutional. The situation would not be different from a person who buys property subject to a restrictive covenant that reduces the value of the property but the purchaser thinks that covenant is invalid. If the purchaser is able to persuade a court to invalidate the restrictive covenant, the purchaser wins.

If Ms. Baker, in our hypothetical, could not sue, and the state's regulations are invalid, then the state would get the windfall, because it engaged in a taking and did not have to compensate anyone for its taking. That, ultimately, is the question: should the state get the windfall if it enacts regulations that amount to a taking for which the state does not grant compensation? Or should the owner of the land receive just compensation, whether he is the original owner or a later one?

None of the Justices in *Palazzolo* considered the last issue that we set out in the hypothetical: whether the prohibition of any use of some part of a parcel of land should be analyzed as a *per se* taking under *Lucas,* or, in the alternative, a diminution in the total value of the total parcel of land. Kennedy's majority opinion found that the Court did not need to address this issue because of the way in which the petition for certiorari had been worded. Kennedy noted that some of the Court's decisions indicated that actions that removed one aspect of a land's value simply required that the impact of the regulatory action be measured against the value of the whole parcel of property, but that the Court had "at times expressed discomfort with the logic of this rule" because such a rule might allow for the total deprivation of the value of a distinct parcel of land. Kennedy's majority opinion omitted any reference to the easement cases, which established the principal that changing the occupation rights to property would constitute a *per se* taking.

The property owner whose land becomes subject to wetlands regulation that prohibits any improvement of part of his land asserts that the government has effectively taken an easement over a strip of his land. From the perspective of the property owner it is irrelevant that this easement allows birds, rather than human beings, to use of the land.

Justice Breyer argued that there should be no difference in the ability of an individual to make a claim regarding total deprivation of value simply by having structured transactions to isolate the portion of the land that was subject to the regulations. Breyer did not take a position on whether such wetlands or coastal protection legislation would constitute a taking of property. He simply indicated that, in a case like our hypothetical, either Mr. Able should or should not receive compensation because the law made 20 acres of his land totally unusable. The takings clause determination should not rest on whether Mr. Able brought the action while he owned the entire 100 acres, or whether he sold the 20 unusable acres to another person who would then bring the takings claim.

Physical Occupations as Per Se Takings. The Court will allow governmental entities to regulate either real or personal property for the public good without the requirement of compensation so long as the action is not an unreasonable infringement of the rights of the private property owner. The government, however, is not free to transfer property rights from one group of owners to another or to take and use private property for the public good (1) unless the action is justified by emergency conditions, or (2) unless compensation is paid.

A permanent physical occupation of private property by the government or a government regulation that allows someone other than the property owner to have permanent physical occupation of a definable part of a piece of property should constitute a taking.

For example, in *Loretto v. Teleprompter Manhattan CATV Corp.* (1982), Justice Marshall, for the Court, invalidated a city ordinance that required a landlord building owner to allow installation of cable television receiver on apartment building and denied the landlord the ability to demand payment in excess of $1. The Court held that this physical intrusion constitutes a compensable taking because the ordinance allowed for "permanent physical occupation" of a small part of the building.

In *Brown v. Legal Foundation of Washington* (2003), the Court was sharply divided in ruling on a variety of takings clause issues. *Brown* involved state regulation of the accounts held by attorneys and escrow services for clients, and the government's use of the interest on those funds. Attorneys often have to hold money for a client on a temporary basis. Rules of professional responsibility prohibit a attorney from co-mingling client funds with the attorney's own money or from taking the interest if the money is put in a interest-bearing account. Sometimes, attorneys hold an amount of money for a client that is so large that the attorney will place the funds into an account with a financial institution that will generate interest. That interest, of course, belongs to the client. Attorneys may hold money for clients in small amounts that would not generate interest, and these small amounts of money are normally placed in accounts that will not produce any interest. The attorney has no incentive to pool the money into a larger account that would produce interest, because he cannot take that interest. It belongs to the clients, and it would probably take computer programs to determine how much any particular client receives for having small amounts of money kept for short periods of time.

During the last part of the twentieth century every state enacted laws or court rules that required lawyers to place all of the funds of their clients that would not otherwise generate interest into single accounts of a type that would generate interest. While the interest created by funds is considered the property of the clients (they own the funds from which the interest grows), nevertheless, each state required the attorneys to turn over the interest from the combined small accounts to fund various government projects, subsidized legal services for low-income persons.

Federal and state governments may take property for public use. Although the Court has not interpreted the public use requirement to be a significant hurdle, the government taking of property, even with compensation, must be done to produce some type of social benefit. In *Brown v. Legal Foundation of Washington* (2003) (5 to 4), Justice Stevens, for the Court, held that the public use requirement is satisfied so long as the taking of property, if any, is rationally related to promote any legitimate public interest. Providing legal services for low-income persons meets this test.

Stevens' concluded that the government *regulation of trust accounts* is not a taking of property under the factors following the "ad-hoc approach applied in *Penn Central Transportation* ... because [the owners of the money put into the combined accounts] had suffered neither an actual loss nor interference with any investment-backed expectations...."

The more interesting question was the government *taking of the interest*. The government requirement that attorneys transfer the interest on the combined small accounts to the fund for legal services was the equivalent of a direct government confiscation of that interest. Therefore, Stevens ruled that the required transfer of the interest income constituted a taking of property, based under the cases that found that government's physical occupation of property was a taking that required compensation.

Because the government took property, it owed just compensation to the owners of the property. These persons were the beneficial owners of the small amounts of money held by an attorney who was required to place their money into an interest generating account with the funds of other clients. The Justices divided 5 to 4 over the question of what amount of compensation was owed to those persons.

The Supreme Court had long held that, when the government takes property, it owes the individual what is the property owner's loss, rather than the value of the property after the government took it. For example, if the government took a piece of land that was worth $100,000 and then combined it with other land owned by the government, the value of the individual piece of land might have escalated from $100,000 to $1,000,000, because it is now part of a large development. However, the government would only owe $100,000 to the individual whose property was taken (the value of the property before it was taken by the government and converted to public use).

Applying the loss to the property owner concept in *Brown*, Justice Stevens' majority opinion found that no monetary compensation was due to the owners of small amounts of money that had been combined into accounts that generated the interest that was transferred to the fund to subsidize legal services for low income persons. The owners of small amounts of money held by attorneys would not have received any interest prior to the law allowing for the combination of funds into an interest bearing account. In other words, the net earnings for each client who had money being held by an attorney would have been zero before the enactment of the state statute (*and* the change in federal law that allowed such accounts). Therefore, the loss to each such person was, in the view of the majority, zero dollars; the amount of compensation they were to be paid also was zero.

If an individual client of an attorney had an account that was so large that it would produce interest by being placed into a separate account, even prior to the legal services funding statute, the government would owe the interest amount to the property owner if it took that interest for a public use.

The dissent argued that the total amount raised by these programs is millions of dollars and that if the government "takes" millions of dollars, the fair market value, e.g., of $55 million is $55 million.

Limitations on the Owner's Right to Exclude Others. *Kaiser Aetna v. United States* (1979) held that the application of the federal navigational servitude to a lagoon on the island of Oahu constituted a taking for which compensation was required. Historically, the pond in question was considered private property. It was leased, along with the surrounding land, to a resort and private housing developer. The developer converted the pond into a marina, and dug channels connecting it with a bay which allowed ships to travel from the lagoon into the bay and the ocean. The federal government claimed that the connection of the waterway to the bay made it a "navigable water" of the United States and therefore subject to regulation by the Corps of Engineers and open to public use.

The Supreme Court found that the lagoon was a navigable waterway and subject to regulation by the United States government and the Corps of Engineers acting under the commerce power. However, the government could not require the owners and lessees of the marina to allow the public free access without invoking the eminent domain power and paying them compensation. Although the government could have refused to allow connection of the lagoon to the bay or regulated use of the lagoon in any arguably reasonable manner, it could not simply convert private property into public property without paying just compensation.

The state's removal of a property owner's right to exclude others under certain circumstances does not necessarily constitute a "taking" in the constitutional sense. In order to determine whether or not such a limitation of property rights constitutes a taking, a court must consider the character of the government's action in terms of the degree to which it (1) promotes legitimate social goals, (2) diminishes the value of the private property owner's economic interest, and (3) interferes with reasonable expectations regarding the use of the property.

For example, in *PruneYard Shopping Center v. Robins* (1980), the Court upheld a decision of the California Supreme Court that ruled that the California constitution prohibited the owners of private shopping centers from excluding persons who wish to engage in non-disruptive speech and petitioning activities. Although the state had eliminated part of the shopping center owner's right to exclude other persons, the owners did not suffer a taking in the constitutional sense because they could not demonstrate that an unchecked right to exclude others was a basic part of the economic value of the shopping center. The state court ruling was seen as a reasonable government regulation of the use of property normally open to members of the public and not a taking of property.

Another example of the difficulty of determining when a legal restriction on a property owner's right to exclude others from using his property constitutes a taking is provided by *Nollan v. California*

Coastal Commission (1987) (5 to 4). The Court held that a condition of a building reconstruction permit that required a public easement across beach property constituted a taking of property for which compensation was due. The issue was a restriction placed on beachfront property in California. The owners wished to demolish a small building on the property and replace it with a larger structure. The Coastal Commission granted the construction permit *on the condition* that the owners allow the public to pass across the beach area of their property. This easement would allow members of the public to cross the private property when traveling between two public beach areas which were separated, in part, by the beachfront lot.

Although this point may be subject to some debate, it appears that the Court determined it was irrelevant whether the easement granted to the public ran from the street to the beach across the part of the property that abutted the house or merely across the beach portion of the property providing "lateral access" to the public beaches. There simply was no purpose supporting the required grant of a public easement, other than facilitating public travel across private property. This was not an illegitimate interest; the state could pursue it by condemning a portion of the land for the easement and paying just compensation to the property owner.

Justice Scalia's opinion for the Court in *Nollan* stated, in dicta, that a zoning commission might condition a waiver of a zoning regulation regarding the size of buildings near a beach that would allow the construction of a new building blocking the public's view of the beach if the owner agreed to provide a limited public access area on the property for passers-by to view the beach. In other words, since a limitation on the size of buildings for aesthetic purposes would be permissible (so long as it did not unreasonably diminish the economic value of the property), granting of access to the property for the purpose of providing the public the ability to see the beach should be permissible (unless the amount of required access constituted a substantial diminishment in the value of the property). However, the easement at issue in the *Nollan* case was not related to preserving the aesthetic quality of the beachfront area or the public's ability to view the beach. The permit system in *Nollan* in effect created a continuous strip of publicly accessible beach by granting to the public the use of privately owned property.

Conditional Development Permits—A Special Type of Spot Regulation. Most of the Supreme Court's decisions concerning whether a government property use regulation constitutes a taking of property have involved general regulations over all similarly situated property. One type of general regulation case involves a zoning law that defines and limits the types of property uses that will be allowed within an area of a city. Another type of general regulation case involves the regulation of all business entities of a certain type, such as coal mines. In these general regulation cases, the Court has given a great deal of deference to judgments made by legislatures or administrative entities.

When the government regulates a specific piece of real property, rather than regulating all similarly situated property within the jurisdiction, the government regulation is sometimes referred to as "spot zoning" or "spot regulation." In spot regulation cases there is often less reason than in general regulation cases for judicial deference to the legislative judgment. When the government regulates only a specific parcel of property, the individual property owner whose land is regulated cannot join with, or rely on, the owners of similar property to influence the government decision-makers to give fair treatment to the economic interests of the land owner. Nevertheless, the Supreme Court has not established separate standards for the review of spot regulation.

If the government regulates a specific piece of property for the purpose of stopping the property owner from harming other persons, it would be hard, if not impossible, for the property owner to show that the special regulation of his property constituted a taking. A government action prohibiting a property owner from engaging in activities that created a significant risk of harm to other persons is not a taking of property. In such a circumstance, even a form of judicial review that gave no deference to the legislative or administrative decision-making authorities would find that the government had not unjustly extracted an economic benefit from the property owner. Such a government regulation reasonably relates to legitimate government interest.

A government entity may require a property owner to receive a permit to develop real property or to improve the structures on it. The governmental authority charged with the responsibility for operating the permit system may require the property owner to meet certain conditions in order to obtain a permit. Typical permit conditions require the property owner to demonstrate that the property development will be in accordance with all building regulations and environmental laws. Although a permit system conditions the ability of an individual to place improvements on property he owns, it will not result in a judicial finding that the regulation constitutes a taking so long as the permit conditions are reasonable regulations of property use. The Supreme Court has described a permit requirement that is conditioned upon compliance with laws of general applicability as follows: "[A] requirement that a person obtain a permit before engaging in a certain use of his or her property does not itself 'take' the property in any sense: after all, the very existence of a permit system implies that permission may be granted, leaving the landowner free to use the property as desired. Moreover, even if the permit is denied, there may be other viable uses available to the owner. Only when a permit is denied and the effect of the denial is to prevent 'economically viable' use of the land in question can it be said that a taking has occurred." *United States v. Riverside Bayview Homes, Inc.* (1985).

However, when the government requires a property owner to get a permit in order to develop the land and imposes conditions on the granting of the permit that are not applicable to all similarly situated pieces of land within the jurisdiction, there should be a special concern as to whether the conditions on the permit constitute a taking. In this situation, the government is extracting a cost from a particular property owner that it is not imposed on other persons.

If the government conditions the granting of a development permit on the requirement that the property owner transfer the rights to a portion of the property to the government, or on the requirement that the property owner open the property to the public, the government must demonstrate that these conditions are reasonably related to legitimate public interests. If the government fails to justify the access condition, the Court will find that the government's conditional permit is a taking of property. A government law that would simply grant the public an easement to use a part of privately owned real property would be subject to the "per se rule" that forced changes in occupation rights constitute a taking for which just compensation is due. Making the individual give up her right to exclude others from her property in order to gain a development permit is an "unconstitutional condition" unless the government can demonstrate that the condition is reasonably related to promoting legitimate government ends.

Nollan v. California Coastal Commission (1987) did not give a detailed explanation of the way in which the government might prove that requiring the property owner to open his property to public access might be a reasonable condition for a development permit. In that case, it was clear to the Court that the government's attempt to secure a public easement across the beach had no possible relationship to any legitimate government interest. Therefore, the majority in *Nollan* found that the government was simply trying to secure a public easement across a privately owned beach without having to pay the owner for that taking of property rights.

Dolan v. City of Tigard (1994) established a standard for the review of a building permit condition requiring the dedication of privately owned land for public use. The property owner in *Dolan* owned a store with a gravel parking lot and that bordered a creek. The city had some problems with the creek overflowing in earlier years; it had adopted a drainage plan that involved improvements to the creek basin and recommendations that land immediately adjacent to the creek be used only as "greenways". The property owner sought a permit to increase the size of her store and to increase, and pave, the parking lot. She was informed that she would be denied this permit unless she met conditions that required her (1) to dedicate the portion of her property line immediately next to the creek for a greenway that could be used by the public, and (2) to dedicate a fifteen foot strip of land across her property for use as a pedestrian and bicycle pathway. The property owner claimed that these two conditions for her development permit constituted a taking of her property and could not be imposed upon her without just compensation.

Dolan ruled (5 to 4) that the conditions imposed on the store owner constituted a taking of property that required the city to pay just compensation to the property owner. *Dolan* requires courts to go through a two-step process to determine whether a permit condition requiring dedication of private land for public use constitutes a taking of property. First a court must determine whether there is an "essential nexus" between the permit condition and a legitimate interest of government. Second, if such a nexus is found to exist, a court must determine whether there is rough proportionality between the condition requiring the property owner to dedicate a portion of the property to public use and the impact of the proposed development on governmental and social interests. In making this determination, the court should place the burden on the government to demonstrate that there is a reasonable relationship, or "rough proportionality," between the permit condition and the nature of the proposed land development.

Applying this two-step analysis, and the rough proportionality test, *Dolan* found that the conditions placed on the store owner's development permit constituted a taking of property. Preventing flood damage along the creek and reducing traffic congestion were legitimate interests that arguably might be impaired by the property owner increasing the size of her store and parking lot. However, the city had failed to demonstrate that requiring the property owner to dedicate a portion of her property to be a public greenway, which might be used by pedestrians, was related to the government interest in controlling flood damage along the creek. If the city had simply forbid the owner from building on the part of the property closest to the creek, without requiring that she make that public greenway available to public use, the Court might uphold the condition as being reasonably related to the legitimate public interest in flood control. But, requiring the property owner to open the greenway to the public was not proportional to, or reasonably related to, the effect of her proposed development on flood control within the city.

The city had argued that the increase in the size of the store would result in increased traffic. But the Court found that "on the record before us, the city has not met its burden of demonstrating that the additional number of vehicle and bicycle trips generated by [the store owner's proposed development] reasonably relate to the city's requirement for a dedication of the pedestrian-bicycle pathway easement."

Under *Dolan*, courts should not give great deference to the decision of the government to require a property owner to grant public access to the property as a condition for a building or development permit. Instead, the courts must independently determine whether the asserted government interests are legitimate and whether the access condition is reasonably related to those interests. To justify such a condition the government must demonstrate that the required dedication of private property for public use is "roughly proportional" to the adverse impact of the proposed development on legitimate public interests.

The rough proportionality test is used only for determining the constitutionality of conditioning a building or development permit on the transfer of an easement or the right to occupy the property. The proportionality test is not appropriate for an examination of governmental regulations of property use.

Utility Rate Regulation. Virtually all governmental entities that have conferred the right to be a legal monopoly on a private utility company have regulated the utility's charges to its customers. The regulation of the amounts that utilities may bill for their services is a regulation of the property of the utility owners. So, if the government sets the utility's charges, and the rate of return on the owners' investment, at a level that is judicially determined to be unjust and confiscatory, the rate regulation will constitute a taking of the property of the utility.

In *Duquesne Light Co. v. Barasch* (1989) a Pennsylvania utility company asserted that the method used to determine the amount of its rates and rate increases constituted a taking of property because state law prohibited including in the rate base (the value of the utility that would be used for determining the rates and rate of return) the amount of money that the utility invested in initial stages of construction for four power plants that were cancelled prior to being put into use. Because the investments in these power plants were "prudent" when the initial investments were made, the utility claimed that the method for calculating the rate of return was a violation of the takings clause because the state disregarded the historical cost of the utility. However, the utility did not claim that Pennsylvania's rates resulted in a total return on the utility's investment that was unjust or unreasonable. The Court held that the utility rate regulation is not a taking of property so long as the rate of return was not so unreasonable and unjust as to be considered "confiscatory."

Shortly after the Supreme Court began to examine utility rate regulations, in *Smyth v. Ames* (1898), it indicated that rates and charges should be set according to the present value of the assets employed by the utility, so as to determine whether the rate was reasonable by examining it as a return on the "fair value" of the utility. Justice Brandeis, in the 1920s, had noted the difficulty of attempting to establish the "fair value rule" as a constitutional requirement. Brandeis believed that the Constitution allowed utility rate regulations to be set with a system that would compare the utility's rate of return to the value of the capital that had been prudently invested in the utility throughout its history.

The Supreme Court eventually adopted the position that Brandeis advocated, which is sometimes called the "prudent investment" or the "historical cost" principle, in *Federal Power Commission v. Hope Natural Gas Company* (1944). That case held that the fair value rule, previously adopted in *Smyth,* was not the only method for constitutionally setting utility rates and allowed state lawmakers to use the historical cost or prudent investment rule.

Duquesne Light Co. held that the Constitution does not mandate any one formula for fixing utility rates. So long as the utility's rate of return is not so unjust as to be confiscatory, the Court will not invalidate due to the method by which the state law had set the rate structure. If a utility company challenged a rate as being "confiscatory", the Court can examine the value of the company and the return upon prudent investments to determine if the rate was confiscatory.

(c) Emergency Actions

Authorities have long stated that in time of extreme emergency, the government, if the need arises, may take or even destroy private property. As a general rule, the Supreme Court has been reluctant, during the time of emergency, to find that the government must compensate the injured property owner.

Courts often hold that military actions taken in time of war are not compensable emergency measures. *United States v. Caltex, Inc.* (1952) held that the Army had not "taken" property that the military had destroyed to prevent enemy forces from capturing it. The Army, in late 1941, destroyed the claimant's oil facilities in Manila as Japanese troops were entering the city. After the war, the owner of the facilities demanded compensation for all the property destroyed by the Army. The government agreed to pay for all the petroleum products used or destroyed but refused to pay for the destroyed terminal facilities. The Court, upholding the army's refusal, held that the destruction of private property during battle is a cost that the individual owners must bear.

In *United States v. Central Eureka Mining Co.* (1958), another case arising from government action during World War II, the Court refused to find that a War Production Board order requiring nonessential gold mines to cease operation amounted to a taking of the mines. The government had in no way taken physical possession of the affected mines, and the order was a reasonable means of conserving equipment needed to promote the war effort. War, stated the Court, "demands the strict regulation of nearly all resources. It makes demands which otherwise would be insufferable."

The Court reaffirmed these principles in *National Board of Young Men's Christian Associations v. United States* (1969). Looters in the Panama Canal Zone destroyed its building because American troops had taken shelter there. The Court, concluding that the presence of the troops in the area had been for the landowner's benefit, found that "fairness and justice" did not require that the government bare the loss. The Marines had not planned to take over the building but only sought its temporary use in an emergency.

The type of emergency situation that may enable the state to destroy property, without payment of compensation, is not limited to wartime conflict. *Miller v. Schoene* (1928) involved the Virginia's destruction of a large number of ornamental red cedar trees. The trees were infected with cedar rust, a disease highly dangerous to apple trees. The only effective means of controlling the disease is to destroy all infected red cedars growing within two miles of any apple orchards.

Schoene held that the state could destroy the trees without incurring any constitutional duty to compensate the injured landowner. The Court observed that apple production was an important agricultural activity while ornamental cedar trees had only minimal importance. The Court concluded that "[w]hen forced to such a choice, the state does not exceed its constitutional powers by deciding upon the destruction of one class of property in order to save another, which, in the judgment of the legislature, is of greater value to the public."

Dames & Moore v. Regan (1981) upheld the validity of executive agreements suspending claims of United States citizens against the government of Iran in exchange for a return of our citizens who were being held hostage by that country. In so doing the majority opinion by Justice Rehnquist found that the Presidential order nullifying attachments on Iranian assets and allowing a transfer of those assets out of the country did not constitute a compensable taking of property because the President had statutory authority to prevent or condition the allowance of such attachments so that those bringing claims against Iran did not have a property interest in the attachment.

As a part of the agreement with Iran, the President suspended claims of United States citizens pending in United States courts and required their submission to a "claims tribunal." The Court refused to consider whether this suspension of claims constituted a taking of property because the issue was not ripe for review. However, persons whose claims the Presidential order had suspended could bring an action in the Court of Claims to determine whether the suspension had resulted in an unconstitutional taking of property by executive action.

(d) Impairment of Use

The taking issue can arise when the government has neither destroyed nor regulated the use of private property. If the government causes the landowner's use and enjoyment of his property is impaired, there may be a "taking" for which compensation is due.

The Constitution does not require the literal appropriation of property before there is a "taking". *Pumpelly v. Green Bay & Mississippi Canal Co.* (1871) interpreted the "taking" clause of a state constitution and it found that a serious interruption in the use of property might be the equivalent of a taking, so that a government dam flooding land is a "taking".

In this area the Court's rulings have an *ad hoc* quality because individual decisions are based on the degree of loss to the individual and the reasonableness of the government's actions in relation to the private property. For example, in *Peabody v. United States* (1913) the Court faced the issue of whether the placement of a gun battery in the vicinity of the claimant's resort hotel amounted to a Fifth Amendment taking. The resort owners argued that the proximate location of the battery to the hotel property greatly impaired the land's recreational value for all practical purposes. The Supreme Court found no taking, but, in *dicta*, stated that if the government had installed the battery with the intent to practice at will over the hotel property, "with the intent of depriving the owner of its profitable use," such action would constitute an appropriation of property and would require compensation.

After there were addition firings, plaintiffs sued, and again the Court rejected the claims. *Portsmouth Harbor Land & Hotel Co. v. United States* (1919). Three years later the same parties again sought recovery urging that the cumulative effect of subsequent firings had resulted in a taking. This time, the Court, per Justice

Holmes, reversed the trial court's dismissal of the action, and, adopting the theory of *Peabody*, ordered that evidence be heard to determine whether the continued firings were sufficient to prove an intent to create a servitude over the hotel property. *Portsmouth Harbor Land and Hotel Co. v. United States* (1922).

A leading case is *United States v. Causby* (1946). The Supreme Court applied the rationale of the *Portsmouth Hotel* cases to decide whether frequent and regular flights of government planes over the plaintiffs' land created an easement for the benefit of the government. The plaintiffs owned a small chicken farm near an airport used by army and navy planes. The glide path of one of the airport runways passed directly over the property at a height of only 83 feet. The use of the runway greatly disturbed the occupants of the farm and also eventually forced the plaintiffs to give up their chicken business. The Court found that the frequent low altitude flights of government planes over the farm created an easement in the plaintiffs' land. The Court held that the landowner was entitled to as much of the air space over his property as he had been reasonably using in connection with his land, and found that the government's use of this airspace resulted in the imposition of a servitude on the chicken farm.

If government agents or employees intentionally destroy or take a person's property, there should be no question that there has been a "taking" for which just compensation is due, although there may be questions in any given case regarding the adequacy of state administrative or judicial procedures for determining the amount of compensation. *Hudson v. Palmer* (1984).

The Supreme Court later ruled that mere negligence by government agents, which resulted in harm to a prisoner in a penal institution, did not constitute a taking of liberty property without due process, even though state tort law and state sovereign immunity doctrines precluded any compensation for the prisoner. An inmate brought civil rights actions against deputy sheriff to recover for injuries allegedly sustained when he slipped and fell on a pillow that the deputy sheriff left on the jail stairs. The Court said that to hold that a negligent injury is a deprivation within the meaning of the Due Process Clause would trivialize the due process of law. *Daniels v. Williams* (1986), overruling *Parratt v. Taylor* (1981) to the extent that it states otherwise.

In *Daniels v. Williams,* Justice Rehnquist, for the Court, stated: "We conclude that the due process clause is simply not implicated by a negligent act of an official causing unintended loss of or injury to life, liberty, or property." *Daniels* left open the question of whether any type of action by government agents short of an intentional destruction of property (such as the destruction of property though grossly negligent or reckless conduct) could constitute a taking of property.

If taken literally, the quoted statement from *Daniels* would mean that an individual had no constitutional right to just compensation when agents of the state negligently destroyed his property, regardless of the extent of loss or the nature of the state activity.

For example, assume that a state employee negligently drove a truck filled with flammable liquids off the highway and crashed into a house, destroying the house and all persons therein. Could any surviving members of the family that owned the house be denied all compensation for the loss of their property and the lives of their family members due to a state sovereign immunity law? Perhaps the Supreme Court should rule that the judiciary should use a case-by-case approach to determine whether the negligence of government employees had so unfairly shifted social costs (such as the cost for the societal benefit from the state agency that employed the truck driver) to an individual or a limited group of individuals (the property owners and family members in our hypothetical) that the unintended harm to the individual or group of individuals constituted a taking for which just compensation was required. This type of case-by-case approach would eliminate turning all minor tort suits into constitutional issues, while requiring just compensation for those persons who have been severely injured by negligent government actions.

Such a construction of the prisoner's rights cases may be possible, because the Supreme Court in *Daniels* stated: "We need not rule out the possibility that there are other constitutional provisions that would be violated by mere lack of care in order to hold, as we do, that such conduct [causing the minor injury to the prisoner in this case] does not implicate the due process clause of the Fourteenth Amendment." The Court avoided this taking of property question when it ruled executive actions that harm persons or property would be judged by a "shock the conscience" test.

§ 11.12   The "Public Use" Limitation

The government is not entirely free to take a person's property whenever it is willing to compensate him. The individual may not wish to part with his property, and, under both the Fifth and Fourteenth Amendments, property may not be taken by the government, even upon payment of just compensation, unless the property is taken *for a public use*. Like the requirement that that state compensate a landowner when it takes his property, the "public use" limitation has its roots in natural as well as constitutional law. The early interpretation of this public use test was broadly viewed as properly exercisable for "the public good, the public necessity or the public utility."

The leading modern case defining the scope of the public use limitation is the unanimous decision in *Berman v. Parker* (1954). This case involved the constitutionality of the 1945 District of Columbia Redevelopment Act. Under section 2 of that Act, Congress declared it the policy of the United States to eliminate all substandard housing in Washington, D.C. because such areas were "injurious to the public health, safety, morals, and welfare." The Act also created the District of Columbia Redevelopment Land Agency and granted that agency the power to assemble real property for the redevelopment of blighted areas of the city through the exercise of eminent domain. After assembling the necessary real estate, Congress authorized the Agency to lease or sell portions of the land to private parties upon an agreement that the purchasers would carry out the redevelopment plan.

The appellant in *Berman* held property within the redevelopment area where a department store was located. The appellants argued that their property could not constitutionally be taken for the project, first, because the property was commercial and not residential or slum housing, and second, because, by condemning the property for sale to a private agency for redevelopment, the land was being redeveloped for a private and not a public use as required by the Fifth Amendment. The Supreme Court, in an opinion by Justice Douglas, disagreed and upheld the use of the eminent domain power.

Congress has a "police power" over the city of Washington, D.C., which is equivalent to the police power of the individual states, to legislate as necessary for the health, safety and welfare of its residents. Congress was exercising this "police power" in *Berman*. This use of the term "police power" indicated that the federal government is not limited by the enumerated powers when it legislates for the District of Columbia.

Berman confirms that the public use limitation of the Fifth and Fourteenth Amendment is as expansive as a due process police power test. The Court concluded that once the legislature has declared a condemnation to be for a public use, the role of the courts is an extremely narrow one. The Court approved the concept of area redevelopment by holding that the government could take the property that, standing by itself, was innocuous as part of the overall plan. As for the power of the legislature to condemn areas for the purpose of renovation, the Court broadly stated that "[i]t is within the power of the legislature to determine that the community should be beautiful as well as healthy, spacious as well as clean, well-balanced as well as carefully patrolled."

After *Berman*, the public use limitation is not much of a limitation, if the purpose of the action is for the benefit of the health, safety and welfare of its citizens. This public use limitation is met whenever the object of the exercise bears any reasonable relationship to one of its implied or enumerated powers.

The Supreme Court followed the broad public benefit test of *Berman* in upholding the Hawaii Land Reform Act of 1967. Hawaii created a system for taking title and residential real property from lessors, and—after providing the lessors with just compensation—transferring title to the lessee of the property in order to reduce the concentration of land ownership in the state. *Hawaii Housing Authority v. Midkiff* (1984) held that this exercise of the eminent domain power was rationally related to the public purpose of correcting deficiencies in the real estate market and social problems attributed to land oligopoly. The fact that the property was transferred to private individuals did not invalidate the taking. The public use requirement is "coterminous with the scope of a sovereign's police powers."

Governments have the power of eminent domain, which is the power to force a property owner to sell his property to the government at its fair market value. The Fifth Amendment uses the phrase "public use," but, for more than a century, the Court has ruled that the federal and state governments may take property, after paying just compensation, if the property is taken for a public "purpose." The terms "public use" and "public purpose" are now interchangeable in takings clause analysis.

Kelo v. New London (2005) (5 to 4) made clear that once the government takes the property, it may sell or give that property to another private person, so long as the government action has a conceivable public purpose. The property owners admitted that the government may take their homes to build a road or police station, or to eliminate a property use that harms the public (e.g., blighted property), but they argued that it cannot take their property for the private use of other owners simply because the new owners may make more productive use of the property. The Court disagreed. Justice Stevens, for the majority, concluded that the courts should not independently determine whether a taking of property was for a public use or public purpose, if the government paid just compensation and the taking of the property might conceivably promote a legitimate interest of society. The majority opinion stated: "[this] Court long ago rejected any literal requirement that condemned property be put into use for the public." Instead, the court must defer to the city's determination that the area at issue was sufficiently distressed to justify a program of economic rejuvenation.

Four dissenting Justices in *Kelo* argued that the language and original intent of the Fifth Amendment takings clause required judges to determine independently whether a government taking of private property provided a real public benefit. Three of the four dissenters in *Kelo* would not allow the government to use its eminent domain power to take the property unless the judiciary found that a real public benefit resulted from the taking of private property. One of the four dissenters, Justice Thomas, would only allow the government to use its eminent domain power to take property if that property literally would be used by the public. The dissenters claimed that the majority would allow the state (if it pays just compensation) to take the property of *A* and give that property to *B*. Justice O'Connor's dissent argued that the majority effectively eliminated any distinction between private and public use of property, and thus amended the Fifth Amendment to eliminate a public use requirement. She concluded:

"Any property may now be taken for the benefit of another private party, but the fallout from this decision will not be random. The beneficiaries are likely to be those citizens with disproportionate influence and power in the political process, including large corporations and development firms. As for the victims, the government now has license to transfer property from those with fewer resources to those with more. The Founders cannot have intended this perverse result."

Justice Thomas' separate dissent argued that the framers allowed "the government to take property not for 'public necessity,' but instead for 'public use.' " The Court's different phraseology, according to Justice Thomas, enables it to "hold, against all common sense, that a costly urban-renewal project whose stated purpose is a vague promise of new jobs and increased tax revenue, but which is also suspiciously agreeable to the Pfizer Corporation, is for a 'public use.' "

The *Kelo* case need not lead to wholesale use of the use of the government's eminent domain power to take private property of one person (with just compensation) and then to transfer it to another private person The Federal Government(through legislation), or a state government (through state legislation or state constitutional law) may restrict the use of the eminent domain power to circumstances where the property taken must be used by a governmental entity or the public.

§ 11.13 A Brief Note on the Amount of Compensation and Compensable Property Interests

The Fifth and Fourteenth Amendments require that a person receive "just compensation" for property that has been taken by the state or federal government. The Supreme Court has said that the constitutional guarantee of just compensation is not a limitation on the power of eminent domain, but only a condition of its exercise. In determining what is "just compensation" the courts have developed various standards of valuation.

The most basic principle for determining the amount due an individual whose property has been taken is in the often-quoted statement by Justice Holmes that the test is "what has the owner lost, not what has the taker gained." *Boston Chamber of Commerce v. Boston* (1910). The courts normally look to the market value of the property that has been taken. In determining the market value of the land, the court will normally look to the value of the property as if land were applied to its "highest and best" use. The highest and best use of a piece of property is determined by the value of the property in light of its present and potential uses if those uses can be anticipated with reasonable certainty.

The market value test is not, however, a definitive test. *United States v. Fuller* (1973) stated that the overall standard is governed by basic equitable principles of fairness. The government as a condemnor was not required to pay for elements of the property's market value that the government had created by granting the landowner a revocable permit to graze his animals on adjoining Federal lands.

When the Taking Occurs. The fair market value of property must be determined on the date of the taking in order to compensate fully the owner in accordance with the guarantee of the just compensation clause. If there is a difference in value between the date of the taking and the date on which the government will tender payment, the individual will be entitled to interest on the value of the property from the date of the taking or a new valuation of the property if during the delay the value of the property changed materially.

Even when the government seeks to secure title to the property through a judicial "condemnation" proceeding against the property, or through legislative action taking the property, it may be difficult to determine the exact date when the taking occurred. Government actions prior to the formal transfer of title may have made the property virtually valueless to the individual. The Court has found that the same considerations used to determine *whether* a taking has resulted from government actions are to be considered in determining *when* the taking occurred. Thus, courts must determine the time at which the value of the property was so substantially reduced by the government's actions or announcement of intention to take title to the property that a taking occurred at that time.

Inverse Condemnations. Particularly difficult problems arise when a property owner alleges that the government has taken his property by regulatory action or impairment of the value rather than by physically taking possession of the property or court or legislatively transfer of the title to the government. In such situations, the property owner institutes an "inverse condemnation" suit against the government. The individual will be seeking a court determination that a taking of property has occurred so as to force the government to either pay just compensation to the property owner, cease the governmental actions, or rescind the governmental regulation that has caused the diminution of the value of the property and the taking.

If an inverse condemnation proceeding results in a judicial determination that a governmental action or regulation has resulted in a taking of property, the government may seek to limit the property owner's remedy to invalidation of the government action that impaired the value of the property. Once it is determined that the government action constitutes a taking for which compensation is due, the government can choose to continue the action and pay fair market value for the permanent taking of the property.

If the government stops its regulation of the property, a court must determine whether the governmental activity that impaired the value of the property constituted a taking of property for the time period between the initiation of the government action (or regulation) and the time when the government rescinded its action (at the conclusion of the inverse condemnation proceeding). If the court determines that there was a taking of property for that time period, and the government chooses not to exercise its eminent domain power and pay for a permanent taking of the property, the court must order appropriate just compensation for the temporary taking.

In sum, the power of eminent domain extends to tangibles and intangibles, including choses in action, contracts and charters. As with the basic determination of value, this test combines traditional property law interests and equitable principles of fairness.

Chapter 12

STATE ACTION

Table of Sections

§ 12.1 Introduction

(a) Central Theory

Most of the protections for individual rights and liberties contained in the Constitution and its Amendments apply only to the actions of governmental entities. The big exception is the thirteenth amendment, which abolishes the institution of slavery in all its forms. In other words, the Thirteenth Amendment not only bans state-sanctioned slavery but it also forbids any person from having a slave.

Because the Constitution (except for the Thirteenth Amendment) imposes limits only on the state and federal government whenever they have taken actions that have violated the civil or political rights of another, there must be a determination of whether defendant's actions constitute governmental or "state" action of a type regulated by the appropriate constitutional provision.

In many types of constitutional litigation the state action issue is not difficult. When a legislature, executive officer (e.g., the policeman engaging in a search or arrest), or a court takes some official action against an individual, that action is subjected to review under the Constitution, for the official act of any governmental agency is direct governmental action and therefore subject to the restraints of the Constitution. All state officials when acting under "color of state authority" satisfy the state action requirement of the Constitution.

The "state action" issue becomes more complex when the persons or entities alleged to have violated the Constitution are not

299

explicitly acting on behalf of the government. In such a case the persons or entities in question will argue that they are incapable of violating the Constitution because they are not part of the government, raising the question if there is "state action" or what might be called state responsibility.

Actions of any governmental entity give rise to state action for the purposes of constitutional limitations. Any subdivision of a state, an administrative agency, a public school, an independent political subdivision, such as a city, represents government or state authority to a sufficient degree to invoke constitutional restrictions on its actions.

While the cases refer to "state action," the identical issue arises when the *federal* government or its agents are involved in a case. In all cases, the problems relating to the existence of government action—local, state or federal—that would subject an individual to constitutional restrictions come under the heading of "state action."

Beginning in the late 1980s and 1990s, the Supreme Court stated that a court should make two inquiries in determining whether a private actor who has harmed other persons acted with "state action." The court must determine, first, "whether the claimed constitutional deprivation [the harm caused to some private persons by the individual who is alleged to be acting with 'state action'] resulted from the exercise of a right or privilege having its source in state authority [or the authority of the federal government in a federal case] and, second, whether the private party charged with the deprivation could be described in all fairness as a state actor." *Edmonson v. Leesville Concrete Co., Inc.* (1991).

In the first step of the analysis a court asks whether the private actor who caused the harm to another person was acting in conformity with the law of the jurisdiction when he caused the harm. That inquiry may well be of little practical importance in deciding any state action case. If a private actor is breaking the law of the jurisdiction when he harms another individual, it is unlikely that the private actor will be subject to a suit that centers on whether he had state action when he caused the harm.

For example, when a burglar breaks into a house and takes away property, he is not subject to Fourth Amendment limitations on searches and seizures or Fifth Amendment restrictions on the taking of property, because his actions have absolutely no connection to the government. However, if the burglar broke into a house at the direction of state police, who wanted the burglar to seize evidence for the government to use in a criminal investigation, the burglar would be acting with state action because he was in a conspiracy with, and acting at the direction of, the police. Even though the burglar's action in the latter situation violates state or local laws, the burglar would be acting with state authority, at the behest of state actors.

The second question the Court started asking in its decisions in the 1980s and 1990s melds the traditional "public function" and "entanglement" branches of state action analysis from earlier cases. In the second step of the analysis a court should determine whether the actions of the private actor can be described "in all fairness" as the acts of a person acting with state action. In making this determination, the Supreme Court said that a court should examine three factors: "[1] the extent to which the actor relies on governmental assistance and benefits, ... [2] whether the actor is performing a traditional government function.... [3] and whether the injury caused is aggravated in a unique way by the incidence of government authority." *Edmonson v. Leesville Concrete Co., Inc.* (1991).

The second of the three factors listed by the Court in the second step of its analysis is merely traditional public function analysis, which we will examine in the next section of this chapter. The first and third factors are only some of the factors to consider when determining whether the totality of contacts between the government and a private person are such that it is fair, and constitutionally necessary, to restrict the actions of the private person with constitutional limitations. In later sections of this chapter we will examine the types of contacts between the government and a private actor that can be the basis for finding state action when the private actor is not performing a traditional government function.

(b) Origins of the Problem

The issues concerning the applicability of constitutional restrictions and congressional legislation to private conduct did not rise until after the enactment of the Civil War Amendments. At the time of the proposal and ratification of the Thirteenth and Fourteenth Amendments, the Congress passed a wide ranging series of civil rights statutes designed to protect blacks against the actions of both state officials and private persons. In several cases between 1875 and 1882 the Supreme Court indicated that Congress was not empowered to regulate the conduct of private persons simply because that conduct might disadvantage blacks or other persons. In the two most important cases of the period the Court held that federal criminal indictments under the Civil Rights Acts for participation in the lynchings of blacks were unconstitutional as applied to persons who had no connection to state governments and who were not interfering with uniquely federal rights such as the petitioning of Congress. However the issue was not fully examined until 1883 in the *Civil Rights Cases* (1883).

The *Civil Rights Cases* concerned four criminal indictments and one civil action under Section 1 of the Civil Rights Act of 1875. That Act established criminal and civil penalties against anyone who interfered with the "full and equal enjoyment" of public facilities and conveyances by persons because of their race. The five cases were brought against individuals and railroads who had excluded black persons from railroads, hotels and theaters because of their race. The Court reversed the indictments and the civil penalty, because it held that the discrimination did not involve state action, which the Fourteenth Amendment ("nor shall any State deprive ...") requires. The Court also held that the congressional acts could not be justified by the Thirteenth Amendment, because that Amendment only related to abolition of slavery in the United States.

As to the Fourteenth Amendment issue, the Court's basic premise in the *Civil Rights Cases* was that Congress had no power to enact legislation under section 5 of the Fourteenth Amendment unless the law dealt with actions that violated section 1 of the Fourteenth Amendment, and that section only dealt with rights that the *states* must not violate; the fatal flaw of Section 1 of the Civil Rights Act of 1875 was that it had "state action" requirement. So long as neither the state government nor its agencies deprived anyone of rights there is no state violation of due process or equal protection of law. If a private person or a corporation refuses to allow blacks to use public accommodations or public conveyances, they are engaging in private wrongs that had no relationship to a deprivation of rights that the Fourteenth Amendment protects.

The *Civil Rights Cases* also held that these laws should not be upheld under the enforcement clause of the Thirteenth Amendment. That Amendment does not require state action, for it abolishes slavery and involuntary servitude in the United States regardless of whether those conditions are imposed by a government entity or private persons. However, for a law to be a valid enforcement mechanism for this Amendment it would have to relate to the abolition of slavery or the "badges and incidents" of slavery.

There were three distinct holdings in the *Civil Rights Cases*. First, that the guarantees of civil liberties contained in the Fourteenth Amendment applied only to governmental or "state" actions. Second, that the Fourteenth Amendment only empowered Congress to regulate the activities that the Court independently would find to be a violation of section 1 of the Amendment. Third, that the Court will independently review congressional legislation under the Thirteenth Amendment to insure that it was designed to eliminate clear vestiges of slavery.

These three holdings have had varying degrees of acceptance by later Justices and the Court. The modern Court has rejected the final holding relating to the Thirteenth Amendment and now upholds federal based on the Thirteenth Amendment if Congress acted rationally in forbidding the badges and incidents of slavery. E.g., *Jones v. Alfred H. Mayer Co.* (1968).

In 1966, six Justices (some in the majority and some in the dissent) in dictum indicated their belief that Congress could regulate private actions that would have constituted a denial of due process or equal protection if those actions had been undertaken by the state, but these Justices did not state that view in a majority opinion, so it was never a holding of the Court. Later, the Court clearly concluded that Congress could *not* use section 5 of the Fourteenth Amendment to regulate or prohibit the actions of *private* persons merely because those actions would constitute a violation of equal protection if done by the state. *United States v. Morrison* (2000). *Morrison* held, among other things, that Congress did not have the power to give individuals a statutory right to be free from sexual assault by *private* persons, because a private person's sexual attack does not involve state action.

From these early cases to the present, the Court has developed a series of theories to find state action in cases where it is not immediately apparent. The remainder of this Chapter examines and analyzes this question.

§ 12.2 The Public Function Concept

If private persons are engaged in the exercise of governmental functions their activities are subject to similar constitutional restrictions. The state cannot free itself from the limitations of the Constitution in the operation of its governmental functions merely by delegating certain functions to otherwise private individuals. The functions of government that are subjected to these restraints are termed "public functions." But, while this theory is easily justified, it is very difficult to determine what activities should be deemed public functions and subjected to constitutional limitations.

The fact that a private person engages in an activity that could be performed by a state government will not in itself subject him to such limitations, for state governments could engage virtually in any activity. But if activities or functions are traditionally associated with sovereign governments, and are operated almost exclusively by governmental entities, they are public functions subject to due process, equal protection, and so forth. Thus, the operation of election systems, the governance of cities and towns, and, perhaps, the operation of seemingly public facilities such as parks are public functions. Because the Court has given us only the most general guidelines to these determinations, it is important to review the major decisions of the Court in this area.

The First Public Function Cases: The White Primaries. The public function concept originated in a series of decisions relating to the applicability of the Fourteenth and Fifteenth Amendments to primary elections in Texas, which were segregated by race. As early as 1927 the Court held that Texas state laws that excluded blacks from Democratic primaries violated the Fourteenth Amendment. *Nixon v. Herndon* (1927). A few years later the Court held that if state law grants political party committees the authority to determine who is eligible to vote in the primary, then the action of the committees in excluding blacks from voting is state action and violates the equal protection clause. *Nixon v. Condon,* (1932).

In 1935, in *Grovey v. Townsend* (1935), the Court backed away from the logic of these decisions and held that a state political party convention that discriminated on the basis of race was not constitutionally invalid because there was no state action connected to it. However, nine years later in *Smith v. Allwright* (1944) overruled *Grovey.*

Smith held that the white primary system, which a Texas political party convention (not the state of Texas) established, violated the Fifteenth Amendment because the election system and the fixing of qualifications for voters is a public function that is subject to constitutional limitations regardless of who actually conducted the election.

The culmination of these series of cases is *Terry v. Adams* (1953), which found state action in the practices of the "Jay Bird Democratic Association," which was composed of supposedly voluntary clubs of white Democrats in Texas. These clubs held their own private elections of nominees who then ran in the Democratic primaries in Texas—usually unopposed. The Court held that these pre-primary elections constituted state action even though there had been a "complete absence" of formal state connection to any of the activities of the political clubs. There was no majority opinion in this case but the Justices agreed that the relationship between the club practices and electoral system constituted the delegation of a public function to this group so as to subject it to the Fifteenth Amendment. Justice Frankfurter noted that while the state had taken no positive action it had *abdicated* its responsibility of insuring a racially neutral election system and that this abdication was the basis for subjecting the club to the restrictions of the Fifteenth Amendment.

Company Towns and Public Parks. *Marsh v. Alabama* (1946) involved a "company town," which was a *privately owned* area encompassing both residential and commercial districts. The Gulf Shipbuilding Corporation owned and governed this area but it had no formal ties to any state agency or authority. Agents of the corporation had ordered a Jehovah's Witness to leave the privately owned business district and to refrain from distributing religious leaflets within the boundaries of the company town. If the order were valid it would have subjected the leafleter to conviction under state trespass laws for her refusal to leave the area or stop distributing literature. Unquestionably this town would have violated the First Amendment if it were an agency of the state attempting to suppress the distribution of the literature. Thus, the only issue in the case was the applicability of the First and Fourteenth Amendments to the conduct of the corporation that owned the town. The Court held that the First and Fourteenth Amendments applied.

The Court relied on the fact that the state allowed private ownership of land and property to a degree that allowed this corporation to replace all of the functions and activities that would normally belong to a city. The privately owned business area served as the equivalent of a community shopping district in a normal city, so the First Amendment applied in full force to the activities that took place there. Perhaps the most revealing part of the opinion was the statement that, in the determining of the existence of a public function, the Court would "balance the constitutional rights of the owners of property against those of the people to enjoy freedom of press and religion."

Evans v. Newton (1966) involved the exclusion of members of racial minorities from a park in Macon, Georgia. Senator Bacon's will, in 1911, gave the city a public park and required that it be used only by white persons. The city had originally been the trustee and operator of the segregated park until the decision in *Brown v. Board of Education* (1955) (*Brown* II). The city then resigned as trustee and requested the appointment of private persons to take its place.

The Supreme Court held that the park could not be operated with the racial restriction even if the new trustees would have no connection to the city government. The Court seemed to center on the entanglement between the city government and the operation of the park. For example, the city continued to offer certain maintenance assistance to the park even after the substitution of the private trustees. However, the opinion indicated that the park could not be operated on a racially restricted basis even if the city managed to sever all of its ties to the operation of the facilities. Justice Douglas' majority opinion implied that the operation of the park was an essential municipal function that could not be delegated to private persons so as to avoid the restrictions of the Fourteenth Amendment.

Following this decision the local state courts terminated the trust and the land reverted to the heirs of Senator Bacon. *Evans v. Abney* (1970) upheld this reversion to the heirs—for uses other than a racially restrictive park. The divided Court found that the application of property law that ended the trust and returned the land to the heirs did not violate the Constitution because it was not premised on any continuation of racial restrictions. This holding strengthens the theory that the operation of the public park on a racially restrictive basis violated the Fourteenth Amendment because it constituted a public function.

The Shopping Center Cases. The most interesting developments under the public function concept occurred in relation to privately owned shopping centers. In a series of three cases between 1968 and 1976 the Supreme Court wrestled with the problem of whether there was a constitutional right to go into the open areas of privately owned shopping centers to distribute pamphlets on public issues (e.g., anti-war protests) in the same way that one could distribute pamphlets on the public sidewalks. In the final analysis the Court held that there were no First Amendment rights in these areas because the privately owned shopping centers did not constitute a public function and there was no state action that violated the Constitution. See, *Hudgens v. National Labor Relations Board* (1976), holding that privately-owned shopping centers are not company towns and are not state action. This opinion explicitly overruled *Amalgamated Food Employees Union v. Logan Valley Plaza* (1968).

Later *PruneYard Shopping Center v. Robins* (1980) held that *Hudgens* did not preclude a state from granting protection to speech and associational activities at privately owned shopping centers.

Public Utilities. The Supreme Court restricted the scope of public function analysis in *Jackson v. Metropolitan Edison Co.* (1974), which concerned the activity of a privately owned electric utility and the applicability of the due process clause to its termination of services for individual customers. The plaintiff complained that the private-owned utility violated her procedural due process rights when it terminated her electric services without giving her notice and a hearing as if it were a governmental agency that was terminating state benefits to her. The Court found no state action involved in the operation of this utility even though it was given virtually a monopoly status and licensed by the state.

Later, by the way, the Court held that government-operated utility companies must provide their customers with fair notice and billing review procedures prior to termination of service if state law provides for such termination only "for cause." *Memphis Light, Gas and Water Division v. Craft* (1978). *Jackson* indicated that only those activities that are traditionally reserved to state authority or commonly associated with state sovereignty are "public functions."

Self-help Creditor Remedies. *Flagg Brothers, Inc. v. Brooks* (1978) held that a warehouseman's proposed private sale of goods entrusted to him for storage, as state paw *permitted* (the self-help provision of New York Uniform Commercial Code) was not an action properly attributable to state of New York and thus was not "state action" absent allegation of the participation of any public officials.

Flagg Brothers said that its holding did not affect prior rulings finding state action in programs providing incidental aid to segregated schools. The Court also noted that activities such as "education, fire and police protection, and tax collection" might constitute public functions, although his opinion did not resolve these issues. Indeed, in a footnote the majority refused to rule that private control of debtor-creditor disputes could never constitute a public function or state action. "This is not to say that dispute resolution between creditors and debtors involves a category of human affairs that is never subject to constitutional constraints. We merely address the public function doctrine as respondents would apply it in this case."

Flagg Brothers asserted that: "Unlike the parade of horribles suggested by our Brother Stevens in dissent, this case does not involve state authorization of private breach of the peace." The property was already in the hands of the private party and the state law did not authorize any private party to resort to violence (unlike a state statute that "recognized" a right of the strong to take the property of the weak).

The economists would say that the state reserved to itself a monopoly of violence. If the state marshal seized the property, she would have the authority of the state supporting her actions and it would be a crime for anyone to interfere with her. If a private warehouseman already has the property, the state law merely recognizes that. If the debtor has the property, the law recognizes that as well. In both cases, the law will not allow the private warehouseman or the debtor to take the property by force; only the marshal and do that, and when she does, she is engaging in state action.

Thus, *Lugar v. Edmondson Oil Company* (1982), ruled that a debtor could challenge, as a violation of due process, the state procedure by which a creditor secured a pretrial writ of attachment against his property based upon the creditor's ex parte petition. The involvement of the state judicial system in the issuance of the writ, and the involvement of the county sheriff in the execution of the writ, distinguished the *Lugar* case from the *Flagg Brothers* creditor "self help" decision. Thus the debtor in *Lugar* could challenge the debt collection system whereas the debtor in *Flagg Brothers* could not.

If police officers (or other government officials) assist a creditor in seizing the property of an alleged debtor, the joint action of the police and the creditor constitutes state action. The seizure of the alleged debtor's property through joint action of the creditor and police will violate due process and the Fourth Amendment if the seizure was not carried out with the procedural safeguards required for a constitutionally reasonable seizure of property. *Soldal v. Cook County*.

The private party's seizure of an alleged debtor's property is not a public function. If the creditor acts alone in seizing the property, the seizure does not involve state action. The involvement of the police department officers in the seizure gives rise to state action, so as to trigger due process and Fourth Amendment restrictions on both the police officers and the creditor.

The Jury Selection Cases. An attorney participating in jury selection, even when exercising peremptory challenges (i.e., a challenge to a juror without cause), is participating in a traditional public function. The lawyer tells the judge whom he wishes to exclude, but it is the judge who makes the exclusion, and it is state or federal law that allows the lawyer to exercise any peremptory challenges.

Thus, *Edmonson v. Leesville Concrete Co., Inc.* (1991) ruled that a private litigant violates the equal protection guarantee if he used peremptory jury challenges to exclude persons from jury service because of their race. Later, *Georgia v. McCollum* (1992) applied this rule to criminal *defense* counsel (the Court had long before ruled that prosecutors' peremptory challenges are state action). *J.E.B. v. Alabama ex rel. T.B* (1994) held that the intentional use of peremptory challenges by a government attorney to exclude persons of one sex from a jury violated the equal protection clause.

§ 12.3 State Commandment or Encouragement of Private Activities

Other than the public function cases, the determination of state action is based on the relationship between government and the activities of the alleged wrongdoer. There is no formal test for the amount of contacts with government that will subject a private person's activities to the restrictions of the Constitution. The one constant factor in the cases is the Justices' unwillingness to commit to any such test. The Court has stressed continually that it must determine on a case by case basis whether there is state action present by "sifting facts and weighing circumstances." *Burton v. Wilmington Parking Authority* (1961). However, it is possible to isolate certain factors that have caused the Court to make a determination of state action in a particular activity.

One category of cases include cases where the aggrieved party claims that the wrongdoer has been commanded or encouraged by government to engage in the activity that has harmed the aggrieved party.

For example, in *Lombard v. Louisiana* (1963) reversed the trespass convictions of sit-in demonstrators protesting the refusal of privately-owned diners to serve blacks. The protestors would sit in the dinner and refuse to leave until they were served. The city officials, prior to the demonstration, condemned sit-ins and stated that the city was prepared to enforce the law against trespass. These statements were taken to be official encouragement of store owners to use the state trespass laws in a discriminatory manner.

Not every encouragement by state officials will result in a finding of state action if the challenged activities of private persons were themselves worthy of some constitutional deference. For example, the Court might not find sufficient state action if members of the majority race refusing to invite minorities to their homes for private dinner parties simply because the sheriff said, in response to a reporter's questions, that the city will enforce its trespass laws. The importance of private property and associational rights might require that no state action be found unless the racially discriminatory dinner invitations were solely the product of the official encouragement.

The decision of the state courts to enforce a private, racially restrictive real estate covenant is state action. When judges command private persons to take specific actions that would violate the Constitution if done by the State, state action will be present in the resulting harm to constitutionally recognized rights. The classic example is *Shelley v. Kraemer* (1948). A white property owner attempted to sell his property to a black purchaser. The house was subject to a covenant that forbade sales to racial minorities. Third-parties—those persons with an interest in the restrictive covenant—sued to restrain the current owner from violating the covenant by selling to a black. In other words, there was a willing purchaser and a willing buyer, but the state court would enjoin the sale because third parties wanted to enforce the racially restrictive covenant. The Court said that, in such a situation, the state court order would constitute the state action that prevented the willing buyer and willing seller from contracting each other.

In contrast, consider *Moose Lodge Number 107 v. Irvis* (1972). The Moose Lodge refused to serve Irvis, a black guest of a member the lodge, solely because of his race. Irvis contended that the discrimination was state action, and thus violated the equal protection clause, because the Pennsylvania liquor board had issued appellant a private club liquor license.

The Court ruled, first, that Pennsylvania's regulatory scheme, which the state liquor board enforced, did not sufficiently implicate the state in the Moose Lodge's discriminatory guest practices so as to constitute "state action." There is no suggestion in the record that the State's regulation of the sale of liquor is intended overtly or covertly to encourage discrimination. However, and second, the state liquor board's regulation requiring that "every club licensee shall adhere to all the provisions of its constitution and by-laws" in effect placed state sanctions behind the discriminatory guest practices and those should be enjoined to the extent that it requires Moose Lodge to adhere to those practices.

The existence of a state law that recognizes the legitimacy of an action taken by an otherwise private person will not give rise to "state action" being present in the private activity. To imbue an activity with state action there must be some non-neutral involvement of the state with the activity. Thus, *Martinez v. California* (1980) held that a state parole board was not liable under federal civil rights acts for the death of a young girl killed by a parolee, five months after his release because there was no state action that caused her death. The parole board was state action, but a parole board's failure to accurately assess the rehabilitation of prison inmates does not deprive other persons of any constitutionally protected interest, even if the parolee injures or kills those persons.

Another class of cases involves the state's de facto authorization of activities by public officers. When a public officer takes acts relating to his office those actions should be considered to be "state action" even if they exceed the scope of the officer's authority under the law of that jurisdiction. Thus, the Court has held that law enforcement officers who beat a prisoner to death did so under "color of law." *Screws v. United States* (1945) (interpreting and applying Congressional Act passed in pursuance of section 5 of the Fourteenth Amendment that used the phrase "under color of any law").

These cases regarding de facto authorization of public officials' actions should be unaffected by the decisions regarding state "recognition" of otherwise private actions. Were it not for state action, the public official would not have the opportunity to abuse his authority, nor would he be able to represent to the public that his actions were authorized by the government. This fact distinguishes the de facto cases from the state recognition of many private self-help actions because the self-help remedies would exist to some extent even if the state never recognized or authorized those actions. *Flagg Bros., Inc. v. Brooks* (1978).

The distinction between recognition of private action and governmental authorization of activities by public officers is illustrated by comparing two cases. First, *Polk County v. Dodson* (1981) held that a public defender did not act under color of state law when performing a lawyer's traditional functions as counsel to a defendant in a criminal proceeding. The state merely paid the public defender, but did not control the public defender or give her special authority (like the authority the state gives to anyone who wears the policeman's badge). The public defender worked for the client and was serving an essentially private function, adversarial to, and independent of, the state. However, the Court noted, a public defender making hiring and firing decisions on behalf of the state may be a state actor.

Contrast *Lugar v. Edmondson Oil Co., Inc.* (1982). An oil company sued an alleged debtor in Virginia state court and, pursuant to state law, obtained a prejudgment writ of attachment of some of the debtor's property. The county sheriff, an obvious state actor, executed the prejudgment writ. The involvement of state officials in the prejudgment attachment process provided a state action basis for the debtor's claim that he had been deprived of property without due process.

The Court set forth a two part test to determine if deprivation of a federal right may be fairly attributed to the state: "First, the deprivation must be caused by the exercise of some right or privilege created by the state, or by a rule of conduct imposed by the state, or by a person for whom the state is responsible.... Second, the party charged with the deprivation must be a person who may fairly be said to be a state actor [either] because he is a state official, or because he has acted together with or has obtained significant aid from state officials, or because his conduct is otherwise chargeable to the state." *Lugar* satisfied this two part test. While the oil company's *private* misuse of a state statute could not be attributed to the state, *the procedural scheme created by the statute* was state action. Second, the ex parte application of the oil company resulting in attachment of the property by the sheriff made the oil company a joint participant with state officials in the seizure of the property.

§ 12.4 Symbiotic Relationships

In many situations an alleged wrongdoer appears to have a variety of physical and economic contacts to the government even though it is not an agent of the government or part of a regulated industry. These multiple or joint contacts may so intertwine the private actor and the government that the private actor will be treated as a government agent. Even though there is no partnership, these contacts may give the appearance of government action. Where the private actor and government can be said to be in a "symbiotic relationship," the private actor will be subject to constitutional restraints.

This category is, in reality, a "catch all" that may have little, if any, substantive meaning. All that can be said with certainty is that the Court has found some otherwise private actors to have sufficient state action to subject them to constitutional restraints even though no single factor indicated that the government was responsible for their activities. The courts engage in "sifting the facts and weighing the circumstances," as illustrated by the leading case of *Burton v. Wilmington Parking Authority* (1961).

Burton held that a privately owned restaurant that leased space in a government parking facility could not refuse service racial minorities. While the restaurant did not receive any direct aid from the government it benefited from its location within the government facility. The restaurant's location and status as a lessee of the government gave the appearance of government authorization of the practices. While the government and restaurant were not co-venturers, they were in a "symbiotic relationship." The restaurant benefited from its location in the government facility and patronage by government workers. And to the extent the restaurant made improvements to the realty, it enjoyed the parking authority's tax exemption. The government benefited from convenience for its employees as well as the rental monies received. In that sense, the state profited from the decision of the restaurant to discriminate racially in serving its patrons.

There was no single factor that indicated the presence of state action in the challenged practices, the majority concluded that the totality of the circumstances showed sufficient contacts to the government to subject the restaurant's activities to constitutional restraint. When the activities of the government and the private actor become so intertwined for their mutual benefit, the private party has no basis for complaint when his decisions are subjected to constitutional limitations in the same manner as those of the government.

Consider also, *Reitman v. Mulkey* (1967). In this case, the people of California approved an amendment to the state constitution that not only repealed open housing legislation (i.e., legislation preventing private parties from discriminating racially in selling and renting housing) but also prevented the state legislature or local governments from enacting similar legislation. The amendment, in effect, required supporters of open house to pass a special hurdle (a new constitutional amendment) that did not apply to supporters of other, similar legislation. The Court held that this amendment constitutes state action that violates equal protection.

One might argue that the amendment encouraged racial bias in land transactions. However the state's refusal to outlaw *private* discrimination on the basis of race in real estate activities is not encouraging such activity. Such a position would mean that the state could never repeal legislation that protected minority rights. The Supreme Court of California had held that the amendment would cause increased discriminatory practices, and the U.S. Supreme Court said it was defer to that judgment, but that made little sense because federal courts do not defer to state courts on what the federal constitution means. Nor would it make sense to treat the state court conclusion as some sort of "fact," like a trial jury would make. First, the state supreme court is not a jury. Second, to defer would mean that another state court, or even a state court in California at a different time could conclude that a similar amendment did not, as a factual matter, encourage private discrimination and hence is constitutional.

A stronger rationale for *Reitman* is the fact that the ultimate effect of California's constitutional provision was to establish a legal impediment to minority access to legislative remedies for their problems in the real estate market. Thus the Amendment could be considered the direct activity of a state to create a "super-majority" requirement for the passage of laws that would assist racial minorities. Before a city or the state could enact open housing legislation, the state constitution would have to be amended. So viewed the state amendment directly violates the Fourteenth Amendment because it restricted access to legislative remedies based on the race of those seeking legislative action.

Contrast *Washington v. Seattle School District No. 1* (1982) with *Crawford v. Board of Education of Los Angeles* (1982). *Seattle School District No. 1* invalidated a state statute, adopted through voter initiative, that effectively permitted mandatory assignment or transfer of students by local school boards for any reason except for the purpose of desegregating schools. The statute violated the equal protection clause because it used the racial nature of an issue to determine the governmental decision-making structure. The law left student assignment in the power of local school boards *except* when assignment related to desegregation. The law removed assignment of students for desegregation purposes from the power of local boards, and placed at the state level, thus imposing substantial and unique burdens on racial minorities seeking elimination of school segregation.

However, in *Crawford*, the Court upheld a state constitutional amendment providing that state courts could not order mandatory assignment or transportation of students unless a federal court would do so to remedy a violation of the equal protection clause of the Fourteenth Amendment. Stressing that the amendment did not embody a racial classification, the majority opinion held that mere repeal of race-related legislation that was never required by the federal constitution does not violate equal protection. The state constitution did not allocate governmental or judicial power on the basis of a discriminatory principle, nor did it interfere with the school districts' obligation under state law to take steps to desegregate and their freedom to adopt reassignment and busing plans to effectuate desegregation.

In every state action case the question is whether a seemingly private person or entity should be subject to the restrictions of the constitution. The answer to this will be based on whether the conduct of that private person or entity, which allegedly has deprived a person of a constitutional right, should be attributed to governmental action. In *National Collegiate Athletic Association v. Tarkanian* (1988) the Court (five to four) held that the National Collegiate Athletic Association [NCAA] did not violate the due process rights of a basketball coach because it was not a state actor. The NCAA had found that the coach and the basketball program of the University of Nevada, Las Vegas [UNLV] had violated the association's rules in a variety of ways. Consequently, the NCAA took certain disciplinary actions against the school, such as placing the school on probation, and ordering the school to "show cause" why it should not be subject to additional disciplinary sanctions (such as an increase in the number of years in which it would be excluded from the NCAA basketball tournament) unless it removed the coach from all coaching duties at the university during the period of time when the university was on NCAA probation. The fact that the NCAA was made up of both private and state universities did not result in NCAA rules, or their enforcement by an NCAA committee, having the type of "state action" that would subject those rules and enforcement practices to constitutional restraints under the Fourteenth Amendment.

The Court has often found that when a private person engages in a conspiracy with government actors to deprive a person of federal rights that the conspiracy (and actions taken pursuant to it) involve state action by the government official and the private persons in the conspiracy. However, in *Tarkanian* there was no conspiracy or agreement between the NCAA and the state university to deprive the coach of any federal right or take any action against him. In fact, UNLV had supported the coach's position regarding his innocence and the unfairness of punishing him for what UNLV administrators believed were only alleged, but not proven, violations of NCAA regulations. UNLV had not delegated any power to the NCAA; UNLV was free to accept the coach's assertion of his innocence and refuse to take disciplinary action against him. The reason that UNLV chose to take actions against the coach was its desire to avoid having sanctions imposed upon it in its NCAA activities and its decision not to withdraw from the NCAA.

Government Subsidies or Aid. Another set of joint contact cases involves public funding or other direct aid to persons who are alleged to violate the Constitution. In these cases the government is giving direct aid to a person whose activities would violate the Constitution *if* the government itself were engaging in the action.

Two separate questions arise in such cases. First, does state aid to a private party subject that person's activities to constitutional review? Second, even if the private activities are not subject to constitutional limitation, may the government continue to grant the private wrongdoer a subsidy?

For example, assume that an otherwise private school discriminates on the basis of race and also receives a $5,000 yearly grant from the state. If a black student sues to gain admission to the school does the financial support by the state establish his right to entry under the fourteenth amendment? If the court finds that there is insufficient state action present in the school's activities to subject it to constitutional restraint, may the state stop giving that school cash subsidies? There is nothing that requires that these two questions be answered in the same manner, because the second question involves a government program rather than a limitation on the actions of private persons.

When the government provides some direct, specialized subsidy to an entity that impairs fundamental constitutional rights there can be no question but that the government aid program violates the Constitution. Regardless of whether the private party has a right to act free of constitutional restraints, it is clear that the government has no authority to provide specialized benefits to those who effectively burden the exercise of constitutional rights.

For example *Moose Lodge Number 107 v. Irvis* (1972) held that private clubs such as the Moose Lodge have a right—unless there is a law to the contrary—to exist as racially restrictive, private voluntary associations. However, both before and after that decision, lower federal courts held that such clubs could not receive *specialized* tax exemptions that were the equivalent of a cash subsidy. E.g., *Pitts v. Department of Revenue*, 333 F.Supp. 662 (E.D.Wis.1971) (three-judge district court enjoining tax exemptions to organizations that discriminate in their membership on the basis of race). These clubs still can benefit from *generalized* government services such as police and fire protection or general tax exemptions. Regardless of their racially discriminatory acts they have a right to exist in the same manner as any other person or association—generalized government services do not constitute prohibited state action. However, they cannot receive any specialized benefits that would be the equivalent of government support for their racially restrictive practices.

In assessing the quantity of aid and whether it provides support for the challenged activity the Court will consider both the worth of the subsidized activity and the harm to constitutionally recognized rights. Thus, *Norwood v. Harrison* (1973) prohibited the state from granting books to students who attended racially discriminatory schools under a state law that provided free books to all students. The state aid was invalid even though the Court had previously upheld the power of the state to grant textbooks to children who attended *religious* schools under an identical statute. *Board of Education v. Allen* (1968). While the form of state aid to each set of schools was identical, the practice constituted an unconstitutional subsidy only insofar as it aided the racially restricted schools. While the sectarian schools represented the constitutionally recognized values of both free association and the free exercise of religion, the segregated schools represented no similar significant interest.

Consider *Rendell–Baker v. Kohn* (1982). The issue was whether a private school's discharge of its teachers is state action. The Court concluded that the relationship between a private school and its teachers is not changed because the state pays the tuition of most students. "The school . . . is not fundamentally different from many private corporations whose business depends primarily on contracts to build roads, bridges, dams, ships, or submarines for the government. Acts of such private contractors do not become acts of the government by reason of their significant or even total engagement in performing public contracts." Because state regulation and the government funding programs neither commanded nor influenced the school's employment practices, the school's discharge of the teachers did not involve state action.

In other words, the Constitution does not limit the autonomy of private persons or corporations simply because they accept government funds.

Chapter 13

PROCEDURAL DUE PROCESS—
THE REQUIREMENT OF FAIR
ADJUDICATIVE PROCEDURES

Table of Sections

§ 13.1 Introduction

Both the Fifth and Fourteenth Amendments prohibit governmental actions which would deprive "any person of life, liberty or property without due process of law." Due process has several quite distinct meanings.

First, due process restricts the ways in which the government may limit individual freedom. This "substantive" due process may protect certain fundamental rights or void arbitrary limitations of individual freedom of action. Part of the substantive impact of the due process clause of the Fourteenth Amendment is the incorporation of many of the guarantees in the Bill of Rights. Thus state legislatures cannot pass legislation that denies freedom of speech, for to do so would violate due process because part of the liberty that due process protects includes the freedom of speech guaranteed by the First Amendment.

Second, due process also has a procedural aspect in that they guarantee that each person shall be accorded a certain "process" if the government deprives them of life, liberty, or property. When the power of the government is used against an individual, there is a right to a fair procedure to determine the basis for, and legality of, such action. But there is no general requirement that the government institute a procedure prior to taking acts which are unfavorable to some individuals. It is only when someone's "life, liberty or property" is impaired that the government owes that person some type of process for the consideration of his interests. Today the Court defines so as to exclude a variety of personal interests from their scope and protection, even though earlier cases had recognized the phrase as virtually all-encompassing.

If life, liberty or property is at stake, the individual has a right to a fair procedure. The question then focuses on the nature of the "process" that is "due." In all instances the state must adhere to previously declared rules for adjudicating the claim or at least not deviate from them in a manner which is unfair to the individual against whom the action is to be taken. The government always has the obligation of providing a neutral decision-maker—one who is not inherently biased against the individual or who has personal interest in the outcome.

If the government deprives the person of his or her physical liberty for a substantial period of time and penalizes him, due process guarantees that person a trial. The criminal trial process must include all the safeguards of the Bill of Rights as well as being a fair adjudicatory process. When the state penalizes the individual for some infraction of civil law through a judicial action, the trial process must be a fair one, although the Seventh Amendment's guarantee of a jury trial applies only to federal actions.

In a number of other circumstances the government may impair someone's "life, liberty or property" without a trial-type process. These situations involve the regulation of certain specific activities or the denial of some governmental benefits. There are some very specific rulings on the types of procedures that are necessary for the taking of physical property by creditors, but other required "processes" are decided in terms of what procedures are both necessary and affordable for proper resolution of certain types of claims.

The first major section of this chapter we examine what interests the Supreme Court has held to come within the scope of the terms "life," "liberty" or "property," because no process is required if the government actions do not deprive an individual of one of these three interests.

In the second major section, we examine the types of procedures that are due an individual when the government takes an action which deprives him of one of these interests.

§ 13.2 Deprivations of "Life, Liberty or Property" for Which Some Process Is Due

The due process clauses apply only if a government action will constitute the impairment of some individual's life, liberty, or property. Where government actions adversely affect an individual but do not constitute a denial of that individual's life, liberty or property, the government does not have to give the person any hearing or process whatsoever. One might assume (incorrectly as it turns out) that the phrase "life, liberty or property" includes all aspects of an individual's life in society, but the Supreme Court has given the phrase a more restrictive meaning. Since 1972, the Court has continually held that the government need not give someone a procedure to determine the fairness in the treatment of that individual unless its actions fall within distinct rulings as to the meaning of "life," "liberty," and "property."

Erosion of the "Right–Privilege" Distinction. Early in the twentieth century, the Court embraced a distinction in constitutional law between "rights" and "privileges." The government could not deny someone a "right" except for specific reasons that complied with constitutional standards. However, the government could deny anyone a "privilege" for any reason and with no constitutional restrictions. For example, when a policeman lost his job for engaging in political activities, the Supreme Court of Massachusetts upheld the dismissal. Oliver Wendell Holmes, then sitting on the state court, pithily said: "The petitioner may have a constitutional right to talk politics, but he has no constitutional right to be a policeman." *McAuliffe v. Mayor of New Bedford* (Mass. 1892).

The problem with this distinction is that it is conclusory. If the Court decides that you have a "privilege," then you lose. But what test does the Court use to determine if the government is taking away from you a right or a privilege. For example, what if the government said, if you criticize the government, you are ineligible for any government welfare? You have a constitutional right to criticize the government, but you have no "right" to welfare.

The first significant development that eroded the right-privilege distinction was the concept of "unconstitutional conditions." This doctrine recognizes that a state may not do indirectly that which it is forbidden from doing directly. Thus, the government may not deny "privileges" for reasons that violate constitutional guarantees. The state cannot make the gaining or keeping of government benefits conditional upon the recipient's agreement to forego the exercise of constitutional rights. For example, a provision that government-subsidized housing would go only to those who agreed not to speak out against the foreign policy of the federal government would be an "unconstitutional condition;" although there may be no right to housing, the government cannot "buy up" First Amendment freedoms, which it could not restrain directly. The "unconstitutional conditions" may also be a tautology, because it does not tell the Court how to determine if a condition is unconstitutional.

Judicial Definition of "Life, Liberty or Property." Since 1972, the Court, has, in general, treated quite literally the concept that due process applies only to "life, liberty or property." As we shall see, the Court has allowed the government to injure someone's reputation or terminate his employment without a hearing because a majority of the Justices did not find "liberty" or "property" present in the facts of those cases.

The Court no longer embraces the discredited "right-privilege" distinction, but it only requires due process for certain interests defined as life, liberty or property. The distinction is now between life, recognized liberty interests and property "entitlements" as opposed to unprotected interests or "mere expectations." Unless a government action deprives an individual of one of those interests, the Court will not require any "process" or hearing for the individual adversely affected by the action.

When no life, liberty or property interest is at stake, a state is free to deny privileges to individuals without any hearing and, therefore, on an arbitrary basis. Thus, the Supreme Court summarily held, in a per curiam opinion, that out-of-state lawyers seeking to represent defendants in a state criminal proceeding are not entitled to any hearing as to whether or not they may appear *pro hac vice*. *Leis v. Flynt* (1979) held that a lawyer has neither a liberty nor property interest in being admitted on a case-by-case basis to practice in a state in which he or she is not licensed and that there should be no inquiry into whether or not a state trial judge had been totally arbitrary in refusing to admit the attorneys to practice.

§ 13.3 Life

Definition of "Life." While the Supreme Court has never attempted to define the term "life", it has come very close to doing so in its decisions concerning the prohibition of voluntary abortions. In *Roe v. Wade* (1973) the Court held that the term "person" in the Fourteenth Amendment does not apply to an unborn fetus. When combined with the history of abortion practices prior to the adoption of the Fourteenth Amendment, the Court concluded that a fetus was not a constitutionally recognized person. Thus a fetus has no constitutional rights prior to birth, although a state has greater rights to protect "viable" fetuses.

Termination of Life. The Supreme Court has not dealt with the issue of when a person's life ends following a live birth. Given the ability of medical doctors to sustain a person's life for extended periods following what otherwise would be a fatal occurrence of illness or injury, there are various issues, both procedural and substantive, in the "right to die" cases, discussed primarily in the chapter on equal protection

Relationship of Death Penalty Cases to Due Process Analysis. Detailed rules of criminal procedure, and the Court's rulings concerning the procedures that must be used for imposition of the death penalty, are also due process issues, but they are beyond the scope of this book. However, one could turn to multi-volume edition of our Treatise on Constitutional Law: Substance and Procedure.

§ 13.4   Liberty—Generally

(a) Introduction

There are many meanings for the term "liberty." Under the Fourteenth Amendment, "liberty" includes those provisions of the Bill of Rights that the Court deems to be "incorporated" into the due process clause, as well as "fundamental rights," which the Court derives either from the concept of liberty or other constitutional values. These constitute substantive prohibitions of government actions which would violate those rights.

"Liberty" in the due process clauses is also the basis for the "substantive due process" requirement that legislation must relate to a legitimate end of government. In their procedural aspects, the due process clauses of the Fifth and Fourteenth Amendments require that the government not deprive any individual of a constitutional liberty without a fair "process."

There are two distinct ways in which the state can deprive a person of liberty. First, the government might physically restrain him. Second, the government might curtail his freedom of choice and action by making it impossible or illegal for that person to engage in certain types of activity.

This second category can be subdivided into two parts. The government might deny a person the ability to exercise a right that has special constitutional protection (such as the right to free speech or the right to privacy). Or, the government might foreclose an individual from engaging in an action that has no special constitutional status, but is an action in which others may engage without the restrictions imposed on this individual (such as the freedom to engage in a particular business activity). Thus we may subdivide "liberty" into three headings involving governmental restraints on (1) physical freedom, (2) the exercise of fundamental constitutional rights, and (3) the exercise of other forms of freedom of choice or action.

(b) Physical Liberty

The essential guarantee of the due process clauses is that the government may not imprison or otherwise physically restrain a person except in accordance with fair procedures. The first due process clause is a part of the Fifth Amendment, which is primarily concerned with procedures used to convict someone of crime. But the due process guarantee has long been understood to go beyond the criminal justice system; it governs all government deprivations of liberty. Indeed the protection of physical liberty is the oldest and most widely recognized part of the guarantee.

The initial requirement of due process is that there is some fair procedure for determining whether the government has lawfully taken an individual into custody. While an individual may be arrested without prior judicial approval, such an arrest must be based on probable cause for the police to believe that the person has committed a crime. If the arrest was in fact made without a warrant, the law enforcement authorities must make prompt application to a magistrate for a neutral determination that the arrest was made upon probable cause. Custody of the person even then cannot continue except in conformity with the Eighth Amendment's prohibition of excessive bail. The entire process leading towards the trial of a criminal charge must be undertaken in a timely manner in order to comply with the due process and speedy trial guarantees of the Bill of Rights.

The adjudicative process itself is governed by the specific guarantees of the Bill of Rights and an independent concept of fundamental fairness that the due process clause imposes. The reasonable doubt standard is derived from the due process clause and is the historical barrier to arbitrary deprivation of freedom in the criminal justice system. The standard requires, in criminal cases, that the government prove, within a fair procedural framework, that a person is unquestionably guilty of the crime for which he is to be incarcerated. The standard also prohibits the use of any procedure that shifts to the accused the burden of proving his innocence as to any basic element of the criminal charge.

Loss of Liberty Apart from a Criminal Conviction. The due process guarantee also applies to restraints on physical liberty that are imposed in noncriminal settings. While the required procedures may differ depending on the type of action, the government can never impose substantial physical restraints on an individual without establishing a procedure to determine the factual basis and legality of such actions. Thus a child may not be made a ward of the state and subjected to state custody unless the child first receives a fair procedure including a notice of any charges against him and the assistance of counsel. *Application of Gault* (1967).

The state deprives a significant number of people of their freedom of action by involuntarily committing them to state institutions for mental treatment. While the Court has not clearly defined the procedures required, it is clear that the state cannot commit an adult for a treatment of "mental illness" unless there has a fair procedure to determine that the person is dangerous to himself or others. *O'Connor v. Donaldson* (1975).

Addington v. Texas (1979) ruled that the state cannot involuntarily commit an adult to a psychiatric institution on a burden of proof that only requires the state to show, by a preponderance of the evidence, that the person is dangerous to himself or another. Although the Court did not require a "beyond a reasonable doubt" standard, it held that trial courts must at least employ a "clear and convincing" evidence standard.

The Supreme Court has not required states to provide similar due process safeguards for children who are committed to a mental health care facility by their parent or guardian. *Parham v. J.R.* (1979) concluded that the parents decision to voluntarily commit a child to a state-operated mental health care institution, over the child's objection (the state's commitment of the child, if the child is a ward of the state) deprived the child of a liberty interest but that this deprivation did not require a pre-commitment adversarial hearing. The child is only entitled to have a "neutral fact finder" (such as a state-employed social worker or psychologist) determine if statutory criteria for commitment are met in the individual child's case. The Court did not determine whether the parents' commitment of a child to a *private* institution constituted state action that deprived the child of a constitutionally protected liberty interest.

The Supreme Court has found that juveniles have only a limited right to freedom from government custody. For that reason, the Supreme Court has upheld two types of detention programs for juveniles, without indicating whether similar detention programs for adults would meet constitutional standards. *Schall v. Martin* (1984) upheld a pretrial detention system for juveniles accused of serious crimes, because the Court found that the detention program was nonpunitive in nature and that the program protected both society and the well-being of the accused juvenile. In making that finding, the Court noted that "juveniles, unlike adults, are always in some form of custody," such as the custody of parents or school authorities.

Reno v. Flores (1993) relied on *Schall* when it upheld Immigration and Naturalization Service [INS] regulations regarding the custody of alien juveniles who were being held pending deportation proceedings. The INS regulations allowed for the release of alien juveniles awaiting deportation hearings but this release (except in the most unusual and compelling circumstances) was only to relatives or guardians in the United States. The Court found a child did not have a fundamental right to be released into a noncustodial setting in all circumstances even if noncustodial care would be in the child's "best interest." *Flores* was based, in part, on the uncontested finding that the government custodial program was not punitive in nature.

Post-incarceration Deprivations of Liberty—Prisoners' Rights Cases. A court confronting a prisoner's rights claim will examine two questions. First, did the government action about which the prisoner is complaining involve an intentional deprivation of the individual's life, liberty, or property interests? If the court answers "yes," the second question is, was the person whose life, liberty, or property interest the government has taken given a fundamentally fair procedure for determining whether applicable law justified the taking of that interest? In this section, we will examine the prisoner's rights cases to determine what kinds of interest a prisoner might have that require that he be given a fair hearing prior to depriving him of that interest. In a later section of this Chapter, we will examine the question of what type of procedure should be given to a prisoner if prison authorities are depriving him of a life, liberty, or property interest.

Once a person has been incarcerated following a fair procedure, that fact does not completely terminate his or her right to liberty. Persons convicted of a crime may be placed on probation in lieu of being imprisoned or paroled from prison prior to the end of their maximum sentence. If the state seeks to revoke the probation or parole and place the convicted defendant in prison, it must give him a new hearing. While this hearing need not have the safeguards of a criminal trial it must constitute a fair procedure for determining the basis for the revocation of parole or probation. Taking away early release credit from a prisoner also requires a fair procedure, but the state, without a hearing, can deprive prisoners of benefits by transferring them to a different corrections facility.

When the state convicts a person of a crime, he has received the best process that our society offers to justify his liberty loss. A later transfer of the prisoner to differing conditions of confinement does not require a new process unless the new conditions may be said to be outside of the normal range of (or substantive constitutional limits on) the conditions of confinement. Thus, a prisoner who is transferred to a facility for mental treatment is entitled to a hearing. *Vitek v. Jones* (1980). In *Vitek* the state statutes at issue in this case gave rise to a legitimate expectation on the part of the prisoner that he would only be kept in normal prison facilities and not be transferred to a mental hospital for psychiatric treatment without an accurate determination of his need for that treatment. Secondly, the involuntary commitment to a mental hospital, unlike a transfer between normal correctional facilities, involved the loss of a liberty interest because it involved not only a greater degree of confinement but also the imposition of mandatory treatment and a realistic possibility of stigmatizing consequences for the defendant in the future.

However, when the state places a prisoner in administrative segregation or transfers him to a different penal facility, even one in another state, no new process is required because the transfer does not implicate a liberty interest that was not adequately protected by the original criminal process and conviction. *Montanye v. Haymes* (1976).

The administration of antipsychotic drugs to a prison inmate impairs a constitutionally protected liberty interest of the inmate that his criminal conviction does not automatically take away. Therefore, prison regulations regarding the administration of such drugs to a prison inmate without his consent must comply with both substantive and procedural due process principles. *Washington v. Harper* (1990) upheld both the substantive and procedural aspects of a prison regulation that subjected certain inmates to involuntary treatment with such drugs. The regulation allowed prison authorities to administer the drugs to inmates who were dangerous to themselves or other persons if the treatment was in the inmate's medical interest. In the substantive due process portion of its ruling, the Court held that the regulation was reasonably related to legitimate penological interests. The prison regulation in *Harper* provided the inmate with notice and a hearing before a tribunal of medical professionals and prison authorities at which the inmate could challenge the initial decision to give him the drug treatment. This hearing procedure complied with the fair process requirements of the due process clause.

A convicted inmate of a penal institution does not have a constitutionally cognizable liberty or property interest in the possibility of receiving parole release before expiration of his prison sentence. He has only "a hope which is not protected by due process." But state law might create a specific entitlement to release under certain circumstances which would require some minimal procedures to ensure fair decision-making by a parole board. *Greenholtz v. Inmates of the Nebraska Penal and Correctional Complex* (1979).

Based upon the rationale of the *Greenholtz* decision, the Supreme Court ruled in *Connecticut Board of Pardons v. Dumschat* (1981) that a prisoner serving a life sentence had no right to procedural fairness in the review of his request for commutation of his life sentence. Chief Justice Burger, for the Court, argued that, absent a state-created entitlement to fair treatment in the review of his sentence, the due process clause imposed no procedural safeguards against arbitrary treatment of the defendant's request for commutation. The Court refused to find that the prisoner had a constitutionally cognizable interest at stake in the review of his sentence even though the review board commuted most of the life sentences that came before it.

Correctly analyzed, the ruling in this case is no more than a finding that the prisoner's liberty had been properly taken from him through the criminal trial-and-appeal process. The prisoner had no right to a statement of reasons for the denial of his request because it amounted to nothing more than "an appeal for clemency." However, some may mistakenly view the case as propounding the principle that "liberty" as well as "property" is only a creation of state law, but that position has no basis in prior substantive or procedural due process rulings of the Supreme Court.

These cases establish the principle that a prisoner has no liberty interest in release on parole that is protected by the due process clause unless the government (by statute or administrative regulation) creates such a liberty interest. If state law establishes such an interest, then the due process clause will require the state to grant the individual a fair process for the determination of whether he should be released on parole.

Conclusion. Any significant, even though temporary, physical restraint or punishment of a person constitutes a deprivation of liberty which requires some procedural safeguard. *Ingraham v. Wright* (1977) upheld the use of corporal punishment for children by state school teachers so long as the state had some procedure to later determine the propriety of such actions and impose liability for any excessive use of force. But in so doing the Court fully accepted the position that physical restraint constitutes a deprivation of liberty for which some process is due unless it would be of an extremely brief and *de minimis* nature.

The cases examined in this section involve the determination of when the procedural component of the due process clause requires prison authorities to create a fair procedure for determining that an inmate should be subject to some loss of liberty or property. The legitimacy of prison regulations that restrict the activities of all prisoners, or a specific class of prisoners, must be examined under substantive due process and equal protection principles. The Court has ruled that prison regulations that restrict the exercise of fundamental constitutional rights by prisoners should be upheld so long as the prison regulation is reasonably related to a legitimate penological interest.

(c) Fundamental Constitutional Rights

Liberty includes the freedom of choice to engage in certain activities. When those activities have specific constitutional recognition, the due process guarantee protects the liberty to engage in them. In one sense it may be said that all activities or liberty have constitutional recognition because none is singled out for special limitations. Yet, the government has broad powers to curtail individual freedom of action to promote the legitimate ends of society except where there is some specific constitutional limitation on its powers.

Since 1937 and the rejection of the old substantive due process, the Court will actively protect only "fundamental" constitutional rights. These rights are those with textual recognition in the Constitution, or its Amendments, or values found to be implied because they are "fundamental" to freedom in American society. The Court recognized the concept of fundamental rights when it incorporated most of the guarantees of the Bill of Rights into the due process clause of the Fourteenth Amendment and applied them to the states. The most significant implied "fundamental" rights are the right to freedom of association, the right to interstate travel; the right to privacy (including some freedom of choice in marital, family, and sexual matters), and the right to vote.

Procedural due process requires that the government not restrict a specific individual's freedom to exercise a fundamental constitutional right without a process to determine the basis for the restriction. Thus, if a filmmaker is to be subjected to a licensing system to determine whether his film is obscene, the government must establish a prompt and fair procedure to determine its obscenity or allow him to show the film. Whenever the government seeks to restrain speech, there must be a prompt procedure to determine whether the speech may be limited in conformity with First Amendment principles.

(d) Other Rights or Liberties

While the Court has not defined the exact scope of the liberties which are protected by the due process clauses, it is clear that they go beyond mere physical restraint or fundamental constitutional rights. The clauses also guarantee that each individual will have some degree of freedom of choice and action in all important personal matters. The Court has stated that the term "denotes not merely freedom from bodily restraint but also the right of the individual to contract, to engage in any of the common occupations of life, to acquire useful knowledge, to marry, establish a home and bring up children, to worship God according to the dictates of his own conscience and generally to enjoy those privileges long recognized ... as essential to the orderly pursuit of happiness by free men." *Board of Regents v. Roth* (1972). However, the Court was also careful to note that not all areas of human activity could be described as "liberty" for constitutional terms and that individuals in some situations could be adversely affected by government without any substantive or procedural guarantees.

It would appear that whenever the government takes an action which is designed to deprive an individual or a limited group of individuals of the freedom to engage in some significant area of human activity, some procedure to determine the factual basis and legality for such action being taken is required by the due process clause. The primary issues have arisen in terms of restrictions on employment, the granting or withholding of important occupational licenses, and injury to the reputation of an individual.

Professional Licenses. If the government terminates an individual's ability to engage in a profession, it must grant that individual a procedure to determine his fitness to be a member of the profession. Thus, if an agency with governmental authority seeks to revoke the professional status or license of a doctor or lawyer, it must accord that individual a fair hearing.

If someone seeks temporary admission to practice as a licensed professional in a state, state agencies are under no obligation to grant that person a hearing *prior* to denying him or her the opportunity to practice temporarily in the state, if state law has not created an "entitlement" to practice temporarily in the state. Thus, if a state court judge refused to allow attorneys, licensed only in other states, to appear *pro hac vice* in state court proceedings, there is no deprivation of property because there is no entitlement to engage in temporary practice under state law. The denial involved no deprivation of liberty because the attorneys' reputation and ability to practice law in other states, in which they were licensed, were not seriously damaged by the refusal. *Leis v. Flynt* (1979).

Government as Employer. When the government acts as an employer there are special issues regarding the existence of liberty and property rights in employment. If the law does not grant the particular employee a term of guaranteed employment, absent removal for just cause, the employee will have no property right or entitlement to continued employment in that position. *Board of Regents v. Roth* (1972). If the government dismisses the employee (e.g., one whom the relevant statute says may be fired at will before the end of a probationary period), the government firing or dismissal does not amount to any loss of "liberty" either, because he is at liberty to do anything except stay at a job from which he was fired.

If the government bases its termination for cause (e.g., the employee stole money) then the government must provide a fair procedure prior to his determination, in order to determine if the employee actually stole the money. When the employee can make a prima facie showing that he is being dismissed for exercising his right to freedom of speech as protected by the First Amendment, he will be entitled to a hearing to determine the basis for his termination. If the government worker is an at will employee and is terminated, but the employee claims that he was fired because he exercised a constitutional right (e.g., he exercised his right of free speech), he can sue to raise that claim, but his hearing will be a post-termination hearing, because the firing took away neither his property (he was an at-will employee) nor his liberty (he remains free to speak), but the firing did violate his rights of free speech.

Driver Licenses. Because the government has taken control of who may drive automobiles on its highways, when it revokes someone's driver's license, that person is entitled to a hearing to determine the basis for the revocation. *Bell v. Burson* (1971). For example, if the law provides that one loses her driver's license for driving while intoxicated, at the hearing the state will prove that the defendant was driving while intoxicated.

However, if the revocation is based on *prior* judicial determinations of violations of traffic laws, no hearing is necessary for there are not no further factual issues to contest. *Dixon v. Love* (1977). For example, if the law says that a driver loses his license after three moving violations, then there is no need for a hearing when the driver is convicted of the third violation because he has already received the opportunity for full judicial hearings.

Freedom of Action Within the Community. If the government revokes someone's right to engage in an activity it is required to grant the individual a hearing. Thus, if the government labels someone a "drunkard," and state law makes it illegal to sell alcohol to anyone labeled a drunkard, the state must first provide a hearing to determine if it can label a particular person a drunkard. *Wisconsin v. Constantineau* (1971).

Personal Reputation. Government actions that injure a person's reputation within the community do not constitute a *per se* deprivation of property or liberty so as to require that the person be granted a hearing *prior* to the government action. The individual can always sue under state law for defamation, but the government does not have to give a hearing just because a state actor says something about any individual. For example, the policeman may say to a TV reporter, "The victim says that Mr. Jones raped her. If anyone knows where he is, please let us know." The policeman's claim may injury Mr. Jones' reputation, but there is no violation of procedural due process.

In *Paul v. Davis* (1976), a sheriff had distributed to merchants a listing of "active shoplifters." The plaintiff argued that listing him on the sheet violated due process because there was no hearing to determine whether in fact he had engaged in such activities and this resulted in an injury to his reputation. (The plaintiff had been arrested for shoplifting prior to the distribution of the circular but he had not yet gone to trial.) The Court held that the sheriff's label did not constitute a violation of due process. Mere injury to reputation alone was not a deprivation of "liberty" such that it required the sheriff to have a notice and hearing before making the charge. The aggrieved party had no legal impediment to shopping, unlike the aggrieved party in *Wisconsin v. Constantineau* (1971), who could no longer legally buy liquor.

Paul v. Davis (1976) noted that the individual would have the right to sue the government officials who libeled him, in a state court, as a matter of state tort law. If the State had no tort action for libel against such officials—if the State granted its public officials immunity to defame private citizens while otherwise recognizing defamation action—one might argue that the State was depriving someone of liberty or property by allowing the government to damage his name with no hope of rectifying the harm done.

Paul found there was no impairment of a constitutionally protected liberty or property interest. It is not clear whether harm to an individual's reputation by the government could ever constitute a liberty or property deprivation for the purposes of the due process clause. In *Goss v. Lopez* (1975) the Supreme Court ruled that disciplinary action in a government school that resulted in suspending the student from the school, constituted a deprivation of liberty interests, in part because the disciplinary charges and the suspension would damage the students' associational relationships with fellow students and their future educational and employment opportunities. Also, a suspension of three days, deprived the student of three days of education.

Based on *Goss*, one might argue that a person is entitled to some type of fair process from the government to prevent, or remedy, a government action that will harm the individual's reputation so severely that the person will lose a wide range of employment opportunities. However, *Siegert v. Gilley* (1991) held that a discharged employee of the federal government stated no cause of action under the due process clause when he sued his former supervisor for writing a letter to a prospective employer that prevented him from being hired for the new job. The plaintiff in

Siegert had alleged stated that the material in the government supervisor's letter was false and that the supervisor had made the statements maliciously. *Siegert* acknowledged that the plaintiff in *Paul* had not alleged that the government actor who harmed his reputation had malicious intent to do so, and then said: "our decision in *Paul v. Davis* did not turn, however, on the state of mind of the defendant but on the lack of any constitutional protection for the interest in reputation." Recall the previous example, when the policeman told the reporter, "The victim says that Mr. Jones raped her." There was no claim that the policeman spoke with knowing falsity. Thus, it appears that a person's interest in his reputation may be totally unprotected by the due process clause.

Conclusion. Liberty in its most general sense includes the ability of individuals to engage in freedom of action within a society and free choice as regards their personal lives. Of course, not every limitation of individual freedom constitutes a violation of "liberty" in a constitutional sense or requires that the government grant the individual a hearing. When the government acts so as to regulate an area of human activity for all persons, the law will be tested under the substantive restrictions of the due process clause and the specific protections of the Constitution. But unless some specific fundamental constitutional right is involved the government will be able to regulate most areas of human activity. So long as the government does not classify persons in such a way as to violate the equal protection clause, it may also regulate certain classifications of persons.

But the government's ability to regulate or eliminate an area of activity for a general class does not mean that it should be able to single out individuals for special limitations of freedom of action without granting them some process to determine the basis for such an action. For example, while the state need not let anyone purchase alcohol, it cannot single out a specific individual for denial of the right to purchase alcohol without giving that individual a hearing to determine whether such an action is proper. *Wisconsin v. Constantineau* (1971). This principle does not restrict the substantive powers of the state to regulate activities within its jurisdiction, but only recognizes that when the state acts against a specific individual, it must do so in a procedurally fair manner.

§ 13.5 Property

(a) Introduction

In one sense all property is a creature of the state because each government is free, at least initially, to define or limit property rights. The government, for example, might decide to protect trademarks, thus creating a form of intellectual property. However, the ability of either the state or federal governments to limit rights in property is subject to constitutional limitations. There are substantive limitations—such as the First Amendment, the equal protection guarantee and the concept of substantive due process—that limit the ways in which government can define even the most general property rights. For example, the state government could not define or enforce rights in real property as contingent on the provision that the property not be turned over to a member of a racial minority, for this "definition" would violate the equal protection clause. The government must comply with the few substantive guarantees of the Constitution, but otherwise it is free to define property rights as it chooses.

Besides these substantive guarantees, there is still the important procedural requirement that the government may not deprive a person of any property unless it affords him or her "due process."

There are two basic questions concerning the procedural protection for property. First, when is the government depriving someone of property? Second, what constitutes "property"? The first question really is a state action issue: the due process clauses only protect against governmental, rather than private, deprivations of property. This state action issue is examined in chapter. Whenever the government enforces private claims to property of one person against another, it has acted to deprive someone of his property. Thus state must afford the alleged debtor some fair procedure before it decides to take his property and transfer it to another party.

The most difficult issues relate to the definition of property. Certainly all of the traditional forms of real and personal property fall within this definition, but what of governmental distributions that do not fit this classical concept of property ownership? One might think that any recipient of government benefits or largess (welfare, public education, subsidized water for certain farmers) has no property right in the benefit because such a person has no traditionally recognized ownership interest in the largess. Under the old right-privilege distinction the Court would classify the interest of a recipient of welfare payments or a student's interest in receiving public education as an unprotected privilege. Because the government has no duty to create systems of welfare payments or education, one might think that its decision to grant or withhold any such "privileges" is not restrained by constitutional guarantees.

However, the Court no longer embraces the conclusory right-privilege distinction. The government, for example, need not create a public school system, but that does not mean that, once it creates the system, it can dole out the benefits irrationally. Moreover, when the government does establish this system, its own laws limit the discretion of the government workers to distribute the welfare. For example, the aide in the welfare office cannot distribute welfare checks to his friends. The applicants must meet certain criteria and once they do, they have a statutory right to the welfare payments.

If the applicant meets the statutory requirements for welfare, he is, in a sense, "entitled" to it because the statute says that anyone meeting certain characteristics receives the welfare. When the person no longer meets those characteristics, he no longer is entitled to the welfare. When the government acts to dispense these benefits, it must conform to the restrictions of the Constitution, which means that it may not deprive someone of an interest to which they are otherwise entitled without a procedure to determine the basis for the deprivation.

The definition of property since *Board of Regents v. Roth* (1972) has centered on the concept of "entitlement." The Court will recognize interests in government benefits as constitutional "property" if the person is "entitled" to them. Thus, the applicable federal, state or local law that governs the dispensation of the benefit must define the interest in such a way that the individual should continue to receive it under the terms of the law. If the person already receives the benefit (i.e., a previously recognized claim of entitlement) then, before the state can take it way, the state, in general, must provide a *pretermination* hearing, a fair procedure, before it can take away the benefit.

Government employment is another form of property if the law does not give the supervisor the power to fire the subordinate on a whim. A person has an entitlement-property interest in employment with the government if he has already has position and applicable law guarantees him continued employment. However, if the person has not yet been hired, he has no property right that requires a hearing on the refusal to initially employ him. Similarly, if one occupies a position that applicable law defines as terminable for any reason, that person can be discharged without the requirement of fair procedures. *Bishop v. Wood* (1976).

The concept of entitlement does not require a hearing for those interests that are not statutory entitlements or are totally unlike traditional property. Unfortunately this analysis can come very close to the old right-privilege distinction, for states are allowed to define those interests that they will be required to protect under the due process clause. The requirement of present enjoyment also recognizes that the Constitution does not require a hearing for disappointed wishes or expectations but only for property entitlements.

Obviously, the distinction between "entitlements" and "expectancies" offers little guidance to those who need to solve problems relating to the meaning of property under the due process clauses. All that can be said with certainty is that the Supreme Court focuses on local law to determine if a person can be said to have a fair claim to a continuation of the government benefit. If a person has an entitlement to the benefit, he must receive a fair procedure to determine the basis for the government's withdrawal of the benefit.

If he has no claim of entitlement under applicable law there need be no process at all. State law is critical to the determination of whether or not a person has a "property" or "entitlement" interest in a benefit he receives from the government. The state cannot grant persons a right to a benefit that would be an "entitlement" for due process purposes and then, by statutory action or administrative ruling, give recipients fewer procedural safeguards for the termination of that benefit than would be required by a judicial analysis of due process principles. This is an important distinction. Local law provides the basis for the judiciary to determine whether an interest is protected by due process principles. If such an entitlement exists, the judiciary must determine independently whether the procedures that state law authorizes to terminate the entitlement meet the procedural requirements of due process. See *Cleveland Board of Education v. Loudermill* (1985), discussed below.

It is easier to understand these principles if we look at some specific cases. Let us turn to three particular problems in this area: (1) transfer of property in debt actions; (2) termination of government benefits; (3) government employment. In addition, an individual's interest in his or her reputation is reconsidered as a property interest.

(b) Debt Actions

Whenever someone (a creditor) uses the aid of the government to take property away from another person, there is a deprivation of property. The next question is whether the state had provided due process. Some cases are easy. If plaintiff wins a lawsuit against defendant, and the court orders the defendant to pay money to a plaintiff, the state has deprived the defendant of property. In such a situation, however, there is no denial of due process because the defendant received a fair process—the opportunity for a full trial.

A significant due process issue arises where the government aids a party in taking property in the possession of the alleged debtor *prior* to trial. If, prior to trial, the government grants the plaintiff-creditor a writ of replevin, or otherwise assists in the transfer of property to the creditor, there is a deprivation of the debtor's property, requiring that the government establish some sort of fair procedure to determine whether the creditor should receive the use of property and to insure that the debtor's interest in the property will be safeguarded pending the outcome of the litigation. Even though the property of the defendant is only taken for a time (e.g., "frozen" prior to trial) to insure that the asset will be available to any later judgments, there is a deprivation of property. Although the state has not transferred the property, it has deprived the debtor-defendant of its use for a time. Such garnishments or attachments of debtor assets thus require a fair procedure to protect the interests of the debtor-defendant. We examine the procedures required to safeguard these interests in later sections of this Chapter.

Many states have provisions in their commercial codes that allow private repossession of goods from debtors by creditors. While the private repossession constitutes a taking of a debtor's property, only "state action" is regulated by the due process clauses. A state's formal recognition of the "self-help" remedy (as opposed to state aid, by having the sheriff issue a writ) is not sufficient state action to implicate the due process clause. See Chapter 12 on state action.

(c) Government Benefits

"Government Benefits" is a category that includes all forms of benefits that the government dispenses to individuals. Sometimes these benefits are called "transfer payments." The government may pay these in cash (social security payments or farm subsidies), or distributed in kind (housing in publicly-owned facilities), or given in a hybrid form (food stamps, which constitute a subsidy for particular items). Even the most basic governmental services, such as police protection or public primary education, are forms of public welfare benefits.

Because the government is not under a duty to provide these benefits, they are sometimes referred to as government largess. But when the government distributes these benefits, it must do so in accordance with constitutional limitations. This largess is not like the medieval king throwing alms to passers-by as he walks among the multitude. Instead, the statutory law places limits on who receives these benefits, when the state can reduce them, and when the state can take them away.

The Constitution places some substantive limits. The government cannot deny benefits to someone because he or she is a member of a particular race, for that would violate the equal protection guarantee. It cannot deny benefits to people because they engage in speech or associational activities, or religious activity that the First Amendment protects.

Once the government has established a system of benefits, the due process clauses impose some requirement of fairness in the treatment of individual recipients of these goods or services. An important distinction is between *pre*-termination and *post*-termination hearings. The general rule is that if the government *already gives* a person a benefit, it must offer some sort of fair procedure *before* terminating the benefits (a *pre*-termination hearing). In general a person has no property rights in benefits that he has not yet received.

If the person does not have the benefit, the government does not have to start giving him; instead, the general rule is that the person can sue to collect the benefit. If the person's interest in the continuation of the benefit is categorized as a "mere expectancy", there is no loss of *property* that merits the protection of procedural due process. It is only when the person has a "claim of entitlement" that the interest rises to the level of constitutional property. If the person is a government employee at will, the government can fire the person, who does not have a constitutional right to a *pre*-termination hearing. But, if the person claimed he was fired for an unconstitutional reason (he supervisor did not like his religion), then the person can sue after his termination and argue that the firing violated his First Amendment rights (a *post*-termination hearing). The person who was fired is not claiming a loss of property (because he was an employee-at will) but he is complaining about a loss of liberty (the loss of his job because of he engaged in his right of free exercise). The firing does not prevent him from exercising his liberty, but, if his allegations are true, it did punish him for exercising his religious freedom and he has a right to a *post*-termination hearing to make that claim.

If the applicable state or federal law establishes criteria for continued receipt of the benefit that the individual appears to meet, he will have a claim of entitlement to continued benefits. However, if applicable law creates no claim to future payments, the person has only an "expectancy" of continued benefits. Hence, the courts may allow a state to eliminate the need for hearings to determine the basis for termination of benefits if it establishes a system that clearly indicates that there is no right to continuation of benefits.

Consider, for example, *O'Bannon v. Town Court Nursing Center* (1980). This case held that nursing home residents could establish no government-created entitlement to their continued residence at a particular nursing home. Hence, residents had no right to a hearing *before* a government agency revoked the home's certification to receive payments from the Medicare and Medicaid programs. Decertification of a particular nursing home did not terminate a recipient's medical assistance but merely required him to find a different institution which would accept him and which was certified as qualified for the receipt of Medicare or Medicaid funds. While the residents of a particular nursing home might feel that they would be better treated at the former institution or that it would be difficult for them to find comparable care, they had no *government-created* entitlement to continued benefits at a particular nursing home that the government decertified. Only the owners of the nursing home had a right to be heard in the administrative process leading to the decertification.

Goldberg v. Kelly held that state statutes granting welfare benefits create a sufficient entitlement in the continued receipt of public aid or housing payments to require a hearing to determine the basis for termination of these benefits. Similarly, when a state establishes a school system it must grant students a hearing regarding the fairness of dismissing or suspending them from the system. *Goss v. Lopez* (1975).

Government licenses are also a form of property insofar as they constitute an entitlement to engage in a valuable activity. Thus the government must have a fair procedure to determine whether to revoke driver's licenses or occupational licenses. In all of these cases the government had established criteria for the receipt and continuation of the benefit which the individuals appeared to meet. As the individual had present enjoyment of the benefit and a claim of entitlement to its continuation under state law, he had a property interest that the due process clause protects.

In theory the government might be able to reverse the result of these cases by enacting a law that declares that individuals may have benefits (such as welfare payments, public schooling or occupational licenses) terminated for any reason by the government without any process. Our hypothetical law might say, for example, that it is within the whim and discretion of the public aid official to give benefits to whomever she wishes and to stop giving the aid to whomever she wishes with no standards whatsoever. The law might give her the power of the medieval potentate gives alms to whomever she wishes.

The democratic process should prevent such a law from ever being enacted. If it were enacted, we should not be surprised that our public aid official decided to herself give all of state money; she might give it to her near-do-well brother-in-law. The people of the state could not allow the state to enact such laws because the people do not want to give unbridled discretion to state officials to spend their money with no safeguards. Democracy, just like the due process clause, helps protects us from arbitrary government action.

In addition, one might argue that a law that gives arbitrary discretion is susceptible to attack under the substantive due process and equal protection guarantees as totally arbitrary and invidious uses of governmental power.

(d) Government Employment

One form of government benefit to which the Supreme Court has strictly applied the entitlement theory is public employment.

If a person is hired for a government position that the law makes clear is terminable at the will of his superiors, the employee does not have a property interest in the position that mandates a fair procedure for determining the basis for his termination. The President can fire his Secretary of State for no reason or for any reason. The due process clause gives not give any Cabinet official a right to a pretermination hearing.

If the government gives the employee assurances of continual employment or dismissal for only specified reasons (e.g., a civil service position), then it must provide a fair procedure to protect the employee's interests when the government seeks to discharge him from the position. This entitlement also may come from statutory law, formal contract terms, or the actions of a supervisory person with authority to establish terms of employment.

To appreciate the dichotomy between a "claim of entitlement" to employment and a mere subjective expectancy of employment, consider the companion cases of *Board of Regents v. Roth* (1972) and *Perry v. Sindermann* (1972). In *Roth* the school refused to rehire a teacher who had only a one year contract. Applicable state law left the retention of such persons in the total discretion of university officials. *Roth* held that there was no claim of entitlement under local law and no deprivation of property that required a pretermination hearing. *Roth* was the first case to use the entitlement concept to exclude some important individual interests from the concept of "life, liberty or property" because they are not entitlements.

A state junior college professor in *Sindermann* had a contract that the school did not review. He was employed in a state college system for 10 years, the last four as a junior college professor under a series of one-year written contracts. The college declined to renew his employment for the next year, without giving him an explanation or prior hearing. He had a similar lack of express rights under his contract, but in this case the college officials had previously indicated that he had a claim to reemployment under a "de facto" tenure program. The Court looked at the job description and other factors and found that he could continue in the job unless fired for cause. Thus, he had a sufficient claim of entitlement so that the government must offer a pretermination hearing, i.e., hearing prior to the final decision not to renew his contract. The Court agreed that his subjective expectancy of tenure is not protected by procedural due process, but his allegation that the college had a de facto tenure policy, arising from rules and understandings officially promulgated and fostered, entitled him to an opportunity of proving the legitimacy of his claim to job tenure. Such proof would obligate the college to afford him a requested hearing where he could be informed of the grounds for his nonretention and challenge their sufficiency.

In *Arnett v. Kennedy* (1974) the Court upheld the dismissal of a nonprobationary employee by the federal government without a pretermination hearing. Although there was no majority opinion, at least six Justices appeared to agree that the employee had an interest that could not be terminated without due process. The action of the Court seemed to be based on a majority view that *pre*termination review procedures and a post termination hearing constituted a sufficient procedure to safeguard this interest.

Bishop v. Wood (1976) went further and held that the state could define the terms of what appeared to be permanent employment so as to eliminate the need for procedural safeguards. The lower federal courts said that state law provided that a "permanent" employee held his position at the will and pleasure of city, with removal being conditioned only on compliance with certain specified procedures. In that case, the discharge of police officer without a hearing did not deprive him of a property interest protected by the Fourteenth Amendment. Justice Stevens, for the Court, deferred to the district court analysis of state law that the employee held his position at "the will and pleasure" of city officials. The majority then held that the state was free to define the terms of employment so as to preclude claims of entitlement and procedural safeguards.

Arnett and *Bishop* establish that the meaning of local law is important in determining whether a government employee has a job "entitlement" protected by due process. However, state law cannot deny an employee who has an entitlement to her or his job the procedural safeguards against improper termination of employment that are guaranteed by due process. A state may define the procedures for terminating the employment of a government employee who has an entitlement to her job, only if the state procedures meet or exceed the minimum procedural safeguards required by due process. Thus, a state cannot by statute or regulation authorize the termination of employment for such employees without granting an employee a right to respond *prior* to the termination of her or his employment to the charges which are the basis of the job termination. *Cleveland Board of Education v. Loudermill* (1985).

Even those employees who lack any entitlement to continued employment cannot be discharged for reasons that in themselves violate the Constitution. Thus, the state cannot fire nontenured teachers because they engage in speech protected by the First Amendment. *Board of Regents v. Roth* (1972). The discharged teacher can always sue. However, a hearing on the free speech claim will occur after the termination, when the teacher files suit.

§ 13.6 Irrebuttable Presumptions—The "Non" Liberty or Property Due Process Requirement

In a few cases the Supreme Court has held that the government could not establish an "irrebuttable presumption" which classified people for a burden or benefit without determining the individual merit of their claims. These presumptions were said to violate due process because they deprived someone of a governmental benefit without any fair process. Thus the Court struck down a college tuition system that did not allow individuals a fair chance to prove they were residents of a state. E.g., *Vlandis v. Kline* (1973).

Similarly, *Cleveland Board of Education v. LaFleur* (1974) struck down employment restrictions on pregnant teachers when the system made no individualized determination of their ability to continue working during their pregnancy. Indeed, the Supreme Court engaged in one of its rare invalidations of a welfare payment qualification when it struck down a food stamp act provision that disqualified a large class of households without individualized determination as to their need. *United States Department of Agriculture v. Murry* (1973).

In spite of the language of due process, these cases actually rest on an equal protection rationale, for the objectionable portion of each law was the way that it classified individuals. It was the arbitrary classification by previous residency for tuition, by pregnancy for employment, or by income tax status for food stamps that was the impermissible basis of these laws. In none of the cases would a "process" have saved the law because the procedure would only have determined whether an individual fit into one of these arbitrary classifications. The Court consistently upholds classifications that are not invidious against charges that they constitute irrebuttable presumptions.

For example, a state may ban all advertising on trucks that do not advertise the business interests of the truck owner. *Railway Express Agency v. New York* (1949). The classification between "owned" and "rented" advertising is sufficiently related to legitimate governmental concerns to pass review under the equal protection guarantee. No hearing under the due process clause is necessary unless a trucker who is fined for "rented" advertising claims his advertisement represented his own interests. To strike the law as an irrebuttable presumption against those who rented advertising space would resurrect the discredited theory of substantive due process as a check on economic or general welfare legislation.

By masking substantive decisions in procedural language, the Court, in the irrebuttable presumption cases, confused procedural due process and equal protection analysis. Irrebuttable presumption analysis allowed the Court to overturn legislative decisions without having to justify the use of judicial power that is required by use of substantive due process or equal protection analysis. The use of irrebuttable presumption language was a conceptually confused method of justifying non-deferential judicial review of legislative classifications. The declining use of irrebuttable presumption analysis evidences increasing willingness of Justices to address directly the judicial role in reviewing legislatively created classifications.

For example, *Michael H. v. Gerald D.* (1989), without a majority opinion, upheld a state statute that established a presumption that a child born to a married woman was the legitimate child of the woman and her husband. This presumption could only be overcome, in limited circumstances, by either the wife or husband. A man who asserted that he was the biological father of a child born to a woman who was married to another man attacked the law. Justice Scalia wrote for four members of the Court in finding that the statutory classification of the child as the offspring of the married husband and wife did not violate either substantive due process or procedural due process principles. If the state can make the substantive decision that children born to a married couple are to be treated as the offspring of the two parties of the marriage (and the Scalia plurality agreed the state can do this), then there is simply nothing to have a hearing about. The assertion that the state had created an "irrebuttable presumption" was nothing more than an assertion that the substance of the state law should be rejected.

§ 13.7 What Process Is Due? The Procedures Required by the Due Process Clause—Introduction

When a person is deprived of life, liberty or property, there must be some process granted him in order to ensure that the action taken complies with the due process clauses. However, "process" is not a term with a clear definition and the nature of the procedure required to comply with the due process clause depends on many factors concerning the individual deprivation.

In this section we will outline the constitutional framework within which the Supreme Court must determine specific cases concerning the adequacy of procedures granted an individual prior to depriving him of life, liberty or property. Our discussion will be divided into three major parts: first, a brief statement of the general principles that the Court follows in determining the adequacy of any procedure; second, a look at the most significant procedural due process decisions in three areas: deprivations of physical liberty, debtor-creditor relationships and termination of government benefits; and third, a look at access to judicial process.

§ 13.8 General Principles

The Supreme Court has tended to view its decisions on necessary procedures under the due process clause in an essentially utilitarian fashion. The Court has demonstrated a consistent belief that the adversary process is best designed to safeguard individual rights against arbitrary action by the government. The Court determines the scope of trial-type procedures required for any particular deprivation by balancing the worth of the procedure to the individual against its cost to the society as a whole.

The Court uses a balancing test to determine which procedures will be required. In *Mathews v. Eldridge* (1976) the Court stated that it will consider three factors in making this determination:

> First, the private interest that will be affected by the official action; second, the risk of an erroneous deprivation of such interest through the procedures used, and the probable value, if any, of additional or substitute procedural safeguards; and finally, the Government's interest, including the function involved and the fiscal and administrative burdens that the additional or substitute procedural requisites would entail.

There are different elements of the adversary process that may be required as part of the "due process" that the government must afford an individual when it deprives him of life, liberty or property. The essential elements are: (1) adequate notice of the charges or basis for government action; (2) a neutral decision-maker; (3) an opportunity to make an oral presentation to the decision-maker; (4) an opportunity to present evidence or witnesses to the decision-maker; (5) a chance to confront and cross-examine witnesses or evidence to be used against the individual; (6) the right to have an attorney present the individual's case to the decision-maker; (7) a decision based on the record with a statement of reasons for the decision. Additionally there are six other procedural safeguards which tend to appear only in connection with criminal trials or formal judicial process of some type. Those are: (1) the right to compulsory process of witnesses; (2) a right to pre-trial discovery of evidence; (3) a public hearing; (4) a transcript of the proceedings; (5) a jury trial; (6) a burden of proof on the government greater than a preponderance of the evidence standard.

Need for Resolution of a Factual Dispute. The first decision which a court has to make on the due process issue is whether any procedure is required. There is no requirement of a procedure to determine the basis for an action that affects an individual if there are no factual issues in dispute. Thus a discharged government employee has no right to a procedure when he does not challenge the truthfulness of the facts upon which his discharge was based. *Codd v. Velger* (1977) (per curiam). Similarly, there is no right to a hearing to determine whether property previously taken for delinquent taxes can be sold if there was no challenge to the original seizure of the property by the government. *Pearson v. Dodd* (1977).

Cases also arise where the government makes a decision based upon facts that already were determined through some adequate procedural system such as a trial. The individual will have no further right to a hearing if the disputed issues have already been resolved by adequate process. Thus there is no right to a hearing or other procedure in connection with a suspension or revocation of a person's automobile driver's license where the revocation is based on violations of traffic laws which were previously established through the judicial process. *Dixon v. Love* (1977).

Rulemaking–Legislative Process. It is most common for the government to affect the life, liberty or property interest of a great number of people through its legislative functions. When the legislature passes a law that affects a general class of persons, those persons have all received procedural due process—the legislative process. That is the only process that is due. Challenges to such laws must be based on their substantive compatibility with constitutional guarantees. Similarly, an administrative agency may make decisions that are of a legislative or general rulemaking character. When an agency promulgates generalized rules (as opposed to engaging in adjudicative functions) there is no constitutional right to a hearing for a specific individual. The Court has not required procedural safeguards of systemic fairness in this rulemaking or quasi-adjudicative process beyond those established in the Administrative Procedure Act.

Right to a Fair Decisional Process and an Impartial Decision-maker. The essential guarantee of the due process clause is fairness. The procedure must be fundamentally fair to the individual in the resolution of the factual and legal basis for government actions that deprive him of life, liberty or property. Due process only guarantees an individual a fundamentally fair procedure. Nothing in the Constitution guarantees that an individual will have a process that is most likely to result in a favorable ruling for that individual. Neither substantive due process nor procedural due process principles are violated when a government agency (during an investigation of misconduct within the agency) takes an adverse action against a government employee, for false statements the employee made. *LaChance v. Erickson* (1998).

While different situations may entail different types of procedures, there is always the general requirement that the government process be fair and impartial. Therefore, there must be some type of neutral and detached decision-maker, be it a judge, hearing officer or agency. The Court has continually held that "a fair trial in a fair tribunal is a basic requirement of due process." *In re Murchison* (1955). This requirement applies to agencies and government hearing officers as well as judges.

Hence, decision-makers are constitutionally unacceptable where they have a personal monetary interest in the outcome of the adjudication or where they are professional competitors of the individual. *Gibson v. Berryhill* (1973); *Ward v. Village of Monroeville* (1972); *Tumey v. Ohio* (1927).

The democratic process itself may be biased against an individual because a majority of the electorate may be biased, yet the system is "fair" within the meaning of due process. Thus the Court has upheld a requirement that zoning changes be subject to popular referendum, for that does no more than allow the general electorate to determine whether they wish to alter their laws. *Eastlake v. Forest City Enterprises, Inc.* (1976). Yet even this procedure cannot be used to disguise a system that subjects one to a determination of his rights by a group composed of his professional or commercial competitors. Thus the Supreme Court has held that the zoning of a tract of real property cannot be left to the discretionary voting of neighboring property owners with interests adverse to the individual property owner. *Washington ex rel. Seattle Title Trust Co. v. Roberge* (1928).

Notice. Due process requires the government to give notice to individuals of government actions that would deprive those individuals of a constitutionally protected life, liberty, or property interest. When individual interests are adversely affected by legislative action, there is no notice issue, because publication of a statute is normally considered adequate to put all individuals on notice of a change in the law of a jurisdiction. When a government agency or a court (even in a case where no government agency is a party) considers terminating or impairing an individual's constitutionally cognizable life, liberty, or property interest, notice must be given to the individual whose interest is at stake in the proceeding.

The form of the notice and the procedure for delivery or posting of the notice must be reasonably designed to insure that the interested parties in fact will learn of the proposed adjudicative action. "An elementary and fundamental requirement of due process in any proceeding which is to be accorded finality is notice reasonably calculated, under all the circumstances, to apprise interested parties of the pendency of the action and afford them an opportunity to present their objections." *Mullane v. Central Hanover Bank & Trust Co.* (1950).

Form of the Hearing or Process: The Balancing Test. If there is a deprivation of life, liberty or property which is based on disputed facts or issues, then the individual whose interests are affected must be granted a fair procedure before a fair decisionmaker. However this principle does not mean that the individual has the right to a hearing before the action is taken or even to any personal hearing at any time. What is required is a procedure, not necessarily a hearing.

As explained above, *Mathews v. Eldridge* (1976) consider three factors in making this determination as to what process is due:

First, the private interest that will be affected by the official action; second, the risk of an erroneous deprivation of such interest through the procedures used, and the probable value, if any, of additional or substitute procedural safeguards; and finally, the Government's interest, including the function involved and the fiscal and administrative burdens that the additional or substitute procedural requisites would entail.

On the side of the individual, a court must assess two factors: (1) the importance of the individual liberty or property interest at stake; (2) the extent to which the requested procedure may reduce the possibility of erroneous decision-making. On the other side of the balance, the court must assess the governmental interest in avoiding the increased administrative and fiscal burdens which result from increased procedural requirements.

Any balancing test that does not calibrate the scales and tells us how to weigh the elements is, frankly, quite vague. While this test may suit the purposes of the Supreme Court, one cannot accurately predict how any specific case will be decided by using this test for two reasons. First, one cannot weigh the values unless one knows the personal value systems of those doing the balancing. Second, this type of intuitive functionalism disregards a systematic pursuit of due process values.

A court may need to employ the *Mathews v. Eldridge* balancing test in three areas of procedural due process rulings. First, a court should use the test to determine if an individual is entitled to a hearing *prior to* (rather than *after*) a governmental action that would deprive him of a liberty or property interest. The government should be able to act to advance important public interests even though it deprives someone of property or liberty without a prior hearing, so long as adequate post-deprivation process provides the individual with a safeguard against arbitrary governmental actions. The existence of a state court remedy may be sufficient process to protect individuals from improper deprivations of some liberty or property interests by state employees.

In addressing the first procedural due process issue, the Court starts from the premise that an individual should receive notice and some type of a hearing prior to any deprivation of life, liberty, or property by the government. However, the Court has allowed the government to seize property, or temporarily deprive a person of liberty, prior to giving the individual a hearing in exceptional situations where an important governmental interest would be threatened by granting notice and a pre-deprivation hearing to the individual.

The adequacy of the notice given to a person whose liberty or property may be taken by the government is to be determined by this reasonableness test, rather than by use of the multi-factor balancing test that is used to determine the adequacy of the process that is to be afforded that individual.

Second, whether the court decides that the state must offer a pre-deprivation or post-deprivation hearing, it should employ the balancing test to determine the precise procedures to be employed at the hearing. The procedural spectrum will span from requiring only informal hearings to requiring a full adversarial process.

Third, if the court requires a formal adversarial process, it may use the balancing test to determine the standard of proof that the government must meet in order to justify the deprivation of the individual liberty or property interest in the individual case.

§ 13.9 A Summary of the Major Decisional Areas

(a) Loss of Physical Liberty

Overview of Restrictions on the Criminal Process. Before an individual is subjected to punishment upon a criminal charge, he must receive a full trial in conformity with many constitutional safeguards or waive those rights. The primary restrictions on the criminal process are the result of the application of the principles of the Bill of Rights. The guarantees of the Fourth, Fifth, Sixth, and Eighth Amendments restrict the ways in which the government may investigate as well as prosecute someone for a criminal charge. All of these safeguards apply to the criminal process of state and local governments except for the grand jury requirement of the

Fifth Amendment. These specific guarantees include almost all of the procedural safeguards that were mentioned in our general discussion. Specifically, the Amendments require: (1) respect for individual rights to privacy and freedom from self-incrimination in the investigative process; (2) that the person not twice be placed in jeopardy for the same offense; (3) prompt processing of the charges; (4) that the trial of the charges be public; (5) that the charges be tried before an impartial jury; (6) fair notice of the charges and a chance to prepare a defense; (7) the right to confront and cross-examine witnesses; (8) compulsory process to obtain favorable witnesses and evidence; (9) the assistance of counsel; (10) that excessive bail not be used to keep the individual in custody prior to the termination of the prosecution; (11) that the punishment not be excessive or cruel.

Additionally, due process requires that all procedures be fundamentally fair.

For example, when a defendant seeks pretrial suppression of statements or evidence which the government will seek to use against him at trial, his interest in the suppression hearing is of a lesser magnitude than his interest in the trial itself according to the Supreme Court. Therefore, the procedures used at a suppression hearing may be less elaborate than those accorded a defendant at his trial. *United States v. Raddatz* (1980) used the *Mathews v. Eldridge* balancing test in finding that the Federal Magistrates Act adequately protected a defendant's due process rights in a suppression hearing. The Court did not require the federal district judge personally to rehear testimony submitted to a federal magistrate when the judge made a "de novo" determination of the admissibility of evidence.

Appellate Process. Once the criminal trial is over and the defendant has been found guilty, there is no inherent right to appeal. But, while the Court has stated that there is no right to an appellate process, the Justices have never been confronted, at least in modern times, with the situation where a state would not grant some review—either collateral or direct—of decisions which resulted in conviction of criminal charges.

When a state does set up an appellate system, it must design that system to produce a fair review of the original trials of all persons. It may not establish a system that explicitly, or by its impact, affords fair appellate process only to those who can afford to pay for that process. Thus the state is required to waive filing fees and transcript reproduction costs for the appeals of indigent defendants. Similarly, the state must provide defendants with the assistance of counsel for their first appeal as of right in order to insure that all classes of defendants receive a fair review of their trials. *Douglas v. California* (1963). However, the state need not provide counsel for indigent defendants who seek to attack their convictions in later discretionary appeals or collateral attacks, *Ross v. Moffitt* (1974), because the assistance of counsel at trial and on the first appeal of right insures an equality of treatment as to fundamental issues of law and fact. Apparently the Court concludes that later appeals or collateral attack are not so significantly related to fairness as to require that indigent defendants be accorded completely equal access to them.

Parole or Probation Revocation. Following a criminal trial and conviction on a criminal charge, a person may be placed on conditional release from a penitentiary. The system known as probation allows one to forego serving his sentence of imprisonment so long as he meets certain conditions relating to his conduct. A person sentenced to serve a term of imprisonment may be allowed to leave prison prior to the expiration of his maximum term under a system of parole which also conditions continued release on certain standards of behavior. When the state seeks to revoke someone's continued right to parole or probation and place him in prison, it is depriving him of "liberty" within the terms of the due process clauses. However, this fact does not require the government to prove that the conditions of parole or probation have been violated in the same way that it had to prove the initial charge.

The procedures for revoking probation or parole must include: (1) notice of the claimed violation of parole or probation conditions; (2) disclosure of evidence to the defendant; (3) a personal hearing for the defendant; (4) the opportunity to present evidence on behalf of the defendant; (5) the right to confront and cross-examine witnesses against the defendant unless there is specific good cause for avoiding such a confrontation; (6) a written statement by the adjudicator as to the evidence relied on and the reason for revoking the parole or probation status. All of this must take place before a neutral hearing examiner or board.

The previously convicted defendant does not have an absolute right to counsel at either the probation or parole revocation hearing. Instead, the Court has held that the decision as to whether counsel must be allowed at the proceedings must be made on a case by case basis. There will be a need for counsel wherever the charges concerning the parole or probation violation are such that they could not adequately be defended against by the defendant alone.

Prisoners' Rights Cases. An individual does not lose all of his constitutional rights by being imprisoned for commission of a crime. Specifically, if there are further significant deprivations of life, liberty, or property following imprisonment, the prisoner is entitled to a fair procedure to determine the basis for the deprivations. Because of the limited nature of a prisoner's constitutional rights, it is very difficult to determine when there is a constitutionally cognizable interest in life, liberty or property being denied a prisoner.

In *Wolff v. McDonnell* (1974) the Court held that where a state establishes a system of "good time credits" which reduce a defendant's time until possible parole, the state must accord the defendant a fair procedure prior to eliminating his good time credits. This hearing would not be an extensive one and would require only written notice of the violation, an opportunity for the convict to present evidence in his behalf and a written statement as to why the disciplinary action is being taken.

These procedural requirements will not apply to all prison disciplinary actions. *Wolff* indicated that a prisoner is entitled to a hearing whenever disciplinary actions are so serious as to cause a significant change in the individual's circumstances, such as the imposition of a punishment of solitary confinement. However, prisoners could be transferred to "administrative segregation" or to prisons with less favorable conditions without any procedure. Of course, in an emergency situation greater latitude would clearly be allowed to prison authorities to impose order and safe conditions in a prison without engaging in any formalized procedures.

The Court has held that the mere possibility of receiving parole is not a liberty interest protected by the due process clauses and that even a state created entitlement of prisoners to receive parole under specific circumstances requires no more than informal hearings at which a parole board can receive a presentation by the prisoner. *Greenholtz v. Inmates of the Nebraska Penal and Correctional Complex* (1979).

Vitek v. Jones (1980) held that an involuntary transfer of a prisoner to a mental hospital implicated a protected liberty interest and that due process is not satisfied by the mere certification of the need for such treatment by a state-designated physician or psychologist. The transfer constituted a deprivation of liberty both because state statutes at issue in the case gave rise to a legitimate expectation on the part of the prisoner that he would only be kept in normal prison facilities and because this transfer involved a significantly greater degree of confinement, the imposition of mandatory treatment, and a realistic possibility of stigmatizing consequences for the defendant. The state's interest in treating mentally ill patients is strong, but the Court concluded that it was outweighed by the prisoner's interest in not being arbitrarily classified as mentally ill and subjected to treatment.

Five Justices in *Vitek* agreed that due process required: (1) notice to the prisoner of the intended transfer and of his rights to contest that transfer; (2) time for the prisoner to prepare his arguments; (3) a hearing where the prisoner has the opportunity to be heard in person, to present evidence and witnesses, and to cross-examine state witnesses, except where good cause exists for limiting confrontation; (4) an independent decision-maker; (5) a written statement by the decision-maker detailing the evidence and rationale underlying a decision to transfer.

Washington v. Harper (1990) upheld a prison regulation that authorized the administration of antipsychotic drugs to a prisoner without his consent. The Court found that the regulation was reasonably related to a legitimate penological interest and, for that reason, did not violate the substantive component of the due process clause. Procedural due process still applied, and the procedures in this case were adequate. The prison regulation in the *Harper* decision gave the prison inmate notice of the medical professional's intent to administer antipsychotic drugs to him, a hearing before a panel of medical professionals and prison officials who were not involved in the inmate's current treatment, a right to present evidence and to cross-examine persons at the hearing, and judicial review of the hearing committee's decision (if the prisoner filed a petition for judicial review with the trial courts in the state). The Supreme Court used the *Mathews v. Eldridge* balancing test to conclude that these procedures were sufficient procedural due process. The government did not have to provide the prisoner with a hearing before a judge, rather than administrative panel. The prison regulations provided the prisoner with a fair hearing, which was similar to the type of hearing a prison inmate would receive before being transferred to a mental health care facility. Therefore, the Court ruled that the regulation complied with the due process clause.

Loss of Liberty Through Civil Process. When the state seeks to impose physical restraints of significant duration on a person it must afford him fair procedure to determine the basis and legality of such a deprivation of liberty, even when the nature of the state's action may be considered civil rather than criminal. When the state seeks to take custody of juveniles, it must accord the child a fair procedure. *Application of Gault* (1967).

This process includes: (1) adequate notice of the charges; (2) a right to counsel; (3) the appointment of counsel for indigents; (4) the right to confrontation and cross-examination of witnesses and (5) the privilege against self-incrimination. Additionally, when the action is based upon a charge which would constitute a crime if committed by an adult, the state must prove its case beyond a reasonable doubt. The state does not have to grant the juvenile either a jury trial or a public hearing.

Commitment for Mental Care. When the state seeks to commit someone for mental care on an involuntary basis, it must establish a fair procedure for determining that the individual is dangerous to himself or others due to a mental problem.

The Supreme Court has not yet settled many issues concerning the extent of the procedural safeguards that the government must accord a person whom the state seeks to commit for mental care. The Court has held that the state must grant equivalent procedural safeguards to individuals whom it seeks to commit in civil proceedings and who have been found mentally incompetent in connection with criminal trials.

The Court has allowed a state to make a distinction between "mentally ill" and "mentally retarded" persons in civil commitment proceedings. *Heller v. Doe* (1993) upheld Kentucky statutes that made it more difficult for the state to commit a person to a mental health care facility on the basis of mental illness rather than on the basis of mental retardation.

Heller first rejected equal protection attacks on these classifications. The Court found no reason to overturn the legislative decision that the greater difficulty of determining mental illness, as opposed to mental retardation, and the more invasive treatments for mental illness than for mental retardation justified giving greater substantive and procedural protections to persons who might be committed to a health care facility for treatment of mental illness. These classifications were rationally related to legitimate state interests in protecting individuals from erroneous decisions in the civil commitment process.

Heller also ruled that allowing guardians and immediate relatives to participate in commitment proceedings based on mental retardation did not violate procedural due process principles. The Court employed the *Mathews v. Eldridge* test in determining that the participation of family members in the civil commitment process would aid in the accurate determination of whether the defendant was mentally retarded and in need of commitment. The participation of these family members in the process might make it more likely that the person would be committed for care than if they were excluded from such proceedings. Because due process principles only protect the individual's interest in a fair proceeding, rather than an interest in favorable rulings, there was no due process violation.

Although there may be circumstances that would justify the government detaining a person at a mental health care facility for a short time prior to a hearing, due process normally requires that an adult receive notice and a hearing prior to being involuntarily committed to a state mental health facility.

Conclusion. Whenever the government seeks to restrain someone physically, it is depriving him of a constitutionally significant liberty interest so long as the restraint is more than momentary. Where the physical restraint is of a very brief duration, lesser procedures may be required to determine the legitimacy of the action.

Thus when the police arrest an individual without an arrest warrant, the state must seek validation of the arrest from a judicial officer within a relatively short period of time. *Gerstein v. Pugh* (1975). This procedure will amount to no more than an ex parte determination of the officer's probable cause to arrest the defendant. While this procedure is very limited in its scope, it only authorizes the temporary detention of the defendant, who still has the safeguards of the speedy trial and excessive bail provisions to restrict the state's power to subject him to indefinite pretrial incarceration.

Similarly, a public school student is deprived of liberty when he is subjected to physical punishment by school authorities. *Ingraham v. Wright* (1977). However, the Court held that this liberty interest was adequately safeguarded by the creation of a cause of action in tort against teachers who exceeded their authority in imposing physical punishments on the child.

(b) Enforcement of Debtor–Creditor Relationships

When a creditor uses government-enforced procedures to take the property of his alleged debtor, the debtor-defendant is deprived of a constitutionally significant interest in property. This deprivation exists whether the government transfers the property from the debtor to the creditor or merely prevents the debtor from using the property until the termination of the judicial proceeding instituted by the creditor. Of course, once the creditor has established her claim through a trial, the debtor has been accorded due process of law and the state may aid the creditor to enforce her judgment. However, the creditor may wish to have the property kept from the alleged debtor's use prior to trial in order to insure a recovery. When the government assists the creditor prior to trial, it must establish certain procedures to safeguard the interests of the alleged debtor.

The government cannot garnish the wages of an alleged debtor without granting that individual the right to a hearing to determine whether there is a legitimate basis for keeping a portion of his wages from him. *Sniadach v. Family Finance Corp.* (1969) held that garnishing a portion of a wage earner's salary to safeguard the interest of an alleged creditor was impermissible absent either a prior hearing for the debtor or an extraordinary emergency situation that justified foregoing the hearing. The majority opinion did not explain what type of emergency situation might justify garnishing someone's wages without a hearing. While the Court has made many conflicting statements about due process in the years since *Sniadach*, it has not withdrawn the strict requirement of a hearing prior to wage garnishments.

In determining the type of process that must be provided to an individual in connection with a government termination of a liberty or property interest, the Court considers three factors: (1) the nature of the interest that will be impaired by the government action; (2) the extent to which formal procedures, or a specific procedure requested by the individual, might reduce the possibility of erroneous or otherwise improper decisions by the government; (3) and the governmental interest in the process and the burdens that additional or more complex procedures would impose on the government.

A consideration of these factors has led the Court to find that, absent exigent circumstance, an individual should be provided with notice and a hearing *prior* to the time when a state court or administrative agency issues an order that would constitute a pretrial attachment of the individual's property. Thus, *Connecticut v. Doehr* (1991) invalidated a state statute that authorized the prejudgment attachment of real estate without notice and hearing prior to the attachment even though the statute conditioned the issuance of the attachment upon a showing that the person seeking the order had filed a court action against the property owner and that there were grounds to believe that the plaintiff would be likely to prevail at trial on the claim against the property owner.

The Court found that prejudgment attachment orders constituted significant impairments of property interests and that there was a severe risk of erroneous deprivation in such prejudgment attachment processes because there was little assurance that the party seeking the order could prevail on the merits of a tort case. The statute at issue in *Doehr* provided the property owner with a hearing *after* the issuance of the attachment order. The Supreme Court found that there was no governmental or societal interest in having *ex parte* attachments that justified the harm that was caused to individuals by having their property interests frozen prior to the time when they received a hearing. The Supreme Court distinguished the cases in which it had found that a creditor who seeks a pretrial remedy to preserve assets of a debtor, on the basis of the nature of the creditor's interests and the likelihood that a written submission could demonstrate that the creditor would prevail at trial.

A creditor may seek to have assets other than wages of an alleged debtor seized by the government to insure that there will be a source for recovery of later judgments against the debtor. Where the creditor has a specific interest in the property, he may seek return and use of the property prior to trial. These pre-judgment remedies against debtors include procedures such as replevin, attachment of assets and garnishment of property other than wages. For a time it appeared that the Supreme Court would always require a hearing prior to an attachment of the debtor's property; subsequently it appeared that the Court would allow creditors to regain such property with almost no procedural safeguards. In *Fuentes v. Shevin* (1972) (4 to 3) the Court indicated that there would be a requirement of a prior hearing in pre-judgment attachments or replevin just as there was for wage garnishments.

Only two years later the Court held (5 to 4) that a state trial judge could order sequestration of personal property on the application of a creditor with very few safeguards, in *Mitchell v. W. T. Grant Co.* (1974). Indeed, the dissenting Justices in *Mitchell* feared that *Fuentes* had been implicitly overruled. But such was not the case and *Fuentes* was given renewed, if somewhat restricted, life in *North Georgia Finishing, Inc. v. Di–Chem, Inc.* (1975), which invalidated (6 to 3) a statute that allowed the creditor to garnish property of an alleged debtor with certain procedural safeguards but without a hearing prior to the garnishment or attachment of the debtor's assets.

Di–Chem set four requirements for pre-judgment replevin, attachment or garnishment statutes which did not provide a prior hearing for the debtor. If the state gave the debtor a hearing prior to the attachment, it would have met the procedural due process requirement of even the strict *Sniadach* standard. Without such a prior hearing, the statute must have the following four features: (1) the creditor must post a bond to safeguard the interest of the debtor; (2) the creditor or someone with personal knowledge of the facts must file an affidavit which sets out a prima facie claim for prejudgment attachment of the property; (3) a neutral magistrate must determine that the affidavit is sufficient before issuing the writ of attachment or replevin; (4) there must be a provision for a reasonably prompt post-attachment hearing for the debtor.

Emergency Limitation of Due Process Rights. These requirements as to due process in the taking of property may be modified by extraordinary or emergency conditions. Most states have provisions for pre-judgment sequestration or attachment of the assets of an alleged debtor where a creditor can make a prima facie claim that the assets are liable to be hidden or destroyed before the claim can be resolved by the trial process. These provisions would seem to be permissible so long as they are reasonably tailored to dealing with emergency situations rather than merely providing a form for creditors to avoid the pre-trial hearing process.

This theory was carried to its furthest extreme in *Calero–Toledo v. Pearson Yacht Leasing Co.* (1974) when the Court upheld the government seizure of a ship used to transport contraband without a prior notice or hearing. The Court accepted the seizure as serving a significant governmental interest in asserting jurisdiction over a moveable item of property against which the government could legitimately conduct forfeiture proceedings. The Court held that this was an "extraordinary situation in which postponement of notice and hearing until after seizure did not deny due process."

United States v. James Daniel Good Real Property (1993) both clarified and narrowed *Calero–Toledo* when the Court ruled that the federal government must give notice and some type of a hearing to the owner of real property before seizing the real property, which allegedly was subject to forfeiture proceedings. The government, in the *James Daniel Good Real Property* case, had sought to institute forfeiture proceedings against residential property because the owner of the property had been convicted of violating federal drug laws by keeping proscribed drugs on the property, which had resulted in the property owner being convicted of state crimes several years prior to the federal government's initiation of the forfeiture action. The federal government, in an ex parte proceeding, received a warrant from a federal magistrate that allowed seizure of the property; the final disposition of the property would be determined at a later adversary proceeding.

The Supreme Court ruled that the government's use of an ex parte proceeding in these circumstances violated due process. The seizure of a home or other real property constituted a greater deprivation of property interest than the seizure of personal property, an ex parte warrant procedure does not sufficiently reduce the risk of erroneous determinations that the property could be seized, and the federal government had no interest that outweighed the individual's interest in receiving a hearing prior to the seizure. Justice Kennedy, for the Court, distinguished *Calero–Toledo* on the basis that the government had to prevent personal property that might be subject to forfeiture proceedings from being hidden or destroyed. The government did not need to seize real property prior to granting the individual property owner notice and some type of hearing.

(c) Deprivations of Government Benefits

The Justices use a balancing test to determine whether the individual interest merits a specific procedure in view of its cost to the government and society in general. Not surprisingly, this balancing process has yielded varying rules whereby some deprivations of government benefits can only be accomplished with very detailed hearings while others can be summarily terminated. A sampling of the major decisions in this area should give one a feeling for the way in which the current Justices are striking the balance

An interest that requires great procedural protection in the view of the Supreme Court is that of subsistence payments to indigent individuals. In *Goldberg v. Kelly* 1970), the Court required a trial-type hearing (a *pre*-termination hearing) before the state could terminate basic welfare benefits. The Court found that the interest in the termination of basic subsistence benefits was such that it could be likened to a property right. While the Court stated that a "quasi-judicial trial" is not required, it went on to hold that a pre-termination hearing must be granted, including such procedures that one could accurately describe it as a quasi-judicial trial.

The Court required that the welfare beneficiary be granted a hearing that included: (1) adequate notice; (2) an opportunity for oral argument to the adjudicator; (3) a chance to present evidence in his behalf; (4) an opportunity to confront any witnesses who are adverse to his claim; (5) an opportunity to cross-examine those witnesses; (6) disclosure of all evidence against him; (7) a right to have an attorney present his case; (8) a decision based solely on the evidence produced at the hearing; (9) that the decision-maker state the reasons for his determination and the evidence he relied on; and (10) that the decision-maker in fact be unbiased and impartial.

The only basic administrative procedural requirements that the Court left out were the right to a complete record or comprehensive opinion, the assignment of counsel, and a formal finding of fact or opinion. The guaranteed procedures come very close to an administrative trial.

Lying in the middle range of interests, in terms of the procedural safeguards that they require, are terminations of important licenses or liberties. Two of the most important cases in this area involve the suspension of driving privileges and the suspension of students from school. *Bell v. Burson* (1971) invalidated a statute that suspended the licenses of drivers involved in automobile accidents unless they furnished security to satisfy a judgment or gave proof of financial responsibility. The Court held that due process required a prior hearing to determine the probability of a judgment against an individual that would require proof of his financial responsibility. While the Court did not delineate all of the rights that would be involved in such a procedure, the opinion indicated that the procedures would be somewhat less than the administrative trial the *Goldberg* had required. The Court later held that suspension of an individual's driver's license based on the number of times he has been convicted of traffic law violations does not require a hearing as there is no disputed issue of fact. *Dixon v. Love* (1977).

Mackey v. Montrym (1979) upheld a state statute requiring the 90 day suspension of a person's driver's license for failure to take a chemical test or breath analysis test for usage of alcohol while driving a vehicle; the law also provided for a prompt post-suspension administrative hearing. The administrative hearing would determine three issues: (1) whether the police officer who requested the driver to take the test had reasonable grounds to believe that the driver was under the influence of intoxicating liquor; (2) whether the person was in fact arrested by the officer; (3) whether the person in fact refused to take the test. Applying the *Mathews v. Eldridge* balancing test, the Court held that the individual's interest in a *pre*-suspension hearing to minimize the risk of erroneous deprivation of the driver's license for a 90–day period was outweighed by the governmental interest in protecting the safety of the populace through strict drunk driving penalties and prompt procedures for removing the drunk drivers from the highways.

Goss v. Lopez (1975) held that high school students who were suspended for up to ten days were entitled to procedural protections against unfair or illegal suspensions. The applicable state law established an entitlement to attend school so as to create a constitutional property interest. The suspension also impinged upon the "liberty" of the students because it might limit their employment or associational opportunities.

The process that was required to safeguard these interests was less complex than the *Goldberg* administrative trial procedures. The majority opinion indicated that the procedure would require that the student be given some oral or written notice of the charges and an opportunity to explain his position to the school authorities. The Court also noted that in situations that called for immediate action to establish discipline or order within a school, the school authorities could act *prior to* taking any procedures to safeguard the student interest. Later the Court held that school authorities were free to impose physical discipline on children so long as there was some state law limitation of the authority to impose such punishments and the possibility of later judicial actions against teachers who exceeded their authority. *Ingraham v. Wright* (1977).

The Supreme Court dealt with a number of procedural due process issues regarding the dismissal of students from institutions of higher education in *Board of Curators v. Horowitz* (1978). The Court upheld a medical school's dismissal of a student, without a formal hearing, based on low evaluations of her clinical work. As a medical student, the plaintiff had been required to achieve satisfactory evaluations from faculty member doctors regarding her clinical performance in a variety of hospital departments. After a faculty doctor expressed dissatisfaction with her performance in the pediatrics department, a faculty-student council recommended that she be allowed to advance to her second and final year on probationary status. She continued to receive unsatisfactory evaluations of her clinical performance and the Dean notified her of this fact. Later, the council recommended that she not be allowed to graduate and that she be dropped from school unless her performance greatly improved. The plaintiff was allowed to "appeal" from this recommendation by taking a set of oral and practical exams, which were reviewed by seven practicing physicians. Only two of those physicians thought that she should be allowed to graduate on schedule. Following further low evaluations of her clinical work, the council recommended that she not be allowed to re-enroll in the School of Medicine. This recommendation was approved by the Dean and a university provost after review of her academic record. All nine Justices agreed that there had been no deprivation of procedural due process rights in this case.

Because the plaintiff was given a fair procedure, if not a hearing, the Court found it unnecessary to decide whether this student had been denied a "liberty" or "property" interest. Assuming arguendo the existence of a liberty or property interest, the Court found that the student had no right to a formal hearing at which she might challenge the basis for her dismissal. The opinion distinguished *Goss v. Lopez* on the ground that it involved a disciplinary procedure. An informal hearing in *Goss* was necessary to allow a student to present his or her side of a disciplinary issue so as to diminish the possibility of wrongful suspensions. Although the severity of the deprivation might be greater in the academic dismissal situation, under the *Mathews v. Eldridge* balancing test, fewer safeguards were required in *Board of Curators* because there was less chance of wrongful dismissal. All that was required was notice to the student and some form of fair procedure for evaluation and review of the student's academic record. The student in *Board of Curators* had received more than a minimally fair review of the facts upon which her dismissal was based.

The majority opinion noted that the school had followed all of the rules that it had previously established for such cases. The opinion noted that the failure to follow previously established rules would invalidate federal administrative action as a matter of federal administrative law, but the opinion said that this rule was not a constitutional principle binding on the states. However, failure of an institution to follow its own established procedural rules might weigh in the determination of whether or not an individual had been treated in such an arbitrary manner as to constitute a violation of due process.

Board of Curators also found that there was no violation of substantive due process, even assuming that the courts could legitimately review standards for academic dismissals. If the announced basis for reviewing academic performance is arguably reasonable, the courts have no function in reviewing the substantive basis for dismissals under the due process clause unless those dismissals were clearly arbitrary or invidious.

One of the interests that receive fewer procedural protections is the right to a continuation of disability or welfare payments under the Social Security Act. *Mathews v. Eldridge* (1976) held that the government can terminate such benefits terminated under a system that accords the individual no right to a special hearing until *after* the termination of his benefits. The Court found that there were sufficient procedural safeguards other than a pretermination hearing to lessen the chances of improper terminations. The termination was based on medical decisions concerning and the agency would have considered this written evidence prior to the termination decision. The Court also felt that the interest in disability payments was not as significant as that in subsistence payments. Finally the majority simply believed that the benefits to the government and society in general from foregoing these administrative burdens outweighed the interests of the individual recipient of disability payments.

The Court has also been fairly restrictive in its view of what procedures are necessary to safeguard the interest of government employees who are discharged from their positions. A leading case is *Cleveland Board of Education v. Loudermill* (1985). The Court held that a government employee who had an entitlement to his government position under local law could not be dismissed from that position without being given some opportunity to respond to charges that would form the basis for his job termination. Local law provided for no pre-termination hearing for the individual but only a chance to have the job termination reviewed at a later date. The Supreme Court noted that state or local law was only relevant for determining whether the individual had an entitlement to his job. *Loudermill* rejected the view that states could limit the type of procedures necessary for job termination below that required by the due process clause by legislatively deciding that an employee was entitled to few procedural safeguards prior to the termination of his job. In other words, once the statute creates an entitlement, it is the due process clause and not the statute that determines the process that is due.

Cleveland Board of Education held that an employee is not entitled to a pre-termination "hearing" but only "an opportunity to respond" to charges against him prior to his job termination, followed by a post-termination hearing to review the decision of an informal or summary pre-termination process. The Court reached this conclusion by applying the *Mathews* three factor balancing approach. First, the private interest in government employment, for a person who has an entitlement to his employment, is a "significant" interest. Second, employment terminations often involve factual disputes or difficult questions regarding the appropriateness or necessity for a discharge from employment. A *pre-termination* opportunity to respond to charges helps to avoid erroneous or unjustified termination decisions. Finally, the state interest in avoiding the cost and delay of pre-termination proceedings do not outweigh the employee's claim for fair treatment prior to the termination of this interest.

However, the state's interests were sufficient for the Court to rule that "the pre-termination hearing, though necessary, need not be elaborate." If there is a post-termination review of the termination decision, the government can fire an employee with an entitlement to his job following a pre-termination notice of the reasons for his discharge and a pre-termination opportunity to respond to those charges. Thus, the Court gives some pre-termination rights to government employees but it does not required the type of formal pre-termination proceedings for termination of employment that it required for termination of subsistence welfare benefits.

Post–Deprivation Hearings. In some instances due process is fulfilled by a "post-deprivation" hearing or suit. This type of hearing would be in accordance with the utilitarian balancing test and might in fact result in a wider role for due process. It may be that the Court will be less fearful of recognizing a wide variety of interests as life, liberty or property if that recognition does not require universal government hearings *prior* to affecting those interests.

When someone's life, liberty or property interest is going to be taken by the government, procedural due process principles normally will require that the person receive notice and a hearing prior to the deprivation of the constitutionally protected interest. However, it is possible for a court using the *Mathews* balancing approach to determine that some types of deprivations of liberty or property can be justified without a pre-deprivation process, or with very informal or limited pre-deprivation procedures, if the individual whose interest is being taken by the government receives a subsequent (post-deprivation) process for review of the decision and possible restoration of that interest. It would be rare for a court to allow the government to take a person's liberty or property with no prior hearing of any type but a court may approve very informal pre-deprivation procedures if there is a more elaborate post-deprivation process available to protect the individual's interest.

As predicted in the first edition of the treatise on which this book is based, the Court has found that some liberty and property interests are adequately protected by procedures that take place *after* the governmental termination of that liberty or property interest. In these cases the Court rules that the insignificant nature of the individual liberty or property interest at stake, or the magnitude of the government's need to take action without administrative delay, justifies a government action temporarily depriving a person of a liberty in property interest until a "post-deprivation" hearing can be held. In a few cases the Court has ruled that the government need not initiate post-deprivation process because the individual's interest is adequately protected by state law which allows the individual to bring a state court action against the government agency or employees who allegedly wrongfully deprived him of a liberty or property interest.

Consider, for example, *Hudson v. Palmer* (1984), which held that a state need only provide an adequate judicial or administrative post-deprivation remedy for the alleged intentional destruction of property by state employees. *Hudson* examined the claim of a prisoner who argued that state employees had intentionally destroyed his property, including legal papers, during a shakedown search. The Court ruled that the state would have to have a "meaningful post-deprivation remedy," although state procedure need not be like what would compensate an individual as fully in monetary terms as a federal civil rights action. In holding that the state did not have to provide a pre-deprivation remedy, the Court focused on the reasons why some types of property deprivations only require after-the-fact access to judicial or administrative remedies. Takings of property "through random and unauthorized conduct" of state employees are unpredictable so that there is no practical system for pre-deprivation hearings. The inability of the state to control such conduct in advance and the nature of the taking of property are such that the state action regarding the property is not considered "complete until and unless it provides or refuses to provide a suitable post-deprivation remedy."

In contrast to *Hudson*, see *Logan v. Zimmerman Brush Co.* (1982), which held that a state could not refuse to establish a pre-deprivation hearing procedure before taking a property interest where the property deprivation is achieved pursuant to a state statutory system. *Logan* held that a state law violated procedural due process. The Act required that the complainant alleging that he had been improperly fired from his job because of his physical handicap must first file a charge with a state Employment Practices Commission; before he could file suit, the Commission would have to hold a fact finding conference within 120 days of filing the claim. Although in the case before the Court the Commission had admittedly failed to hold the fact finding conference through its own negligence, the state courts had ruled that the 120 day requirement was jurisdictional so that the complainant permanently lost the right to sue.

The Court concluded: the statutory system created an entitlement to bring a fair employment practices suit; the due process clause protected this entitlement; and the possibility of suing the Commission for its negligence was not a sufficient remedy. Instead, the state must allow the complainant to bring suit against the employer. The Court found that the post-deprivation remedy (the possibility of a negligence suit against the Commission) was insufficient to comply with due process because "Logan is challenging not the Commission's error, but the 'established state procedure' that destroys his entitlement without according him proper procedural safeguards."

Logan should not be taken as indicating that a state may never set up a statutory system that grants only a post-deprivation remedy to someone whose property rights the state has taken. *Logan* noted that its prior decisions "suggest that, absent 'the necessity of quick action by the State or the impracticality of providing any predeprivation process', a post-deprivation hearing here would be constitutionally inadequate. That is particularly true where, as here, the State's only post-termination process comes in the form of an independent tort action."

Cleveland Board of Education v. Loudermill (1985) held that the state could not terminate a government employee who, under state law, had an entitlement to his unless it also gave him a pretermination process; it was not sufficient to offer only a post-termination review procedure. The Court employed the *Mathews* balancing approach and held that the state interest in avoiding the costs and delays of pre-termination process did not outweigh the significant individual interest in continued government employment and the value of pre-termination process for avoiding erroneous deprivations of that interest. basic requirement of the due process clause is the opportunity for an individual to receive "notice and a hearing" before he is deprived of a constitutionally protected liberty or property interest. The Court said that this pre-termination process for an individual need not be elaborate; the state need only give the employee a right to respond to charges against him. This type of process could be "something less than a full evidentiary hearing." The post-termination process available to the employee minimized but did not eliminate the need for some type of pre-termination hearing in order to ensure fair treatment for the individual.

Cleveland Board of Education v. Loudermill does not hold that a state always must provide pre-deprivation hearings or procedures. In most circumstances procedural due process principles require the state to provide an individual with notice and a hearing before an impartial decision-maker prior to the deprivation of a life, liberty, or property interest. The government should be able to use an informal or limited form of pre-deprivation process, followed by a post-deprivation review of the government action, if the Court agrees that the government need to act quickly or summarily outweighs the individual interest in retaining the full extent of the liberty or property prior to final administrative resolution of the dispute between the individual and the government. There may be an even more limited group of cases where an individual is entitled to no pre-deprivation process because of the need of the government to act quickly or because there is no reasonable way for the government to establish a pre-deprivation administrative or judicial process to protect the type of interest at stake.

Zinermon v. Burch (1990) provides an example of how the *Mathews v. Eldridge* (1976) balancing test applies to the question of whether a post-deprivation proceeding complies with due process. In *Zinermon*, the question was whether a former patient in a state mental care facility had stated a cause of action, under the due process clause, against state employees who admitted him to the mental health care facility as a "voluntary patient." The plaintiff alleged that he was not mentally competent to sign admission forms at the time of his admission and that he did not meet the criteria for involuntary commitment to the facility. He also alleged that the state hospital employees who admitted him knew, or should have known, that he could not make an informed choice as to whether to commit himself voluntarily. There were provisions in this state's law regarding state mental health care facilities that would have allowed for an emergency admission of a person through either administrative or court processes for a short period of time (up to 5 days) if the person appeared to be mentally ill, in need of mental health care, and likely to injure himself or others. State law provided for a judicial hearing for the indefinite involuntary commitment of an individual.

The mental hospital admitted plaintiff as a voluntary patient, so it did not give him any of the procedures available under state law. He remained in the hospital for five months following his initial admission without receiving any hearing. The Court (5 to 4) held that the complaint did state a cause of action because the plaintiff's allegations, if true, established a violation of procedural due process principles. Recall that he alleged that the state hospital employees who admitted him to the state facility *knew, or should have known*, that he could not make an informed choice to commit himself voluntarily. The *Mathews* analysis should be used to determine whether a post-deprivation process is sufficient to comply with due process. The majority found that under some circumstances, the impairment of liberty interests, like the impairment of property interests, is permissible with only a post-deprivation process.

Zinermon first concluded that the individual's interest in avoiding unjustified commitment is a significant liberty interest. Second, the pre-deprivation process provides a significant safeguard against improper deprivations of that liberty interest.

Finally, *Zinermon* examined the government interests that might support denying an individual a pre-deprivation hearing. The third inquiry under *Mathews* (the inquiry into the government interest) only requires an examination of whether a pre-deprivation process is impractical and whether a post-deprivation process adequately protects the individual liberty interests at stake. Providing the individual with a pre-deprivation process is practical, since state law provided a prompt process for the temporary placement of an individual in the state mental health care facility. Plaintiff claimed in his complaint, the state hospital employees knew, or should have known, that he was incapable of giving consent to a voluntary admission. If that allegation is true, there is no reason why this individual was not provided with the statutory procedural safeguards for an involuntary temporary admission.

The dissent argued that the state's post-deprivation remedy (the ability to sue the state hospital employees) for an improper voluntary admission, when viewed together with the involuntary admission procedures, provided a fair process to each individual. Involuntary patients receive pre-deprivation process; voluntary patients received a post-deprivation process. The post-deprivation state process could redress individual deprivations of liberty. The dissent argued that it would be impractical to require state hospital employees to challenge every individual's voluntary admission by having a hearing concerning whether the individual who wished to be admitted to the state hospital had the capacity to make an informed choice.

The majority in *Zinermon* did not require a true pre-deprivation process for every person admitted to a state mental health care facility. The majority avoided ruling whether the temporary admission provisions of the state law were constitutional. An individual might be temporarily admitted for examination at a state hospital with a prompt post-deprivation process. For example, if the employees whose actions were at issue in *Zinermon* had decided that plaintiff could not give voluntary consent, but that he was in need of mental health care and might pose a danger to himself or others, they could have admitted him to the hospital immediately, detained him for 48 hours based on the decision of a health care professional or for up to 5 days with a temporary court order, under the terms of their state's statutes. Nothing in *Zinermon* indicates that such a process is unconstitutional.

In the late 1990s the Supreme Court unanimously endorsed the balancing test of *Mathews v. Eldridge* (1976) for determining whether a post-deprivation process, rather than a pre-deprivation process, satisfies due process requirements. *Gilbert v. Homar* (1997) held that a security officer for a state university was not entitled to notice and a hearing prior to being suspended from his job after he was charged with a violation of state drug laws. The police arrested Mr. Homar, a police officer at a state university, on private property outside the university and charged him with several felony crimes, including possession of, and intent to deliver, a banned substance. The police filed a complaint and did not secure a grand jury indictment. The University, without giving Mr. Homar a hearing, suspended him without pay after he was charged with the crimes.

In *Gilbert*, Justice Scalia, for a unanimous Court, held that Mr. Homar's temporary suspension without pay did not violate the due process clause. Based on the agreement of all the parties, the Court assumed that the university police officer, who could only have been dismissed from his position for "cause," had a property interest in his government employment. The first *Mathews v. Eldridge* factor, concerning the importance of the interest at stake, weighed in favor of the university because of the government action involved only a temporary suspension without pay, not a more serious deprivation of the property interest of the such as dismissal from his university position. The second factor (the risk of an erroneous deprivation without pre-suspension procedures) also weighed heavily in favor of the state university, because the only issue at a hearing would have been the whether the employee had been formally charged with a felony. The employee admitted that he had been charged; that fact was easily verifiable by the university. The third *Mathews v. Eldridge* factor the government's interest, also weighed against requiring a pre-suspension hearing. The state "has a significant interest in immediately suspending, when felony charges are filed against them, employees who occupy positions of great public trust and high public visibility, such as police officers." Because the university could suspend the officer without a pre-deprivation hearing, the university could deny the individual monetary compensation during the period of his suspension.

Gilbert, assumed that the officer had a right to a post-deprivation hearing, in part because the charges against the police officer were dropped and, "once the charges were dropped the risk of an erroneous deprivation increased substantially." However, it did not reach the question of what type of post-suspension is required, or how soon the university give it.

§ 13.10 The Right to Judicial Process—Access to the Courts

In the cases concerning "procedural due process," the issue is typically whether the government must afford a hearing to a person whom it is about to deprive of life, liberty, or property. In these situations the government is either operating one of its own administrative systems or instituting judicial process against an individual. However, in some instances a person will want access to the judicial process whether or not he or she is about to be deprived of a constitutionally cognizable interest in life, liberty or property. This access normally presents no problem, because individuals are free to file their suits and make use of the judicial process within the generally applicable rules of civil procedure. If state law allows persons to bring suit in state court to redress alleged grievances against public or private agencies, it cannot arbitrarily deny an individual the ability to use those judicial procedures. The arbitrary refusal to allow individuals to use the established state court process is invalid under even the most minimal due process or equal protection standards.

Previous sections of this book discuss this issue. See, in particular, the equal protection rights of indigents who seek access to the courts. However, here we briefly review a few of the major cases.

One category of denial of access to courts are claims that systemic official action frustrates a plaintiff or plaintiff class in preparing and filing suits at the present time. For example, in prison-litigation cases, the remedy often sought is a law library, or a reader for an illiterate prisoner.

Other denial-of-access cases challenge filing fees for plaintiffs who cannot afford to pay. In these cases, the remedy an order requiring waiver of a fee to open the courthouse. Filing fees are the government's a way of allocating the costs of judicial process to a certain class of plaintiffs—those who are willing and able to pay. The government may not impose filing fees that prohibit access to the courts by indigents when that would impair a fundamental constitutional right of the indigent or when the fees are so arbitrary that they invidiously exclude poor persons from the judicial process.

An example of filing fees that restrict a fundamental constitutional right are those imposed before married persons may receive a divorce. In *Boddie v. Connecticut* (1971) the Supreme Court held that the filing fee requirement for divorce actions could not be applied to indigents who sought a divorce. The application of fees to indigent persons would effectively preclude them from exercising their constitutionally guaranteed right of freedom of choice in marital decisions.

United States v. Kras (1973), in a sense, held that one can be too poor to file for bankruptcy. The Supreme Court held that the state can deny access to the bankruptcy courts for those who were unable to pay the $50 filing fee for voluntary bankruptcy. Unlike divorce, bankruptcy is not the only method available for a debtor to adjust his legal relationship with his creditors. The debtor can settle his debts out of court. We no longer have debtor prisons. The Court justified its holding by explaining that a congressional desire to make the bankruptcy system somewhat self supporting is a permissible justification for the fee. Because the bankruptcy process is not essential to the exercise of any fundamental constitutional right, Congress was free to allocate access to the system on such a basis without violating either the due process or equal protection guarantees.

Similarly, the Court has upheld a system which imposed $25 filing fees for appellate court review of welfare eligibility determinations, thereby precluding indigent welfare recipients from receiving judicial review of the termination of their benefits. *Ortwein v. Schwab* (1973) (per curiam). When individuals' welfare benefits are terminated, they are entitled to due process, which include only a fair initial hearing. Because there is no fundamental constitutional right to welfare payments, the state could impose such filing fees on all persons.

The Supreme Court, however, has never determined that legislatures are totally free make determinations over significant rights of individuals without providing for some system of appellate or judicial review. The Court's decision upholding the state procedural system which required a filing fee for appellate review of welfare eligibility determinations might be limited by the fact that the process did not involve fundamental rights and the administrative system met all requirements for procedural fairness.

Christopher v. Harbury (2002) was a different type of case. The plaintiff alleged that federal officials had previously concealed information about the death of her husband, a foreign national, in a country outside of the United States. She alleged that U.S. Government officials intentionally deceived her by concealing information that Guatemalan army officers (paid by the Central Intelligence

Agency) had detained and tortured her husband, a Guatemalan dissident. She also claimed that this deception denied her access to the federal courts by leaving her without the information that she could have used to bring a lawsuit that might have saved her husband's life.

Justice Souter, for the Court, held that the plaintiff failed to state a cause of action against the federal government. First, plaintiff did not identify the underlying cause of action that the alleged deception had compromised. And, second, there was no remedy regarding access to the courts that would have saved her husband's life. Souter agreed that the plaintiff could seek damages for the alleged infliction of emotional distress, but she cannot obtain the order that might have saved her husband's life.

Filing fees for causes of actions that are not essential to the exercise of fundamental rights will still be invalidated if plaintiff can shown that they are totally irrational and can serve no purpose other than to deter suits by poor persons. Thus, *Lindsey v. Normet* (1972) invalidated a requirement that tenants who wish to appeal from summary eviction proceedings post appeal bonds in twice the amount that would be required to safeguard the interests of the landlord. This double bond requirement served no purpose other than to deter appeals by low income tenants, which is why the Court invalidated it.

Bankers Life and Casualty Company v. Crenshaw (1988) upheld a state statute that imposed a 15% penalty against a person who appealed unsuccessfully from a money judgment. Unlike *Lindsey* this penalty was not arbitrary and irrational. It did not single out a narrow class of parties or defendants for discriminatory treatment. The 15% penalty applied to both plaintiffs and defendants and to all money judgments, as well as to a number of other types of judgments whose money value could be determined. There was a rational relationship between the 15% penalty on unsuccessful appeals and the statute's objective of deterring frivolous appeals. Unlike *Lindsey,* the statute in *Banker's Life* was not likely to discourage nonfrivolous appeals.

Chapter 14

EQUAL PROTECTION

Table of Sections

§ 14.1 Introduction to Equal Protection Analysis—Application to State and Federal Acts

The Fourteenth Amendment commands that no person shall be denied equal protection of the law by any state. This clause introduced a new concept into constitutional analysis by requiring that individuals who are similar to each other must be treated similarly. There are similar concepts in the privileges and immunities clause of Article IV, and the commerce clause requirement that states not discriminate against interstate transactions, but these relate only to state treatment of certain specific matters. The equal protection guarantee, however, governs all governmental actions that classify individuals for different benefits or burdens under the law.

In recent years the equal protection guarantee has become the single most important concept in the Constitution for the protection of individual rights. As we have seen, the Justices generally disclaimed substantive due process power after 1937. And the privileges or immunities clause of the Fourteenth Amendment has not been a meaningful vehicle for the judicial review of state actions, although the drafters of the Fourteenth Amendment may have been intended to be a primary safeguard of natural law rights.

Instead, the Court has increasingly focused upon the concept of equal protection to guarantee that all individuals are accorded fair treatment in the exercise of fundamental rights or the elimination of distinctions based on impermissible criteria. It was not that long ago that Justice Holmes could categorize the concept of equal protection as "the last resort of constitutional arguments." *Buck v. Bell* (1927). Now, the equal protection clause has become an important tool of the courts to control the legislative and executive branches.

The equal protection guarantee applies to both the state and federal governments although the restrictions have two totally distinct bases. The equal protection clause of the Fourteenth Amendment by its own terms applies only to state and local governments. There is no equal protection clause that governs the actions of the federal government, but if the federal government classifies individuals in a way which would violate the equal protection clause, the Court has held that it violates the equal protection component of the due process clause of the Fifth Amendment. As we shall see in the following sections, the standards for validity under the implied equal protection guarantee of the Fifth Amendment due process clause and the equal protection clause of the Fourteenth Amendment are almost identical. *Bolling v. Sharpe* (1954).

Whenever "fundamental rights" are limited, the Court holds that any law in question must promote an overriding or "compelling interest" in order to be valid under either clause. When the governmental action relates only to matters of economics or general social welfare, the law need only "rationally relate" to a legitimate governmental purpose. If the law does not classify individuals, the due process guarantee applies. However, if the means the law employs to achieve its end is the classification of persons for differing benefits or burdens, the Court will test the law under the equal protection guarantee (or the equal protection component of the Fifth Amendment). A state or federal law in the area of economics or social welfare that classifies persons is valid under equal or due process so long as the law rationally relates to a legitimate governmental purpose. For simplicity's sake, we will typically refer to both state and federal guarantees as "equal protection."

§ 14.2 Government Classifications and the Concept of Equal Protection

The equal protection clause guarantees that similar individuals will be dealt with in a similar manner by the government. It does not reject the government's ability to classify persons or draw lines in the creation and application of laws, but it does guarantee that those classifications will not be based upon impermissible criteria or arbitrarily used to burden a group of individuals. The Court will uphold a government classification that relates to a proper governmental purpose. Those persons who are treated less favorably by the legislation, by not receiving a benefit given to other persons, are not denied equal protection of the law if they are not similarly situated to those persons who receive the benefit of the legislative classification.

The equal protection guarantee has nothing to do with the determination of whether a specific individual is properly placed within a classification. Equal protection tests whether the classification is properly drawn. It is the guarantee of procedural due process that determines what process is necessary to find that an individual falls within or outside of a specific classification. Equal protection deals with legislative line drawing; procedural due process deals with the adjudication of individual claims, although some courts are a little casual in making these distinctions.

However, it is incorrect to say that equal protection has nothing to do with the application of a law. If the law (on its face or as applied) makes a classification, the litigant can seek to have the courts test it under the equal protection guarantee. The Court will then determine whether the law is valid "on its face." In some instances this judicial review will involve a further inquiry into the nature of the legislative classification and its purpose and effect. For example, a zoning ordinance may constitute an unconstitutional racial classification if, but only if, the purpose and effect of the ordinance is the exclusion of members of a racial minority from a residential area. *Arlington Heights v. Metropolitan Housing Development Corp.* (1977).

In other situations a law may have no impermissible classification by its own terms but it may be applied in such a way as to create a classification. Then the Court will test the law "in its application" to determine whether the classification established by administrative actions is permissible. For example, a law that eliminated the use of wooden buildings for hand laundries constitutes an improper racial classification when all Chinese persons owning such laundries are forced to give up their businesses while all non-oriental persons who had similar laundries have exemptions from the prohibition. *Yick Wo v. Hopkins* (1886). In these cases, equal protection is used to determine whether the classification established by the administrative acts is permissible—not whether a given individual falls within the terms of the classification.

Equal protection is the guarantee that the government will deal with similar people in a similar manner. In reviewing any classification, the courts must first determine whether or not the persons classified by the law for different treatment are in fact "dissimilar." The question relates to the bases upon which the government can distinguish between individuals in society. There is no requirement that government follow natural classifications and it may subdivide persons as it deems proper for the advancement of legitimate governmental purposes.

Conversely, the courts do not test classifications by whether or not the individuals are truly different in some absolute sense from those who receive different treatment. For example, it is undeniably true that men and women are biologically different. However that difference does not mean that sex-based classifications are generally valid, for most often there is no difference between men and women in terms of the promotion of a legitimate governmental end. Thus, sex cannot be the basis for determining whether an individual is able to be the executor of an estate, *Reed v. Reed* (1971), or mature enough to drink alcoholic beverages. *Craig v. Boren* (1976).

Usually one must look to the end or purpose of the legislation in order to determine whether persons are similarly situated in terms of that governmental system. The judiciary need not necessarily review the permissibility of the legislative purpose, but it must decide the purpose end of the legislation to be tested. Once a court has found an end of government that is legitimate, i.e., does not in itself violate the Constitution, it can analyze the way in which the government has classified persons in terms of that end.

Classifications can relate to government "ends" in any one of five ways, any one of which may be determined to be constitutional or unconstitutional depending on the nature of the legislation in the specific case. First, the classification could be perfect in that it treats all similar persons in a similar manner. Second, the classification could be totally imperfect in that it selects exactly the wrong class for a burden or a benefit while excluding the class of persons who do relate to the legitimate purpose of the statute. Third, the classification can be under-inclusive in that it includes a small number of persons who fit the purpose of the statute but excludes some who are similarly situated. Fourth, the classification can be over-inclusive in that it treats in a similar manner not only those persons whose characteristics similarly relate to the purpose of the law but also some additional persons who do not share the legitimately distinguishing characteristic. Fifth, there can be a mixed relation of over-and under-inclusions. Some examples should help to clarify this breakdown of classifications.

The perfect classification involves the legislative use of a classifying trait that exactly fits the purpose of law and treats all similar people in a similar manner. On the other hand, a perfectly bad classification benefits a classification of persons who have no relationship to the legitimate purpose of the statute. Such perfect line drawing, be it good or bad, is a rarity. We may best analyze classifications in terms of the difficult burden of trying to prove such a relationship.

For example, let us assume that a state government passes a law that allows men but not women to be bartenders. We will assume that the permissible purposes of the law are to have efficient bartenders and to avoid disturbances of the peace in establishments serving alcohol. The legislative classification would be perfect if it is a fact that all men would be good bartenders who would maintain discipline and that all women bartenders always caused inefficient service or disturbances of the peace. The classification would be perfectly bad if all women make excellent bartenders but that male bartenders always caused inefficiency or disturbances of the peace. Of course, neither fact situation is correct.

Under–Inclusive Laws. An under-inclusive classification contains all similarly situated people but excludes some people who are similar to them in terms of the purpose of the law. To return to our bartender example, the law could be construed as an under-inclusive burden if no women would be good bartenders and that only some men would be good bartenders. In this situation all the women are similarly situated but a similar group of men is excluded from the imposition of the burden. The same law might be deemed an under-inclusive benefit if some women would not make good bartenders but that all men and some women would provide efficient and peaceful service. In this situation the law is under-inclusive because it fails to extend the benefit of a bartender's license to women who are similar in their abilities as bartenders to the men who receive the license.

Over–Inclusive Laws. A law may be said to be over-inclusive when the legislative classification includes all persons who are similarly situated in terms of the law plus an additional group of persons. In our bartender example the law could be construed as an over-inclusive burden if all men and some women made good bartenders but that a sub-group of women could not be efficient bartenders or created disturbances of the peace. The law would be over-inclusive because it burdened not only the group of women who would be bad bartenders but also those who would provide efficient service and avoid disturbances of the peace. The same law might be construed as an over-inclusive benefit if only a small group of men could give efficient bartender service and maintain the peace in these establishments. Were that the case, the law would be over-inclusive as a benefit measure because it gave the benefit of a bartender license to *all* men, not just qualified men.

Laws That Are Both Under– and Over–Inclusive. Many classifications can be a mix of both over- *and* under-inclusions. The ease with which we could change labels by viewing the statute as one dispensing benefits or burdens in our bartender example should highlight the fact that many classifications can have this mixed quality. Thus, in our bartender example, it would be easiest to construe the statute as being both under- and over-inclusive, because some women and some men make good bartenders while some women and some men do not give efficient service or control discipline within the establishments. In other words, we cannot identify the class of persons who will promote the end of the statute by the characteristic of sex. Thus, men and women are similarly situated in terms of their abilities to be bartenders. The Court, in fact, once upheld a law that denied bartender licenses to all women except the wives or daughters of male owners of bars. *Goesaert v. Cleary* (1948), but that case should no longer be good law.

It is important to analyze classifications in terms of their relationship to the legitimate purposes of the statute. This analysis will be the basis for determining whether the classification has a sufficient relationship to a proper governmental purpose so as to withstand a challenge under the equal protection guarantee. However, the labeling of a classification as over-inclusive or under-inclusive will not establish its compatibility with the equal protection clause.

It is sometimes said that under-inclusive burdens are not reviewed as strictly by the Court because those burdened by the classification are properly identified as deserving the burden or regulation and that the legislature may seek to solve social problems "one step at a time." As the foregoing examples demonstrate, almost any classification can be alternatively analyzed as over-inclusive or under-inclusive depending on one's view of the statutory system and the facts developed in the course of a challenge to the statute. Very few classifications will be either a perfect promotion of an articulated governmental purpose or a clearly irrational mismatch of classifications with the purpose of the statute, its ends. The key factor in reviewing classifications is the degree of correlation between the means and the ends that is required by the judiciary and the extent to which the judiciary will analyze the permissible purposes of the legislation.

If the Court is more likely to uphold under-inclusive classifications it is because they tend to be "economic" or "social welfare" regulations where the Court does not require the legislature to demonstrate a very close relationship between its classifications and the purposes of the statute. It was on this basis that the Supreme Court, in 1948 to uphold a law that excluded some women from being bartenders in a case very close to our example. However, today the Court would look at the classification as discrimination based on sex, not as economic legislation, and thus it would not uphold the sex discrimination. *Goesaert v. Cleary* (1948). Thus a key factor in equal protection analysis is whether the Court will review the government classification as economic regulation (where the Court defers to the legislature) or as a classification that affects a suspect class or other classification over which the Court exercises more active review (race, sex, and so forth) or a classification based on fundamental rights (such as voting, free speech, right to travel, and so forth).

§ 14.3 An Introduction to Standards of Review Under the Equal Protection Guarantee

(a) Overview

The degree to which a classification can be said to meet the equal protection guarantee depends on the purpose that one attributes to the legislative act and the determination whether there is a sufficient degree of relationship between the asserted governmental end and the classification. It is rare that a classification is so artfully drawn that it can be said to promote perfectly any but the most peculiar or narrowly defined ends. Thus the ultimate conclusion as to whether a classification meets the equal protection guarantee in large measure depends upon the degree of independent review that the courts exercise over the legislative line-drawing in the establishment of the classification.

To the extent that the Court defers to the legislature's choice of goals or its determination of whether the classification relates to those goals, it takes the position that it is the function of the legislature, rather than the judiciary, to make the equal protection determination as to the particular law. To the extent that the Court independently determines whether the law has a purpose which conforms to the Constitution and whether the classification in fact relates to that purpose, the Court takes the position that it is best able to assess these issues in a manner superior to, or at least different from, the legislative judgment. Thus the Court must decide whether it will engage in an active scrutiny of legislative classifications, and thereby assume the power to override democratic process, or whether, by deferring to that process, it will limit the judicial function.

The Court's institutional decision as to the degree of unique judicial function and the amount of deference that should be paid to legislative policy decisions in equal protection issues has mirrored the role of the Court in dealing with substantive economic due process. As we saw in Chapter Eleven, from 1887 to 1937, the Court used both the equal protection and due process clauses to invalidate those social welfare or economic legislation with which it was in fundamental disagreement.

When the Court renounced the theory of substantive due process, it also rejected the claim to an institutional ability to determine the reasonableness of economic classifications when reviewing laws under the equal protection guarantee. However, the Court did not reject its function of protecting fundamental constitutional values, such as free speech, freedom from state-imposed racial discrimination.

Thus, in the post 1937 period we have a dichotomy between the judicial review of classifications employed in economic and general social welfare regulation and review of classifications that either touch upon fundamental constitutional values or use a criterion for classification that itself violates a fundamental constitutional value. The Court will uphold classifications of the first type so long as they arguably relate to a legitimate function of government. As for classifications of the second type, however, the Court will subject them to independent judicial review, which means that the Court will not give great deference to the legislature. In those cases, the Court will use a different, and more strict "standard of review."

It is possible to rationalize all equal protection decisions as judicial determinations of whether the government has fairly classified persons and argue that there is only one equal protection standard of review. However, such an argument fails to recognize that the Supreme Court performs quite different functions when it: (1) virtually prohibits governmental use of some classifications, (such as racial classifications); (2) independently examines the reasonableness and legitimacy of some classifications (such as sex classifications); and (3) presumes that some classifications are within the constitutional prerogative of the legislature (such as classifications relating to economic or social welfare matters).

There are at least three standards of review that may be employed in equal protection decisions.

The Rational Relationship Test. The first standard of review is the rational relationship test, which the post–1937 Supreme Court uses for both equal protection and substantive due process issues. The Court will not exercise any significant review of legislative decisions to classify persons in terms of general economic legislation. In this area the Court has concluded that it has no unique function to perform. It has no special institutional capability or superior ability to assess the legislative judgment as to the scope of legitimate governmental ends or the reasonableness of economic classifications. Thus, as to these classifications, the Court will ask only whether it is conceivable that the classification bears a "rational relationship" to an end of government that the Constitution does not prohibit. So long as it is arguable that the other branch of government had such a basis for creating the classification a court will not invalidate the law.

The Strict Scrutiny Test. The second type of review under the equal protection guarantee is generally referred to as "strict scrutiny". This test means that the Court will not defer to the decision of the other branches of government but will instead independently determine the degree of relationship that the classification bears to a constitutionally compelling end. The Court will not accept every permissible government purpose as sufficient to support a classification under this test, but will instead require the government to show that it is pursuing a "compelling" or "overriding" end.

Even if the government can demonstrate such an end, the Court will not uphold the classification unless it independently reaches the conclusion that the classification is necessary, or "narrowly tailored," to promote that compelling interest. The Court will require the government to show a close relationship between the classification and promotion of a compelling or overriding interest. If the classification need not be employed to achieve such an end, the law will be held to violate the equal protection guarantee.

Under the due process guarantee, the Court often employs the "strict scrutiny-compelling interest test" in reviewing legislation that limits fundamental constitutional rights. However the Court will also use this standard of review under the equal protection guarantee in two categories of civil liberties cases: first, when the governmental act classifies people in terms of their ability to exercise a fundamental right; second, when the governmental classification distinguishes between persons, in terms of any right, upon some "suspect" basis.

Equal protection problems generally involve restrictions on the government's power to classify rather than the government's power to limit the rights of all persons. On the other hand, all legislation, in a sense, makes some classification. If the Court will strictly scrutinize *all* legislative classifications of persons for that would merely return us to the pre–1937 general review of economic and social welfare legislation. The Court will only employ the strict scrutiny standard to review the legitimacy of classifications when they are based upon a trait that itself seems to contravene established constitutional principles so that any use of the classification may be deemed "suspect"—a phrase that originated in *Korematsu v. United States* (1944).

Laws that classify persons on the basis of either their race or on the basis of their national origin (ancestry) are suspect and subject to this strict standard of review. In 1995, the Supreme Court ruled that the government's benign use of racial classifications (affirmative action) is also subject to strict scrutiny and is upheld unless the racial classification is narrowly tailored to a compelling interest. *Adarand Constructors, Inc. v. Pena* (1995).

The Court has also held that state or local laws that classify persons in terms of alienage, by treating resident aliens less favorably than citizens, are also suspect and subject to this test. However, as discussed later in this chapter, the Court does not enforce this test quite as strictly.

The Intermediate Test. At the close of the 1960's it was still possible to do a detailed analysis of all Supreme Court equal protection decisions in terms of a "two-tiered" model involving recognition of only the two previously described standards of review.

During the last third of the twentieth century, the Supreme Court adopted an intermediate standard of review that is not as difficult for the government to meet as the compelling interest test, but that involves far less judicial deference to the legislature than does the rationality test. Under the intermediate standard of review, the Court will not uphold a classification unless it finds that the classification has a "substantial relationship" to an "important" government interest. The Supreme Court has used this intermediate standard of review in cases involving sex classifications and illegitimacy classifications.

Sometimes the Court is not as clear as we would like in explaining what test it is using. Although some majority opinions continue to invoke strict scrutiny—compelling interest language in fundamental rights cases, it has been common for the Court to decide fundamental rights cases without stating a clear standard of review.

For example, the Court has found the right to vote to be fundamental but has in some cases upheld regulations of voting rights or the rights of candidates without requiring that the government formally demonstrate a compelling interest. In those cases the Court seems to exercise independent judicial review in order to insure that the regulation of the voting process reasonably promotes important ends (such as the governmental interest in running efficient and honest elections) and does not unreasonably restrict the voting rights of any class of individuals. That would appear to involve a middle-level standard of review that neither prohibits all regulation of the right to vote nor presumes that the government is free to limit voting rights as it would be under the traditional rational basis standard of review.

The Court has established a separate standard of review for prison regulations that limit fundamental constitutional rights. Courts will uphold prison regulations that significantly limit fundamental rights of prisoners, such as the right to marry or to receive news publications, so long as they are reasonably related to a legitimate penological interest. *Turner v. Safley* (1987); *Thornburgh v. Abbott* (1989). Nevertheless, any use of a racial classification by prison authorities will violate equal protection, unless the government can prove that the use of a racial classification is necessary to promote a compelling interest. *Johnson v. California* (2005).

(b) Is the Rationality Test Changing?

Historians can look at a period of time and classify it as transitional. In a sense, the law is always in some sort of transition period. As we see later in this chapter, the Court may sometimes be using the language of "rationality" but exercising a more active review. The rationality test is easy to state: the classification need only have a rational relationship to any legitimate governmental interest in order to comply with the equal protection guarantee. However, the meaning of that test is not clear. Few things are clearly "irrational," but the Court sometimes invalidates a law under that standard.

The mere existence of the cases invalidating classifications under the rationality standard leads one to question whether the Supreme Court is slowly changing that standard. The Supreme Court continues to state that, when it is applying "minimal judicial scrutiny" (which is another way of describing the "rational basis" or "rationality" test), it will not second guess legislative judgments.

Allegheny Pittsburgh Coal Co. v. County Commission (1989), held unanimously that an assessment system used to value real property for tax purposes violated the equal protection clause. The tax assessor valued the petitioner's real property on the basis of its recent purchase price, but made only minor modifications in the assessments of land that had not recently been sold, with the result of gross disparities in the assessed value of generally comparable land. A state, the Court said, "may divide different kinds of property into classes and assign to each class a different tax burden so long as those divisions and burdens are reasonable. But West Virginia did not draw such a distinction. The result subjected the petitioners to "intentional systematic undervaluation by state officials" of comparable neighboring property in the same county. The state assessed their property at about 8 to 35 times more than comparable neighboring property. If "general adjustments are accurate enough over a short period of time to equalize the differences in proportion between the assessments of a class of property holders, the Equal Protection Clause is satisfied." But here, the County's adjustment policy would take more than 500 years to equalize the assessments.

City of Cleburne v. Cleburne Living Center (1985) another example of where the Court may be putting new wine into the old label of "rationality." The Court unanimously invalidated a city zoning ordinance insofar as it prohibited the operation of a group home for the mentally retarded. The Court emphasized that it was reviewing this law under the mere rationality test. Yet the Court invalidated the law because it said that the denial of a permit for a group of mentally retarded persons to live together could not in any conceivable way promote any interest other than the desire to exclude mentally retarded persons from the city. The city zoning ordinance that authorized denying a "special use permit" for mentally retarded persons to live together in a group home in this case would have allowed an identical number of unrelated people to inhabit an identical house or apartment building if those persons were not mentally retarded. The city could not exclude mentally retarded persons based on an unsubstantiated fear or negative attitude about such persons. The Court concluded that the desire to discriminate cannot constitute a legitimate end that will supports a discriminatory classification.

§ 14.4　Establishing and Testing Classifications of a Law—"On Its Face," in Its "Application," or in Its "Purpose and Effect"—The Problem of Statistics

In order to subject a law to any review under the equal protection guarantee, one must be able to demonstrate that the law classifies persons in some manner. This first step will not be of much help to a person challenging a classification in the area of "economics or social welfare" for the Court does not subject those classifications to a very meaningful form of judicial review. Thus, the person challenging the law will need to show either that it classifies persons in terms of their ability to exercise a fundamental right or establishes a classification on the basis of race, national origin, alienage, illegitimacy, or sex.

In the course of litigation, questions may often arise as to whether such a classification exists; if it does not the law will not be subjected to strict scrutiny. For example, the law, on its face, may not have a racial classification, but, *in practice*, it does discriminate on the basis of race. This issue may often involve difficult problems of proof and intricate statistical demonstrations. The details of those litigation problems are beyond the scope of this book, but we do wish to introduce the basic concepts of how a court determines the existence of a classification.

A classification within a law can be established in one of three ways. First, the law may establish the classification "on its face."

This means that the law by its own terms classifies persons for different treatment. In such a case there is no problem of proof and the court can proceed to test the validity of the classification by the appropriate standard.

Second, the law may classify in its "application." In these cases the law either shows no classification on its face or else indicates a classification that seems to be legitimate, but persons challenging the legislation claim that the governmental officials who administer the law are applying it with different degrees of severity to different groups of persons who are described by some suspect trait. Here the challengers must establish that there is an administrative classification used to implement the law that merits some heightened review.

Finally, the law may contain no classification, or a neutral classification, and be applied evenhandedly. Nevertheless the law may be challenged as, in reality, constituting a device designed to impose different burdens on persons who should be treated similarly. If plaintiffs can prove this claim the Court will review this law as if it established a classification on its face. However, because all laws are susceptible to having their impact analyzed in a variety of ways, it is very difficult to establish this claim for the purpose of seeking strict judicial review of a legislative act.

The approach that the Court has taken on these issues over the years has not changed abruptly but many of its recent results may seem inconsistent with earlier decisions. One reason for this apparent inconsistency is that the Court also reviews classifications under statutes that allow for easier proof as to the existence of discriminatory classifications than would be acceptable if the Court is only enforcing the equal protection guarantee.

Any law may be applied in a manner that creates a classification. For example, let us assume that it could be proven that a local police force only enforces an anti-littering ordinance against members of a minority race. This evidence would establish that the law as applied involved a racial classification so that enforcement of the law could be enjoined, at least until such a time as the authorities could show that there would be no further discriminatory application.

The first, and the leading, case in this area is *Yick Wo v. Hopkins* (1886), which held unconstitutional the enforcement of a San Francisco ordinance banning the operation of hand laundries in wooden buildings. The facts showed that Chinese residents owned and operated the vast majority of such laundries. Moreover, all non-oriental launderers who applied for an exemption from the statute received one, while the authorities granted no Chinese applicant any exemption. This discriminatory application of the law constituted an invalid racial classification.

The statistical evidence was quite impressive. Of the 320 laundries in the city, Chinese owned and operated about 240; approximately 310 were constructed of wood, the same material used for 90% of the houses in the city. The board in charge of licenses had denied the application of all the Chinese (approximately 200) who had applied for licenses, all of whom had occupied and used the houses for laundries for more than 20 years. With one exception the board had granted the applications of all the non-Chinese who had applied, about 80. The facts demonstrated an administration directed so exclusively against a particular class of persons as to warrant and require the conclusion, that, whatever may have been the intent of the ordinances as adopted, they are applied by the public authorities charged with their administration, and thus representing the State itself, with a mind so unequal and oppressive as to amount to a practical denial by the State of that equal protection of the laws" that the Fourteenth Amendment guarantees. The Court added:

> "Though the law itself be fair on its face and impartial in appearance, yet, if it is applied and administered by public authority with an evil eye and an unequal hand, so as practically to make unjust and illegal discriminations between persons in similar circumstances, material to their rights, the denial of equal justice is still within the prohibition of the Constitution."

Yick Wo demonstrates, the Court cannot turn a blind eye to laws that are administered with "an evil eye and an unequal hand." The Court's treatment of statistics is complex and certainly open to criticism from those who desire a single standard for testing the impact of all rules that might have differing effects on racial or sexual classifications of persons.

§ 14.5 Classifications Based on Race or National Origin: Introduction

Today the equal protection clause of the Fourteenth Amendment mandates that no governmental entity shall burden persons, or deny a benefit to them, because they are members of a racial minority. After many years of indifference to the use of racial classifications, the Supreme Court, since 1954, enforced the constitutional principle of racial equality. Of course, there was no such principle prior to the Civil War when slavery existed with constitutional and Supreme Court sanction. Following that War, the states ratified the Thirteenth, Fourteenth and Fifteenth Amendments as part of an effort to grant constitutional equal rights to the freeman. Although, at the outset, it appeared as though the Supreme Court might strongly enforce the equal protection guarantee, the Court initially endorsed racial segregation of public facilities and functions, other than overt discrimination in jury selection, by adopting the concept of "separate but equal."

Following 1930 the Court began to evidence a growing distaste for having to place a constitutional imprimatur on racial discrimination. In the mid 1940's, the Court upheld the wartime restrictions on persons of Japanese ancestry but indicated that classifications based on race or national origin would not be consistent with constitutional principles absent the most important justification. Finally the Supreme Court began to enforce the concept of equal protection by forbidding the establishment of separate educational facilities for blacks. Thereafter the Court was to strike down every form of government action that discriminated against members of a minority race or segregated public facilities by race.

Classifications based on race or national origin have been held to be "suspect," that is, the Court will use "strict scrutiny" to determine whether the law is invidious. The use of these classifications will be invalid unless they are necessary to promote a "compelling" or "overriding" interest of government. Burdening someone because of his national origin or status as a member of a racial minority runs counter to the most fundamental concept of equal protection. For this reason the Court has not approved of racial classifications burdening minorities for many years. However, the Court has not yet held that all government acts must be race-neutral (or "color-blind") and so that sometimes the Government can use racial classifications for benign purposes, *i.e.*, affirmative action.

§ 14.6 The Civil War Amendments and Racial Discrimination—An Introductory Note

The Civil War changed the basic features of the Constitution just as it altered the country's political and social structure. These three Amendments—the Thirteenth, Fourteenth, and Fifteenth—are often referred to as the Civil War Amendments because they are the direct outgrowth of the war and its political aftermath.

The Thirteenth Amendment, which the states ratified in 1865, consists of two sections, the first of which prohibits "slavery" and "involuntary servitude" throughout the United States or its territories. This prohibition applies to all persons subject to the jurisdiction of the United States. It proscribes slavery even by private persons who have no connection to the government. The only exception is that made by section one for the punishment of properly convicted criminals. Section two of the Amendment grants Congress the power to make laws to enforce section one.

The Fourteenth Amendment, which Congress proposed in 1866 and the states ratified in 1868, has five sections dealing with separate issues. Section one is the provision that has been the source of most civil rights rulings by the Supreme Court. It consists of two sentences containing a total of four clauses. Sentence one grants citizenship to everyone "born or naturalized in the United States, and subject to the jurisdiction thereof, . . ." The three clauses of sentence two grant important individual rights, but they require "state action," that it, they secure these rights only against interference by the states. Thus sentence two is inapplicable to the actions of private persons or the federal government. The first clause of sentence two prohibits the states from abridging "the privileges or immunities of citizens of the United States." The second clause mirrors the language of the Fifth Amendment due process clause and prohibits the states from depriving anyone of "life, liberty or property, without due process of law." The last clause of section one contains the only equal protection clause in the Constitution, and it prohibits the states from depriving anyone of "the equal protection of the laws."

Section two of the Fourteenth Amendment altered the regulation of the electoral franchise in two ways. First, it counts blacks as full citizens for purposes of representation in the Congress by replacing the provisions of Article I Section two, which counted only three-fifths of "all other persons" (meaning "slaves"—a word the Constitution's drafters avoided). Second, it provides that representation in the federal Congress is reduced for those states that deny any adult male citizen the right to vote except for "participation in rebellion, or other crime. . . ." In these ways the drafters of the Amendment hoped to encourage the states to grant universal male suffrage without direct federal action.

Sections three and four of the Fourteenth Amendment relate to political problems of the period. Section three bars from federal office, except by vote of Congress, any previous government office holder who participated in a rebellion or gave aid to the enemies of the United States. Section four insulates the government debt, including the Union war debt, from legal attack. It also insures that the federal government would never pay any of the Confederate debt.

Section five of the Fourteenth Amendment gives Congress the power to enforce the Amendment.

The Fifteenth Amendment, which Congress proposed in 1869 and the states ratified in 1870, enfranchised blacks by prohibiting both the state and federal governments from denying anyone the right to vote "on account of race, color, or previous condition of servitude." Section two of the Amendment grants Congress the power to enforce section one.

Although there were many economic or political influences that took part in causing the war, the Northern Abolitionists and their goals of abolishing slavery and providing for the freed blacks were of critical importance in shaping postwar history.

While the three Amendments were not part of a preconceived legislative package or plan, they represent the natural progression of the abolitionist goals as these goals were represented in Congress by the "Radical Republicans." Each of the Amendments can be traced in part to particular political considerations. Most of the leading Republican members of Congress were confirmed abolitionists. A large part of the population, at least in the North, shared their desire to secure freedom and safety, if not social equality, for freed blacks.

During this period, there were times in which the ardor people of the northern states waned. Many want all reconstruction issues to end and the southern states to be "readmitted" to the Union. Indeed, the continued discrimination against black persons in the northern states gives one cause to doubt the popular strength of the abolitionist movement after the War. Yet the continued mistreatment of freed blacks in the South also resulted in renewed dedication of many Northerners to the abolitionists' goals. Thus, after a period of seemingly lessening Northern interest, the people ratify the Fifteenth Amendment in 1870.

Congress passed the major civil rights act in 1871 because it realized that the passage of the Amendments alone would not secure equality for blacks or stop the atrocities committed against them. As news of lynchings and other violent acts against blacks reached Washington, northern congressmen sought new legislation, which led to the Civil Rights Act of 1871, known at the time as the "Ku Klux Klan Act." It was designed to civilly and criminally punish those who acted to deprive others of their civil rights. The Act granted sweeping presidential powers to use the armed forces to enforce its provisions and even to suspend the right to habeas corpus when necessary to restore order to areas dominated by violent organizations. Although these provisions were the focus of most of the debate in Congress, the most important section was to be the civil penalty provision. Now usually referred to as simply "section 1983", that section today provides the cause of action and general basis for federal courts to protect individual civil rights.

§ 14.7 Classifications Based on Race or National Origin Following the Civil War

(a) Introduction

The Fourteenth Amendment prohibits states from denying any person the "equal protection of the laws." Whenever any governmental entity classifies persons by their race for dispensation of benefits or burdens, it probably has violated the equal protection clause, which requires that similar persons be dealt with in a similar manner. Therefore, it must be determined when, if ever, the government may rule that a person is "dissimilar" from others for the purpose of a law because of that person's race.

The Supreme Court has considered race and national origin classifications together for they both involve the government's treatment of persons on the basis of their ethnic ancestry rather than individual actions. Classifications based on alienage—the status of not being a citizen—relates to the personal attributes of citizenship rather than ancestry alone and they are dealt with in a separate section.

Today classifications based on race or national origin are "suspect." Courts will make an independent and active inquiry to determine whether the laws are invalid as "invidious" discrimination. These classifications are permissible only if necessary to promote a compelling or overriding interest of government. This conclusion requires a judicial finding that the use of the classification is so important that it outweighs the central purpose of the Amendment. But the Court went through a long period of allowing the use of racial classifications, such as state-segregated public facilities, before it reached that conclusion.

The Thirteenth Amendment has not served as a significant prohibition of racial discrimination absent congressional action. The Amendment prohibits "slavery" or "involuntary servitude" throughout the United States or any territory under its jurisdiction.

The Supreme Court acknowledged shortly after the ratification of the Amendment that it prohibited systems of peonage as well as the type of slavery that existed prior to the Civil War. However, only a few years later the Court held that racial discrimination by private persons did not violate the Thirteenth Amendment because it did not involve imposition of the incidents of slavery upon those against whom the discriminatory actions were taken nor did it involve a slavery or peonage system. By ruling that "mere discriminations on account of race or color were not regarded as badges of slavery," the Court restricted the application of section one of the Thirteenth Amendment to a prohibition of peonage or slavery. However, in the next century the Supreme Court would rule that Congress has the power under section two of the Amendment to outlaw by statute almost any form of racial discrimination even though section one of the Amendment did not in itself outlaw such discrimination.

(b) The First Cases—Institutional Uncertainty

Shortly after the ratification of the Fourteenth Amendment, the Court, in *Strauder v. West Virginia* (1879), held that a state statute that excluded blacks from juries violated the equal protection clause. A West Virginia statute provided that only white male citizens were eligible to serve on juries. The Court held that the defendant, a black citizen, had the right to trial by a jury selected without discrimination against persons of his race or color.

As the Court specifically noted, the question was not whether the defendant had the right to have persons of his own race serve on the jury but, rather, whether the law might exclude all blacks solely because of their race or color.

The opinion next discussed the meaning and the effect of the Amendment. The Court found that laws must be the same for all persons, black or white, and prohibited discrimination against blacks because of their color. The prohibitory language of the Amendment contained a necessary implication of a right for blacks—the right to be exempt from unfriendly legislation, to be exempt from legal discriminations, "implying inferiority in civil society, lessening the security of their enjoyment of the rights which others enjoy," and "which are a step toward reducing them to the condition of a subject race." The exclusion from juries is invalid discrimination because it expressly denied blacks the right to serve as jurors because of color. However, the Court would not strike down a conviction where a black defendant had been tried before an all white jury if blacks were not excluded from jury service. *Virginia v. Rives* (1879).

Yet, *Pace v. Alabama* (1883) upheld an Alabama statute that provided for more severe penalties for adultery and fornication if the couple were a white person and a black person than if the couple were of the same race. The Court upheld the law, at this early period in our history, because, it argued, the law applied to both races equally. Yet, the law discriminated on the basis of color, because it made a criminal penalty more severe for interracial couples.

In 1964, the Court overruled *Pace* in *McLaughlin v. Florida* (1964). The Court did not directly rule on interracial marriage prohibitions until 1967, when it invalidated all such laws. *Loving v. Virginia* (1967).

In 1883, the Court struck down certain federal civil rights laws as beyond the power granted to Congress by the Civil War Amendments, in the *Civil Rights Cases* (1883), which held that Congress could not impose sanctions against private persons for interfering with the civil liberties of the rights of black citizens.

In 1886 the Supreme Court again prohibited racial discrimination, in *Yick Wo v. Hopkins* (1886). A San Francisco ordinance prohibited the operation of laundries in wooden buildings without the consent of a board of supervisors. The authorities denied permission to defendant and all other Chinese persons to operate such laundries, while granting permission to virtually all non-Chinese persons operating laundries in wooden buildings. The facts established "an administration directed so exclusively against a particular class of persons as to warrant and require the conclusion, that, whatever may have been the intent of the ordinances as adopted, they are applied ... with a mind so unequal and oppressive as to amount to a practical denial by the State of [equal protection]." The state could show no reason for the discrimination could be shown other than hostility against the Chinese. Therefore, the ordinance could not be enforced.

(c) 1896–1954: The "Separate but Equal" Doctrine and Its Limitation

From 1896 to 1954 there existed a concept known as "separate but equal." Under this principle, the state could require separate services or treatment to blacks so long as it was "equal" to that provided for whites. Of course this rule amounted to no more than the Court giving racial discrimination a constitutional imprimatur.

The leading case is *Plessy v. Ferguson* (1896). A Louisiana statute required that all railway companies provide "equal but separate accommodations" for black and white passengers, imposing criminal penalties for violations by railway officials. Plessy, who alleged his ancestry was seven-eighths Caucasian and one-eighth African, attempted to use the coach for whites. The Louisiana Supreme Court denied his request for a writ of prohibition against the judge who was to try him for a violation of the statute. The Supreme Court affirmed and held that the statute did not violate of the Fourteenth Amendment.

The majority in *Plessy* summarily dismissed the equal protection claim: "The object of the Amendment was undoubtedly to enforce the absolute equality of the two races before the law, but in the nature of things, it could not have been intended to abolish distinctions based upon color, or to enforce social, as distinguished from political equality, or a commingling of the two races upon terms unsatisfactory to either." Laws requiring racial separation, according to the Court, did not necessarily imply the inferiority of either race and, in the view of the majority, were therefore permissible. The majority held that the state could legally classify and treat blacks in such a manner because of their race because, in the view of the majority, the classifying law was a reasonable exercise of the police power. The opinion added: "if the two races are to meet upon terms of social equality, it must be the result of natural affinities, a mutual appreciation of each other's methods and a voluntary consent of individuals."

Only Justice Harlan dissented in *Plessy*. He viewed the Civil War Amendments as together removing "the race line from our governmental systems." In the opinion of Harlan, the Constitution was now "color-blind" so that government could not use a person's color to determine his rights. Justice Harlan was an accurate prophet when he viewed *Plessy's* approval of separate but equal as a doctrine that "will, in time prove to be quite as pernicious as the decision made by this tribunal in the *Dred Scott* Case."

Although the facts of the separate but equal doctrine in *Plessy* applied to accommodations on public conveyances, states and court decisions used it to justify widespread segregation in public schools and other state institutions as well as state and local laws that required segregation of privately-owned business, such as restaurants. The Court did not fully reconsider the validity of the separate but equal doctrine again until 1954.

The Court was willing to invalidate segregation laws when it could not accept the separation as incident to a valid police power end. Accordingly, *Buchanan v. Warley* (1917) unanimously struck down an ordinance that prohibited a black from moving into a neighborhood that was predominantly white at the time the ordinance was passed and vice versa. The Court held the law violated due process because it arbitrarily eliminated the right to acquire, use, and dispose of property. The Court distinguished this case from *Plessy* because that case did not deprive blacks of transportation; the law merely required them to conform to "reasonable rules" concerning the separation of races. In *Buchanan*, however, the statute effectively deprived persons of the right to acquire land in a neighborhood predominated by members of the other race or to dispose of their property to a member of the race which was not predominant.

Buchanan can best be explained by the desire of the Justices, during this era, to protect property rights, given the fact that Court at this time in our history did little else to promote racial desegregation.

Beginning in 1938, there were a series of cases in which the Court, without re-examining the separate but equal doctrine, found that the black plaintiffs were entitled to relief because they had not in fact been offered "equal" educational opportunities. First, there was *Missouri ex rel. Gaines v. Canada* (1938), the school denied an admittedly qualified black applicant admission to the state law school solely because of his color. Because there was no state law school for blacks in Missouri, the state sought to fulfill its obligation to provide blacks an education that was "substantially equal" to the education provided whites by paying plaintiff's tuition at a comparable out-of-state school that did admit blacks. The Court, however, held that this procedure did not satisfy the state's duty—the question was not whether the legal education a black could receive at the out-of-state school was equal to the legal education received at the Missouri school, but what opportunities Missouri provided for whites, but not blacks, solely on the basis of color.

In subsequent cases, the Court began to examine intangible as well as tangible factors in determining if the educational opportunities offered to blacks were equal. *Sweatt v. Painter* (1950) involved a black petitioner seeking admission to a law school that turned him down solely on the basis of race. The trial court recognized that this situation denied equal protection, but, instead of ordering the school to admit petitioner, it continued the case to allow the state to supply substantially equal facilities. The state created a school for blacks while petitioner's appeal was pending and, as a result, the case was remanded. The trial court found the new school for blacks was "substantially equivalent", and did not order the white state school to admit him. The U.S. Supreme Court reversed.

The Court expressly reserved the question of the validity of the separate but equal doctrine, holding only that the newly established law school was not substantially equal. The white law school had a better faculty, a better offering of courses, a better library, and a wider range of activities than the law school established for blacks. Furthermore, the white school possessed those qualities that are immeasurable but make a superior law school, e.g., reputation of the faculty, position and influence of alumni.

In *McLaurin v. Oklahoma State Regents for Higher Education* (1950), decided the same day, the issue was whether a state—after admitting a black graduate student to its university—can treat him differently because of his race. The previously all-white state school required McLaurin to sit at a desk in a classroom anteroom behind a railing with a sign "for colored's only," to sit at a designated desk on the mezzanine floor of the library, and to eat at a different time and at a specified table in the cafeteria. During the course of litigation, the school changed the requirements so that it allowed him a seat in the classroom but in a special row set aside for black students. It also assigned him a special desk on the main floor of the library, and allowed him to eat at the same time as the white students but at a different, specified table.

The Court held that such state-approved restrictions based on race produced inequality in educational opportunities that violated even the separate but equal test. The restrictions impaired and inhibited "his ability to study, to engage in discussions, and exchange views with other students, and in general, to learn his profession." As in *Sweatt*, the Court relied on intangible factors in making its determination that the state did not offer blacks equal educational opportunities. The students might treat McLaurin differently even in the absence of state-approved restrictions but that was immaterial. There was a vast difference—a constitutional difference—between a *state*-imposed prohibition of commingling of students and the voluntary refusal of individuals to commingle.

(d) The Modern Position on Racial Restrictions

(1) The World War II Japanese Restriction Cases—A Turning Point for "Suspect Classifications." Out of an alleged fear of espionage by Japanese persons in the United States or an invasion by Japanese military, the government placed severe restrictions on the rights of persons of Japanese ancestry during World War II. Our Western states detained Japanese persons, whether aliens or citizens, in guarded camps. As a security measure, President Roosevelt issued an executive order authorizing military commanders to exclude persons from vast areas. Congress then made it a federal crime to violate military orders made pursuant to this authority.

Hirabayashi v. United States (1943) upheld an 8 p.m. to 6 a.m. curfew requirement as within the discretion granted the executive to wage war. *Korematsu v. United States* (1944) was the start of a revolution in constitutional analysis of equal protection issues. The Court (6 to 3) upheld the temporary exclusion and detention of persons of Japanese ancestry. The opinion gave great deference to the combined war powers of the president and Congress as these detentions far exceeded anything necessary to protect the country.

The dissenting Justices would not have tolerated any but the most necessary restrictions to promote the war effort. Indeed, the three dissenting opinions are classic statements warning of the false security that results from using war powers to burden minorities.

The majority agreed with the dissent as to the general unconstitutionality of imposing burdens on a person because of his race but still concluded that the needs of the nation, as perceived at the start of the war, justified these measures. Justice Black's majority opinion, while ruling against the Japanese–American citizens, did establish a new constitutional standard of review of race classifications:

"It should be noted, to begin with, that all legal restrictions which curtail the civil rights of a single racial group are immediately *suspect*. That is not to say that all such restrictions are unconstitutional. It is to say that courts must subject them to the *most rigid scrutiny*. Pressing public necessity may sometimes justify the existence of such restrictions; racial antagonism never can." (emphasis added).

This opinion established three points for future analysis of classifications based on race or national origin. First, these classifications are "suspect," which meant, at a minimum, that they were likely to be based on an impermissible purpose. Second, these classifications are subject to independent judicial review—"rigid scrutiny." Third, such classifications are invalid if based on racial antagonism and upheld only if they are based on "public necessity." From this opinion came the concepts of "strict judicial scrutiny" and the requirement that some restrictions on liberty must be necessary to promote "compelling" or "overriding" interests. Subsequent cases often cite this case with approval, but the portion cited is the part dealing with treating racial classifications with the *most rigid scrutiny*. If you only read the cases citing *Korematsu*, and not *Korematsu*, itself, you would never know that Mr. Korematsu lost.

(2) The Rejection of Separate but Equal and Establishment of Racial Equality as a Constitutional Principle.

The *Brown* Decision. In 1954, the Court in *Brown v. Board of Education* (1954), for the first time since *Plessy*, fully examined the validity of the separate but equal doctrine. The Court did not expressly overrule *Plessy* (although it is often assumed that it did so) but held simply that the separate but equal doctrine has no place in education. *Brown* involved four consolidated cases focusing on the permissibility of local governments conducting school systems which segregated students by race. In each case blacks sought admission to public schools on a nonsegregated basis and in each the state court based its decision upon the separate but equal doctrine. The plaintiffs challenged the validity of the doctrine, arguing that segregated schools were not "equal" and could not be "equal."

The case was briefed and argued at two successive terms of Court. The reargument before the Supreme Court centered largely on the circumstances surrounding the adoption of the Fourteenth Amendment and the intentions of its framers. Because it was a constitutional Amendment rather than a statute that the Court was interpreting, the search for the intent of the framers had two facets: whether the drafters contemplated that the Amendment would immediately abolish segregation in public schools and, if not, whether the Amendment was to embody a principle that would allow Congress or the judiciary to abolish segregation in the future.

The Court in *Brown* could not "turn the clock back to 1868 when the Amendment was adopted, or even to 1896 when *Plessy v. Ferguson* was written." It stated the question presented as: "Does segregation of children in public schools solely on the basis of race, even though the physical facilities and other 'tangible' factors may be equal, deprive the children of the minority group of equal educational opportunities?" The Justices unanimously held that it did and, in so doing, sounded the death knell for legally enforced segregation.

The Court said, "that in the field of public education the doctrine of 'separate but equal' has no place." The opinion referred to the earlier recognition in *Sweatt* and *McLaurin* that intangibles played a considerable role in the value educational opportunities offered. Although all tangibles such as faculty, books, or buildings were "equal", a difference in "intangibles" caused by separation would render a school unequal. To separate black children "from others of similar age and qualifications solely because of their race generates a feeling of inferiority as to their status in the community that may affect their hearts and minds in a way unlikely ever to be undone."

The Court stated that this finding was "amply supported by modern authority" and in a footnote cited findings of sociologists, anthropologists, psychologists, and psychiatrists who had done work in race relations. Commentators later criticized the Court's citation on social science data.

The Federal Government's Denial of Equal Protection. On the same day it decided *Brown*, the Court invalidated segregation of public schools in the District of Columbia in *Bolling v. Sharpe* (1954). Because the equal protection clause of the Fourteenth Amendment, upon which *Brown* was based, is inapplicable to the federal government, the Court held that racial segregation also violated the due process clause of the Fifth Amendment.

After *Brown*, it was unthinkable that the Constitution would impose a lesser burden on the federal government. Today it is accepted that the due process clause imposes an equal protection guarantee on the federal government.

Immediate, Post-*Brown* Rulings. The rulings that followed *Brown* made clear what we take for granted today—no governmental entity may segregate or burden people because of their race or national origin. In a series of short, per curiam opinions or orders, some without any citation and other merely citing *Brown*, the Court invalidated state-sponsored segregation in public beaches and bathhouses, municipal golf courses, buses, parks, public parks and golf courses, athletic contests, airport restaurants, courtroom seating, and municipal auditoriums. Through *Brown* and these subsequent cases the Court abandoned the entire separate but equal doctrine, required that all racial classifications be subject to "strict scrutiny," and thus prohibited state-sponsored racial segregation.

In 1964 the Court also rejected the limited view of equal protection that had allowed the use of racial classifications to determine whether certain activity was criminal so long as the same sanctions were given members of each race. *McLaughlin v. Florida* (1964) invalidated a statute prohibiting a white person and black person from living together or occupying the same room at night. The law did not prohibit the same behavior between persons of the same race. *McLaughlin* stated that, while the Court would normally uphold statutory classifications if they were not totally arbitrary, when the classification are drawn on the basis of race the legislature lacked its normally wide discretion. The Court would uphold the statute only if the state were able to show an overriding purpose requiring proscription of the specified conduct when engaged in by members of different races but not when engaged in by persons of the same race. Because the state could show no such purpose, the Court invalidated the statute.

Justices Douglas and Stewart concurred in *McLaughlin* but objected to the implication that it might be possible for a state to show an overriding purpose which would validate such a statute. In their view, *any* statute that made the color of the actor the test for whether his conduct was criminal is invidious discrimination and *per se* unconstitutional.

It was not until 1967 that the Supreme Court invalidated antimiscegenation statutes, *i.e.*, laws that prohibit interracial marriage. *Loving v. Virginia* (1967) ruled that antimiscegenation statutes violated both equal protection and due process. The Court rejected the notion that the mere "equal application" of a statute containing a racial classification is enough to remove the classification from the Fourteenth Amendment's proscription of racial classifications.

Conclusion. The Supreme Court appears to treat the phrases "racial classifications, ""ancestry classifications," and "ethnic classifications" as interchangeable. In *Rice v. Cayetano* (2000), the Court held that the Fifteenth Amendment prohibited Hawaii from limiting the vote for members of the board that administered programs to benefit native Hawaiians (a term defined by State law) to persons who were native Hawaiians. *Rice* ruled that the law constituted an ancestry classification, and that, at least in this instance, "ancestry can be a proxy for race."

Racial classifications that burden individuals because of their race or ethnic background or that have a stigmatizing effect, run contrary to the fundamental goal of racial equality that the Supreme Court has come to recognize as a core value of both the equal protection clause of the Fourteenth Amendment and the equal protection component of the Fifth Amendment due process clause. The Court, in recent years, has stressed that such classifications require that the government demonstrate both a compelling interest and that the classification is truly necessary to promote that interest. *Palmore v. Sidoti* (1984) invoked this test as when it unanimously held that a state court could not remove an infant child from the custody of its natural mother, otherwise found to be an appropriate person to have custody, simply because she had married a person of a different race.

Palmore recognized that racial and ethnic prejudices might affect the couple and the mother's child from a previous marriage but held that "the reality of private biases and the possible injury they might inflict" are not permissible considerations for removal of the child from the custody of the mother. Because "[c]lassifying persons according to their race is more likely to reflect racial prejudice than legitimate public concerns" it is necessary to have "the most exacting scrutiny" in order to insure that a classification of this type is justified by a compelling interest and is indeed necessary to the accomplishment of that interest. Under this test, it is difficult to hypothesize what circumstances would ever justify a state in using a racial classification to burden members of minority races or ethnic groups.

The prison authorities do not have the right to temporarily segregate new prisoners by race based on the assertion that the policy will promote peaceful conditions in the prison. The Court will uphold such a government policy only if the government can prove that the temporary segregation of prisoners by race is, in fact, necessary to promote a compelling interest. *Johnson v. California* (2005). Prison authorities should be able to make race-conscious decisions when temporary segregation of prisoners is necessary to quell violence that has resulted from racial tensions within the prison. However, a policy separating incoming prisoners on the basis of racial stereotypes is unlikely to survive strict judicial scrutiny.

The government appears to have some right to know the racial impact of its actions. Thus, the government can compile racial information so long it does not use them to burden anyone because of race. The government has to compile racial statistics when issues of racial discrimination in public services are litigated. Although statistics on racial impact do not decide substantive issues regarding discrimination, the information is relevant to determine government purposes.

We discuss the question of benign racial classifications, often called reverse discrimination or affirmative action, later in this chapter. First, let us explore the implementation of the desegregation rulings.

§ 14.8   Implementation of the Desegregation Decisions

(a) Desegregation of the Schools

(1) The Rise and Fall of "All Deliberate Speed." In 1954 the Court decided *Brown v. Board of Education* (*Brown I*), which held that segregated school systems violated the equal protection guarantee. But that decision postponed any ruling as to the relief to be granted in the cases. The Court heard new arguments concerning the proper scope of its decree in the next term. In *Brown v. Board of Education* (*Brown II*) (1955) the Supreme Court addressed the question of the manner in which relief should be accorded black students who previously had been found to have been denied equal protection of the laws due to the segregation of public schools.

Generally when a court finds a constitutional violation, it will order an immediate end to the unconstitutional practice. *Brown II*, however, because of the complexities the Court anticipated would occur nationwide in the transition to a system of public education freed of racial discrimination, the Court required only that school authorities dismantle segregated school systems with "all deliberate speed." The Court required a "prompt and reasonable start toward full compliance." Once the school started complying, the courts might permit school authorities additional time to comply if "necessary in the public interest" and "consistent with good faith compliance at the earliest practicable date."

The Court assumed faith in state and lower federal courts that, because of their proximity to local conditions, were best suited to perform the duty of insuring good faith implementation of the decision. The Court gave the lower courts and the school authorities no specific guidelines. They were to consider equitable principles, which traditionally had been characterized by practical flexibility and facility for balancing public and private needs. Unfortunately, local courts did not measure up to this task.

Brown II met with massive resistance. The tactics in opposition to desegregation included inaction, defiance by political leaders, vigorous defensive action in the legislatures, including attempts to punish civil rights attorneys, and violence. The resistance was typified by the occurrences in Little Rock, Arkansas, in 1957. School authorities developed a plan for desegregation, but the legislature engaged in a program to perpetuate racial segregation. When the governor sent state troops to prevent blacks from entering the previously white high school, the Court enjoined him from further interference. To enforce the constitutional ruling, the federal government sent federal troops to allow the blacks to attend the schools. School authorities requested postponement of their desegregation plan because they believed that the extreme public hostility caused by the actions of the governor and the legislature made it impossible to maintain a sound education program with the black students in attendance.

Cooper v. Aaron (1958) denied the city any additional time to comply with the ruling. The opinion was signed by all nine Justices of the Court to emphasize the strength of the ruling that was to "unanimously reaffirm" the holding in *Brown*. The Court accepted without reservation the assertions that the school board had acted in good faith and that the educational process of all students would suffer if the prevailing conditions of the previous year continued but stated that the rights of black children were not to be sacrificed to violence and disorder engendered by the actions of state officials. *Brown* could not be nullified either "openly and directly by state legislators or state executive or judicial officers" or "indirectly by them through evasive schemes for segregation whether attempted 'ingeniously or ingenuously.' "

Many school districts persisted in the use of dilatory practices to avoid complete desegregation. As time passed and no appreciable progress toward integration was made, the Court manifested its impatience. In 1963, the Court noted that "the context in which we must interpret and apply this language to plans for desegregation has been significantly altered." The following year, *Griffin v. Prince Edward County Board of Education* (1964) held: "the time for mere deliberate speed had run out." Later, *Green v. County School Board* (1968) stated that "[t]he burden on a school board today is to come forward with a plan that promises realistically to work, and promises realistically to work now."

By 1969, the Supreme Court was no longer willing to tolerate any delay. Reviewing a Fifth Circuit decision granting more time for the desegregation of a public school system, *Alexander v. Holmes County Board of Education* (1969) (per curiam), held: "the Court of Appeals should have denied all motions for additional time because continued operation of segregated schools under a standard of allowing 'all deliberate speed' for desegregation is no longer constitutionally permissible. Under explicit holdings of this Court the obligation of every school district is to terminate dual systems at once and to operate now and hereafter only unitary schools." Acknowledging the Court's holding, the Fifth Circuit nevertheless permitted a one semester delay in implementing a desegregation order because the order was issued in the middle of the school year. The Supreme Court summarily reversed in a per curiam opinion. Two concurring Justices thought that the time between a finding of noncompliance and the effective date of the remedy, including any judicial review, should not exceed eight weeks. Four other Justices thought that even that delay would be too long.

(2) Institutions Subject to the Desegregation Principle

(a) **The De Jure–De Facto Distinction.** Neither *Brown I* nor later decisions of the Supreme Court require all public schools to be racially integrated. Rather, the decisions require that public schools not racially desegregated. School systems that have not been segregated *by law* (de jure) need not take steps to integrate their school system even though their individual schools have racially unbalanced student populations. However, if a school district has operated a racially segregated system, it must entirely eradicate that practice by integrating its schools. These historical differences are the core of the *de jure-de facto* distinction.

De jure ("by law") segregation is racial separation that is the product of some purposeful act by government authorities. De facto ("by the facts") segregation occurs because of multiple private housing and migration patterns and is unconnected to any purposeful *governmental* action to racially segregate schools. If a school system involves de jure segregation, it violates the equal protection guarantee; the courts will intervene if necessary to remedy this situation. The short statement of the rule is that if a school district is unintentionally (de facto) segregated, there is no constitutional violation and the courts will not intervene. Of course, it is not always easy to determine if the resulting segregation is truly de facto, for the government may aid private discrimination in subtle ways, thus converting de facto into de jure segregation.

In the South, it was easy to show schools had been segregated by law, so courts issued desegregation orders and compliance followed, albeit slowly. In the North and West, however, where there were no express *statutory* provisions authorizing segregation of schools, plaintiffs faced the more difficult task of showing purposeful discrimination in school assignments even where segregation resulted from discriminatory housing practices or gerrymandering of school districts. As a result, in 1970 in the South only 39.4% of black students attended predominantly minority schools, while in northern and western states the figure was 57.6%.

Today a central issue in school desegregation suits is whether the school system constitutes de jure rather than de facto segregation. Mere statistics showing an imbalance between the racial make-up of individual schools will not in itself be sufficient, for such an imbalance could have arisen unintentionally from housing and migration patterns. The Supreme Court has held that de jure segregation is only present when there has been "segregative purpose or intent" and government action to maintain segregated schools. *Keyes v. School District No. 1* (1973).

Proving Discriminatory Purpose. In 1973 in *Keyes v. School District No. 1* the Court for the first time considered a charge of racially discriminatory behavior against a school system in a large metropolitan area outside the South. The Denver school district had never operated under a constitutional or statutory provision that explicitly required or permitted racial segregation in the public schools. However, there was proof that at least some of the schools had been used to isolate blacks and Hispanic–Americans. The Court adopted the de jure-de facto analysis and held that there was a constitutional violation to the extent there was "segregative purpose or intent" in school board actions.

The Court first discussed the method of defining a "segregated school." Because the Court found Hispanic–Americans and blacks suffer identical discrimination in treatment when compared to whites, schools with a combined predominance of blacks and Hispanic–Americans may be considered "segregated" schools.

The Court went on to find that government-designed segregation as to a substantial portion of the school system should not be viewed in isolation from the rest of the district. If plaintiffs prove that school authorities have carried out a systematic program of segregation affecting a substantial portion of the students, schools, teachers, and facilities within the school system, it is logical to assume there is a predicate for a finding of the existence of a dual school system. Normally, racially discriminatory actions will have an impact beyond the particular schools. However, it is possible that the school board might be able to show that the segregated portion did not directly affect the other schools.

Even if the board were able to prove this contention, finding intentional segregation on the part of the school board in one portion of the school system is highly relevant to the question of the board's intent with respect to other segregated schools in the system. A "finding of intentionally segregative school board actions in a meaningful portion of a school system, as in this case, creates a presumption that other segregated schooling within the system is not adventitious." Such a finding establishes a *prima facie* case of unlawful segregation and shifts the burden to school authorities to prove that other segregated schools are not also the result of deliberate racial discrimination. In discharging this burden, the school board must do more than simply offer some allegedly logical, racially neutral explanation for their actions. They must produce proof sufficient to support a finding that segregative intent was not among the motivating factors for their actions. If segregative intent has been shown, the board can rebut the prima facie case only by showing that past discriminatory acts did not create or contribute to the current segregated condition of the schools.

Inter-District Integration Problems. Courts may not order suburbs with de facto segregation to integrate with a neighboring system (a different school district) involving de jure segregation. In *Milliken v. Bradley* (1974) the question, as the Court phrased it, was "whether a federal court may impose a multidistrict, area-wide remedy to a single-district de jure segregation problem absent any finding that the other included school districts have failed to operate unitary school systems within their district, absent any claim or finding that government authorities had established boundary lines of any affected school district with the purpose of fostering racial segregation in public schools, absent any finding that the included districts committed acts which effected segregation within the other districts, and absent a meaningful opportunity for the included neighborhood school districts to present evidence or be heard on the propriety of a multidistrict remedy or on the question of constitutional violation by those neighboring districts." Perhaps as indicated by the manner in which the Court stated the question, its answer was no.

In *Milliken* case, the Court found that the Detroit public schools were unlawfully segregated. The federal district court adopted a metropolitan, inter-school district plan that included fifty-three Detroit suburbs in the "desegregation area." The Supreme Court, however, found it impermissible for the lower court to decree inter-district relief simply to produce area-wide integrated schools.

While school district lines are not sacrosanct, local autonomy in education is of great importance. In determining the validity of a court decree requiring cross-district or inter-district consolidation in order to remedy segregation found in one district, the controlling principle is that the scope of the remedy must be determined by the extent and the nature of the constitutional violation. "Before the boundaries of separate and autonomous school districts may be set aside by consolidating the separate units for remedial purposes or by imposing a cross-district remedy, it must first be shown that there has been a constitutional violation within one district that produces a significant segregative effect in another district." Thus, inter-district relief is appropriate where plaintiffs show either that the racially discriminatory acts of one district affect an adjacent district or where district lines have been drawn according to race. A court cannot order inter-district relief unless it makes such a finding.

Four of the Justices dissented. Although their opinions differed in part, they all believed that once there has been a finding of state-imposed segregation, it becomes the duty of the state to remove all traces of racial segregation. They would have held that the constitutional rights of black students were too fundamental to be abridged on such grounds.

School Districts With Continuing or Recurring Segregation. *Pasadena City Board of Education v. Spangler* (1975) invalidated the district court's requirement as a part of a desegregation plan that the composition of the student body of particular schools fit a certain ratio every year. Because the system involved de jure segregation, the initial use of a statistical goal for racial integration was proper, but once the court remedy establishes a racially neutral school system, the lower court exceeded its authority in requiring annual readjustment to racial balance. Later changes in racial mixture were not caused by segregative acts of school or state authorities and, therefore, the new racial imbalance constituted only de facto segregation.

(b) The Desegregation Principle and Private Schools. Private schools that segregate on the basis of race do not violate the Constitution unless they have sufficient contacts with the state or the federal government to allow description of their acts as "state action," because the equal protection clause of the Fourteenth Amendment applies only to the states and the due process clause of the Fifth Amendment applies only to the federal government. Thus, private segregated schools present a classic "state action" issue and under traditional analysis, they are not subject to constitutional restraint absent further contacts with the government. However, the government may not give any aid to these schools because that would constitute government support for and facilitation of racial segregation. Therefore, these schools could be put to an election between receiving assistance from the government and maintaining the segregative practices.

(c) Colleges and Universities. The Court never applied the "all deliberate speed" principle to state universities. The desegregation of higher education had begun prior to *Brown* in a series of Court decisions finding that educational facilities and opportunities afforded blacks were not equal. These holdings resulted in the mandate of immediate admission of black students to previously white universities and law schools on a nonsegregated basis.

Following *Brown II*, the Supreme Court rejected all attempts to apply the "all deliberate speed" doctrine, holding that qualified blacks seeking to enter colleges, graduate or professional schools were entitled to prompt relief. *Florida ex rel. Hawkins v. Board of Control* (1956).

In some states, the task of remedying unconstitutional race discrimination in higher education is more complex because some of those states had created colleges for minority race students that are now termed "historically black colleges." Some historically black colleges are state universities that are excellent educational institutions.

United States v. Fordice (1992) took a limited step towards clarifying the approaches that state officials and courts should take in the desegregating of state university systems that had given rise to historically black state colleges. *Fordice* examined the state university system of the State of Mississippi. The state university system in Mississippi had been run on a racially segregated basis, by way of statutes and purposeful discriminatory administrative actions, through most, if not all, of the 1960s. In the 1970s, the state board with authority for the state university system submitted plans for compliance with the constitutional desegregation principle and federal statutes. The lawsuit that resulted in the Supreme Court case began in 1975; plaintiffs claimed that the state had maintained the racially segregated school system by allowing its effects to continue. They claimed that the state colleges that once had been officially for white students only remained an institution with very few minority students. The state colleges that had once been for minority students only remained as schools with primarily minority race students.

The lower federal courts ruled that Mississippi's financial and educational policies since the late 1970s were racially neutral (including the student admission policies at the state universities) and that the state had met its obligation to dismantle its racially segregated university system. The United States Supreme Court disagreed with the lower courts, holding that state university systems were under the same obligation to eliminate the effects of de jure segregation as public grade schools and high schools. Mere elimination of prior segregation, and ending racially discriminatory policies, did not meet this obligation. The state does not discharge "its constitutional obligations until it eradicates policies and practices traceable to its prior de jure dual system that continue to foster segregation."

Some racially segregated practices of states (in areas outside of education) could be remedied merely by a court ordering a state to cease its racial segregation. Thus, a court could end racial segregation regarding physical facilities such as parks or hospitals by simply ordering an end to racially discriminatory practices. But education is different. In *Fordice* Justice White stated:

"If the State perpetuates policies and practices traceable to its prior system that continue to have segregative effects—whether by influencing student enrollment decisions or by fostering segregation in other facets of the university system—and such policies are without sound educational justification and can be practicably eliminated, the state has not satisfied its burden of proving that it has dismantled its prior system."

The majority opinion went on to find that Mississippi's current admissions policies (which required higher test scores for state universities that happened to be historically white institutions) and the widespread duplication of educational programs at historically white and black colleges appeared to perpetuate the effects of past discrimination. The lower federal courts, on remand, should examine the basic question of whether all eight of the state's higher educational institutions had to be continued in operation. If the continuation of all eight schools was a perpetuation of the prior racially discriminatory system, the courts would have to consider whether one or more of the schools should be closed or merged. If the courts fully adopted the standards used in public school desegregation cases when examining state university systems, it might be that there could be no justification for the continuation of some state universities that operated with racially neutral admissions policies but continued to be institutions that served almost solely racial minority students. On the other hand, it might be that the interest in providing an educational atmosphere conducive to minority race students at a historically black college might at the current time (rather than at the time the institution was started) be designed to advance the educational interests of minority race students.

Justice Thomas, who concurred in the opinion and judgment of the Court in *Fordice,* stated:

> "We do not foreclose the possibility that there exists 'sound educational justification' from maintaining historically black colleges as such. Despite the shameful history of state-enforced segregation, these institutions have survived and flourished ... think it undisputable that these institutions have succeeded in part because of their distinctive history and traditions ... obviously, a state cannot maintain such traditions by closing particular institutions, historically white or historically black, to particular racial groups. However, it hardly follows that a state cannot operate a diverse assortment of institutions— including historically black institutions—open to all on a race-neutral basis, but with established traditions and programs that might disproportionally appeal to one race or another."

Fordice held that the lower federal courts were in error when they accepted the adoption of race neutral policies by the state university system as the equivalent of dismantling the former segregated system of public universities in Mississippi. However, near the end of the majority opinion, Justice White added:

"If we understand private petitioners to press us to order the upgrading of [the historically black state universities in Mississippi] solely so that they can be publicly financed, exclusively black enclaves by private choice, we reject that request. The state provides these facilities for all its citizens and it has not met its burden under *Brown* to take affirmative steps to dismantle its prior de jure system when it perpetuates a separate, but 'more equal' one. Whether such an increase in funding is necessary to achieve a full dismantlement under standards we have outlined [requiring the state to make sure that student choices regarding which state institutions to apply to and attend were truly free of the effects of past segregation] is a different question, and one that must be addressed on remand."

The principles employed in school segregation cases following *Brown* require states to dismantle racially discriminatory state university system as fully as they would dismantle racial segregation in a public grade school or high school system. Whether some historically black state universities and colleges will be able to retain their educational character is a question for future cases.

(3) State School Programs Relating to Desegregation. In connection with massive resistance, school authorities and state legislatures often adopted various creative measures in an attempt to evade compliance with *Brown*. When faced with desegregation orders, some authorities reacted by closing public schools and giving financial support to private schools; others attempted to form new school districts. In other cases, school authorities superficially indicated compliance with the desegregation mandate but adopted desegregation plans that did not effectively integrate schools. These included freedom-of-choice plans or grade-a-year plans. State legislatures attempted to evade *Brown* by passing statutes that prohibited school busing evening when the busing was necessary to desegregate past de jure segregation. The Supreme Court invalidated all of these methods when used in an attempt to perpetuate segregated school systems. The law now requires that states eliminate de jure segregation root and branch.

(4) Federal Court Remedial Powers. In the years immediately following *Brown*, little progress was made toward the desegregation of schools, and the Supreme Court said little about what form judicial relief should take. The result was confusion. The problems encountered by judges of the lower federal courts made clear their need for guidance from the Supreme Court as to the scope of federal court powers to dismantle de jure segregated school systems. That guidance came in *Swann v. Charlotte–Mecklenburg Board of Education* (1971), which laid out in more precise terms

the scope of the duty of school authorities and district courts to fashion an end to racially segregated school systems.

Swann explained that a federal court has no power to require school authorities to take any action until it finds de jure segregation. If there is a showing of purposeful discrimination in a substantial portion of a school district is there a presumption of intentional discrimination in the rest of the district. The school can rebut the presumption only by showing that no such intent existed.

Even when the court finds there has been purposeful discrimination, it should give school authorities the opportunity to submit a plan for desegregation. If they fail to submit an adequate desegregation plan, the does the district court then has the authority to order specific steps to desegregate the schools.

Swann explained that the existing policy and practices with regard to faculty, staff, transportation, extracurricular activities, and facilities are among the most important indicia of a segregated school system. If it is possible to identify a school as a white school or a black school by the racial composition of the faculty and staff, the quality of the school buildings or equipment, or the organization of sport activities, then there is a prima facie case of an equal protection violation.

When there has been a violation of equal protection the first duty of school authorities is to eliminate all invidious racial discriminations. The action should be immediate with respect to transportation, supporting personnel, extracurricular activities, maintenance of buildings and distribution of equipment. Faculty assignment and the construction of new schools offer easy, flexible ways to achieve integration. *Swann*, therefore, upheld the district court's use of a fixed ratio in making faculty assignments to achieve an initial degree of desegregation and correction of the de jure segregation. Because the location of school buildings may determine the racial composition of individual schools, the courts and school authorities must give particular care to prevent the use of future school construction and abandonment to perpetuate or re-establish the dual system.

Swann then turned its attention to the question of remedies for the de jure racial segregation of students. Where such practices have existed, the school must terminate them and establish a nondiscriminatory school system. *Swann* gives the school authorities an opportunity to correct the system by presenting an effective plan for desegregation. Grade-a-year plans, freedom-of-choice plans, or other remedies that do not truly reverse the segregation are inadequate. In such situations, the district court is forced to use student remedies.

Swann discussed the extent to which courts may alter attendance zones as a remedy. The redesign of school districts and attendance zones has been one of the tools most frequently used that school planners and courts use to eliminate dual systems. Courts have the power, as an interim measure, to use tools such as the creation of attendance zones neither compact nor contiguous. If all things are equal, students should be assigned to the school closest their homes. But *Swann* emphasized, all things are not equal in a deliberately segregated school system; the court, to desegregate the system, must mix students formerly segregated. Although the remedy may be administratively awkward or burdensome for some students, some reasonable amount of inconvenience or burden cannot be avoided in the transition from segregation to integration. In determining the validity of a particular attendance plan the lower court should make its decision in light of the objective sought and its knowledge of local conditions. The Supreme Court will approve of reasonable lower court decrees.

Swann also discussed busing, an important tool for the desegregation of schools. If, as in *Swann*, the assignment of students to the schools nearest their homes will not effectively dismantle the segregated school system, the court may order the assignment of some students to schools at a distance which requires the provision of some transportation for students. Because of the infinite variety of local problems and conditions, *Swann* did not set rigid guidelines. It simply stated that neither the time nor the distance involved should be so great that it risks the health of the children or significantly impinges on the educational process. The age of the children is probably the primary factor for courts to consider in determining the limits on travel time. Very young children should not be assigned to schools far from their homes. Older children, such high school students, can ride buses to school with little impact on their education.

Hence, if a school district has engaged in de jure segregation and has refused to submit an effective plan to end segregation, the district court must fashion a remedial decree to end segregation. The district court may decree that some students be assigned to schools other than those closest to their home in order to desegregate the student bodies of the schools. If the reassignment is beyond normal walking distance for a child, the court may order the school district to provide transportation for the students. Often this reassignment has been linked in public debate to some concept of judges imposing statistical ratios. However, statistical imbalance alone will not establish de jure segregation, though the extent to which children are reassigned to eliminate segregation does involve the use to statistics.

Swann upheld the use of an *initial* statistical ratio for faculty assignment. The limited use of mathematical ratios in student assignment is valid, especially if the school board fails to submit an effective plan. But there is no requirement that every school reflect the racial composition of the school system as a whole. Indeed, *Swann* held that there was no absolute requirement that every one-race school be eliminated. Schools whose students are all, or virtually all, of the same race require close judicial scrutiny, but their existence alone is not a sufficient indication of a segregated system.

Because the goal is to end de jure segregation, school and judicial authorities are necessarily concerned with the elimination of such schools. Yet, federal courts cannot require schools to maintain a certain racial balance but, instead, must tailor their decrees to provide a reasonable remedy. A district court should not require an annual adjustment in the student ratios in the absence of a showing that the shift in racial balance was the result of purposeful discrimination. The court ordered remedy should be terminated when the effects of de jure discrimination have been eliminated.

The Scope of a Remedial Order—Inter–District Remedies. The final, and most important, limit on federal court remedial powers arose in *Milliken v. Bradley* (1974). That case prohibited district courts from fashioning remedies that included more than one school district unless it first found that the other school districts failed to operate unitary, integrated school systems or that the state fashioned the boundary lines of the affected school districts with the purpose of fostering racial segregation.

In *Milliken v. Bradley (Milliken II)* (1977), the Court held that a federal district court could order the State of Michigan to pay a share of the cost of compensatory and remedial educational programs because they are necessary to correct the effects of past de jure discrimination in the establishment and maintenance of the Detroit school system for which the State had some responsibility. The order violated neither the Tenth nor Eleventh Amendments because it required prospective compliance with the requirements of the Fourteenth Amendment.

In *Dayton Board of Education v. Brinkman* (1977) the Court unanimously held that, if the evidence in the record supported a finding of segregation throughout the school system, the judge may order system-wide busing if it did not impair educational interests. If the segregation in fact occurred only in a part of the system, the court must limit the remedy to that area.

Following the remand of the *Dayton* case, the district court found that there was a violation of the Constitution as to only a limited number of schools in the district, but the court of appeals reversed and held that the proof of purposeful discrimination as to a selected group of schools gave rise to an inference of area wide discrimination and that the school board had failed to meet its burden of showing that it had not engaged in area wide discrimination.

The Supreme Court upheld the court of appeals and found clear proof that the Dayton school board had intentionally discriminated against black students and operated segregated schools in 1954, that the board had never taken any action to dismantle its dual school system, and that the board had simply refused to attempt to integrate the school system which had been admittedly segregated in the past. The clear establishment of a continuing violation as to a few schools gave rise to an inference of area wide discrimination, and the school board could not rebut that inference; it did not show that its policies had been clearly designed to achieve important educational goals rather than to maintain the segregated school system.

Court Orders Requiring Governmental Units to Implement a Desegregation Decree. After a federal court has found that a school district has engaged in unconstitutional racial segregation, and that it has failed to remedy that segregation, the court will issue an order directing the school district to take appropriate actions to end the segregation in the school system and to eliminate the effects of the unconstitutional segregation. The Supreme Court has approved lower court orders requiring cities and school districts to provide appropriate educational resources to school systems, and to individual schools, in order to end the effects of unconstitutional racial discrimination. The state government, as well as a city or school district, will be required to provide resources for the implementation of a school desegregation decree, if the federal court finds that the state government bears responsibility, in whole or in part, for the creation or maintenance of the racially segregated school system.

If a unit of local government, such as a city, refuses to implement the federal district court's desegregation decree, the district court may hold the city in contempt of court, and impose monetary fines on the city. If a local government asserts that it lacks the monetary resources to comply with the remedial order, the federal district court may order local taxing authorities to provide the financial resources for implementation of the desegregation decree.

However, a federal district court should not itself order an increase in local or state taxes. The district court should, instead, order the appropriate taxing body (most commonly a city or a school district) to increase its tax levy in a manner sufficient to fund the actions required by the remedial order. If state statutes prevent a local taxing district from increasing its tax levy in the manner required to fund the remedial order, the district court may enjoin the state from enforcing its statutes. Such court action is necessary to ensure that the local school district will comply with the command of the Fourteenth Amendment to remedy the effects of its prior unconstitutional racial discrimination. *Missouri v. Jenkins* (1990). Federal courts have broad authority to fashion remedies for the correction of de jure racial segregation in a school system. Nevertheless, a federal court may not issue orders that are designed to affect more than one school district, if there was no finding that multiple school districts were involved in the unconstitutional racial segregation.

It is important to keep in mind that the underlying issue in cases wherein the district court has ordered the enactment of legislation (including tax increases) is whether the initial remedial order issued by the district court was proper. If the initial district court order was narrowly tailored to correct prior unconstitutional racial segregation (in accordance with the principles established by the Supreme Court) then the district court has the power to force the city and state governments to provide the resources to implement its desegregation order.

(b) Desegregation of Other Facilities

Although the Supreme Court delayed implementation of public school desegregation, it did order an immediate end to state-imposed racial segregation in other public facilities. In the decade following *Brown I*, primarily in a series of per curiam decisions, the Court invalidated the segregation of public beaches and bathhouses, golf courses, buses, parks, athletic contests, public restaurants, auditoriums, and courtroom seating. The lower courts followed suit so, there racial segregation in contexts other than public education, the courts ordered immediate relief so long as there was state action. However, many of the public facilities that excluded or segregated blacks were privately owned and, therefore, not subject to the restrictions of the equal protection clause.

Congress responded by enacting the Civil Rights Act of 1964, which prohibits racial discrimination in "establishments affecting interstate commerce or supported in their activities by State action as places of public accommodation, lodgings, facilities principally engaged in selling food for consumption on the premises, gasoline stations [and] places of exhibition or entertainments." The Court upheld this law as a valid exercise of federal power to regulate interstate commerce. Similarly, the Court has upheld and applied statutes passed pursuant to the Congressional power under the Thirteenth Amendment to eliminate racial discrimination in property sales and business contracts.

Palmer v. Thompson (1971) faced the issue of the constitutionality of a city shutting down city pools allegedly in response to a court decree that pools could not be racially segregated. The Court affirmed the lower court's decision that closing the pools did not violate the equal protection clause. The city had no affirmative duty to operate any swimming pools. One pool that the city previously leased from the YMCA apparently was being run by that organization for whites only and another pool that the city previously owned was now owned and operated by a predominantly black college. However, there was no evidence to show the city was directly or indirectly involved in the funding or operation of either pool. The dissent in *Palmer* disagreed with the assertion that it was impermissible to find invidious purpose on the facts in the case. The pool closings came only after a desegregation order and the dissent believed the ruling came dangerously close to allowing a town to evade the mandate of the Fourteenth Amendment.

Interdistrict relief problems have also arisen apart from school integration. In *Hills v. Gautreaux* (1976) the question before the Court was the appropriateness of interdistrict relief in the context of public housing, not schools. The Court distinguished *Milliken v. Bradley* (1974) and held that district court should consider the possibility of ordering a metropolitan area remedy. The Court rejected HUD's contentions that *Milliken* barred the adoption of a metropolitan area plan and held that the district court had the authority to order remedial action by HUD outside the city limits. The courts found that HUD, unlike the suburban school districts in *Milliken*, violated the Constitution, thereby providing the necessary predicate for the entry of a remedial order against HUD. Following the finding of a constitutional violation, the district court has broad authority to provide for an effective remedy. Nothing in *Milliken* suggested the federal courts lack the authority to order parties guilty of unconstitutional behavior to undertake remedial efforts beyond the boundaries of the city where the violation occurred. Rather, they lacked the authority to interfere with the operations of governmental units that were not implicated in any wrongdoing.

In contrast to the *Milliken* desegregation order, a metropolitan relief order would not consolidate or restructure local political units. The decree would have the same effect as a discretionary decision by HUD to offer alternatives to the segregated Chicago public housing system created by CHA and HUD.

§ 14.9   Benign   Racial   Classifications—Affirmative Action Programs

(a) Overview

(1) Introduction. In the previous sections of this chapter we saw that the Supreme Court had held that racial classifi-

cations that discriminate against racial minorities are inherently "suspect" and subject to "strict scrutiny". Such a classification are upheld only if it is necessary to promote a "compelling" interest. In 1989, a majority of Supreme Court Justices found that a racial classification used by the state for "affirmative action" purposes (a classification designed to aid members of racial minorities) is also subject to strict judicial scrutiny and invalidated unless it is narrowly tailored to promote a compelling governmental interest. *Richmond v. J.A. Croson Co.* (1989), invalidating a city's plan for increasing the number of minority owned businesses who were awarded city construction contracts.

In 1995, the Supreme Court ruled that any federal law that created a racial classification, regardless of whether it benefitted or burdened minority race persons, are subject to strict judicial scrutiny, and will not be upheld unless the government demonstrates that the racial classification is necessary to promote a compelling interest. *Adarand Constructors, Inc. v. Pena* (1995), overruling *Metro Broadcasting, Inc. v. FCC* (1990).

While it is clear that a majority of Justices will use the strict scrutiny-compelling interest test in state and local government racial affirmative action cases, the meaning of that test is not entirely clear. *J.A. Croson* examined a Richmond, Virginia ordinance that created a plan for awarding city funded construction contracts. As a part of that plan, 30% of the dollar amount of each city funded construction contract had to be awarded by the prime contractor to subcontractor businesses that members of racial minorities owned. Richmond argued that this plan was remedial in nature, because a very low percentage of construction related businesses in the Richmond area and in the nation are owned by minority race persons. The Court held that correcting "societal discrimination" was not a compelling interest that would justify the use of a racial classification. If a state or local government attempts to defend its use of a racial classification on the basis that the classification is "remedial", the governmental entity must be able to show that the racial classification is narrowly tailored to correct past discrimination by the governmental entity itself or by private sector entities within its jurisdiction.

Fourteen years after *J.A. Croson*, Justice O'Connor wrote a majority opinion finding that, at least in some contexts, the creation of a racially diverse student body in institutions of higher education (post-secondary education) would be a compelling interest and that race-conscious admissions policies that were narrowly tailored to that interest would be upheld. *Grutter v. Bollinger* (2003) (5 to 4) upheld the race conscious admissions policy of the University of Michigan Law School. O'Connor's opinion concluded that the law school's admissions policy was narrowly tailored to promote a compelling interest in creating a racially diverse student body in the law school. O'Connor joined the majority opinion in the companion case of *Gratz v. Bollinger* (2003), which invalidated the University of Michigan's admissions policy for undergraduate students, because the majority found that the undergraduate admissions system was not tailored to the compelling interest in creating a racially diverse student body.

There are an enormous number of cases in this area. Let us turn to just the highlights, including *Grutter* and *Gratz* and the major legal issues.

Quota Issues. In judging the constitutionality of affirmative action programs, there is a distinction between two basic forms of affirmative action. A quota may be set reserving a specific number of places for minority members (here the law or regulation or rule typically lists the favored minorities) and a specific number for nonminority (i.e., majority race) members. Alternatively, the law or regulation or rule may impose separate standards for preferential treatment to minority members without using a quota.

The case law concludes that quota programs are difficult, if not impossible, to defend. When the government distributes benefits under a strict quota system, it totally disregards individual circumstances and also burdens members of minority races. For example, if a government housing project consists of 100 units to be assigned 50% to white families and 50% to black families, the fifty-first black family to apply will be denied housing because of its race (because the family it black) even if there are housing units available. This system disregards both the need for benefits and the availability of government benefits. The fact that the program burdens both white and black persons is irrelevant given past decisions of the Supreme Court. *Loving v. Virginia* (1967) (striking miscegenation statute though state argued it limited the marital rights of both black and white persons).

Nonetheless the second circuit *upheld* such a system because the quota prevented "white flight" from public housing. *Otero v. New York City Housing Authority* (2d Cir.1973). Yet a majority race member's dislike of living near a large number of minority persons hardly seems to be a sufficient reason for refusing to extend benefits to a black person. Indeed, this use of the quota system stands integration on its head; it becomes a tool for limiting the rights of minorities by accepting the bias of members of the majority race. Indeed, *Cooper v. Aaron* (1958) held that violent reaction of white persons does not justify a delay in integrating schools.

Richmond v. J.A. Croson Company (1989) held that a state or local government's affirmative or benign use of race is subject to strict judicial scrutiny and only justified by a compelling government interest. A true quota system, under which the government allocates welfare benefits, such as housing units, on racial criteria for no purpose other than to achieve a racial mix in the recipient population is difficult to justify under the strict scrutiny approach. In order to justify the use of a racial quota, a court would have to find that the goal of integration, even in the absence of proof of prior discrimination, is so compelling as to justify denying benefits to some people (including some minority race persons) solely because of their race.

When a program gives members of minority races preferential treatment, such as guaranteeing them a minimum (but not fixed) share of benefits, the problem becomes more complex. Here the goals of racial equality for the minority and racial integration both seem to be more effectively promoted by the affirmative action program. The issue is whether the use of a racial classification is prohibited because the Constitution is color-blind and forbids the government from limiting opportunities of anyone on the basis of race.

(2) Involuntary Affirmative Action—Remedying Proven Racial Discrimination.

The Supreme Court has ruled that Fourteenth Amendment not only permits but mandates the use of racial classifications by school authorities to implement desegregation of an intentionally segregated school system. See *Swann v. Charlotte–Mecklenburg Board of Education* (1971). Similarly, the Court has approved, in the field of employment, giving preference to qualified minority employees to remedy past discriminatory practices. While the Court has not upheld using minimum quotas for hiring new employees where past discrimination is found, it has upheld other remedial practices under the civil rights acts. *United Steelworkers of America v. Weber* (1979).

The judiciary may issue decrees that use race-cognizant remedies to correct discrimination against members of a racial minority, if the plaintiffs have proven prior discrimination in court. However, neither the judiciary nor any other governmental entity has an open-ended power to use racial classifications by merely asserting that its use of race is remedial. The identification of the prior illegal or unconstitutional race discrimination only justifies a race-conscious remedial order that is narrowly tailored to correct the past discrimination.

United States v. Paradise (1987) upheld a district court order that set a numerical goal for the promotion of black troopers in a state police department. The relevant government agency was the Alabama Department of Public Safety. The first district court issued its first order finding systematic exclusion of blacks from employment or promotion in the Department had in 1972. In 1983, the district court found that the selection and promotion procedures of the department continued to have an adverse impact on black persons, despite virtually continuous litigation and attempts at court monitoring of the hiring and promotion practices of the Department. The district court then entered an order that required the promotion of one black person for every white person promoted in the department (to a specific rank), if there were qualified black candidates for the position, if the rank to which the persons were being promoted had fewer than 25% black persons, and if the Department failed to provide the district court with an adequate alternative promotion plan. Although there was no majority opinion for the Supreme Court, the Justices appeared to be unanimous in accepting the proposition that a narrowly tailored order to correct past governmental racial discrimination is not truly an affirmative action program or, in the alternative, that a judicial order of that type will be considered as necessary to promote a compelling or overriding government interest. Justice Brennan announced the judgment of the Court in *Paradise* in a plurality opinion for four Justices. He stated that the Court did not have to address the appropriate constitutional analysis for true affirmative action programs because "we conclude that the relief ordered survives even strict scrutiny analysis." According to the Brennan plurality, "the government unquestionably has a compelling interest in remedying past and present discrimination by a state actor."

(3) *Voluntary Affirmative Action Programs—Statutory Rulings.*

The Supreme Court has ruled that Title VII of the Civil Rights Acts, which literally forbids race discrimination in private employment, did not prohibit a private employer from adopting a voluntary affirmative action program. *United Steelworkers of America v. Weber* (1979). The Court interpreted Title VII to permit such programs, voluntarily adopted by employers or bargained for by employers and unions, because the Congress, which adopted the statute, was concerned with discrimination against members of minority races, there was no evidence that Congress would have prohibited these programs, and the statute only stated that it did not "require" such programs, thus leaving open the possibility of voluntary programs. But the majority opinion in *Weber* was careful to note that the case did not involve a challenge to an affirmative action program undertaken with state action so that there was no need to consider the constitutionality of such programs. In *Weber* the Court held only that Title VII did not prohibit employers or unions from seeking to remedy racial imbalances in traditionally segregated job categories.

(4) Voluntary Remedial Measures—Constitutional Issues.

A difficult question arises where there has been no finding of de jure segregation and such remedial measures are undertaken voluntarily. The Supreme Court has suggested, in dictum, that a school board does have the *authority to use racial classifications to produce a mixed student body which reflects society. Swann v. Charlotte–Mecklenburg Bd. of Education* (1971):

> "School authorities are traditionally charged with broad power to formulate and implement educational policy and might well conclude, for example, that in order to prepare students to live in a pluralistic society each school should have a prescribed ratio of Negro to white students reflecting the proportion for the district as a whole. To do this as an educational policy is within the broad discretionary power of the school authorities; absent a finding of a constitutional violation, however, that would not be within the authority of a federal court."

Voluntary measures to end de facto school segregation in elementary and high schools may be differentiated from preferential admissions to professional schools because the state gives all students a public education and no one has a right to attend segregated schools (even if state action does not cause the segregation).

(b) Supreme Court Decisions

(1) The J.A. Croson Decision and an Overview of the Supreme Court's Rulings Regarding State and Local Governments' Racial Affirmative Action Programs.

A governmental entity that has not previously been found guilty of illegal or unconstitutional racial discrimination may employ a race based classification to benefit members of a minority race. Such an affirmative action program may be invalid under the equal protection clause of the Fourteenth Amendment (for a state or local governmental program) or the equal protection component of the Fifth Amendment due process clause (for a program of the federal government).

In 1989, in *Richmond v. J.A. Croson Company* (1989) held that a court must review racial classification in an affirmative action program with "strict scrutiny" and such a classification, like racial classifications that burden minorities, will be upheld only if it can be shown to be necessary (or narrowly tailored) to the promotion of a compelling interest.

In *J.A. Croson,* the Supreme Court examined and invalidated a plan adopted by the City of Richmond for awarding city construction contracts. The plan required the primary contractor on a city awarded construction contract to subcontract at least 30% of the amount of the contract to subcontractor businesses that were owned by members of certain minority racial groups. The minority groups were identified in the statute as persons who are "black, Spanish-speaking, Orientals, Indians, Eskimos, or Aleuts." The plan allowed a prime contractor to seek a waiver of the 30% requirement in "exceptional circumstances" (when the 30% minimum could not reasonably be fulfilled).

Six Justices voted to invalidate Richmond's affirmative action plan. Justice O'Connor announced the judgment of the Court in *J.A. Croson* in an opinion that was, in part, a majority opinion and, in part, a plurality opinion. When the portion of Justice O'Connor's opinion regarding the standards of review, which was joined by Chief Justice Rehnquist and Justice White, is combined with the concurring opinions of Justice Kennedy and Justice Scalia, we know that five Justices voted to subject all racial classifications, including those classifications that appear in affirmative action programs, to the strict scrutiny-compelling interest standard. Of the six Justices who voted to invalidate the law, only Justice Stevens found it unnecessary to address the standard of review question. Justice Marshall, in a dissent joined by Brennan and Blackmun, noted that this case marked the first time that a majority of the Court voted to employ the strict scrutiny-compelling interest standard to the review of racial classifications that aided members of a racial minority.

In *J.A. Croson*, the City of Richmond asserted that its affirmative action plan for minority owned businesses was designed to remedy past discrimination against minorities in construction businesses. A majority of the Justices found that a state or local governmental entity only had a compelling interest in remedying past discrimination if the governmental entity could identify past discrimination against a racial minority within its jurisdiction. Cities and states may not justify a racial affirmative action plan on the basis that they are correcting "societal discrimination." In other words, a city must identify past governmental or private sector discrimination within the city in order to create a plan that seeks to remedy that discrimination. The affirmative action program of either a state or local government must be narrowly tailored to correct the identified discrimination.

What type of proof is required to identify past discrimination? *J.A. Croson* did not make clear how a lower court should determine if a city or state government has established a factual basis for showing prior governmental or private sector discrimination that might justify an affirmative action plan. A majority of the Justices found that the statistics showing that, in Richmond, there was a very low percentage of construction business owners or subcontractors who were members of a minority race was not sufficient to show racial discrimination within construction industry in the city. If the Court allowed a statistical showing of under-representation of minority races in a job category or business activity to prove past illegal or unconstitutional discrimination, the ruling might allow state and local governments to use affirmative action racial classifications whenever the government chose, because minority race persons may be under-represented in many jobs or businesses due to the effects of societal discrimination against members of racial minorities.

Note that the Richmond plan was designed, in part, to help Aleuts, but it is safe to say that Richmond presented no evidence that it ever discriminated against Aleuts, who are members of an indigenous people who live in the Aleutian Islands and southwestern coastal Alaska, many thousands of miles from the capital of Virginia.

Justice O'Connor's opinion in *J.A. Croson* was, in part, a plurality opinion and, in part, a majority opinion. In a portion that was a majority opinion, she appears to set out conflicting approaches to the use of statistics for identifying past racial discrimination. She stated that the disparity between the number of minority businesses that had received city construction contracts or subcontracts in previous years and the percent of minority race members in the city population would not demonstrate identifiable racial discrimination against minority race members in the construction business. In this portion of the opinion, she also stated that the city, and the district court that had upheld the city's plan, had wrongly relied on evidence that minority owned businesses were statistically under-represented in a local contractors' association. The disparity between the number of minority owned construction businesses and minority participation in the contractors' association, (like the disparity between the percentage of city residents who are members of a minority race and the percentage of construction contracts awarded to minority race members) could be attributable to a variety of reasons, including generalized societal discrimination against minorities. These statistics did not identify past illegal or unconstitutional racial discrimination against minority owned construction businesses or against minority race persons who desired to establish a business that might be eligible to receive city construction contracts. When Justice O'Connor discussed the need to identify past private or public sector discrimination against minority businesses, she cited cases in which the Supreme Court had examined the use of statistical evidence to establish a prima facie case of employment discrimination. Her citations to those cases may mean that a court should examine the evidence put forward by the city or state to justify its affirmative action program in terms of whether that evidence would be sufficient to establish a prima facie case of identified discrimination if the case had been brought under a civil rights statute.

In a portion of her opinion that was a majority opinion, O'Connor noted that the low representation of minority owned businesses who did business with the city might help an individual city in a particular case to show past private sector discrimination. O'Connor stated: "For low minority representation in these associations [groups of contractors in a city who often dealt with city contracts] to be relevant, the city would have to link it to the number of local MBEs [Minority Business Enterprises] eligible for membership. If the statistical disparity between eligible MBEs and MBE membership [in the trade association] were great enough an inference of discriminatory exclusion would arise. In such a case the city would have a compelling interest in preventing its tax dollars from assisting these organizations and maintaining a racially segregated construction market." In other words, if the city can make a prima facie case of past private or public sector discrimination against minority owned businesses of a certain type, the city has a compelling interest in creating a program to correct that racial discrimination. If the racial discrimination related to businesses to which the city awards contracts, the city could adopt an affirmative action plan that was narrowly tailored to ensure that future city contracts would be awarded to a racially diverse group of contractors or subcontractors.

Even if city or state can identify prior illegal or unconstitutional discrimination within its boundaries, the affirmative action plan adopted by the governmental entity must be narrowly tailored to correct the identified discrimination. *J.A. Croson* found that, even if Richmond had identified past discrimination against minority owned construction businesses in the city, its use of a 30% quota for subcontracts to minority owned businesses, which provided for only limited waivers from the quota system, showed that the plan was not narrowly tailored to the correction of prior discrimination.

In a portion of her opinion that was joined by Chief Justice Rehnquist, and Justices White and Kennedy, Justice O'Connor stated: "nothing we say today precludes a state or local entity from taking action to rectify the effects of identified discrimination within its jurisdiction." According to the plurality, to justify a plan for awarding construction contracts or subcontracts in a manner that preferred businesses owned by minority race members, a city might be able to rely on "an inference of discriminatory exclusion" that would arise from a "significant statistical disparity" between the number of qualified minority contractors in the city and the number of minority contractors who had been employed by the jurisdiction in prior years. "In the extreme case [O'Connor's plurality opinion concluded], some form of narrowly tailored racial preference might be necessary to break down patterns of deliberate exclusion.''

In *J.A. Croson,* the Supreme Court created a framework for determining the constitutionality of racial affirmative action programs that are "remedial" in nature. However, in that case, the Court did not tell us whether there are other interests that would be sufficiently "compelling" to justify a racial classification that favored members of a minority race.

In *Regents of the University v. Bakke* (1978) the Supreme Court invalidated a state medical school admissions program that set aside places in an entering class for members of racial minorities in order to ensure that there would be a certain minimum number of racial minority persons in each entering class. Although there was no majority opinion and the decision interpreted a federal civil rights statute, the *Bakke* decision appeared to allow university and professional school admissions officers, or admission committees, to consider an applicant's race for the purpose of ensuring racial diversity in the student body if, but only if, the admissions system promoted diversity without using racial quotas and without imposing burdens on individuals because of their race.

Wygant v. Jackson Board of Education (1986), with no majority opinion, invalidated a school board's action that laid off white teachers from their jobs, before laying off black teachers, for the purpose of maintaining a racially integrated faculty. Justice O'Connor, concurring, indicated that a majority of Justices might uphold a governmental program of hiring (rather than firing) teachers that took cognizance of the race of an applicant for a teaching position in order to have a racially diverse faculty in grade schools and high schools within the school board's jurisdiction.

For fourteen years following *J.A. Croson,* lower courts were left with no guidance regarding whether they should use the form of analysis adopted by Justice Powell in his plurality opinions in *Bakke* when reviewing race conscious admissions policies of educational institutions. In 2003, in a majority opinion written by Justice O'Connor, the Court adopted Justice Powell's analytical framework, and ruled that the University of Michigan Law School's race conscious admissions policy was narrowly tailored to a compelling interest. *Grutter v. Bollinger* (2003).

On the same day, Justice O'Connor joined a majority opinion written by Chief Justice Rehnquist, which ruled that the race conscious admissions policy employed by the University of Michigan for its undergraduate studies program was not narrowly tailored to a compelling interest. *Gratz v. Bollinger* (2003). Let us now turn to those cases.

(2) Race Conscious Government Policies Designed to Promote Educational Diversity—The Bakke, Wygant & Bollinger Decisions.

In a quarter-century (from 1978 to 2003), the Court decided several important cases concerning government policies designed to create racial diversity in schools. This era began with *Regents of the University v. Bakke* (1978), a case where Justice Powell, in part of his opinion that was not joined by any other Justice, set forth an analytical framework for determining the constitutionality of admissions programs for higher education. The era ended in 2003 when, in two separate cases, a majority of the Court adopted Powell's analysis; upheld a race conscious admissions program for the University of Michigan Law School; and invalidated the University of Michigan's policy for admitting students to its undergraduate studies program. The 2003 decisions left unresolved questions concerning the creation or maintenance of racial diversity in primary and secondary school faculties, which the Court had dealt with in *Wygant v. Jackson Board of Education*.

Regents of the University v. Bakke. Allan Bakke was denied admission to the Medical School of the University of California at Davis in both 1973 and 1974 because the admissions committee did not believe that his qualifications justified admitting him under the general admissions program, even though his academic qualifications were substantially equivalent to those of other students being admitted under the program at that time. However, during each of those years Davis operated a special admissions program to consider the applications of candidates who asked to be considered as "economically and/or educationally disadvantaged," or as members of a "minority group."

Under the Davis program, membership in certain racial or ethnic minorities—African–American, Mexican–American, Asian, or American Indian—qualified one for consideration under the special admissions program. Bakke was not a member of the specified racial minority groups and, therefore, was not eligible for consideration for admission under the special admissions program. Since a certain number of places in the class were reserved for minority or disadvantaged students, Bakke contended that the refusal to admit him was the result of the special admissions program.

Bakke brought suit in state court alleging that the Davis special admissions program caused him injury by effectively excluding him from the freshman medical classes during 1973 and 1974 and that the Davis program violated the constitution of the state of California, Title VI of the Federal Civil Rights Act of 1964, and the equal protection clause of the Fourteenth Amendment. The state trial court held that the Davis program violated all three provisions, and, on appeal, the California Supreme Court avoided ruling on either the state constitutional issue or the applicability of Title VI of the Civil Rights Act to the Davis program. It held that the Davis admissions program violated the equal protection clause of the Fourteenth Amendment because the government could not take cognizance of race in dispensing governmental benefits. The state supreme court therefore ordered the admission of Mr. Bakke to the Medical School.

The U.S. Supreme Court agreed that Bakke should be admitted but disagreed on numerous issues. Four Justices—Chief Justice Burger and Justices Stewart, Rehnquist, and Stevens—concluded that the Davis program violated Title VI of the Federal Civil Rights Act. They found that the application of Title VI to the admissions program made it unnecessary to reach any constitutional issue. Four Justices—Brennan, White, Marshall and Blackmun—were of the opinion that Title VI was meant to bar only such racial discrimination as the Fourteenth Amendment prohibited and that the Davis program did not violate either the equal protection clause or Title VI. Thus, the ruling of the case turned on the vote of Justice Powell, even though no other justice agreed with his analysis.

Justice Powell argued that the equal protection clause and, therefore, Title VI, required invalidation of the Davis program. But Powell was of the opinion that neither provision requires the invalidation of all race conscious affirmative action programs. He therefore voted with the group of four Justices who ruled only on the Title VI issue to the extent of finding the Davis program a violation of Title VI and ordering Davis to accept Mr. Bakke into the medical school. However, Powell voted to reverse the California decision insofar as it required state governmental units to avoid all consideration of race in affirmative action programs. Only two portions of Powell's opinion were joined by four other Justices: the statement of facts and the paragraph in which he stated that not all racial classifications were invalidated by the Fourteenth Amendment. Nevertheless, he cast the fifth vote that resulted in affirming the order that required Davis to accept Mr. Bakke while allowing it and other educational institutions to make some use of race conscious admissions criteria.

The *Bakke* decision means that an admissions program of an institution receiving federal funds that uses clear, strict racial preferences, such as that of the Davis Medical School, will violate Title VI of the Civil Rights Act because five Justices would find it to be a Title VI violation, although for differing reasons. A program of admissions to institutions of higher education that allows admissions officers to consider race as an affirmative factor without using clear racial preferences will violate neither the equal protection clause nor Title VI because a different alignment of five Justices would vote to uphold such programs. In *Bakke,* five Justices, with no majority opinion, did vote for the proposition that Title VI bars only such racial discrimination as would violate the equal protection clause if it involved state action.

Bakke left many important issues regarding racial preferences unsettled. There was no ruling on the constitutionality of any affirmative action program other than those relating to admission to higher education. The Court did not determine whether other federal civil rights acts can, or do, mandate or restrict the use of such benign classifications; the statutory ruling involved only Title VI.

Justice Powell found that all racial classifications are inherently suspect and subject to the strictest judicial scrutiny. Powell also found that there was no difference between setting racial quotas and establishing "goals" of minority representation; in so doing he took the position that he would subject any use of racial criteria to the most strict equal protection test because, he argued, application of the strictest equal protection test to racial and ethnic classifications is required by the "constitutional and demographic history" of the country. He concluded that it was "far too late to argue that the guarantee of equal protection to all persons permits the recognition of special wards entitled to a degree of protection greater than that accorded others."

In reaching the conclusion that all racial and ethnic classifications should be subjected to the most exacting scrutiny, Powell distinguished three groups of prior decisions. First, that the school desegregation cases were not relevant to the affirmative action decision because they involved only remedies designed to redress specific constitutional violations. Second, the employment discrimination cases decided under Title VII of the Civil Rights Acts were not relevant because the affirmative action remedies were ordered in such cases only after a judicial or administrative finding of discrimination against a racial minority in a particular business or industry. Third, he argued that sex-based classification cases was irrelevant to the race affirmative action question because sex-based discrimination is not tested by strict scrutiny, and that r there are only two sexes while there are many races. The special societal and constitutional history of race discrimination in America made racial classification qualitatively different, he argued. In addition, sex-based classifications, which involve only two possible groups, justified the greater use for remedial purposes by government units.

Powell applied strict scrutiny-compelling interest to the Davis program and found it wanting. First, the school could not assert as a legitimate purpose the attainment of a minimum specified percentage of a particular racial or ethnic group in the class; in Powell's view, that purpose is "facially invalid." Second, he recognized that the state had a legitimate interest in eliminating the effects of "identified discrimination," but this end would only support programs that were judicially, legislatively, or administratively found to be necessary to remedy violations of the constitution or statutes which had been passed to promote constitutional purposes. Because the University could not claim any ability, or any state granted authority, to make findings of particular discrimination in its or other educational programs, the University's special admissions program do not further the governmental interest in ending the effect of prior acts of racial discrimination.

Third, Powell found that the program was not a reasonably necessary way of improving health care for communities that currently did not receive adequate medical services. Even assuming that in some situations an interest in health care might be compelling, he found that there was no proof that the Davis program would in fact substantially increase the number of doctors or the quality of health care available to economically deprived citizens.

Fourth, Justice Powell found that the attainment of a "diverse student body" would be a compelling interest under some circumstances. He argued that the attainment of a diverse student body related to "academic freedom," and that, in turn, is related to the guarantees of the First Amendment dealing with academic freedom. Because Powell believed that this interest embodied a value of independent constitutional importance, he would consider it compelling under some circumstances.

In graduate and professional schools, as well as undergraduate colleges, a faculty could attempt to insure that students and teachers would be exposed to a wide variety of diverse social and political interests. Powell announced that the use of racial or ethnic classifications, whether described as "goals," quotas or something else, did not further this goal, however, because it set aside places in the class for persons solely on this basis, without regard to whether the acceptance or rejection of specific individuals on the basis of their race was promoting true diversity within the university. "The diversity that furthers a compelling state interest encompasses a far broader array of qualifications and characteristics of which racial or ethnic origin is but a single though important element."

Thus, Powell found that strict racial track programs for admission, no matter how many special groups they might include, did not further a compelling interest. Instead, if a university wished to assert this compelling interest to justify its admissions program, it would have to establish an admissions procedure that would consider all facets of an applicant's background when that applicant was considered for admission on the basis of particular personal characteristics, or for the attainment of diversity in the student body. In attaining this diversity the educational institution, in Justice Powell's opinion, may consider or give positive weight to virtually any personal characteristic of the applicant. "An otherwise qualified medical student with a particular background—whether it be ethnic, geographic, *culturally advantaged or disadvantaged*—may bring to a professional school of medicine experiences, outlooks and ideas that enrich the training of its student body and better equip its graduates to render with understanding their vital service to humanity."

Justice Powell did not limit consideration of these personal factors only to a member of a racial or disadvantaged minority rather than an educationally advantaged member of a racial majority. Indeed, his statement regarding "cultural advantage or disadvantage," and his statement that "the weight attributed to a particular quality may vary from year to year depending upon the 'mix' both of the student body and the applicants for the incoming class," make it appear that Powell would allow a university to give a "plus" to economically advantaged *white* students over minorities once it had, in its view, a sufficient mix of minority members. While it seems hard to believe that he meant to approve of systems that subtly disadvantaged a minority member because of his or her race, his opinion provides little basis for limiting this use of the diversity goal.

Justice Powell acknowledged that some persons claimed that such discretionary programs could be a subtle means of employing a racial preference. Yet he said that there would be no "facial infirmity" in such programs and that the Court, in his view, would not allow such an admissions program to be challenged on the basis of its disparate impact on persons of similar races because "good faith would be presumed" in the absence of a showing of a discriminatory purpose.

Justice Powell concluded that affirmative action programs would be constitutional if they followed the race consciousness approach without the use of predetermined racial classifications preferences, quotas, or goals. For this reason he voted with Justice Brennan and the other Justices who would have upheld the Davis program in total, but he did so only to the extent of reversing the California Supreme Court ruling that race could never be considered in educational admissions programs. The only portion of Justice Powell's opinion concerning the constitutionality of racial classifications that received five votes was the following paragraph:

> In enjoining petitioner from ever considering the race of any applicant, however, the courts below failed to recognize that

the State has a substantial interest that legitimately may be served by a properly devised admissions program involving the competitive consideration of race and ethnic origin. For this reason, so much of the California court's judgment as enjoins petitioner from any consideration of the race of any applicant must be reversed.

In *Richmond v. J.A. Croson Co.* (1989) the Supreme Court ruled that a state or local government could not use a racial affirmative action classification unless the classification was narrowly tailored to promote a compelling interest. A racial classification could only be justified as narrowly tailored to promote the compelling interest of remedying racial segregation or discrimination if the state or local governmental entity could show that its affirmative action racial classification was narrowly tailored to correct past discrimination by that governmental entity itself or by private sector persons entities within its jurisdiction. The opinion of Justice O'Connor in *J.A. Croson,* which was in part a plurality opinion and in part a majority opinion, did not explain which, if any, government goals other than remedying identified past discrimination would be sufficiently compelling to justify the use of a racial affirmative action classification.

The *Wygant* Decision—Maintenance of a Racially Integrated Faculty. *Wygant v. Jackson Board of Education* (1986) invalidated an attempt by a local school board to maintain a racially integrated faculty, at a time when the school board had to reduce the number of faculty members that it employed, through the means of laying off white teachers before laying off black teachers with less seniority. There was no majority opinion.

All of the Justices in *Wygant* seem to agree that the problem had its roots in community racial tension on a variety of topics, including education. In 1972, negotiations between the Jackson Board of Education and the teachers' union, which objected to changes in the seniority system for faculty benefits and job protection, resulted in the addition of a layoff provision to the collective bargaining agreement between the Board and the union. This agreement provided that, if it was necessary to lay off teachers, layoffs would be done on a seniority basis (the last hired would be the first laid off) "except that at no time will there be a greater percentage of minority personnel laid off than the current percentage of minority personnel employed at the time of the layoff." In other words, layoffs would be made proportionally among nonminority and minority teachers so that layoffs would not result in increasing the disparity between the percentages of minority and nonminority faculty members. This system resulted in the layoff of some nonminority teachers with more seniority than some minority teachers who were not laid off.

The Court (5 to 4) held that the layoff of nonminority race teachers solely because of the race of the individual teachers violated the equal protection clause. However, there was no majority opinion. Even the four Justices who dissented could not agree on a single standard of review.

The school could have provided for a lay-off of teachers by lot instead of last-hired, first-fired. That way, the number of minority teachers, on the whole, should not change with lay-offs. That system would be color-blind and achieve the school's goal of not reducing the number of minority teachers.

Justice Powell wrote the plurality opinion announcing the judgment of the Court in *Wygant*. Powell's opinion was joined by Chief Justice Burger and Justice Rehnquist and, in part, by Justice O'Connor. Powell's plurality opinion found that a racial classification, regardless of whether it aided or burdened the members of a minority racial group, would be invalid unless it was narrowly tailored to promote a compelling interest. This formulation is similar to the position Powell had taken in earlier affirmative action cases and is quite close to the formulation used in cases examining racial classifications that burden members of minority races, although the compelling interest test is often stated in terms of whether a law is "necessary" to promote a compelling or overriding government interest. Powell found that a goal of remedying societal discrimination would not in itself be sufficient to support this racial classification.

Powell did not exclude the possibility that maintaining a diverse and racially integrated faculty could be a compelling interest. Regardless of the legitimacy or compelling nature of that interest, Justice Powell's plurality opinion found that a layoff plan that imposed the burden of achieving racial equality on particular nonminority individuals, (who were to be laid off or fired despite their seniority) was not narrowly tailored to the promotion of that interest.

Justice Powell's plurality opinion concluded that there was no evidentiary support for the assertion that the remedial program was adopted to correct past governmental discrimination. "[E]videntiary support for the conclusion that remedial action is warranted" was required in order to assure that governmental entities would not merely assert fictitious past discrimination as a basis for justifying racial preferences that otherwise would be invalid under the equal protection clause.

Diversity in Education—A Compelling Interest After All. In the quarter century between 1978 and 2003, lower courts were left with virtually no guidance regarding how they should assess the constitutionality of the university's consideration of race in an admissions process. No other Justice had joined Powell's constitutional analysis in *Bakke*. In 2003, Powell's views in *Bakke* attracted a five-person majority in *Grutter v. Bollinger* (2003), which upheld the University of Michigan's Law School's race conscious admissions policy. The *Grutter* ruling was a narrow one; it is difficult for state universities to establish race conscious admissions programs that would comply with the Powell standards, as they were understood by a majority of the Justices in *Grutter*. On the same day that *Grutter* was decided, the Court, in *Gratz v. Bollinger* (2003) invalidated the University of Michigan's policies governing the admission of students to its undergraduate programs.

In *Grutter* Justice O'Connor wrote the five to four opinion the Court. The law school's admission system did not guarantee admission to the Law School for anyone based on their numerical scores on a standardized test or their numerical grade point average in an undergraduate or graduate degree program. Instead, according to the Law School, it individually evaluated each applicant in an effort to find a diverse student body for the purpose of having a "critical mass" of persons from under represented minority races and from persons with various points of view so that the Law School could best train future leaders in society, as well as future attorneys.

Justice O'Connor acknowledged that some statements in majority, plurality, and concurring opinions since *Bakke* might have lead lower courts to believe that diversity in education was not a compelling interest. She said that it was unnecessary "[to] decide whether Justice Powell's opinion [had been] binding" because *Grutter* had decided independently "[to] endorse Justice Powell's view that student body diversity is a compelling state interest that can justify the use of race in university admissions."

Having found that diversity in education was a compelling governmental interest, the majority opinion went on to consider whether the University of Michigan's Law School admission program was narrowly tailored to promote that compelling interest. The majority opinion, like the four dissenting Justices in *Grutter*, agreed that the use of race in admissions, to any extent, constituted a racial classification that had to be reviewed under "strict scrutiny" and that "this means that such classifications are constitutional only if they are narrowly tailored to further compelling governmental interest." However, the majority found that this test was not "fatal" and that "context matters when reviewing race-based governmental action."

Although O'Connor found that some deference or latitude had to be given to educational decision makers, she stated that the dissenters in *Grutter* were wrong when they accused the majority of abandoning the Court's historic position of "strictly scrutinizing" (that is, taking a very close look at) any race-based classification that the government claimed was narrowly tailored to advance a compelling interest. The *Grutter* majority opinion found that the University of Michigan Law School did not use a quota system, made a truly individualized consideration of each application, and did not set aside any seats simply for minority race persons. The fact that Law School officials had stated that the faculty wanted a "critical mass" of minority race students did not make the program invalid.

The majority in *Grutter* recognized that the Law School had not examined every race neutral alternative method of achieving student body diversity, but it said that the "narrow tailoring [requirement of the strict scrutiny test] does not require exhaustion of every conceivable race-neutral alternative."

Near the close of O'Connor's opinion, she stated that race based policies designed to achieve a compelling interest, including racial diversity in institutions of higher education, should be limited in time in order to qualify under the narrow tailoring requirement of the strict scrutiny standard. Her majority opinion stated "we expect that 25 years from now, the use of racial preferences will no longer be necessary to further the interest approved today." Two of the concurring Justices believe that this statement in the majority opinion did not, in fact, place a 25 year time limit on the use of a race conscious admissions program, but only expressed the hope that a future generation would not need to use race based policies to achieve true equal opportunity. However, at least some of the dissenting Justices believed that the majority opinion had placed a 25 year time limit on race-conscious Law School admissions program.

Chief Justice Rehnquist, joined by Justices Scalia, Kennedy, and Thomas, filed a strong dissent. Rehnquist said that the use of race conscious decision-making in government might be allowed in some circumstances, but he did not specifically endorse or reject the majority's conclusion that diversity in education might be a compelling interest and under certain circumstances would support a race conscious admissions policy for a state operated institution of higher learning. Rehnquist believed that the majority had failed to truly scrutinize the University of Michigan's Law School admissions program and that a close scrutiny of that program would demonstrate, that the law school was in fact operating an admissions policy that simply set aside some places for minority race applicants by giving those applicants admission based solely upon their race. The dissenters believed that the majority had not really used a true strict scrutiny test, because it had not demanded that the government show that its Law School admissions policy was necessary to promote a compelling interest. Chief Justice Rehnquist set out facts regarding the University of Michigan's Law School's admissions from the years 1995 through 2000 to demonstrate why the dissenters believed that the Law School in fact was operating a program that set quotas based on race. He believed a true quota system is not narrowly tailored to a compelling interest.

No other Justice joined Justice Kennedy's dissent in *Grutter*. Kennedy accepted Justice Powell's method of analysis in *Bakke*. In *Grutter* Kennedy took the position that a university's admissions policy that had numerical goals for enrollment of minority race students could never be considered narrowly tailored to a compelling interest. Kennedy objected to the majority failure "to apply meaningful strict scrutiny." He quoted the law school administrator who had directed the admissions process for over a decade. That person had "testified that faculty members were 'breathtakingly cynical' in deciding who would qualify as a member of underrepresented minorities. An example he offered was faculty debate as to whether Cubans should be counted as Hispanics: "One professor objected on the grounds that Cubans were Republicans."

Justices Scalia and Thomas, in their two dissenting opinions, argued that the University of Michigan was using a quota system that is not narrowly tailored to a compelling interest. The difference between the Scalia and Thomas dissenting opinions appears to be Justice Thomas seemed to accept the fact that some types of race conscious admissions policies for state operated institutions of higher education would stand for a 25 year period.

On the same day that the Court upheld the University of Michigan's Law School admissions policy, the Supreme Court, in *Gratz v. Bollinger* (2003) invalidated the admissions policy used by the University of Michigan for students seeking admittance to its *undergraduate* degree programs. Chief Justice Rehnquist wrote a majority opinion (6 to 3).

After finding that the plaintiffs had standing to challenge the University's undergraduate admissions policy, the Chief Justice did not question the District Court's ruling that the system of admissions used by the University of Michigan through 1998, which involved totally separate consideration of applications by racial groups, was unconstitutional. The majority in *Gratz* focused on the most recent version of the University's undergraduate admissions system, which awarded 20 points extra towards an admissions score for students if they are members of certain racial or ethnic minorities.

Without endorsing the ruling in *Grutter*, from which he had dissented, the Chief Justice, in *Gratz*, acknowledged that the Court in *Grutter* rejected the argument that educational diversity is never a compelling interest.

Having assumed that the interest in educational diversity is a compelling interest, the Chief Justice in *Gratz* looked at the relationship of the University of Michigan's undergraduate admissions scoring system and found that its admissions policy was not narrowly tailored to a compelling interest in racial diversity. Therefore, the current admissions policy violated the equal protection clause, and related statutes.

In *Gratz*, Chief Justice Rehnquist referred to Justice Powell's opinion in the *Bakke* case to explain why the current University of Michigan's undergraduate admissions policy could not be considered narrowly tailored to promote racial diversity. Rehnquist agreed with Powell that the equal protection clause demanded that each individual application be given individualized consideration in the sense that one's race could not be used as an automatic basis for admission for a program to be narrowly tailored to promote educational diversity in a college or university. The University of Michigan system (unlike the law school) did not provide individualized consideration of each student, even though there was the possibility that some students who were not members of a minority race might be considered for admission if their score was below the normal point score for admitted students. The applications of students who were not members of designated racial minorities, under the University of Michigan program, would not receive individualized consideration until after the University had made most of the decisions regarding admissions. In contrast to other applicants, members of the favored racial minorities were automatically given 20 points towards the minimum score needed for admission, which virtually guaranteed that every student in the designated minority group who met absolute minimum standards would be automatically admitted. However, the students who were not members of a designated racial minority group would not receive automatic admission to the University of Michigan even though they also met minimum admissions standards.

In short, students in the racial groups that were not favored by the University of Michigan would have to have test scores, grade point averages from their high school, and points awarded for other factors (such as state of residency, alumni relationships or personal achievement) that would raise their admissions score close to, or over, 100 points. But a minority race student, whose grades and test scores were at the minimally acceptable level, would have a point score near, or over, 100 points once they were given the automatic 20 points for being a member of a racial or ethnic group favored by the University of Michigan for diversity purposes.

Gratz acknowledged that it might be difficult, if not impossible, for a large university such as the University of Michigan to give truly individualized consideration to each of the thousands of applications that it receives for its undergraduate program. But, "the fact that the implementation of a program capable of providing individualized consideration might present administrative challenges does not render constitutional an otherwise problematic system." For that reason, the majority held that the University of Michigan's system of awarding automatic points to members of minority races for the purposes of meeting scores needed for admission could not be necessary or narrowly tailored to promoting educational diversity. The admissions polices failed the strict scrutiny test, because the system was not narrowly tailored to a compelling interest.

O'Connor, who had authored the majority opinion in *Grutter* upholding the Law School's admissions policy, wrote an opinion concurring in both the judgment and opinion of the Court in *Gratz.* Breyer joined the entirety of O'Connor's concurring opinion except for the last sentence of her opinion (the sentence that stated O'Connor concurred in Chief Justice Rehnquist's opinion). O'Connor thought that her analysis was entirely consistent with the majority opinion. Justice Breyer agreed entirely with O'Connor's analysis, but he must have thought that her analysis was inconsistent with the majority opinion written by Chief Justice Rehnquist.

Justice O'Connor based her vote to invalidate the University of Michigan's undergraduate admissions policy on the basis that the mechanical assignment of a great number of points towards an admissions score merely for membership in a racial minority was not tailored to achieve racial diversity. Instead, according to O'Connor, the Michigan undergraduate admission system was nothing more than a quota system or a set aside of some places in the class for minority race students.

Justice Thomas concurred in the judgment and opinion of the Court. His opinion in *Gratz* emphasize that "a state's use of racial discrimination in higher education admissions is categorically prohibited by the equal protection clause." He referred to his dissenting opinion in *Grutter,* in which agreed with the first Justice Harlan that the Constitution should be "color-blind."

Justice Ginsburg dissented in *Gratz* in an opinion that Souter joined and Breyer joined in part. Breyer agreed with Ginsburg to the extent that she found government programs designed to undo the harmful effects of a racial caste system that existed for much of our country's history would comply with equal protection principles. In the part that only Souter joined, she concluded that the undergraduate admissions policy was narrowly tailored to remedying the effects of racial discrimination in our society by the creation of a diverse student body. She believed that the University of Michigan system was of necessity somewhat mechanical because of the great number of applications for admissions to an undergraduate program that would be received by a high quality state operated institution in a large state.

Only Justices Kennedy and Scalia joined the Chief Justice's opinion in *Gratz* without writing separate opinions. Scalia predicted that the Court left the lower courts with no guidance in this area and that the Court's 2003 decisions would simply be the catalyst that would start a new era of litigation concerning the constitutionality of such educational policies.

The Supreme Court did provide lower courts with the answer to at least one question: could the achievement of racial diversity in colleges, universities, and professional schools be a compelling interest? The Court's answer, in 2003, was yes. When lower courts review challenges to race conscious admissions policies of those types of educational institutions, the lower courts will focus their attention on the question of whether a particular institution's admissions policy is narrowly tailored to the compelling interest in racial diversity. By tracking Justice Powell's analysis in *Bakke*, O'Connor's opinion in *Grutter*, and the Chief Justices' opinion in *Gratz*, provide some guidance to lower courts assessing the narrow tailoring issue.

Lower courts now know that it is the University's obligation to demonstrate that individualized consideration is given to all of the persons in the applicant pool and that there can be no setting aside of some places in the class for members of minority races whether that set aside is done through quotas, or systems that are effectively mechanical in nature in their granting of preferences to members of minority race groups.

The 2003 cases left open some many questions. For example, *Grutter* and *Gratz* did not explain whether the achievement of racial diversity in faculties, at any level of education, would constitute a compelling governmental interest.

The 2003 cases concerned only education and, therefore, the majority opinions in these cases did not give any clear indication as to whether the government could seek to achieve racial diversity outside of the educational arena. The 2003 cases did not modify other Supreme Court decisions concerning government programs designed to encourage the creation of minority race owned businesses that would participate in government funded projects, or government employment policies designed to achieve a racially diverse public sector work force. These issues are examined in other sections of this Chapter.

(3) *Federal Affirmative Action Programs—The Adarand, Metro Broadcasting, and Fullilove Decisions.*

The Supreme Court has examined the constitutionality of federal racial affirmative action plans in three cases. *Fullilove v.*

Klutznick (1980) upheld a federal law that gave a preference to minority race businesses in securing contracts for federal public works projects, but there was no majority opinion and both the standards used and the rationale for upholding the law were unclear.

A decade later, in *Metro Broadcasting, Inc. v. Federal Communications Commission* (1990), the Court (5 to 4) ruled that federal racial affirmative action programs are valid so long as the benign racial classification have a substantial relationship to an important interest. Using that standard, the Court upheld preferential treatment for certain race minority persons in the awarding of television and radio broadcast licenses.

Only five years later, the Supreme Court overruled the *Metro Broadcasting* decision. In *Adarand Constructors, Inc. v. Pena* (1995), the Supreme Court (also by a 5 to 4 vote). The Court gave us two important rulings. First, it held that the equal protection component of the Fifth Amendment due process clause requires the Court to use the same standards when reviewing federal racial classifications that it uses to review state or local classifications under the equal protection clause of the Fourteenth Amendment. Second, *Adarand* held that any law using a racial classification (including the benign use of a racial classification in a federal affirmative action program) is invalid unless the government can demonstrate that the classification was narrowly tailored to promote a compelling interest.

In *Adarand*, Justice O'Connor announced the judgment of the Court and delivered an opinion that was, in part, a majority opinion and, in part, a plurality opinion. In the portions of her opinion that were written for a majority, O'Connor ruled that any government classification that was based on race is subject to strict judicial scrutiny and invalid unless the classification is narrowly tailored to a compelling governmental interest.

Although a majority of the Justices in *Adarand* ruled that the federal affirmative action program had to be subjected to strict judicial scrutiny, the Court did not rule on whether the federal statutes and agency regulations that gave a preference to minority race contractors would survive that standard of review. Two of the five Justices (Scalia and Thomas) took the position that the government would never have a compelling interest in using racial classifications to remove the effects of generalized racial discrimination. However, both Scalia and Thomas joined the part of O'Connor's majority opinion where she stated that the majority "wish[ed] to dispel the notion that strict scrutiny is strict in theory but fatal in fact ... when race-based action is necessary to further a compelling interest, such action is within constitutional constraints if it satisfies the narrow tailoring test this Court has set out in previous cases."

The *Adarand* decision settles some questions and leaves others open. The Court has settled, at least temporarily, the standard of review to be used by the judiciary when reviewing a federal racial affirmative action programs. All racial classifications, including benign racial classifications in federal racial affirmative action programs, must be narrowly tailored to serve a compelling governmental interest. The Court left open the question of what, if any, governmental interests might be deemed "compelling."

(4) Race–Conscious Legislative Districting.

When, if ever, can a government entity take into account the race of voters when establishing district lines for those elections? The leading cases would include: *Gomillion v. Lightfoot* (1960); *Mobile v. Bolden* (1980); *Rogers v. Lodge* (1982); *Shaw v. Reno I and II* (1993 and 1996); *Miller v. Johnson* (1995); *Bush v. Vera* (1996); *Hunt v. Cromartie I and II* (1999 and 2001). The principles that tie all of the cases together remain the same.

First, a court will automatically subject to strict judicial scrutiny any government entity's use of an explicit racial classification; the government action will violate equal protection unless the government can prove that its use of the racial classification is necessary to promote a compelling interest. *Rice v. Cayetano* (2000).

Second, if voters challenge a legislative districting map as being race-based, and the challenged laws do not involve explicit racial terminology, those voters must prove that racial considerations were the primary motivating factor for the creation of one or more legislative districts. If a government entity, such as a state legislature, merely considered the race of possible voters along with a variety of other considerations, (such as the political affiliation of all possible voters), when creating a district map, the Court may rule that the legislative district map was not based on race. If the Court does not find that the creation of a legislative district map was primarily motivated by racial considerations, it will not apply the strict judicial scrutiny used in race classification cases. (*Hunt II*)

Sometimes the determination that voting districts or boundaries were established for racial reasons will be easy, based on a long history of the government's attempts to diminish or eliminate the voting power of minority race residents. *Gomillion v. Lightfoot* (1960). The identification of race-based districting is also easy when a state legislature is redrawing a legislative districting map only because the United States Attorney General, pursuant to the Voting Rights Act, required the state legislature to create additional legislative districts in which minority race voters would control the outcome of some elections. (*Shaw I and II*) In some cases, it will be difficult to determine whether race neutral language in statutes creating legislative districts or voting boundaries was primarily the result of legislative purpose to strengthen or weaken the power of voters of a certain race. Compare the *Mobile* and *Rogers* cases, and *Hunt I and Hunt II*].

If a government entity, such as a state legislature, merely considered the race of possible voters along with a variety of other considerations, (such as the political affiliation of all possible voters), when creating a district map, the Court may rule that the legislative district map was not based on race. If the Court find that the creation of a legislative district map was not primarily motivated by racial considerations, the Court will not apply the strict judicial scrutiny used in race classification cases. (*Hunt II*)

THIRD, the desire of government entities (even popularly elected ones) to increase the voting power of one racial group (even a minority racial group) within a state, is not a compelling interest that justifies race-based legislative districting. The Supreme Court has invalidated the legislative districting map in every case where it found that race was the primary motivating factor for drawing legislative district lines. Without a majority opinion, a fragmented Court upheld a redistricting plan that seemed to be race motivated in *United Jewish Organizations v. Carey* (1977) [*U.J.O.*]. Today, a majority of the Justices would likely consider *U.J.O.* case as one in which ethnic and religious considerations were merely some of the factors that motivated the government's creation of legislative districts that were designed to avoid serious diminution of the voting power of a distinct ethnic group.

FOURTH, legislatures and courts have a compelling interest in correcting specific, unconstitutional acts of racial discrimination in voting regulations. Thus, legislatures and courts may adopt race conscious remedies that are narrowly tailored to eliminate race-based voting laws and race-based districting. *Rogers v. Lodge* (1982); *Gomillion v. Lightfoot* (1960).

FIFTH, Congress has some power to regulate state and local elections for the purpose of eliminating racial discrimination in those election systems, although the extent of this power is not clear. Congress has the power to prohibit state and local voting practices that the Court would rule unconstitutional. The Court has also recognized that Congress, due to its greater fact-finding powers, may discover, and create congruent and proportional remedies for racially discriminatory voting practices that have avoided judicial invalidation. Thus, Congress could eliminate the use of literacy tests as a condition of voting, even though the Court had never held that literacy tests constituted a per se violation of equal protection. *South Carolina v. Katzenbach* (1966); *Oregon v. Mitchell* (1970). However, the federal government may not demand that state and local governments create legislative districts that are designed to ensure control of district elections by minority race voters, unless such districts necessary to remedy prior unconstitutional racial discrimination against minority race voters within that state. *Miller v. Johnson* (1995).

§ 14.10 General Status of Aliens—Citizenship, Immigration, Deportation, Naturalization, and Expatriation

Many types of laws or executive actions may distinguish between citizens of the United States and noncitizens. Such actions raise the question of the constitutionality of classifications based on "alienage", the status of being a noncitizen.

Aliens do not receive the protection of constitutional guarantees that by their terms apply only to "citizens," for example the Privileges or Immunities Clause of section 1 of the Fourteenth Amendment applies only to "citizens." However, the clauses of the Constitution that apply to "persons," protect aliens, such the protection of the Bill of Rights, including the Fifth Amendment due process clause, and the Fourteenth Amendment due process and equal protection clauses.

The Fourteenth Amendment both defines and confers citizenship. Section one states: "All persons born or naturalized in the United States, and subject to the jurisdiction thereof, are citizens of the United States and of the State wherein they reside."

The Court has not really limited Congressional ability to set standards for naturalization of aliens. However, the Fourteenth Amendment grant of citizenship contains no provision for termination of citizenship. Thus problems have arisen as to expatriation—the termination of a person's citizenship. In 1868, for example, Congress declared in a statute that "the right of expatriation is a natural and inherent right of all people." The Court has already agreed that a person may voluntarily renounce his or her citizenship.

The Court has stricken several congressional attempts to provide for involuntary termination of citizenship. Thus, the Court has held that persons could not be deprived of their citizenship because of refusal to serve in the armed forces or for voting in a foreign election. See *Afroyim v. Rusk* (1967), holding that a statute providing for the expatriation of citizen for voting in a foreign election is unconstitutional, overruling *Perez v. Brownell* (1958).

There may still be a question as to whether Congress may require a person to elect to reject his citizenship for an act totally opposed to that status, such as service in the armed forces of a nation at war with the United States. While the Court has taken the position that Congress is without power to deprive a person of citizenship because the Fourteenth Amendment was meant to be an irrevocable grant of citizenship to certain persons, it might be argued that at some point a person's actions might constitute voluntary expatriation. Or, one might argue that the person is still a citizen but the act in question (voluntarily fighting in a foreign army against the United States) is an act of treason.

In *Vance v. Terrazas* (1980) the Court held that an individual cannot be deprived of his United States citizenship unless the government demonstrates not only that he *voluntarily* took an action that Congress has deemed to be expatriating, but also that he *intended to renounce* his citizenship when he took that action. The government, however, need only prove the elements of voluntariness and specific intent by a preponderance of the evidence.

The Court has extended the protection of the Fourteenth Amendment equal protection clause to illegally resident aliens but, in so doing, it did not impliedly limit the power of the federal government to exclude or deport such persons. Thus, when we examine the rights of an alien in this country we are really looking primarily at the rights of lawful resident aliens apart from questions of immigration, deportation, or naturalization. The ability of the government to treat resident aliens differently from citizens depends on the degree to which alienage is relevant to legitimate goals of government programs. It is this problem of classification and discrimination that is the subject of the next subsection.

§ 14.11 Classifications Based on Alienage

Aliens are persons, so they receive the protection of the due process clauses and the equal protection clause. While the equal protection clause does not apply to the federal government, the Fifth Amendment's due process clause guarantees equal protection in the application of federal law. State classifications that treat aliens differently on the basis of that status are reviewed under the equal protection clause of the Fourteenth Amendment while federal acts are subject to the due process clause of the Fifth Amendment.

The equal protection guarantee requires that the government treat similar persons in a similar manner. When testing a classification based upon alienage the issue is whether the status of being a United States citizen differentiates persons in terms of a proper governmental purpose. If not, it should be invalidated as an arbitrary refusal to accord equal treatment to lawfully resident persons who are not citizens. The Supreme Court has refused to enunciate a single test to be used when determining the compatibility of alienage classifications with the equal protection guarantee of the Fourteenth Amendment equal protection clause or the Fifth Amendment due process clause.

All of the Court's decisions since 1970 on this issue would appear to be consistent if the Court is using an intermediate standard of review—between the traditional rational basis test and the strict compelling interest test—which required the government to demonstrate that a citizenship classification bore a reasonable and substantial relationship to an important government interest.

Since state and local governments have no interest in foreign affairs, the Court can consider their use of alienage classifications differently. The Supremacy Clause or federal preemption may invalidate some state rules governing aliens because the federal interest in aliens is different than the state interest in aliens.

Federal laws imposing citizenship classifications are almost always upheld because they bear a substantial relationship to an important interest standard. The federal interest in international affairs, as well as the federal power over immigration and naturalization, should justify the use of alienage classifications. So long as a federal alienage classification is not a totally arbitrary means of disfavoring lawfully resident aliens, the courts are likely to uphold the classifications. The Court tends to give the federal government freedom to pursue national goals without simultaneously granting it a virtually unchecked power to make use of arbitrary and invidious classifications burdening noncitizens. Unfortunately, the Court has chosen not to analyze all alienage classifications in terms of a single standard of review, which makes the analysis more complicated. Instead, the Court has divided alienage cases into three categories.

First, when state or local laws classify persons on the basis of U.S. citizenship for the purpose of distributing economic benefits, or limiting the opportunity to engage in private sector economic activity, the law is subject to strict judicial scrutiny. In this situation, the Court recognizes that classifications based on alienage should be deemed "suspect" and upheld only if necessary to promote a compelling or overriding interest. *Ambach v. Norwick* (1979). Until recently, the Court upheld alienage classifications whenever it believed that the state had a "special public interest" in granting privileges only to citizens. Now that the Court subjects these economic citizenship classifications to strict scrutiny, the state must demonstrate a compelling purpose for treating aliens in a less favorable manner than citizens. This test makes it quite difficult for the state to meet the burden because in almost all instances the lawfully resident noncitizen is subject to federal and state taxation just as is the resident citizen. The lawfully resident alien is not reasonably distinguishable from the citizen in terms of legitimate, nondiscriminatory economic goals of the state.

Second, the Court will uphold an alienage classification created by state or local law that relates to allocating power or positions in the political process under the traditional rational basis test. The Court recognizes that a state has a legitimate interest in reserving positions in the self-governance process for United States citizens. The state need not allow noncitizens the right to vote or hold elective office. Indeed, it appears that the state need not allow the noncitizen to hold an important governmental position of any type. *Cabell v. Chavez–Salido* (1982). The Supreme Court has created a "political function" exception to the strict scrutiny of state alienage regulations so that local governments may require citizenship as a condition of obtaining a government position "intimately related to the process of democratic self-government." If a government position is related to the self-governance process, involves a significant policy-making function, or requires the exercise of important discretionary power over citizens, the state or local government may reserve that position for a United States citizen. However, states may not use a United States citizenship classification to exclude lawfully resident aliens from employment in government positions which are purely functionary and are not related to the interest in self-governance.

The trait of being an United States citizen does define a class of persons, in the view of the Court, who have a special affiliation to both the federal and state governments and, therefore, who may be given a priority for employment in governmental positions that are related to the self-governance process and involve the exercise of important powers in our democratic system. A political, as opposed to economic, alienage classification will be upheld so long as it is rationally related to the state interest in preserving the governmental process for citizens. Even in the political area, a state may not be totally arbitrary in its use of the alienage classification. Thus, *Sugarman v. Dougall* (1973) held that a state's total exclusion of noncitizens from state civil service position is invalid.

If the alienage classification does not relate to this self-governance interest, the state classification is tested under the strict scrutiny standard. Because states may not pursue foreign policy objectives (that is a federal function) state classifications must relate to a legitimate state interest, not an interest relating to foreign affairs. The Court will not intrude into the foreign relations interests of the United State and any state law regulating what might interfere with federal policy in this area is void under the supremacy clause or preempted by federal law. Thus, *Toll v. Moreno* (1982) held that a state university may not deny in-state tuition status to nonimmigrant aliens who are state residents and have valid federal visas for employees of international organizations, for that violates the supremacy clause of Article VI by interfering with federal policy.

Third, *federal* alienage classifications are subjected to only the rational basis standard of review. Although the Court has not been clear in identifying the proper standard of review to be employed in these cases, it would appear that the federal government may use a citizenship classification so long as it reasonably relates to a federal interest. Although some judicial opinions read as if every federal alienage classification will be upheld, a federal alienage classification should be invalid if it is an arbitrary and invidious classification designed only to burden a disfavored group of persons. Most, if not all, federal alienage classifications are upheld under any standard of review other than the strictest form of the compelling interest test.

The proper differentiation between federal and state laws in this area is not in terms of the standard of review to be employed, but in the nature of the governmental interest which justifies the classification. The federal government, unlike state government, has an important interest in foreign affairs and foreign relations. The federal government should be allowed to classify persons by their citizenship when that classification is arguably related to foreign policy interests. The federal government may treat aliens differently than U.S. citizens for the purposes of increasing bargaining power with other governments, or for purposes of national security, or simply because it wishes to create an image that it wants to present to the world. However, if the federal government does not appear to be pursuing such ends, it should not be allowed the freedom to engage in invidious classification of aliens and such a federal action should be invalidated as a totally arbitrary imposition of burdens on a group of persons whom the federal government has allowed to remain in this country.

Supreme Court Decisions After 1970.

In *Graham v. Richardson* (1971) the Court held that the equal protection clause prevented a state from conditioning welfare benefits either upon the possession of United States citizenship or residence in this country for a specified number of years. The opinion noted that prior decisions had equated classifications based on alienage with those based on race or national origin and declared that such classifications are inherently suspect and subject to close judicial scrutiny. The classification is valid only if it is necessary to promote a compelling state interest.

The Court stated further: "we conclude that a state's desire to preserve limited welfare benefits for its own citizens is inadequate to justify Pennsylvania's making noncitizens ineligible for public assistance, and Arizona's restricting benefits to citizens and long time resident aliens."

Graham also held the statute invalid because it interfered with the exclusive exercise of the federal government's control of aliens. Congress has broad powers to determine who may enter and reside in this country and Congress has not barred any aliens who become indigent after entry into the country. Thus the opinion found that "state laws that restrict the eligibility of aliens for welfare benefits merely because of their alienage conflict with these overriding national policies in an area constitutionally entrusted to Federal Government."

The Court went further in requiring only narrow uses of alienage classifications in *Application of Griffiths* (1973), which invalidated a state court requirement of citizenship for admission to the bar. The Court found it did not denigrate lawyers' high responsibilities to observe that their duties hardly involve matters of high state policy or acts of such unique responsibility so as to entrust them only to citizens. The possibility that some resident aliens are unsuited to the practice of law cannot be a justification for a wholesale ban. Since the state could not demonstrate that the classification was a narrow means of promoting a compelling or "substantial" end, the rule was invalid.

While the Court has been quite strict in recent years in prohibiting the use of alienage classifications in the economic area, it has allowed the states much wider latitude to use alienage classifications which are related to the self-governance process. When the government claims that an alienage classification serves political goals, the Court must determine whether the classification is so overinclusive or underinclusive that the claim should not be believed. When the state uses such a classification to exclude noncitizens from holding government employment, the Court should ask whether the positions from which the noncitizens are excluded relate to the self-governance process.

Sugarman v. Dougall (1973) invalidated a law making citizenship a requirement for any position in the competitive class of a state civil service system. The competitive class included all positions for which it was practicable to determine merit by a competitive exam and reach various positions in nearly the full range of governmental services. The state asserted that its goal was to employ only persons with undivided loyalty, but this prohibition was applicable to many positions whose function had no relationship to the loyalty, or citizenship, of the individual excluded.

The Court noted that its holding was a narrow one: it did *not* hold that "on the basis of individualized determination, an alien may not be refused, or discharged from, public employment, even on the basis of noncitizenship, if the refusal to hire, or the discharge rests on legitimate state interests that relate to qualifications for a particular position or to the characteristics of the employee." In later cases, the Court upheld laws that reserved positions in state governmental agencies for citizens.

Thus, *Foley v. Connelie* (1978) upheld a state law that excluded aliens from appointment as members of the state police force. The majority opinion by Chief Justice Burger stated that the earlier cases "generally reflect a close scrutiny" of alienage classifications, at least when they are used by state governments, but that the Supreme Court "never suggested that such legislation is inherently invalid, nor ... held that all limitations on aliens are suspect." Of course, this statement is incorrect to the extent that it would deny that alienage classifications have been held to be "suspect." The statement is correct to the extent that prior cases make it clear that alienage classifications are not to be reviewed as strictly as the suspect classifications of race or national origin.

The majority opinion noted that the Court has recognized that obtaining the status of a citizen is a significant act because many rights relating to self-government may be properly reserved to citizens. In this way Chief Justice Burger is able to harmonize the substance of prior cases even though prior opinions use inconsistent language. Prior cases have recognized that reasonable alienage classification may be employed to pursue substantial state interests, such as that of self-governance, although prior "strict scrutiny" language has clouded these rulings. The majority in *Foley* believed that the great discretion granted police officers made individual officers important components of the system of government. Thus, the Court concluded that the state could reserve these positions for those who have a right to participate in the governance process.

In recent years, the Supreme Court sought, perhaps unsuccessfully, to add some framework to its alienage decisions of the 1970's. *Ambach v. Norwick* (1979) upheld a state law prohibiting the employment as a teacher, in any *publicly* operated grade school or high school, of any person who was not a citizen of the United States unless that person had manifested an intention to apply for citizenship or was not yet eligible for citizenship. Justice Powell, for the Court, admitted that the Supreme Court decisions regarding alienage classifications "have not formed an unwavering line over the years."

Ambach raised two important issues: first, whether public school teachers are a part of a governmental function; second, whether the classification is rationally related to that function. The majority found that the role of teachers in publicly-funded and operated grade schools and high schools constituted a significant governmental function. Teachers in these schools were employed, in part, to prepare young persons for participation in the governance process as citizens. Public school teachers were also to foster and preserve many societal values, including those relating to self-governance. The majority found that standardization of teaching materials would not fulfill this important role because teachers served as a "role model" of persons involved in the American democratic system. This opinion does not allow the state to require private schools to hire U.S. citizens. For example, a state law could not prohibit a private school from hiring a lawfully resident Spanish citizen to teach Spanish.

Having found that teachers were a part of a government function, the majority upheld the alienage classification as rationally related to the promotion of a self-governance, or governmental, function. For the majority this distinguished the teacher and police officer cases from the earlier cases finding that aliens could not be excluded from becoming licensed attorneys or engineers. The attorney and engineer positions were not positions of government employment and the exclusions of aliens from those professions, therefore, was not related to a governmental function. The majority noted that the state had not attempted to bar aliens from positions as teachers in public institutions of *higher* education or from any teaching positions in private schools. It would be most difficult to uphold the bar of aliens as teachers in private schools, if they met educational requirements, because those teachers are not public employees and those schools do not perform the same government function as do publicly operated schools.

Although the dissenters may have been correct in finding the restriction unreasonable; a majority of the Justices rejected the dissenter's claim that it was "logically impossible" to differentiate this case from those striking the exclusion of aliens from practice as attorneys or engineers. The majority opinion found that the dissenters "missed the point" by failing to ask first if the public employment position were a part of a governmental (in the sense of self-governance) function. An affirmative answer to that question, for the majority, allows the state to use any classification that will pass a rational basis test.

It now appears that state governments cannot employ alienage classifications in a burdensome manner in their police power regulations or their granting of social welfare benefits but they will receive greater latitude in excluding aliens from public employment as well as from direct participation in the governance process. While the states will not be allowed to have a blanket exclusion of aliens from public employment, they will be able to exclude aliens from positions that are part of a governmental function.

The Supreme Court appears to require a judicial determination of whether a state or local law requiring United States citizenship for government employment is reasonably related to the government's interest in allocating power in our democratic system of governance. However, the Court also appears to give a significant degree of deference to the decision of legislative bodies. The Court upheld the ability of states to require that a person be a citizen of the United States to be a "peace officer" even though the state defined that term so that it included a wide variety of persons employed in the criminal justice process. Thus *Cabell v. Chavez–Salido*, (1982) held that the California statutory requirement that peace officers be citizens was not unconstitutional and that it could be applied to exclude lawfully resident aliens from holding positions as deputy state probation officers. After reviewing the decisions noted previously in this section, the majority opinion by Justice White stated, "while not retreating from the position that restrictions on lawfully resident aliens that primarily affect economic interest are subject to heightened judicial scrutiny ... we have concluded that strict scrutiny is out of place when the restriction primarily serves a political function."

There is an exception to the general principle that state and local laws employing alienage classifications are subject to strict scrutiny. "This exception has been labeled the 'political function' exception and applies to laws that exclude aliens from positions intimately related to the process of democratic self-government." *Bernal v. Fainter* (1984). The state may exclude noncitizens from elected government positions and also from those positions that are related to the democratic process, involve a significant policy-making function, or require the exercise of important discretionary governmental powers over citizens. If the alienage classification relates to self-governance or to positions that go to "the heart of representative government," the Court will uphold the classification with a deferential standard of review. If the classification does not relate to the self-governance process and, therefore, does not come under the political function exception, it will be subjected to strict scrutiny and invalidated unless it is narrowly tailored to promote a compelling state interest.

Federal Laws. The Supreme Court has employed a lenient standard of review when examining federal laws which employ citizenship classifications. The Court has not clarified the standard of review to be employed when examining federal alienage classifications but it seems apparent that most, if not all, such classifications will be upheld under any but the strictest form of judicial review. Because of the important nature of the federal interest in foreign affairs and foreign relations, as well as the federal power to regulate immigration and naturalization, the Court will defer to the

Congress and uphold alienage classifications so long as they are not clearly an arbitrary and invidious imposition of burdens upon a politically powerless group.

In *Mathews v. Diaz* (1976) the Court held that Congress could condition an alien's eligibility for participation in a federal medical insurance program on continuous residence in the United States for a five-year period. The Court noted that Congress had no duty to give all aliens the full benefits of citizens. Illegal or temporary resident aliens could present no substantial legal claims, so the question was whether Congress could impose a durational residency requirement in order to define who was eligible for the benefits. Because some line had to be drawn, the opinion held it reasonable for Congress to make an alien's eligibility for benefits depend on the "character and the duration of his residence." The determination of precisely where to fix the line for eligibility was for Congress, as any cutoff would produce some apparently arbitrary consequences for those falling slightly short of the requirement.

While *Diaz* makes it clear that the federal government may use alienage classifications to a greater degree than classifications based on the other suspect criteria of race or national origin, this decision is not inconsistent with recent alienage cases. Classifications based on race, national origin or alienage are "suspect," because they are highly likely to be used to arbitrarily disadvantage these groups. The history of the Civil War Amendments and post-war racial discrimination justify a judicially imposed prohibition against using race and national origin to disfavor these minorities.

However, aliens bear a relationship to this country that is in fact different from that of citizens. They have yet to establish a permanent commitment to this country and they retain the obligations and benefits of citizenship in another nation. Another nation continues to have a legitimate interest in their treatment by this government.

These factors may distinguish them, for some government programs from citizens. These differences, however, relate only to national citizenship. The states, unlike the federal government, have no interest in regulating aliens and their legitimate local interests do not relate to national citizenship. Thus, the states are rarely able to show that they need to distinguish between aliens and citizens to promote substantial state interests. States may restrict the employment of those who are not lawful residents of the United States. *DeCanas v. Bica* (1976).

Only the federal government may conduct foreign relations activities. Therefore, it alone has a need to distinguish between citizens and aliens. Since the treatment of aliens is intertwined with our relations with foreign nations, distinguishing aliens and citizens does not demonstrate prejudice against aliens or an arbitrary treatment of them. Thus the federal government has a "substantial" or "compelling" interest in the conduct of foreign relations and it may make reasonable use of alienage classifications to promote those ends.

Because the national treatment of aliens is interwoven with foreign policy the Supreme Court will grant Congress some deference in its use of alienage classifications even though they are suspect. Where, as in *Mathews*, the classification appears to relate to national policy and is not based on a prejudice against aliens the Court will uphold the classification, if the government agency making the distinction has the authority to do so. Consider *Hampton v. Mow Sun Wong* (1976), which held unconstitutional a regulation of the United States Civil Service Commission barring resident aliens from employment in the competitive federal civil service.

The majority did not invalidate the regulation on the grounds that Congress could not delegate this authority. Instead, it only held that the regulation appeared to exceed the actual grant of authority that Congress gave to the Commission. In other words, the Court simply concluded that Congress did not delegate this power. After this case, President Ford, by executive order, barred most resident aliens from employment in the competitive federal civil service. On remand the trial court upheld this executive order. *Mow Sun Wong v. Hampton* (N.D.Cal.1977). Now it was clear that the government wanted to bar most resident aliens from the federal civil service.

One should compare *Hampton v. Mow Sun Wong* (1976) to *Nyquist v. Mauclet* (1977). The *Mauclet* case invalidated a *state* law that granted aid for higher education to citizens and resident aliens who were or would be applying for citizenship. The Court (6 to 3) found no compelling state interest in encouraging citizenship or limiting general programs to those who determine its policy. States simply do not have the same authority to regulate aliens as the federal government has.

The most important point of the decision is not the result of the case, which is in complete conformity with earlier rulings, but a statement in the majority opinion that "classifications by a state that are based on alienage are inherently suspect and subject to close judicial scrutiny." In an accompanying footnote to this statement Justice Blackmun stated that the Court used "relaxed scrutiny" in upholding the federal welfare requirements in *Diaz* because "Congress, as an aspect of its broad power over immigration and naturalization, enjoys rights to distinguish among aliens that are not shared by the states." It would have been analytically and historically more sound for the Court to distinguish state from federal power in this area by grounding its decisions on the Supremacy Clause and implied federal preemption of state laws that affect alien rights contrary to what Congress intended.

§ 14.12 Classifications Burdening Illegal Aliens and Undocumented Citizens

Congress has virtually plenary power to define the class of persons (other than citizens of the United States) who may lawfully reside in this country. A person who is born in the United States and subject to the jurisdiction thereof, is a U.S. citizen at birth, due to the first sentence of the Fourteenth Amendment. Congress has no constitutional authority to take away the citizenship of any anyone who is a citizen under the terms of the Fourteenth Amendment. A person may be a U.S. citizen, because she was born in the U.S., although she lacks documents that would prove the place of her birth and, therefore, her citizenship. Such a person is not an illegally or unlawfully resident alien. Rather, she is a citizen of the United States. Such a person should be referred to as an "undocumented person," rather than as an illegal or unlawful alien. There are other persons who are, in fact, illegal aliens. They also lack the documents to prove their citizenship because those documents do not exist.

The Court has long held that all persons within the country are protected by the due process guarantee; any person within the jurisdiction of the United States is entitled to a fair process to determine whether he may be deported from, or prohibited from returning to, the United States for violation of a federal statute or regulation. The Court has not yet imposed any substantive restrictions on the ability of Congress to define the class of persons who may lawfully reside in the country or the ability of Congress to disfavor unlawfully resident persons in the distribution of federal benefits.

In 1982, the Court (5 to 4) for the first time extended the scope of the equal protection clause to give *unlawfully* resident aliens limited protection from state or local laws which arbitrarily denied them benefits or imposed burdens upon them. *Plyler v. Doe* (1982). The Court employed a middle level standard of review (as if the world needed yet another test) that required the state to demonstrate that a classification burdening the children of illegal aliens in fact furthered a substantial goal of the state. The Court indicated that states might be given greater leeway in burdening unlawfully resident aliens when they were acting pursuant to authority given them by the federal government or promoting a federal policy. Indeed, the Court did not prohibit states from taking other actions that give preferential treatment to citizens and lawfully resident aliens in the dispensation of governmental benefits.

Plyler v. Doe held that a Texas statute that withheld from local school districts any state funds for the education of children who were not "legally admitted" into the United States, and that authorized local school districts to deny enrollment in their schools to children who were not "legally admitted" to the United States, violated the equal protection clause of the Fourteenth Amendment. Texas had argued that the equal protection clause was not applicable to this law and that it only protected those persons lawfully within the state.

The majority opinion rejected that argument. There was nothing in the history of the Fourteenth Amendment or its language that indicated that the scope of the equal protection clause is meant to be narrower than that of due process.

The majority opinion by Justice Brennan noted that the state punishing the children for the conduct of their parents. "Even if the state found it expedient to control the conduct of adults by acting against their children, legislation directing the onus of a parent's misconduct against his children does not comport with fundamental conceptions of justice."

The Court refused to recognize illegal aliens as a suspect class, which would have required that laws burdening this class of persons be subject to strict judicial scrutiny. The majority opinion also refused to find that all laws burdening illegal aliens should be subject to a strict or active form of judicial review, such as laws that employed sex or illegitimacy classifications, because the status of being an undocumented alien was not "an absolutely immutable characteristic since it is the product of conscious, indeed unlawful, action." The fact that the Texas law at issue was directed against the children of those persons who entered the country illegally required, in the majority's view, some realistic examination of whether it was arbitrary to penalize these children for the actions of their parents.

The federal government might exclude or deport these children, but the law that the Court invalidated was a state law, not a federal one. Later *Reno v. Flores* (1993), upheld Immigration and Naturalization Service regulations that required the federal government to retain custody of alien children who were being held pending deportation proceedings in almost all instances when there were no relatives or guardians in the United States to whom the children could be released. The majority opinion held that the INS regulations did not violate the substantive or procedural guarantees of the due process clause of the Fifth Amendment or the implied equal protection guarantee of the due process clause of the Fifth

Amendment. The children held in custody argued that the government regulations must be narrowly tailored to serve the best interest of a child and that the government must release a child into the custody of non-relatives when the best interest of the child would be served by such a release. The majority opinion rejected that argument. The children did not have a fundamental right to be placed in a noncustodial setting or a right to have the government make decisions in "the best interest of the child." Because there was no fundamental right involved in this case, there only had to be a "reasonable fit" between the regulation and legitimate government interest. The federal regulation had to meet "the (unexacting) standard of rationally advancing some legitimate government purpose." The regulations rationally related to the *federal* government purposes in securing the appearance of the children in the deportation proceedings while providing them with adequate care.

§ 14.13   Illegitimacy Classifications: Introduction

An illegitimate child is one whose parents were not lawfully married to each other at the time of his birth. Historically, some statutes accorded more favorable treatment to legitimate children than to illegitimate children, particularly when dispensing benefits following the death or disability of one of the children's parents. Although the modern Court has not held that legitimacy classifications are "suspect," they now receive a meaningful review under the equal protection guarantee. The Court does not apply the compelling interest test to these classifications, but it will independently review the basis of these classifications to determine if they substantially advance an important government purpose. The Court has stated that "imposing disabilities on the illegitimate child is contrary to the basic concept of our system that legal burdens should bear some relationship to individual responsibility or wrongdoing." *Weber v. Aetna Casualty & Surety Co.* (1972).

Under the modern cases, the courts will uphold a governmental use of a classification based on the status of a person having been "legitimate" or "illegitimate" at birth only if the classification is "substantially" related to an "important" government interest.

This standard of what is often called "intermediate scrutiny" or the "middle tier" because it falls between the rational relationship test and the strict scrutiny test in terms of the strictness of the judicial review of the classification. The Court did not formally adopt this test for illegitimacy classifications until 1988. The case was the unanimous decision in *Clark v. Jeter* (1988).

Jeter invalidated, as a violation of equal protection, a Pennsylvania law that ordinarily required an illegitimate child to establish paternity within six years of the illegitimate child's birth, while a legitimate child could seek support from his or her parents at any time. The unanimous Court concluded that the six-year statute of limitations was not substantially related to Pennsylvania's interest in avoiding stale or fraudulent claims because in some other cases it places no limit on when the paternity issue may be litigated (e.g., at any time, under the intestacy statute, if there is "clear and convincing evidence that the man was the father of the child"), and because "increasingly sophisticated tests for genetic markers permit the exclusion of over 99% of those who might be accused of paternity, regardless of the age of the child."

The Court summarized the modern day test to determine if an illegitimacy classification violates the Equal Protection Clause:

> "[W]e apply different levels of scrutiny to different types of classifications. At a minimum, a statutory classification must be rationally related to a legitimate governmental purpose. Classifications based on race or national origin, and classifications affecting fundamental rights, are given the most exacting scrutiny. Between these extremes of rational basis review and strict scrutiny lies a level of intermediate scrutiny, which generally has been applied to discriminatory classifications based on sex *or illegitimacy*.

> "To withstand *intermediate scrutiny,* a statutory classification must be *substantially related to an important governmental objective.*" (emphasis added).

Classifications that distinguish illegitimate from legitimate children may be upheld if the Court finds that they advance permissible government purposes and are not burdens placed on the illegitimate child because of his status. Neither state nor federal laws may use these classifications to punish the parent's behavior for giving birth to an illegitimate child. Nor can illegitimate children be burdened on the theory that unfavorable treatment of them will encourage legitimate family relationships. Legitimacy classifications created for impermissible reasons constitute the arbitrary burdening of the child or his parents rather than mere regulation of activities that the state has a right to proscribe.

The state may not disadvantage illegitimate children in the dispensation of government benefits, or of property rights from their parents, merely because the problem of proving parentage may be difficult. Statutes must include procedures to resolve questions of parentage; difficulties of proof may not be used as a barrier to the rights of illegitimate children. But the government need not give all children an equal presumption of a support or dependency relationship to their parents if that classification is not based on the status of illegitimacy.

Governmental benefit systems designed to give support to those children dependent upon a parent who is deceased or disabled may presume dependency for legitimate children and certain classes of illegitimates who have a relationship to the parent that indicates a support obligation from the parent to the child. This classification will be valid even though it excludes from the presumption some classes of illegitimate children. However, to survive scrutiny under the reasonable basis test, the classification must be narrowly drawn to identify those with a likelihood of dependency upon the parent, and it must grant a presumption of dependency to illegitimate children whose personal circumstances indicate that they have been acknowledged or supported by the parent. Furthermore, these laws should also permit other illegitimate children to prove their actual entitlement to benefits because of their continuing relationship to the parent, even though they do not have a presumption of dependency.

Because the decisions on illegitimacy have been made under a "middle level" scrutiny test for validity of classifications, they have a certain *ad hoc* quality. The Court's rulings on the permissibility of a classification depends in part on the Justices' view of the purpose of the classification and whether it is used to invidiously burden illegitimate children.

It is helpful to note the range of results in the illegitimacy decisions before examining them individually. Statutes granting causes of action for wrongful death cannot deny a right of recovery to either illegitimate children or to their mothers. *Levy v. Louisiana* (1968); *Glona v. American Guarantee & Liability Insurance Co.* (1968). The Court has held that such actions should be unrelated to the fact of illegitimacy and should depend upon the continuing relationship between the child and the mother.

However, statutes may prohibit *fathers* of illegitimates from suing for the wrongful death of an illegitimate child unless the father has legitimated or formally acknowledged the child during the child's lifetime. *Parham v. Hughes* (1979). These laws burden the father, not the child, and encourage the father to formally acknowledge his child.

Neither the Social Security System, *Jimenez v. Weinberger* (1974) nor state worker's compensation provisions may deny benefits to all illegitimate children. *Weber v. Aetna Casualty & Surety Co.* (1972). *Weber* invalidated a Louisiana workers' compensation law that granted full recovery for injury to parents by legitimate and acknowledged illegitimate children but limited benefits to unacknowledged illegitimates. The Court held that when unacknowledged children had been dependent upon the injured parent, there was no basis for denying them full benefits.

The state must base this type of law on the relationship between the child and the parent and cannot arbitrarily exclude all illegitimates because of the status of their birth. If a state grants legitimate children a right of support from either their mothers or their fathers, it must grant similar support rights to illegitimates who can prove their parentage. E.g., *Mills v. Habluetzel* (1982). The fact that it will be difficult for the state to create systems for proving parentage does not excuse it from its obligation of treating illegitimates in a fair manner. *Trimble v. Gordon* (1977).

For a time the Court held that illegitimate children could be treated less favorably than legitimate children in the property distribution from the estate of a male parent who died without a will. The Court then adopted the position that illegitimate children cannot be arbitrarily excluded from inheriting from either their mother or their father, even though allowing inheritance rights to illegitimates will raise problems of proof of parentage. *Trimble v. Gordon* (1977). However, the Court upheld a state law that excluded illegitimates from inheriting from their fathers' estate unless a judicial proceeding had already determined them to be the children of the decedent father during his lifetime. *Lalli v. Lalli* (1978).

The Supreme Court appears to have employed the intermediate standard of review when examining classifications based on gender or legitimacy and both state and federal laws with one possible exception: federal immigration and naturalization laws. The Court has upheld the federal immigration laws that placed special restrictions on the ability of a U.S. citizen-father, as opposed to a U.S. citizen-mother, to receive an immigration preference for an illegitimate child who was born in another country. *Fiallo v. Bell* (1977). The Court has also upheld federal naturalization laws that require the United States citizen-father of a child born out of wedlock to take certain steps *prior* to the child's receiving citizenship, while the same statutes granted immediate citizenship to a child born out of wedlock to a United States citizen-mother who was outside the country. *Tuan Anh Nguyen v. I.N.S.* (2001). The Court found the sex and illegitimacy classifications of these immigration laws related to establishing that the male United States citizen was in fact the parent of the child. The dissenting Justices in these cases argued that the generalized classifications were difficult to describe as being substantially related to an important government interest.

Although the Court held that these classifications were substantially related to an important governmental interest, one should not assume that the Court would be so lenient when examining sex or illegitimacy classifications in areas unrelated to immigration and naturalization.

The Court has looked with disfavor upon laws based on an arbitrary view of the worthiness of the parents of illegitimate children or family units containing illegitimate children to receive governmental benefits or equal treatment of laws relating to family matters. For example, the law cannot disqualify households from receiving benefits because they contain illegitimate children. *New Jersey Welfare Rights Organization v. Cahill* (1973) invalidated a program providing welfare to low-income family units consisting of married couples with either natural or adopted children. The opinion held that the states could not deny benefits to family units simply because they contained illegitimate children. The effect of the statute was to punish illegitimate children by denying benefits to them and their families. That is not an acceptable justification for distinguishing between legitimates and illegitimates when the purpose of the benefits should be to support needy persons rather than single out a class of children as unworthy because of their status at birth.

Contrast, *Mathews v. Lucas* (1976), which held that the Social Security Act could condition the eligibility for survivor's benefits of certain illegitimate children upon a showing that the deceased wage earner was both the child's parent and was supporting the child at the time of his death. The Court examined the law under the Fifth Amendment equal protection guarantee. The federal law granted a presumption of dependency to legitimate children and illegitimates who were entitled to inherit from the decedent under state law. Other illegitimate children were allowed to establish their dependency upon the deceased wage earner and to collect survivor's benefits, but they had to produce evidence of their dependency.

Mathews upheld the law because it found that the reduction in administrative problems and expense in avoiding a proof of dependency requirement for all children could support this classification. The classification was not strictly a division between legitimate and illegitimate children because those illegitimate children whose circumstances indicated that the children were dependent on the wage earner were treated in a manner similar to legitimate children. Illegitimate children were entitled to a presumption of dependency if they could inherit personal property from the parent under state law, if their parents had ever gone through a purported marriage ceremony or had acknowledged the children, if they had been decreed by a court to be the wage earner's children, or if the wage earner had ever been ordered by a court to support the children. Thus, only a small group of illegitimate children were not entitled to a presumption of dependency upon the death of their parents. Furthermore, the remaining children were allowed to prove their dependency, in which case they would be qualified for benefits. The law was upheld because it was not an attempt to burden illegitimate children but only a narrow way of easing administrative problems for the establishment of dependency.

Califano v. Boles (1979) held that a Social Security Act provision that restricted surviving parent benefits to persons who have been lawfully married to a deceased wage earner prior to the wage earner's death does not discriminate against illegitimates. In 1976 the Supreme Court held that the Social Security Act could condition the eligibility for survivor's benefits of certain illegitimate children upon a showing that the deceased wage earner was both the child's parent and was supporting the child at the time of his death.

States may not presume that the father of an illegitimate child is unfit to take custody of the child but must allow fathers some opportunity to retain custody following the death of the child's mother. *Stanley v. Illinois* (1972).

Similarly, the Court overturned a statute that required the consent of the mother but not the father of illegitimate children prior to their adoption, at least insofar as the statute excluded the known or ascertainable fathers of older children. *Caban v. Mohammed* (1979) invalidated a New York law that required the consent of the mother of an illegitimate child prior to its adoption but which did not give equal consent rights to the father of the child. The majority found that the law constituted an impermissible form of sex-based discrimination between the parents of illegitimate children, although the majority did not reach the question of whether such discrimination would be allowed when the father of the child was not readily ascertainable or during the period when the child was in its infancy.

Caban indicates that fathers of illegitimate children should be given notice and a hearing before the child can be adopted by another person, at least where the natural father can be located and identified without unreasonably complicated or expensive administrative systems. However, a father who fails to take any steps toward acknowledgment of his paternity and does not seek to establish a relationship with his illegitimate child can be denied a right to veto the adoption of that child even though a veto power is granted to other parents.

Michael H. v. Gerald D. (1989) fits with this line of cases, although there was no opinion of the Court Justices Scalia, O'Connor, and Kennedy, and Chief Justice Rehnquist found that a male had no constitutionally protected interest in establishing a relationship with a child born to a woman who was married to another man, regardless of whether he could prove that he was the biological parent of the child. Justice Stevens, concurring in the judgment, found that the male had no constitutionally protected interest in being declared the "father" of a child born to a married couple but assumed for purposes of the case that the male in this situation had a constitutionally protected liberty interest in establishing a personal relationship with the child. Justice Stevens found that interest was sufficiently protected by a related state statute that allowed any person who had an interest in the well-being of a child to seek a court judgment that the individual should be allowed visitation rights.

Lehr v. Robertson (1983) helped clear up the confusion when it held that the state was *not* required by due process or equal protection to provide notice and a hearing to the putative father of a two year old illegitimate child when the father had never sought to establish a substantial relationship with, or accept responsibility for, the child. In *Lehr* the state allowed a man who claimed to be the father of an illegitimate child to file a statement to that effect in the "putative father registry." That registration would guarantee that the man received notice of future adoption proceedings. Due process did not require a more extensive system to identify or notify fathers who had never claimed responsibility for the child; equal protection did not require that such fathers be granted rights equal to those who had established a substantial custodial, legal, or financial relationship with the child.

§ 14.14 Illegitimacy Classifications: Conclusion

The Court will invalidate state laws that place unnecessary roadblocks to proof of paternity. For example, under the state statute at issue in *Mills v. Habluetzel* (1982) the failure of an illegitimate child (with his guardian) to file a paternity suit within the first year of the child's life resulted in the illegitimate being forever barred from the right to sue his natural father for support. In that case, the Court also required that restrictions relating to illegitimacy must be substantially related to a legitimate state interest. The Court rejected the state assertion that legitimacy classifications promoted the continuation of the institutions of family and marriage; the Court repeated that imposing disabilities on the illegitimate child is contrary to the basic principle of our law that burdens should bear some relationship to individual responsibility or wrongdoing. However, this unanimous judgment of the Court was made in the context of a strict and substantial restriction on the rights of illegitimates to obtain parental support. Restrictions of lesser magnitude on the rights of an illegitimate child to seek support from his or her natural father may result in a divided Court upholding or striking a particular illegitimacy classification based on the Justices' differing views of the purpose and effect of the restriction.

Following *Mills,* the Court unanimously invalidated a two-year statute of limitations on paternity actions brought by illegitimate children in *Pickett v. Brown* (1983) and invalidated a six-year statute of limitations on paternity actions by such children in *Clark v. Jeter* (1988). This statute of limitations was not substantially related to the important governmental objective of avoiding stale or fraudulent claims in the courts. The distinction in these statutes of limitations between support cases that legitimate children bring and that that illegitimate children bring did not withstand any form of judicial review beyond the most deferential rational relationship test. The Court's opinions in these cases establish the principle that any law that burdens a classification of persons solely because of the status of being illegitimate will be upheld only if the government can demonstrate that the use of the illegitimacy classification is substantially related to an important government interest.

§ 14.15 Gender or Sex Classifications: Introduction

Men and women were not originally considered to stand as equals before the law. The married woman in particular was subject to severe legal disabilities at common law. The passage of the Fourteenth Amendment had no immediate effect upon the use of sex-based classifications. States continued to pass, and courts continued to uphold, legislation which reflected traditional beliefs of sex-defined roles and provided distinct treatment for men and women, notably in regard to employment opportunities and jury duty.

The earliest challenge to unequal treatment of women arose under the privileges and immunities clause of the Fourteenth Amendment. These challenges were unsuccessful chiefly because of the narrow construction given to this phrase by the Supreme Court. The clause was construed to encompass only those privileges or immunities which resulted from national, as opposed to state, citizenship.

Although the equal protection clause was soon found to apply to other arbitrary classifications besides race, prior to 1971 sex-based classifications were treated exactly as were general economic regulations. When the Court was taking an active role in the evaluation of economic regulation under substantive due process, it took a correspondingly active role in the evaluation of statutes which treated women differently from men. The Court generally upheld these statutes because it agreed with the legislatures that it was necessary to give women special treatment; however, where the Court found special treatment was not needed, it struck the legislation. Following the repudiation of substantive economic due process, the Court treated all economic and social welfare legislation—

including all sex-based classifications—with great judicial deference.

Bradwell v. Illinois (1873) was the first case in which the constitutionality of different treatment for men and women was challenged. Relying upon the privileges and immunities clause of the Fourteenth Amendment, Bradwell challenged the refusal of the Illinois Supreme Court to grant her a license to practice law solely because she was a woman. On appeal to the United States Supreme Court, Bradwell maintained that she was entitled to a license to practice because the Fourteenth Amendment "opens to every citizen of the United States, male or female, black or white, married or single, the honorable professions as well as the simple enjoyments of life." The Supreme Court rejected this argument, affirming the state court decision with but one dissent. The concurring Justices upheld the different treatment of women because it was mandated by "the law of the creator." Job opportunities for women were necessarily more limited than for men, the justices argued, and women were not suited for occupations with highly special qualifications and responsibilities. The "paramount destiny and mission of womanhood are to fulfill the noble and benign offices of wife and mother." The views quoted here were representative of the attitudes women met when they attempted to challenge sex-based classifications.

Finally, *Reed v. Reed* (1971) broke from this tradition and engaged in the independent judicial review of a statute that discriminated between persons on the basis of sex, without declaring sex to be a suspect classification. It soon became clear that the Court would no longer treat sex-based classifications with the judicial deference given economic regulations; however, it became equally clear that such classifications are not subject to the "strict scrutiny" given to truly suspect classifications such as those based upon race. For a five year period, the Court struggled with the appropriate standard or review to be applied in sex-based discriminations.

§ 14.16 Gender Classifications: Finding a Test— From *Reed v. Reed* to *Craig v. Boren*

Reed v. Reed (1971) was the first case that offered realistic protection against sex discrimination under the equal protection guarantee. *Reed* involved a challenge to an Idaho statute which established a scheme for the selection of the administrator of an intestate estate. Under the statute eligible persons were grouped into eleven categories by their relationship to the decedent and the categories were ranked in an order which was to be determinative if it was necessary to select between two competing applicants. The challenged portion of the statute provided that if it was necessary to select between two competing applicants in the same category the male was to be preferred over the female. As construed by the Idaho Supreme Court, the statutory preference for males was mandatory and was to be given effect without regard to individual qualifications.

The Supreme Court unanimously held that the arbitrary preference for males could not withstand constitutional attack. The opinion did not find sex classifications to be "suspect" and there was no direct challenge to a legislature's power to classify persons by gender. But the opinion impliedly challenged the power to provide different treatment of persons on the basis of their sex when that was unrelated to the legitimate objective of a statute. "A classification must be reasonable, not arbitrary and must rest upon some ground of difference having a fair and substantial relation to that object of the legislation, so that all persons similarly circumstanced shall be treated alike."

The question thus presented in *Reed* was whether the difference in the sex of the administrator had a rational relationship to some permissible objective of the statute. While the objective of reducing the workload by eliminating one class of contests is not without some legitimacy, the crucial question is whether the preference of males advances that objective in a manner consistent with the command of the equal protection clause. The Court's conclusion was that it did not. "To give a mandatory preference to members of either sex over members of the other, merely to accomplish the elimination of hearings on the merits, is to make the very kind of arbitrary legislative choice forbidden by the Equal Protection Clause of the Fourteenth Amendment; and whatever may be said as to the positive values of avoiding intrafamily controversy, the choice in this context may not lawfully be mandated solely on the basis of sex."

Under the rationality test used in prior cases, the statute could have been found to be related to the administrative convenience. It is easier and less costly for the probate courts to choose administrators if one class of claimants (women) were eliminated. The Court, however, held that the manner by which the objective was accomplished was arbitrary. Clearly the statute was not designed to pick the most competent administrators unless it was based on a theory that women were not as capable as men to administer the estate; the Court's refusal to defer to the use of such an assumption allowed it to find the classification arbitrary. The Court determined that the state's interest in judicial efficiency was less important than the interest of women in equal treatment with respect to the purpose of choosing qualified administrators of decedents' estates.

In the term following *Reed* the Court in *Frontiero v. Richardson* (1973) faced a question concerning the rights of a female member of the uniformed services to claim her spouse as a "dependent" for the purposes of obtaining increased quarters allowances and medical and dental benefits. A serviceman could automatically claim his wife as a dependent without regard to whether she was in fact dependent upon him; a servicewoman had to show her husband was in fact dependent upon her for over half of his support. The question before the Court was whether this difference in treatment constituted a violation of the due process clause of the Fifth Amendment. The Court found it was.

Brennan, in a plurality opinion, stated that sex was a suspect class, finding implicit support in the unanimous decision in *Reed*. Because this opinion was only a plurality, there was no holding that sex is suspect. The Court agreed on a standard in *Craig v. Boren* (1976), which invalidated an Oklahoma law that permitted the sale of 3.2% beer for off-premises consumption to women at age eighteen but required males to be twenty-one. The Court noted that previous cases had established the principle that to withstand constitutional challenge, classifications by gender must serve important governmental objectives and must be substantially related to the achievement of those objectives. A majority of the Justices now had agreed upon a specific definition for the *intermediate* level of review applied in gender discrimination cases.

Indeed, the Court's agreement on a standard of review was much more important than the holding in *Craig*. Under almost any form of realistic judicial review, the classification examined in *Craig* could not withstand analysis. The Court accepted traffic safety as the goal of the legislation, but the statistical evidence could not support a conclusion that the classification reasonably served to achieve that objective. The relationship between traffic safety and the gender classification was too tenuous. While more teenage males were involved in car accidents than females, and that more teenage males were arrested for driving while intoxicated than were teenage females, there was no evidence that would substantiate the claim that a person's sex made him or her more or less likely to become a drunken driver. The classification was based upon a stereotype perception of teenage males and females. It was not *substantially* related to the important state interest in traffic safety.

§ 14.17 Gender Classifications: Decisions Under the Intermediate Standard of Review

Under an intermediate standard of review, the test neither prohibits the use of all sex classifications but invalidates some of them. The Court's decisions sometimes appear to be *ad hoc* based upon Justices' perceptions of the gender classification at issue in each case.

The major emphasis of the post-*Craig* cases has been the elimination of governmental classifications that arbitrarily burden one gender in terms of economic rights. Such laws are almost always viewed as based upon little more than sexual stereotypes. When the government employs a gender classification that does not allocate economic rights, the Court has a difficult time analyzing the constitutionality of that gender classification.

Benign Classifications. Not all laws which allocate economic rights on the basis of gender will be invalid. Those laws that appear to be a reasonable means of compensating women as a class for past economic discrimination will be upheld. Thus, the Court was unanimous in upholding a now superseded provision of the Social Security Act that allowed women to compute their benefits with a more favorable formula relating the past earnings than could be used by men at retirement. *Califano v. Webster* (1977). The Court also upheld a provision of the Act that provided greater secondary benefits for a woman married to a retired wage earner than for divorced spouse of wage earner. *Mathews v. de Castro* (1976). Giving women some preference on a scale for retirement benefits that was keyed to earnings was reasonable because it compensated for the fact that discrimination in the employment market might have kept many women from achieving their highest potential in terms of earnings and contributions to the Social Security System.

Conversely, the Court will strike down laws giving preference to women in the economic area if those laws are not reasonable means of compensating for past discrimination against women as a class. Thus, the Court struck down a provision of the Social Security System that required male, but not female, spouses of deceased wage earners to prove actual dependency in order to receive survivor's benefits. *Califano v. Goldfarb* (1977).

Marital Property—Alimony. *Orr v. Orr* (1979) employed the "substantial-relationship-to-an-important-governmental-interest" standard as it struck down a state law that provided that the state courts could grant alimony payments only from husbands to wives and never from wives to husbands. The majority opinion rejected the permissibility of any goal of the state related to insuring that the husband was allocated primary responsibility for the family. The Court has consistently rejected any state interest in keeping men in a role of primary responsibility in the family.

The majority opinion did note that there were two possible objectives for such laws that might be considered sufficiently important to support a gender based classification: providing help for needy spouses and compensating women for past economic discrimination. However, the law was impermissible because the classification did not substantially promote either important governmental interest. Indeed, the opinion noted that the Court did not have to engage in an analysis that would require it to determine if this sex-based classification was a "sufficiently accurate proxy" for need, or for compensating women as a class for past societal discrimination, because the state system in fact could not promote either purpose.

Alabama, like virtually all other states, required an individualized court hearing at which the parties' financial circumstances were examined before the court entered an alimony order. Because the state required individualized hearings there was no demonstrable need to use the gender based classification as a proxy for need or as compensation for past discrimination. It would cost the state nothing to determine, at that hearing, whether the woman was financially secure and the husband in need of financial support. Because there was no state goal that could not be achieved by applying a sex neutral rule at the hearing, the statutory classification was invalid.

Family Welfare Systems. The Court employed the substantial relationship-important interest test in *Califano v. Westcott* (1979) to invalidate a gender based classification used to allocate benefits to families with dependent children. The Social Security Act system of aid to families with dependent children provided benefits to families with children deprived of parental financial support because of the unemployment of the father only; no benefits were paid when support was lost due to the unemployment of the child's mother. Although the government claimed that there was no "gender bias" in the statute because it always affected a family unit with a male and a female parent and one or more children, the Justices unanimously found that the law discriminated against mothers who in fact were the primary economic providers for their families. The classification was invalid under the equal protection component of the Fifth Amendment because it did not substantially advance the government interests in identifying children in need of support or reducing the unemployed father's incentive to desert his family, which had been encouraged by earlier federal aid programs.

Westcott concluded that the program should be extended to all families where a parent was unemployed. Although the decision as to extension of benefits or termination of the program is a nonconstitutional one, as invalidating the statute also would eliminate the unconstitutional classification, a majority of the Justices concluded that the congressional objective of providing for needy children and families would be best effectuated by extension of benefits in this case.

Worker Dependents' Benefits. *Wengler v. Druggists Mutual Insurance Co.* (1980) invalidated a state worker's compensation law that provided death benefits (upon the work-related death of a spouse) to a widower only if he was mentally or physically incapacitated or could prove actual dependence on his wife's earnings, but automatically granted such benefits to a widow. The Court found that the statute discriminated against both men and women. The Court has consistently used a middle level standard of review in cases where discrimination is said to exist against working women because lesser benefits are granted to their spouses or dependents than are granted to the spouses or dependents of their male counterparts. Justice Stevens, in a concurring opinion, thought that the statute only discriminated against men, but he believed that the statute should still be subjected to the middle level standard of review.

The majority opinion stated that, "[h]owever the discrimination is described in this case, our precedents require that gender-based discriminations must serve important governmental objectives and that the discriminatory means employed must be substantially related to the achievement of those objectives." Providing benefits for needy spouses of deceased workers is an important government objective, but that objective could have been achieved in a non-discriminatory manner by giving benefits only to widows and widowers who could demonstrate need. The state made only a generalized claim of administrative convenience for employing the classification, asserting that it might result in the savings of dollars that could then be used to pay benefits. It "may be that there are levels of administrative convenience that will justify discriminations that are subject to heightened scrutiny under the equal protection clause, but the requisite showing has not been made here by the mere claim that it would be inconvenient to individualize determinations about widows as well as widowers."

It seems difficult to believe that a showing of administrative convenience will ever be found sufficient to support a gender-based discrimination because the state could always be charged with finding some way to determine need as regards beneficiaries and challenged worker's compensation systems and doing so in a manner that would not seriously deplete the resources available for paying benefits under those systems. In *Wengler* the Supreme Court remanded the case to the state supreme court for a determination as to whether the classification should be made equal by granting benefits to all widows and widowers automatically or by requiring proof of dependency or need from all widows and widowers following the work-related death of their spouses.

Property Rights—Control of Marital Property. Laws that allocate property or economic rights on the basis of gender should be invalidated under the intermediate level of review. *Kirchberg v. Feenstra* (1981) invalidated a Louisiana statute that gave a husband, as "head and master" of the family, the unilateral right to dispose of property jointly owned with his wife without her consent. Because neither the state nor the husband who was a party to the case could identify any important state interest that was in fact promoted by such a law, this granting of special rights to men violated the equal protection clause. Louisiana statutes allowed a wife to take steps to protect her property interest and avoid some of the discriminatory impact of the statute, but this fact could not save the gender-based classification because the degree of burden placed upon women is irrelevant when the sex-based classification fails to serve any important governmental objective.

Parental Rights—Illegitimacy Cases. The Court has had a great deal of difficulty in analyzing the constitutionality of a sex classification when the classification at issue does not allocate property or economic rights. While the Court in these cases also applies the "substantial-relationship-to-an-important-interest" test, the outcomes of the cases vary with the judicial assessment of the asserted governmental interests.

In two cases that involved combined gender and illegitimacy classifications the Court applied this standard in differentiating between the rights and duties of fathers and mothers of illegitimate children. *Caban v. Mohammed* (1979) invalidated a state law that granted a veto power over the adoption of such children to all mothers but no fathers because the state failed to show that such discrimination was necessary to achieve important interests in the facilitation of adoptions of illegitimates. But in *Parham v. Hughes* (1979), a 5 to 4 decision with no majority opinion, the Court allowed the state to deny the father (but not a mother) the right to sue for the wrongful death of his illegitimate child if the father had failed to acknowledge the child during its life. The state's the interest in determining paternity before the death of the child, as well as encouraging fathers to legitimate their children, supported the distinction. In a related illegitimacy case the Court upheld the exclusion of illegitimates from the intestate estates of their decedent fathers if they failed to get a judicial order of paternity before the death of the father. The difference in the difficulty of proving paternity, as opposed to maternity, justified the state's desire to have such suits settled before the death of the father. *Lalli v. Lalli* (1978).

Combined Illegitimacy and Gender Classifications in Immigration and Naturalization Laws. *Fiallo v. Bell* (1977) upheld federal statutes that granted an immigration preference to the illegitimate children of foreign national women who were lawfully living in the United States that was denied to the children of a foreign national father who was lawfully living in the United States. Under the immigration laws in force at the time of the *Fiallo* litigation, any permanent lawful resident parent could bring her or his legitimate child, who resided in another country, to the United States without that child being subject to certain immigration quotas. A permanent lawful resident foreign national woman was also allowed to have her illegitimate child come to the United States without being subject to immigration quotas. However, a lawfully resident foreign national father could not bring his child to the United States unless the child's admission fit within the quota limits for immigrants from the country where the illegitimate child resided.

The majority in *Fiallo* did not examine the government's use of a gender basis separately from its use of the illegitimacy basis for this classification in this immigration preference law. Rather, it simply stated that the Supreme Court traditionally had given great deference to Congressional decisions concerning immigration and that the Justices were "no more inclined to reconsider this line of cases" than they had been in prior years.

Fiallo concluded that the statute's use of a combined illegitimacy and gender classification was related to the government interest in avoiding fraud, because a foreign national father in the United States might be able to easily fraudulently claim that many children were his illegitimate children so that they could avoid United States Immigration preferences. However Justice Powell was unclear concerning which standard of review should be applied to gender classifications in immigration and naturalization laws.

The Court's lack of clarity might be attributable to several reasons. First, the Court, throughout our history, has given great deference to Congress in immigration naturalization laws. Second, the intermediate standard of review had been adopted only one year prior to the *Fiallo* case, and the Justices may have been unwilling to explore the meaning of the intermediate standard for the first time in an immigration setting. Third, the Court had not adopted a clear standard of review for illegitimacy classifications in 1977. Despite all of the ways in which we can recast *Fiallo* in terms of modern equal protection standards, the *Fiallo* majority opinion seems to reject all basis for independent review of illegitimacy and gender classifications in immigration laws. The majority's refusal to subject the law to any meaningful form of judicial review was challenged only by Justices Marshall, Brennan, and White, who dissented in *Fiallo*.

Miller v. Albright (1998), without a majority opinion, avoided ruling on the constitutionality of a gender classification in a naturalization statute, while the Justices upheld the use of the illegitimacy trait for establishing classification. Under the federal law, an illegitimate child born to an unmarried American citizen *female* outside the country received citizenship at birth so long as the mother had one year of continuous residence in the United States. A child born out of wedlock to a U.S. citizen *father* and a non-citizen woman outside of the country would receive citizenship that related back to the date of birth if, but only if, the father had resided in the United States for at least 2 years after the age of 14 and if the father took several steps to acknowledge the child's eighteenth birthday.

Miller involved a woman who was born in the Philippines to a non-U.S. citizen mother; she did not receive the acknowledgment of her father until after she was 18 years old. Because Ms. Miller had not been "acknowledged" by her father prior to the time she was 18, the Secretary of State refused her citizenship request. Ms. Miller claimed that the distinction between illegitimate children born to a U.S. citizen mother, and those with a U.S. citizen father denied violated the equal protection principle of the due process clause of the Fifth Amendment.

In *Miller v. Albright*, seven Justices believed that Ms. Miller could raise the issue of discrimination against U.S. citizen fathers, as opposed to U.S. citizen mothers, as well as discrimination against a certain classification of illegitimate children, to which she belonged (the class of children whose fathers were U.S. citizens and who had not received acknowledgment prior to their 18th birthday). Five Justices considered the constitutionality of the gender classification in a meaningful way; three of these five voted to invalidate the statutory distinction between illegitimate children born to United States citizen mothers and those born to United States citizen fathers. Nevertheless, *Miller* did not invalidate the classification in the naturalization law because of the division of the Justices' votes on both jurisdictional issues and equal protection claims.

Miller turned on the votes of four Justices who refused to give independent judicial review to Ms. Miller's gender discrimination claim. Two of these Justices, Scalia and Thomas, refused to review of the classifications in the naturalization law because they believed that the Court had no power to invalidate a portion of a naturalization law to give United States citizenship to any person who did not completely fulfill the requirements created by Congress.

Tuan Anh Nguyen v. Immigration and Naturalization Service (2001) involved a citizenship question that arose during deportation proceedings. In 1969, Joseph Boulais, who was a United States citizen working in Vietnam for a private corporation, fathered a child with a woman who was a Vietnamese citizen. In 1975, Mr.

Boulais brought the child, Tuan Anh Nguyen, to the United States. Mr. Boulais did not technically legitimate the child, acknowledge his paternity in writing and under oath, or establish paternity through the ruling of a competent court before the child was 18. When Nguyen was 22, he was convicted, based on a guilty plea, of two crimes that would have made him deportable. It was not until Nguyen's appeal of a deportation order that Mr. Boulais obtained a DNA test showing that Nguyen was his child; he then received a state court order establishing paternity. Because these actions were not completed until Nguyen was 28 years old, Nguyen did not have citizenship under the terms of the federal statutes.

In other words, the statutory system granted immediate citizenship to the child of a U.S. citizen woman who gave birth to a child outside of the United States and who was not married, so long as the woman and the child met certain requirements concerning residency in the United States. Nguyen would have been a citizen of the United States if his one U.S. citizen parent had been a female. Mr. Boulais and Mr. Nguyen both appealed from a ruling of the Board of Immigration Appeals that rejected Nguyen's claim to United States citizenship.

Five Justices in *Tuan Anh Nguyen* ruled that the sex classification in the statute did not violate the equal protection guarantee of the Fifth Amendment due process clause. Justice Kennedy's majority opinion stated that the Court was using the intermediate protection standard that had been used in other gender classification cases, and was requiring the government classification to be substantially related to important governmental interests. Therefore, according to Justice Kennedy, the Court did not have to consider either whether Congress should be given special deference regarding immigration and naturalization classifications, or whether a court could have granted citizenship to someone who did not meet the statutory standards, if those standards were invalidated. Justice Kennedy's opinion asserted that the majority had applied the identical intermediate standard of review used in all other gender classification cases during the past quarter century.

The sex classification in the naturalization statute was substantially related to two important government interests. First, Justice Kennedy found that the law was tailored to "assuring that a biological parent-child relationship exists." According to the majority, the United States citizen mother status of a child for immigration and naturalization purposes would be easily verifiable at birth, whereas other standards would be needed to determine that the alleged U.S. citizen father who claimed eligibility for citizenship was in fact the parent of the child.

The persons challenging the law had claimed that the law was not substantially related to that interest because other means, such as DNA testing, could establish paternity as easily, and with greater certainty, than the statutory legitimization or affirmation requirements. Kennedy rejected that argument. Justice Kennedy stated that the Constitution did not require Congress to choose one particular method for requiring fathers to establish paternity and that such requirements would not solve any gender classification problems because the paternity tests would still only be required of one gender.

The Court concluded that the need to assure the biological relationship would result in Congress at least requiring fathers, but not mothers, of children to take DNA tests, and that a gender classification would necessarily appear in the statutory system. The "use of gender-specific terms takes into account a biological difference between the parents. The differential treatment is inherent in a sensible statutory scheme, given the unique relationship of the mother to the event of birth."

Kennedy also said that the government had an important interest in ensuring that the United States citizen parent and the child born out of wedlock in another country had the opportunity to have a meaningful relationship before the child was an adult. The majority opinion admitted that the statutory scheme making the father take certain steps before the child was 18 or 21 would not guarantee that the United States citizen father would in fact establish a personal relationship with the child. According to the majority, however, the law was sufficiently tailored to that end so it survived the substantial relationship to an important interest standard.

The cases involving combined illegitimacy and gender classifications in immigration and naturalization laws should not be seen as or changing the intermediate standard of review used under the equal protection guarantee of the Fifth Amendment that is normally used to review gender or illegitimacy classifications in federal statutes or regulations. Although *Tuan Anh Nguyen* claimed that it was using the "conventional" standard, Justice Kennedy was writing for a majority, rather than a plurality, of Justices only because he obtained the votes of Justices Scalia and Thomas, who clearly stated their view that "the Court lacks power to provide relief of the sort requested in this suit—namely conferral of citizenship on a basis other than that prescribed by Congress." In cases involving sex discrimination in areas other than immigration and naturalization laws, Kennedy and Stevens have voted to require the government to demonstrate with an exceedingly persuasive justification when the government asserted that a gender-based classification in fact was substantially related to an important governmental interest. It appears that the Court in fact was applying a very deferential standard of review in these immigration and naturalization cases, rather than applying an intermediate equal protection standard that would have required independent judicial review of congressional judgments in this area.

Statutory Rape. *Michael M. v. Superior Court* (1981), without a majority opinion, upheld California's "statutory rape" law which defined as unlawful sexual intercourse "an act of sexual intercourse accomplished with a female not the wife of a perpetrator, where the female is under the age of 18 years." Although the statute provided only for the punishment of males who engaged in sexual intercourse with minor females and not for females who engaged in sexual activity with minor males, the Court did not overturn the statute.

Justice Rehnquist, writing for four members of the Court, found that the state had an important interest in preventing illegitimate pregnancies and that the gender-based classification was sufficiently related to that end "[b]ecause virtually all of the significant harmful and inescapably identifiable consequences of teenage pregnancy fall on the young female."

Justice Stewart, in a concurring opinion, noted that there was a variety of statutes in California which made unlawful various types of sexual activity with both males and females below specified ages; the statutory rape law was merely the imposition of an additional sanction which promoted the state's interest in avoiding illegitimate teenage pregnancies and the unique harm caused by them to young females.

Justice Blackmun, concurring in the judgment, applied the substantial relationship-important state interest test. He believed that the law was valid because it substantially promoted the interest in the avoidance of illegitimate teenage pregnancies.

Justice Brennan, in a dissent joined by White and Marshall, believed that the Court had either not applied or misapplied the intermediate standard of review.

Military Service—The Selective Service Case. The Supreme Court upheld the constitutionality of the military selective service act, which exempted women from the draft registration process, in *Rostker v. Goldberg* (1981). The majority opinion stated that the Court should accord Congress great deference when reviewing laws having to do with the establishment or regulation of the military, but went on to find that the gender-based classification would survive scrutiny under the substantial relationship-important interest test.

The majority ruled "the government's interest in raising and supporting armies" was an important governmental interest. The majority opinion found that Congress could conclude that men and women, because of the combat restrictions on women, were not similarly situated for purposes of a draft or registration for a draft. For this reason the congressional decision to authorize only the registration of men did not violate the equal protection component of the Fifth Amendment due process clause. The majority found that "the exemption of women from registration is not only sufficiently but closely related to Congress' purpose in authorizing registration."

Educational Programs. The uncertain meaning of the intermediate standard of review employed in gender discrimination cases was demonstrated in *Mississippi University for Women v. Hogan* (1982). Mr. Hogan was a registered nurse in Mississippi who did not hold a baccalaureate degree in nursing. He applied for admission to the Mississippi University for Women [MUW] School of Nursing, which offered a four-year baccalaureate program in nursing and a graduate program. Although Mr. Hogan was otherwise qualified for admission, the state school denied him admission solely because of his sex. Mississippi statutes, which included the charter of the university, limited the enrollment at Mississippi University for Women to women. The Court invalidated the exclusion of males from the state nursing school. Indeed, the majority opinion left open the question of whether the Mississippi University for Women could deny admission to men because of their sex to schools within the university other than the school of nursing.

Mississippi University for Women said: "That this statute discriminates against males rather than against females does not exempt it from scrutiny or reduce the standard of review." Mississippi justified the single sex admissions policy on the basis that it compensated for discrimination against women. However, the fact that women were not under-represented in the field of nursing undercut the reasonableness of the state's argument. Indeed, "rather than compensate for discriminatory barriers faced by women, MUW's policy of excluding males from admission to the school of nursing tends to perpetuate the stereotyped view of nursing as an exclusively woman's job."

The majority was unwilling to take a broad position against the dispensation of educational benefits by gender. Justice O'Connor's opinion, in a footnote, stated: "we decline to address the question of whether MUW's admissions policy, as applied to males seeking admission to schools other than the school of nursing, violates the Fourteenth Amendment." It might be that one or more Justices in the five member majority would view the limiting of admissions to other schools in the university, or other types of state supported schools, to one gender as being a permissible means of compensating for past discrimination against persons of one gender or to achieve some other asserted governmental interest in the education process.

Four Justices dissented in *Mississippi University for Women*. They believed that the fact that the state offered some coeducational nursing programs at other state schools justified limiting this nursing program or that the entire university to a single gender.

Fourteen years later, in *United States v. Virginia* (1996), the Court held that a male-only state college [the Virginia Military Institute] violated the equal protection clause when it excluded females. Justice Ginsburg wrote a majority opinion for six of the seven Justices. Chief Justice Rehnquist concurred only in the judgment of the Court. Justice Scalia dissented in the V.M.I. case. Justice Thomas did not participate in the case.

Justice Ginsburg's opinion in the V.M.I. case acknowledged that the Court had not yet equated gender classifications "for all purposes, to classifications based on race or national origin." However, Virginia had failed to meet the intermediate standard of review, which required invalidation of a law unless the government could demonstrate that the gender classification was substantially related to an important interest. Because the state case was unable to meet the intermediate standard in the V.M.I. case, the majority did not have to address the question of whether gender classifications in education should be reviewed with strict judicial scrutiny, and invalidated if they were not narrowly tailored to a compelling interest.

Some language in Justice Ginsburg's majority opinion made the intermediate standard seem more difficult for the government to meet than it had been in the 1970s and 80s. The majority opinion stated:

> "To summarize the Court's current directions for cases of official classification based on gender: focusing on the differential treatment or denial of opportunity for which relief is sought, the reviewing Court must determine whether the proffered justification is exceedingly persuasive. The burden of justification is demanding and it rests entirely on the state ... the state must show at least that the [challenged] classification serves important governmental objectives and that the discriminatory means employed are substantially related to those objectives.... The justification must be genuine, not hypothesized or invented *post hoc* in response to litigation. And it must not rely on overbroad generalizations about the different talents, capacities, or preferences of males and females."

The intermediate standard of review allows judges to engage in a bit of ad hoc decision-making. The Justices must make a case-by-case evaluation of the evidence that the government has presented in its attempt to demonstrate that there is a distinction between males and females that is not based on stereotypes and that substantially relates to an important governmental interest. Ginsburg's opinion in the V.M.I. case is instructive concerning the government's burden of proof and the types of justifications that can be used by governmental entity in a gender classification case. Her opinion described the government's burden in a gender classification case in the following terms:

"The heightened review standard our precedent establishes does not make sex a proscribed classification. Suppose inherent differences are no longer accepted as a ground for race or national original classifications.... Physical differences between men and women, however, are enduring ... Inherent differences between men and women are enduring: the two sexes are not fungible.... [gender classification based on alleged differences between men and women may not be used] for denigration of the members of either sex or for artificial constraints on an individual's opportunity. Sex classifications may be used to compensate women for particular economic disabilities ... [and] to advance full development of the talent and capacities of our Nation's people. But such classifications may not be used ... to create or perpetuate the legal, social, and economic inferiority of women."

This portion of Ginsburg's opinion indicates that any governmental entity will have a difficult burden in demonstrating that a gender classification is based upon real differences between men and women rather than stereotypes or traditions. The history of discrimination against women in our society may provide a constitutionally sufficient basis for benign (or so-called affirmative action) classifications that aid women. A benign gender classification would have to be tailored to remedying past social or governmental discrimination against women in order to be upheld as being substantially related to an important interest.

As an alternative to admitting female students to the Virginia Military Institute, the State of Virginia sought to provide specialized "leadership" education for women by creating, and paying for, the "Virginia Women's Institute for Leadership," an educational program that would be provided at a private college for women. Six of the seven Justices voting on the V.M.I. case found that this alternative educational program did not give female students the same types of education and career advantages that the Virginia Military Institute provided for male students.

Justice Scalia, the sole dissenter in the V.M.I. case, believed that the majority opinion had altered the intermediate standard by making it extremely difficult for the government to provide exceedingly persuasive proof that might justify gender classification. However, most of his dissent attacked the Court's interference with what Scalia believed are educational and social policies that should be within the discretion of state and local governments. Scalia asserted that there was no basis for the creation of the principles in the majority opinion that would make it impossible for states to have single sex schools and impossible for states to provide any type of significant financial or tangible aid to single sex schools.

The Supreme Court has not yet ruled on whether any governmental entity might provide some type of "separate but equal" elementary or high school courses for male and female students. Perhaps the Court might allow single-sex elementary or high schools, or some one sex courses in elementary or high schools. Then, one would expect that the Court will have to travel the road of an earlier era, when it tried to determine if the separate schools are "separate but equal." Ginsburg's majority opinion leaves that question open, although her opinion will make it difficult for the government to meet its burden of proof even under the intermediate standard. After the V.M.I. case, a government entity attempting to provide one sex schools at the grade school, high school or college level will have to provide an "exceedingly pervasive justification" for the separate but equal educational program. It will be the government's burden to prove that its one sex educational program is substantially related to an important educational interest. Such a burden will be difficult, if not impossible, for the government to meet.

Conclusion. The Court's adoption of the "substantial-relationship-to-an-important-governmental-interest" standard has settled, at least formally, the issue of the proper definition of a middle level standard of review for gender classifications. However, that standard of review is hardly a litmus test. Yet, the test does make some cases easy ones. For example, it is easy to predict the result in *J.E.B. v. Alabama ex rel. T.B.* (1994), which held that the intentional use of peremptory challenges to exclude men from a jury violate the equal protection clause.

§ 14.18　Gender Classifications: Pregnancy Classifications and Irrebuttable Presumptions

Cleveland Board of Education v. LaFleur (1974) ruled that mandatory maternity leaves for teachers violated due process. Under the Cleveland rule, a pregnant teacher had to take a maternity leave beginning five months before the expected birth of her child and could not return without a doctor's certificate of physical fitness or until the semester which began after her child had reached the age of three months. A Virginia rule, which was challenged in a companion case, required a woman to leave four months before the expected birth, but guaranteed her re-employment the first day of the school year after she had received a doctor's certificate of physical fitness and could assure the school that child care would not interfere with her teaching.

The mandatory maternity leave provisions involved in these cases placed a heavy burden on a woman's exercise of her freedom of personal choice in matters of marriage and family life, a fundamental right. The question was whether there was a state interest sufficient to justify the rules. The firm cut-off dates were claimed to be necessary to maintain the continuity of classroom instruction.

The Court assumed arguendo that some pregnant teachers became unfit to teach during the latter stages of pregnancy. However, this rationale could not justify the "irrebuttable" presumption that every pregnant teacher reaching the fifth or sixth month of pregnancy was physically incapable of teaching. Later, the Court retreated from deciding such cases on supposedly procedural grounds of "irrebuttable" presumptions. All laws classify to some extent. Any law that draws a line (one has to be 21 years old to drink alcohol) can be recast as an "irrebuttable" presumption. The law simply draws a line and the real issue is whether that line violates equal protection. This case is still good law, but the rationale nowadays would be that the law violates equal protection.

Not all laws that make distinctions on pregnancy violate equal protection. That same year, *Geduldig v. Aiello* (1974) rejected the claim that a California disability insurance system that covered all disabilities of a prescribed duration subject to various exceptions was unconstitutional. One of these exceptions excluded disabilities from normal pregnancies. That exclusion did not violate equal protection. The Court said that the program might rightfully exclude some risks and the exclusion of pregnancy served a legitimate interest in keeping costs low. The majority rejected the contention that this exclusion was a sex-based classification, stating there was no evidence that the selection of risks that were covered harmed any definable group "in terms of the aggregate risk derived by that group or class from the program." There were no risks from which men were protected that women were not and vice versa.

Justices Brennan, Marshall, and Douglas dissented. The program paid for disabilities regardless of whether they were costly, voluntary, as with cosmetic surgery, unique to one sex such as prostatectomy or hemophilia, or statistically more likely to occur to one race, such as sickle-cell anemia, or the result of a preexisting condition. Despite this otherwise broad coverage, the program denied compensation for disabilities suffered in connection with "normal pregnancy", disabilities unique to women. Women suffering such disabilities had equivalent medical and economic needs as persons suffering from disabilities covered by the program. The dissent therefore would have found that the sex-based discrimination violated the equal protection clause.

General Electric Co. v. Gilbert (1976) rejected a suit attacking a similar provision under Title VII. Relying on *Geduldig,* the Court held that excluding pregnancy from a disability benefits plan providing general coverage is not a sex-based distinction. Congress later amended Title VII so that discriminatory treatment of employees on the basis of pregnancy is now prohibited by statute.

§ 14.19   Classifications Based on Wealth

One can describe the constitutional protection for classifications burdening poor persons, sometimes called wealth classifications, as nothing more than the protection that the Court gives to any other classification of persons or business entities that are based on criterion that are not suspect. The Court will uphold legislative actions that burden poor persons as a class under the equal protection or due process guarantee if the actions have any rational relationship to a legitimate end of government. So long as these laws do not involve the allocation of fundamental rights (a topic considered later in this chapter) the Court will treat them the way it treats economic and social welfare policy. In other words, unless the classification is truly irrational, the Court does not invalidate the legislative classifications.

Classifications based on wealth and poverty do not merit active judicial review under the strict scrutiny-compelling interest standard. However, the Court will actively review classifications that burden the exercise of fundamental rights (e.g., voting) when such classifications are based upon wealth.

The Supreme Court has consistently held that the government is not permitted to restrict the ability to engage in fundamental constitutional rights on the basis of individual wealth. However, the Court has held that the state need not subsidize the financing of abortions for women who lack the economic resources to obtain an abortion during the first two trimesters of their pregnancy. E.g., *Maher v. Roe* (1977). This distinction is based upon the Court's view that the right to privacy concerning abortions involves only the absence of express governmental limitations on the abortion decision and that the failure to subsidize these practices constitutes no more than a policy choice not to give increased wealth or welfare benefits to a class of people who are not described by any suspect trait.

In a series of decisions in the 1960's concerning rights to fair treatment in the criminal process, *Douglas v. California* (1963), voting rights, *Harper v. Virginia State Board of Elections* (1966), and interstate travel, *Shapiro v. Thompson* (1969), the Court had indicated that classifications that burden the poor are reviewed under an increased standard of review as suspect classifications. However, the Court only grants this heightened review when it deals with a law that combines discrimination based on poverty *and* a fundamental right such as voting.

For example, *Dandridge v. Williams* (1970) upheld a statute that set a formula for the provision of aid to families with dependent children that, in effect, did not offer any benefits for children born to families over a certain size. Because the Court has never recognized the interest of an individual in government subsistence benefits as a fundamental constitutional interest, there was no fundamental right present in this case. The majority opinion then upheld the law under a rational relationship test, finding an arguable basis for relating the classification to the state interest in economy and the provision of certain families.

The Court has consistently followed this position, holding that there is no basis for using any form of strict scrutiny, or increased standard of review, to test legislation that burdens classifications of poor persons in the receipt of other forms of welfare benefits, public housing, or access to the judicial process when no fundamental right is involved.

A leading case is *San Antonio Independent School District v. Rodriguez* (1973), which upheld the constitutionality of a property tax system that financed primary and secondary education in school districts in a manner that created large differences in the amount of money spent on the education of individual children. The Court found nothing in the allocation of educational opportunities based on the wealth of the district in which a child resided that furnished a constitutionally cognizable basis for close judicial supervision of legislative policies in this area. In so doing the opinion noted that in no case had the Court ever engaged in an active standard of review solely because the law burdened poor persons in the allocation of benefits which could not be deemed to be fundamental constitutional rights.

The rule is different if the government uses poverty in its classification of a fundamental right. Thus, *Harper v. Virginia State Board of Elections* (1966) held that the government cannot restrict assess to the ballot by imposing any form of voter tax or poll tax. The right of an individual to stand for elective office is also part of that fundamental right. The state may impose filing fees on candidates who can afford to pay them, for this is a reasonable means of determining which candidates are seriously interested in running for office, but the same filing fees cannot be applied to a person without the funds to pay them. *Lubin v. Panish* (1974). Similarly the state cannot establish residency requirements for government benefits it that would penalize the right to interstate travel for poor persons. *Shapiro v. Thompson* (1969). If access to the courts is necessary to protect one of these fundamental rights, the process may not bar litigants because of their inability to pay filing fees. *Boddie v. Connecticut* (1971).

The issue in fundamental rights cases is whether the individual statute constitutes a limitation of the fundamental right that violates the Constitution and not whether it is fair or unfair to poor persons.

§ 14.20   The Right to Privacy: Introduction

The "right to privacy" has varied meanings. In the common law of torts, the right encompasses a freedom from intrusion by others into privately owned areas as well as freedom from disclosures of information about an individual's private life. The phrase also has several meanings in terms of constitutional analysis. The oldest constitutional right to privacy is the Fourth Amendment's restriction on governmental searches and seizures. The First Amendment also protects some rights to privacy in speech or association. The Court has also confronted the tort right to privacy in determining when suit may be brought against a person whose speech has invaded the privacy of another.

But in terms of due process and equal protection the "right to privacy" has come to mean a right to engage in certain highly personal activities. More specifically, it currently relates to certain rights of freedom of choice in marital, sexual, and reproductive matters. Even this definition may be too broad, for the Court still has not recognized any general right to engage in sexual activities that are done in private. Instead, the Justices have acknowledged the existence of a "right" and defined it by very specific application to laws relating to reproduction, contraception, abortion, and marriage.

This general constitutional right to privacy may have had its inception in an influential article Samuel Warren and Louis D. Brandeis wrote in 1890, *The Right of Privacy*, 4 Harvard Law Review 193 (1890). The article attacked intrusions by newspapers into the private affairs of individuals and advocated the protection of the "inviolate personality" of each person. In contemporary terms Warren and Brandeis were advocating protection, under the law of torts, for dissemination or use of facts relating to an individual's private life. They did not consider the problem of government intrusion into sexual autonomy or the "inviolate personality" of each individual, but they did help to establish recognition in American legal thought that each person had a cognizable legal interest in a private life, both physical and emotional.

Later, as a Justice of the Supreme Court, Brandeis advocated a wide reading of the Fourth Amendment in order to insure that government did not intrude into the "privacy of the individual." Justice Brandeis did not foresee the issue of government restrictions or decision-making in private matters, he laid the basis for the modern right when he recognized a right to protection of one's private life from government intrusion or "the right to be let alone—the most comprehensive of rights and the right most valued by civilized man." *Olmstead v. United States*, (1928) (Brandeis, J., dissenting).

§ 14.21 Sterilization and Contraception

The development of the contemporary concept of a constitutionally protected "right of privacy" in sexual matters can be traced to the Supreme Court's decision in *Skinner v. Oklahoma* (1942). This case used the equal protection clause to invalidate a statute that authorized the sterilization of persons previously convicted and sentenced to imprisonment two or more times of crimes "amounting of felonies of moral turpitude" in the state. The statute did not apply to persons convicted of "offenses arising out of the violation of the prohibitory laws, revenue acts, embezzlement, or political offenses." A person was subjected to sterilization only if her or his crimes were classified (perhaps arbitrarily) as ones involving moral turpitude. Under this system a person convicted three times of larceny could be subjected to sterilization while the embezzler was free from sterilization no matter how often he committed the crime or how large the sum of money appropriated.

The Court did not "stop to point out all the inequities of the Act," but instead rested the decision upon the artificiality of the distinction drawn between larceny and embezzlement, crimes of intrinsically the same nature. Despite the broad police powers of the state, this classification violated the equal protection clause because it could not withstand the scrutiny to which the fundamental nature of the right involved demanded it be subjected. The Court noted that the Act dealt with "one of the basic civil rights of man. ... Marriage and procreation [were] fundamental to the very existence and survival of the race." This fact required strict scrutiny of the classification for "[w]hen the law [laid] an unequal hand on those who [had] committed intrinsically the same quality of offense and sterilize[d] one and not the other, it [made] as invidious a discrimination as if it had selected a particular race or nationality for oppressive treatment." In this way the Court went beyond traditional rational relationship standard of review.

This rationale first, established the basis for "fundamental rights" analysis under the due process and equal protection guarantees by finding that some rights deserved special judicial protection from the majoritarian process. Second, while the opinion never mentioned a "right of privacy" relating to sexual matters, it announced that interests in marriage or procreation as ones of special constitutional significance.

The Supreme Court, oddly enough, has not ruled that involuntary sterilization is *per se* unconstitutional. *Skinner* was an equal protection ruling where the Court held that classifications of persons who were sterilized would be subjected to strict scrutiny. This holding therefore does not establish a constitutional prohibition of all such statutes. Previously, *Buck v. Bell* (1927) had upheld a sterilization statute. In that case, Justice Holmes spoke for the Court, and said that the legislature was the branch of government most suited to defining the necessity of these procedures. It is doubtful that the Supreme Court would follow *Buck v. Bell* today, although Justice Blackmun, speaking for the Court, cited it with apparent approval in *Roe v. Wade* (1973). However, if the Court finds no compelling interest to justify the prohibition of abortions, any state interest in sterilization should similarly be found wanting.

Justice Harlan, in his dissent in *Poe v. Ullman* (1961) also focused on a right to privacy. *Poe* was a case involving birth control. The majority did not reach the merits because it found no justiciable controversy. Harlan dissented on this issue and then argued that the statute that restricted married persons from using birth control devices violated the due process clause because the regulation invaded marital "privacy." In his opinion, he explained that the statute intruded upon "the most intimate details of the marital relation" and prosecution under the statutes would require disclosure of those relationships.

Later, *Griswold v. Connecticut* (1965) held the same Connecticut statutes invalid because they restricted the right of married persons to use contraceptive devices. The appellants in this case, a doctor and executive of the Planned Parenthood League, were convicted for giving information and medical advice to married persons concerning means of preventing conception.

Justice Douglas, speaking for the Court, found that the statute impermissibly limited the right of privacy of married persons. The law violated the due process clause because it deprived these married persons of the liberty protected by this fundamental right.

There was some confusion caused by Douglas' attempt to find a specific textual basis for a "right of privacy" that would include the right of married persons to use contraceptives, but it should be realized that this confusion was not the sole fault of the Douglas opinion, for the Court continued to formally reject the substantive due process decisions of the first part of the century.

Douglas repudiated *Lochner v. New York* (1905) and emphasized that the Court "did not sit as a super-legislature." It was too close—in terms of decisional, if not calendar, time—to the period of substantive due process for the Court to protect some individual rights against government intrusion in much the same manner as the Court had done in *Lochner*. Douglas argued that the "penumbras" and "emanations" of several guarantees of the Bill of Rights established this right to privacy.

It is fair to say that *Griswold* created the modern right of privacy The Connecticut legislature banned the use of contraceptives by married persons, which contravened the established values of privacy in three ways: (1) it regulated a personal marital relationship without an identifiable, legitimate reason; (2) it gave government the right to inquire into these private marital relationships; (3) prosecution under the statutes would often require husbands and wives to testify to the intimate details of their relationship.

Separate concurring opinions articulated other reasons for judicial protection of these privacy values against legislative or executive actions. Justice Goldberg took the position that it was the function of the Court to defend certain fundamental rights under the due process clause even though these rights were not expressed in the first eight Amendments. Goldberg was of the opinion that the Ninth Amendment evinced the historic belief that certain fundamental rights could not be restricted by the government even though it did not create specific rights. The Court should look to the "tradition and [collective] conscience of our people" to determine if a right was fundamental and one which should be judicially protected from infringement by other branches of government. "Marital privacy" was such a right because there were clear historic values in freedom of choice in marital relationships. Justice Goldberg argued that if a law required husband and wives to be sterilized after having two children, any Justice would have held it unconstitutional absent the most compelling justification regardless of the "implied" nature of the guarantee.

Justice Harlan concurred in the decision, also finding that the due process clause protected fundamental liberties that were not expressed in the Bill of Rights. Like his dissent in *Poe v. Ullman* (1961) he found that marital privacy was a basic part of the liberty "protected by the Fourteenth Amendment." Harlan argued that it was the role of the Justices to decide when legislation violated "basic values 'implicit in the concept of ordered liberty.' "

Justice White's concurrence argued that no legitimate end of government could support this law. The state claimed that the statute was to deter illicit sexual relationships but there was no likelihood that a ban on contraceptives for married persons would promote that end.

Justices Black and Stewart dissented in *Griswold*. They could find no basis for judicial protection of a right to privacy, and they objected to the Court following in the steps of the substantive economic due process decisions by enforcing values that had no textual basis in the Constitution. By the time of abortion cases in 1973, Justice Stewart had come to accept this decision as a permissible use of substantive due process theories.

Later, *Eisenstadt v. Baird* (1972) invalidated a statute that prohibited distributing contraceptives to unmarried persons on the grounds that this separate treatment of unmarried persons violated the equal protection clause. *Eisenstadt* did not explicitly rely on the fundamental rights-strict scrutiny analysis. Instead, it simply said that there was no rational or legitimate way for the legislature to distinguish between contraceptives used by married or unmarried persons.

While the majority opinion, by Justice Brennan, purported to apply only the traditional equal protection standard of review, the majority clearly employed some form of independent judicial scrutiny. After *Griswold* and *Eisenstadt,* it was clear that states may not prohibit adults from using contraceptives because the state simply objects to contraceptive use. However, the states should be able to restrict the manufacture and sale of contraceptive devices to insure that the products meet health and safety standards. Yet, mere assertion of police power ends will not justify limitation of the right to privacy.

Carey v. Population Services International (1977) invalidated a law that allowed only pharmacists to sell nonmedical contraceptive devices to persons over 16 years of age and prohibited the sale of such items to those under 16. As to the general restriction, a majority agreed that the burden on an adult's freedom of choice could only be justified by a compelling interest and distribution only through pharmacists did not advance such an end. The Court struck the restriction on children without a majority opinion.

Writing for four members of the Court, Brennan implied that even young persons have some rights to freedom of choice in these matters. The other three Justices voting to strike the law wanted to avoid any implication of a right of minors to engage in sexual activity. They would allow a law to prohibit sexual activity but seemed to conclude that the state could not enforce this restriction by requiring them to bear the risk pregnancy and disease. Thus when these three are combined with the two dissenting Justices, a majority would allow statutes that regulate the sexual activity of minors but not allow the state to enforce those laws by forcing the minors to bear children.

Lawrence v. Texas (2003) later held that a state law prohibiting sodomy between persons of the same sex violated the due process clause, because it would not further a legitimate interest of government that would justify a severe intrusion into an area of personal privacy. *Lawrence v. Texas* (2003), overruled *Bowers v. Hardwick* (1986).

§ 14.22 Marriage, Family Relationships, and Sexual Activity as a Part of the Right to Privacy

A case of special significance in establishing marriage as a fundamental right is *Loving v. Virginia* (1967), which invalidated a statute prohibiting interracial marriage. The Court said that the law violated equal protection because it rested solely upon distinctions drawn according to race. The Court went on to say that the law also denied due process, for it deprived each individual of significant freedom of choosing whom to marry. Because the Court said marriage is a fundamental right, the state could not restrict the right to marry for less than compelling reasons.

Later, the Court held that it was unconstitutional to deny a person access to appellate review of a trial court decision permanently terminating her parental right simply because she could not afford to pay for a transcript of the trial court record. *M.L.B. v. S.L.J.* (1996). The ex-husband sought to terminate his former wife's relationship to the children so that those children could be adopted by his new wife. The ex-husband won in the trial court. The biological mother of the children could not appeal solely because she could not pay for record preparation fees *M.L.B.* the Supreme Court held that using the state rule to prohibit the mother's appeal violated both due process and equal protection.

Yet *Califano v. Jobst* (1977) upheld provisions of the Social Security Act that terminated the benefits of a disabled person who had received benefits as a disabled dependent child of a deceased wage earner—this person lost benefits when he or she married someone who was not receiving Social Security benefits. The Court upheld the law, which denied money to those disabled children who married other persons entitled to benefits under the Social Security Act. Justice Stevens, for a unanimous Court, held that the traditional rational relationship test applied because the law was not based on "stereotyped generalization about a traditionally disadvantaged group, or as an attempt to interfere with the individual's freedom to make a decision as important as marriage."

It was, in short, not irrational for Congress to terminate secondary benefits for the disabled children of deceased social security wage earners when those children married, even if termination created financial hardship for these persons. Congress sought to alleviate the hardship on some persons dependent upon deceased wage earners and social security benefits by exempting those whose spouse was also entitled to benefits under the Social Security Act. The legislative exemption was not irrationally underinclusive.

In a ruling similar to *Jobst,* the Supreme Court in *Lyng v. Castillo* (1986) upheld provisions of the Federal Food Stamp Act that gave lesser food stamp benefits to nuclear families than to nonrelated persons or extended families living together.

Contrast *Zablocki v. Redhail* (1978). This case invalidated a law that restricted the ability of economically poor persons to marry. The Justices had considerable difficulty in deciding why the law violated the equal protection clause. The Wisconsin statute in question prohibited any Wisconsin resident from marrying without court permission if that person had minor issue who were not in his custody and whom he was required to support according to a court order or judgment. A state court could grant such persons permission to marry only if they submitted proof of compliance with the support obligation and demonstrated that the children covered by the court order were not likely to become "public charges."

Justice Marshall wrote a majority opinion for five members of the Court and argued that the statute requiring permission to marry was invalid because it prevented a person's marriage but it did not assure support for the children from that person's prior marriage. Yet it left the exact nature of the standard of review employed in this case unclear, but that has been true in many of the "fundamental rights" cases.

The concurring opinion of Justice Stevens argued that the classification based on marital status in *Califano v. Jobst* simply was not as significant a burden on the right to marriage as was the law reviewed in this case. Justice Powell concurred in the judgment in *Zablocki,* although he felt the majority opinion swept too broadly by indicating that there might be strict scrutiny of a variety of traditional marriage regulations. He mentioned laws prohibiting marriages that involve incest, bigamy, and homosexuality had been assumed to be within the constitutional scope of state powers. Powell based his decision on the fact that the state had been unable to establish any reasonable basis for foreclosing marriage to citizens who were willing but unable to make payments to meet their previous child support obligations.

Justice Stewart would have abandoned the equal protection rationale because he did not believe that this law created any testable classification. He viewed the decision as one based on the concept of substantive due process. Stewart voted to strike the law examined in *Zablocki* because it contained no exception for those who were truly indigent and could not afford to pay their child support obligations. Only Justice Rehnquist would have upheld the law in *Zablocki*.

From these cases it appears that the relationship between parent and child is a fundamental aspect of liberty. The government may terminate, or significantly impair, such an interest, if it is acting pursuant to a law that is narrowly tailored to promote a compelling or overriding interest. For example, a law authorizing a government agency to terminate a parent-child relationship on the basis that the parent is unfit, because the parent is placing the child in harm's way or hurting the child, the law might well be narrowly tailored to the compelling or overriding interest in the protection of the child. In such a case, the law would withstand substantive review under due process and equal protection. Nevertheless, when the state sought to severe the parent-child relationship, the parent has a due process right to some type of fair proceeding, under the procedural aspect of the due process clause.

The Court has not defined the nature of family relationships that constitute fundamental aspects of liberty nor has it defined with preciseness the relationships between a child and other relatives of the child such as grandparents. *Troxel v. Granville* (2000) held that a state statute granting visitation rights to grandparents and other persons was so broad that it could not be used, due to the circumstances of the case, to override a mother's decision to limit paternal grandparent visits to her children. However, there was no majority opinion in *Troxel*, in part because the Justices could not agree on how to define the nature of the family relationships that were fundamental constitutional liberties.

In *Troxel* the courts had to deal with a situation in which there was a conflict between the mother and paternal grandparents of children. The mother and the father of the children had not been married. The father of the children had committed suicide. The mother of the child sought to limit, but not terminate, the visits of the paternal grandparents to the children. Then the grandparents sought, and received, visitation rights under a Washington state statute that allowed a state court to grant visitation rights to any person whenever "visitation may best serve the interests of the child."

Justice O'Connor announced the judgment in *Troxel*, in a plurality opinion that was joined by Chief Justice Rehnquist and Justices Ginsburg and Breyer. The plurality opinion noted the parent-child relationship was the most long recognized fundamental aspect of liberty, by Supreme Court cases going back to the 1920s. O'Connor questioned the breadth of the statute, in light of its broad intrusion into the parent-child relationship, but the plurality only voted to invalidate the application of the statute in the particular case.

Justice Souter concurred in the judgment of the Court, but he would have preferred an opinion even more narrow than the plurality opinion. Justice Thomas concurred in the judgment with a brief opinion that assumed for purposes of the case that substantive due process was a legitimate tool of analysis, because the issue of whether the Supreme Court should reject substantive due process had not been presented by the parties to the case.

There were three dissenting Justices in *Troxel*, none of whom joined the opinion of any of the other dissenters.

§ 14.23   Abortion

(a) An Introductory Note

The formal tests that should be employed by a court that is reviewing the constitutionality of any type of abortion regulation are not very clear. In *Roe v. Wade* (1973) the Supreme Court held, for the first time, that a woman's right to choose to have an abortion was a part of the fundamental constitutional right of privacy. Yet its rationale was not that clear. After establishing that fundamental constitutional principle, *Roe* ruled that a government regulation of abortion practices could be upheld only if it was narrowly tailored to promote a compelling interest. The *Roe* majority opinion said that the government had a compelling interest in protecting the health of the woman who was having the abortion after the first three months of the pregnancy, and that the government had a compelling interest that would justify prohibiting all abortions (except those that were necessary to protect the life or health of the woman) after the fetus became viable.

Roe apparently concluded that a fetus was not a person for purposes of the Fourteenth Amendment. Had the *Roe* Court ruled otherwise, and found that a fetus was a person, states might have been required to have laws that provided some sort of procedural due process before an abortion so as to avoid denying these persons life without due process of law.

The Court has never ruled that a state cannot treat a fetus as if it were a child for purposes unrelated to preventing a woman from exercising her freedom of choice to terminate her pregnancy. None of the abortion regulation cases hold that the government could not make it a crime for an individual to beat a woman without her consent for the purpose of causing her to have a miscarriage. The *Roe* line of cases, particularly the more recent ones, focus on the woman's right to choose. If the law makes it a crime for someone to kick a pregnant woman and thereby cause her to lose the fetus, the law is not interfering with the woman's choice; the law is implementing the woman's choice, because it is the woman and not an angry boyfriend who should have the ultimate decision to terminate her pregnancy.

Roe majority opinion has often been described as establishing a "trimester" analysis for determining what types of government regulations of abortion are constitutional. Yet, the Supreme Court seemed to abandon a strict trimester analysis within a few years after *Roe*. *Webster v. Reproductive Health Services* (1989) rejected the trimester analytical structure but it did not do so in a majority opinion. All of the post-*Roe* cases, including *Webster,* might be rationalized by the following principle. Even though the Court has never adopted this test, it does explain a lot of the modern cases:

> A state abortion regulation will be upheld if it is a reasonable effort to (1) protect the woman's health, (2) ensure that minors make responsible decisions, or (3) protect a viable or possibly viable fetus. A health regulation may not unduly burden the right to abortion. Statutes protecting possibly viable fetuses must not be so vague as to deter abortions of nonviable fetuses and must allow abortions when a physician finds a significant threat to the life or health of the woman. So long as the law does not impose a significant barrier to, or penalty for, abortions, the state may take other steps to discourage women from choosing to have an abortion.

This reasonableness principle is only an aid to understanding the Court's rules.

(b) The Cases

(1)(a) *Roe v. Wade.* *Roe v. Wade* (1973) overturned a Texas statute that prohibited procuring or attempting the abortion of a human fetus except when necessary to save the life of the mother. The Court held that the statute violated the due process clause of the Fourteenth Amendment as an unjustified deprivation of liberty in that it unnecessarily infringed on a woman's right to privacy.

Justice Blackmun, speaking for the Court, discussed the broad range of decisions involving the right to privacy. With virtually no further explanation of the privacy value, he found that the right of privacy, regardless of exactly what constitutional provision it was ascribed to, "is broad enough to encompass a woman's decision whether or not to terminate her pregnancy." Because this right was now a part of the liberty protected by the Fourteenth Amendment, the state could not restrict it without due process of law.

Normally the legislature may regulate activities so long as the legislation has some rational relationship to a legitimate state interest. However, where the legislation restricts the exercise of fundamental constitutional rights the Court will uphold it only if it is necessary to promote a compelling state interest. In this case the Court found that the right to an abortion was not absolute and so it could be limited in some circumstances. But the majority found the right to privacy that included the woman's right to an abortion was "fundamental." Thus, the Court held that limitations on the woman's right to have an abortion would only be upheld where they furthered a "compelling state interest."

There were two state interests that the Court found might support some limitations on the right to an abortion—the interest in the health of the mother and in the life of the fetus. The only interest that might have supported a total ban on abortion was the protection of the fetus as a human life. But the majority found no basis, apart from certain philosophies or religions, for calling the fetus a person. While this argument did not establish the invalidity of the Act, the refusal of the Court to recognize this interest required the states to demonstrate some independent interest in the life of the mother or the fetus. There would be a "compelling interest" in the mother's life where restriction on the right was needed to protect her life or safety. There would be a "compelling interest" in the fetus when the state could show a viable life that it had an interest to protect.

Through approximately the first third of a pregnancy, abortion performed under a doctor's care was as safe, if not safer, for a woman's health as was completion of the pregnancy. Thus the opinion held there could be no significant restriction on the right of the woman to have an abortion during the first trimester of the pregnancy. The woman was free to have an abortion during this time subject only to her ability to find a licensed physician who would perform the operation. The state could require a few minimal medical safeguards during this period such as requiring that the abortionist be a licensed medical doctor.

The risk to the pregnant woman's health increased after the first trimester. Thus the Court found a "compelling interest" in establishing further medical regulations on abortions performed after that stage of the pregnancy. Later decisions made it clear that the reasonableness of these restrictions would be subjected to independent judicial review and that only those regulations of abortion procedures that the Justices would find to be reasonable and narrowly tailored to protect the health of the woman during a second trimester abortion would be upheld.

With respect to the state's interest in the existence of the fetus, the majority found that the state had a "compelling interest" when the fetus became viable—normally considered to be the beginning of the third trimester (end of the sixth month) of the pregnancy. At this point the fetus could have "meaningful life" outside the mother and the state could demonstrate an important interest in its existence apart from moral philosophy concerning the beginning of life. The Court held that after the time of viability the legislature could prohibit abortions except where necessary to protect the life or health of the mother. It should be noted that all of the opinions have assumed that an exception would be made to such a proscription to secure the mother's life or prevent serious injury to her health.

The separate opinions of individual Justices foreshadowed the continuing debate over the legitimacy of these decisions. In concurring opinions, Justice Stewart accepted this ruling as a permissible use of the substantive due process theory and Justice Douglas elaborated on the concept of unwritten fundamental values recognized by the Ninth and Fourteenth Amendments.

There were only two dissents but they touched on the points that would lead to later criticism of the decisions. Justice White explained that there was no basis for finding that the judiciary should make decisions concerning the competing values of the mother and the potential life of the fetus. He saw the decision as the "exercise of raw judicial power" rather than the protection of clear constitutional values. Justice Rehnquist noted the similarity with the use of substantive due process between these decisions and the now-repudiated position of the Court in *Lochner v. New York* (1905).

(1)(b) *Webster v. Reproductive Health Services*—Limiting the *Roe v. Wade* Analytical Structure.

The *Roe v. Wade* (1973) majority opinion appeared to establish a rigid "trimester" structure for the judicial examination of abortion regulations. Virtually no regulations would be upheld that related to first trimester abortions; any regulation of abortions performed between the end of the first trimester and the time when the fetus was viable (as determined by an attending physician) would be upheld only if the regulation was narrowly tailored to protect the health of the woman. Abortions could be outlawed after the fetus was viable, although the ban on post-viability abortions, and all other abortion regulations, would have to include an exception for abortions performed to protect the life or health of the woman.

In *Webster v. Reproductive Health Services* (1989) a majority of Justices appeared to reject the *Roe v. Wade* formal "trimester" analytical structure although they did not at that time replace the *Roe* analysis with any new test for the judicial review of abortion regulations.

In *Webster,* the Court examined the constitutionality of four provisions of Missouri state law: (1) a statutory preamble stating that "the life of each human being begins at conception"; (2) a prohibition against public employees performing abortions or public facilities being used for abortions; (3) a prohibition of public funding of abortion counseling; (4) a set of requirements regarding physician's use of certain medical tests to determine whether a fetus was viable.

First, the statutory preamble, which included the legislative determination of when life begins, did not present a ripe constitutional question. There was no indication that this legislative preamble would in any way limit a woman's ability to have an abortion in the state.

The Court upheld the second provision at issue on the basis of earlier Court cases that had held that the state's refusal to subsidize abortions did not restrict a woman's right to privacy. In those cases the Court had found that the right to privacy included a woman's decision to have an abortion without interference by the state but did not include a right of a woman to receive abortion services or funds for such services. See, e.g., *Maher v. Roe* (1977).

Webster noted that the state law restrictions on public employees performing abortions did not appear to impose restrictions on the performance of abortions by persons employed by the state if the person was acting on his own time (not during the time when he was employed by the state) and at private hospitals. If a state attempted to prohibit doctors who performed abortions on their own time at privately owned medical facilities from using public medical facilities for any purpose, that prohibition might violate women's right to privacy because it restrict a women's ability to have an abortion, rather than merely refuse to subsidize abortions.

The Court also upheld the third portion of the statute at issue in *Webster,* which prohibited public funding of abortion counseling. The Court accepted the state's assertion that the statute did nothing other than prohibit the use of public funds for abortion counseling and regulated only those persons responsible for spending public money. The parties attacking the statute admitted that they would not be adversely affected by a statutory prohibition of expending public money for abortion counseling, so long as it did not restrict public employees from speech or associational activities outside of the scope of their employment. For that reason, six Justices found that any previous controversy regarding the abortion counseling provision of this statute was moot.

The final provision of the Missouri statute at issue in *Webster* required a physician, before performing an abortion on a woman whom the physician had "reason to believe is carrying an unborn child of twenty or more weeks of gestational age," to determine if the fetus was viable by using the degree of care that would normally be exercised by a "prudent physician." The statute went on to say that, in making the viability determination, "the physician shall perform or cause to be performed such medical examination and tests as are necessary to make a finding of the gestational age, weight, and lung maturity of the unborn child." If the statute had been read to create a presumption that every fetus of twenty or more weeks was viable, the statute would have directly conflicted with the analytical structure established by *Roe v. Wade.* However, the parties attacking the statute did not appeal the portion of a lower court decision upholding the statutory provision and finding that the presumption did not restrict abortion rights. Therefore, *Webster* made no ruling on whether a state could establish statutory criteria that would bind individual physicians in the viability determination.

Five Justices upheld the portion of the statute regarding viability determination tests, though without majority opinion. Though the Rehnquist plurality did not use a compelling interest test, the Chief Justice's opinion appears to reaffirm the *Roe* holding that the potential life of the fetus and the health of the woman were both compelling interests that would justify abortion regulations. The plurality opinion stated that the Missouri statute should be upheld as "reasonably designed to ensure that abortions are not performed where the fetus is viable—an end that all concede is legitimate—and that is sufficient to sustain its constitutionality."

Justice O'Connor concurred in the Court's ruling that the viability testing provision was constitutional. Unlike the other Justices in the majority, she did not believe that the viability provision conflicted with earlier decisions of the United States Supreme Court. Of the five Justices in the majority, only Justice Scalia expressly favored overruling *Roe.* The dissenting Justices believed that the ruling in *Webster v. Reproductive Health Services* impaired the fundamental constitutional right of privacy.

(1)(c) *Planned Parenthood v. Casey*—**Reaffirming and Modifying** *Roe v. Wade.*

In 1992, a majority of the Justices, in a majority opinion, reaffirmed the ruling of *Roe* that recognized a woman's fundamental right to choose to abort a nonviable fetus. But seven Justices, though not in a majority opinion, rejected the *Roe* trimester analysis. *Planned Parenthood v. Casey* (1992) upheld most, but not all, provisions of a Pennsylvania abortion statute. Justice O'Connor, in *Casey,* announced the judgment of the Court in an opinion that was, in part, a majority opinion, and in part a plurality opinion. Justice O'Connor wrote for a majority of the Court in finding that a woman's right to choose to have an abortion of a nonviable fetus was grounded in the concept of liberty protected by the due process clause of the Fourteenth Amendment. Justices Blackmun and Stevens as well as by Justices Kennedy and Souter joined this portion of O'Connor's opinion. The "essential holding" of *Roe* was reaffirmed on the basis of an independent analysis of the concept of "liberty" and on the basis of stare decisis. Justice O'Connor wrote:

> "It must be stated at the outset and with clarity that Roe's essential holding, the holding we reaffirm, has three parts. First is a recognition of the right of the woman to choose to have an abortion before viability and to obtain it without undue interference from the State ... Second is a confirmation of the State's power to restrict abortions after fetal viability, if the law contains exceptions for pregnancies that endanger a woman's life or health. And third is the principle that the State has legitimate interest from the outset of the pregnancy in protecting the health of the woman and the life of the fetus ... these principles do not contradict one another...."

Hence, while four Justices dissented from the majority's position concerning a woman's right to an abortion, it seems unlikely that the basic principle established by *Roe* will be overturned.

In addition to its reaffirmation of a woman's constitutional right to choose an abortion the Court reaffirmed the state's power to prohibit abortions of a viable fetus, so long as the prohibition allowed an abortion to be performed when the continuation of the pregnancy would "endanger a woman's life or health." *Casey* did not involve statutes that defined viability and, therefore, the Court did not have occasion to clarify the concept of viability or to explain the types of dangers to a woman's life or health that might require exceptions from a prohibition on the abortion of viable fetuses.

Justice Blackmun, the author of the majority opinion in *Roe,* was the only Justice in *Casey* who wished to reaffirm not only what O'Connor called the basic holdings of *Roe* (set forth in the above quotation from her majority opinion) but also the use of a compelling interest test tied to trimester analysis. Justice Stevens favored using a case-by-case test that focused on whether particular abortion regulations promoted societal interests that were so compelling as to outweigh the woman's liberty interest.

With four Justices wishing to reject *Roe* in its entirety, and two Justices wishing to uphold both *Roe*'s basic principle and some elements of the compelling interest test, the outcome of the Court's decision in *Casey* rested with Justices O'Connor, Kennedy, and Souter. O'Connor wrote for herself and Justices Kennedy and Souter in finding that a state regulation of abortions of nonviable fetuses would be permissible only so long as it did not impose an "undue burden" on the woman's freedom to choose to have an abortion. This "undue burden" test had its roots in Justice O'Connor's separate opinion in *Webster v. Reproductive Health Services.* (1989).

O'Connor's plurality opinion in *Casey* clarifies the undue burden test. After finding that the right to choose to abort a nonviable fetus, like other fundamental aspects of liberty, is not an absolute right and that this right can be subject to state regulations that promote constitutionally valid ends that had only incidental effects of making it more difficult or expensive to exercise the right, the plurality rejected the "rigid trimester framework of *Roe v. Wade*". Justice O'Connor then tried to explain the meaning of the undue burden test:

> "A finding of an undue burden is a shorthand for the conclusion that a state regulation has the purpose or effect of placing a substantial obstacle in the path of a woman seeking an abortion of a nonviable fetus. A statute with this purpose is invalid because the means chosen by the State to further the interest in potential life must be calculated to inform the woman's free choice, not hinder it. And a statute that, while furthering the interest in potential life or some other valid state interest, has the effect of placing a substantial obstacle in the path of a woman's choice cannot be considered a permissible means of serving its legitimate ends.... Some guiding principles should emerge. What is at stake is the woman's right to make the ultimate decision, not a right to be insulated from all others in doing so. Regulations that do no more than create a structural mechanism by which the State, or the parent or guardian of a minor, may express profound respect for the life of the unborn are permitted, if they are not a substantial obstacle to the woman's exercise of the right to choose ... Unless it has that effect [the effect of creating a substantial obstacle] on her right of choice, a state measure designed to persuade her to choose childbirth over abortion will be upheld if reasonably related to that goal. Regulations designed to foster the health of a woman seeking an abortion are valid if they do not constitute an undue burden.... unnecessary

health regulations that have the purpose or effect of presenting a substantial obstacle to a woman seeking an abortion impose an undue burden on the right.''

The most important part of the plurality's undue burden test may be the "purpose or effect" aspect of the test. Because the plurality in *Casey* endorsed the purpose branch of undue burden analysis, lower court judges reviewing abortion regulations may not be able to uphold an abortion regulation merely by finding that it is a reasonable health law. But perhaps the purpose branch of undue burden analysis will not be very difficult for judges to apply. It may be that any law that is demonstrably related to protecting the health of the female patient will have a legitimate purpose that would withstand constitutional scrutiny, even though some legislators might have voted for the law for a variety of purposes (including the purpose of making it more difficult for a woman to obtain abortions).

It is the effect branch of the undue burden test that is most likely to have meaning for future cases and lower court rulings on new types of abortion regulations. According to the plurality opinion, if an abortion regulation has the effect of placing a "substantial obstacle in the path of a woman seeking an abortion of a nonviable fetus" it will be invalid. However, if regulations are designed to protect the health of a woman, to give the woman complete information concerning abortion choices, or to protect the variety of interests in children that might be present when a minor pregnant female seeks an abortion, the law will be seen as only an incidental burden on women who seek abortions rather than an impermissible substantial obstacle.

The meaning of the undue burden test may be clarified by looking at the specific types of abortion regulations before the Court in *Casey*. The Pennsylvania statute in *Casey* defined "medical emergency" as a condition that the physician in good judgment could determine "so complicates the medical condition of a pregnant woman as to necessitate the immediate abortion of her pregnancy to avert her death or for which a delay will create serious risk of substantial and irreversible impairment of a major bodily function." The lower courts had interpreted the statute to include a variety of circumstances so that "compliance with [the state's] abortion regulations would not in any way pose a significant threat to the life or health of the woman." With that understanding of the statute, a majority had approved the definition of a medical emergency.

Several types of consent and recordkeeping provisions were before the Court in *Casey*. Justice O'Connor wrote for a majority in striking down a provision of the Pennsylvania law that required, except in emergency cases, a physician to refrain from performing an abortion on a married woman absent a statement that the woman had notified her spouse about her decision to have the abortion. O'Connor held that Supreme Court decisions had invalidated father-husband consent requirements and that, because these requirements place a substantial obstacle in the path of women choosing to have an abortion, they cannot be justified now that society had rejected the common law view of the status of married women as being subservient to their husbands.

The state's recordkeeping requirements applied to both state funded institutions and privately funded institutions that performed abortions. Records were kept regarding the number of abortions, the specific circumstances surrounding each abortion, and the types of procedures used. Although information from state funded institutions became public, O'Connor found that, as to both public sector and private sector reporting, "the identity of each woman who has had an abortion remains confidential." In accordance with earlier Court rulings, the plurality found that these record keeping requirements, with their provisions for confidentiality, did not constitute an undue burden on a woman's right to choose to have an abortion of a nonviable fetus. However, the Justices did vote to strike down the part of the state recordkeeping regulation that required reports on whether a married woman had given notice to her husband. The failure of the husband consent requirement meant that this recordkeeping requirement placed an undue burden on the woman's choice.

Casey upheld a portion of the Pennsylvania statute that prohibited a doctor from performing an abortion on an unemancipated pregnant female under the age of 18 years unless she and one of her parents, or her guardian, had consented to the abortion 24 hours before the procedure was performed unless (1) there was a medical emergency that required the abortion or (2) the minor pregnant female had received court authorization to have the abortion. The plurality found that this parental consent provision had the type of "judicial bypass procedure" that protected the well-being of the pregnant minor so that the requirement did not impose an undue burden on that minor's freedom of choice. Earlier Supreme Court case law had upheld similar parental consent laws.

The only pre–1992 rulings of the Supreme Court that were overturned in *Casey* related to (1) formalities imposed by the state for the demonstration of a female patient's consent to an abortion and (2) the imposition of a 24 hour waiting period between the time when a woman consented to have an abortion and the time when the abortion was performed. The State of Pennsylvania required a physician or a trained physician's assistant, health care worker, or social worker to provide the woman patient with information regarding the nature and risks of the proposed medical treatment, the probable gestational age of fetus, medical risks associated with carrying the child to childbirth, printed material describing abortion alternatives, information regarding medical assistance benefits for childbirth and child care. Some of this information had to be provided to the woman by the physician. A woman's consent would not be valid unless these informational provisions had been complied with 24 hours prior to the time the abortion was performed. Under state law both the information component of the consent requirement and the 24 hour waiting period could be disregarded when there was a "medical emergency."

Earlier cases had invalidated the requirement that a medical doctor personally provide the woman with the information prior to an abortion and requirements that kept an adult female from having an abortion for a set time period after she gave consent. Justices Stevens and Blackmun thought that those cases should be followed; they believe that there was no interest of sufficient constitutional importance to interfere with the doctor-patient relationship concerning abortion or to deter a woman's ability to have an abortion. The four Justices who voted to overrule *Roe* also voted to uphold the entirety of the Pennsylvania statute, including the consent provisions.

Thus, the three Justices who used the undue burden test were left to decide the constitutional fate of the informed consent provisions, and concluded that the informed consent provisions should be upheld because these provisions did not place an undue burden on a woman's ability to choose to have an abortion. Critical to the plurality's decision was a provision of the Pennsylvania law that allowed doctors to disregard the requirements when in good faith they believed it was necessary to do so to protect the life or health of the woman. With that medical emergency exception, the regulation provided complete information to the woman that might be of assistance to her in making the abortion-childbirth choice. The plurality believed that the informed consent provision was "a reasonable measure to insure an informed choice.... this requirement cannot be considered a substantial obstacle to obtaining an abortion, and, it follows there is no undue burden."

The 24 hour waiting period presented a more difficult issue for the plurality. On one hand, the 24 hour waiting period promoted and informed deliberative choice by the woman medical patient. On the other hand, it was possible that the 24 hour waiting period might be onerous to women who had to travel a great distance to receive abortion services or to women who were in a geographic and social situation where multiple visits to the doctor who would perform an abortion might involve multiple public encounters with persons who sought to block or stop legal abortion services. The plurality found that there was nothing about a 24 hour waiting period that inherently imposed an undue burden on a woman's right to an abortion because on its face the regulation was designed to promote an informed choice by the woman. However, O'Connor's plurality opinion left open the possibility that, in the future, in a case where there was proof that a 24 hour waiting period did create real obstacles to a woman's right to choose to abort a nonviable fetus, the Court might find that the purpose or effect of the regulation violated the undue burden standard. At least O'Connor implied as much when she stated that "a particular burden is not of necessity a substantial obstacle ... the District Court did not conclude that the waiting period is such an obstacle even for the women who are most burdened by it. Hence, on the record before us, and in the context of this facial challenge, we are not convinced that the 24–hour waiting period constitutes an undue burden."

The *Casey* decision is the logical outcome of the Court's gradual, but meaningful, shift concerning a woman's right to an abortion between the early 1970s and the early 1990s. The Court has consistently protected the basic right of a woman to choose to abort a nonviable fetus but it has also consistently upheld regulations of a woman's freedom of choice that the Court believed were tailored to promote state interest in the health of the woman or the protection of the viable fetus. Over two decades the Court has come to do less second guessing of medical regulations or regulations designed to express a state's preference for childbirth over abortion. But the Court has invalidated those regulations of abortions that the majority sees as being road blocks to a woman's exercise of her constitutional right. The plurality's adoption of an undue burden analysis, and its recognition of the general state interest in the potential life of the fetus, does very little to change the outcome of the previous Supreme Court cases. The ad hoc nature of the Court's rulings requires a separate analysis of Court decisions examining each type of abortion regulation. It is to those cases that we now turn.

(1)(d) *Stenberg v. Carhart*—"Partial Birth Abortion"

The Court's first encounter with a law restricting what many people call "partial birth abortions" was *Stenberg v. Carhart* (2000). The law at issue in *Stenberg* did not prohibit abortions. Rather, it addressed the manner in which a woman could have an abortion, assuming that she was in compliance with other laws. The statute, which applied to pre-viability as well as post-viability abortions, stated that "no partial-birth abortion shall be performed in this state unless such procedure is necessary to save the life of the mother whose life in endangered by a physical disorder, physical illness, or physical injury including a life endangering physical condition caused by or arising from the pregnancy itself." The statute then defined partial-birth abortions as "an abortion procedure in which the person performing the abortion partially delivers vaginally a living unborn child before killing the unborn child and completing the delivery.''

Writing for five members of the Court, Justice Breyer stated that, the majority was using the undue burden standard set forth in the *Casey* plurality opinion. Under this standard, any law that imposes an undue burden on the woman's decision before fetal viability should be ruled unconstitutional. Subsequent to viability a state could proscribe or regulate abortions, assuming that there was an exception for the preservation of the life or health of the mother.

The Court's opinions concerning abortion regulations, including *Stenberg*, accept both the protection of the viable fetus and the protection of the pregnant woman's health as compelling governmental interests. An abortion regulation that is narrowly tailored to protect those interests should be upheld. On the other hand, any law that is not narrowly tailored to protect those interests constitutes an undue burden on a woman's choice to have a pre-viability abortion will be ruled unconstitutional. Further, all abortion regulations must have an exception that would allow medical personnel judgment to disregard the regulation when necessary to preserve the life or health of the pregnant woman.

For the *Stenberg* majority, the statute was unconstitutional because of its failure to allow an exception to protect the health (rather than merely the life) of the pregnant woman. Justice Breyer explained that the procedure that was prohibited by the statute was less safe for pregnant women under a variety of circumstances. The statute could not, in the opinion of the majority, force doctors to use a procedure that was less safe for the pregnant woman. The fact that the law applied to pre-viability abortions, as well as post-viability abortions presented a significant problem for the Court. Justice Breyer's majority opinion stated that ''the state's interest in regulating abortion pre-viability is considerably weaker than post-viability.''

The *Stenberg* majority opinion clarified, to a slight extent, the nature of the exception that states must have to protect pregnant women. Justice Breyer noted that the state could not limit the protection of the woman exception to circumstances in which it was absolutely necessary to disregard a regulation to save the life of the mother. Although the majority opinion said ''by no means must a state grant physicians unfettered discretion in their selection of abortion methods,'' it did not explain how a state might limit a physician's authority to disregard the abortion regulation whenever the physician might claim that following the law might impair the health of the woman patient.

Among the questions unanswered in *Stenberg* are whether states must grant an exception from abortion regulations if the doctor believes that following the regulation would harm the psychological, as opposed to physical, health of the woman. Also unanswered is whether the law must allow a physician to perform an abortion, and disregard regulations, for health risks that might not be either life-threatening or cause a permanent impairment to the woman's physical health.

Four Justices dissented in *Stenberg*. Three of them, who had dissented in earlier abortion rulings, believed that the Court did not have a legitimate basis for invalidating regulations of abortions under the due process clause. Justice Kennedy, who had joined plurality opinions striking other types of abortion regulations dissented because he believed that the Court misinterpreted the statute and was unjustified in striking a law that allowed women to have abortions and only restricted one particular procedure that he believed was "dehumanizing" and ran contrary to basic societal values. The statutory ban of one particular procedure did not deprive any woman of a safe abortion. He explained: "Dr. Carhart has no specialty certifications in a field related to childbirth or abortion and lacks admitting privileges at any hospital."

(2) Regulations of Abortion Procedures.

Since *Roe v. Wade* (1973) government regulations of abortions have been subject to independent judicial review. Since *Roe,* the Court has regarded a woman's right to choose to abort a nonviable fetus as a fundamental constitutional right that the state cannot abrogate. The state can only regulate this right if the regulation is tailored to promote some societal interest that outweighs the incidental impairment of the woman's ability to choose to have the abortion.

The plurality in *Casey* rejected the trimester analysis of *Roe,* but it is not clear that the Court ever used a strict trimester analysis. For example, although the Court in *Roe* discussed first trimester abortions in terms that would make the reader of the opinion believe that no government regulation of an abortion in the first trimester would be valid, the Supreme Court in the 1970s upheld first trimester abortion regulations that were tailored to protect the health of the woman. The Court upheld regulations requiring the abortionist to be a licensed medical doctor and regulations requiring a hospital to keep accurate records of all abortions performed in the hospital, even though those laws applied to first trimester abortions. *Connecticut v. Menillo* (1975) (per curiam), held that it is constitutional for a state to prosecute a nonphysician for performing an abortion; *Planned Parenthood of*

Central Missouri v. Danforth (1976), upheld record-keeping requirements even though they applied to first trimester abortions.

As indicated in *Roe,* and cases subsequent to it, the state may prohibit post-viability abortions *except* where there is a threat to the life or health of the woman. The state may have regulations of abortion procedures that are designed to protect the existence of a viable fetus if, but only if, the judiciary determines that the regulation is narrowly tailored to that end and does not create any significant health risk to the woman.

Because the Court has decided to make each regulation of abortion procedures subject to this type of active judicial review, these rulings have an *ad hoc* quality. The nature of principles enforced by the Court can best be understood by briefly reviewing a few of the major decisions regarding abortion regulations.

Roe must to be read in conjunction with *Doe v. Bolton* (1973), which examined procedural requirements of abortion statutes. *Doe* invalidated a number of procedural restrictions on the woman's ability to secure an abortion because the Court concluded that they unnecessarily restricted the woman's right to an abortion. One requirement was that the abortion be performed in a hospital accredited by a special committee although the state imposed no such requirement for nonabortion surgery. The State failed to show why the abortion should have to be performed in a licensed hospital rather than some other appropriately licensed institution. The statute also required the approval of two other physicians, despite the fact the performing physician had already been required to exercise his "best clinical judgment" in determining that an abortion was necessary. For almost identical reasons, the Court struck the requirement that the physician's decision to abort be approved by a committee of at least three hospital staff members.

In *Planned Parenthood of Central Missouri v. Danforth* (1976), the statute was challenged on the basis of its definition of viability and its prohibition of the use of saline amniocentesis as a means of abortion after the first twelve weeks. The statute defined viability as "that stage of fetal development when the life of the unborn child may be continued indefinitely outside the womb by natural or artificial life support systems." The Court upheld this definition, finding it consistent with *Roe v. Wade*. The Court said that viability is basically a medical term, and as such it need not be defined as occurring at a specific point in the gestation period but may be left to the judgment of the attending physician.

The Court invalidated the ban on saline amniocentesis because it could not be shown, as required by *Roe*, to be a restriction reasonably related to the preservation and protection of *maternal* health, though it was related to fetal health.

Planned Parenthood of Central Missouri v. Danforth upheld a statutory provision that required a woman to give written consent to the abortion and that required the hospital to keep records of abortions performed because these regulations were reasonably narrow means of protecting the health of the woman patient. The valid regulations were similar to state regulations of a wide variety of surgical procedures.

The *ad hoc* nature of the strict scrutiny test used to examine governmental regulations of abortion procedures was well demonstrated on a single day in 1983 when the Supreme Court decided three separate cases involving several different types of abortion regulations. *Akron v. Akron Center for Reproductive Health, Inc.* (1983); *Planned Parenthood v. Ashcroft* (1983); *Simopoulos v. Virginia* (1983). Because the six Justices who exercise strict judicial scrutiny when reviewing abortion regulations sometimes split over the constitutionality of a specific regulation, some of the decisions in the cases turned on the fact that two or more of those six Justices joined with Justices O'Connor, Rehnquist and White to uphold specific regulations.

In two cases the Court invalidated laws that required all abortions after the first trimester to be performed in a full service hospital, because a majority of the Justices found that this law was not reasonably designed to protect the health of the woman. In contrast, the Court in another case upheld a law requiring that the abortion be performed in a "hospital" when, under state law, that term included "out-patient clinics" that met certain criteria designed to protect the health of women patients, because this law did not unreasonably deter abortions.

Akron v. Akron Center for Reproductive Health (1983) ruled that a medical consent law that included a 24–hour waiting period was not narrowly tailored to protect the health of the woman patient and that it intruded on the decision of the patient and physician to have the abortion performed in a manner, and at a time best suited to the well-being of the patient.

However, in *Planned Parenthood v. Casey* (1992), a majority of the Court, though not in a majority opinion, upheld a law that prohibited doctors from performing an abortion on an adult woman until 24 hours after the doctor had received the woman's "informed consent" to the abortion procedure except in those cases where a "medical emergency" justified the doctor in disregarding the waiting period requirement. The plurality found that, on its face, a law requiring a 24–hour waiting period between the woman's "informed consent" and the abortion was tailored to the interest in ensuring that each woman made an informed, reflective decision concerning abortion. However, the plurality opinion noted that it was only ruling on a challenge to the statute on its face. There was no evidence in the record before the Court that the law had placed a substantial obstacle to women's constitutional rights, and an undue burden on their freedom of choice, by subjecting them to serious costs or personal burdens. Thus, it is possible that, in a future case involving a state law requiring a waiting period, the Court would invalidate a waiting period requirement if there is a showing that women have very great difficulty in receiving abortion services in the state because the law imposes serious financial burdens on them (more than merely a slight increase in costs of an abortion caused by two office visits rather than one) or serious personal burdens (by subjecting women to having to cross privately erected picket lines or barriers to abortion clinics).

Thornburgh v. American College of Obstetricians and Gynecologists (1986) invalidated statutes that required a woman to give "informed consent" as a condition to receiving abortion services. The Court found that these statutes did not merely require a woman to sign a consent form similar to the consent forms that would be required for other medical procedures. The statutes at issue in *Thornburgh* required that the physician give the woman printed material concerning abortion procedures and fetus development; the woman was also required to wait 24 hours after a physician gave her the information before her consent would be valid. *Thornburgh* found the informed consent requirements invalid for two basic reasons: the Court viewed the consent requirements as an attempt to deter women from deciding to have an abortion; the statutes intruded into the physician-patient relationship by requiring a physician personally to provide information that a physician might not deem to be in the woman's best interest. The Court later overruled this portion of *Thornburgh* decision in *Planned Parenthood v. Casey* (1992).

The informed consent statutes at issue in *Casey* required a doctor or other health care professional to provide the woman with information regarding the abortion procedures, the risks from the abortion procedures, the probable gestational age of the fetus, abortion alternatives, the risks of carrying a child to full term (child birth) and the types of medical and financial assistance that might be available for the woman if she chose child birth rather than abortion. Some of the information had to be given to the woman by the physician personally. The plurality believed that these regulations were designed to allow a woman to make a truly informed decision. The regulations allowed physicians to disregard the information and waiting period requirements whenever necessary to avoid serious risks to the life or health of the woman patient. Without that exception, the plurality would have voted to invalidate the law. The plurality found that there was no physician-patient right that derived from the first or Fourteenth Amendments that would prevent a state from having consent requirements that were designed to give the woman complete information about her abortion and childbirth options or to express the state's preference for childbirth. Therefore, the plurality Justices voted with the four Justices who believed there was no right to an abortion to uphold the particular Pennsylvania laws before the Court in *Casey* and to overrule the previous Supreme Court decisions that had invalidated similar informed consent requirements.

Thornburgh also invalidated two provisions of the Pennsylvania statutes requiring a doctor to report the basis upon which he or she determined that the fetus to be aborted was not viable. The Court did not find that the state had improperly attempted to dictate to the doctor the criteria by which she or he would determine that the fetus was viable. Any attempt to do so might have been held invalid as a legislative restriction on a woman's fundamental right to have an abortion or an attempt to deter doctors from performing abortions in situations where a woman had a right to have the fetus aborted. The statutes in *Thornburgh* required a report regarding the abortion and the viability determination. The Court found that these statutes were invalid because they created a record system open to the public that included detailed information that could be used to identify women having abortions. A limited record keeping requirement that related to the state interest in monitoring medical practices within the state might be upheld. The statute allowing public disclosure of detailed information might lead to harassment of women who had abortions or doctors who performed abortions. This statutory system was not narrowly tailored to serve a compelling interest.

The final set of statutes at issue in *Thornburgh* involved restrictions on post-viability abortions. These statutes required that, in post-viability abortions, the doctor exercise the degree of care necessary and reasonable to preserve the life and health of the unborn child. The statutes also required that there be a second physician present at an abortion when viability is possible, to take control of and provide care for the child if the fetus proved to be viable. The Court found that, in demanding that the doctor attempt to save the fetus, the statute did not allow doctors a reasonable opportunity to protect the health of the woman in a post-viability abortion. *Roe* had allowed states to prohibit post-viability abortions only if there was no serious threat to the life or health of the woman. *Thornburgh* found that these statutes required a "trade-off" between the women's health and fetus survival and thus were invalid because they failed to provide that maternal health should be the physician's paramount consideration. The second physician requirement was invalid because, as written or interpreted, it did not contain an exception allowing a single doctor to perform a post-viability abortion when the life or health of the mother was at stake. *Thornburgh* distinguished earlier cases where the Supreme Court had upheld second doctor requirements in post-viability abortions and mandatory care for a fetus that might be saved in a post-viability abortion on the basis that the earlier decisions had involved statutes with an emergency exception to the second physician requirement.

Webster v. Reproductive Health Services (1989) upheld a state law that required a physician to use prudent judgment when deciding whether certain medical tests should be used to determine if a fetus is viable. There was no majority opinion regarding the constitutionality of this legislative attempt to protect a viable fetus.

Vagueness of Abortion Regulations—Definitions of Viability. *Colautti v. Franklin* (1979) held void for vagueness a Pennsylvania abortion regulation that required a doctor to make a determination of viability prior to performing an abortion. If the doctor determined that the fetus was "viable", or if there was "sufficient reason to believe that the fetus may be viable," the doctor was required to "exercise that degree of professional skill, care and diligence to preserve the life and health of the fetus that such person would be required to exercise in order to preserve the life and health of a fetus intended to be born." The statute required that the doctor aborting such a fetus use the abortion technique that "would provide the best opportunity for the fetus to be aborted alive so long as a different technique would not be necessary in order to preserve the life or health of the mother." The statute also stated that a doctor who failed to make the viability determination, or to exercise a required degree of care, would be subject to the same criminal or civil liability as would apply if the fetus had been intended to be born alive.

Colautti found that this statute was unconstitutionally vague: the requirement that the doctor determine if there was sufficient reason to believe the fetus may be viable was vague, and the standard of care that the doctor must use, including the guidelines for choosing between a technique to save the fetus and one to protect the health of the mother, also was vague. Unfortunately, the majority opinion itself was less than a model of clarity and it is difficult, if not impossible, to decide what, if any, principles are established by this opinion.

Little can be gained, in the terms of definite rules, from this opinion. It would appear that the state may not define the point of viability other than by stating that a fetus is viable when it has the potential to live outside of the mother's womb in the judgment of the attending physician. Perhaps a state might be able to define more clearly what abortion techniques might be used after the time of viability, as determined by the attending physician. However, given the Court's prior invalidation of a ban of saline abortions in *Planned Parenthood* and the analysis used in *Colautti*, it would seem virtually impossible for a state to eliminate any form of abortion that was safe for the woman prior to the time of viability.

The dissent by Justice White noted that a requirement that physicians know that the fetus is viable when they abort it, in order to make their actions criminal, will mean that it will be practically impossible to convict many physicians who commit criminal abortions by aborting viable fetuses. There may be many instances when most doctors would have determined that the fetus was viable but where a particular physician will assert that he believed that the fetus was not viable when he performed the abortion.

Because "strict" judicial scrutiny of abortion regulations involves *ad hoc* decision-making, the determination of whether any specific regulation of abortion procedures is constitutional will depend on whether a majority of the Justices believe that the regulation is reasonably designed to protect the health of women or only intended to deter abortions. As a part of this strict judicial scrutiny, a majority of the Justices will require that statutes regulating abortion procedures, particularly those statutes that involve criminal penalties, give a physician very clear notice of the permissible scope of physician activities so that the physicians will not be deterred from performing constitutionally protected abortions by vague statutes. For this reason, the Court has invalidated as unconstitutionally vague a statute requiring physicians, after performing an abortion, to dispose of the fetal remains in a "humane and sanitary manner." *Akron v. Akron Center for Reproductive Health, Inc.* (1983).

In *Webster v. Reproductive Health Services* (1989) the Court, without a majority opinion as to this point, upheld a state law that required a physician to exercise reasonable judgment in determining whether a fetus that was 20 or more weeks of gestational age was viable and to use a variety of age, fetal weight, and lung capacity tests for determining the viability of such a fetus. Both Chief Justice Rehnquist's plurality opinion and Justice O'Connor's concurring opinion found that the statute did not require the use of the viability tests in circumstances where the physician did not believe that the tests were necessary for a viability determination. Because of the history of this litigation, the issue of whether a state could establish a presumption of viability for all fetuses after a certain number of weeks of gestation was not before the Supreme Court. A majority of Justices believed that the statute was tailored to protect a viable fetus and, therefore, was not unconstitutional.

(3) Spouse or Parent Requirements.

Husband–Father Consent Requirements. The Court has held unconstitutional state laws that require a woman to secure the consent of the father of the fetus that is to be aborted *Planned Parenthood of Central Missouri v. Danforth* (1976).

Parental Notification or Consent Requirements. States may place some limitations on the ability of an unemancipated pregnant minor to consent to an abortion. The Supreme Court has not explained, in a majority opinion, the precise extent to which a minor female's abortion choices can be subject to a requirement of parental notification or parental consent. However, the rulings of the Supreme Court provide some guidance as to the types of parental notification or parental consent laws that will be upheld or invalidated.

Before examining the rulings, we should explain the terminology describing state laws regarding abortions for minors. A "consent requirement" is a law that requires one or both parents give actual consent to the minor's decision to have an abortion. A "notification requirement" statute does not require parental consent but it does require the physician (or in some statutes another health care provider) to notify one or both of the parents of the minor at some time prior to the abortion. Notification requirement statutes often require the minor to wait for 24 or 48 hours after the notification before she can have the abortion.

When courts refer to a "judicial bypass procedure," they are referring to a process by which the minor may avoid the consent or notification requirement by seeking a ruling from an adjudicatory tribunal. The tribunal may be a judge of a court of general jurisdiction, a juvenile court judge, or an administrative panel that state law authorizes to make decisions concerning abortions for minors. The judicial bypass procedures that have survived Supreme Court review will allow a minor to have the abortion without notification to, or consent of, either of her parents *if* the judge or tribunal finds either (1) that the minor is sufficiently mature to make her own decision regarding the abortion, or (2) that the best interests of the minor are served by her obtaining the abortion without parental notification even though she is not sufficiently mature to make her own decision regarding the abortion.

Parental Consent or Notification Laws—Overview of the Supreme Court's Cases and Standards. The rulings of the Supreme Court allow the state to require a minor to receive the consent of one parent prior to having the abortion *if*, but only if, the state has established a judicial bypass procedure.

The judge in the bypass procedure must decide whether the minor should receive the abortion without notification to her parent because she is mature enough to make the decision herself or because the abortion is in her interests. The bypass procedure must operate in a timely manner (so as to avoid an undue burden on the minor's rights due to delay). The bypass procedure must guard against disclosure of the minor's identity (although there is no requirement that the state guarantee complete anonymity).

It appears that a state may also require a minor to receive the consent of both parents prior to an abortion if it has established a judicial bypass procedure that meets the foregoing standards, although the constitutionality of this type of law is not entirely clear. A state may not require that both of a minor's parents receive notification prior to the minor having an abortion, unless the state has provided a constitutionally adequate judicial bypass procedure. A two-parent notification requirement without a judicial bypass procedure is unconstitutional.

It is not clear whether a state may require that one of a minor's parents be notified of her intent to have an abortion, if the state does not provide a judicial bypass procedure. It is arguable that a state may require a doctor to give notice to one of the minor's parents, without a bypass procedure, if the doctor is only required to make a reasonable effort to notify one parent and if the doctor is allowed to perform the abortion without notification when waiting for actual notification to the parent would endanger the health or safety of the minor.

If a state law establishes a parental consent or notification requirement that meets constitutional standards (because it has a judicial bypass procedure) then the state may require the minor to wait for 48 hours after her parents have been notified before the abortion is performed. It is unclear whether a waiting period (following a constitutional notification procedure) that is greater than 48 hours would be permissible.

In the cases that established the foregoing guidelines, a majority of Justices, although without majority opinions, have found that the government can take reasonable steps to protect minors and family units without impairing any fundamental constitutional value. Legal systems often require notification to, or consent of, a parent or guardian before a child receives significant medical treatment, as a means of protecting an immature child from making a choice that will be physically or psychologically harmful to the child. An abortion notification statute may also protect a legitimate societal interest in promoting a family unit (though not necessarily a "traditional" or "nuclear" family) as a basic component of the social structure.

The Supreme Court has not issued a majority opinion that identifies these interests as the justification for statutory limitations on a minor female's ability to have an abortion. In each of the cases in which the Supreme Court has examined a parental notification or consent requirement, the Justices have divided into three groups. One set of Justices would invalidate almost any restriction on a minor female's ability to choose to have an abortion; a second group would be so deferential to this state that they would appear to uphold a parental "veto" over the choices of their minor children. The third group of Justices provided the swing votes. This division of the Justices continued in *Planned Parenthood v. Casey* (1992).

Lambert v. Wicklund (1997) (per curiam) suggests that the Court would uphold a state statute requiring a minor to prove *both* that the abortion would be in her best interest, *and* that avoiding parental notification would be in her best interest. *Lambert* upheld a statute that required an unemancipated minor either to notify one of her parents or to prove that the abortion was in her best interest. The Court said that its prior case law assumed that "a judicial bypass procedure requiring a minor to show that *parental notification is not* in her best interests is equivalent to a judicial bypass procedure requiring a minor to show that *abortion without notification* is in her best interests." (emphasis in original). Three concurring Justices in *Lambert* believed that the state statute before the Court did not require a minor to prove both that the abortion was in her best interest and that notification was not in her best interest. The concurring Justices asserted that the Supreme Court had not resolved the question of what the minor must prove regarding the abortion, parental notification, and her best interest.

(4) Public Funding of Abortions. The Court defines a woman's right to an abortion in terms of her freedom to make a decision free of governmental restraints. The Court refuses to accept governmental attempts to demonstrate a societal interest in preserving a fetus that would limit the woman's freedom of choice. Yet the Court has found that indigent women have no claim of right to public funding for abortions. The woman's right includes only her own decision to attempt to secure an abortion in the private sector. The Court will not issue a ruling that requires public funding, even though it will leave some women without a realistic chance to secure the abortion that they have a fundamental right to choose.

Maher v. Roe (1977) held that the Constitution did not require either the state or federal governments to subsidize non-therapeutic abortions (i.e., not necessary to preserve the health of a pregnant woman). *Maher* ruled that the equal protection clause permits a state participating in the Medicaid program to refuse to pay the expenses incident to non-therapeutic abortions for indigent women although it paid expenses incident to childbirth. The majority saw these programs as merely encouraging childbirth rather than penalizing those who sought abortion but could not afford to pay for them. The three dissenting Justices viewed this case as a retreat from the recognition of the right as truly fundamental. But the majority was unconvinced that the right to privacy included a right to government benefits in order to procure an abortion.

Three years later, *Harris v. McRae* (1980) upheld the federal government's decision to exclude from federal medical benefits programs the funding for abortions for indigent women even when a woman's attending physician had determined that an abortion was medically necessary to safeguard her health. The Court found that the law in question (the "Hyde Amendment") not only eliminated federal funding for almost all abortions, but also freed the states of any duty to fund abortions that were not funded by the federal Medicaid program.

Justice Stewart for the majority said that the Court's previous decisions in the area of abortion established only a fundamental right of a woman to be able to choose to have an abortion without direct government interference. The government could not attempt to limit a woman's right to an abortion by imposing an artificial definition of the time when a fetus became viable or by enacting regulations designed to inhibit a woman's access to abortion services, because such laws interfered with a woman's fundamental right and were not supported by a compelling government interest. But, Justice Stewart reasoned, the Hyde Amendment "places no governmental obstacle in the path of a woman who chooses to terminate her pregnancy, but rather, by means of unequal subsidization of abortion and other medical services, encourages alternative activity deemed in the public interest." The Court argued that a woman could not exercise her fundamental right to secure an abortion in the private sector because her inability to exercise her freedom of choice was the result of her own lack of resources rather than government action.

The Court also quickly dispensed with the claim that the Hyde Amendment violated the religion clauses of the First Amendment. The fact that the Hyde Amendment coincided with the doctrines of certain religious sects did not provide a basis for its invalidation because the Amendment has a secular purpose of encouraging childbirth. To use the establishment clause to prohibit laws that have an ethical basis in some religion would be to deprive the government of an ability to act in many areas traditionally recognized as being within the police power of the state. Further, no plaintiff attacking the validity of the Hyde Amendment had standing to claim that the law violated the free exercise clause because, not unexpectedly, none could demonstrate that they must procure an abortion under compulsion of their religious beliefs.

When the government has not monopolized the provision of abortion services, it is not required to fund abortions. Thus, *Rust v. Sullivan* (1991) upheld the Department of Health and Human Services' regulations that prohibited private doctors who received federal funds for "family planning services" from giving abortion information to a woman client of the federally funded family planning service except when an individual woman might need an abortion to prevent a serious threat to her life. These regulations did not impair a woman's right to choose whether to terminate a pregnancy. Earlier cases established that "the government has no constitutional duty to subsidize an activity merely because the activity is constitutionally protected and [the government] may validly choose to fund child birth over abortion." The Court explained that a pregnant woman who visited a federally funded family planning clinic that did not provide her with information concerning abortions was "in no worse position than if Congress had never enacted Title X," the act that provided family planning services grants.

§ 14.24 Emerging Issues Regarding the Right to Privacy

(a) Accumulation and Distribution of Data Concerning Individual Citizens

The Supreme Court has not yet held that the right to privacy limits governmental powers relating to the collection of data concerning private individuals. In *Whalen v. Roe* (1977) the Court unanimously upheld a New York law that required physicians and pharmacists to forward to state authorities copies of prescriptions for medicines containing certain narcotics. The majority opinion by Justice Stevens held that the statute was valid even if the right to privacy places some restriction on the ability of government to collect data concerning individual citizens. The New York law related to the legitimate goal of controlling illegal drug distribution and reasonable in its limitations on the use and distribution of the collected data. The mere possibility that the data would be used improperly did not void the law. Stevens noted, however, that government data collection did threaten individual privacy, and, for that reason, that the right to collect such data normally would be limited by a duty to avoid unwarranted disclosure of the information collected. The majority opinion stated that this duty "arguably has its roots in the Constitution," but did not rule on this issue.

(b) The Right to Die

One can divide the "right to die" cases into two categories. First, there is the case when a mentally competent adult makes a decision to refuse life sustaining medical treatment based on the most complete information that he can receive. The second type of case is what Professor Yale Kamisar has called the "right to kill," which is when an individual who is not competent to make a decision regarding her own medical treatment (perhaps because she is in a coma) and the issue is whether the patient's doctor, family, or a designated surrogate should determine whether life support systems should be employed for a comatose individual.

If a state authorizes a person other than the individual patient to make a decision to refuse or terminate life sustaining treatment for that individual, the state should create some procedure to protect the life, liberty, and property interests of the patient whose medical treatment will be terminated. The due process clause of the Fourteenth Amendment (applicable to states) or the due process clause of the Fifth Amendment (applicable to the federal government) should be considered when determining whether the government may create a system that authorizes one person to terminate the life of another. A decision to terminate life support for a comatose individual will involve "state action" if the decision is made pursuant to a state law or court order or if the individual is treated at a government hospital. The due process clause should require a process that fairly determines whether the interests of the individual who is to die (after the termination of the life sustaining treatment) have been fairly appraised. If a doctor at a state hospital withdraws life sustaining treatment or nutrition from a comatose patient pursuant to a law, the government has taken the life of the individual. There should be some fair process to determine that the decision to withdraw life support was not made arbitrarily or for malevolent purpose (such as a decision by a family member who desires to inherit the property of the comatose individual).

The question whether the Constitution of the United States limits the government's ability to require doctors and hospitals to take all means to sustain the life of an individual, when that individual or his family objected to the medical treatment, is of recent origin. Some judicial rulings on the free exercise of religion might be interpreted to give support to the argument that the government could not force an individual to accept medical treatment that violated the principles of his religion. Before 1990, there was no indication that there was any substantive constitutional right, apart from the religion clauses, to refuse life sustaining medical treatment.

Cruzan v. Director, Missouri Department of Health (1990) (5 to 4) upheld a state's ability to require family members to prove by clear and convincing evidence that an incompetent person desired the withdrawal of life sustaining treatment. The ruling was a narrow one, and language in Justice O'Connor's concurring opinion, and dicta in the majority opinion, gave states little guidance whether there is a right to refuse life sustaining medical treatment.

The *Cruzan* decision involved a state law that the Missouri Supreme Court had interpreted to require a hospital to give life sustaining treatment to an individual (at least when the individual was under the control of the government) unless: (1) the individual was a mentally competent adult who refused the medical treatment on the basis of adequate information or, (2) the guardian (or close family members) of an incompetent patient could prove by "clear and convincing evidence" that the incompetent patient would have rejected life sustaining treatment under the circumstances present in the case.

The U.S. Supreme Court held that the state law, as interpreted, was constitutional. The Court assumed for the purposes of the case (but did not decide) that the "liberty" protected by the due process clauses of the Fifth and Fourteenth Amendments included a right of mentally competent individuals to refuse life saving or life sustaining medical treatment. Even assuming that such a right existed, the Court held that the importance of the interest at stake (the termination of the individual's life) justified the state's decision to use a standard of proof ("clear and convincing evidence") that reduced the chance for error. The state could refuse to make an independent judgment about the quality of a life. The Constitution did not require the state to accept decisions of family members that the best interest of the patient would be saved by terminating medical treatment. The state could prefer the preservation of life over other interests asserted on behalf of the individual, at least in a situation where the patient herself had not made the decision to reject life sustaining treatment.

Cruzan did not decide whether a competent adult could designate another person to make decisions regarding life sustaining or lifesaving medical treatment for her, if she was in a condition that made her incompetent to make that decision herself. Of course, if there is no right to reject lifesaving treatment, there would be no right to appoint a surrogate decision-maker. The four dissenters in *Cruzan* believed that an individual had a right to control the decision to reject life sustaining treatment through the appointment of a surrogate. Justice O'Connor's concurring opinion indicated that she might agree with that view.

Justice Scalia's concurring opinion in *Cruzan* argued that if an individual has a constitutionally protected right to refuse lifesaving medical treatment and life sustaining nutrition, it would seem to be unconstitutional for a state to make it a crime for that person to take active steps to terminate his life. If an individual has a right to refuse life sustaining nutrition, and, thereby, starve to death, then it is hard to understand why the decision to commit suicide could be a basis for committing the person to a mental health care facility.

One answer to the questions raised by Justice Scalia is that only a mentally competent adult would have a constitutional right to refuse medical treatment. Some state laws allow for involuntary commitment of an adult to a mental health care facility if the government, or other persons, can prove that the individual represents a danger to himself. Are these commitment statutes constitutional? But, if there is a "right to die" how could a court order mental health care for a person whose only "abnormal behavior" is his stated desire to kill himself? A court would be unable to determine whether such a person was a "competent adult" or an "incompetent adult" unless the court decided whether the individual had correctly decided that the continuation of his life was not worthwhile. In other words, if there is a constitutional right to die, it would seem difficult for courts to avoid making quality of life decisions when determining whether an individual could be held in a mental health care facility solely because he might kill himself.

Or, the Court might decide that there is no constitutional right to suicide but only a right of a competent adult to refuse life-saving medical treatment. One might make a distinction between acts (to kill) and omissions (to refuse to undergo life-saving surgery). Or, the law might distinguish between heroic or invasive medical procedures versus more ordinary procedures.

In two companion cases in 1997, the Court refused to extend *Cruzan.* The Court held that state statutes prohibiting a person from assisting another person to commit suicide do not violate substantive due process or equal protection. While the Justices were unanimous in upholding the statutes on their face, the decisions left open questions concerning the extent of a terminally ill patient's constitutional right to choose, and a physician's right to provide, medical treatment that would relieve the patient's pain, even thought it might (or would) hasten the patient's death.

Washington v. Glucksberg (1997) rejected a substantive due process challenge to a state law prohibiting anyone from aiding another person to commit suicide. The Ninth Circuit had ruled that the plaintiffs, who had alleged that they were in terminal phases of painful illnesses, were denied liberty without due process by a statute that prohibited them from receiving assistance in terminating their life as they wished. The Supreme Court unanimously overruled the Ninth Circuit and held that the statute, on its face, did not violate due process.

Vacco v. Quill (1997) rejected a claim by physicians that New York statutes that made it a crime for them to assist persons in the commission of suicide during a terminal illness violated equal protection. The statutes allowed mentally competent terminally ill persons to refuse, or direct the removal of, life support systems but did not allow terminally ill persons to receive medical assistance to hasten their death by other means (such as a lethal dose of medication). The Second Circuit argued that the statutory classifications violated equal protection, and the Supreme Court, unanimously, reversed, holding the distinction between suicide and refusing lifesaving medical support does not violate equal protection.

Because *Glucksberg* and *Vacco* both held that there is no fundamental right to commit suicide, it used the rational basis standard to find that: (1) the prohibition on assisted suicides did not violate substantive due process; and (2) the distinction between allowing individuals to refuse life support and the prohibition of suicide did not violate equal protection.

Washington v. Glucksberg held that an individual does not have a fundamental constitutional right to terminate his or her life. Rehnquist, speaking for the majority concluded that the history of legal treatment of suicide in the United States, and the difficulty of precisely defining a "right" to commit suicide, led to the conclusion that "the asserted right to assistance in committing suicide is not a fundamental liberty interest."

The Court had no difficulty in upholding the ban on assisted suicides under the rationality test, because the states have legitimate interests in the preservation of human life, the integrity of the medical profession, and the protection of vulnerable groups of persons who might feel pressured to terminate their lives.

The majority opinion in *Vacco v. Quill* (1997) tracked the reasoning of *Glucksberg*. The State of New York allowed mentally competent adults, under certain circumstances, to refuse life sustaining medical treatment although the state prohibited anyone from aiding another person to commit suicide. Physicians asserted that the statutes prohibiting a terminally ill patient from receiving assistance in suicide while allowing other patients to refuse life sustaining medical treatment created an arbitrary classification that violated the equal protection clause. The New York statute did not employ traits such as race, sex, or illegitimacy that would have justified a more active judicial review of the classification.

Vacco then ruled that there is no fundamental right to commit suicide, and, therefore, that the distinction between allowing a patient to refuse medical treatment and prohibiting a patient from receiving assistance in committing suicide is subject only to the rational basis test. The distinction in the statutes is rationally related to the state's interests in the health and welfare of individuals and the ethics of the medical profession. Indeed, the law treats each person in New York in an identical manner in the sense that every person has the right under state law to refuse unwanted life saving medical treatment and no person is allowed to assist in the commission of a suicide. The statute's distinction between suicide and refusal of life support followed longstanding "legal principles of causation and intent" long used in the law. Thus, the statutory classifications are rationally related to legitimate state interests.

The Justices were unanimous in upholding the Washington and New York statutes prohibiting assisted suicide on their face. Nevertheless, the concurring opinions in *Glucksberg* and *Vacco* demonstrated that there were at least four Justices who believed that, in a future case, the Supreme Court might rule that a person facing imminent death has a fundamental right to receive medical treatment that eases his pain even though it would invariably hasten his death.

For example, Justice O'Connor concurred in the majority opinions written but she also wrote a concurring opinion in *Glucksberg* and *Vacco*. She asserted that the majority had not addressed, and there was no need to reach, "the question of whether suffering patients have a constitutionally cognizable interest in obtaining relief from suffering" that might hasten their deaths.

§ 14.25   The Right to Vote: The Electoral Franchise as a Fundamental Right

(a)(1) Introduction

The Constitution initially contained two provisions that related to the exercise of the electoral franchise. Article I, section two mandates that electors for members of the House of Representatives shall meet the same qualifications as "Electors for the most numerous Branch of the State Legislature." Article II, section one and the Twelfth and Twentieth Amendments, establish the procedure to select members of the Electoral College, who in turn select the President and Vice–President. The Supreme Court has used these provisions to support the proposition that the states, because of this inherent constitutional authority to control the electoral process, can require persons to meet certain reasonable requirements before they vote in state or national elections.

However, later Amendments to the Constitution place restrictions on the ability of states to impose franchise requirements. The Fifteenth Amendment, for example, prohibits the states from impairing the franchise on the basis "of race, color, or previous condition of servitude." The Nineteenth Amendment forbids discrimination in voting by sex. The Twenty–Fourth Amendment prevents the states from imposing "any poll tax or other tax" on a person before that person can vote for a candidate for a federal office. The Twenty–Sixth Amendment grants the right to vote to all citizens of the United States who are eighteen years of age or older.

Besides these explicit constitutional requirements, the Court has held that the Fourteenth Amendment restricts the power of the states to place qualifications on the exercise of the franchise. The Court has used the Fourteenth Amendment to fashion a "fundamental right" to vote. The right to vote is "fundamental" because it "is preservative of other basic civil and political rights." Therefore, any alleged impairment of the right is subjected to "strict scrutiny" and must not violate equal protection. *Kramer v. Union Free School District* (1969).

In addition, the Court has recognized that Congress has some power to legislatively override the states' authority to govern the exercise of the franchise, pursuant to its power under section 5 of the Fourteenth Amendment, a topic considered in Chapter 15.

While the right to vote is fundamental and subject to "strict scrutiny," in this context "strict scrutiny" means only that Court must independently review voting regulations. If restriction is in fact related to important or overriding state interests, the Court will sustain that regulation or restriction. For example, the Court has upheld reasonable age, citizenship, and residency requirements, such as a 50 day residency requirements for voting in local elections. *Marston v. Lewis* (1973); *Burns v. Fortson* (1973).

A government regulation restricting the ability of citizens to nominate or vote for the candidate of their choice restricts their First Amendment right of political association and also raises equal protection problems concerning any classifications contained in, or created by, the regulation. Voting regulations regarding the ability of an individual voter to participate in an election often are examined under the equal protection guarantee because these regulations classify or separate those who my or may not vote in an election. Or, the restriction dilutes the voting power of a particular class of persons.

Under either equal protection or First Amendment analysis, a restriction on the right to vote is subject to "strict scrutiny." However, strict scrutiny analysis in this area is not invariably fatal to the law. In general, the state only has demonstrate that its regulation is narrowly tailored to promote an interest that is significant enough to outweigh any incidental restriction on the right to vote or the right of political association. Laws that totally prohibit a class of persons from voting in a general election or laws designed to restrict the voting power of a particular class of persons in a general election are unlikely to survive such a standard. Laws that regulate the electoral system to promote substantial state interests in the conduct of efficient and honest elections need to be examined on a case-by-case basis.

Burdick v. Takushi (1992) openly adopted this case-by-case balancing approach to voting rights issues and upheld the State of Hawaii's prohibition on write-in voting. Justice White wrote for a majority of the Court in holding: "The rigorousness of our inquiry into the propriety of a state election law depends on the extent to that a challenged regulation burdens First and Fourteenth Amendment rights. . . . when those rights are subjected to 'severe' restrictions the regulation must be narrowly drawn to advance a state interest of compelling importance . . . but when a state election law provision imposes only 'reasonable, nondiscriminatory restrictions' upon First and Fourteenth Amendment rights of voters the state's important regulatory interests are generally sufficient to justify the restrictions."

Burdick found that Hawaii's prohibition of write-in voting limited the ballot to persons with some demonstrated political support so as to avoid "unrestrained factionalism" and to facilitate the workings of the democratic process. These state interests outweighed the desire of the voter to add a name to the ballot, when the person for whom he wished to write-in a vote had not gone through the primary system and, therefore, had no demonstrated public support.

The Court reaffirmed the case-by-case balancing approach in *Timmons* v. *Twin Cities Area New Party* (1997), which upheld a state law prohibiting candidates from appearing on a ballot as a candidate for more than one political party. Chief Justice Rehnquist, writing for the majority, stated that, in election law cases, the Court would "weigh the character and magnitude of the burden, the state's ruling imposes on those rights [First and Fourteenth Amendment association rights] against the interest the State contends justify that burden . . . severe burdens on plaintiffs' rights must be narrowly tailored and advance a compelling state interest. Lesser burdens, however, trigger less exacting scrutiny and a state's important regulatory interest will usually be enough to justify reasonable, nondiscriminatory restrictions."

Hunter v. Underwood (1985) unanimously invalidated a provision of the Alabama Constitution, adopted in 1901, that denied the vote to persons convicted of "any crime . . . involving moral turpitude". The plaintiffs had demonstrated that this provision was adopted for the purpose of disproportionately disenfranchising black persons and that the law continued to have that effect into modern times. Although this provision was, on its face, racially neutral, it was clear that the original enactment was motivated by the desire to discriminate against blacks on account of race and this provision had had a racially discriminatory impact since its adoption. Justice Rehnquist, for the Court, held that section two of the Fourteenth Amendment "was not designed to permit the purposeful racial discrimination" that was the true motivating force of this provision. In response to the state's argument that the Tenth Amendment should protect state autonomy in regulating voting privileges, Rehnquist responded: "The Tenth Amendment can not save legislation prohibited by the subsequently enacted Fourteenth Amendment."

The Court's rulings concerning the right to vote are written in terms of equal protection, because the Court had held that the right to vote is constitutionally "fundamental" and subject to active judicial review. However, many of these decisions may best be described as a form of substantive due process because they are based on an analysis of the importance of that right. The Court ruling restricts the substance of legislation regulating the exercise of the electoral franchise.

(a)(2) The 2000 Presidential Election and the Right to Vote

Introduction. The actions of the United States Supreme Court that effectively ended the long count and thus decided the 2000 presidential election undoubtedly will be the subject of debate for many years. While unofficial media recounts of the Florida election later showed that George Bush still would have won a recount by a slim margin, reasonable (or unreasonable, for that matter) persons may debate the wisdom and, indeed, legitimacy of the Court's rulings in *Bush v. Gore* (2000) (per curiam). Yet, the basic legal issues that the Court addressed were fairly straightforward. In order to understand those rulings one must review the constitutional provisions that might be at issue in voting cases, in general, and the controversy concerning the naming of the State of Florida's presidential and vice presidential electors, in particular.

Article II of the Constitution, and several Amendments, govern the election and terms of the President and Vice President of the United States. Section 1, Clause 2, of Article II gives each state the power to appoint "in such manner as the Legislature thereof may direct," a certain number of electors, equivalent to the state's congressional delegation and sets the terms for electors. Although states are given a plenary power in the naming of electors, Article II Section 1, Clause 4, gives Congress power to determine the time when states choose electors and the date when electors should submit their votes for President and Vice President. The Twelfth Amendment superseded Article II Section 1, Clause 3 regarding the procedures by that electors cast their ballots, and the role of the Congress in choosing a President and Vice President when no individual receives a majority of the electoral votes for those positions. The Twelfth Amendment was modified by Amendment Twenty, which establishes the starting date for the terms of the President and Vice President (as well as Congress), and established a provision for dealing with a situation in that a President-elect shall have died at the time for the beginning for his or her term of office. Amendment Twenty–Two establishes a two-term limit on the Presidency. Amendment Twenty–Five provides rules concerning succession of the President and Vice President. Amendment Twenty–Three gives residents of the District of Columbia the power to name electors for President and Vice President.

No single provision of the Constitution or its Amendments actually establishes a right of individuals to vote, except for Article I, § 2, which gives the people of each state the same right to vote for members of the House of Representatives as their states grant them for the most numerous house of the state legislature, and Amendment Seventeen, which transferred the election of Senators from state legislatures to individual voters. Instead, the most important provisions of the Constitution place limits on the power of the state to deny the vote once it creates it. For example, if the state has an election, it cannot deny the vote on account of race or sex. And, it cannot violate the one person, one vote principle.

In a long series of decisions (many discussed later in this chapter), the Court had held that once a state decides to choose an office by election, the courts must treat the right to vote as a fundamental right whose abridgement requires close judicial scrutiny. The equal protection clause of the Fourteenth Amendment has been the basis for a wide variety of Court rulings prohibiting discrimination concerning the right to vote.

One particular aspect of equality in voting is the so-called one person-one vote rule that requires mathematical similarity between districts that are created for the purpose of electing individuals to a body with rule making power over persons in those districts. The requirement of mathematical similarity between the population of districts for congresspersons is derived from Article I, § 2, rather than the equal protection clause.

The First Round of Litigation: The *Bush I* Decision. The public voting for the 2000 presidential election was held on November 7, 2000. The Presidential candidate of the Republican Party was then Governor George W. Bush of Texas, and the Presidential candidate of the Democratic Party was then-Vice President Albert Gore. Gore received a majority of the popular vote on a nation-wide basis, but lost the electoral vote to the Republican nominee. The vote in several states was close, but Florida was enough to change the result and Gore sued for a recount.

Following litigation in the state trial court, the Florida Supreme Court ruled that the Secretary of State had the power and duty to ignore some of the state statutory deadlines, and accept some county manual recounts that took longer than normally allowed under Florida statutes.

Bush challenged the Florida Supreme Court's interpretation of the Florida statutes, allowing the Secretary of State to accept late recount totals on two bases: first, the Florida Supreme Court had changed the law that had existed prior to the time fixed for the appointment of the state electors in violation of *federal* statutes and Article II; and, second, the Florida Supreme Court violated the equal protection clause of the Fourteenth Amendment by creating a system that would treat similarly situated voters in a disparate and arbitrary manner.

In its first ruling on the Florida election, *Bush v. Palm Beach County Canvassing Board*, [*Bush I*] (Dec. 4, 2000) (per curiam), the Court unanimously vacated the judgment of the Florida Supreme Court. In a per curiam opinion, the United States Supreme Court required the Florida Supreme Court to clarify its decision, because "We are unclear as to the extent to that the Florida Supreme Court saw the Florida Constitution as circumscribing the legislature's authority under Article II, § 1, clause 2 [the provision of the U.S. Constitution granting the legislature of the state the authority to appoint electors in presidential and vice-presidential elections]. We are also unclear as to the consideration the Florida Supreme Court accorded to 3 U.S.C. § 5 [the statute providing a safe-harbor for the slate of state electors so long as the contests were decided by a law enacted prior to the time when the electors were chosen].

The Second Round of Litigation: The *Bush II & Bush III* Decisions. On November 26, the Florida Election Canvassing Commission certified the Florida election results so that Governor Bush would receive Florida's 25 electoral votes. The next day, Vice President Gore contested that certification in a Florida trial court. This litigation was technically separate from the litigation that had led to the Palm Beach County decision by the United States Supreme Court on December 4.

In the second round of litigation, the state trial court found that the Democratic candidates had failed to provide a sufficient basis for rejecting the certification of the vote issued by the Florida Elections Canvassing Commission. On appeal, the Florida Supreme Court modified the trial court's ruling and held that the trial court had properly rejected Gore's challenge to certified results in one county and his allegation that certain votes cast in Palm Beach County were not "legal votes." The Florida Supreme Court ruled, however, that Gore had met the burden of proof in challenging

Miami–Dade County's failure to include in a recount 9,000 ballots that had not registered a vote when they were put through the election machines [so-called "undervotes"]. The Florida Supreme Court ordered a hand recount of the 9,000 ballots, and, also ruled that the trial court could order a manual recount of undervotes in all counties that had not conducted a manual recount. The Florida Supreme Court ordered the trial court to accept votes that had been tabulated after a November 26 deadline in two counties [Palm Beach County and Miami–Dade County], even though the manual vote recounting teams in those counties had used different standards to recount the ballots, with some teams counting (and other not counting) both under-votes and over-votes. Indeed, the standards used to count a vote changed several times during the course of the recount. An over-vote was the term used for a ballot on that the voter punches through two chads, or marked two spots on a card ballot, indicating that the voter may have been attempting to vote for two candidates for the same office.

The Florida Supreme Court's ruling effectively required a state-wide manual recount of ballots that had not been counted by the machines [because the voter had failed to entirely punch through a portion, or chad, of the ballot next to the presidential candidate's name or had made a mark or punched the place next to more than one presidential candidate's name]. The Florida Supreme Court ruled that the persons conducting the manual recount were to examine each ballot that had been legally cast [though not counted by a machine] to determine the intent of the voter who cast the ballot, if possible.

Bush v. Gore [*Bush II*] (per curiam) (Dec. 9, 2000) (5 to 4) stayed Florida Supreme Court ruling requiring the manual recount of legally cast undervotes, and set oral arguments for the next day, which was Sunday, December 10. Justice Stevens, joined by Justices Souter, Ginsburg and Breyer dissented from the Court's ordering a stay of the Florida Supreme Court's ruling.

In *Bush v. Gore* [*Bush III*] (per curiam) (Dec. 12, 2000), the Court made two basic rulings. First, the system for the recounting of ballots established by the Florida Supreme Court violated the equal protection clause of the Fourteenth Amendment. As the per curiam opinion noted: "As seems to have been acknowledged at oral argument, the standards for accepting or rejecting contested ballots might vary not only from county to county but indeed within a single county from one recount team to another." Because no standards existed to count votes manually, the per curiam concluded: "This is not a process with sufficient guarantees of equal treatment."

Second, the Court ruled that all recounting of Florida ballots had to be stopped, so that the state's electoral vote could be certified and cast in a manner that would grant Florida the benefit of the safe harbor provision of 3 U.S.C. § 5. Chief Justice Rehnquist, and Justices O'Connor, Scalia, Kennedy, and Thomas joined this per curiam opinion.

There were three basic issues that faced the Court in *Bush v. Gore*, two concerning substantive provisions of the Constitution, and one concerning any further proceedings in the case.

The first issue, which the Supreme Court did not decide, was whether the Florida Supreme Court's interpretation of state statutes violated Article II, § 1, clause 2 because the state court was preventing the state legislature from effectively exercising control over the system for the appointment of electors and the casting of electoral votes for the President and Vice President of the United States. A related issue was whether the state court ruling conflicted with 3 U.S.C.A. § 5 because it deprived the state from using the safe harbor provision by altering the state law that had existed on Election Day, when Florida voters voted. Because the Court ruled that the state supreme court recount system violated the equal protection clause, *Bush v. Gore* never ruled on the Article II and the related statutory issues.

However, Chief Justice Rehnquist, joined by Justices Scalia and Thomas, not only joined the per curiam opinion (which decided the case on equal protection grounds) but decided this Article II issue. Rehnquist's concurrence argued that the Florida court ruling violated the provision of the U.S. Constitution granting the state *legislature*, rather than the state courts, authority over the appointment of electors. Rehnquist said that, in order "to determine whether a state court has infringed upon the legislature's authority, we necessarily must examine the law of the State as it existed prior to the action of the court." He argued that in some cases the federal courts will not defer to the state court interpretation of state law. He cited several cases, such as *NAACP v. Alabama ex rel. Patterson* (1958), where the state argued that the U.S. Supreme Court had no jurisdiction because the petitioner had not pursued the correct appellate remedy in Alabama's state courts. Rehnquist said of *Patterson*: "We found this state-law ground inadequate to defeat our jurisdiction because we were" unable to reconcile the procedural holding of the Alabama Supreme Court "with prior Alabama precedent." He could also have cited *Indiana ex rel. Anderson v. Brand* (1938), where the U.S. Supreme Court rejected the state court's interpretation of state law, explaining: "[W]e are bound to decide for ourselves" the nature of the contract, "in order that the constitutional mandate may not become a dead letter."

The second issue before the Court was whether the system that the Florida Supreme Court mandated for manually recounting ballots, which allowed canvassing boards to determine voter intent without any objective guidelines to limit their determinations, violated the due process or equal protection clauses by giving unequal treatment to similarly cast ballots by similarly situated voters. The per curiam opinion (joined by five Justices) concluded that a system for counting votes that did not have any objective standards violated the equal protection requirement that similarly situated voters (and their votes) be treated in a similar manner.

The per curiam opinion concluded that the Florida procedures allowed identical ballots to be treated differently, valuing one person's vote differently than another person's ballot. In addition, by counting all overvotes and undervotes in some counties (or parts of some counties) and only undervotes in other counties, the Florida Court was skewing the election results by favoring some counties over others.

The Court said that it is only deciding the issue presented— whether the Florida Supreme Court's procedures for conducting the recount violate equal protection. The Court explained that its ruling is limited to this issue: "Our consideration is limited to the present circumstances, for the problem of equal protection in election processes generally presents many complexities." Some critics have argued that this language meant that the Court was telling us that this case is unique and not precedent. The Court did not say that; not even the dissent made that claim. A fair reading of the quoted language simply states that the Court is not deciding an issue that is not part of this case—whether a state can use different types of voting mechanisms in different parts of the state when electing someone to a state-wide office (e.g., punch cards in some counties, optical character readers in other counties).

Justices Stevens, Souter, Ginsburg, and Breyer all dissented, but Souter's and Breyer's dissents agreed with the Court's conclusion that the recount system that the Florida Supreme Court created violated the equal protection clause.

Souter's opinion, joined by Breyer, acknowledged:

"It is true that the Equal Protection Clause does not forbid the use of a variety of voting mechanisms within a jurisdiction, even though different mechanisms will have different levels of effectiveness in recording voters' intentions; local variety can be justified by concerns about cost, the potential value of innovation, and so on. But evidence in the record here suggests that a different order of disparity obtains under rules for determining a voter's intent that have been applied (and could continue to be applied) to identical types of ballots used in identical brands of machines and exhibiting identical physical characteristics (such as 'hanging' or 'dimpled' chads).''

The, after quoting from the trial transcripts, Souter, joined by Breyer, concluded: "I can conceive of no legitimate state interest served by these differing treatments of the expressions of voters' fundamental rights. The differences appear wholly arbitrary."

However, Justice Souter, joined by Justice Breyer, argued that there could be enough time for the state court to fashion a different recount system that would not violate equal protection:

"electoral votes are due to be cast in six days. I would therefore remand the case to the courts of Florida with instructions to establish uniform standards for evaluating the several types of ballots that have prompted differing treatments, to be applied within and among counties when passing on such identical ballots in any further recounting (or successive recounting) that the courts might order. Unlike the majority, I see no warrant for this Court to assume that Florida could not possibly comply with this requirement before the date set for the meeting of electors, December 18."

Justice Breyer, in a portion of his dissenting opinion that was joined by Justice Souter, concluded that "basic principles of fairness may well have counseled the adoption of a uniform standard to address the problem [of recounting votes]."

However, these two justices did not label their opinions as "concurring in part and dissenting in the judgment." They simply dissented.

Only Justices Stevens and Ginsburg believed that the system established by the Florida Supreme Court for the manual recounting of ballots did not violate the equal protection clause. Justice Stevens did not address the equal protection issue in his opinion, but he joined Ginsburg's opinion, which stated that there was no substantial equal protection issue in the case.

The third issue was whether the United States Supreme Court should remand the case to the state court for further action and recounting of ballots, or whether the United States Supreme Court should simply end the litigation by ruling that the state court lacked any power to alter the results that had been certified by the state board and the Florida Secretary of State.

The Court's ruling effectively rejected any argument that electoral college issues are entirely political questions to be resolved by Congress in the vote counting process set out in Article II and Amendments Twelve and Twenty. However, all the Justices recognized that the ultimate determination of the legitimacy of each state's votes for the President and Vice President of the United

States would rest in the hands of the U.S. House of Representatives and Senate.

Although the majority opinion in *Bush III* described the right to vote as a fundamental constitutional right, it did not set out a specific standard of review when judging legislative classifications that relate to voting rights. The reason for the Court's failure may be a simple one. The five Justices who joined the per curiam opinion, and two concurring Justices, believed that a system for manually recounting votes that had no objective standards to guide the search for voter intent by different vote counters was totally arbitrary and that the disparate treatment of similarly cast votes was not related to any legitimate governmental interest. Because the Court was reviewing a government action that could severely impair a fundamental right (the right to vote) the Court would not grant a presumption of constitutionality to the system that the Florida court established. Rather, seven Justices chose to independently examine the standardless recount procedure to determine if it would create arbitrary classifications and disparate treatment of similarly situated voters, in violation of the basic command of equal protection, which requires that similarly situated persons be dealt with in a similar manner by the government.

First, the Court noted that "the standards for accepting or rejecting contested ballots might vary not only from county to county but indeed within a single county from one recount team to another." In other words, with no objective guidelines, one recounting team might count a ballot in that the area to be punched out next to a candidate's name [a "chad"] was only partially indented but not punched through could be counted in one county but not another. In this way, two similarly situated voters [both of whom had cast ballots with the chad partially punched or indented in an identical manner] might be treated differently, with one vote counting and one not counting, solely because of the views of individual counting teams. This unrestrained discretion on the part of counting teams was not related to any legitimate end of government. The Court cited cases related to the one person one vote principle for the principle that a state could not accord "arbitrary and disparate treatment to voters in its different counties."

The Court majority noted that the state supreme court ruling exacerbated the equal protection problem by requiring early recount totals from two counties to be considered in the new certified vote and allowing for the recount totals from a third county even though none of the counties had been ones in that Vice President Gore had contested the election totals. Those three counties had used differing standards when recounting all of the ballots in their districts, not just those that had failed to record a vote on the voting machines on November 7 or 8. This resulted in a great number of ballots being subject to the open-ended discretionary recount system. Additionally, the state supreme court order included a partial recount in a county even though the total recount could not be done within the time limits established by the state supreme court.

Bush III concluded that the system adopted by the Florida Supreme Court was "inconsistent with the minimum procedures necessary to protect the fundamental right of each voter in the special instance of a statewide recount under the authority of a single state judicial officer." The Court, in *Bush III* did not establish a general rule for the standards that a state would have to adopt when conducting manual recounts of votes, but stated that its consideration was limited only to the particular standardless system adopted by the Florida Supreme Court.

Only Justices Stevens and Ginsburg believed that the recount system adopted by the Florida Supreme Court did not present a substantial question under the equal protection clause. Stevens stated that any problems created by recounting teams using differing standards would be "alleviated—if not eliminated—by the fact that a single impartial magistrate will ultimately adjudicate all objections arising from the recount procedure." Ginsburg found no significant equal protection problem because she believed that the recount procedure adopted by the Florida court was not "any less fair or precise than the certification that had preceded the recount [and that had been admittedly conducted in accordance with Florida statutes]."

Justices Souter and Breyer agreed with the majority's conclusion concerning the equal protection flaws in the recount system adopted by the Florida Supreme Court. Nevertheless Breyer and Souter dissented from the majority's decision to block any further recounting of the ballots cast in Florida. Souter and Breyer wanted the case remanded to the Florida Supreme Court to give that Court an opportunity to create a recount system that had objective standards that might limit the discretion of voting recount teams so as to eliminate the arbitrary treatment of similarly situated votes. They would have allowed the recount to continue at a time that would have gone past the time established for the state to make use of the so-called safe harbor provision of federal law so long as the state could complete its recount *prior* to the time when its electors had to be named and their electoral votes cast for the presidency and vice presidency.

The per curiam opinion in *Bush III* decided against a remand the Florida Supreme Court had earlier said that the relevant state statutes demonstrated a legislative desire to have the all contest to vote totals concluded by December 12, the date that would be the final time for making use of the federal safe harbor provision. Therefore, *Bush III* ruled that implementation of any recounts under state court authority should end, so that the Florida Secretary of State could certify the vote totals and the electors be appointed in a manner that came within the time frame established by the federal safe harbor provision and Florida legislation.

Justice Breyer's dissenting opinion came the closest to stating that the Article II question was a political question issue, although he did not explicitly take that position. Breyer, in a portion of his opinion that was joined by Stevens and Ginsburg, stated: "The Twelfth Amendment commits to Congress the authority and responsibility to count electoral votes. A federal statute, the Electoral Act, enacted after the close 1876 Hayes–Tilden Presidential election, specifies that, after states have tried to resolve disputes (through 'judicial' or other means), Congress is the body primarily authorized to resolve remaining disputes."

Souter, like Breyer, agreed that there were equal protection problems with the way in that the Florida implemented its recount. Like Breyer, he preferred to remand the case to the Florida courts so that they might develop standards for guiding the persons conducting the manual recount so as to avoid totally arbitrary and disparate treatment of similarly situated voters' ballots. He was unclear as to whether he would have reviewed the final recount by Florida, or whether he would have left the entire determination to Congress.

Justice Stevens argued that the majority of the U.S. Supreme Court must have been based their entire decision on "an unstated lack of confidence in the impartiality and capacity of the state judges." He believed that viewpoint undermines faith in the judiciary.

Justice Ginsburg's dissenting opinion, however, unlike the Stevens opinion, recognized that there were some circumstances where federal courts must reject state interpretations of state law: "Unavoidably, this Court must sometimes examine state law in order to protect federal rights."

(b) Restricting the Ballot to Interested Voters

Kramer v. Union Free School District (1969) invalidated a New York state law that provided that residents of a school district either had to own or lease taxable property or had to have children enrolled in the district's schools before they were eligible to vote in school district elections. The appellant in *Kramer*, a resident of the school district, was a bachelor who lived with his parents and neither owned nor leased any property. He argued that, as a resident of the district, any decisions made by the local school board would affect him, and, consequently, he and the class he represented suffered discrimination that violated equal protection. The state responded that it had an interest in limiting the election to interested persons because they would have a better understanding of the complexity of school affairs.

The Supreme Court reviewed the New York law under strict scrutiny, because it denied some persons the fundamental right to vote. The Court was willing to assume, arguendo that a state constitutionally could limit the election to interested voters. Nevertheless, this particular method was unconstitutional because it failed to achieve the purpose for that it was designed "with sufficient precision to justify denying appellant the franchise." The statute was both underinclusive and overinclusive because it drew lines that excluded interested persons and included persons who only had "a remote and indirect interest in school affairs." Therefore, the law violated the equal protection clause.

The state could, of course, limit the vote to residents. *Kramer* suggested that in some situations a state legitimately could limit an election to interested voters. Such a law would have to restrict the election precisely to those voters that would be primarily affected by the election. In *Salyer Land Co. v. Tulare Lake Basin Water Storage District* (1973) the Court encountered such a law. Certain landowners, lessees, and residents of a water storage district in California attacked the constitutionality of the voter qualification provision of the district. They contended the statute violated the equal protection clause because it allowed only landowners to vote in the water storage district elections.

The Court, however, believed that the *Kramer* analysis was inappropriate for this case. It observed that the water storage district possessed only limited authority and did not provide general public services like schools or housing. Moreover, the district's operations affect primarily the land within the district, and not residents as residents. Therefore, because the district served a special purpose that had a disproportionate effect on landowners the state could legitimately impose a landownership restriction as a means to establish a demonstrated interest in the election.

It is not easy to reconcile *Kramer* with *Tulare Lake Basin Water Storage District*. But the functions of the water storage district were more specialized than those of a school board and *Hill v. Stone* (1975) found this distinction important.

Hill examined the Texas "dual box" voting technique for bond elections. Property owners would place their ballots in one ballot box, and voters who did not own property would place their ballots in another. Before a bond issue could pass, it must receive not only a majority of the total votes cast but also a majority of the votes cast by property owners. The Court declared this scheme unconstitutional.

The Court stated that, if the election is of special interest, the state can limit the election to those who will be primarily affected. If "the election in question is not one of special interest, any classification restricting the franchise on grounds other than residence, age, and citizenship cannot stand unless the district or State can demonstrate that the classification serves a compelling state interest." In a previous case the Court had declared that a general obligation bond issue is of general interest. *Phoenix v. Kolodziejski* (1970). Similarly, the bond election at issue in *Hill* failed to serve a compelling state interest, and the dual box voting device violated the equal protection clause.

Ball v. James (1981), another water case, allowed Arizona to create a system for electing directors of a water reclamation district that limited voting eligibility to land owners who were otherwise eligible to vote and that apportioned voting power according to the amount of land owned by each voter. The Arizona system was in essence a one acre, one vote system. Persons who owned less than an acre of land within the district received fractional votes; tenant farmers had no votes. State law authorized the water district to generate and sell electric power to a large portion of the state and distribute water to urban areas as well as farming areas. It could also issue tax exempt bonds, but it had no general taxing power.

Unfortunately, the Court has failed to define exactly the nature of a special interest election, but it has stated that it will sustain a "demonstrated interest" restriction for such elections as long as a reasonable basis exists for the limitation. On the other hand, the Court will review strictly any "demonstrated interest" requirement for general interest elections.

If a state cannot convince the Court that it has created only a limited purpose governmental entity, or that one group of citizens is distinctly affected by the action of a governmental entity, it will be able to limit the vote to a group of interested voters only if the law bears a reasonable relationship to important statutory objectives.

(c) Voting or Poll Taxes

The Twenty-fourth Amendment prohibits the states from imposing a poll tax as a prerequisite for voting in presidential and congressional elections. The Amendment does not apply to local or state elections. Nevertheless, *Harper v. Virginia State Board of Elections* (1966), held that poll taxes for state and local elections violate equal protection.

Harper recognized that the Constitution did not grant an expressed right to vote in state elections, but the Court said that once the state grants the franchise, it must follow the dictates of the equal protection clause. The Court argued that the ability to vote has no relationship to wealth, so any impairment of the voting right based on wealth should violate the Fourteenth Amendment. A state "violates the equal protection clause of the Fourteenth Amendment whenever it makes affluence of the voter or payment of any fee an electoral standard."

(d) Literacy Tests

Historically, the most common restriction on the franchise was the literacy test. The Court considered the constitutionality of literacy tests in *Lassiter v. Northampton County Board of Elections* (1959). The appellants, black citizens from North Carolina, asked the Court to declare unconstitutional on its face a state statute that required a person to pass a literacy test before he could vote in state elections. The Court previously had held literacy tests constitutional in *Guinn v. United States* (1915), which it refused to overrule. *Lassiter* believed that the states have broad power to establish requirements that a person must meet before exercising the franchise. As long as the states do not administer literacy tests in a racially discriminatory way, the Court will not ban them under the Fourteenth Amendment. The Court added that the ability to read and write has a direct relationship to the intelligent use of the voting right, and, therefore, classifications based on literacy are neutral.

Congress later enacted a statute prohibiting state from using literacy tests as a voting requirement. Congress began the process of outlawing literacy tests with the 1965 Voting Rights Act. In a series of cases, the Court sustained the Act as within Congress' power to enforce the Fourteenth and Fifteenth Amendments.

(e) Physical Access to Polling Places—Inmates of Correctional Facilities

Inmates, in a series of cases, have challenged a state's authority to restrict the franchise based on a physical ability to go to the polls. *O'Brien v. Skinner* (1974) involved imprisoned persons who were either awaiting trial or convicted of misdemeanors. None was subject to any voting disability under state law.

The New York election and correctional officials refused either to issue ballots, to establish registration or voting facilities within the jail, or to transport the appellants to the polls. The Court found that the decision as to who would receive absentee ballots, as the state's election statutes were construed by its highest courts was "wholly arbitrary." For example, those held in jail awaiting trial in a county other than their residence were permitted to register by mail and vote by absentee ballot, but if a person was confined for the same reason in the county of their own residence, he would be denied the ballot. The state cannot, the Court concluded, deny voters "any alternative means of casting their vote although they are legally qualified to vote."

It is unclear how broadly one should read *O'Brien*. The basis of the Court's decision was not that absentee ballots are constitutionally required but that if the state has this absentee procedure it cannot be "wholly arbitrary" in deciding what classes of voters may use it. But the majority's broad concluding dictum supports a view that a state cannot refuse to provide means for qualified citizens to exercise the franchise who are physically unable to get to the polls.

In any event, this line of cases does not involve the power of the state to deny completely the ballot (absentee or otherwise) from certain classes of voters, for example, convicted felons. *Richardson v. Ramirez* (1974) sustained the states' authority to deny the vote to convicted felonies even though they had completed serving their sentences. The Court found support in section two of the Fourteenth Amendment.

(f) Residency Requirements

The Supreme Court has recognized that the state may qualify the voting right with reasonable residency restrictions. *Carrington v. Rash* (1965), for example, declared unconstitutional a Texas statute that prevented members of the armed services who moved to Texas from voting in state elections regardless of the length of time they had lived in Texas or their status as property-owners. The Court held that the law violated equal protection, and that Texas must develop a more precise means to determine the validity of a claim of residency than the challenged statute's classification scheme.

Some states have imposed *durational* residency requirement. Congress, however, abolished residency requirements for presidential elections with the 1970 Voting Rights Act, and the Court sustained it in *Oregon v. Mitchell* (1970). Nevertheless, the Voting Rights Act allowed the states to place a durational residency restriction on the right to vote in state elections.

Dunn v. Blumstein (1972) considered the constitutionality of Tennessee's durational residency requirement. Tennessee law provided that before a person could vote in state elections that person not only had to meet age and citizenship requirements but also had to be a resident of the state for one year and of the county for three months. Although the *Dunn* Court acknowledged that the states can require their voters to be residents, the Court invalidated this particularly long durational requirement because it impaired both voting rights and the right to travel. The Court reasoned that other means were available to determine bona fide residence and that with the prevalence of mass communications, citizens who have moved into an area can learn about local affairs quickly.

The Court's test appears to be one of reasonableness. It has upheld a fifty-day durational restriction. A Court has concluded that a restriction of less than two months may be necessary to verify voter lists or records and prevent fraud. *Marston v. Lewis* (1973); *Burns v. Fortson* (1973).

Holt Civic Club v. Tuscaloosa (1978) approved a municipality's exercise of extra-territorial jurisdiction over nonresidents who could not vote in municipal elections. Holt, an unincorporated community, was three miles from Tuscaloosa, Alabama. Alabama statutes subjected Holt residents to the police and sanitary regulations of Tuscaloosa, a major municipal entity. Under these statutes, Tuscaloosa could license certain businesses, trades, and professions in Holt, however, the license fees that it collected from businesses in an unincorporated community could not exceed one-half the fee charged similar businesses in the city. Holt residents argued that Tuscaloosa's jurisdiction over them was unconstitutional because they were not given the opportunity to participate in elections for city officials. They wanted the Court either to invalidate the extra-territorial powers of the city or, in the alternative, to give them the right to vote in municipal elections if they are subject to the municipality's jurisdiction.

Holt rejected both the equal protection and due process claims of the Holt residents. First, the Holt residents could not vote because they were not residents of Tuscaloosa. Using residency as a requirement for voting was permissible because using a governmental "impact analysis" to determine who should vote in city elections is unworkable. Municipal actions often affect many persons living immediately outside city boundaries in a variety of ways. The Court therefore concluded that "the line heretofore marked by this Court's voting qualification decision coincides with the geographical boundary of the governmental unit at issue."

Secondly, there was no other equal protection problem because the classification was rational: the Alabama legislature might have believed that extending the city jurisdiction was a reasonable way to facilitate possible future annexation of territory to cities, to assure that the population outside of the cities do not go without basic municipal services, and to regulate businesses outside the cities without extracting onerous license fees.

Finally, *Holt*, found no due process claim to participate in the election because the classification was not totally arbitrary. Justice

Brennan, joined by Justices White and Marshall in dissent, would have found that the Alabama system violated the equal protection clause.

In contrast, a state cannot exclude people living within a federal enclave (the National Institute of Health) within the state from voting in state elections if a federal law provides that they are state residents. *Evans v. Cornman* (1970). Federal law, after all, is the supreme law of the land.

(g) Restrictions Based on Party Affiliation

States often conduct primary elections before the final general election. To prohibit voters who belong to one political party from voting for a weak candidate in another party's primary, the states may restrict a person's ability to vote in party primary elections. Thus, *Rosario v. Rockefeller* (1973) upheld a New York law that required voters to register with the state and to select their party thirty days before the November election to be eligible to vote in the next primary. This registration deadline generally occurred eight to eleven months before the primary. Plaintiffs challenged this primary registration statute because it placed a limitation on the right to vote. The Court rejected the challenge because the law furthered the legitimate state goal of preventing party raiding. The time limit bore a reasonable relationship to that goal because a voter probably would not register in one party when he intended to vote the other party's ticket in the November election.

In contrast, *Kusper v. Pontikes* (1973) invalidated a party affiliation that prohibited a person from voting in the primary election of one political party if that person had voted in another party's primary election anytime within the previous twenty-three months. This time limit was too long; it locked-in a voter into a party affiliation and the only way to break free was to forego voting in primaries for almost two years. Illinois could use less drastic alternatives to prevent party raiding.

Timmons v. Twin Cities Area New Party (1997) upheld a state "antifusion law" that prohibited any person from appearing on a ballot as a candidate for more than one political party. Although an antifusion law makes it more difficult for minor parties to nominate a candidate who had a realistic possibility of being elected, the Court concluded that they were not that severe The court did not require Minnesota to justify its law with a compelling interest; the law only had to be related to an important state interest. Chief Justice Rehnquist ruled that the antifusion law was related to, and justified by, the state's interest in "protecting the integrity, fairness, and efficiency" of their election process and the "stability of [the state's] political systems." See also, § 16.20.

(h) Racial Restrictions

The Court has invalidated laws regulating the right to vote whenever the law is designed to deny the right to vote to persons because of their race or to dilute the voting strength of a racial group.

A series of cases commonly called the *White Primary Cases* clearly established that a state could not exclude a minority race from the franchise. The first of the *White Primary Cases*, *Nixon v. Herndon* (1927), declared unconstitutional a Texas law that expressly excluded blacks from voting in the Democratic primary. The law violated the Fourteenth Amendment because it impaired the right to vote on account of race or color. Later primary cases declared unconstitutional other schemes that states adopted in attempts to circumvent this holding.

Not only does the Constitution prohibit the states from expressly infringing on the right to vote on the basis of race, but it also prohibits the states from applying facially neutral laws to disenfranchise on account of race. Thus, *Gomillion v. Lightfoot* (1960) invalidated an Alabama statute that altered the city limits of Tuskegee from a square to a twenty-eight sided figure. This change removed nearly 400 black voters but no white voters from the city. This affirmative legislative action deprived citizens of the vote on the basis of race and thus violated the Fifteenth Amendment. The Court recognized the invalid racial purpose of the law.

Mobile v. Bolden (1980) invalidated a city commission system, a type of election in which there was an at-large election of all three members of the city's governing body. Black voters claimed that the city's refusal to elect commission members by district ensured that no black person could ever be elected to city government. The Court rejected the claim because the plaintiff failed to prove that the at-large voting system was created or maintained for a "racially discriminatory purpose." Statistical proof of the racially discriminatory impact of a voting regulation is relevant but one still needs to show that the government acted with the *intent* to discriminate when a party claims a violation of the Fourteenth or Fifteenth Amendment.

Contrast *Rogers v. Lodge* (1982), which upheld lower court rulings that found an at-large county commission election system violated the equal protection clause. In this case, plaintiffs had proven that the voting system was maintained for a racially discriminatory purpose. First, no black person had ever been elected to the county board of commissioners; second, the evidence showed bad intent—the system was maintained by those holding political power so that they could consistently disregard the interests and concerns of members of racial minorities within the county.

(i) Adjusting the Majority Requirement

The Court has recognized that the states legitimately may require more than a simple majority of the vote cast before the government can adopt certain programs. In *Gordon v. Lance* (1971), for example, voters challenged the constitutionality of a provision in the West Virginia Constitution that prevented political subdivisions from incurring bonded indebtedness unless sixty percent of the voters approved the bond issue in a referendum. They contended that the provision violated the Fourteenth Amendment; the Court rejected the contention. The state constitutional scheme did not single out any discrete or insular minority. Although "any departure from strict majority rule gives disproportionate power to the minority," the Constitution fails to contain any requirement that a simple majority must always prevail.

§ 14.26 The Right to Be a Candidate

(a) Introduction

The Constitution contains no express provision that guarantees the right to become a candidate. The states are free, therefore, to create restrictions on the ability to become a candidate, but the restrictions must not violate provisions of the Constitution that are of general application. States have justified their right to create conditions on the right to candidacy for several reasons. First, the restrictions help the state to limit the size of the ballot, and thus reduce the potential for voter confusion. Second, limiting the number of potential candidates helps assure that the candidate who eventually wins will have received a majority of the popular vote. Restricting the right to candidacy also helps reduce frivolous candidacies and thus preserves the integrity of the electoral process. The Supreme Court has recognized these reasons as legitimate interests of the states and as acceptable justification for some restrictions on access to the ballot.

The states have used several methods to qualify the right to become a candidate. These methods include: (1) wealth restrictions; (2) residency restrictions; (3) property ownership requirements; (4) party affiliation and demonstrated support limitations; and (5) racial classifications. With respect to category 5, obviously, any law that is a purposeful discrimination against minority race candidates or dilution of minority race voting power will be found to be a violation of equal protection and, perhaps, the Fifteenth Amendment. However, the Court has not yet adopted clear guidelines concerning when government may consider race for benign purposes, that is, in order to create electoral districts where members of racial minorities will be more likely to control the outcomes of elections and elect members of their racial group.

Although the Court has recognized the power of the states to control the electoral process in some ways, it also has used various constitutional provisions to limit the state's power to regulate access to the ballot. Ballot access restrictions, for example, must follow the dictates of the equal protection clause as well as other provisions of the Constitution, including the free speech clause, which includes a right to associate, which the Court also uses at time to void state restrictions on the right to become a candidate.

Although the Court recognizes that basic constitutional rights are intertwined in the electoral process, it also acknowledges that elections are largely political creatures and that the courts should refrain from getting too involved in basically political decisions. Nonetheless, the courts must independently scrutinize the basis for legislation to assure that ballot access restrictions are a reasonable, nondiscriminatory means of promoting important state interests.

(b) Wealth Restrictions

Many states require potential candidates for public office to pay a filing fee before the state will place their names on the ballot. In *Bullock v. Carter* (1972) the appellees challenged the constitutionality of the Texas filing fee requirement. They met all the other qualifications necessary to become candidates for public office but could not afford to pay the requisite fee of $1000. These candidates contended that the fee requirement violated the equal protection clause. Because the filing fee requirement affected the fundamental right to vote, the Court would use strict scrutiny to review the Texas law.

The state argued that the fee was necessary to limit the size of the ballot to frustrate frivolous candidates, and to help finance the election. The Court acknowledged the state's legitimate interest in protecting the integrity of the ballot, but the Court also observed that appellees were not unwilling to pay the fee but simply were unable to pay. Hence, the filing fee requirement excluded legitimate as well as frivolous candidates. It is rationale to use a filing fee to help finance elections, but under the strict scrutiny test, the state failed to show that the fee requirement was necessary to finance elections. Moreover, the state's financing argument was diluted by the fact that the state charges candidates for statewide office a lower fee than candidates for local office. Hence, *Bullock* held that the Texas filing fee requirement violated the equal protection clause.

Lubin v. Panish (1974) considered a California filing fee requirement, which equaled two per cent of the annual salary of the state office sought. The Court held that this violated equal protection insofar as it applied to indigent candidates. A minimum wealth requirement does not reflect a potential candidate's popular support or the seriousness of the candidacy. Hence, the state must provide alternative means for indigent candidates to qualify for a ballot position.

(c) Residency Restrictions

Frustrated candidates for elective office face a major constitutional obstacle whenever they challenge durational residency requirements. The Constitution itself requires candidates for federal elective office to meet certain residency standards. Art. I, §§ 2, 3 and Art. II, § 1. Therefore, unless the residency requirement is patently unreasonable in length for the particular elective office the lower courts usually have sustained such qualifications. The Supreme Court has not explained what constitutes a reasonable and constitutional residency requirement.

(d) Property Ownership Requirements

The Court invalidated a property ownership requirement for appointment to a "Board of Freeholders" in *Quinn v. Millsap* (1989). The Court said that it need not make a determination of the appropriate standard of review for all voting and candidacy rights cases in order to invalidate a state law requiring the ownership of real property as a condition for being appointed to a government board that could recommend a plan of governmental reorganization to the electorate of a city and county. There was no rational relationship between property ownership and the ability of persons to understand issues in the community; individuals who did not own real property could not be presumed to be persons who lack knowledge about issues or who lacked true attachment to the community and its well-being.

(e) Party Affiliation and Demonstrated Support Requirements

A party affiliation qualification gives various advantages to persons who run for elective office as a member of major political parties. Typically, the major parties are assured ballot access without having to circulate petitions to show demonstrated support. In addition, people are more likely to vote for candidates who carry the label or brand name of one of the two major parties. The advantages of party affiliation have led to a number of lawsuits. The Court, in general, allows reasonable restrictions but does not allow restrictions that discriminate too severely against independent candidates. Let us look at a few of the major cases.

Storer v. Brown (1974) upheld a California law that prohibited independent candidates from running in the general election if the candidates either had voted in an immediately preceding party primary or had registered their party affiliation with a qualified party within one year of the primary. Because Storer had been a registered Democrat, the state had disqualified him from running as an independent candidate. He contended that the provision violated his First Amendment and Fourteenth Amendment rights.

The Court held that the Constitution did not prevent California from adopting a party affiliation statute. The state, however, must adopt reasonable alternative means for independent candidates and minor political parties to get a ballot position, and the alternative means must not place too heavy a burden on the right to vote and the right to associate.

The state has an interest in imposing some candidate qualifications to avoid voter confusion, to prevent burdening the election process, and to facilitate the election winner receiving a majority. The California party affiliation restriction helped achieve these goals because it kept a loser in the party primary from running in the general election. Therefore, the state reduced the potential for political factionalism and splintered parties, and prevented the general election ballot from becoming a forum for intra-party feuds. Moreover, the state provided the necessary alternative means for ballot qualification. A party member who intended to run as an independent could disaffiliate himself from the party before the deadline and, by using the alternative methods to a primary election, gain a position on the general election ballot. Consequently, the Court found the California party affiliation provision constitutional.

The Court has considered several challenges to the constitutionality of demonstrated support requirements. A leading case is *Williams v. Rhodes* (1968). Members of a minor political party contended that the Ohio demonstrated support statute strongly favored the established political parties, and thus violated equal protection. Ohio required new political parties to submit petitions with signatures of qualified voters equaling in number fifteen percent of the number of votes cast in the last gubernatorial election. Ohio also imposed an early filing deadline for the petition. However if the party received ten percent of the vote in the previous gubernatorial election it has ballot access without the need for a petition.

The Court reviewed the requirements under the strict scrutiny standard because it burdened both the right to vote and the right to associate. The Court held that the proffered state interests were less than compelling. Ohio's law assured the election of majority candidates but it did so by suppressing the growth of new parties. The statute helped avoid voter confusion, but the means Ohio chose to achieve this goal were not necessary to that end. Under this strict level of review the Court found that the Ohio law violated the equal protection clause.

A demonstrated support statute may discriminate against some voters as well as some candidates. *Moore v. Ogilvie* (1969) dealt with an Illinois law that required independent candidates for President and Vice President to submit petitions with signatures from 25,000 qualified voters. At least 200 signatures had to come from each of 50 different Illinois counties out of the state's 102 counties. The Court held that the law discriminated against the more populous counties. Nearly 94% of Illinois voters, who lived in only forty-nine counties, could *not* form a new party, but 6.6% of the voters in the remaining 53 counties could form a new party. The law violated the principle of equality among voters and was an unreasonable burden on candidates.

After *Moore v. Ogilvie*, the Illinois election code required that new political parties and independent candidates obtain the signatures of 25,000 qualified voters to appear on the ballot for statewide elections. However, independent candidates, or candidates of new parties, for offices of political subdivisions in Illinois had to receive signatures from at least five percent of the number of people who had voted in the previous election of that particular subdivision. The distinction in the statute, as applied to City of Chicago or Cook County elections, meant that candidates needed substantially more signatures to gain access to the Chicago or Cook County ballots than would similar independent candidates for statewide office. Thus, an independent candidate would need 35,000 signatures for inclusion on the ballot in a Chicago election, while a candidate for statewide office needed only 25,000 signatures. *Illinois State Board of Elections v. Socialist Workers Party* (1979) unanimously held that this political subdivision requirement violated equal protection.

Not all demonstrated support statutes are unconstitutional. The Supreme Court sustained Georgia's demonstrated support requirement in *Jenness v. Fortson* (1971). Georgia law required candidates for elective office who ran without winning a primary election to file petitions with signatures from qualified voters equaling five percent of the vote cast in the last general election for that office. If the candidate belonged to a political party that received more than twenty percent of the votes in the last gubernatorial election, the state relieved the candidate of the petition requirement. Unlike *Williams* and the Ohio statute invalidated there, Georgia not only permitted independent candidates but also did not require any unreasonable early filing deadline. Moreover, the five percent Georgia requirement was not a "suffocating" restriction like the fifteen percent Ohio requirement. Further proof that the Georgia rule did not "suffocate" was the historical fact that George, unlike Ohio, often had independent candidates running for election office. The Georgia election scheme violated neither the First Amendment nor equal protection.

A demonstrated support statute may be unconstitutional if it limits too narrowly the pool of available voters who can sign the required petition, or if it limits too severely the time period to submit the petition.

Anderson v. Celebrezze (1983) invalidated a state statute that required an independent candidate for President to file his nominating petition in March, prior to the general election in November. This March filing date came before the time when major political parties, which had sufficient demonstrated support to reserve a place on the ballot, named their candidates. The state could justify some date certain cut-off for candidate filing but not one so far in advance of the general election. The Court said that judges, in reviewing such a restriction, must balance the degree to that the regulation impaired free speech and equal protection against the degree to that the regulation advanced important state interests. The Court concluded the early filing date did not sufficiently advance the interests in political stability, voter awareness, or equal treatment of candidates to justify such a significant restriction on the voter's freedom of choice and freedom of association.

In the demonstrated support cases, the Court has not rigidly applied a compelling interest standard. Rather, the Court has found that the states have interest in running efficient and honest elections that justify some candidate regulations. In some of these cases, such as *Anderson*, the Supreme Court seems to have openly balanced the burden imposed on the First and Fourteenth Amendment rights of the candidate and voters against the degree to which the regulation advanced legitimate and important state interests. In other cases, the Court has indicated that it would uphold demonstrated requirements so long as the requirement is reasonably tailored to promote the state interest in efficient and honest elections and does not create an unreasonable barrier to ballot access for independent candidates and minor political parties.

Burdick v. Takushi (1992) upheld Hawaii's total ban on write-in votes at primary and general elections by finding that important state interests in stopping unrestrained factionalism at the general election and inter-party raiding outweighed any minor restrictions on a voter's ability to vote for candidates of his choice. Critical to the *Burdick* decision was the Court's finding that Hawaii's primary system allowed persons to qualify for partisan and nonpartisan ballots very easily. Persons who wished to be in the nonpartisan primary could qualify with petitions that needed only 15 or 25 signatures from registered voters. Because there was no regulation of political association or political expression, there was no real First Amendment restriction. Because of the open primary system, the law did not significantly limit voters' choices. Therefore, the state did not need an interest of compelling importance to justify its ban on write-in voting.

(f) Racial Classifications

Any state law that impairs a person's ability to become a candidate for elective office because of that person's race is unconstitutional under the Fourteenth and Fifteenth Amendments. The Constitution prevents the states from directly dictating, casually promoting, or facilitating a distinction in the treatment of persons solely on the basis of race." A state may not designate the race of a candidate on a ballot. *Anderson v. Martin* (1964). Such a racial designation requirement facilitates private discrimination by voters. And, it has no rational relationship to the determination of a person's capabilities to function in public office.

§ 14.27 Judicial Control of Political Parties

Cousins v. Wigoda (1975), arising out of a 1972 credentials challenge to Mayor Daley's Illinois delegation at the Democratic National Convention, suggests that the Court is reluctant to take too active a role in regulating national political party conventions. In 1972, the Democratic Convention's Credential's Committee refused to recognize the credentials of Mayor Daley and his loyalists. The Court held that the national interest in selecting candidates for *national* office and the party members' freedom of association overcame an admitted *state* interest in the integrity of its election process. Thus, national party rules on delegate selection may legitimately disqualify delegates who had been selected according to state law.

Cousins should not be read too broadly. It really limited the extraterritorial power of the state. *Cousins* does not prohibit, nor does it even reach the question of, state laws regulating state parties or federal law regulating the national party convention. Moreover, the Court was careful to point out that no one claimed that the party delegate selection rules violated the Constitution. If the party rules involved racial discrimination as in the *White Primary Cases*, then *Cousins* does not preclude the Court from acting. As the Court said:

> "[W]hatever the case of actions presenting claims that the Party's delegate selection procedures are not exercised *within the confines of the Constitution—and no such claims are made here*—this is a case where 'the convention itself [was] the

proper forum for determining intra-party disputes as to that delegates [should] be seated.' "

The Court followed the implications of *Cousins* in *Democratic Party v. Wisconsin ex rel. LaFollette* (1981). Wisconsin tried to impose its *state* rules on the *national* party convention. Though National Democratic Party rules provided that only those willing to affiliate publicly with the Democratic Party may participate in the process of selecting delegates to the party's national convention, Wisconsin state law allowed anyone to vote in the state primary without requiring a public declaration of party preference. In this "open" primary, Wisconsin voters did not vote for delegates but only expressed their choice among the Democratic Party presidential candidates. Later, the Democratic Party caucuses, made up of people who had publicly stated their affiliation with the Democratic Party, selected the delegates to the National Convention. Wisconsin law then purported to bind these delegates to vote at the National Convention in accord with the results of the open presidential preference primary.

Although Wisconsin's open presidential preference primary did not itself violate national party rules, the state's mandate that the results of the primary must determine the allocation of votes cast by the state's delegates at the national convention did violate the Democratic Party rule that the procedure that binds convention delegates must be limited to those who have publicly declared their Democratic Party preference. The Court held that *Cousins* foreclosed any issue as to the validity of this type of state law, with its extraterritorial effects. The Court broadly stated in dictum: "[T]he freedom to associate for 'the common advancement of political beliefs' necessarily presupposes the freedom to identify the people who comprise the association, and to limit the association to those people only."

A different question—not considered in *LaFollette*—is raised by federal regulations of national political party conventions. A related question—also not decided by *LaFollette*—is raised by state regulation of state political party conventions. Whether the Court approves of such regulations should be a function of the extent to that they interfere with the freedom of association. There is certainly no absolute right of the political party to control its membership in all circumstances. The *White Primary Cases* and open primary cases are proof of that.

§ 14.28 The Reapportionment Cases and the Rule of One Person, One Vote: The Creation of Justiciability

Colegrove v. Green (1946) was the first major case to reach the Supreme Court claiming that election districts for the House of

Representatives were malapportioned because they lacked compactness of territory and approximate equality of population. A majority of Justices dismissed the suit, but there was no majority for treating reapportionment as a political question. Justice Frankfurter in an opinion concurred in by only Justices Reed and Burton argued that "due regard for the effective working of our Government revealed this issue to be of a peculiarly political nature and therefore not meet for judicial determination." He strongly urged that "Courts ought not to enter this political thicket." Three Justices found jurisdiction and one concurred on nonjurisdictional grounds.

The next major case was *Gomillion v. Lightfoot* (1960). The Court ruled for the plaintiffs, but on a narrow ground. Justice Frankfurter wrote the opinion for the Court. Black voters, who had been residents of the City of Tuskegee, complained after the Alabama legislature enacted a statute redefining the City of Tuskegee by altering its shape from a square to a strangely shaped twenty-eight-sided figure. Plaintiffs relied on the equal protection guarantees of the Fourteenth Amendment and the right to vote under the Fifteenth Amendment, and claimed that the state created the gerrymandered boundaries solely for the purpose of fencing out black voters from the town in order to deprive them of the preexisting right to vote in the municipal election.

The Court agreed that the claim was justiciable, relying only on the Fifteenth Amendment. By placing the case on such grounds, Frankfurter perhaps hoped to isolate it from a more general precedent. Justice Whittaker's concurrence was analytically more satisfying; he relied on equal protection:

> It seems to me that the "right ... to vote" that is guaranteed by the Fifteenth Amendment is but the same right to vote as is enjoyed by all others within the same ... political division. ... But ... "fencing Negro citizens out of" Division A and into Division B is an unlawful segregation of races of citizens, in violation of the Equal Protection Clause of the Fourteenth Amendment. ...

Finally, *Baker v. Carr* (1962) held that reapportionment cases are justiciable, based on the more general equal protection clause of the Fourteenth Amendment. The Court held that debasement of a person's vote by malapportionment is a violation of the equal protection guaranty of the Fourteenth Amendment. The Court did not base the right on race; in other words, all persons have an equal protection right to vote.

After *Baker*, malapportionment claims were now before the Court, but it had not yet decided what the nature of the constitutional right would be.

§ 14.29 The Origins of One Person, One Vote

Reynolds v. Sims (1964) created the one person, one vote principle. But two prior cases laid the groundwork: *Gray v. Sanders* (1963), and *Wesberry v. Sanders* (1964).

Gray invalidated the county unit system of nominating the Governor and other officials of Georgia. Under the Georgia law, each candidate in the primary election who won a plurality of the popular vote in any county was entitled to *all* of the county's electoral "units." A majority of the county unit votes nominated the Governor and the United States Senator; the other nominees needed only a plurality of unit votes. Although the units were not assigned among counties according to population, the Court suggested that apportionment of units on a one person, one vote basis could not cure the constitutional flaws of the unit system because the winner of a county won all of its unit votes.

Using the entire state as the appropriate geographic unit, the Court interpreted the Constitution to require the addition of a minority candidate's votes in one county to the votes he received in the other counties:

> Once the geographic unit for which a representative is to be chosen is designated, all who participate in the election are to have an equal vote—whatever their race, whatever their sex, whatever their occupation, whatever their income, and wherever their home may be in the geographic unit. This is required by the Equal Protection Clause of the Fourteenth Amendment.

Wesberry required that congressional districts be apportioned equally, but the Court did not base its holding on the equal protection clause but rather it used Article I, section 2, which requires that Representatives be chosen "by the People of the several States." That clause, said Justice Black speaking for the Court, "means that as nearly as practicable one man's vote in a congressional election is to be worth as much as another's. ... To say that a vote is worth more in one district than in another would not only run counter to our fundamental ideas of democratic government; it would cast aside the principle of a House of Representatives elected 'by the People'. ..."

In *Reynolds v. Sims* the Court faced a challenge to the malapportionment of the Alabama state legislature. This time, relying on the equal protection clause, Chief Justice Warren formulated the broad one person, one vote rule:

> Legislators represent people, not trees or acres. ... And, if a State should provide that the votes of citizens in one part of the State should be given two times, or five times, or 10 times the weight of votes of citizens in another part of the State, it

could hardly be contended that the right to vote of those residing in the disfavored areas had not been effectively diluted ... the Equal Protection Clause requires that the seats in both houses of a bicameral state legislature must be apportioned on a population basis.

In one of the companion cases the Court struck down an election apportionment scheme in that one house was malapportioned by use of an area representation system analogous to the U.S. Senate. *Lucas v. Forty–Fourth General Assembly* (1964). Even though state voters in every county of the State had approved of their malapportioned State Senate, the malapportionment was still flawed: "An individual's constitutionally protected right to cast an equally weighted vote cannot be denied even by a vote of a majority of a State's electorate. ..." The majority cannot waive the rights of the minority, nor should the majority be able to waive the rights of future generations of voters.

Although the Supreme Court made the issue of malapportionment subject to judicial review, it did not authorize federal courts to create new legislative districts merely because the federal court disagreed with the legislative apportionment scheme established by the state legislature or the state courts. A federal court should only intervene in the state legislative districting process if the court finds that the legislative districts drawn by the local or state governmental units do not meet the constitutional standards established by the Supreme Court.

§ 14.30 The Application of the One Person, One Vote Principle

(a) To the Appointment of the State Governor and Other Such Officials

Fortson v. Morris (1966) upheld the election of Georgia's Governor by the state legislature. When no candidate had received a majority of the votes cast in the state's general election, the state constitution allowed the General Assembly to elect the Governor from the two front runners. The voters of each legislative district elected the state representatives who in turn elected the Governor. *Fortson* approved one major procedural defect struck down in *Gray v. Sanders* (1963)—not adding a minority candidate's votes in one part of the state to the votes he receives in other parts—as it applied to the "delegates" who elect another person. The case indicates that the equal protection principle underlying *Gray* and other reapportionment cases should be inapplicable to voting by bodies that, like party conventions, perform a deliberative, but non-legislative function.

Gray and *Fortson* are in one sense difficult to reconcile with one another. On one level they appear directly contradictory. *Gray*, on the one hand, seems to hold that where the voters are asked or required to participate, equal protection mandates that each vote be counted equally. *Fortson*, on the other hand, upholds the selection of a state official by what had earlier been ruled to be a malapportioned legislature. On another level, however, *Fortson* sanctions a representative process in the performance of a nonlegislative task, after the voters have exercised untrammeled their right to choose first-tier spokesmen. *Fortson* and *Gray* together thus appear to permit selection of an officer through indirect "election"—i.e., appointment—by a state legislature, but not by a mechanical unit system.

The *Fortson-Gray* theory permits multi-stage representative selection of delegates to the national conventions. A majority of the registered voters in a particular area—a county, for example—could constitutionally elect a delegate to a state convention, which in turn chooses the national delegates. The minority voters in the county are not disenfranchised, as they would be under a unit system, because they will be represented at higher levels by a delegate who, though committed to a differing point of view, can think, compromise and change in the deliberative process, the purpose of that is to select the "best man" for the office.

Pragmatic reasons may also explain *Fortson:* Georgia already had two primaries, one general election, and still failed to choose a governor. Justice Black argued that "Statewide elections cost time and money and it is not strange that Georgia's people decided to avoid repeated elections."

In any event, *Fortson*, at the least, shows that the Constitution does not require that the governor of a state be popularly elected. The state can choose to appoint members to an official position rather than elect them. If there is no popular election, the one person, one vote rule does not apply.

(b) To Local Government Elections

Hadley v. Junior College District (1970) dealt with the trustees of a junior college district. The trustees in *Hadley* could levy and collect taxes, issue some bonds, hire and fire teachers, perform other activities and manage the junior college. The Court found the governmental powers general enough and of sufficient impact to justify the one person, one vote rule. But the decision appeared to find crucial another factor:

> [While] the case now before us ... differs in certain respects from those offices considered in prior cases, it is exactly the same in one crucial factor—*these officials are elected by popular*

vote. .... If there is any way of determining the importance of choosing a particular governmental official, we think the decision of the State to select that official by popular vote is a strong enough indication that the choice is an important one. (emphasis added).

The Court refused to distinguish (for purposes of the apportionment rule) between elections for "legislative" officials and those for "administrative" officials. It offered this general test:

> [A]s a general rule, whenever a state or local government decides to select persons by popular election to perform governmental functions, [equal protection] requires that each qualified voter must be given an equal opportunity to participate in that election, and when members of an elected body are chosen from separate districts, each district must be established on a basis that will insure, as far as is practicable, which equal numbers of voters can vote for proportionally equal numbers of officials. It is of course possible that there might be some case in that a State elects certain functionaries whose duties are so far removed from normal governmental activities and so disproportionately affect different groups that a popular election in compliance with [one man, one vote] might not be required.

In short, the general rule is that once the government chooses a popular election mechanism, then one person, one vote must apply. If an official is appointed to a position, then one person, one vote need not apply.

However, the Court has found, in conformity with the *Hadley* principle, that some elected entities are so specialized that the one person, one vote rule need not be applied to them. In several cases the Court upheld the restriction of votes to elected members of a water storage district that gave the franchise only to local owners and weighted the votes according to the amount of property the individuals held. While not a classic districting case, these franchise restrictions did allow for differing degrees of voter participation. The activities of the water storage district fell disproportionally on the landowners as a group. The Court upheld this deviation from the one person, one vote principle because in these cases the restrictions furthered the interest of insuring that land owners controlled the limited water supply in these areas. E.g., *Salyer Land Co. v. Tulare Lake Basin Water Storage District* (1973).

The Supreme Court, without explanation, has affirmed lower court rulings that refused to apply the one person, one vote principle to the election of judges. However, a local government should not be able to insulate a system for the election of officials with general governmental powers merely by describing those officials as "judges". If so-called "judges" have some type of general governmental powers, beyond those normally associated with the judiciary, the election of those "judges" should be subject to the one person, one vote principle. The Court has held that the Voting Rights Act applies to judicial elections. *Chisom v. Roemer* (1991).

(c) Mathematical Precision

(1) In Federal Elections. Wesberry v. Sanders (1964) required states to draw their congressional districts so that *"as nearly as is practicable* one man's vote in a congressional election is to be worth as much as another's." In subsequent litigation the Court has had occasion to explain what it meant, and the Court has literally required, one person, one vote.

Kirkpatrick v. Preisler (1969) struck down a congressional districting plan where "the most populous district was 3.13% above the mathematical ideal, and the least populous was 2.84% below." The Court found no justification for even this small deviation and explicitly rejected any argument that there is any variance small enough to be considered de minimis. Moreover, it was no justification that the State attempted to avoid fragmenting political subdivisions by drawing the Congressional districts along existing county lines or other political subdivisions. In districting for the House of Representatives, the State must "make a good-faith effort to achieve precise mathematical equality."

White v. Weiser (1973) invalidated a reapportionment plan where the differences were even smaller than *Kirkpatrick*. In *White* the average deviation of all districts from the ideal was .745%; the largest district exceeded the ideal by 2.43% and the smallest district under the ideal by only 1.7%. The Court rejected that plan in favor of one where the largest district exceeded the ideal by .086% and the smallest was under the ideal by .063%.

Although the Supreme Court formally bases congressional redistricting principles on article I, § 2 of the Constitution, the underlying principle that justifies judicial scrutiny of such state activity is one of guaranteeing equality in the power of voters within a state. The Court has not ruled out all deviations from mathematical equality between congressional districts within a state, even though it has found that no deviation in this area is so small that it may be considered *de minimis* and permissible under Article I, section 2 without any justification. The Court, in reviewing congressional district maps, first requires those attacking the districting plan to demonstrate that the population differences between congressional districts could have been reduced or eliminated by a good faith effort to draw districts of equal population. If a plaintiff can demonstrate that the population differences are not a product of a good faith effort to achieve equality, the state will be required to prove that each significant variance between districts was necessary to achieve some legitimate goal.

There will be fewer legitimate reasons for population variances between congressional districts than for variations in state or local legislative districts. States may have more legitimate reasons for wishing to keep voter groups in county or other political subdivisions when voting for state legislative positions. Such political divisions often have political powers as units of local government. States may also wish to guarantee representation to small counties because the state legislative system may act on matters that clearly effect different counties in different ways and in that legislative input from all counties or political subdivisions is important. County and other political subdivision lines are less relevant to the determination of congressional districts because persons in Congress are not primarily concerned with legislation that effects specific counties within a state.

(2) In State Elections. While the one man, one vote mandate for Congressional districting is based on Article I, section 2, the apportionment in elections for state or local offices is justified by the Equal Protection Clause. Thus the strict application of the one man, one vote standard for Congressional districting does not require a similar rule for other elections, where the Court has been more flexible. *Abate v. Mundt* (1971) allowed deviations in a County Board of Supervisors election where the most underrepresented town deviated from the ideal by 7.1% and the most overrepresented deviated 4.8%. The Court found justification in the "long tradition of overlapping functions and dual personnel in Rockland County government and on the fact that the plan before us does not contain a built-in bias tending to favor particular political interests or geographic areas."

The Court has held that de minimis variations require no justifications at all: in a case where the most overrepresented district exceeded the ideal by 5.8% and the most underrepresented was under by 4.1%, for a total variation of 9.9%, the Court held that 9.9% total variation does not make out a prima facie case and does not require any special justification. *White v. Regester* (1973). However, deviations of up to 16.5% for state senate districts and 19.3% for state house of representative districts do violate the one person, one vote principle. *Connor v. Finch* (1977).

The Supreme Court allows greater deviations from mathematical equality between districts for districting plans for state or local legislative bodies, as opposed to congressional districts. This difference is not based solely on the technical distinction that congressional districting is reviewed under article I while local apportionment is reviewed under the Fourteenth Amendment equal protection clause. The substantive policy justification for allowing greater leeway in local legislative maps is that the government has a wider range of legitimate reasons for deviating from population equality when it creates local or state wide legislative maps. State or city legislative entities often have the power to pass laws that have a particular effect on a limited number of counties or other political subdivisions within the jurisdiction; ensuring that persons within each county or political subdivision are grouped together to elect representatives to the legislative body is a legitimate concern. Because of the regional nature of much state or local legislation, keeping state or local legislative districts compact so that persons are grouped in small geographic districts is also a legitimate concern. Many state constitutions require legislative districts be both contiguous and compact. A state may even go so far as to guarantee every county, or relevant political subdivision, at least one representative in the legislature in order to ensure that persons from that political subdivision have some voice in legislation that affects counties in different ways throughout the state.

(3) Who Counts? The Court has not created a rule that sets a fixed requirement of who must be counted to determine the equality of representation. In general the cases have required that the apportionment be made on the basis of total population even though the actual voters may be apportioned differently because of peculiar distribution of persons of certain ages or other characteristics that may properly preclude them from voting. Thus, the Court has not required the states to "include aliens, transients, short-term or temporary residents, or persons denied the vote for conviction of crime, in the apportionment base by that their legislators are distributed...." However the state cannot reduce the voting strength of an area because it contains military personnel. "The difference between exclusion of all military and military-related personnel and exclusion of those not meeting a State's residence requirements is a difference between an arbitrary and constitutionally permissible classification" because the former discriminates on the basis of employment while the latter does not offer voting strength to those who validly do not have the vote. *Burns v. Richardson* (1966).

(d) Multimember Districts

The Court early held that the equal protection clause does not require that even one house of a bicameral state legislature consist of single-member election districts. But multimember districts will be invalidated if they are designed to, and in fact do, "minimize or cancel out the voting strength of racial or political elements of the voting population." *Burns v. Richardson* (1966). Multimember districts are not per se unconstitutional, and the State may use such multimember districts in one part of the state and single member districts in other parts.

(e) Political Gerrymandering

The one person, one vote principle is not the only criteria for challenging or evaluating the district lines drawn for municipal, state, or federal elections. Even though a legislative districting map complies with the one person, one vote principle, it will be invalid if drawn upon the basis of constitutionally improper criteria.

If the district lines were drawn for the purpose of diluting the voting strength of minority racial or ethnic groups, the law would violate the equal protection clause.

The equal protection principle that prohibits purposeful dilution of the voting strength of racial minorities should also prohibit legislative districting or apportionment maps that are created for the purpose of diluting the voting power of a religious group. Indeed, this principle should prohibit the legislature, or other districting authority, from singling out any group of persons, whether or not they constitute a "suspect classification," for disenfranchisement through the creation of electoral districts that would dilute their voting strength and eliminate their representation in a legislative body.

In 1986, the Supreme Court for the first time held that a claim that a legislative districting map was politically gerrymandered so as to seriously dilute or eliminate the voting power of persons affiliated with a particular party, was an equal protection issue that the courts could resolve. *Davis v. Bandemer* (1986) ruled that claims of unconstitutional political gerrymandering were not political questions. While six Justices agreed that the courts could adjudicate this equal protection claim, there was no majority opinion regarding the standards to be used in determining whether a particular state districting plan was an unconstitutional political gerrymander. Indeed, only two Justices believed that the particular state districting plan at issue in *Davis* so diluted the voting power of an identifiable political group as to violate the equal protection clause.

Later, *Vieth v. Jubelirer* (2004) affirmed a three judge district court upholding a congressional redistricting map that plaintiffs challenged on the ground that the Pennsylvania General Assembly had engaged in unconstitutional political gerrymandering. Justice Scalia (joined by Chief Justice Rehnquist and Justices O'Connor, and Thomas) concluded that the political gerrymandering claim was nonjusticiable because there was no judicially discernable and manageable standard to apply. They would overrule *Davis v. Bandemer*. Kennedy concurred in the judgment. While he agreed that "great caution is necessary when approaching this subject, I would not foreclose all possibility of judicial relief if some limited and precise rationale were found to correct an established violation of the Constitution in some redistricting cases." After this decision, it is highly unlikely that the Court would find that a legislative redistricting map amounted to unconstitutional political gerrymandering. Stevens, Souter, Ginsburg and Breyer dissented.

(f) Departures From Strict Majority Rule

Gordon v. Lance (1971) upheld a West Virginia law requiring a 60% vote requirement before political subdivisions of the State incurred bonded indebtedness or increased tax notes above a certain amount. The 60% vote requirement constituted no geographic discrimination unlike the typical reapportionment case. The Court also appeared not to disapprove a requirement that more than a majority vote be assembled for some issues in a state legislature or that a given issue be approved by a majority of all registered voters. "[T]here is nothing in the language of the Constitution, our history, or our cases that requires that a majority always prevail on every issue."

Gordon explicitly did not consider whether a provision requiring unanimity or giving a veto to a "very small group" would be constitutional, or whether it was proper to require "extraordinary majorities" to elect public officers.

§ 14.31   The Right to Travel Abroad

The right to travel abroad pits the constitutional right of travel against the broad power of the government in the international area. Just as the equal protection rights of illegitimates are significantly lessened in the context of the government's foreign affairs power over immigration, so also when the right to travel is exercised in the context of international travel, governmental power frequently overcomes this right.

The Court's rulings upholding government restrictions on the ability to engage in international travel (except in those cases when the government action is totally arbitrary or endangers a specific constitutional right) indicate that there is no fundamental right to engage in international travel.

Kent v. Dulles (1958) ruled that the Secretary of State had improperly denied passports to two persons on the basis of their alleged association with the Communist Party. The Court based its ruling on an interpretation of federal statutes. While Justice Douglas's majority opinion included *dicta* supporting a right to international travel, the Court based its ruling on statutory grounds.

Aptheker v. Secretary of State (1964) quoted with approval the broad language of *Kent*, but again its decision rested on narrower grounds. In this case several ranking officials of the Communist Party of the United States had their passports revoked. This time there was no question of whether Congress had delegated such power to the Secretary of State. Section 6 of the Subversive Activities Control Act of 1950 provided that it was unlawful for any member of a Communist organization that was registered or under a final order to register, to use, apply for, renew a passport if the applicant had knowledge or notice that the organization is registered or that an order to register was final.

Aptheker actually decided the case on a more narrow ground. Given the importance of the right to travel, the degree of the legislative abridgement must be restricted to the least drastic means of achieving the same purpose. In this case, Section 6 was overbroad on its face because it applied whether or not the member actually knew or believed he was associated with what was deemed to be a communist-action or communist-front organization. The section also included both knowing and unknowing members. For these and similar reasons the Court held this section unconstitutional on its face, but it did not hold that Congress could not enact a more narrowly drawn statute.

In *Zemel v. Rusk* (1965), the Court faced an explicit, narrow Congressional prohibition of travel to Cuba. Chief Justice Warren, writing for the Court, upheld the prohibition. First, that Congress had authorized the Secretary of State to refuse to validate American passports for travel to Cuba—where the United States had broken diplomatic and consular relations—and second, that the exercise of that authority is constitutional. The Court admitted that the legislative history of the basic passport act does not affirmatively indicate an intention to authorize area restrictions on travel abroad, but "its language is surely broad enough to authorize area restrictions. . . ."

The Court upheld the constitutionality of the Secretary's decision by relying on the foreign policy context of the case. "That the restriction that is challenged in this case is supported by the weightiest considerations of national security is perhaps best pointed up by recalling that the Cuban missile crisis of October 1962 preceded filing of appellant's complaint by less than two months." The majority again cited with approval the *Kent* dictum that the right of travel is a part of the liberty cannot be deprived without due process, but it pointedly noted that the fact "a liberty cannot be inhibited without due process of law does not mean it can under no circumstances be inhibited." In this case, the inhibition was proper.

Later, *Califano v. Aznavorian* (1978) unanimously upheld restrictions on the payment of certain Social Security benefits. The restrictions limited payments to those who, in certain circumstances, exercised their right to engage in international travel. The law said that the Social Security Act benefits would not be paid to a recipient residing outside of the United States for 30 days until that person once again had been a resident of this country for 30 days.

The Court first found that the constitutionality of welfare legislation should be upheld if a *rational basis* existed for the classification; the Court did not use strict scrutiny. The right to travel *abroad* is not judged by the same standards applied to laws that directly burden the right of *interstate* travel by use of durational residence requirements.

In *Haig v. Agee* (1981), the Court, relying on *Zemel v. Rusk*, upheld the powers of the Secretary of State to revoke the passport of one Philip Agee, an American residing abroad, on the grounds that his activities caused or were likely to cause serious damage to American national security or foreign policy. In *Agee*, however, unlike *Zemel* the Court did not rely on prior administrative *practice* but rather on administrative *policy*.

Agee was a former employee of the Central Intelligence Agency who had been trained in clandestine operations. In 1974 he publicly announced his intention to expose CIA officers and agents. "He recruit[ed] collaborators and train[ed] them in clandestine techniques designed to expose the 'cover' of CIA employees and sources."

In 1979 the Secretary of State revoked Agee's passport, pursuant to departmental regulations and based on a determination that his activities "are causing or are likely to cause serious damage to the national security of the United States." Agee sued claiming that Congress had not authorized the regulation and that it was unconstitutional. He moved for summary judgment and for "purposes of that motion, Agee conceded the Government's factual averments and its claim that his activities were causing or were likely to cause serious damage to the national security or foreign policy of the United States."

The Court first concluded that although the Passport Act of 1926 "does not in so many words confer upon the Secretary a power to revoke a passport," the fact that there was no evidence that Congress intended to repudiate the prior administrative construction led the Court to find that Congress, in 1926, adopted the previous assertions of executive power. An "unbroken line of Executive Orders, regulations, instructions to consular officials, and notices to passport holders" evidenced the prior interpretation.

Agee responded that in order for the Executive to establish implicit congressional approval it must show "longstanding and consistent *enforcement* of the claimed power: that is, by showing that many passports were revoked on national security and foreign policy grounds." The Court simply rejected that argument. "[I]f there were no occasions—or few—to call the Secretary's authority into play, the absence of frequent instances of enforcement is wholly irrelevant." It is enough that the Executive's announcement of policy was " 'sufficiently substantial and consistent' to compel the conclusion that Congress has approved it."

The majority also rejected the other grounds that Agee raised and found no violation of the freedom to travel abroad because the restriction on travel served a reasonable, indeed compelling, governmental interest: protecting the security of the nation.

The Court then quickly turned to and rejected without any substantial discussion Agee's other constitutional arguments that the passport violated his free speech and constituted a taking of his liberty interests without procedural due process. Agee responded by securing a new passport from Grenada; he then announced that he would continue his activities against the CIA.

The Supreme Court's decisions since *Zemel* may be categorized as showing a high degree of deference to the executive branch both in terms of finding statutory authority for executive branch actions regarding foreign affairs and in imposing only minimal constitutional restraints on executive actions taken with Congressional authority.

This reluctance to interfere with executive decisions regarding foreign policy, absent an express Congressional restriction on executive power, provided the basis for *Regan v. Wald* (1984). A Treasury Department regulation effectively eliminated travel from America to Cuba except for certain types of travel, such as official visits, news gatherings, professional research, and visits to relatives located in Cuba. *Regan v. Wald* held that there was no reason to require the Executive or Legislative Departments to demonstrate that there was some danger to national or foreign policy interests presented by travel to Cuba in the 1980's that was similar to the basis for the government actions following the Cuban missile crisis in the 1960's. *Zemel*, in the Court's view, did not rest upon an analysis of the foreign policy interest that supported the restriction on travel but was, rather, "merely an example of this classical deference to the political branches in matters of foreign policy." The decision of the State Department and the Treasury Department that it was contrary to the national interest for American travelers to provide hard currency to Cuba was sufficient to restrict whatever travel rights might be created by the due process clause of the Fifth Amendment "given the traditional deference to executive judgment" regarding foreign policy.

Thus, while it would seem that the Fifth Amendment does grant some protection to arbitrary restrictions on the ability of American citizens to travel to other countries, the Court will uphold those restrictions whenever the Executive Department can reasonably argue that the restrictions are related to our foreign policy interest and there is no clear basis for finding that Congress has restricted Executive authority.

§ 14.32   The Right to Interstate Travel

Introduction–Summary. The Supreme Court has established a "right to travel" within the United States, but the scope of that right is less than clear. Defining the right to travel is difficult because state or local laws may interfere with several aspects of an individual's ability to travel; the Supreme Court has used several provisions of the Constitution, and its Amendments, in cases that might be described as right to travel cases. State or local laws that restrict travel by restricting transportation between and among the states might be challenged under the commerce clause of Article I, the privileges and immunities clause of Article IV, or all three clauses of the second sentence of the Fourteenth Amendment—the privileges or immunities clause, the due process clause, and the equal protection clause.

When a law is challenged under the due process clause or the equal protection clause, the Court will uphold the law so long as it is rationally related to any legitimate end, *unless* the law substantially impairs a fundamental right or employs a classifying trait (such as race, ancestry, gender or illegitimacy) that justifies independent judicial review. A law that restricts the movement of persons between states is not subject to independent judicial review under the due process or equal protection clause *unless* the law regulates the "right to travel," which the Supreme Court has found to be a fundamental constitutional right. A law that substantially impairs the ability of all persons to engage in the right to travel would be tested under the due process guarantee; a law that restricts the right to travel of one class of persons will be subject to review under the equal protection guarantee.

Separating the types of laws that relate to the fundamental constitutional right to travel from the types of laws that restrict transportation or travel of persons is not easy. A state law that restricts interstate movement of individuals or products, but neither restricts the ability of individuals to establish residency in the state nor treats newly arrived residents less favorably than long time residents, should not be seen as an impairment of the fundamental right to travel. For example, a state license fee for trucks that travel through a state certainly restricts travel (in the sense of reducing the amount of transportation through a state), but it does not impair the right to travel. The Court has not subjected truck license fees to strict judicial scrutiny under the due process or equal protection clauses. If the state's truck license fee discriminates against interstate commerce, the licensing fee would be invalidated under commerce clause principles.

The privileges and immunities clause of Article IV protects citizens as they travel to states other than the state in that they reside. That clause prohibits state and local governments from restricting certain basic rights, such as the ability to engage in private sector commercial activity or the ability to exercise a constitutionally protected liberty, to permanent residents of the state or local jurisdiction. Thus, for example, a state cannot require a person to be a resident of the state in order to engage in private sector activities, including being an attorney, in the state. However, this clause protects only citizens, not persons who are not citizens of the United States. In contrast, equal protection and due process protects "persons," not just "citizens."

When we look to the Supreme Court's Fourteenth Amendment decisions for a definition of the right to travel, we find that the Court has focused on the protection of the right of individuals, particularly United States citizens, to establish residency in a state and to be treated in the same manner as persons who have been long time residents of the state. The Court has not engaged in independent judicial review of laws that are designed to encourage a person to establish residency within a state or that discourage a person from traveling out of the state after becoming a resident.

The Supreme Court has ruled that states do not have to give a welfare benefit (any type of property, money or service that goes directly from the government to the individual) to persons who are not bona fide residents of the state. A person who is receiving subsistence welfare benefits from a state may lose those benefits if he changes his residency to another state, because states are not required to provide benefits to persons in other jurisdictions. Based on that principle, a state can refuse to employ a person in a government job if the person does not reside within the state boundaries. *McCarthy v. Philadelphia Civil Service Commission* (1976). Similarly, a city or state can refuse to provide a public school education to a child who is merely a temporary resident in the jurisdiction. *Martinez v. Bynum* (1983). The Court also upheld a law making a parent's abandonment of a child a more serious crime if the parent leaves the state after abandoning the child. *Jones v. Helms* (1981). None of these laws were subjected to strict judicial scrutiny, because these laws had the effect of encouraging people to remain within the state, rather than deterring migration into the state.

Although a state can require an individual to be a bona fide resident in order to receive government benefits, the Court has invalidated a variety of *durational* residency requirements. A simple residency requirement in a state law would allow an individual to have the government benefit as soon as the individual entered the state, so long as the individual could in good faith assert that he was now a resident of the state for the indefinite future and for all purposes. On the other hand, a durational residency requirement that requires an individual to be in the jurisdiction for a certain amount of time before he can receive the government benefit or engage in some activity. The waiting period established by a durational residency requirement has an impact on the fundamental constitutional right to travel.

There are two ways in that a durational residency requirement may impair the right to travel. First, whenever the government requires an individual to be in the state for a period of time prior to being able to exercise a basic constitutional right or prior to receiving some government benefit, the law may deter migration into the state.

The standard used by the Supreme Court to review durational residency requirements is less than clear. The Court has stated that a waiting period for the granting of basic welfare benefits must be narrowly tailored to a compelling government interest. *Shapiro v. Thompson* (1969).

However, the Court has also indicated that waiting periods that do not deter migration into the state might be upheld either on the basis that the law does not impair the constitutionally protected right to travel, or because such a law will survive some type of intermediate scrutiny (such as being related to an important government interest). It is possible that the Court may engage in a type of ad hoc balancing when reviewing durational residency requirements, by balancing the degree to that the law will deter migration into the state against the nature of the interests that are advanced by the waiting period. Most of the Supreme Court's right to travel cases, which are examined in this Section, have involved durational residency requirements that might deter the right to travel. In those cases, the Court has upheld laws that seemed to be narrowly tailored to ensure that persons claiming benefits are good faith residents of the state. The Court has invalidated durational residency requirements that were not tailored to the state's interest in insuring that it is not giving benefits to persons who are fraudulently claiming state residency.

The second way in that a durational residency requirement can impair the right to travel results from a law that distributes government benefits based on length of residency. Such a law distributes benefits based on the duration that each individual has lived within the state. If a law grants $100 per year to each individual who resides in the state, the law would not involve a *durational* residency requirement, because every person who is a bona fide resident of the state would receive the same amount of money in each year. A person who remained in the state for 10 years would ultimately receive more than a person who resided in the state for only a single year, but that result would not be a function of a law distributing benefits based on the length of each person's residency. On the other hand, a law that gave $100 to each resident for every year that they had lived in the state prior to the passage of the law would involve a durational residency classification. The person who arrived in the state only two years ago would receive only $200, while the person who had arrived twenty years ago would receive $2,000, even though both persons were bona fide residents of the state at the time the law was passed. Once a state determines that a person is a bona fide resident, the state must treat the new resident the same as long-time residents of the state. *Zobel v. Williams* (1982).

Let us now turn to some specific problem areas. And let us start with the leading modern case, *Shapiro v. Thompson* (1969), the case that ushered in the era of strict scrutiny.

The Era of Strict Scrutiny. The landmark decision concerning the right to travel and the permissible scope of the burdens on that right that result from residency requirements came in *Shapiro v. Thompson* (1969). The Court invalidated two state statutes and a District of Columbia statute that denied welfare benefits to persons who had not resided within the jurisdiction for at least one year. The Court found that the state statutes violated the equal protection clause of the Fourteenth Amendment and the District act violated the equal protection guarantee of the due process clause of the Fifth Amendment.

The basis for this equal protection ruling was the conclusion that a residency requirement has the effect of deterring the entry of indigent persons into these jurisdictions, thereby limiting their rights to engage in interstate travel. The majority opinion held that, because the right limited was a fundamental constitutional right, the classification had to be invalidated unless it was "shown to be necessary to promote a *compelling* governmental interest." The state's argument that it was attempting to deter indigents who entered the state solely to obtain larger benefits would not be permissible because the states had no right to exclude poor persons from their borders. It was impermissible for the state to try to distinguish between old and new residents when that distinction burdened fundamental rights. While the state might impose some requirement that the persons be residents at the time they applied, they could not create subclasses of citizens based on the duration of time that persons had been residents of the state. There was also no proof that the system significantly promoted the budgeting process of the state and the Court found that administrative efficiency was not such a compelling interest as to support the limitation of a fundamental right.

Justice Harlan's dissent attacked not only the Court's strict protection of the right to travel but the entire fundamental rights branch of equal protection analysis. He found no basis for elevating the right to travel to strict scrutiny, and he believed that protecting rights in this way allowed the Court to sit as a super legislature.

The *Shapiro* analysis has spawned a series of cases dealing with durational residence requirements. These statutes require not only that persons declare themselves to be residents of the state but that they maintain that residency status for a set duration of time prior to being eligible to receive some benefit or exercise some right. The right involved need not be a fundamental right in order to require the strict scrutiny analysis, for the right to travel that is itself a fundamental right. Thus, any classification that burdens that right will be subject to strict judicial scrutiny.

In many of these cases the Court has invoked the language of the "compelling interest" test to indicate that these laws must meet a high standard before the Justices will uphold them. However, in other cases the Court has issued rulings both upholding and striking residency requirements that indicate that the Court may only be employing some form of true "reasonableness" test or an *ad hoc* balancing test when deciding whether these laws serve legitimate governmental purposes that justify a limitation of the right to travel.

The Supreme Court has never held that a state or local government is prohibited from requiring persons to be residents of that location in order to receive government benefits. The state may restrict some welfare benefits to *bona fide* residents. Thus, *Martinez v. Bynum* (1983) upheld a state statute that permitted a school district to deny tuition free education to a child who lived apart from his parent or lawful guardian if the child's presence in the school district was "for the primary purpose" of attending school in the district. "A bona fide residence requirement, appropriately defined and uniformly applied, furthers the substantial state interest in assuring that services provided for its residents are enjoyed only by residents."

The *Shapiro* rationale only requires close judicial scrutiny of durational residency requirements, a distinction between new and old residents. Each jurisdiction has a right to limit voting to residents of that jurisdiction, and the state can require public employees to be residents of a specific area. *McCarthy v. Philadelphia Civil Service Commission* (1976). The Court has never foreclosed the possibility that some residence requirement for securing benefits may violate the right to travel, but neither has it indicated that a resident would be entitled to keep any form of state dispensed benefit when leaving the state.

The Supreme Court has dealt with the right to travel in terms of restrictions on voting eligibility in several cases. In these cases it has stricken the residency requirement whenever it was a period beyond that which is truly reasonable or necessary to protect the electoral process from fraudulent practices or administrative breakdowns. E.g., *Dunn v. Blumstein* (1972) struck down a state law that required a voter to be a resident of the state for one year and the county for three months before he could vote. Of course, this line of cases involves two fundamental rights, voting and interstate travel.

The Court will protect the right to travel even when no other fundamental right is involved. This point became clear in *Memorial Hospital v. Maricopa County* (1974). An Arizona statute required one year residence in a county as a condition to receiving nonemergency hospitalization or medical care at public expense. The Court held that this classification impinged upon interstate travel and, in so doing, found that it was irrelevant that the classification also burdened travel by persons within their own state. This fact could not protect the discrimination against the interstate traveler any more than discrimination against some in-state businesses could justify discrimination against interstate commerce.

The Court has never found medical care to be a fundamental right just as it has never found that any form of necessary welfare assistance payment or general government benefit constitutes such a right. But the majority held that it must use the compelling interest test to protect the right to interstate travel in this setting. With an analysis similar to that employed in *Shapiro* the opinion found that denying medical services to indigents from other states constituted a severe penalty on their right to engage in interstate travel. This "basic necessity of life" is such a severe burden on the right to travel that it could not be justified by the state's interest in administrative efficiency or general pursuit of economic policies. The Court said it might not scrutinize so strictly residency requirements for all government benefits, but that where the state burdened the right to travel by denial of benefits that were essential to the daily life of the new indigent in the state, the Court would require that the state meet this "heavy burden of justification."

State Education Benefits. As indicated in the *Memorial Hospital* opinion, the Court does not apply the strict scrutiny analysis of *Shapiro* to every durational residency requirement. The Court has not prohibited states from charging lower tuition at state universities for persons who have been residents for some significant period. Medical care, unlike tuition payments, are a "basic necessity of life."

In *Vlandis v. Kline* (1973) the Court invalidated a Connecticut statute that *permanently* barred a non-resident student from becoming an in-state resident for the purposes of lower tuition rates in the state university system of higher education. However, *Vlandis* cited with approval its decision in *Starns v. Malkerson* (1971), which had summarily affirmed a decision upholding Minnesota's requirement that students be residents of the state for one year prior to qualifying for lower tuition. One may conclude that there will be a reasonableness test for durational residency requirements in the area of education that will be similar to the test that the Court has used in the primary election cases.

Martinez v. Bynum (1983) upheld a state statute that permitted a school district to deny tuition-free education to a child who lived apart from his parent or lawful guardian if the child's presence in the school district was "for the primary purpose" of attending school in the district. "A bona fide residence requirement, appropriately defined and uniformly applied, furthers the substantial state interest in assuring that services provided for its residents are enjoyed only by residents." The statute at issue in *Martinez* was a bona fide residence requirement because it provided free education for all children who resided in the school district with the intent to remain in the district indefinitely.

Residency Requirements for Divorce. The Supreme Court has indicated that some burdens on the right to travel will be upheld so long as the Court finds them not to be arbitrary in fact. In *Sosna v. Iowa* (1975) the Court upheld a one year residency requirement for parties seeking a divorce from state courts. The Court found that there was no due process violation here because there was no deprivation of access to the state courts but only a delay before they could be used by the parties. This delay was justified by the state's interest in ensuring that it had a real interest in those who sought to use its courts to alter fundamental family relationships and by a desire to insulate state divorce decrees from successful collateral attacks. The opinion distinguished *Shapiro, Dunn*, and *Memorial Hospital* on the basis that this classification did not prevent the woman who sought the divorce from receiving support or functioning as a citizen of the state during this period.

Distributing Benefits Based on Length of Residency.
Zobel v. Williams (1982) the Court (8 to 1) invalidated a statute
that distributed state money to residents based upon the length of
their residency in the state. The Court did not in this case attempt
to define the appropriate standard of review for this type of law.

In *Zobel*, an Alaska statute distributed money from a state
fund that enriched by the state's share of oil exploration revenues.
Under the statutes, each citizen of the age of 18 years or more
received one "dividend unit" for each year of residency after 1959,
which was the first year of Alaska's statehood. The statute fixed the
value of each unit at $50 so that a one-year resident would receive
$50 while a resident of Alaska since 1959 would receive $1,050
yearly. Only Justice Rehnquist's dissent argued that the Court
should defer to the legislative judgment to prefer old residents over
new residents in this case.

The *Zobel* majority opinion, by Chief Justice Burger, asserted
that the Court would not in this case define the appropriate
standard of review for right to travel cases, but that Alaska's
statutory scheme failed even the minimum rationality standard. It
is difficult to conceive of situations where the state would have a
legitimate interest in granting benefits to citizens based solely upon
their length of residency in the state. While new residents are, by
definition, different from old residents, that difference must relate
to some legitimate purpose of the government if it is used as a basis
for distinguishing between groups of persons for the dispensation of
governmental benefits or burdens.

Hooper v. Bernalillo County Assessor (1985) invalidated a state
statute that granted a property tax exemption to honorably discharged veterans of the armed forces who had served in the
military during the Vietnam War era and who had become residents of the state before May 8, 1976. Chief Justice Burger again
wrote the majority opinion. Again he concluded that this statutory
scheme cannot even pass the minimum rationality test. The Court
said that the state could give a tax benefit to all of its bona fide
resident veterans because that action would constitute the dispensation of economic benefits, which do not involve fundamental
rights, on a nonsuspect basis.

Hooper did not address the question of whether the state had a
special interest in granting benefits to persons who had been
residents of the state during the time when they were called away
for military service. The tax classification at issue in *Hooper* granted a tax benefit to a person who resided in the state as an infant
before May 8, 1976, then moved to another state and served in the
armed forces, and then returned to the state after 1976. But it
denied a tax exemption to a person who had served in the military
service for the same period of time but who had never resided in

the state until a May 9, 1976. The law, "by singling out previous residents for the tax exemption, rewards only those citizens for their 'past contributions' toward our nation's military effort in Vietnam. *Zobel* teaches that such an objective is not a legitimate state purpose."

In *Hooper*, Chief Justice Burger, writing for the Court, stated: "The State may not favor established residents over new residents based on the view that the state may take care of 'its own' if such is defined by prior residence. Newcomers, by establishing bona fide residence in the state, become the state's 'own' and may not be discriminated against solely on the basis of their arrival in the state after [a specific date]." The basic concept of equality between citizens requires that the state not define citizens as deserving of more or less favorable treatment merely because of the length of their residence in the state.

Attorney General of New York v. Soto–Lopez (1986) invalidated state constitutional and statutory provisions that gave a preference in civil service employment to residents of the state who were veterans of the armed services and who had lived in the state when they entered the military service. These laws denied a similar preference to veterans who were current residents of the state and in all respects similar to the preferred veterans but for the fact that they did not live in the state when they entered military service. The Justices could not agree on a standard of review in this case, so there was no majority opinion.

The Privileges and Immunities Clause. All of the decisions where the Supreme Court held that state distribution of benefits based upon the length of a person's residency violated the equal protection clause appear to involve rather straightforward forms of equal protection analysis even though the Court was often not clear about the standard of review it used. The basic guarantee of equal protection is that similar people will be dealt with in a similar manner. Once the Court took the position that a state did not have a legitimate interest in rewarding long time residents simply because they were long time residents the Court removed any legitimate interest the State might have asserted in distributing benefits based on a person's length of residency. In other words, these laws had no rational relationship to a legitimate interest because there was no legitimate reason for the state to give lower benefits to some persons simply because they were new residents in the state.

In *Saenz v. Roe* (1999) is different because when it struck down a law that accorded benefits based on the length of residency, it used the privileges or immunities clause of the Fourteenth Amendment. California, which has the sixth highest welfare benefit levels in the country, amended its Aid to Families with Dependent Children (AFDC) program in 1992 by limiting new residents, for the first year they live in the State, to the benefits they would have received in the state of their prior residence. The Secretary of Health and Human Services approved this change, but the Court invalidated it.

Justice Stevens, for the Court, held that the state statute violated the Fourteenth Amendment's right to travel, and the federal statute authorizing California to impose durational residency requirements did not validate state statute. Stevens based the holding on the privileges or immunities clause, which allowed *Saenz* to avoid any discussion of equal protection standards of review. In the future, the Court may determine that the length of residency cases that were decided on equal protection grounds were, in fact, based on the privileges or immunities clause of the Fourteenth Amendment.

§ 14.33   The Guarantees of the Bill of Rights as Fundamental Rights for Equal Protection Analysis: Introduction

The Court has applied most of the provisions of the Bill of Rights to the states because it found them to be fundamental to the American system of government and inherent in the concept of liberty under the due process clause. These rights also are also fundamental rights for the purposes of equal protection analysis.

However, laws that classify persons in terms of their abilities to exercise rights that have specific recognition in the first eight Amendments usually are not analyzed as equal protection issues. In these instances the Court is likely to hold that the denial of the right to one class of persons is a violation of the specific guarantee without any need to resort to equal protection analysis. Thus, if the state or federal government were to deny to a specific class of persons the right to bail upon certain criminal charges, the classification should be analyzed to determine the compatibility of the law with the substantive guarantees of the Eighth Amendment prohibition of excessive bail, although it could be analyzed as an equal protection issue.

There are two areas of rights that deserve some specific mention because they have been the subject of particular interest in terms of the government's ability to establish laws that burden particular classes of persons in the exercise of these rights. The areas involve the exercise of First Amendment rights and the concept of fairness in the criminal justice system, which is derived from the various restraints placed upon the criminal process by the Bill of Rights.

§ 14.34   First Amendment Guarantees

Each of the guarantees of the First Amendment has been held to be a fundamental right and made applicable to the states through the due process clause of the Fourteenth Amendment. Thus whenever a state burdens the freedom of religion, speech, press, assembly, or petition the law must be analyzed under the strict scrutiny required by the First Amendment as well as the general guarantees of the due process and equal protection provisions. The right of freedom of association is not mentioned in the First Amendment but is implied by its provisions and analyzed in the same manner as those specific guarantees.

Whenever a state law impermissibly burdens the exercise of one of these rights, it also violates due process. Because those provisions are applicable to the states through the due process clause, state laws that burden these rights constitute a denial of liberty protected by that clause. Because the interpretation of the substantive guarantees of the First Amendment are the same, regardless of whether the provisions are being applied to state or federal actions, there is little need to discuss substantive due process guarantees in these cases. This same analysis applies in equal protection cases.

Although analyzing First Amendment issues under the equal protection guarantee is not common, the Court sometimes uses this mode of analysis. First Amendment rights are fundamental; therefore, the Court will subject to strict judicial scrutiny any classifications that affect the ability to exercise those rights.

For example, *Police Department of Chicago v. Mosley* (1972) invalidated a statute that prohibited pickets and demonstrations within 150 feet of local schools during school hours, but that exempted "peaceful picketing" by a labor dispute within the school. The Court found that the classification regarding permissible picketing was a violation of the equal protection guarantee for there was no overriding state interest to support a distinction between labor pickets and other forms of speech. While local governments might create laws to protect schools from disruption that were compatible with both the First and Fourteenth Amendments they could not classify the ability to speak in a manner that was not supported by overriding interest. In this case the Court specifically found that where statutory classifications affected conduct within the protection of First Amendment rights, it would be inappropriate to review them under traditional rational basis standards of the equal protection guarantee.

§ 14.35 Right to Fairness in the Criminal Justice System

There is no single decision of the Court that specifically recognizes a "fundamental right" to fair treatment in the criminal justice system for purposes of equal protection analysis. However, the Court has established this right through a series of related decisions. Most of the guarantees of the Bill of Rights concern fairness in the investigation and adjudication of criminal charges against individuals. All of these provisions, except for the grand jury clause of the Fifth Amendment are fundamental and applicable to the states through the due process clause of the Fourteenth Amendment. The Court has also found that the concept of due process itself requires the establishment of procedures that will result in the fair treatment of individuals when the state seeks to prosecute them on criminal charges. In cases dealing with required filing fees or other practices that hamper the review of criminal convictions, the Supreme Court has established a right of access to courts to vindicate claims of mistreatment of individuals within the criminal justice system. Taken together these cases recognize fairness in the criminal justice system as a fundamental right of each individual.

It was not until 1956 that the Court used equal protection analysis to require the government to provide a guaranteed minimum form of fairness to all defendants, regardless of whether the claim related to a right with specific recognition in the first eight Amendments. In *Griffin v. Illinois* (1956) the Supreme Court held that the state had to provide a defendant with a stenographic transcript of criminal trial proceedings where that was necessary to his appeal. The state could not limit these transcripts to a small class of defendants or to those who offered to pay for them. The Court said that all defendants are entitled to some form of "equal justice." Although the state may not be required to provide an appellate system, once it did so, equal protection required it to grant access to the system in ways designed to ensure fair treatment of individuals. In the years since *Griffin* the Court has ruled that indigents must be provided with transcripts, or their functional equivalent, for appeal and post conviction proceedings.

Mayer v. Chicago (1971) held that the state must waive transcript fees required for appeal even in cases that do not involve incarceration of the defendant. The unanimous Court held that the state's fiscal and other interests do not justify eliminating access to basic review procedures for indigent defendants. The *Mayer* Court explained: "*Griffin* does not represent a balance between the need of the accused and the interest of society; its principle is a flat prohibition against pricing indigent defendants out of as effective an appeal as would be available to others able to pay their own way."

The Court has recognized that part of the right to fair treatment in the criminal justice system is a right of access to review procedures. The state may not impose burdens on the indigent's right to access to courts unless it can demonstrate some truly compelling interest in the limitation. The state may not require defendants to pay filing fees in order to have access to appellate courts or even as a requirement for post conviction proceedings following appeals.

Even after the defendant's right to counsel has expired, states may not take other actions to limit his access to the court. Thus the Court has held that where the state does not provide counsel to defendants for collateral attack proceedings, the state cannot prohibit prisoners from assisting each other with the preparation of papers seeking further review of their criminal convictions. *Johnson v. Avery* (1969). The Court has extended this principle to include a right of access to the courts to contest deprivations of rights while in prison. Thus the states cannot prohibit inmates from providing assistance to each other in the filing of civil rights actions while they were in prison. *Wolff v. McDonnell* (1974).

This right of access to courts includes a right to the materials that are necessary to prepare and file documents seeking review of criminal convictions or civil rights actions. States must also provide prisoners with adequate legal research materials for these purposes. *Bounds v. Smith* (1977).

The Court has not guaranteed that all defendants will be able to present their defense or prosecute their appeals with equal resources, for it is incapable of leveling the economic ability of some defendants to pay for superior legal or investigative services that may be of some assistance to them. However, the Court has sought to guarantee a basic level of fair treatment as a fundamental constitutional right. This distinction between insuring required fair treatment and leveling economic distinctions is the basis for the Court's rulings concerning the scope of counsel following a criminal conviction.

Douglas v. California (1963) held that a state could not dismiss the appeals of indigent criminal defendants with a separate system that did not include counsel to represent the defendant. While the state might not be required to establish an appellate system, it cannot grant appellate review on the basis of the wealth of the individual defendants. Thus equal protection required the state to provide counsel for indigent defendants in their first appeal as of right in order to grant them a meaningful form of judicial review.

However, states need not provide attorneys for indigent defendants in *discretionary* appeals or *collateral* attack proceedings following their first appeal as of right. *Ross v. Moffitt* (1974) held that these proceedings were not so essential to a fair determination of the individual criminal defendant's claims regarding his trial that they required the assistance of counsel. Furnishing the individual defendant with counsel and transcripts during his first appeal as of right sufficiently enabled him to receive fair treatment in the process of applying for discretionary appeals or collateral review of his conviction.

The Court has not fully considered the extent to which the right to fairness in the criminal process requires states to provide indigent defendants with access to other forms of assistance, or aid to present a defense or to prosecute an appeal. *Ake v. Oklahoma* (1985) held that, under the due process clause, an indigent defendant who makes a preliminary showing that his sanity at the time of the alleged offense is likely to be a significant factor at his trial is entitled to access to a state-provided psychiatrist. This psychiatrist will examine him and assist in the evaluation, preparation, and the presentation of his defense. In addition, at the sentencing phase of a capital case, if the state introduces evidence of the future dangerousness of the indigent defendant, then the defendant is entitled to similar state-supported assistance. In addition to the unresolved equal protection issues there are also questions as to whether the Sixth Amendment right to compulsory process of witnesses might include some right to state assistance to secure expert testimony to aid in the presentation of a defense.

Equal protection issues arise where indigent defendants are incarcerated because they cannot pay a fine. The Court uses equal protection analysis rather than the Eighth Amendment prohibition of excessive fines to determine the constitutionality of these procedures. It has held that the inability to pay a fine cannot be used to extend the prison term of a defendant beyond the maximum period fixed by statute. If a fine is the only punishment, the state cannot impose any incarceration on individuals too indigent to pay the fines. *Williams v. Illinois* (1970); *Tate v. Short* (1971) (incarceration in lieu of fine invalid).

The rights in the criminal justice system relate either to specific guarantees or to fairness in the system of investigating and adjudicating individual claims. The Court has not held that the government is required to grant economic benefits to indigent criminal defendants. Thus, the Court has upheld statutes that require convicted indigents to repay the state for the services of counsel that were provided them at trial or on appeal; the statute in question gave the defendant the opportunity to show that state's recovery of legal defense costs would impose hardship. *Fuller v. Oregon* (1974). That law requires convicted defendants who are indigent at the time of the criminal proceedings against them but who subsequently acquire the financial means to do so, to repay the costs of their legal defense.

But the Court will invalidate statutes that subject persons to arbitrary classifications in the enforcement of debts. Thus *Rinaldi v. Yeager* (1966) held that the legislative decision to tax those confined to prison but not those who are also convicted but given a suspended sentence, probation, or a fine without imprisonment is invidiously discriminatory and thus violates equal protection.

§ 14.36　Welfare Payments

There is no constitutional right to receive subsistence payments or welfare benefits. Instead Court has considered such programs as general economic and social welfare measures that are reviewed under the basic rationality standard of the due process and equal protection guarantees. However, the Court will subject these laws to strict scrutiny if they dispense the benefits based on suspect criterion. Similarly, the Court will subject these laws will be subject to the strict scrutiny test if the welfare system has limitations that burden other fundamental constitutional values such as the right to travel.

Where the state has declared that someone is "entitled" to receive these benefits, the individual has a right to a hearing, in accordance with the procedural due process guarantee, prior to their termination. But even in the area of procedural due process the Court has left the states free to determine the basis upon that they will grant these benefits and the definition of those persons who are entitled to receive or retain them.

The most vivid example of this type of analysis is *Dandridge v. Williams* (1970), which upheld a state law for the administration of Aid to Families with Dependent Children (AFDC) that, in effect, put an upper limit on the number of children for whom any family could receive subsistence payments. Justice Stewart, for the Court, not only upheld the law but found that it was one concerning only "economics and social welfare." The Court stated that although the classification "involved the most basic needs of impoverished human beings," it could find "no basis for applying a different constitutional standard."

There are two cases where the Court did invalidate provisions of the Food Stamp Act under what seemed to be a more meaningful standard of review than the basic rationality test, *United States Department of Agriculture v. Moreno* (1973), and a companion decision, *United States Department of Agriculture v. Murry* (1973). In the first case, the Court invalidated a section of the Food Stamp Act that made any household comprised of unrelated individuals ineligible to receive food stamps. In the second case it invalidated a section of the act that disqualified any household that included a member who was over 18 years of age and who had been claimed as a tax dependent by a nonmember of the household in the previous year.

Unfortunately, in these two cases, the Court did not indicate why it was employing an increased standard of review, or, indeed, if it even appreciated that it was going beyond the rationality test. These cases have not spawned a line of precedent, although the Court has never explicitly overruled them.

§ 14.37 Housing

The Supreme Court has never found that there is any right to government assistance to secure adequate housing or other forms of shelter. Indeed, the Court has not subjected government actions that might burden persons' abilities to find adequate private housing to any standard of review above the rationality test of the due process and equal protection guarantees. Of course, if these laws involve the use of suspect classifications or burden fundamental rights they will be subjected to the strict scrutiny standard of review.

§ 14.38 Education

The Supreme Court has not held that publicly financed primary or secondary education is a fundamental right. It has avoided the ultimate issue, but it has refused to impose upon the states the requirement that they provide equal access to high quality forms of education. The leading case is *San Antonio Independent School District v. Rodriguez* (1973). However, the Court has held that once the state grants educational rights, it cannot terminate without procedural due process safeguards, although these safeguards will not preclude the individual student from certain actions, such as physical punishment, within the school system. standards.

In *San Antonio Independent School District v. Rodriguez* the Supreme Court (5 to 4) upheld the state's use of local property taxes to finance primary and secondary education, even though this tax system allowed areas within a single school district to have great disparities in the amount of money spent per student on educational programs and resources.

The majority opinion, by Justice Powell, applied the standard of minimal scrutiny; it found it arguably reasonable for the legislature to use local property taxation to advance goals of local control over schools. The Court accepted these interests at face value and never inquired whether the system in fact bore a rational relationship to a state interest of a quality sufficient to justify the lower standard of education for children in the least wealthy districts. The majority opinion never found it necessary to inquire as to whether the state's legitimate goals would still be met if an equal amount of money was expended on the education of each child in the state. The Court found that no suspect classification was involved since there was no correlation in this case between district wealth and race.

Because education is not a "fundamental right," most laws that regulate access to education or allocate differing amounts of educational benefits to different classes of persons will not be subject to strict judicial scrutiny. However, if a state singles out a class of children and denies them all educational opportunity, that classification should be subject to some form of independent judicial review. The basis upon which the class is defined need not be suspect if singling out of an identified class of children for complete denial of this important governmental benefit is irrational or arbitrary on its face.

For example, if a state denied all state funded education to left-handed children or red-haired children, the law would be subject to some meaningful form of judicial review and the Court will not simply presume that the legislature was acting within its constitutional authority by refusing to grant any educational benefits to these children.

§ 14.39 Government Employment

So long as the government does not employ suspect criteria or burden fundamental rights, the Court defers to legislative and executive judgments concerning the terms of public employment in the same way it treats other forms of economic and social welfare legislation. Thus, the Court has upheld mandatory retirement from government service at age 50 since classifications by age are not "suspect" or of special constitutional significance. *Massachusetts Board of Retirement v. Murgia* (1976).

Vance v. Bradley (1979) upheld a requirement that participants in the foreign service retirement system retire from their government positions at age 60. The plaintiff employees argued that the distinction between the mandatory retirement at age 60 for their job classifications and the general federal requirement of retirement at age 70 for the federal Civil Service Retirement System personnel violated the equal protection component of the Fifth Amendment.

The Court held that the retirement classification did not violate the equal protection guarantee. White's opinion stressed that the federal judiciary should not actively review classifications that do not involve fundamental rights or suspect classifications.

Chapter 15

CONGRESSIONAL ENFORCEMENT OF CIVIL RIGHTS

Table of Sections

§ 15.1 Introduction

This Chapter provides an overview of the power granted to Congress to enforce Amendments 13, 14 and 15, which are commonly known as the Civil War Amendments. For a more complete examination of these congressional powers, the reader should consult our multi-volume Treatise.

The Thirteenth Amendment, ratified in 1865, expanded the effect of the Emancipation Proclamation by making slavery and involuntary servitude illegal throughout the United States and property under its control. Section 2 of the Thirteenth Amendment gave power to Congress to enforce the Amendment "by appropriate legislation." The Civil Rights Act of 1866, which was passed over President Andrew Johnson's veto, gave all citizens the same rights "as enjoyed by white citizens" regarding a wide variety of activities. Questions were raised in Congress, and in public debates, regarding whether the Thirteenth Amendment was sufficient to justify the Civil Rights Act of 1866.

The Fourteenth Amendment was ratified in 1868. Section 1 of the Fourteenth Amendment: defined citizenship; protected the privileges or immunities of citizenship; and gave all persons a right to due process and equal protection. Sections 2, 3 and 4 of that Amendment address issues of national importance in the 1860s regarding voting, representation in Congress, and Civil War debts.

Section 5 gave Congress "power to enforce, by appropriate legislation, the provisions" of the Fourteenth Amendment.

Despite the ratification of the Thirteenth and Fourteenth Amendments, a number of states continued to refuse to recognize the rights of minority race persons to vote. In 1870, the country ratified the Fifteenth Amendment. Section 1 of that Amendment prohibited denying or abridging the right to vote on the basis of "race, color or previous condition of servitude" by the United States or by any state or local government. Section 2 of the Fifteenth Amendment gave Congress the power to enforce the Amendment "by appropriate legislation."

Any federalism limitations on the scope of congressional power established in the original Constitution of 1787, or by the Tenth and Eleventh Amendments, could be overridden by legislation passed pursuant to the Thirteenth, Fourteenth or Fifteenth Amendments. However, a federal statute will only be valid under the Civil War Amendments, and only capable of overriding earlier limits on congressional power, if the Supreme Court decides that the statute is within the scope of power given to Congress by the Thirteenth, Fourteenth or Fifteenth Amendments.

At the time when the Civil War Amendments were ratified, the sentiment of the country, at least in the victorious Union states, may have favored granting Congress significant new powers through the enforcement clauses of the Civil War Amendments. Be that as it may, in the last quarter of the nineteenth century, the Supreme Court took a narrow view of the power granted to Congress by the Thirteenth, Fourteenth and Fifteenth Amendments. During the last years of the Warren Court, and throughout the Burger Court years, the Supreme Court appeared ready to expand the scope of congressional power under those Amendments. However, by the start of the twenty-first century, the Rehnquist Court would endorse the narrow view of congressional power under the Fourteenth Amendment that had been used by a majority of the Justices in the late nineteenth century.

In Chapter 12 of this text, concerning the subject of state action, we set forth the holdings of the *Civil Rights Cases* (1883). In that decision, the Supreme Court read section 1 of the Thirteenth Amendment quite narrowly, and ruled that section 2 of the Thirteenth Amendment did not give Congress the power to make illegal any activities that were not made unconstitutional by section 1 of that Amendment. The majority in the *Civil Rights Cases* also ruled that section 5 of the Fourteenth Amendment did not give Congress the power to make illegal any activity that the Court would not have found unconstitutional under section 1 of the Fourteenth Amendment.

The Supreme Court at the start of the twenty-first century: (1) grants Congress significant deference concerning the use of its Thirteenth Amendment section 2 power to eliminate racial discrimination; (2) prohibits Congress from using its section 5 Fourteenth Amendment powers to expand the rights and liberties protected by section 1 of that Amendment; and (3) is unclear concerning the scope of congressional power to enforce the Fifteenth Amendment.

§ 15.2   The Thirteenth Amendment

Section 1 of the Thirteenth Amendment constitutes an absolute bar to slavery or involuntary servitude in the United States (and in any property or territory under the control of the United States government). An individual who has no connection to government, and who lacks "state action," can violate section 1 of the Thirteenth Amendment. If a private person forces another individual to work for him in a condition of slavery or peonage that person has violated section 1 of the Thirteenth Amendment.

It might be advantageous for the reader to reflect on a difference between the Thirteenth Amendment and the commerce clause. Congress can regulate private activity under the commerce clause, even though a private individual cannot violate the commerce clause. For example, an individual who takes heroin across a state line is not violating the commerce clause. Nevertheless Congress, under the commerce power granted to it by Article I, Section 8, can make the interstate transportation of heroin a federal crime.

In contrast with the commerce power situation, the person who forces another individual into slavery or peonage violates section 1 of the Thirteenth Amendment. We need not worry about what types of penalties might have been imposed on an individual who violated section 1 of the Thirteenth Amendment if there had been no federal statutes to enforce that Amendment. Since the ratification of the Thirteenth Amendment, the federal government has had statutes punishing individuals who force other persons into involuntary servitude or peonage.

Section 1 of the Thirteenth Amendment, absent any expansion through Congress's power under section 2 of the Amendment, only forbids slavery or peonage. In *Bailey v. Alabama* (1911) the Supreme Court said: "The state may impose involuntary servitude as a punishment for crime, but it may not compel one man to labor for another in payment of a debt . . .". In *Butler v. Perry* (1916) the Court noted that the Thirteenth Amendment "was not intended to interdict enforcement of those duties which individuals owe to the state, such as services to the Army, Militia, or on the jury, etc." The Court has upheld military draft laws that require labor from both soldiers and conscientious objectors. In *International Union v.*

Wisconsin Employment Labor Relations Board (1949) the Court ruled that injunctions in certain labor disputes do not involve involuntary servitude.

§ 15.3   Congressional Power to Expand the Impact of the Thirteenth Amendment

In the *Civil Rights Cases,* the Court stated that section 2 of the Thirteenth Amendment gave Congress the "power to pass all laws necessary and proper for abolishing all badges and incidents of slavery ..." Initially, the reader might believe that the Court was granting Congress significant powers to abolish race discrimination. However, a majority of the Justices, in that case, decided that the Court should give virtually no deference to congressional decisions regarding which types of racial discrimination constituted the badges and incidents of slavery. These Justices took unto themselves the power to determine those types of race discrimination that Congress could outlaw through the use of its Thirteenth Amendment power.

The federal government, in the *Civil Rights Cases,* argued that, while Section 1 of the Thirteenth Amendment only made true slavery or peonage unconstitutional, Congress could make other activities illegal by using the power granted to it by section 2 of the Thirteenth Amendment. The Court rejected that argument in the *Civil Rights Cases,* when it invalidated a federal statute that would have prohibited individuals from denying persons access to public facilities or public conveyances because of their race.

Decisions of the Supreme Court in the late nineteenth century undercut many of the civil rights laws passed by the Reconstruction Congress. The Thirteenth Amendment power of Congress, and legislation passed pursuant to that power, lay dormant for many decades. It was not until the end of the 1960s that the Supreme Court began to give full effect to the grant of power to Congress contained in section 2 of the Thirteenth Amendment.

In 1968 and 1969 the Supreme Court upheld, as valid Thirteenth Amendment legislation, 42 U.S.C.A. § 1982, which guarantees to every person in the United States the same right "as is enjoyed by white citizens" regarding rights and interests in real and personal property. In *Jones v. Allfred H. Mayer, Co.* (1968) the Supreme Court, based on the legislative history of that 1866 statute, ruled that § 1982 prohibited private persons, as well as government entities, from engaging in racial discrimination related to the sale of property. The Supreme Court in *Jones* overruled an early twentieth century decision that had ruled that the Thirteenth Amendment did not allow Congress to regulate private rights that were not connected with institutionalized slavery. [*Hodges v. United States* (1906), overruled by *Jones v. Allfred H. Mayer, Co.* (1968)]

In *Jones*, the Court held that, to be within Congress's Thirteenth Amendment power, a federal statute only had to have some arguably rational connection with the eradication of the badges and incidents of slavery. The *Jones* Court found that the judiciary must defer to a congressional judgment that an outlawed form of private discrimination might constitute a remnant of this country's experience as being one in which slavery had once been lawful. In *Sullivan v. Little Hunting Park, Inc.* (1969) the Supreme Court extended *Jones*, as the Court held that § 1982 of the Civil Rights Act invalidated racial discrimination in community facilities connected to the rental of real property. Later, the Court would hold that § 1982 can be used by any persons who are members of any racial or ethnic group.

In the 1970s, the Supreme Court consistently upheld statutes banning racial discrimination that arguably were based on Congress's power to enforce the Thirteenth Amendment. The Court never backed away from the rulings of the 1960s, which held that Congress needed only a rational argument that forms of racial discrimination that were outlawed by federal legislation might be connected to the history of a society that once condoned slavery.

Because the Thirteenth Amendment applies to private action, statutes based on the Thirteenth Amendment can apply to either private persons or government entities. *Griffin v. Breckenridge* (1971) ruled that 42 U.S.C. § 1985 could be used by minority race persons to seek damages from individuals who had stopped their car on a highway and then severely beat them with clubs. The racially motivated assault, which was connected to a conspiracy to interfere with the rights of these persons to travel, was actionable under § 1985. The Justices in *Griffin* ruled unanimously that § 1985, and its application to these facts, was within the power granted to Congress by the enforcement clause of the Thirteenth Amendment. Also in *Griffin*, by a vote of 8 to 1, the Justices held that the statute, as applied, was a constitutionally valid exercise of a congressional power to protect a fundamental right of interstate travel.

42 U.S.C.A. § 1981 prohibits racial discrimination in connection with the making and enforcement of contracts, and many other rights. The Supreme Court, in *Runyon v. McCrary* (1976), found that § 1981 was a valid use of the power granted to Congress by the Thirteenth Amendment. Therefore, a minority race family could use § 1981 to recover damages from a private school that had refused to admit their child because of the child's race. However, the Court left open the question of whether § 1981 applied to

schools that discriminated on the basis of race solely for religious reasons. The *Runyon* Court ruled that: (1) absent a possible exception for certain types of religious schools (which it was not addressing in the case), any school that advertised and offered services to members of the general public was offering to enter into a contractual relationship; and (2) § 1981 prohibited race discrimination in such contracting activities. Later Supreme Court decisions interpreting § 1981 found that any person (regardless of her or his ethnic background) could bring suit under the statute if he or she had suffered discrimination related to contracts that were based on race.

In *Patterson v. McClean Credit Union* (1989) the Court interpreted § 1981 so that it would not prohibit racial harassment related to contracts if the harassment occurred after the formation of the contract. This statutory interpretation, which flew in the face of the Burger Court rulings, was quickly rejected by the other branches of the federal government. Congress [at the request of President G.H.W. Bush, and with the approval of President Clinton] amended § 1981 to make it clear that the statute applied to such racial discrimination.

§ 15.4 Congressional Power to Enforce the Fourteenth Amendment

The Court's position regarding the scope of congressional power under § 5 of the Fourteenth Amendment in the early twenty-first century is as narrow as the position the Court took in the *Civil Rights Cases* (1883). The following statement would come very close to the Court's position both in the late nineteenth century and in 2004: Section 5 of the Fourteenth Amendment gives Congress only the power to discover, regulate, prohibit, and remedy activities that the Justices [if they had known the facts considered by Congress] would have found to be a violation of section 1 of the Fourteenth Amendment.

For a time, in the twentieth century, it appeared that the Court might expand Congress's power to enforce the Fourteenth Amendment and allow Congress to expand the scope of civil liberties protected from both public and private interference by using its Fourteenth Amendment power. In *United States v. Guest* (1966) the Court found that a law passed in 1870 outlawing interference with the exercise or enjoyment of any "right or privilege" protected by federal law could be applied to punish private individuals (unconnected to any governmental activity) who had conspired to intimidate minority race persons in order to prevent those persons from using facilities of interstate commerce within the State of Georgia. The majority opinion in *Guest* expressly stated that it was not going to address "the question of what kinds of other broader legislation Congress might constitutionally enact under section 5 of the Fourteenth Amendment." The majority in *Guest* was unclear regarding whether the law could be justified by section 5 of the Fourteenth Amendment alone or by some inherent congressional power to protect certain uniquely federal rights (such as the right to engage in interstate travel). In separate opinions in *Guest*, six Justices indicated that they would have voted (on that day in 1966) to allow Congress to expand civil liberties, with its section 5 power. However, those statements were not contained in a majority opinion. In 2000, the Court rejected the views of the *Guest* concurring Justices.

In *United States v. Morrison* (2000) the Supreme Court ruled that Congress could not regulate private action under the powers granted to it by section 5 of the Fourteenth Amendment. The Court returned to the position of the *Civil Rights Cases*, when it held, in *Morrison*, that congressional power under section 5 of the Fourteenth Amendment is limited to regulating the action of state or local governments or persons who are acting in a way that justifies treating their activity as "state action."

Morrison invalidated a section of a federal statute that was popularly called the Violence Against Women Act, although the act simply prohibited sex-based violence and did not single out women for special protection. The law allowed a person who was the victim of a "crime of violence motivated by gender" to bring a civil action against a person who had attacked her or him. The Supreme Court, in *Morrison,* ruled that the law could not be justified by section 5 of the Fourteenth Amendment because it regulated private action, rather than state action. Additionally, as we saw in Chapter Four, the Court in *Morrison* ruled that the statute did not come within the Article I commerce power of the federal government, because the statute neither regulated activities that involved interstate activity nor a class of activity that had a substantial effect on interstate commerce.

If Congress wishes to protect civil rights from private interference, it will need to find a basis for justifying the law under a federal power that can govern private activity, such as the commerce clause. As we have seen, Congress can regulate many types of racially discriminatory activities under its Thirteenth Amendment power.

Some Justices, and professors, have argued that Congress should be able to expand the nature of rights that the Fourteenth Amendment protects from governmental interference. These persons believe that the Supreme Court should view the power granted to Congress by section 5 of the Fourteenth Amendment in the same way as it looks at the power of state or local governments to protect civil liberties. The Constitution, and its Amendments, establish the minimum scope of civil liberties that state governments must respect. However, a state is always free to expand the scope of civil liberties under its state law. Thus, for example, the United States Supreme Court has held that, under certain circumstances, state police officers may search an automobile without a search warrant. Despite that holding of the U.S. Supreme Court, a state would be free to adopt a state law that prohibited state police officers from ever searching an automobile without a valid search warrant with a similar approach to congressional power, a court would rule: that section 1 of the Fourteenth Amendment protected a certain minimum level of civil liberties, which Congress could not decrease; and that section 5 of the Fourteenth Amendment gives Congress the power to expand the scope of civil liberties protected against state and local government interference. Despite the popularity of that argument in academic circles, the Supreme Court has rejected that argument.

Through a series of cases, spanning roughly thirty years, culminating in *City of Boerne v. Flores* (1997), the Court effectively has restricted Congress to the role of discovering violations of section 1 of the Fourteenth Amendment that might have escaped judicial notice (because of Congress's greater fact-finding powers) and remedying those violations of section 1.

The *Morgan* Case. *Katzenbach v. Morgan* upheld the constitutionality of section 4(e) of the Voting Rights Act of 1965. That section provided that no person who has completed the sixth grade in a Puerto Rican school (where the predominant classroom language was not English) may be denied the right to vote in any election because of his or her inability to read or write English. The statute *pro tanto* prohibited enforcement of New York law requiring an ability to read and write English as a condition of voting. The question in *Morgan* was whether Congress could prohibit enforcement of the state law by legislating under section 5 of the Fourteenth Amendment, regardless of whether the Court would find that the equal protection clause itself nullified New York's literacy requirement.

The Court utilized a two-part analysis to uphold the federal statute. It first construed section 5 as granting Congress, when enforcing the Fourteenth Amendment, the same broad powers it has in the necessary and proper clause. The Court held Congress has the power to determine that the Puerto Rican minority needed the vote to gain nondiscriminatory treatment in public services and that this need warranted federal intrusion on the states. The Court reached the same result in the second part of its analysis. Because it "perceived a basis" on which Congress might reasonably predicate its judgment that the New York literacy requirement was invidiously discriminatory, the Court was willing to uphold the law.

In *Oregon v. Mitchell* (1971), the Court evaluated the constitutionality of provisions of the Voting Rights Act Amendments of 1970, which lowered the minimum voting age in state, local, and federal elections from 21 to 18, barred the use of literacy tests under certain circumstances, and forbade state imposition of residency requirements for presidential and vice-presidential elections. If *Morgan* granted Congress *carte blanche* to enact legislation remedying what Congress regards as denials of equal protection, the Court would have upheld the federal statute on that basis. Instead, the Court, in five separate opinions, struck down the section of the Act that authorized 18 year-olds to vote in state and local elections.

Four Justices—Douglas, Brennan, White, and Marshall—maintained that Congress had the power under section 5 to determine what are the equal protection requirements as applied to the voting rights of 18 to 21 year-olds in state, local, and federal elections. Brennan argued that because Congress had sufficient evidence to conclude that exclusion of such citizens from the franchise was unnecessary to promote any legitimate state interest, it could properly extend the franchise, regardless of the Court's view of the matter. None of the other Justices of the fragmented Court saw Congress' role as that extensive.

Justice Stewart, joined by Chief Justice Burger and Justice Blackmun, found that Congress could not usurp the role of the courts by determining the boundaries of the equal protection clause. Rather than reading *Morgan* as granting Congress power to define the reach of the equal protection clause, Stewart argued that the Court in *Morgan* only accepted an undoubtedly correct congressional conclusion, that a state statute denying a racial group the right to vote amounts to invidious discrimination under the equal protection clause.

Justice Harlan agreed that Congress could not define the reach of equal protection because, in his view, any other position would allow Congress to change the meaning of the Constitution.

Justices Black and Douglas disagreed on the validity of the Voting Rights Act Amendments of 1970 based on their views of the reach of the equal protection clause, but each assumed that the legal question was for the courts, not Congress, to decide.

Although the Court was splintered, a majority of the Justices did reject the contention that section 5 authorizes Congress to define the substantive boundaries of the equal protection clause by invalidating state legislation. *Oregon v. Mitchell* laid the groundwork. Then came the *Boerne* decision.

City of Boerne v. Flores In *City of Boerne v. Flores* (1997) when it ruled that Congress exceed its powers under section 5 of the Fourteenth Amendment when it enacted the Religious Freedom Restoration Act ("RFRA").

Congress enacted RFRA to overturn *Employment Division, Department of Human Resources of Oregon v. Smith* (1990). In *Smith*, the Court had upheld state power to enforce generally applicable neutral laws (in that case, a law banning the use of peyote, an illegal drug) even if the law was applied to deny unemployment benefits to individuals who lost their job because of the illegal peyote use, where the users were members of a Native American Church, and they claimed that they used peyote as a sacrament and the law interfered with their free exercise of religion.

RFRA, in contrast to *Smith*, provided that both the state and the federal government cannot "substantially burden" a person's exercise of religion, even under a rule of general applicability, unless the government demonstrates that the burden (1) furthers a "compelling governmental interest;" and, (2) is the "least restrictive means of furthering" that interest. RFRA, in short, sought to overrule *Smith*.

In *Boerne*, local zoning authorities denied a church a building permit to enlarge a church because the enlargement, in the view of the Historical Landmark Commission, conflicted with an historical preservation plan. Archbishop Flores then sued under RFRA. Justice Kennedy, for the Court, held that RFRA was unconstitutional and not justified by section 5 of the Fourteenth Amendment. While Congress has section 5 power to enforce the Free Exercise Clause, its power is the power only to "enforce." Its power is preventive, remedial. Relying on *Oregon v. Mitchell*, the Court said that this section does not give Congress the right to decree the substance of what the First Amendment means. "Legislation which alters the meaning of the Free Exercise Clause cannot be said to be enforcing the Clause."

Congruence & Proportionality. The line between remedial legislation and legislation that makes a substantive change in the law may not always be clear. The Court will give Congress "wide latitude" to decide where to draw the line. However, there must be "congruence and proportionality between the injury to be prevented or remedied and the means adopted to that end."

For example, when Congress enacted (and the Supreme Court in *Katzenbach* later upheld various provisions of) the Voting Rights Act of 1965, there was a long and widespread record before Congress and in the case law documenting racial discrimination in voting. But when one turns to RFRA, there is no evidence of any generally applicable law enacted because of religious bigotry in the last 40 years. There was only evidence of laws that placed incidental burdens on religion, and these laws were not enacted or enforced because of animus or hostility to religion nor did they indicate that there was any widespread pattern of religious discrimination in this country. RFRA, in short, was a major federal intrusion "into the States' traditional prerogative and general authority to regulate for the health and welfare of their citizens."

The "congruence and proportionality" standard does not apply outside the § 5 context. For example, "it does not hold sway for judicial review of legislation enacted, as copyright laws are, pursuant to Article I authorization."

Reaffirming *Boerne*. In a trio of cases decided the same day during the 1998–1999 Supreme Court term, the Court reaffirmed *City of Boerne*, agreed that section 5 of the Fourteenth Amendment gives Congress the power to create causes of action against the state to enforce the Fourteenth Amendment, but then held that this power had not been properly exercised. A different Justice wrote the majority in each of these opinions (all decided by the same five to four vote).

In *Florida Prepaid Postsecondary Education Expense Board v. College Savings Bank* (1999), Chief Justice Rehnquist spoke of the Court. Congress enacted a statute expressly abrogating the states' sovereign immunity from lawsuits for patent violations. Then College Savings Bank sued the Florida State Board for patent infringement, arguing that Congress has properly exercised its powers under section 5 of the Fourteenth Amendment to protect the due process property guarantees of a patent holder. The Court found that section 5 did not authorize this abrogation of Florida's sovereign immunity from suit in federal court.

The Court agreed that Congress—by using its power under section 5 to enforce section 1 of the Fourteenth Amendment—can abrogate a state's sovereign immunity rights and its Eleventh Amendment immunity. The Court also readily agreed that patents are property, that section 1 does protect the right to property, and that the state cannot take this private property without paying just compensation.

However, because Congress' enforcement power is remedial, Congress must carefully tailor its legislative scheme to remedying or preventing the particular conduct that violates the Fourteenth Amendment. That was not done in this case because this legislation did not enforce the just compensation clause. First, neither the language of the statute nor the legislative history indicated that Congress was trying to enforce the Just Compensation Clause;

second, the United States specifically declined to defend the law as based on the Just Compensation Clause.

The law was also not justified on the basis that it protected procedural due process, because the state had already provided a fair judicial remedy for a takings or conversion claim. The federal statute merely offered a different procedure, but the state already offered a procedure was adequate for Constitutional purposes.

The federal statute's aim was to provide a uniform procedural remedy for patent infringement and to place states on the same footing as private parties. These are proper Article I concerns, the Court agreed, but Article I does not authorize Congress to abrogate state immunity from suit, and Article I cannot justify action under the Fourteenth Amendment. Hence, the legislation was not "appropriate" under section 5, and was therefore unconstitutional.

In *College Savings Bank v. Florida Prepaid Postsecondary Education Expense Board* (1999), a companion case, plaintiff sued Florida for false and misleading advertising under the Federal Trademark Act of 1946 (the Lanham Act). The Trademark Remedy Clarification Act ("TRCA") subjected states to suit in federal court. The plaintiff argued that Congress' abrogation of sovereign immunity in the TRCA was constitutional on the grounds that it enforced the guarantee found in section 1 of the Fourteenth Amendment that a state will not deprive anyone of property without due process. Justice Scalia, for the Court, rejected that argument.

The Court explained that laws enacted pursuant to § 5 must be for the purpose of remedying or preventing constitutional violations. But the TRCA did not enforce property rights.

First, there is no "property" because the hallmark of a constitutionally protected property interest is the right to exclude others.

Second, a business's assets, including its good will, are property, and any state taking of those assets is a "deprivation" of property. However, the state action in this case did not take the petitioner's "property." Business, "in the sense of *the activity of doing business, or the activity of making a profit* is not property in the ordinary sense—and it is only *that*, and not any business asset, which is impinged upon by a competitor's false advertising."

The third case was *Alden v. Maine* (1999). In that case, the Court held that Congress, using its Article I powers, could not subject a state to suit in *state* court by private parties without the state's consent, just as Congress could not subject a state to suit in *federal* court in similar circumstances. However, the Court expressly declared that this prohibition did not apply when Congress properly exercises its power under § 1 of the Fourteenth Amendment: "Congress may authorize private suits against nonconsenting States pursuant to its § 5 enforcement powers."

In 2000, the Court invalidated another federal effort to revoke the Eleventh Amendment rights of the states. The Age Discrimination in Employment Act (ADEA) clearly stated that it was subjecting the states to the ADEA and taking away their Eleventh Amendment immunity. However, *Kimel v. Florida Board of Regents* (2000) held that Congress could not constitutionally use section 5 in this manner because the abrogation exceeded federal power under section 5. Age is not a suspect class under the equal protection clause and therefore an age classification is constitutional if it is rational. Congress cannot annul the states' Eleventh Amendment immunity merely by stating that it is enforcing the Fourteenth Amendment; the law must actually enforce (not redefine) section 1.

The Hibbs Case. In *Nevada Department of Human Resources v. Hibbs* (2003) the Court applied the methodology of the prior cases and, this time, upheld the law, which it found to cover a protected class (sex-based discrimination) and it was congruent and proportional to the constitutional injury that the law sought to prevent.

Mr. Hibbs, an employee of the Nevada Department of Human Resources, sought leave to care for his ailing wife under the Family and Medical Leave Act of 1993 (FMLA), which entitles an eligible employee to take up to 12 work weeks of unpaid leave annually for the onset of a "serious health condition" in the employee's spouse and for other reasons. The FMLA creates a private right of action to seek both equitable relief and money damages "against any employer (including a public agency) in any Federal or State court of competent jurisdiction," if that employer interferes with, restrains, or denies the exercise of FMLA rights. Chief Justice Rehnquist, for the Court, held that employees of the State of Nevada may recover money damages in the event of the state's failure to comply with the family-care provision of the Act.

Quoting *City of Boerne*, the Court said that laws passed under § 5 "reaching beyond the scope of § 1's actual guarantees must be an appropriate remedy for identified constitutional violations, not 'an attempt to substantively redefine the States' legal obligations.'" Congress, in the exercise of its § 5 powers, may "do more than simply proscribe conduct that we have held unconstitutional."

The Court summarized the evidence on which Congress based its law. For example, parental leave for fathers is rare, and even where it exists, "men, *both in the public and private sectors*, receive notoriously discriminatory treatment in their requests for such leave." These differential leave policies were based on the "pervasive sex-role stereotype that caring for family members is women's work."

Discrimination in the case of age based classifications is not judged under a heightened review standard, and passes muster if there is "a rational basis for doing so at a class-based level." In contrast, a sex-based classification must do more than meet than the rational-basis test—it must "serve important governmental objectives" and be "substantially related to the achievement of those objectives." Hence, it is "easier for Congress to show a pattern of state constitutional violations."

By creating an across-the-board, routine employment benefit for all eligible employees, Congress sought to ensure that family-care leave would no longer be stigmatized as an inordinate drain on the workplace caused by female employees, and that employers could not evade leave obligations simply by hiring men. By setting a minimum standard of family leave for all eligible employees, irrespective of gender, the FMLA attacks the formerly state-sanctioned stereotype that only women are responsible for family caregiving, thereby reducing employers' incentives to engage in discrimination by basing hiring and promotion decisions on stereotypes.

Conclusion: Case-by-Case Determination. The Court's decisions regarding the Congress's use of its Fourteenth Amendment, section 5 power appear to be ad hoc rulings. it is difficult to determine in advance whether a majority of the Justices will find that a specific federal statute is a congruent and proportional method of preventing or remedying a violation of section 1 of the Fourteenth Amendment. For example, *Board of Trustees v. Garrett* (2001) ruled that Title I of the Americans with Disabilities Act [ADA], which allows a disabled person to sue an employer for money damages under certain circumstances cannot be used to sue a state employer for money damages. *Garrett* ruled that Title I could be justified only by Congress's Article I commerce power, and not by Congress's Fourteenth Amendment power; and, therefore, that Title I did not override the state's Eleventh Amendment immunity. In contrast, *Tennessee v. Lane* (2004) ruled that Title II of the ADA, which prohibits the exclusion of disabled persons from public services or programs, was a valid exercise of Congress's Fourteenth Amendment power at least insofar as it was applied to state practices that excluded persons from exercising a "fundamental right of access to courts." Therefore, a paraplegic plaintiff could receive money damages from the state, based on the state denying the plaintiff physical access to a state court.

§ 15.5 Congressional Enforcement of the Fifteenth Amendment

With the enactment of the Fifteenth Amendment in 1870, the Reconstruction Congress did not sit on its haunches. It was not content to rely on its self-executing section 1, but passed implementing legislation pursuant to section 2. The Enforcement Act of 1870 made it a criminal offense for either public officials or private persons to obstruct the right to vote. The next year Congress tightened that law by careful federal supervision of registration through the certification of election returns. But as the "years passed and fervor for racial equality waned, enforcement of the laws became spotty and ineffective, and most of their provisions were repealed in 1894."

Portions of the country responded by vigorous efforts to disenfranchise minority race persons through the use of grandfather clauses, procedural hurdles, primary elections open only to whites, improper voting challenges, racial gerrymandering, and discriminatory application of voting tests, all struck down in a long series of Supreme Court opinions. In 1965, Congress again entered the battle in a major way with a new weapon, the Voting Rights Act of 1965.

South Carolina v. Katzenbach (1966) upheld various challenged portions of the Voting Rights Act of 1965. South Carolina brought this original case in the Supreme Court pursuant to Article III, section 2. All states were invited to submit amicus briefs and a majority did so, some supporting South Carolina and others supporting the Attorney General.

Chief Justice Warren, writing the opinion for the Court, observed that Congress, prior to passage of the Voting Rights Act, "explored with great care the problem of racial discrimination in voting." This Congressional investigation showed, first, that certain parts of the country had long used various means to defy the command of the Fifteenth Amendment, and that, second, stronger federal legislative remedies were in order. For example, in spite of previous court actions and earlier federal legislation, the registration of voting age blacks in Mississippi rose from only 4.9% to 6.4% between 1954 and 1964.

One of the sections attacked was the Act's coverage formula. This formula provides coverage as to any state, county, parish, or similar political subdivision, that the Attorney General has determined that on November 1, 1964, maintained a "test or device" to qualify voting rights and, that the Director of the Census has determined that less than 50% of its voting age residents were registered on November 1, 1964, or voted in that year's presidential election. The term "test or device" is defined as any requirement that the registrant be able to read or interpret any matter, or demonstrate any educational achievement or knowledge of any particular subject, or possess good moral character, or prove his voting qualifications by the voucher of registered voters or others.

No court may review the findings of the Attorney General or the Census Director under these sections. Such statutory coverage is terminated if the area persuades a court to grant it a declaratory judgment that tests and devices have not been used within the last five years to abridge the vote on racial grounds. This declaratory judgment must be obtained from a particular court, a three judge court of the District Court for the District of Columbia, with a direct appeal to the Supreme Court.

As long as the statutory coverage is effective, the state or political subdivision is barred from enforcing its tests or devices. Also, before the state or political subdivision may change its election qualifications or procedures, it must submit its changes to the Attorney General for approval or obtain a declaratory judgment from a three-judge court of the District Court for the District of Columbia, with direct appeal to the Supreme Court.

If the Attorney General certifies certain facts to the Civil Service Commission, it must appoint voting examiners. The Attorney General's certification is either that he or she has received meritorious written complaints alleging racial discrimination in voting from at least twenty residents or that the appointment of the examiners is otherwise necessary to implement the guarantees of the Fifteenth Amendment. These certifications are also not reviewable in any court. These examiners test the voting qualifications of applicants; any applicant meeting the nonsuspended portions of state law is to be promptly placed on the list of eligible voters.

The Court quickly rejected the argument that the Act violated the due process rights of the states by employing an invalid presumption: the word "person" in the due process clause of the Fifth Amendment does not include the states of the Union. The Court also dismissed the objection that the statutory bar to judicial review of administrative findings constituted an unconstitutional bill of attainder and violated the separation of powers by adjudicating guilt through legislation, because these principles apply only to protect individual persons and private groups, not the state. Nor does a state have standing to invoke these provisions on behalf of its citizens.

The Supreme Court next rejected the argument that only the judiciary may strike down state statutes and procedures. Section 2 of the Fifteenth Amendment contemplates a role for Congress. "As against the reserved powers of the States, Congress may use any rational means to effectuate the constitutional prohibitions of racial discrimination in voting." To determine if this Congressional legislation is valid, the basic test is to apply Chief Justice Marshall's test for the validity of legislation under the necessary and proper clause.

Let the end be legitimate, let it be within the scope of the constitution, and all means which are appropriate, which are plainly adapted to that end, and which are not prohibited, but consist with the letter and spirit of the constitution, are constitutional.

The majority opinion in *Katzenbach* found that it was a legitimate response for Congress to prescribe voting discrimination remedies without going into prior adjudication given the ample evidence showing that case-by-case litigation was inadequate to combat the persistent discrimination. The fact that the remedies were confined to certain locations did not affect the validity of the statute because Congress had learned that the problem was localized and in these areas immediate action seemed necessary. "The doctrine of the equality of States, invoked by South Carolina, does not bar this approach, for that doctrine applies only to the terms on which States are admitted to the Union and not to the remedies for local evils which have subsequently appeared."

It was also proper for Congress to limit litigation under challenged provisions of the Act to a single court in the District of Columbia. The Court also concluded that the District Court's opinions issued under the Act are not advisory, because the state seeking to change its voting laws has a concrete controversy with the federal government. The appointment of federal examiners and the expeditious challenge procedure of those whom the examiners list as qualified to vote are also an appropriate response to the problem. Thus, the majority upheld all of the provisions of the Voting Rights Act challenged in that case.

Allen v. State Board of Elections (1969) held that private litigants may invoke the jurisdiction of the district court to assure that their political subdivision complies with the requirement of section 5 of the Act, which provides that no person shall be denied the right to vote for failure to comply with an unapproved new enactment subject to section 5. "Congress intended to reach any state enactment which altered the election law of a covered State in even a minor way."

Georgia v. United States (1973) held that reapportionment plans come within section 5 of the Voting Rights Act. *Beer v. United States* (1976) held that the Voting Rights Act does not permit implementation of a reapportionment plan that "would lead to a retrogression in the position of racial minorities with respect to their effective exercise of the electoral franchise."

During the past several decades the Supreme Court has confronted a wide variety of issues concerning the interpretation and application of the Voting Rights Act, which has been amended during that time. References to many of these Supreme Court cases are contained in the longer versions of this text.

Chapter 16

FREEDOM OF SPEECH

Table of Sections

§ 16.1 Introduction and Chapter Summary

This introductory section summarizes most of the major topics that later sections of this Chapter examine in greater detail.

The Court has used the Fourteenth Amendment to incorporate all of the First Amendment freedoms to be applicable to states and local governments. Thus, the scope of First Amendment freedoms protect individuals from actions by local and state governments, as well as from actions by the federal government.

Government punishment or restriction of expressive activities has been the focus of almost all of the Court's free speech jurisprudence. For that reason, this Chapter focuses on various types of government restraints on expressive activities. In a few instances, the government has attempted to influence expressive activities by granting and denying monetary benefits, which is the focus of a separate section in this Chapter.

The bulk of this Chapter considers how the Court deals with specific types or categories of speech in concrete situations, such as subversive speech; obscene speech; the speech of the broadcast media and of the traditional print media; libelous speech; speech affecting associational rights; speech before hostile audiences; symbolic speech; speech that affects the right to a fair trial; and speech associated with rights of assembly and petition.

These categories are neither exhaustive nor airtight, but they are useful, because the Supreme Court often develops different tests when it evaluates the permissible scope of restrictions on the various categories of speech. This difference in treatment is expected because the relevant interests of one type of speech, e.g., political speech, may vary from those of another, e.g., obscene speech. Moreover, the Court applies the techniques of reviewing alleged restrictions on speech (overbreadth, vagueness, and so on) differently to each category, either consciously or unconsciously.

Content–Based and Viewpoint–Based Laws. In examining government restrictions on expressive activities, an initial question is whether the government regulation is based on the content of the expression or the idea being promoted by an association. The Court often says that content-based restrictions on speech are subject to strict scrutiny, whereas non-content based restrictions are subject to a more lenient form of judicial review. However, that simple distinction between content-based restrictions and content-neutral restrictions on speech is probably too simplistic. We need to subdivide content-based restrictions on speech in order to understand the Court's approach to various types of government restraints on expressive activity.

There are two types of content-based restrictions. First, the government may want to totally ban some type of speech based on its content. Second, the government may wish to impose time, place or manner restrictions on certain types of speech.

A government action that totally bans a certain type of expressive activity due to its content will be subject to strict judicial scrutiny. Strict judicial scrutiny means that the Court will not uphold a true ban on a certain type of expression (based on the language used or the idea conveyed in the expression) unless the government can bear the burden of proving that its action is narrowly tailored to a compelling interest.

The government meets this strict scrutiny test for punishing certain types of categories of speech. The Supreme Court has allowed the punishment of speech based on content if the content is being punished through a clear and narrow regulation that is limited to the proscription of: (1) speech that incites imminent lawless action; (2) speech that triggers an automatic violent response (so-called "fighting words" or the related "hostile audience" problem); (3) "true threats;" (4) obscenity, (which the Court narrowly defines to exclude much material that the popular press often describes as pornography); (5) child pornography (a limited category of speech involving photographs and films of young children); (6) certain types of defamatory speech; and (7) certain types of commercial speech (primarily false or misleading speech connected to the sale of a service or product, or offers to engage in illegal activity).

If the government wants to punish speech based on its content apart from these categories, the government bears a heavy burden of proving that its regulation is one that is narrowly drawn to promote what the Court concludes is a compelling government interest. The government has met this strict scrutiny test (apart from the punishment of speech that fits within one of the previously mentioned categories) only in a few instances, such as where the Court has allowed some limits on campaign financing.

Content-based government restrictions are different than viewpoint-based government restrictions. The fact that the Court has allowed the government to punish certain categories of speech does not mean that the Court will allow the government to punish individuals because they hold points of view that differ from those of the government.

All of the clauses of the First Amendment are tied together by the concept of a freedom of belief. Although the freedom of belief, or freedom of thought, is not explicitly mentioned in the First Amendment, it is the core value of all of the clauses of the First Amendment. In the middle of the last century, Justice Jackson explained that the freedom of belief was inviolate. Today we would say that the government may not punish an individual for holding a viewpoint opposed to any view or theoretical position taken by government officials, The modern Court may leave open a situation where the government could restrict a viewpoint if the government action was truly necessary to promote what the Court calls "a compelling interest." However, the Court has never openly approved a government action punishing an individual merely on the basis that the government's views of a particular issue differed from those of the individual.

Not all content-based punishment involves viewpoint-based punishment. Yet all viewpoint-based punishment involves content-based punishment. For example, a law that bans all obscene movies is content-based, but a law that bans obscene movies that make fun of the President is both content-based and viewpoint-based. Similarly, if an obscenity law banned only movies with graphic sexual scenes that were critical of the government's war activities, the ban would constitute viewpoint discrimination.

Content–Neutral Regulations. The Court often says that the government can place reasonable time, place and manner restrictions on speech without regard to content. For example, the government can place reasonable restrictions on parades—there cannot be two parades on the same street at the same time. But the government cannot ban an anti-war parade because that is a restriction on the content or message of the parade.

Determining if a restriction is content-based is not always obvious. If we were told that an individual was arrested because he was giving a speech criticizing the city mayor, we might first assume that the government had violated the First Amendment. Details regarding that arrest might change our position. Assume that the person making the speech was doing so at 2:00 a.m., while trespassing on someone else's privately-owned parking lot next to a private hospital, and using a bullhorn to amplify his speech. The First Amendment does not prevent the government from controlling speech at that time (2:00 a.m.), place (the private property next to a hospital), or manner (the use of the bullhorn in a way that disturbed the hospital patients).

Time, place, and manner regulations have the incidental effect of limiting the amount of speech in our society. However, some time, place, or manner regulations must exist if we are to have any semblance of order in our society. Because regulations of this type are not designed to suppress any particular message they are not subject to the strictest form of judicial scrutiny. In other words, time, place, and manner regulations do not have to be narrowly tailored to a compelling interest.

While time, place, and manner regulations of speech are not subject to the compelling interest test, the Court will not merely rubber-stamp the validity of any law that the government asserts to be a time, place, or manner regulation. In due process and equal protection cases, when no fundamental right or special classification is involved in a case, the Court upholds a law so long as it is rationally related to any legitimate interest. If the Court were to approve all time, place, or manner regulations under a rationality standard the government might be able to greatly suppress the amount of speech in our society. For that reason, the Court has adopted an intermediate approach (between the mere rationality and compelling interest standards) to time, place, or manner regulations. This approach involves greater scrutiny of the law than would the Court's approach under the mere rationality test, but this approach does not involve the strict judicial scrutiny that is used to examine laws subject to the compelling interest standard.

The intermediate approach (or intermediate judicial scrutiny) that the Court uses in a time, place, or manner case involves a three-part test. To be upheld as a time, place, or manner regulation of speech, the regulation must be narrowly tailored to promote an important or significant government interest that is unrelated to the suppression of expression. This principle, which was first developed in so-called symbolic speech cases, becomes a three-part test when it is used to examine a specific time, place, or manner regulation. To be upheld, a time, place, or manner regulation of speech or other First Amendment activity (such as assembling or gathering to protest) must: (1) be content-neutral; (2) be narrowly tailored to an important or significant government interest; and (3) leave open adequate alternative channels of communication.

The most important part of the time, place, or manner standard is the requirement that the law be content-neutral both as written and applied. A law that is not neutral regarding content cannot be upheld as a time, place, or manner regulation. A law that is not content-neutral will only be valid if it can survive strict judicial scrutiny.

Several related examples demonstrate this point. Let us assume that a city law bans all signs on front lawns of single family homes that are larger than four square feet. Such a law might or might not be a valid time, place, or manner law, depending on whether it is content-neutral, and narrowly tailored to serve an important or significant government interest that left open alternative channels of communication. In other words, because the law is content-neutral it would only have to survive the intermediate form of judicial review. The Court usually states that such a law is upheld if it is narrowly tailored to promote a significant interest unrelated to the suppression of expression.

Now, let us assume that the city law banned all signs on the front lawns of privately owned homes if the sign included material that is "obscene." If the city's law as written and applied only prohibited signs with words or pictures that met the Supreme Court definition of obscenity the law is valid even though it is not content-neutral. The Court has held that "obscenity" is not speech and the state can ban it. This law, by definition, is narrowly tailored to a compelling interest if it punishes only the category of speech that the Supreme Court has determined to be "obscene."

Now, let us turn to a third example, a city law that bans "for sale" signs. The Supreme Court has invalidated a city law that banned all for sale signs on private homes. This law was content-based, not content-neutral, because it banned signs based on the content of the message displayed on the sign. For this content-based law to be valid, the government would have had to establish either that the law fell within the narrow lists of proscribable categories of speech (e.g., it is obscene) or that the law was narrowly tailored to a compelling interest. But when a homeowner truthfully states that her house is for sale, that is not misleading and so is not the type of commercial speech that the government can prohibit. The prohibition of truthful information about houses being sold is not narrowly tailored to promote a compelling government interest.

A law that is content-neutral on its face will be treated as a law that is content-based if the individual whom the government wants to punish can show that the government only enforces the law so as to prohibit one type of content or viewpoint. Consider laws that are enforced in a discriminatory way.

Let us return to our example of a city that bans all signs on private property that are larger than four square feet. Assume that an individual is charged with a violation of the law after he places a sign that exceeds the limit on his property that states: "Vote for

Jane Jones for Mayor." If the individual charged with violation of the law can demonstrate that the police had not enforced the size restriction against persons who put up signs that exceeded four square feet so long as those signs promoted the mayoral candidacy of Sam Smith (the incumbent Mayor), the person charged with the violation of the law will have shown that the law, as applied, is both content-based and viewpoint-based. The Court will invalidate this type of viewpoint discrimination under the strict scrutiny standard. After the defendant showed that the seemingly content-neutral law was being used to punish a particular content or viewpoint, the government could not win unless it demonstrated that the selective use of the law against certain content or certain viewpoints was narrowly tailored to a compelling government interest—and one cannot expect the government to meet that strict test.

If the Court finds that a law is content-neutral, as written and as applied, the Court is likely to uphold the law as a valid time, place, or manner regulation. The basic principle employed by the Court in such cases requires that all such regulations must be narrowly tailored to promote an important or significant interest *unrelated to the suppression of the content of the speech.*

If a law is found to be truly content-neutral, the law is unrelated to the suppression of expression. The Court will still determine whether the content-neutral law is narrowly tailored to promote an important or significant interest. The Court breaks down this part of the time, place, or manner standard into two formal inquiries, though those inquiries seem to be closely linked. First, the Court requires that the content-neutral law be narrowly tailored to promote an important or significant interest. Second, the Court requires that the law be one that leaves open adequate channels for communication.

The Court employs the concept of narrow tailoring into both of the last two branches of the test for the validity of time, place or manner laws. If a content-neutral law does not leave open adequate or ample alternative channels of communication, then the Court will strike the law as not being narrowly tailored to a significant interest. Conversely, if the Court rules that the law is narrowly tailored to promote an important or significant interest, the Court will rule that the law leaves open adequate alternative channels of communication.

When the Court employs the narrow tailoring requirement in time, place, or manner cases, the Court is not requiring the government to use the least restrictive means of advancing the asserted significant or important government interest. Rather, the Court is merely exercising a form of ad-hoc independent judicial review, sometimes termed "intermediate scrutiny," to determine whether the law is a reasonable means of advancing an important societal interest.

The manner in which the Court decides whether the asserted interests of the government constitute important or significant interests is uncertain. The Court has never yet found that any interest asserted by government to justify a time, place, or manner regulation of expressive activity was so insignificant that it did not qualify as an "important" or "significant" interest. However, the Court has invalidated a number of laws on the basis that these laws were not narrowly tailored to the interest that the government asserted.

It may well be that the Court is employing an ad-hoc balancing test in time, place, and manner regulation cases. If the Court engages in ad-hoc balancing, then the Court, in each case, would determine whether the extent to which the time, place, or manner law lessened the amount of expressive activity in society was justified by the degree to which the law promoted a significant societal interest. If the Justices believed that the promotion of societal interests outweigh any incidental burden on speech caused by the content-neutral law, they would find that the time, place, or manner regulation is narrowly tailored to a significant or important government interest and that it leaves open adequate alternative channels of communication. If they believed to the contrary, they would invalidate the law.

The problem with ad hoc judgements, or weighing the interests is that we (and the lower courts) do not know how cases will come out until the Court decides the cases. Granted, the open use of a balancing test for the judicial review of truly content-neutral laws explains easily the results in some cases, because one can always decide that the balance should tilt one way or the other. For example, the interest in the esthetic quality of a city may justify some limited restrictions on handing out leaflets for the size or type of signs on privately owned property. However, those same interests are not sufficient to justify a total prohibition in handing out leaflets within an entire town or the total prohibition of all signs on residential property. When the burden on speech is small, the government interest in the esthetic quality of the city is sufficient to justify the law. But the interest in esthetic quality is not sufficiently important to justify the banning of all leaflets or signs.

Symbolic Speech. Non-verbal activity can be speech. Symbolic speech is simply a phrase used to describe non-verbal activity that is treated as if the activity were speech. If people understand that waving a red flag is a call to action, then waving a red flag is a form of speech. The question is when the state can ban or regulate symbolic speech.

The problem of symbolic speech is intertwined with the problems presented by time, place, or manner regulations of expression. Indeed, the only difference between a symbolic speech case and a time, place, or manner regulation case is the need to determine (in a so-called symbolic speech case) whether non-verbal activity should be treated as if it is speech.

The general rule is that the government may restrict speech if it meets a four-part test: [1] if it is within the constitutional power of the Government; [2] if it furthers an important or substantial governmental interest; [3] if the governmental interest is unrelated to the suppression of free expression; and [4] if the incidental restriction on alleged First Amendment freedoms is no greater than is essential to the furtherance of that interest. The crucial fact, in symbolic speech cases is part 3: *if the governmental interest is unrelated to the suppression of free expression.*

For example, the government can prohibit burning draft cards because its rationale is unrelated to the content of the act. The government will argue that the draft cards are useful as a backup copy of each person's status under the draft laws. That purpose is unrelated to the suppression of free expression. However, if the government banned public draft card burning, or burning a draft card "with contempt," that ban does not fit within the rationale proffered, to have a backup copy of each person's status under the draft laws. The government is seeking to ban a symbolic act because it communicates a particular message, opposition to war.

Assume that Mr. Adam Adams lives in a small town that has recently made it illegal to burn leaves, or any other items, outside of enclosed furnaces. Adams is very upset with the law because he previously had burned his leaves on his driveway every Autumn. Adams, in private, tells his spouse that he is going to burn leaves on the sidewalk "as a means of demonstrating my protest against this unjust limitation of my liberty."

The intention of the actor who engages in the non-verbal conduct cannot in itself determine whether the conduct is the equivalent of speech. In other words, the fact that we know that Adam intended to convey a message by his leaf burning does not, in itself, mean that the judiciary would have to treat his leaf-burning as speech. There is some indication in the cases that, to be considered as speech, non-verbal activity must be of a type that a reasonable onlooker would understand as conveying some type of message. However, in cases involving restrictions on nude dancing, the Court has assumed that nude dancing constitutes some form of expression, even though it is not clear exactly what message one conveys by dancing naked (as opposed to dancing with some minimal clothing).

What is significant is the intention of the government—a law prohibiting only *public* draft card burning would, by its own terms, establish that the government is concerned with the message of the burning, not the need to have every draft-eligible person keep a copy of his draft status. A law prohibiting leaf-burning, even on private property, is a law unrelated to the freedom of expression because its purpose relates to the pollution from the act and not the message conveyed by the speaker when he performs the act.

The Court has described the time, place, or manner principle as involving intermediate judicial scrutiny because, once the Court determines that the non-verbal activity constitutes expression, it will not merely approve the law and the prosecution with the mere rationality standard. So long as the Court finds that the law is not content-based, the law will apply to time, place or manner standard rather than engaging in strict judicial scrutiny. In other words, if a law restricting the symbolic speech is content neutral, the Court will not require the government to demonstrate that the law is narrowly tailored to promote a compelling interest.

The Court has often been able to avoid deciding whether particular non-verbal action involved in a case constitutes speech by looking at the nature of the government regulation involved in the case. Many times the government regulation that is being applied to the non-verbal activity is clearly designed to suppress a certain type of expressive message. In such a situation, the non-verbal activity must be considered to be speech, because the only possible interest in the government regulation would be to suppress content of expression. The cases involving flag burning have been ones in which nonverbal activity are treated as speech, because the law punishes the flag-burner because of his or her motive when burning the flag. The typical statute banning flag-burning makes it a crime to desecrate the flag, such as burning it out of disrespect. The traditionally correct way to handle a flag that has become too worn is to burn the flag in a respectful manner.

The government could not defend the flag desecration laws as being content-neutral. These laws did not ban the destruction of all red, white and blue cloth, and if it did, one wonders what rational justification the government had to create such a law. The law did not ban burning of any cloth item either. Indeed, these laws did not ban all burning of flags; these laws allowed a flag to be burned in a respectful manner as a means of disposing of a used flag. Because laws banning desecration of the flag involve symbolic speech and are content related, the Court invalidated them. The government could not show that such laws were narrowly tailored to a compelling interest. The Court refused to add flag destruction to the limited number of categories of speech, such as obscenity, that the government can prohibit.

In *Virginia v. Black* (2003), a majority of the Justices upheld a Virginia statute that banned burning a cross with the intent to intimidate another person. The statute banning cross burning with intent to intimidate could not be defended as a content-neutral law, because the statute was aimed at banning a certain type of expression: a threat designed to intimidate another person. The cross-burning law had to be treated as a law restricting symbolic speech because the only reason for banning the cross burning was to suppress a true threat. The Court upheld this law, although it was content-related, because a majority of the Justices found that it was narrowly tailored to serve a compelling interest—true threats against specific individuals. This threat or specific intimidation was a form of "fighting words" that presented a danger that can be totally banned without undercutting the basic values of the First Amendment.

The government can impose reasonable regulation of time, place, or manner regulation *without* regard to content regardless of whether the speech is symbolic or verbal speech.

Let us assume that an individual wishes to burn the American flag in protest of an American foreign policy decision. This person burns the flag in the street while proclaiming that she is doing so as a sign that she is no longer proud of being a United States citizen. If she is arrested for desecrating the flag, she could not be punished because flag-burning is constitutionally protected symbolic speech. However, she could be punished under a content-neutral environmental law that banned the burning of any item in the public streets. In other words, an individual has no right to disregard the anti-air pollution ordinance merely because she chooses to burn the flag rather than trees leaves. Because flag burning is speech, the Court would ask whether the environmental regulation was narrowly tailored to promote an important or significant government interest *unrelated to the suppression of expression*. The Court would uphold the environmental regulation, and the conviction for air pollution by the flag burner, if the Court found that: (1) the law as written and applied was truly content-neutral; (2) the law banning the burning of all items in the public streets was narrowly tailored to promote a significant or important interest (in health or environmental matters); and (3) people had ample alternative means to express anti-government viewpoints and messages without having to violate smoke reduction ordinances.

Hybrid Problems Involving Aspects of Content and Non–Content Based Programs. The Court sometimes indicates that all laws regulating speech must be either reasonable time, place, or manner regulations that are content-neutral, or laws that are content-based but are narrowly tailored to promote a compelling government interest. However, at various points in this Chapter, we will see the Court uphold a law that appears to be content-based, but does not totally proscribe a message, or a law deals only with the effects of a certain type of content on a specific environment.

For example, the Court has allowed the prohibition of certain types of speech related to sexual activity broadcast over radio and television channels at times when children might be watching or listening to the broadcast. These cases can best be understood by recognizing that the technical aspects of broadcasting make it difficult, if not impossible, for the government to keep minors from seeing or hearing material that it may declare unfit for minors over the broadcast airwaves. The government interest in protection of children is like an interest in protecting an environment. The unfiltered speech over broadcast airwaves at times when children will be watching and listening has a specific impact on the environment. The government will not be able to totally outlaw such speech, but it will be able to restrict the speech so as to further the societal interest in the protection of children.

The Court has upheld laws that establish separate areas in a city or town for adult entertainment. In these cases, the Court claims that laws creating separate zoning requirements for adult entertainment are content-neutral. But the determination that entertainment is "adult entertainment" means that the government has to look at the content. The concept of content-neutrality in a zoning law that regulates the places for certain types of entertainment based on whether the entertainment involves sexual material is a complete legal fiction. If a movie theater owner in a town with such zoning wishes to know where he can place his theater he will have to first determine the content of the movies he is going to show in order to understand whether he is restricted to those areas zoned for adult entertainment or whether he can build his theater in areas zoned for general business and general entertainment purposes.

In these zoning cases, the Court has emphasized that the adult content of the speech has a different effect on government interests unrelated to the suppression of expression, namely, the property values of parcels of property near the entertainment establishment. Any type of activity will have a secondary economic effect of influencing prices on real estate surrounding the site of the economic activity. Placing an adult theater in a neighborhood demonstrably has a more serious effect on real estate values of nearby residential property than would placing a theater for showing only movies that are fit for children. In these zoning cases, the laws did not completely prohibit the message conveyed in the adult entertainment. Despite the majority's content neutrality language, the Court was upholding a limited form of content regulation.

In a few situations, the Court has allowed the government to restrict speech in a particular environment because the content of the speech has a special effect on that environment, even though the Court has not clearly established any guidelines for deciding when content can be regulated because of its impact on interests unrelated to the suppression of expression. The Court will use some form of judicial review more lenient than strict judicial scrutiny where a government action is content-based, but is designed to deal with the impact of the content on a certain type of environment, and does not involve a true government proscription of some type of speech or message.

For example, the Court has allowed the government to ban demonstrating or speaking near a court house with the intent of interfering with, obstructing, or impeding the administration of justice, even though it has not allowed the government to ban all speech from the sidewalks near the Supreme Court of the United States. Unfortunately, the Supreme Court opinions did not carefully explain the difference between speech near normal courthouses and speech near the United States Supreme Court. The rulings might be tied together by finding that speech advocating that juries or lower courts might change their verdicts to accord with public opinion, whereas messages regarding the public's view of United States Supreme Court rulings are not at all likely to influence the outcome of Supreme Court decisions. In the first case the Court did say, "There can be no question that a State has a legitimate interest in protecting its judicial system from the pressures which picketing near a courthouse might create. Since we are committed to a government of laws and not of men, it is of the utmost importance that the administration of justice be absolutely fair and orderly."

Distinguishing Different Types of Forums (or Fora). When government restricts speech on property that it owns (the streets, public buildings), or in a medium of communication its owns (such as a public school newspaper or a public school campus mail system), the Court will analyze the restrictions on speech in terms of the type of forum that is involved in the problem. Forum analysis applies only to government-owned property or government-owned channels of communication. Forum analysis should not apply to speech on privately owned property or privately owned channels of communication.

The Court has divided all types of government owned property into three types of fora (or forums). Government owned property may be described as a public forum, a limited public forum, or a nonpublic forum.

A public forum is a type of government property that has traditionally been open to public discourse, such as public sidewalks and public parks. When controlling speech in a public forum, the general rule is that the government may impose content-neutral time, place, or manner regulations.

In addition, the government may restrict speech in a public forum if the speech (like other categories of speech) falls into one of the categories of speech that the Court has held that the government may prohibit; or if the government proves that the restriction is necessary to promote a compelling interest.

The phrases "limited public forum," "designated public forum," and "part-time public forum" are really interchangeable. Courts and commentators may use any of these terms to refer to a government-owned channel of communication, or government-owned property, that is not traditionally open to public discourse but a governmental entity has chosen to throw open this channel or property to public discourse for a time. This type of public forum is usually not as difficult to identify as the previous sentence might indicate. A limited public forum is simply a place or channel of communication that the government owns and that (given our history and traditions) you would not expect to be open to public discourse. Nevertheless, the government entity that owns and controls that property has chosen to open it to public speech.

For example, when the classrooms in a government-owned school are not in use for class purposes, the government might keep those classrooms closed and the public would have no right to use those classrooms. However, if the government entity that controls the public school chooses to allow the public to use those classrooms when school is not in session, then the government has turned those classrooms into a limited public forum.

The government cannot close traditional public forums; but the government can simply close a limited public forum so long as it does so in a way that does not discriminate based on content.

The government has no greater power to have content-based regulations of speech in a limited public forum than it does in a public forum. If the government does discriminate on content, it can do so for the same reason it can prohibit any speech based on content, that is, the speech is in a category that the Court has ruled the government may prohibit, such as the speech is obscene, or the regulation is narrowly tailored to promote a compelling government interest.

For example, the government cannot exclude religious groups from using the public school classrooms for after-hours meetings *if* the government has opened these classrooms to general public discourse. If the government opens up the public school classroom for use by the registered student groups after school hours (e.g., the chess club), then it cannot ban the speech of a registered student religious group because that would be based on the content of the speech (religious oriented speech).

The last type of government owned property or government owned channel of communication is a non-public forum. A non-public forum is government property, or a government-owned channel of communication that has not traditionally been open to public discourse and that the government has chosen not to throw open to public discourse. Examples of a nonpublic forum would include a public school classroom when class is in session or a courtroom.

There are three ways that the government may control speech in a nonpublic forum, two of which mirror the government's powers over a public forum. First, as with a public forum or limited public forum, the government may employ content-neutral time, place, or manner regulations. Second, as with the public forum and limited public forum, the government may prohibit speech that falls within a proscribed category of speech, or that is subject to a regulation that is narrowly tailored to a compelling interest.

Third, the government may regulate speech in a non-public forum if the regulation is: (a) reasonable (in light of the uses and purpose of the non-public forum); and (b) viewpoint-neutral (in the sense of not being a regulation designed to punish or suppress a viewpoint with which the government disagrees). It is common for courts and commentators to simply say that the government may control speech in a nonpublic forum with a regulation that is reasonable and viewpoint-neutral. That statement is correct, although one should remember that the government's power to enact reasonable, viewpoint-neutral regulations of expressive activity in a non-public forum is in addition to the powers the government would have over speech in a public forum or a limited public forum.

The government is not allowed to engage in viewpoint punishment in a nonpublic forum (or anywhere else). For example, the government could choose to close all public school classrooms when classes are not in session. When a class is in session, it can limit the speech in ways that are content-based but not viewpoint-based; for example, the government can reserve the American history classroom for the teaching of American history when the American history class is in session (the content is American history, not mathematics). But the government cannot engage in viewpoint-based discrimination (the government cannot prohibit the teacher or students from saying something critical of government policy).

Or, let us assume that a public school teacher dismisses two students from mathematics class because they were talking about baseball during class. This restriction of speech is content-based because it separates baseball speech from mathematics speech. Although the government cannot ban speech about baseball from the public streets, it can ban it from the mathematics classroom because of its impact on the teaching environment. But the government could not engage in viewpoint-based punishment: if the two students were having their baseball discussion because one of them was a Chicago Cubs fan, and one was a St. Louis Cardinals fan, the public school teacher and school would be violating the First Amendment if they chose only to punish one student (the student whose team the school favored).

"Facial" and "as Applied" First Amendment Challenges.

In several topic areas, you will see cases in which Justices struggle over the question of whether they should invalidate a law "on its face" or merely leave the law subject to "as applied" challenges. If the Court invalidates a law "on its face," it will totally invalidate a law. When a defendant challenges a law on its face the defendant is, in effect, saying: "The law I have been charged with is totally invalid, so that it cannot be used to punish anyone, under any circumstances. You should rule that I cannot be punished because the statute is totally invalid, even though my words might have been punished consistently with the First Amendment, if the State had a better drafted statute."

When the Court determines whether a law is invalid on its face, it looks at not only the statutory language but also the way the courts and enforcement authorities have interpreted the language. The Court will strike a law on its face if it is vague (a concept that may meld due process and First Amendment concerns) or substantially overbroad (because the law punishes speech that cannot be punished consistently with the First Amendment, even though the law make criminal some speech that could be punished consistently with the First Amendment).

If a law is not invalid on its face, the litigant can still argue that it invalid as applied in a specific case. In an "as applied" challenge to a law, a defendant charged with violating the law is, in effect, saying "Even if the law is constitutional on its face, I cannot be convicted under this law for what I did."

Let us assume that the Illinois has a law that states: "Dirty movies are illegal; Any theater owner who shows a dirty movie to the public will be subject to a $1,000 fine and 3 months in jail." The state convicts a theater owner for showing a movie with explicit nudity in it, even though he presented evidence that the movie was critically acclaimed and even won the Academy Award. The state supreme court affirmed the conviction and the U.S. Supreme has accepted certiorari.

At the trial and appellate levels, the movie theater owner would challenge the law both on its face and as applied. If the Illinois Supreme Court had not clarified the law to explain that "dirty movies" meant "obscene movies" as the United States Supreme Court has defined the term, the law will be invalid on its face, as either vague (because the law did not give clear notice to persons regarding what types of movies are illegal) or overbroad (because it punished sexually related movies that are not "obscene"), or both.

If the law is invalid on its face, the state cannot use it to convict anyone for showing a movie, even if the movie is really "obscene." However if the state court had interpreted the "dirty movies" to mean precisely what the U.S. Supreme Court means by "obscene," then the law is not invalid on its face. As construed by the state court, the law would not be vague or overbroad because the law would be clear (when understood in light of the state court cases) and narrowly tailored to punish only material that was truly obscene under Supreme Court rulings (because of the state court interpretations of the statute).

Even if the law is constitutional on its face, the theater owner would still have an "as applied" challenge, arguing that the movie displayed in his theater won an Academy Award for Best Picture of the Year and cannot be so lacking in value as to come within the Supreme Court's definition of "obscenity." The Illinois Dirty Movies Law would be valid on its face, but invalid insofar in so far as it was applied to the movie that won the Academy Award, a movie that clearly, when taken as a whole, had serious artistic value.

A Final Word Regarding Prior Restraints. Government will encounter special problems if it seeks to use a "prior restraint" which is a formal government mechanism to prevent speech from being distributed, published, spoken, or otherwise put into the marketplace of ideas and given to persons other than the speaker.

A large penalty for speech that is deemed illegal may deter people from speaking, but subsequent punishment for speech is different from a prior restraint that prevents the speech from ever being uttered. Let us suppose that a state imposes a fifty-year sentence on any movie theater owner who shows an obscene movie. The possibility of being subject to a half-century of incarceration will deter movie theater owners from showing any movies other than those that they are sure are not obscene under the terms of Supreme Court rulings. That law, nevertheless, would not be a prior restraint in legal terminology.

A prior restraint would occur if the law prohibited the theater from showing the movie until it was first approved by a government administrative panel. A court injunction prohibiting someone from showing the movie is another form of prior restraint.

Prior restraints, more than subsequent punishment, effectively prevent ideas from being sent to the public. Further discussion of prior restraint will appear at various points in this Chapter.

§ 16.2 The Overbreadth Doctrine

Two closely related doctrines particularly important in dealing with free speech issues are the prohibitions against overbreadth and vagueness. Because of the importance of the free speech guarantee, even when the state does have the power to regulate an area, it must exercise that power very carefully, so as not, in accomplishing a permissible end, unduly infringe on a protected freedom. This section considers the overbreadth doctrine, and then turns to the vagueness doctrine.

An overbroad statute—a statute that is written too broadly, or more broadly than necessary—is one that is designed to burden or punish activities that are not constitutionally protected, but its flaw is that, as drafted, it also punishes activities protected by the First Amendment. In the case of a statute that is overbroad on its face, a carefully drawn statute could have reached the conduct. Nevertheless the Court will invalidate the statute if the Court rules that it is "substantially overbroad."

Overbreadth and Standing Compared. When the Court examines a claim that a statute should be invalidated as being an unconstitutionally overbroad regulation of speech, it is easy to confuse standing and First Amendment issues.

Justices who argue against use of the overbreadth doctrine to strike a statute on its face have often asserted that the individuals before the Court lacked standing to raise the rights of hypothetical persons to whom the statute could not be applied without violating the First Amendment. Nevertheless, it is easy to become confused if one thinks of an overbreadth problem as a form of standing or as a justiciability issue.

Rather, one should recognize that when the Court is asked to strike a law on its face as being overbroad, the individual is asserting that no one—including persons whose speech is unprotected by the First Amendment—can be subjected to punishment under a statute so sweeping that it could include both protected and unprotected speech within its scope. If the Court believes that the statute is so sweeping that it would deter persons from engaging in protected speech, or that the statute may be used on an arbitrary basis against unpopular viewpoints, the Court will strike the law as overbroad. If the Court believes that there is little chance that the statute will deter constitutionally protected speech, or will be used in a selective manner to punish unpopular speech, it will uphold the law and allow it to be applied on a case-by-case basis.

§ 16.3   The Void–for–Vagueness Doctrine

Closely related to the overbreadth doctrine is the void for vagueness doctrine. The problem of vagueness in statutes regulating speech activities is based on the same rationale as the overbreadth doctrine and the Supreme Court often speaks of them together.

Vagueness and Criminal Laws Generally. The void for vagueness doctrine applies to all criminal laws, not merely those that regulate speech or other fundamental constitutional rights. All such laws must provide fair notice to persons before making their activity criminal and also to restrict the authority of police officers to arrest persons for a violation of the law.

Vagueness and the First Amendment. When a law criminalizes conduct that relates to speech, to the normal concerns of every criminal law, we have to add the value of free speech.

Several rationales justify special judicial strictness to insure that laws that regulate speech, a fundamental constitutional right, are not vague. First, the requirement that a law place persons on notice as to precisely what activity is made criminal is particularly important when the activity relates to a speech. To the extent that the law is vague, it might have an *in terrorem* effect and deter persons from engaging in protected activities. An unclear law, a law that does not draw bright lines, might regulate (or appear to regulate) more than is necessary, and thus deter or chill persons from engaging in protected speech.

In contrast, an unclear law relating to merely economic matters, such as an unclear negligence law, would chill activity that does not have special First Amendment significance. The lessened risk to the constitutional values makes more palatable the wait until such time as the statute is clarified by the appropriate courts. Indeed, the vagueness, in the non-speech area, may be both necessary and advantageous. For example, if a law that forbids reckless driving causes people to be more cautious than absolutely necessary while driving, that is a good thing, not a bad thing. We are not concerned that the law will "chill" people's ability to drive as recklessly as possible without crossing the line from legal to illegal.

Another rationale for the void for vagueness doctrine is to require that there be clear guidelines to govern law enforcement. Without these guidelines, law enforcement officers have too much discretion to enforce the statute on a selective basis. This discretion is most dangerous when the law regulates a fundamental right, such as speech, so that the officers might be subjecting persons to arrest and prosecution because they disagree with the message that the person wishes to convey, or for some other constitutionally suspect reason.

§ 16.4 Government Prescribed Speech, Government Subsidies for Speech, Unconstitutional Conditions, and Equal Protection Analysis

Almost all First Amendment cases that have reached the United States Supreme Court involve governmental attempts to regulate speech. In this section we discuss the more rare situation, where a government enters the First Amendment marketplace to advance messages favorable to the government.

Government Speech and Propaganda. The most direct way for government to enter the political marketplace is to have government officials or agencies issue messages or reports designed to convince the public to support governmental positions on domestic or foreign policy. To date the Supreme Court has not restricted government speech, unless the governmental action violates the Establishment Clause.

However, if the government were to use subsidies to private speakers in order to suppress some anti-government messages, the governmental attempt to foreclose opposing views may be seen as a violation of the First Amendment.

Federal Communications Commission v. League of Women Voters (1984) invalidated a section of the Public Broadcasting Act that prohibited any noncommercial educational broadcasting station receiving a grant from the Corporation for Public Broadcasting from engaging in editorializing or the endorsement of candidates. The four dissenting Justices believed that the prohibition on editorializing protected the public from having stations writing editorials favorable to the government so as to increase their prospects for receipt of public funding. The majority believed that the ban was not narrowly tailored to providing a balanced presentation of issues to the public, but only suppressed the role of such stations in bringing matters of public concern to the attention of the public. All nine Justices, however, recognized that the government was not free to subsidize speech that favored governmental policy on publicly owned stations while refusing to fund speech adverse to governmental interests.

Government Required Speech. The government may not enter the political marketplace by forcing private persons to subscribe to or advance messages favorable to the government. Such activity is inconsistent with the fundamental freedom of belief that lies at the core of all First Amendment guarantees. The government should not be able to force a person who objects to a position to endorse that position absent the most unusual and compelling circumstances, none of which have appeared in the cases to date.

For example, in *West Virginia State Board of Education v. Barnette* (1943) the Court prohibited states from requiring children to pledge allegiance to the country at the start of the school day. The children who objected to taking the oath were members of a religious sect that objected to such practices, but the majority opinion by Justice Jackson was careful not to limit the decision by basing it on the religion clauses of the First Amendment alone. All students have a First Amendment right to refuse to pledge allegiance to the country or its symbols because of the freedom of thought and belief that is central to all First Amendment freedoms.

Similarly, *Wooley v. Maynard* (1977) prohibited a state from punishing a person for making illegible a portion of his automobile license plate that the state required him to put on his car. This portion made illegible was the state motto "Live Free or Die." A Jehovah's Witness objected to carrying this message based on his religious belief. However, the Court based its decision on the free speech clause, not the free exercise clause. *Wooley* held that no private person could be required to broadcast governmental symbols or to endorse governmental positions absent the most compelling circumstances. A person will not have the right to deface the numbers on his license plate that identify his vehicle, or the right to mutilate American currency that has the motto, "In God We Trust." *Wooley* recognized that some government regulations are necessary to advance societal interests that have nothing to do with censorship or propaganda, such as the identification of vehicles in traffic accidents and the need for a uniform monetary system.

Compelled Subsidization of Advertising Generic Goods. *Glickman v. Wileman Brothers & Elliott, Inc.* (1997) upheld a federal statutory scheme that required certain farm producers to pay for advertising promoting generic goods. The Secretary of Agriculture, pursuant to statute, issued various orders that imposed assessments to cover the cost of generic advertising of California nectarines, plums, and peaches. Growers, handlers, and processors of California tree fruits challenged the validity of these orders, claiming that their forced subsidization of such generic advertising violated their rights of free speech.

The Court (5 to 4) rejected these challenges, noting that these marketing orders are a form of economic regulation that has displaced competition in certain markets. The marketing orders must be approved by affected producers who market at least two-thirds of the volume of the commodity. Among the collective activities that Congress authorized is any form of marketing promotion including paid advertising. This advertising serves the producers' and handlers' common interest in selling particular products. Various regulations seek to minimize the risk that the generic advertising might adversely affect the interests of any individual producer.

Glickman acknowledged that there is a free speech right not to be compelled to contribute to an organization whose expressive activities conflict with one's freedom of belief. For example, in *Abood v. Detroit Board of Education* (1977) the Court ruled that the state can compel union members to pay dues to support activities related to collective bargaining, because those costs are germane to an otherwise lawful regulatory program, but the state cannot compel union members to make contributions for political purposes unrelated to collective bargaining.

The Court limited *Glickman*, in *United States v. United Foods, Inc* (2001). The Mushroom Promotion, Research, and Consumer Information Act, required fresh mushroom handlers to pay assessments that were used primarily to fund generic advertisements promoting mushroom sales. United Foods claimed that its branded mushrooms are better, and argued that the First Amendment prohibited this assessment.

In *United Foods*, unlike *Glickman*, almost all of the funds collected under the mandatory mushroom assessments had but one purpose: generic advertising. "Beyond the collection and disbursement of advertising funds, there are no marketing orders that regulate how mushrooms may be produced and sold, no exemption from the antitrust laws, and nothing preventing individual producers from making their own marketing decisions." The expression that the statute requires United Foods to support is not germane to a purpose related to an association independent from the speech itself. Hence, it is unconstitutional.

The Supreme Court has not placed any constitutional restrictions on the government's speech, apart from limitations that arise from the establishment clause. Government speech, like all the activities of government entities, is funded through taxes (sometimes called fees or assessments) on individuals and economic entities such as corporations. The fact that a taxpayer disagrees with a government speech that, at least in part, is funded by the taxpayer's money does not violate the First Amendment.

If the government requires an individual to fund the speech of other *private* persons, there is a significant question regarding whether the government violated the First Amendment by making the individual subsidize a message with which she does not agree. *United Foods* assumed that the money collected from the growers was used to fund private speech, rather than government speech.

On that basis the Court found that a mandatory collection of assessments from growers who did not agree with the advertisements violated the First Amendment.

In contrast with *United Foods*, the Court in *Johanns v. Livestock Marketing Association* (2005) upheld a federal statute that imposed an assessment on the sale of all domestically grown or imported cattle and used the proceeds to fund generic advertising promoting the purchase of beef products. The majority opinion in *Johanns* found that the Court in *United Foods* had not addressed the question of whether the generic advertising should be considered government speech.

The *Johanns* Court saw the beef marketing advertisements as being true government speech. Although private persons designed the beef advertising campaign, the Secretary of Agriculture appointed those persons to a board; the Secretary maintained control over which messages would be funded with the proceeds from the assessment. Hence the majority found that the advertisements constituted true government speech, and were not subject to First Amendment scrutiny. The fact that the government funded this government speech through a targeted assessment on a certain group of taxpayers was irrelevant for First Amendment analysis.

In considering the impact of the *Johanns* decision, one must not forget the Court's ruling in *Wooley*, discussed previously in this section. If the government says "buy more beef," the government has not violated the First Amendment. However, if the government says "Professors Nowak and Rotunda want you to eat more beef," those professors would have a First Amendment claim that the government was, in effect, forcing them to speak (if the professors did not want to be associated with the pro-beef message). In the *Johanns* case, the majority opinion noted that there was no significant evidence that persons who viewed any of the ads for beef would associate that message with particular beef producers.

Subsidization and Unconstitutional Conditions. Another way that the government participates in political expression is to subsidize persons on the condition that they engage in, or refrain from engaging in, a certain type of speech or association. This type of governmental activity is often said to be subject to the principle of no "unconstitutional conditions." Some discussions make it appear that any conditions on the granting of government benefits are invalid but that is not the case. In each instance, courts must examine the substance of the condition to determine whether it violates constitutional principles.

For example, it would be permissible for the federal government to condition a grant to a farmer on a requirement that the farmer not plant more than a specific acreage of a commodity because, under its commerce power, Congress could directly limit agricultural production. On the other hand, an agricultural grant conditioned on a farmer's promise not to criticize government farm policy would be an invalid penalty on speech protected by the First Amendment.

Similarly, the government cannot grant money to a research scientist on the condition that the scientist refrain from criticizing the government. But the government should be able to fund advocacy research. For example, it could grant money to the scientist to investigate only the harmful (or only the beneficial) effects of marijuana. If the scientist took the grant on the condition that he investigate the benefits of marijuana, the government should be able to discipline the grantee if he used the money to explore the harmful effects of marijuana, just as it ought to be able to discipline the grantee if he took the money and used it to investigate wine.

The difficulty in assessing the constitutionality of a condition to receiving a government grant that is related to speech may be seen by contrasting several cases.

Regan v. Taxation with Representation of Washington (1983) unanimously upheld a portion of the Internal Revenue Code that granted a special tax exempt status to organizations that did not use tax deductible contributions for lobbying activity. A pivotal factor in this decision was that a companion section of the Internal Revenue Code granted a slightly different type of tax exempt status to organizations that did use nondeductible contributions for lobbying activities. The law did not penalize persons for engaging in speech, the lobbying of governmental organization. Rather, Congress only refused to subsidize lobbying activities. There is no unconstitutional condition when Congress refuses to subsidize certain political activities.

Rust v. Sullivan (1991) upheld federal regulations that prohibited recipients of Title X grants from engaging in abortion related activities where abortion is a method of family planning. Nothing in the Title X program provided for post-conception care, including abortion (which obviously occurs after conception). Title X required that its funds could only be used to support pre-conception family planning, population research, infertility services, and related services. The regulations expressly prohibited a Title X project from referring a pregnant woman to an abortion provider as a method of family planning. Federal funds could not be used to "promote or advocate" abortion as a "method of family planning."

Rust emphasized that the government was simply refusing to fund activities (including speech that promoted those activities) when the scope of the project excluded such activities. Petitioners argued that the regulations prohibited a Title X project from referring a woman to an abortion service even if her pregnancy placed her life in imminent danger, but the Court specifically rejected that interpretation of the regulations. The regulations only prohibit abortion as a "method of family planning." Referring a woman who needs an abortion for medical reasons is not equivalent to referral for purposes of family planning.

In *Legal Services Corporation v. Velazquez* (2001), clients and others challenged the constitutionality of federal funding restrictions on the Legal Services Corporation (LSC). The Supreme Court invalidated the federal restriction, which prohibited local recipients of LSC funds from engaging in representation involving efforts to amend or otherwise challenge validity of existing welfare laws.

The situation in *Velazquez* was different than the facts of *Rust* because the Government in *Velazquez* was hiring people, such as lawyers, to represent other people's interests, not its interests. When the Government spends money to facilitate private speech it does not have the same latitude to engage in viewpoint discrimination because it is not promoting the *Government's* speech. For example, even though the Government pays the salaries of public defenders, they represent their clients, not the Government, which is represented by its own prosecutors. The purpose of the public defender program is not to transmit information about Government programs. The public defender does not speak on behalf of the Government. Where private speech is involved, even Congress' antecedent funding decision cannot be aimed at the suppression of ideas thought inimical to the Government's own interest.

Government Subsidization of the Arts. *National Endowment for the Arts v. Finley* (1998) upheld as facially constitutional the "decency and respect" standard that Congress imposed for NEA grants. In this case various artists' organizations and performance artists sued the NEA claiming that the denials of their applications for NEA grants violated their First Amendment rights. The statute in question required the NEA, in distributing grants, to take into consideration general standards of "decency and respect" for diverse beliefs and values. The language is "advisory" and it "admonishes the NEA merely to take 'decency and respect' into consideration...." Justice O'Connor, for the Court, avoided deciding the case on broad grounds and only held this statute did not so inherently interfere with First Amendment so as to be facially invalid. The government does not discriminate on the basis of viewpoint if it merely chooses to fund one activity instead of another.

In addition, the statute was not constitutionally vague. The statute merely added some imprecise considerations to an already subjective selection process. When the Government is acting as a patron of the arts rather than acting as a sovereign, the consequences of statutory impression are not constitutionally severe.

Equal Protection. Whenever a statute allows some persons to speak or assemble, but not others, or grants a subsidy for some types of speech activities to a limited group of persons or entities, the statute at issue can be analyzed under equal protection as well as First Amendment principles. Generally, the government may classify persons for the receipt of benefits or burdens so long as there is a rational relationship between the classification and a legitimate end of government. However, if the law employs suspect criteria, such as race, to establish the classification, or if the law creates a classification that allocates the ability to exercise a fundamental constitutional right, then the Court will strictly scrutinize the basis for that classification.

It is difficult to describe the exact standard of review in these cases, but it is often said that when a law regulates the ability to engage in a fundamental constitutional right, the courts must determine whether the classification is narrowly tailored to promote a compelling or overriding governmental interest. All First Amendment rights are fundamental rights and, therefore, classifications relating to them are subjected to this compelling interest standard.

Whenever the Court finds that a classification violates the First Amendment, it alternatively could rule that the classification violated equal protection. For example, if a city ordinance allowed distribution of leaflets by persons who favor the policies of the mayor, but prohibited distribution of leaflets on public streets by persons who opposed the mayor, the law could be stricken under First Amendment principles as the suppression of content that did not create an imminent danger of inciting lawless action. Alternatively, the statute could be held invalid under equal protection because the classification regarding who could use the sidewalks to engage in a fundamental constitutional right was not narrowly tailored to promote a compelling governmental interest. The equal protection argument does not make the analysis any easier, because the Court is really applying First Amendment principles, dressed up in equal protection garb.

§ 16.5 The Advocacy of Violence or Other Illegal Conduct

From the time the First Amendment was ratified until just prior to World War I the Supreme Court had little exposure to freedom of expression issues. The United States involvement in World War I met with vocal resistance. During this period there was the "Red Scare," a general concern about Socialists, Bolshevists, anarchists, and revolutionaries.

Congress, in response to domestic political unrest, passed the Espionage Act of 1917 and the Sedition Act of 1918.

The *Schenck* Case. In *Schenck v. United States* (1919), the Court affirmed appellants' conviction for conspiracy to violate the Espionage Act of 1917. Appellants had mailed leaflets to men eligible for military service asserting that the draft violated the Thirteenth Amendment. These leaflets, the government argued, were prohibited by provisions in the Espionage Act forbidding obstruction of military recruiting.

Justice Holmes, writing for the Court, upheld the convictions and the restraint on freedom of expression as necessary to prevent grave and immediate threats to national security. Ordinarily, Holmes, believed, the leaflets would have been constitutionally protected but:

> The most stringent protection of free speech would not protect a man in falsely shouting fire in a theater and causing a panic. It does not even protect a man from an injunction against uttering words that may have all the effect of force.... The question in every case is whether the words used are used in such circumstances and are of such a nature as to create a clear and present danger that they will bring about the substantive evils that Congress has a right to prevent. It is a question of proximity and degree.

Holmes concluded that First Amendment protection should not be extended during wartime to protect speech hindering the war effort.

The *Abrams* Cases. Holmes, dissenting in *Abrams v. United States* (1919), further explained his "clear and present danger" test. The Government had convicted the appellants of conspiracy to violate the Espionage Acts amendments, which prohibited speech encouraging resistance to the war effort and curtailment of production "with intent to cripple or hinder the United States in the prosecution of the war." They had distributed pamphlets criticizing the United States' involvement in the effort to crush Russia's new Communist Government.

The majority in *Abrams* was unimpressed with Holmes' clear and present danger test as outlined in *Schenck*. Because of the "bad tendency" of the defendants' speech, the majority affirmed, even though the defendants' sentences were twenty years. Under the bad tendency test, speech could be prohibited if it was of a type that would tend to bring about harmful results.

Holmes criticized the Court's decision to uphold the conviction, arguing that it was ridiculous to assume these pamphlets would actually hinder the government's war efforts in Germany. He contended that the government could only restrict freedom of expression when there was "present danger of immediate evil or an intent to bring it about.... Congress certainly cannot forbid all effort to change the mind of the country."

The *Gitlow* Case. The Court continued to use the bad tendency test and remained reluctant to apply the clear and present danger test to protect defendants. The defendants in *Gitlow v. New York* (1925) were convicted of violating New York's "criminal anarchy statute," which prohibited advocating violent overthrow of the government. They had printed and circulated a radical manifesto encouraging political strikes. There was no evidence that the manifesto had any effect on the individuals who received copies.

Gitlow upheld the conviction under the statute. In *Gitlow*, the Court noted, the legislature had already determined what utterances would violate the statute. The government's decision that certain words are likely to cause the substantive evil "is not open for consideration." The government must then show only that there is a reasonable basis for the statute. It is irrelevant that the particular words do or do not create a "clear and present danger."

Holmes and Brandeis dissented. Holmes wrote that if the "clear and present danger" test was properly applied it would be obvious there was no real danger that the appellants' boring pamphlets would instigate political revolution. If the manifesto presented an immediate threat to the stability of the government then, Holmes admitted, there would be a need for suppression. But in the absence of immediate danger, Holmes concluded, the appellants were entitled to exercise their First Amendment rights.

The *Whitney* Case. *Whitney v. California* (1927) affirmed the conviction of Mrs. Whitney for violating the California Criminal Syndicalism Act by assisting in the organization of the Communist Labor Party of California. The statute defined criminal syndicalism as any doctrine "advocating teaching or aiding and abetting ... crime, sabotage ... or unlawful acts of force and violence" to effect political or economic change.

Whitney maintained that, at the organizing convention, she only advocated political reform through the democratic process. The majority of the convention, however, supported change through violence and terrorism. She said that she had not assisted the Communist Party with knowledge of its illegal purpose. The state convicted her because of her mere presence at the convention and, consequently, she alleged deprivation of liberty without due process. But the Court affirmed the conviction, holding that the jury had resolved the question of facts regarding her participation at the convention, that the united action of the Communist Party threatened the welfare of the state, and that Mrs. Whitney was a part of that organization.

Justice Brandeis wrote a concurring opinion (which Holmes joined). While the opinion was labeled a "concurrence" it read like a dissent. Brandeis specifically objected to any notion, first presented in *Gitlow*, that the enactment of a statute foreclosed the application of the clear and present danger test by the Court. "[T]he enactment of the statute cannot alone establish the facts which are essential to its validity."

Brandeis explained that the framers "valued liberty both as an end and as a means. They believed liberty to be the secret of happiness and courage to be the secret of liberty." Free speech is not merely useful. More than the metaphor of a market place supports it. Free speech is a good in and of itself.

Brandeis placed strong emphasis on the state's need to show *incitement*. Only when speech causes unthinking, immediate reaction is the protection of the First Amendment withdrawn.

Brandeis then said that Mrs. Whitney should have argued her conviction was void because no "clear and present danger" of a serious evil resulted from the convention activities. However, she had not challenged her conviction on that basis, so Brandeis said that he was unable to pass on the "clear and present danger" issue. Because of this procedural technicality, Brandeis concurred. His concurrence was a dissent in all but name, upholding the conviction only on this narrow procedural ground.

The 1950s & 1960s Decision. In the early 1950's the Supreme Court decided to reexamine the Holmes–Brandeis "clear and present danger" doctrine.

The federal government convicted the defendants in *Dennis v. United States* (1951) of violating the Smith Act by conspiring to organize the Communist Party of the United States. The party's goal allegedly was to overthrow the existing government by force and violence.

The Court affirmed, but with no majority opinion. Chief Justice Vinson, writing for himself and three other Justices, indicated Congress possessed the power to promulgate laws restricting speech. The Vinson reformulation of the clear and present danger test contained two steps. First, the Government had to show a substantial interest in limiting the speech. Congress, the Court held, did have a substantial interest in preventing violent overthrow of the government. Second, the words or actions restricted in the legislation must be shown to constitute a "clear and present danger."

The Vinson plurality opinion relied on the lower court's interpretation of the rule, quoting Chief Judge Learned Hand:

In each case [courts] must ask whether the gravity of the "evil," discounted by its improbability, justifies such invasion of free speech as is necessary to avoid danger.

In other words, the greater the gravity of the act advocated, the less clear and present danger is needed to justify governmental intrusion. Advocacy of revolution is fairly grave, so the danger need not be that clear or that present. So rephrased, the clear and present danger test became a disguised balancing test that weighed the seriousness of the danger against competing interest in free speech.

Justice Frankfurter concurred in the affirmance but he also criticized the clear and present danger test as too inflexible.

Yates v. United States (1957) retreated from the broad doctrine of the *Dennis*. Yates and other Communist party officials were convicted for conspiring to "advocate and teach the necessity of overthrowing the federal government by violence" and organizing the Communist party to carry out this revolution in violation of the Smith Act. The Supreme Court held that the trial court had incorrectly interpreted the *Dennis* precedent.

Justice Harlan, in the majority opinion in *Yates*, observed that the District Court had "apparently thought that *Dennis* obliterated the traditional dividing line between advocacy of abstract doctrine and advocacy of action." The essence of the *Dennis* holding, Harlan stated, was that teaching and preparing a group for immediate or future violent action are not constitutionally protected, if it is reasonable to believe based on the circumstances, size, and commitment of the group that the action or revolution will occur. Harlan concluded that the petitioners' statements advocated a philosophy and did not incite action. Without evidence of any actual action or possibility of action, the Court would not affirm the convictions.

Yates did not spell the end to Communist membership prosecutions. In *Scales v. United States* (1961) the Court affirmed the petitioners' conviction for violating the membership clause of the Smith Act. The trial court found the petitioners were active members of the Communist Party who were aware of the illegality of their teachings and advocated violent revolution and overthrow of the government "as speedily as circumstances would permit."

Justice Harlan, again writing the Court's opinion, upheld the lower court's findings, indicating that its interpretation of the membership clause did not impute "guilt to an individual merely on the basis of his associations and sympathies."

After *Dennis* and *Yates*, an individual cannot be punished for membership in an association unless the government proves: the association had an illegal end; and that the individual knowingly participated in the association with the intent to promote its illegal end.

The Holmes and Brandeis "clear and present danger" theory evolved during the late 1960's, as the Court focused on protecting the advocacy of unpopular ideas. Traces of a modified "clear and present danger" analysis are evident in *Watts v. United States* (1969). In a per curiam opinion the Supreme Court reversed the appellant's conviction for violating a statute prohibiting persons from "knowingly and willfully ... threat[ening] to take the life of or to inflict bodily harm upon the President." Watts, during a public rally in Washington, D.C., stated he would not report for his scheduled draft physical, continuing:

If they ever make me carry a rifle the first man I want to get in my sights is L.B.J. They are not going to make me kill my black brothers.

On its face the statute was held constitutional. The nation certainly has a valid interest in protecting the President, but a statute criminalizing certain forms of pure speech must be interpreted with the First Amendment in mind. "What is a threat must be distinguished from what is ... protected speech."

The Court held that Watts' statement was "political hyperbole" and not a true threat. In context, the conditional nature of the remarks and the fact the listeners had laughed at the statement indicated to the Court that the words could only be interpreted as an expression of political belief. Had the circumstances of the speech amounted to a literal *incitement* of violence, the Court's decision would have been different. In context, there was no danger of incitement.

The *Brandenburg* Test. *Brandenburg v. Ohio* (1969) may have been influenced by the reasoning of "clear and present danger," but *Brandenburg* has crucial differences in phrasing and emphasis to assure that its free speech protections remain undiluted.

Brandenburg overruled *Whitney* and, significantly, it never explicitly referred to the "clear and present danger" standard. However it rejected the deference to the government that had prevailed in the "bad tendency" and "balancing" years.

Brandenburg reversed the conviction of a Ku Klux Klan leader for violating Ohio's Criminal Syndicalism statute. The appellant had been charged with advocating political reform through violence and for assembling with a group formed to teach criminal syndicalism. A man identified as the appellant arranged for a television news crew to attend a Klan rally. During the news film made at the rally, Klan members, allegedly including Brandenburg, discussed the group's plan to march on Congress.

Brandenburg adopted a new test to judge laws that restrict speech that advocates unlawful conduct: "[The state may not] forbid or proscribe advocacy of the use of force or of law violation except where such advocacy is directed to inciting or producing imminent lawless action and is likely to incite or produce such action." The *Branderburg* test, though less than clear, has been the standard for reviewing punishment of advocacy of illegal conduct since 1969.

Criminal syndicalism, as defined in the Ohio statute, could not meet the *Brandenburg* test. The statute forbade teaching of violent political revolution with the intent of spreading such doctrine or assembling with a group advocating this doctrine. At the appellant's trial no attempt was made to distinguish between incitement and advocacy. Therefore, the statute violated the First and Fourteenth Amendments. Any law punishing mere advocacy of Ku Klux Klan doctrine and assembly of Klan members to advocate their beliefs was unconstitutional.

Brandenburg's new formulation offers broad new protection for strong advocacy. A post-Warren Court decision, *Hess v. Indiana* (1973) indicates that the Court is serious and literal in its application of the test proposed in *Brandenburg*. Hess had been arrested and convicted for disorderly conduct when he shouted "we'll take the fucking street later (or again)" during an antiwar demonstration. Two witnesses testified that Hess did not appear to exhort demonstrators to go into the street just cleared by the police, that he was facing the crowd, and that his tone of voice was not louder than any of the other demonstrators, although it was loud. The Indiana Supreme Court upheld the trial court's finding that the remarks were in fact intended to incite further riotous behavior and were likely to produce such a result.

The United States Supreme Court reversed, and in a per curiam opinion stated:

> At best ... the statement could be as counsel for present moderation; at worst it amounted to nothing more than advocacy of illegal action at some indefinite future time. This is not sufficient to permit the state to punish Hess' speech. Under our decisions, "the Constitutional guarantees of free speech and free press do not permit a state to forbid or proscribe advocacy of the use of force or of law violation except where such advocacy is directed to inciting or producing *imminent* lawless action and is likely to incite or produce such action."

The Court concluded that because Hess' speech was "not directed to any person or group of persons" Hess had not advocated action that would produce imminent disorder.

The *Brandenburg* test—a test more vigorously phrased and strictly applied than the older clear and present danger test—remains the proper formula for determining when speech that advocates criminal conduct may constitutionally be punished.

§ 16.6   The Distinction Between Prior Restraint and Subsequent Punishment of Speech

Since the expiration of the English licensing system in 1695, under which nothing could be published without prior approval of the church or state authorities, prior restraint has been considered a more drastic infringement on free speech than subsequent punishment.

The Special Problem of Obscenity. In modern times prior restraint usually takes the form of court injunctions rather than a system of licensing by a Board of Censors. The only major exception is the case of allegedly obscene speech. Another section of this Chapter discusses prior restraint of allegedly obscene speech. Here we are primarily concerned with the prior restraint of other types of speech.

Prior Restraint and Subsequent Punishment Compared. If a given utterance may be punished, is there any real difference if one is enjoined from making the speech or whether one is punished *after* having made the speech? Historically, prior restraint has always been viewed as more dangerous to free speech, but why? The marketplace theory of free speech supports this historical distinction between prior restraint and subsequent punishment. While subsequent punishment may deter some speakers, at least the ideas or speech at issue can be placed before the public. But prior restraint limits public debate and knowledge more severely. Punishment of speech, after it has occurred, chills free expression. Prior restraint freezes free speech.

Disobeying Court Orders and Violating Statutes, Compared. Courts usually treat violations of prior restraint orders as a more serious offense than deliberate refusals to abide by a statute. A significant illustration of this principle is found in a comparison of two Supreme Court cases. In *Shuttlesworth v. Birmingham* (1969), the Court reversed the conviction of civil rights demonstrators who had been convicted of violating an ordinance found to be unconstitutionally vague. The ordinance forbade issuance of a license for a protest march if "the public welfare, peace, safety, health, decency, good order, morals or convenience" require that it be refused. Justice Stewart for the Court said that "a person faced with such an unconstitutional licensing law may ignore it and engage with impunity in the exercise of the right of free expression for which the law purports to require a license."

In *Walker v. City of Birmingham* (1967), the Court, earlier, had upheld the conviction of marchers who violated that same statute *after* the statute had been copied verbatim into an ex parte injunction. In short, while one is free to violate an unconstitutional statute restricting free speech, one is not free to violate the same words when written as a court injunction.

Distinguishing Content–Based from Content–Neutral Injunctions. Obviously, an injunction against speech is a prior restraint. But if a court enjoins conduct and the injunction also has an incidental and limited effect on speech, the issue is more complicated. *Madsen v. Women's Health Center, Inc.* (1994) considered this issue. An injunction that is not based on the content of speech will be upheld if the injunction is narrowly tailored to promote an important interest unrelated to the suppression of a message. This standard sounds like, but is applied more strictly than, the test for time, place and manner regulations. The divided Court upheld portions of a Florida state court injunction involving an abortion clinic that was the target of protests that made it difficult for patients and staff to enter the clinic. Given the lower court's specific factual findings, the Court upheld an injunction that created a 36 foot buffer zone prohibiting picketing. The purpose of this buffer zone was to allow access to the clinic. The Court invalidated other portions of the injunction. The Court also used this standard in *Schenck v. Pro–Choice Network* 1997.

§ 16.7 Content–Based Injunctions: From *Near* to the Pentagon Papers and Beyond

Near v. Minnesota (1931) involved a state statute that permitted the state courts to enjoin as a nuisance any "malicious, scandalous and defamatory newspaper, magazine or other periodical." Defendant published "The Saturday Press" and had printed articles with strong antisemitic overtones critical of local officials. The Supreme Court ruled that enforcement of the statute through an injunction against defendant was an infringement of the liberty of the press as guaranteed in the First and Fourteenth Amendments. To reach this conclusion, the Court accepted a major initial postulate: the chief purpose of the freedom of the press and speech clauses is to prevent prior restraints on publication. Thus, there could be very few exceptions to the principle of immunity from previous restraint.

In dictum, the Court listed three "exceptional cases" that *might* justify previous restraint: (1) if it were necessary so that "a government might prevent actual obstruction to its recruiting service or the publication of the sailing dates of transports or the number and location of troops;" (2) the requirements of decency could justify prior restraint on obscene publications; (3) if it were necessary to avoid "incitements to acts of violence and the overthrow by force of orderly government."

The Pentagon Papers Case. *New York Times Co. v. United States* (The Pentagon Papers Case) (1971) involved a leak of secret government documents. The *New York Times*, then the *Washington Post*, and then other newspapers, received volumes of a secret government study of the Viet Nam war, which was still going on while the newspapers published the Pentagon Papers.

The Court dismissed temporary restraining orders and stays against the *New York Times* and the *Washington Post,* and refused to enjoin the newspapers from publishing this classified study on United States policy-making in Viet Nam. The fragmented Court decided the case in nine separate opinions. There was a six to three majority, but all nine Justices agreed on two general themes—any system of prior restraint of expression bears a heavy presumption against its constitutional validity, and the Government carries a heavy burden to justify any system of prior restraint.

The opinions in this case can be grouped in three categories: Justices Black and Douglas maintained that there can never be prior restraint on the press; Justices Brennan, White, Stewart and Marshall maintained that there could be prior restraint on the press in some circumstances but not in this case; and Justices Burger, Harlan, and Blackmun, maintained that the prior restraint was appropriate in this case.

Justice Brennan did leave open the possibility of some constitutional prior restraints, but his test was so strict that none might pass any realistic review. Brennan first pointed out the impropriety of granting injunctive relief in the instant case. The basis of the Government's argument was that publication might damage the national interest but, according to Brennan, "the First Amendment tolerates absolutely no prior judicial restraints of the press predicated upon surmise or conjecture that untoward consequences may result."

Brennan did find one situation that would justify an exception to the First Amendment ban on prior restraint, when the nation is at war. However, Brennan invoked a high standard for imposition of prior restraint even then. The Government must allege and prove that the publication of information must "inevitably, directly, and immediately" cause the happening of an event such as nuclear holocaust. Thus, although Brennan conceptually allowed the possibility of prior restraint, his test is so strict as to be virtually a prohibition.

Justice Stewart argued that prior restraint imposed by the Executive could be justified in order to maintain internal security, because the Executive has a constitutional obligation to preserve the confidentiality required to effectively perform its duties related to national defense and foreign affairs. However, the Executive must show that disclosure of information will result in "direct, immediate, and irreparable damage to our Nation or its people," and the Government did not meet this test for all the documents involved in the instant case.

Even though he was convinced disclosure of the material would do substantial damage to the public interest, Justice White concurred in the Court's judgment because the Government did not satisfy the "very heavy burden" it must meet to justify prior restraint.

Justice Marshall based his concurrence on the absence of Congressional authorization for prior restraint in this situation. He argued that it would be against the separation of powers concept for the Court, through use of the contempt power, to restrain actions Congress has chosen not to prohibit.

The remaining three Justices dissented. Chief Justice Burger did not speak directly to the merits of the case, arguing instead that undue haste in the proceedings removed any possibility of orderly litigation of the proceedings. Justice Blackmun included a strong attack on the newspapers and concurring Justices who comprised the majority of the Court.

Unlike Justice Marshall, Justice Harlan used the theory of the constitutional separation of powers to justify prior restraint of the Pentagon Papers. Harlan argued that the Executive has constitutional primacy in the field of foreign affairs and that it is not within the power of the Court to redetermine the probable impact of disclosure on national security once this decision has been made by the Executive.

The Government lost its injunctive suit and the newspaper proceeded to finish publishing the excerpts of the Pentagon Papers that they had secured by an unauthorized leak from a former government employee, Daniel Ellsberg. The Government did prosecute Daniel Ellsberg. Ellsberg, however, was never convicted. The trial judge directed a verdict of acquittal for Ellsberg because of various prosecution improprieties.

The *Snepp* Case. In *Snepp v. United States* (1980), the Supreme Court, in a per curiam opinion held that a former agent of the Central Intelligence Agency breached his fiduciary obligation and his employment contract when he failed to submit for prepublication review a book concerning the CIA, even though the Government conceded, for the purposes of the case, that the book divulged no classified information. Therefore, the Court put into constructive trust for the Government all the profits from Snepp's book.

The majority explained that the proper procedure that Snepp should have followed, in light of his explicit employment agreement to submit all material to the CIA for prepublication review, would be to submit the material so that the Agency could determine if it contained harmful disclosures. If Snepp and the CIA failed to agree on this issue, the Agency would have the burden to seek an injunction against publication. Without any further discussion the Court appeared to approve of what amounts to prior restraint in those special cases where former CIA employees have been in a position of trust and have signed employment contracts accepting prepublication review of information dealing with the CIA.

Snepp should stand only for the proposition that the government may condition the use of information disclosed to persons who have no constitutional right of access to that information, such as the government's employees: (1) when those persons in fact agree not to discuss or disclose such information; (2) when the governmental interest supporting the condition is significant; (3) when that interest is truly unrelated to the suppression of expression; and (4) when the agreement is a narrow means of promoting governmental interests unrelated to censorship goals. *Snepp* does not give the government the right to condition all government employment on the employee's waiver of free speech rights.

§ 16.8 A Right of Access to the Press

(a) The Fairness Doctrine and the Regulation of the Broadcast Media

The Court, in general, has accepted the argument that the unique nature of broadcast media and the present state of the art mean that there is no comparable right of everyone to broadcast on radio and television what one could speak, write, or publish elsewhere. Frequencies presently available for wireless broadcast are finite, and when some are given the privilege to use some bands of the airways, others must be denied. No particular licensee has a First Amendment right to broadcast and his existing privilege may be qualified through reasonable regulation. Therefore, the government may subject award of a broadcast license to reasonable regulation with goals *other than the suppression of ideas.* This regulation is permissible because the Court considers the right of the listeners and viewers to be paramount, not the rights of the broadcasters.

National Broadcasting Co. v. United States (1943) first recognized that, because no one has a First Amendment right to a radio license or to monopolize a radio frequency, to deny a station a license on the grounds of public interest is not a denial of free speech.

The extent of the right of the government to control the electronic media was not made clear by *NBC*, but it was brought into sharp focus by *Red Lion Broadcasting Co. v. Federal Communication Commission* (1969), which challenged the right of the FCC to require broadcasters to follow a "fairness doctrine." The fairness doctrine required broadcasters to allow reply time to the public in cases involving personal attacks or political editorials. The case was the first time that the Supreme Court ruled on a challenge made to the FCC's fairness doctrine on constitutional grounds.

In *Red Lion*, the petitioner operated a radio station under FCC license. During a broadcast on the station the Reverend Billy James Hargis verbally attacked author Fred J. Cook. Cook demanded free reply time and, when the station refused, he filed a formal letter of complaint with the Federal Communications Commission. The Commission deemed the incident a "personal attack" and ordered the station to grant Cook the time requested.

The broadcasters challenged the fairness doctrine and its specific manifestations in the personal attack and political editorial rules on conventional First Amendment grounds.

The Justices in *Red Lion* unanimously rejected the argument that broadcasters have a free speech right that is identical to published or spoken speech.

The Court reasoned that the fiduciary nature of the relationship between the licensee and the general public put those who hold a license in no more favored position than those to whom licenses are refused. Where the public interest requires, the government could demand that a licensee fulfill his obligation "to present those views and voices which are representative of his community and which would otherwise, by necessity, be barred from the airwaves." Because of this fiduciary role, the rights of the broadcasters must be subordinate to the right of viewers and listeners to suitable access to ideas and information.

It is important to note that the *Red Lion* case only upheld a Federal Communication Commission rule.

While the fairness doctrine regulations do not constitute a prior restraint in the classic sense, they do place a recognizable burden on broadcaster programming discretion. *Red Lion* Court spent little time discussing the competing considerations involved in placing this additional burden. The broadcasters' claims that they would be forced into self-censorship and would substantially curtail coverage of controversial issues under a right-to-reply rule was summarily dismissed as "at best speculative." The Court did admit that if the rules should result in such a reduction of coverage, then "there will be time enough to reconsider the constitutional implications".

No General Right of Access. The generally broad language of *Red Lion* led some commentators to argue that there is a constitutional right of individual access to the airwaves beyond the scope of the fairness doctrine. The Democratic National Committee (DNC) and an anti-war group called the Business Executive's Movement for Vietnam Peace (BEM) tried to establish the existence of a constitutional right of access in *Columbia Broadcasting System v. Democratic National Committee* (1973).

The issue in *CBS* was whether "responsible" groups have a constitutional right under the First Amendment to purchase air time for the presentation of advertisements and programs in order to make known their views about controversial issues of public importance. The two groups claiming such a right, DNC and BEM, were challenging separate decisions of the FCC. In the case of BEM, the FCC had held that a radio station acted within its authority in refusing to air BEM's spot advertisement opposed to the Vietnam conflict; in the case of DNC the FCC had held that as a general matter the DNC did not have a right to purchase time to air its views on controversial public issues.

The Supreme Court upheld the FCC ruling in both cases and said that there is no such right of access under the Constitution. Though the Court divided on several issues, six Justices agreed that the First Amendment would not require the sale of time to responsible groups even if state action was involved.

The opinion of the Court emphasized that a balancing of the First Amendment interests must be carried out within the framework of the regulatory scheme already imposed by Congress on the broadcast media. The Court concluded that an unlimited right of access would not best serve the public interest. The views of the affluent could still prevail because they could purchase more time to air their views. The Court was reluctant to allow full access by individuals who had no responsibilities or accountability to act in the public interest.

The Right of Access of Political Candidates. In *CBS, Inc. v. FCC* (1981), the Court upheld, as consistent with the First Amendment, the power granted to the FCC under 47 U.S.C.A. § 312(a)(7). This law offered legally qualified candidates for federal elective office an affirmative, promptly enforceable right of reasonable access, to purchase broadcast time without reference to whether an opponent has secured time. Violation of this section authorizes the FCC to revoke a broadcaster's license. The Court emphasized that it was not approving any *"general* right of access to the media." The Court ruled that the statute at issue properly balances the First Amendment rights of the public, the broadcasters, and the candidates because it "creates a *limited* right to 'reasonable' access that pertains only to legally qualified federal candidates and may be invoked by them only for the purpose of advancing their candidacies once a campaign has commenced."

Note that in *CBS, Inc. v. Democratic National Committee* the Court refused to create a right of access. In *CBS, Inc. v. FCC*, on the other hand, the Court upheld the constitutionality of a carefully drawn statute providing for limited access.

Arkansas Educational Television Commission v. Forbes (1998) involved a state-owned public television broadcaster (AETC), which sponsored a debate between the two major party candidates for the 1992 election in the Third Congressional District in Arkansas. AETC denied Ralph P. Forbes, a third-party candidate with little popular support, permission to participate in the televised debate. Forbes filed suit claiming that the First Amendment gave him a right to participate in the debate. Justice Kennedy's opinion for the Court held that the televised debate was a nonpublic forum from which the broadcaster could exclude a candidate in the reasonable, viewpoint-neutral exercise of its journalistic discretion. In this case, the jury made express findings that AETC's decision to exclude Forbes had not been influenced by political pressure or by disagreement with his views. The Court ruled that the candidate debate was a nonpublic forum, from which AETC could exclude Forbes in the reasonable, viewpoint-neutral exercise of its journalistic discretion.

Censorship and "Adult" Language. The First Amendment rights of free speech in a broadcasting context raise questions not only of access but also of censorship. In *FCC v. Pacifica Foundation* (1978) a sharply divided Court upheld the power of the FCC to regulate "adult speech" over the radio air waves, at least in some limited circumstances. The Court held that the FCC does have statutory and constitutional power to regulate a radio broadcast that is "indecent" but not "obscene" in the constitutional sense and also does not constitute "fighting words" in the constitutional sense, at least under circumstances when the indecent broadcast would be available to a high percentage of children.

In this case a radio station broadcast for nearly 12 minutes a record of a George Carlin humorous monologue. This broadcast occurred in the early afternoon when the Court assumed that children were likely to be in the audience. (The Court did not explain why it did not assume that children old enough to understand the Carlin monologue were more likely to be in school in the early afternoon.) During this monologue Carlin repeatedly used various words referring to sexual and excretory activities and organs, and mocked middle class attitudes toward them.

The FCC, after having received one complaint, from a man who had heard the broadcast with his son on the car radio, issued a "Declaratory Order" against Pacifica. While the FCC did not impose formal sanctions it did add the complaint to the station's license file and noted that, if subsequent complaints were received, the FCC would then decide whether to utilize any of the sanctions it has, ranging from issuing a cease and desist order or imposing a fine, to revoking the station's license.

In *Pacifica*, five Justices agreed that broadcasting receives "the most limited" free speech protections of all forms of communication because it is "a uniquely pervasive presence in the lives of all Americans" and "is uniquely accessible to children, even those too young to read." But they could not agree any further on the constitutional rationale for their holding.

Justice Stevens, joined by Chief Justice Burger and Justice Rehnquist, thought that "indecency is largely a function of context ..." and that "a broadcast of patently offensive words dealing with sex and excretion may be regulated because of its content."

Justice Powell, joined by Blackmun, wrote a separate opinion. They specifically rejected Stevens' view that the Court is free to decide "on the basis of its content which speech protected by the First Amendment is most valuable.... The result turns instead on the unique characteristics of the broadcast media, combined with society's right to protect its children from speech generally agreed to be inappropriate for their years, and with the interest of unwilling adults in not being assaulted by such offensive speech in their homes."

Justices Stewart and White dissented on statutory grounds and did not read the constitutional issues. Justice Brennan, joined by Justice Marshall, did reach the constitutional issues and strongly dissented. They argued that when an individual turns to a radio station or any transmission broadcast to the public at large, there is no fundamental privacy interest implicated. The listener has, by tuning in, decided to take part in an on-going public discussion. Neither, they believed, was the FCC regulation justified by the need to protect children.

The five member majority emphasized that their decision was very narrow, not involving a two-way radio conversation, an Elizabethan comedy, a closed-circuit transmission, or an occasional expletive. The time of day and the content of the program in which the language is used may also be relevant, as well as the type and amount of punishment imposed.

Censorship and Bans on Editorials by Public Broadcast Stations. In *Federal Communications Commission v. League of Women Voters* (1984) the Court (five to four vote) invalidated a section of the Public Broadcasting Act that forbade any nonprofit educational broadcasting station that receives a grant from the Corporation for Public Broadcasting to engage in editorializing or endorsing candidates for political office. Writing for the majority, Justice Brennan concluded that restrictions on the electronic media have been upheld only when the restriction is narrowly tailored to further a substantial governmental interest, "such as ensuring adequate and balanced coverage of public issues."

The statute at issue in *League of Women Voters* was invalid under Justice Brennan's test because it was not narrowly tailored to further the substantial interest in presenting balanced information to the public. The interest in providing balanced coverage could be advanced by other less, restrictive means such as the requirement that opposing viewpoints be broadcast free of charge. Indeed, the majority found that the structure of the system for financing public broadcasting already operated to insulate local stations from governmental interference. The majority did agree with the dissenters that Congress could avoid funding that portion of a noncommercial educational broadcasting station's budget that was used for editorials or candidate endorsements. Although Congress could refuse to fund speech activities of this type, it could not punish a station that engaged in editorializing by terminating all federal funding for the station.

Cable Television & Monopoly Restitution. In *City of Los Angeles v. Preferred Communications, Inc.* (1986) the Court rejected a city's claim that its refusal to grant a franchise to a cable television company raised no First Amendment concerns. The applicant had not participated in an auction for a single franchise, but the city did not dispute that there was excess physical capacity that would allow more than one cable television franchise. The Court readily concluded that the cable operator's claims raised valid First Amendment issues but also decided that they could not be resolved solely on the basis of the complaint, so it remanded and directed the trial court to balance the First Amendment values against competing societal interests, after a full development of the disputed issues. Beyond that, *Preferred Communications* offered no hint of the ultimate resolution of the controversy except to emphasize that the city ordinance will not be saved merely because it is rational.

The "Must–Carry Provisions" of Cable Regulation. In *Turner Broadcasting System, Inc. v. FCC* (1994), the Court continued its tentative exploration of the free speech rights of cable operators in light of the developing technology. In 1992, Congress enacted the Cable Television and Consumer Protection and Competition Act. Sections 4 and 5 required cable television systems to devote a portion of their channels to the transmission of local broadcast stations, in an effort, according to the sponsors of the legislation, to aid the competitive viability of broadcast television. In the view of the Court, the law regulated cable speech in two major ways: first, it reduced the number of channels over which the cable operators exercised unfettered control; and, second, it made it more difficult for cable programmers to compete for carriage on the limited number of channels remaining.

Cable operators sued, claiming that these "must-carry" provisions violated the First Amendment. The three–judge district court, over dissent, granted summary judgment for the United States, but Justice Kennedy, for the Court, vacated that judgment and remanded for further proceedings.

First, the *Turner* Court ruled that it should not use the less rigorous standard of review reserved for broadcast regulation because the problems of scarcity of broadcast frequencies and signal interference do not apply in the context of cable; "soon there may be no practical limitation on the number of speakers who may use the cable medium." Second, the Court would not apply strict scrutiny to the must-carry rules because they are content-neutral: the must-carry rules, on their face, impose burdens and confer benefits without reference to the content of speech.

Justice Kennedy conceded that, unlike cable programming, "broadcast programming, is subject to certain limited content restraints imposed by statute and FCC regulations." But, he rejected the argument that the preference for broadcast stations *"automatically* entails content requirements." In his view, the congressional purpose was to ensure that broadcast television will retain a large enough potential audience to earn necessary advertising revenue, not to control content: "Congress' overriding objective in enacting must-carry was not to favor programming of a particular subject matter, viewpoint, or format, but rather to preserve access to free television programming for the 40 percent of Americans without cable."

The Court then announced that it should use the intermediate level of scrutiny that applies to content-neutral restrictions that impose an incidental burden on speech. The government need not impose the least restrictive means of advancing its interests, but the regulation must promote "a substantial government interest that would be achieved less effectively absent the regulation."

In a portion of Justice Kennedy's opinion that was a plurality opinion and not an opinion of the Court, Justice Kennedy emphasized that on remand the government "must demonstrate that the recited harms are real, not merely conjectural, and that the regulation will in fact alleviate these harms in a direct and material way." The government must show, for example, that the economic health of local broadcasting is in genuine jeopardy and in need of the protection afforded by "must-carry." While Congress' predictive judgments are entitled to "substantial deference," they are not "insulated from meaningful review altogether." The dissent was more protective of the free speech and would have held the regulations content-based and invalid.

Three years later, in *Turner Broadcasting System, Inc. v. FCC* (1997), Justice Kennedy again spoke for the Court. He upheld the "must-carry" provisions [sections 4 and 5] of the Cable Television Consumer Protection and Competition Act of 1992. Based on the more full factual record that had been developed on remand, the Court affirmed the majority of the three-judge district court. Kennedy concluded that the congressional interests in preserving free, over-the-air television broadcasts, promoting numerous sources to broadcast information, and promoting fair competition in the television broadcasting market justified the congressional decision to impose the must-carry rules. The factual record—in the view of the majority but not the dissent—supported the congressional judgment that cable systems would refuse to carry a significant number of broadcast stations in the absence of the must-carry rules, and that the local broadcast stations that were not carried would be at serious risk of financial difficulty.

The Court concluded that the must-carry provisions, in this context, met the intermediate scrutiny under the First Amendment. That is, the regulations were content-neutral and advanced important governmental interests in a direct and effective way; they where unrelated to the suppression of free speech, and they did not burden substantially more speech than was necessary to further these governmental interests.

(b) Media Other Than the Broadcast Media

In *Miami Herald Publishing Co. v. Tornillo* (1974), a unanimous Court struck down a Florida statute that required newspapers to give free reply space to political candidates whom they had attacked in their columns.

Miami Herald firmly established that the right of newspaper editors to choose what they wish to print or not to print cannot be abridged to allow the public access to the newspaper media. There is a "virtually insurmountable barrier" that the freedom of the press erects between governmental regulation and the print media.

An important distinction between the fairness doctrine as applied to electronic media and the fairness doctrine that cannot be applied to the print media is that the former enjoys a legal monopoly, which serves to justify FCC regulations requiring "fairness." There is no *legal* monopoly of—and no technological justification for a legal monopoly of—newspapers. Laws may not require people to get a license or a certificate of public convenience and necessity before starting up a new newspaper.

No Right of Access to City–Owned Media. In the same term with *Miami Herald* the Court considered another access case, this time not involving the private press but rather the use of billboard space on a city-owned public transportation system. In *Lehman v. Shaker Heights* (1974), a divided Court held that a city that operates a public rapid transit system does not violate the First or Fourteenth Amendments by selling commercial advertising space for cigarette companies, banks, liquor companies, churches, and public service groups on its vehicles while refusing to accept any political advertising on behalf of candidates for public office or public issue advertising.

The essential problem in *Lehman* was not a pure right to access, but rather a right of equal access. Plaintiffs argued that, by making the advertising space available for some uses, the city had created a public forum and could not now censor the content of speech in that forum by banning political advertisements. The majority of the Court, without a majority opinion, rejected the contention that space on a city transit system is to be deemed a public forum. The city acted properly to minimize chances of abuse, the appearance of favoritism, and the risk of imposing on a captive audience.

No Right of Access to Utility Company's Billing Envelopes. In *Pacific Gas & Electric Co. v. Public Utilities Commission* (1986), a fragmented Court, with no majority opinion, held that the California Public Utilities Commission may not require a privately owned utility company to include, in its billing envelopes, the speech of a third party (in this case, a private group called TURN, "Toward Utility Rate Normalization") with which the utility disagreed. Justice Powell's plurality opinion concluded that the utility's newsletter is "no different from a small newspaper." Its stories ranged from energy-savings tips to wildlife conservation to billings to recipes. The Utility Commission could not, consistently with the First Amendment, force the utility to grant TURN access to the utility's newsletter.

§ 16.9 Right of Access by the Press and Public?

Does the press generally, or the institutional press in particular, have any preferred rights under the First Amendment? Does the press clause guarantee the press any rights of access that is different from, or greater than, the rights that any individual might have under the free speech clause?

Thus far, when the Court has guaranteed a right of access—as the right of access to a criminal trial, the right of a public trial—it has granted this right to all; the right is not limited to the press.

Prisons. In *Pell v. Procunier* (1974) and *Saxbe v. Washington Post Co.* (1974), the Court rejected claims by prisoners and the press that the First Amendment guaranteed a right of access to newspapers to interview individual prisoners. It upheld California and federal prison regulations that prohibited face-to-face interviews between prisoners and members of the news media.

Saxbe did not explore the constitutional right of inmates to seek individual interviews with members of the press because inmates were not a party to the litigation. *Pell v. Procunier*, however, explored this aspect of the First Amendment in light of the prisoners' unique position in society. Justice Stewart, writing for the majority in *Pell*, noted that while an absolute ban on interviews applied to the public at large would clearly involve a freedom of speech issue, but the right to hold a press conference does not necessarily survive incarceration.

The Court placed great emphasis on the fact that the prisoners had alternative means of communication with the press.

The Court admitted that the availability of such alternatives are unimpressive as justification for governmental restriction of personal communication among members of the general public. However, the fundamental rights of prisoners may be limited by reasonable prison regulations.

Both *Pell* and *Saxbe* considered whether this limitation on press interviews violates freedom of the press as guaranteed by the Constitution. The press contended that, irrespective of any First Amendment rights of the prisoners, members of the press have a constitutional right of access to interview any willing inmate. The Court rejected this argument in both cases.

In *Houchins v. KQED, Inc.* (1978), the Supreme Court reversed a lower court injunction ordering prison officials to grant the press access to certain prison facilities. The seven-member, fragmented court could produce no majority opinion. The plurality found that there is no First or Fourteenth Amendment right of access to government information or sources of information within the government's control. Further, the press has no greater right of access than that of the public generally.

Because there was no majority opinion and two Justices— Marshall and Blackmun—did not participate, the *Houchins* decision probably will not end litigation over public access to prisons in cases where there is only limited access to parts of the jail. However, the seven justices did agree that the press has no greater right of access to prisons than the public generally. The Court, once again, rejected the notion that the institutional press has greater First Amendment rights than the public generally.

Access to Trials. The press has no constitutional right of access to evidence given at trials greater than that of the general public. *Nixon v. Warner Communications, Inc.* (1978), held that neither the First Amendment guarantee of free speech and press nor the Sixth Amendment guarantee of a public trial gives the press the right to copy evidence given at trial. News organizations sought to copy several Watergate tapes that had been introduced at the trial of several defendants, but the Court held that the opportunity to listen to the tapes at trial and to receive transcripts of them had satisfied both constitutional guarantees. The Court held that within the courtroom, the press enjoys no greater rights than does the public, but that the press is free, within broad limits, to report what its representatives have seen at the proceeding.

Publication of Rape Victim's Name. While the press has no greater rights than the general public, neither should it have any less. *Florida Star v. B.J.F.* (1989) invalidated a Florida statute that made a newspaper civilly liable for publishing the name of a rape victim. The press had obtained this name from publicly released police reports. The Court concluded that if a newspaper publishes information that it has lawfully obtained, the state may impose punishment, if at all, only when the law is narrowly tailored to a state interest of the highest order. The facts of this case did not meet that test. Justice Scalia, concurring in part and in the judgment, astutely noted that Florida limited the press, but it placed no limits at all on gossip by the victim's neighbors. Thus it discriminated against the press. "This law has every appearance of a prohibition that society is prepared to impose upon the press but not upon itself."

§ 16.10   The Press and the Tax Laws

The Government may not impose taxes that serve as a condition to a person exercising a right guaranteed by the Bill of Rights. Thus, *Follett v. McCormick* (1944) struck down a *flat license* tax as applied to one who earns his livelihood as an evangelist or preacher. Those who preach, "like other citizens, may be subject to general taxation [but that] does not mean that they can be required to pay a tax for the exercise of that which the First Amendment has made a high constitutional privilege."

The Court has also invalidated discriminatory taxes on the dissemination of news. *Grosjean v. American Press Co.* (1936) struck down a state tax (which was a tax in addition to other taxes of general applicability) on 2% of the gross receipts of advertising in those newspapers with circulation of more than 20,000 copies per week. The tax is invalid because it was designed to punish a newspaper that opposed government policy.

Minneapolis Star and Tribune Co. v. Minnesota Commissioner of Revenue (1983) interpreted *Grosjean* as dependent on the legislature having improper censorial goals or motive. However, even without such improper goals, a tax may be invalid. In Minnesota, the state's general sales and use taxes exempted periodic publication, but the state had a special "use" tax on the cost of paper and ink products consumed in the production of periodic publications after the first $100,000 worth of ink and paper consumed in a calendar year.

The economic result of this tax was to discriminate against larger publishers, and to favor smaller ones. *Minneapolis Star* correctly invalidated this tax, which singled out the press for special tax burdens.

In *Arkansas Writers' Project, Inc. v. Ragland* (1987) the Court ruled that a state may not constitutionally levy a sales tax on certain types of magazines based on the content of those magazines—the state sales tax in question applied to general interest magazines but exempted newspapers and certain types of magazines (any religious, professional, trade or sports periodical was exempted, but not a general interest magazine).

In *Leathers v. Medlock* (1991), the Court held that Arkansas could extend its generally applicable sales tax to cable television services and satellite services while exempting the print media. The tax in question covered *all* tangible personal property and a broad range of services. Thus it did not single out the press and threaten its role as a watchdog of government activity. Furthermore, the tax did not target cable television in a purposeful attempt to interfere with free speech.

The "Son of Sam" Law. *Simon & Schuster, Inc. v. Members of the New York State Crime Victims Board* (1991), invalidated New York's "Son of Sam" statute, so-called because it was enacted in response to a criminal who called himself the "Son of Sam." This law required that any income of an accused or "convicted" person derived from works describing his crime be deposited in an escrow account, where they were available to victims of the crime and the criminal's creditors. The statute treated as "convicted" any person who admitted to a crime, even if that person had not been prosecuted.

The law was the functional economic equivalent of a tax because it imposed a financial disincentive to create or publish works with a particular content. Justice O'Connor, for the Court, ruled that the statute was overbroad and regulated speech based on content. A statute that imposes a financial burden on speakers because of the content of their speech is "presumptively inconsistent with the First Amendment...." To justify such differential treatment, the regulation must be "necessary to serve a compelling state interest and narrowly drawn to achieve that end."

The state has a compelling interest to insure that criminals do not profit from their crimes and in compensating victims by using the fruits of the criminal's crime, but the statute was not narrowly tailored to that objective. The statute was over inclusive because it applied to works on any subject, whenever the author expresses thoughts or recollections about a crime, however tangentially. The law, as written, would even apply to the *Confessions of Saint Augustine,* (where Saint Augustine, the author, deplores his "past foulness," including his theft of pears from a neighbor's vineyard) and *The Autobiography of Malcolm X* (which described crimes committed before Malcolm X became a religious and social leader).

§ 16.11　Fair Trial versus Free Press

(a) The Reporter's Privilege

In *Branzburg v. Hayes* (1972), a bare five to four majority rejected a reporter's claim that the flow of information available to the press would be seriously impeded if reporters are compelled to release the names of confidential sources for use in a government investigation. The Court also rejected the claim that the First Amendment embraced a reporter's privilege to refuse to divulge confidential sources.

Though the issue before *Branzburg* has far-reaching implications, Justice White, for the Court, phrased the question and holding more narrowly: "The issue in these cases is whether requiring newsmen to appear and testify before state or federal grand juries abridges the freedom of speech and press guaranteed by the First Amendment. We hold that it does not."

Justice Powell, who cast the crucial fifth vote, struck a somewhat problematic note for future litigation relying on *Branzburg.* Because he believed that the "state and federal authorities are not free to 'annex' the news media as 'an investigative arm of government,'" he urged, in his concurrence, a broader test than mere "good faith" for assessing the need to disclose confidential sources. In his view:

> [I]f the newsman is called upon to give information bearing only a remote and tenuous relationship to the subject of the investigation, or if he has some other reason to believe that his testimony implicates confidential source relationships without a legitimate need of law enforcement, he will have access to the Court on a motion to quash and an appropriate protective order may be entered.

The ambiguity surrounding "a legitimate need of law enforcement" suggests an approach not too dissimilar to that rejected in the majority opinion due to inherent administrative difficulties. Indeed, Justice Stewart's dissent interpreted this ambiguity as offering "some hope of a more flexible view in the future."

State Shield Laws. Despite intensive lobbying efforts, Congress has enacted no federal bill that would provide a statutory privilege for newsmen. However, several states have enacted "state shield" laws that offer varying protection, depending on the statutory language and state court interpretation. Under the supremacy clause of the Constitution such state shield laws could not apply to limit the power of federal courts exercising jurisdiction over federal questions.

State shield laws may vary greatly in how they are applied in state cases to prevent a state court from subpoenaing information from a reporter when such information may be helpful to a criminal defendant.

A Reporter's Privilege and Civil Cases. In *Herbert v. Lando* (1979) the Court refused to grant members of the press immunity from pretrial discovery in a civil case.

Search Warrants of Newsrooms. *Zurcher v. The Stanford Daily* (1978) refused to create any special protections for newspapers that might be searched by government authorities pursuant to a search warrant based on probable cause to look for evidence of a crime. The majority quickly dismissed arguments based on the need to protect confidential sources.

(b) Judicial Protective Orders and the Press

The commitment to an "uninhibited, robust, and wide-open" discussion of public issues in a free press may sometimes conflict with the commitment to a criminal process in which the conclusions to be reached in a case are based on only evidence and argument in open court. A major question is the extent to which a trial judge may insulate his or her courtroom procedures from the intrusion of outside prejudice caused by publicity surrounding the case. In this area the rights of the press may conflict with the rights of the accused.

Pre–Trial Publicity, Cameras in the Courts, and Court Orders Against the Press. The first reversal of a state conviction due to prejudicial pre-trial publicity occurred in 1961 in *Irvin v. Dowd*. In that case, ninety percent of the venire and eight of the twelve members of the petit jury admitted that they had formed opinions based on the publicity surrounding the murder, and this result was obtained *after* a change of venue to an adjoining county. Justice Clark, for a unanimous Court, found a due process violation.

Rideau v. Louisiana (1963) found that a denial of a request for change in venue offended due process when a local television had broadcast a film of the defendant confessing to the crimes in response to leading questions by the sheriff. The opinion indicates that the Court's reaction may be attributable to the coercive and pervasive nature of the television medium and the apparent complicity of the state in the broadcast.

This view of the case is buttressed by the result in *Estes v. Texas* (1965), which held that the presence of television cameras recording the trial for rebroadcast over the defendant's objections was so inherently intrusive that a violation of due process was inevitable.

In *Chandler v. Florida* (1981) the Court held that there is no per se constitutional prohibition against a state providing for radio, television, and still photographic coverage of a criminal trial for public broadcast, notwithstanding the objection of the accused.

In *Chandler*, Chief Justice Burger for the Court, first concluded that *Estes* did not establish a per se rule. The Court held that due process did not require any per se prohibition against broadcasting of criminal trials. Because the defendants did not demonstrate with "specificity that the presence of cameras impaired the ability of jurors to decide the case on only the evidence before them or that the trial was affected adversely by the impact on any of the participants of the presence of cameras and the prospect of broadcast," the Court affirmed the convictions.

In *Sheppard v. Maxwell* (1966), the Court held that the trial judge had failed to properly protect the defendant, jurors, and witnesses from the firestorm of publicity, much of which was erroneous and prejudicial. The Court then reversed the conviction. *Sheppard* noted that there were more than adequate procedures at the judge's disposal to prevent a murder trial from being converted into a "carnival." In particular, the Court emphasized stricter control over the activities of the press within the courtroom and provision for the insulation of witnesses and jurors.

The *Nebraska Press* **Decision.** The Supreme Court focused on the overuse of judicial restraining orders against the press in *Nebraska Press Association v. Stuart* (1976). Members of the state press association challenged a restraining order prohibiting them from publishing confessions by an accused in a murder trial (except those made directly to members of the press) as well as other facts "strongly implicative" of the accused. In this case, the press itself was directly challenging the validity of a judicial order in light of the hostility of the First Amendment toward prior restraints. The Court unanimously held the order invalid, but there were five separate opinions.

The Chief Justice, speaking for the Court, narrated the history of those cases invalidating prior restraints, and characterized them as follows:

> Prior restraints on speech are the most serious and least tolerable infringement on First Amendment rights.... A prior restraint ... has an immediate and irreversible sanction. If it can be said that a threat of criminal or civil sanctions after publication "chills" speech, prior restraint "freezes" it at least for the time.

The trial court in *Nebraska Press* had not made a showing that the entire panoply of procedures outlined in *Sheppard* would be insufficient to forestall this occurrence. Such procedures include, for example, continuance, change of venue, intensive voir dire examination, sequestration of the jurors, instruction on the duty of each juror to decide the issues on the evidence, and restraining orders on the parties involved and their attorneys in discussing issues with the press. In the absence of such a showing, the imposition of a protective order could never overcome the heavy presumption against constitutionality that inevitably attaches to prior restraints.

The *Gentile* **Case—Controlling Lawyers and the "Substantial Likelihood of Material Prejudice" Test**

A practical result of the *Nebraska Press Association* case may be the increasing use of restraining orders on the parties under the trial court's control: the attorneys, the police, and witnesses.

Courts also try to control trial and pretrial publicity by enforcing attorney ethics rules. But such "silence orders" will not be upheld, unless there is a substantial likelihood of material prejudice. The "substantial likelihood" test is the rule after *Gentile v. State Bar of Nevada* (1991). This test is less strict than *Nebraska Press Association*.

Attorney Gentile held a press conference a few hours after Nevada had indicted his client. Gentile made a brief statement, and gave a sketch of his client's defense, stating that Nevada sought the conviction of an innocent man as a "scapegoat," and it had not "been honest enough to indict the people who did it; the police department, crooked cops." He declined to answer reporters' questions seeking more detailed comments. Six months later, a jury acquitted Gentile's client of all counts.

Then the Nevada State Bar filed a complaint claiming that Gentile had violated Nevada's Supreme Court Rule 177, governing pretrial publicity. This ethics rule was almost identical to the American Bar Association's Model Rule 3.6, of the ABA Model Rules of Professional Conduct. (The ABA later amended that rule in response to *Gentile*.) Rule 177(1) prohibited a lawyer from making "an extrajudicial statement that a reasonable person would expect to be disseminated by means of public communication" if a reasonable lawyer would know that it "will have a substantial likelihood of materially prejudicing an adjudicative proceeding." Rule 177(3) purported to provide a "safe harbor," listing statements that can be made (e.g., the general nature of the defense, information in a public record) "notwithstanding" previous subsections of the Rule.

In a portion of the opinion of the Court that Justice Kennedy wrote, the Court held that Rule 177, as interpreted by the state court, was unconstitutionally vague. The "notwithstanding" language misled Gentile into thinking that he would give his press conference if complied with Rule 177(3).

Chief Justice Rehnquist authored another portion of the Opinion for the Court in *Gentile*. The Chief Justice's opinion approved of the Rule 177's general test, prohibiting lawyers from publicly disseminating information that one reasonably knows has "substantial likelihood of materially prejudicing an adjudicative proceeding." This test is neutral as to points of view and does not forbid the lawyer from speaking but only postpones it until after the trial.

It is important to note that the Nevada Rule, like the ABA Model Rule, allows an attorney to say what is in a public record. As a constitutional matter, it should be easy to justify allowing an attorney to reveal what is already in a public record. However, this public records exception—not merely found in the ethics rules but an inherent byproduct of the First Amendment—provided an important exception, because of the tendency of prosecutors and defense counsel to tell a story when they file pleadings. An indictment, for example, need not be limited to the bare bones. The prosecutor may describe the alleged crime in detail, may refer to unindicted alleged co-conspirators and what they may have said or done, and so forth. One defendant claimed that "he had never known that his nickname was 'The Snake' until he saw it stated as an alias in an indictment—and then heard the prosecutor repeatedly calling him that on television." (It should not be too controversial to suggest that "the Snake" has pejorative connotations.) Defense counsel, as well, can file pleadings, such as bail motions or other pretrial motions, that tell a detailed story and make detailed allegations that become part of the public record.

***Gannett* and the Right to a Public Trial.** To cope with problems of pretrial publicity, courts at times have sought to close portions of the proceedings to the public, because where the press lawfully obtains information the court cannot thereafter prohibit the press from publishing it. In *Gannett Co., Inc. v. DePasquale* (1979), the Supreme Court upheld this practice under the narrow circumstances of that case. The Court held, by a five to four vote, that neither the public nor the press has an independent constitutional right to insist on access to a *pretrial* suppression hearing, *if* the accused, the prosecutor, and the trial judge all agree that the proceeding should be closed in order to assure a fair trial.

There were various suggestions in *Gannett* that the opinion should be read narrowly. The majority emphasized that any denial of public access was only temporary, because once the danger of prejudice had dissipated the court made available a transcript of the suppression hearing. The majority also discussed the dangers of pretrial publicity in this particular case.

The *Richmond* Case. A narrow interpretation of *Gannett* limited to pretrial hearings is supported by the decision shortly thereafter in *Richmond Newspapers, Inc. v. Virginia* (1980). The fragmented Court, with only Justice Rehnquist dissenting (and Justice Powell not participating), rejected the asserted power of a state trial judge to close a criminal trial.

Chief Justice Burger, joined by Justices White and Stevens, relied on the First and Fourteenth Amendments to give the public the right of access to criminal trials. There is a "presumption of openness," and that "[a]bsent an overriding interest articulated in findings, the trial of a criminal case must be open to the public."

Justice Brennan, joined by Justice Marshall, concurred in the judgment, though they did not appear to disagree with any of the substance of Chief Justice Burger's opinion. They noted that mere agreement of the trial judge and parties cannot constitutionally close a trial to the public in light of the First Amendment guarantees. And, because the state statute in this case authorized the trial judge and parties to engage in trial closures with unfettered discretion, "[w]hat countervailing interest might be sufficiently compelling to reverse this presumption of openness need not concern us now. . . ."

The *Globe Newspaper* **Ruling.** In *Globe Newspaper Co. v. Superior Court* (1982) the Court produced a majority opinion, elaborated on the meaning of *Richmond Newspapers*, and invalidated a state statute, unique to Massachusetts, that *required* trial judges to exclude the press and general public from the courtroom during the testimony of the victim in cases involving certain specified sexual offenses. Although the Court invalidated the mandatory state law (which required no particularized determinations in individual cases), it left open the possibility that under appropriate circumstances and in individual cases the trial court could exclude the press and public during the testimony of minor victims of sex crimes.

Justice Brennan, for the Court, explained that under *Richmond Newspapers* the First Amendment, as applied to the states, grants to the press and general public "a right of access to *criminal trials*" because historically such trials have been open and such openness aids in the functioning of the judicial process and the government. Thus states may deny access only if denial serves "a compelling governmental interest, and is narrowly tailored to serve that interest."

Protecting minor victims of sex crimes from further trauma and embarrassment was compelling, but it did "not justify a *mandatory*-closure rule, for it is clear that the circumstances of the particular case may affect the significance of the interest." The judge should consider the minor victim's wishes regarding disclosure, as well as the victim's age and maturity, the interests of relatives, the nature of the crime, and so on.

Voir Dire Proceedings: The *Press–Enterprise* **Test.** In *Press–Enterprise Co. v. Superior Court* (1984), the Court held that the First Amendment protected a right of access to voir dire proceedings for the screening of potential jurors. Chief Justice Burger, for the majority opinion, found that the history of open jury selection and First Amendment values justified the conclusion that these pretrial proceedings should come within the presumption of openness that had been established in *Richmond Newspapers* and *Globe Newspaper*. Burger then embraced a standard for lower courts to follow when determining whether a portion of the trial process should be closed: "The presumption of openness may be overcome only by an overriding interest based on findings that closure is essential to preserve higher values and is narrowly tailored to serve that interest. The interest is to be articulated along with findings specific enough that a reviewing court can determine whether the closure order was properly entered."

Publication of Rape Victim's Name. In *Cox Broadcasting Corp. v. Cohn* (1975) the Court held that the state, even in a right to privacy action, may not impose sanctions on the accurate publication of a rape victim's name obtained from public records open to public inspection.

The issue came up again in *Florida Star v. B.J.F.* (1989). The Court held that a Florida statute could not make a newspaper civilly liable for publishing the name of a rape victim, a name that the newspaper had obtained from a publicly released police report. However, the majority did not hold broadly that the state may never punish truthful publication; rather, its ruling was more narrow. Where a newspaper publishes truthful information lawfully obtained, the state may lawfully impose punishment, if at all, only when the statute is "narrowly tailored to a state interest of the highest order, and that no such interest is satisfactorily served by imposing liability" under the facts of this case.

Juvenile Proceedings. *Oklahoma Publishing Co. v. Oklahoma County District Court* (1977) found that it is unconstitutional for a court to issue a pretrial order enjoining the media from publishing the name or photograph of an 11–year-old boy in connection with the child's juvenile proceeding that reporters had attended.

Witnesses' Disclosure of Their Own Testimony Before the Grand Jury. In *Butterworth v. Smith* (1990), the Court invalidated a Florida statute that, with certain limited exceptions, prohibited a grand jury witness from ever disclosing testimony that he gave before the grand jury. A unanimous Court held that insofar as the Florida law prohibits a grand jury witness from disclosing his own testimony after the term of the grand jury has ended, it violates the First Amendment. The state's interest in preserving grand jury secrecy is either not served by, or insufficient to warrant, proscription of truthful speech on matters of public concern.

Protecting Pre–Trial Discovery. Although the Supreme Court has consistently invalidated judicial protective orders that prohibited newspapers from publishing information about trial proceedings, in *Seattle Times Co. v. Rhinehart* (1984), the Court upheld a protective order restricting the use of information gained through pretrial civil discovery by a newspaper that was a party to the litigation.

Trial courts have the power to order parties to civil litigation to disclose a wide range of information to opposing parties that is of possible relevance to the preparation for trial of the lawsuit. In *Seattle Times*, the Court examined a trial court order restricting a newspaper, which was a defendant in a defamation action, from publishing information gained from the plaintiff. The order allowed the newspaper to publish identical information if it could show that it had received that information from a source independent of the pretrial discovery proceedings. The Supreme Court found that this order constituted neither a true prior restraint of speech nor any other impermissible prohibition of speech or suppression of publications. Nonetheless, the Court was unanimous in finding that the order should be upheld only if it was narrowly tailored to promote an important or substantial governmental interest—an interest that must be unrelated to the suppression of expression. The government's interest in protecting the privacy rights of parties to litigation and operating a system of truly open pretrial discovery that would facilitate the adjudicatory process were both substantial and unrelated to any governmental interest in suppressing or punishing speech. The order in this case allowed publication of the information if it were gained from an independent source, so it was not unnecessarily restrictive of the newspaper's rights.

Public Disclosure of Recordings of Private Telephone Calls. *Bartnicki v. Vopper* (2001) considered the constitutionality of state and federal wiretap laws applied in an unusual circumstance. An unknown third party intercepted and taped a cellular telephone conversation of the plaintiffs. This third party gave the tapes to media defendants who broadcasted the tape. The plaintiff sued the media, asserting claims under federal and Pennsylvania wiretapping acts. In the facts of this case, the Court held that the statutes were unconstitutional as applied. The holding is narrow, so it is important to understand the facts.

Bartnicki, held, first, the prohibitions of the wiretap acts against intentional disclosure of illegally intercepted communication that the disclosing party knows or should know was illegally obtained are content-neutral laws of general applicability; and, second, the application of those provisions against these defendants violated their free speech rights, because the tape concerned a matter of public importance and the defendants had played no part in the illegal interception.

This case began when an unidentified person intercepted and recorded a cell phone conversation between a chief union negotiator and a union president engaged in labor negotiations with a local school board The president said: "If they're not gonna move for three percent, we're gonna have to go to their, their homes.... To blow off their front porches, we'll have to do some work on some of those guys." After the union signed a contract, respondent Vopper, a radio commentator, played a tape of this conversation on his public affairs talk show in connection with news reports about the settlement. Petitioners filed this damages suit under both federal and state wiretapping laws, alleging that their conversation had been surreptitiously intercepted by an unknown person; that another respondent (who said he found the tape in his mail box) intentionally disclosed it to media representatives; and that they repeatedly published the conversation even though they knew or had reason to know that it had been illegally intercepted.

Under the relevant statutes, an individual violated the law by intentionally disclosing the contents of an electronic communication when he or she knows or has reason to know that the information was obtained through an illegal interception, even if the individual was not involved in that interception. The issue before the Court was the constitutionality of these statutes as applied to this case, where the Court assumed that, first, respondents played no part in the illegal interception; second, they lawfully obtained access to the tapes, although someone else had obtained the tapes unlawfully; and third, the subject matter of the conversations "were a matter of public concern," that is, that they were "newsworthy".

Justice Stevens, speaking for the Court, held the statutes unconstitutional on these facts and emphasized the narrowness of the ruling. He began by noting that *New York Times v. United States* had upheld the right of the press to publish information of great public concern obtained from documents stolen by a third party. The general rule, said the Court, is that "state action to punish the publication of truthful information seldom can satisfy constitutional standards."

The first interest that the federal and state statutes served is in removing an incentive for parties to intercept private conversations. This interest did not justify the statutes' restrictions as applied to those who were not involved in the initial illegality because the government may still prosecute the person who acted illegally.

The second interest, minimizing harm to persons whose conversations have been illegally intercepted, is considerably stronger, but still does not justify the statute in this case, because "privacy concerns give way when balanced against the interest in publishing matters of public importance." The Court did not reach the question whether the law would be constitutional as applied to "disclosures of trade secrets or domestic gossip or other information of purely private concern."

§ 16.12 Commercial Speech

(a) An Introduction

Commercial speech, such as advertising, has always been subject to substantial governmental regulation. Until the early 1970s the Court simply excluded all commercial speech, from the coverage of the First Amendment. Now commercial speech appears to be vested with extensive First Amendment protection. However, commercial speech still does not have the full First Amendment protection of political speech. The state can issue reasonable time, place, or manner regulations of commercial speech. In addition, the state has a broader power to regulate misleading commercial speech than its power to regulate political speech.

Commercial speech may be understood as any form of speech that advertises a product or service for profit or for business purpose. Commercial speech proposes a commercial transaction. This definition is not precise, and courts have not consistently applied it. Neither is it self-evident why this category of speech should be treated differently from other types of speech.

In *Valentine v. Chrestensen* (1942), an entrepreneur in New York City distributed a leaflet containing on one side an advertisement for a commercial exhibition of a former Navy submarine and on the other side a message protesting the City's denial of wharfage facilities for the exhibition. The entrepreneur was convicted of violating a sanitary code provision forbidding the distribution of advertising matter in the streets.

The Supreme Court upheld the conviction unanimously, even though, three years earlier, the Court had struck down several municipal ordinances applied to severely restrict the distribution of political or religious handbills in the streets or in house-to-house canvassing. The Court earlier had stated that "the public convenience in respect of cleanliness of the streets does not justify an exertion of the police power which invades the free communication of information and opinion secured by the Constitution." But the Court had carefully noted that it had not held "that commercial soliciting and canvassing may not be subjected to such regulation as the ordinance requires."

Chrestensen stated:

> This Court has unequivocally held that the streets are proper places for the exercise of the freedom of communicating information and disseminating opinion and that, though the states and municipalities may appropriately regulate the privilege in the public interest, they may not unduly burden or proscribe its employment in these public thoroughfares. We are equally clear that the Constitution imposes *no such restraint on government as respects purely commercial advertising*.

For many years cases relied on this simple pronouncement to exclude completely so-called "commercial speech" from any protection of the First Amendment.

The validity of *Chrestensen's* commercial speech theory was controversial, a controversy encouraged by uncertain and confusing tests used to determine when speech is commercial.

(b) The *Central Hudson* Test

The Four–Part Test of *Central Hudson*. In *Central Hudson Gas & Electric Corporation v. Public Service Commission* (1980), the Court developed an approach to commercial speech issues that the Court has employed for a quarter-century.

Central Hudson invalidated a Public Service Commission regulation that completely banned all public utility advertising promoting the use of electricity.

The Commission argued that such promotional advertising discouraged conserving energy. The Court, per Justice Powell, applied a four-part analysis to the question:

> At the outset we must determine whether the expression is protected by the First Amendment. For commercial speech to come within that provision, it at least must concern lawful activity and not be misleading. Next we ask whether the asserted governmental interest is substantial. If both inquiries yield positive answers, we must determine whether the regulation directly advances the governmental interest asserted, and whether it is not more extensive than is necessary to serve that interest.

Applying this test the *Central Hudson* Court invalidated the New York regulation. Promotional advertising is lawful commercial speech; the state interests in conservation are substantial; the ban on promotional advertising advances this ban; but the state's complete suppression of speech was more extensive than necessary to further energy conservation. For example, some promotional advertising would cause no net increase in energy use. Also more limited restrictions might promote conservation sufficiently. The state could "require that the advertisements include information about the relative efficiency and expense of the offered service, both under current conditions and for the foreseeable future."

The four-part test of *Central Hudson* is based on a two-step method of analysis synthesized from the modern commercial speech cases. First, a court must determine whether the speech is truthful, nonmisleading speech concerning a lawful commercial activity. Promotion of illegal activity therefore is not protected advertising. If the government is attempting to deter or punish false or misleading advertising it will not be subjected to overbreadth analysis and therefore will not be required to demonstrate that its law is no more extensive than necessary to achieve that goal. Second, after finding that the government regulation restricts nonmisleading commercial communications, a court must determine whether the government regulation directly advances a substantial government interest without unnecessary restrictions on the freedom of speech. The government regulation will fail if the interest is not sufficiently substantial to justify a restriction on speech or if the means used to advance a substantial interest either do not directly advance the government interest or do so with an unnecessary burden on the ability to communicate the commercial message.

The Court has often cited and applied this four-part test. However, some Justices have questioned whether it is sufficiently protective of free speech interests.

The "Least Restrictive Means" Test. The Court has refined the four-part *Central Hudson* test by amending the "least restrictive means" test so that, in commercial speech cases, the government need only show that there is a "reasonable" fit between the governmental ends and the means chosen to accomplish those ends.

Board of Trustees of the State University of New York v. Fox (1989) ruled that it was error to apply the "least restrictive means" test to commercial speech cases. Cases like *Central Hudson* do not require that government restrictions on commercial speech be "absolutely the least severe that will achieve the desired end." Rather, there must be only a "reasonable" fit—a "fit that is not necessarily perfect"—between the governmental ends and the means chosen to accomplish those ends. So long as the means are "narrowly tailored" to achieve the desired objectives, it is for the government decisionmakers to judge what manner of regulation may best be employed. The government, however, has the burden to show that its goal is "substantial" and that "the cost [has been] carefully calculated."

(c) Specific Problem Areas

ADVERTISING ILLEGAL ACTIVITIES.

In *Pittsburgh Press, Co. v. Pittsburgh Commission on Human Rights* (1973) a newspaper was charged with violating an ordinance prohibiting sex-designated help-wanted advertisements except where the employer or advertiser would be free to make hiring decisions on the basis of sex. The newspaper argued that the advertisements involved the exercise of editorial judgment as to where to place the advertisement. Therefore the advertisements, it was argued, were sufficiently noncommercial to fall within the ambit of the First Amendment. The Supreme Court disagreed.

Discrimination in employment is not only commercial activity, it is *illegal* commercial activity under the Ordinance. We have no doubt that a newspaper constitutionally could be forbidden to publish a want ad proposing a sale of narcotics or soliciting prostitutes. Nor would the result be different if the nature of the transaction were indicated by placement under columns captioned

"Narcotics for Sale" and "Prostitutes Wanted" rather than stated within the four corners of the advertisement.

The Court, while not yet rejecting *Chrestensen*, relied on a much narrower and more concrete test: if an activity is illegal, the state may prohibit advertising or touting that activity. The negative implication of this reasoning is that if the activity is legal, the state may not prohibit advertising the activity.

ADVERTISING LEGAL ACTIVITIES.

Advertisements for Abortions. *Bigelow v. Virginia* (1975) established a corollary principle that was implicit in *Pittsburgh Press*: If an activity is legal, the state cannot prohibit advertising it. In *Bigelow* a newspaper publisher had been convicted of violating a state statute outlawing advertisements that "encourage or prompt the procuring of abortion." The advertisement in question had been placed by a profit-making organization, located in New York, that had offered to arrange for legal abortions in New York. The Court held that the publisher could not be punished.

However, the Court did not rule that the advertisement was sufficiently editorial or noncommercial in nature to fall outside the ambit of *Chrestensen*. Instead, *Bigelow* reinterpreted *Chrestensen*:

> the holding [in *Chrestensen*] is distinctly a limited one: the ordinance was upheld as a reasonable regulation of the manner in which commercial advertising could be distributed. The fact that it had the effect of banning a particular handbill does not mean that *Chrestensen* is authority for the proposition that all statutes regulating commercial advertising are immune from constitutional challenge.

Advertising Prescription Drug Prices: The *Virginia Pharmacy* Case. In *Virginia State Board of Pharmacy v. Virginia Citizens Consumer Council, Inc.* (1976), a consumer group claimed that the First Amendment invalidated a statute making illegal the advertisement of prescription drug prices. The statute was defended on the grounds that it was a permissible regulation of commercial speech that had the effect of maintaining professional standards of pharmacy. Justice Blackmun, writing for the majority, held that the consuming public had a protected First Amendment interest in the free flow of truthful information concerning lawful activity.

The *Virginia State Board of Pharmacy* opinion reaffirmed the states' authority to issue regulations of the time, place, and manner of speech, if such restrictions are justified without reference to the content of the speech, serve a significant governmental interest and leave open other channels of communication. Also, the Court indicated that the government could prohibit false or even misleading speech.

In disposing of the claim that the advertising prohibition protected professional standards, the Court rejected the rationale that banning advertising was justified by the alleged salutary results—more small pharmacies, less demand for potentially dangerous drug consumption, and high public esteem for the pharmaceutical profession. Conceding the desirability of those results, the Court rejected the advertising ban as a paternalistic means of securing them. In essence, the state was taking away the consumer's ability to choose among economic decisions (where to shop, what prescription to request, and so on) by depriving him of the information needed to make these decisions intelligently. The Court did not use classical, laissez-faire economic thinking to restrict the government's ability to regulate industry, only to show that the government could not accomplish these ends by suppression of First Amendment freedoms.

After *Virginia State Board of Pharmacy* the state may reach the same policy goals as it chose to reach before, but it may not use the means of prohibiting the dissemination of truthful information about lawful activity.

Advertising Compounded Drugs. A provision of the Food and Drug Administration Modernization Act (FDAMA) prohibited advertising and promoting particular compounded drugs. Drug compounding occurs when a pharmacist or doctor combines, mixes, or alters ingredients to create a medication tailored to an individual patient's needs. Licensed pharmacies challenged this section on free speech grounds. In *Thompson v. Western States Medical Center* (2002), the Supreme Court agreed that these advertising and solicitation restrictions violated the First Amendment. Justice O'Connor, speaking for the Court, found that forbidding the advertisement of compounded drugs would prevent pharmacists with no interest in mass-producing medications, but who serve clienteles with special medical needs, from truthfully informing doctors treating those clients about the alternative drugs available through compounding.

Gambling and the *Posadas* Case. In *Posadas de Puerto Rico Associates v. Tourism Company,* Justice Rehnquist, for a bare five-Justice majority, upheld the constitutionality of a Puerto Rican statute that restricted local advertising inviting the residents of Puerto Rico to patronize gambling casinos but that did not restrict local advertising targeted at tourists, even though the local advertising aimed at the tourists may incidentally reach the hands of a resident. In fact, during oral argument before the Supreme Court, counsel for Puerto Rico said that a casino advertising in a Spanish Language Daily, with ninety-nine percent local circulation would be permitted, so long as the advertising "is addressed to tourists and not to residents." The plaintiffs attacked the statute on its face and the court rejected this facial attack.

The Court said that it applied the general principles identified in *Central Hudson*. The commercial speech in *Posadas* "concerns a lawful activity and is not misleading or fraudulent," hence, it met the first prong of the four-part test of *Central Hudson*. The governmental interest in reducing the demand for casino gambling by Puerto Rican residents because of the legislature's apparent belief that excessive casino gambling would seriously harm the health, safety, and welfare of Puerto Rican citizens is "substantial," however, and the majority believed that the challenged restrictions "directly advance" Puerto Rico's asserted interest because "the legislature's belief is a reasonable one."

The majority was unpersuaded that the challenged advertising was underinclusive merely because other kinds of gambling (such as horse racing, cockfighting, and the lottery) may be advertised to residents of Puerto Rico. First, the advertising restrictions " 'directly advance' the legislature's interest in reducing demand for games for chance," and second, the legislative interest "is not necessarily to reduce demand for all games of chance, but to reduce demand for casino gambling." That is, the majority thought that the legislature must have felt that the risks associated with casino gambling are greater because these other forms of gambling " 'have been traditionally part of the Puerto Rican's roots.' " The majority did not otherwise elaborate on why casino gambling may be different in kind from other games of chance. Nonetheless, the law, in the view of the majority, met the second and third prongs of the *Central Hudson* test.

Then, the Court turned to the fourth prong: are the restrictions no more extensive than necessary to serve the state's interest? The Court concluded that the fit between the legislature's ends and its means was close enough. The restriction, limited to advertising aimed at residents of Puerto Rico, was no more extensive than necessary to serve the governmental interest.

The majority cited with approval lower court cases approving of advertising restrictions on smoking and alcohol, and sought to distinguish *Carey v. Population Services International* (1977) (advertising of contraceptives is protected speech), and *Bigelow v. Virginia* (1975) (advertising of abortion clinic is protected speech) as cases where underlying conduct that was the subject of the advertising restrictions was constitutionally protected. "Here, on the other hand, the Puerto Rico Legislature surely could have prohibited casino gambling by the residents of Puerto Rico altogether. In our view the greater power to completely ban casino gambling necessarily includes the lesser power to ban advertising of casino gambling, and *Carey* and *Bigelow* are hence inapposite."

The *Posadas* decision has not been overruled. However, the Court never again upheld a complete ban on truthful advertising.

Restrictions on Cigarette and Tobacco Advertising. Dictum in *Posadas* may (but need not) be read to suggest that legislatures could similarly engage in a limited restriction of advertising of other subjects that the Court views as harmful, even though the activity itself may not be illegal in the particular jurisdiction, such as advertising of cigarettes, alcohol, and legal prostitution. However, the extent to which this dictum is valid is unclear.

In *Lorillard Tobacco Co. v. Reilly* (2001), manufacturers and sellers of cigarettes, smokeless tobacco products, and cigars challenged Massachusetts regulations restricting sale, promotion, and labeling of tobacco products. The purpose of these various restrictions on truthful tobacco advertising was to dampen demand for the product, particularly by minors by restricting information about it.

Justice O'Connor, writing for a majority of the Justices, concluded that: (1) the Federal Cigarette Labeling and Advertising Act (FCLAA) preempted state regulations governing outdoor and point-of-sale cigarette advertising; (2) regulations prohibiting outdoor advertising of smokeless tobacco or cigars within 1,000 feet of school or playground violated the First Amendment; (3) regulations prohibiting indoor, point-of-sale advertising of smokeless tobacco and cigars lower than 5 feet from floor of retail establishment located within 1,000 feet of school or playground violated the First Amendment; but (4) regulations requiring retailers to place tobacco products behind counters and requiring customers to have contact with salesperson before they are able to handle such products did not violate First Amendment.

In *Rubin v. Coors Brewing Co.* (1995) the Court (with no dissent) invalidated, under the First Amendment, a law that prohibited beer labels from displaying alcohol content. The government argued that the labeling ban was necessary to suppress "strength wars," whereby brewers would brag, in their advertisements, about the alcohol content of their beers. In a footnote that may overshadow the rest of the opinion, the Court acknowledged *Posadas,* found that the "greater includes lesser" argument to be mere dictum, and then specifically rejected the government's claim that "legislatures have broader latitude to regulate speech that promotes socially harmful activities, such as alcohol consumption than they have to regulate other types of speech."

Radio and Television Broadcasts of Lottery Results. *United States v. Edge Broadcasting Co.* (1993) upheld the constitutionality of federal statutes that prohibit the broadcast of lottery advertising by a broadcaster licensed in a state that does not allow lotteries; however, the federal statutes allowed such broadcasting by a broadcaster licensed in a state that sponsors a lottery, even if that signal reached into a state where lotteries were illegal.

Edge Broadcasting is a radio station licensed in North Carolina, which has no state-sponsored lottery. Indeed, participating or advertising any nonexempt raffle or lottery is a crime in that state. However, over 90% of Edge Broadcasting's listeners live in Virginia, which does sponsor a lottery. The Edge radio station, on the border between the two states, wanted to broadcast Virginia lottery advertisements.

Justice White, for the Court, applied the four-part test of *Central Hudson* and upheld the law.

First, the majority assumed, that Edge, if permitted, would broadcast nonmisleading information about the Virginia lottery, a legal activity. Second, the Court was "quite sure" that the federal government has a substantial interest in supporting the policies of nonlottery states while also not interfering with the policies of lottery states.

The third and fourth factors under *Central Hudson* basically require the court to consider the fit between the legislature's ends and the means chosen to accomplish those ends. In *Edge Broadcasting*, the majority said that "[w]e have no doubt that the statutes directly advanced the governmental interest at stake in this case." Indeed, the majority announced, without elaboration, that Congress "might have continued to ban all radio or television lottery advertisements, even by stations in States that have legalized lotteries." Applying the fourth prong of *Central Hudson*, the majority concluded that the regulations at issue were not more extensive than necessary to serve the governmental interest because, the fit, while "not necessarily perfect," was "reasonable."

Liquor Advertisements. In *Rubin v. Coors Brewing Co.* (1995) the Court invalidated a federal law that prohibited beer labels from displaying alcohol content. (This labeling law provided that it was inapplicable if state law required disclosure of alcohol content.) Justice Thomas, for the Court found that the commercial speech concerns a lawful activity and is not misleading. The Court did agree that the government has a substantial interest in the health, safety, and welfare of citizens by preventing "strength wars," among brewers competing based on the potency of their beers. However, the federal law did not "directly and materially advance" that interest because of its "overall irrationality." For example, the federal law allows disclosure of alcohol content on the labels of wine and hard liquor, and even compels disclosure for wines of more than 14% alcohol.

In *44 Liquormart, Inc. v. Rhode Island* (1996), the Court invalidated a state law banning advertisements of accurate information about retail liquor prices except at the point of sale. The Court was fragmented as to its reasoning, but no Justice dissented. Part of Justice Stevens' opinion was the opinion of the Court and part was a plurality opinion. Stevens (joined by Kennedy, Souter & Ginsburg) recognized that bans on "truthful, nonmisleading commercial messages rarely protect consumers" from deception or overreaching, but often serve only to obscure an "underlying governmental policy" that could be implemented without regulating speech. For example, in this case, the state could have promoted temperance by imposing higher taxes on liquor or by instituting educational campaigns to promote temperance. Under either alternative, there would have been no need to restrict any speech. Stevens cautioned: "The First Amendment directs us to be especially skeptical of regulations that seek to keep people in the dark for what the government perceives to be their own good."

Justice Thomas, concurring in the judgment and in parts of the Opinion of the Court, warned that when "the government's asserted interest is to keep legal users of a product or service ignorant in order to manipulate their choices in the marketplace, the balancing test" of *Central Hudson Gas* should not be applied. That asserted interest is *"per se* illegitimate" and should not be able to justify regulation of commercial speech any more than it can justify regulation of noncommercial speech.

Compelled Subsidization of Generic Advertising. In *Glickman v. Wileman Brothers & Elliott, Inc.* (1997), the Court upheld federal rules that imposed assessments on farmers and others to cover the cost of generic advertising of California nectarines, plums, and peaches. The marketing orders, pursuant to the federal law, had to be approved by affected producers who marketed at least two-thirds of the volume of the commodity. Among the collective activity that Congress authorized is any form of marketing promotion including paid advertising. Congress had concluded that this advertising served the producers' and handlers' common interest in selling particular products. Various regulations minimized the risk that the generic advertising might adversely affect the interests of any individual producer. "The central message of the generic advertising" is that "California Summer Fruits" are "wholesome, delicious, and attractive to discerning shoppers." Growers, handlers, and processors of California tree fruits challenged the validity of these orders, claiming that their forced subsidization of such generic advertising violated their rights of free speech.

The Court rejected these challenges, concluding that these marketing orders are a form of economic regulation that has displaced competition in certain markets. It was error, said the majority, to apply *Central Hudson* to this generic advertising. It was irrelevant that the Federal Government had failed to prove that generic advertising was more effective than individual advertising in increasing demand for California nectarines, plums, and peaches.

Glickman should not be read broadly. In *United States v. United Foods, Inc.* (2001) the Court agreed with mushroom producers who challenged an assessment that the Secretary of Agriculture imposed pursuant to the Mushroom Promotion, Research, and Consumer Information Act. The purpose of the assessment was to fund generic advertisements promoting mushroom sales. The Court held that the assessment requirement violated the First Amendment, where the assessments were not ancillary to a more comprehensive program restricting market autonomy, and the advertising itself was the principal object of the regulatory scheme. United Foods claimed that its branded mushrooms were better, refused to pay the assessment, and argued that the First Amendment prohibited it. The U.S. Supreme Court agreed, holding that *Glickman* did not control because the mandated payments in this case were not part of a comprehensive statutory agricultural marketing program.

As we saw in § 16.4, the speech of government entities is not subject to any First Amendment scrutiny, apart from the establishment clause. In the *United Foods* case the Court assumed that the money taken from the mushroom producers was being used to fund the speech of a private entity that promoted generic sales. The Court in *United Foods* held that the objecting growers had a right not to fund speech by private persons with which the objecting growers disagreed.

However, if the government collects taxes from the producers of a commodity, it may use the tax revenues to engage in its own speech about the commodity. One can assume that the government will take that approach, and avoid the issues that were raised in the *United Foods* case, after *Johanns v. Livestock Marketing Association* (2005). That case considered a beef promotion statute that was almost identical to the mushroom promotion statute in *United Foods*. However, as Justice Breyer said, concurring: "The 'government speech' theory the Court adopts today [in *Johanns*] was not before us in *United Foods*, and we declined to consider it when it was raised at the eleventh hour." In *Johanns* the Court accepted the argument, holding that generic advertising funded by targeted assessment on beef producers was 'government speech,' not susceptible to a First Amendment compelled-subsidy challenge.

Johanns found that the promotional campaign for beef products was true government speech, due to the Secretary of Agriculture's control over the promotional speech. Hence, beef producers had no First Amendment right to refuse to pay the assessment on cattle. In the view of the majority, the fact that the money for the beef promotional campaign came through a "targeted assessment" on those who sold cattle was irrelevant.

Attempts to Ban for Sale Signs. In *Linmark Associates, Inc. v. Township of Willingboro* (1997). The Court ruled that the First Amendment did not permit a municipality to prohibit by ordinance the posting of "For Sale" or "Sold" signs even though the town acted to stem what it perceived as the flight of white homeowners from a racially integrated community.

The *Linmark* Court was unwilling to regard the governmental objective of assuring that Willingboro remains an integrated community as sufficient to justify the ordinance. The Court rejected this rationale on two grounds, one very narrow and one much broader. First, the Court concluded that the record before it did not support the township's fears that it was experiencing panic selling by white homeowners because of a belief the township was changing from a white to a black community. More broadly, the Court found the defect in the ordinance "more basic" because if "dissemination of this information can be restricted, then every locality in the country can suppress any facts that reflect poorly on the locality, so long as a plausible claim can be made that disclosure would cause the recipients of the information to act 'irrationally.' "

In *City of Ladue v. Gilleo* (1994), Justice Stevens, for a unanimous Court, invalidated a city ordinance that banned all residential signs subject to certain exceptions: the law, for example, allowed small residential signs advertising that the property is for sale, signs for churches and schools, commercial signs in commercially zoned districts. The ordinance in question did not allow Margaret Gilleo to display an 8.5 by 11 inch sign in her window, stating: "For Peace in the Gulf." Gilleo opposed the Persian Gulf War of 1990 to 1991. The City justified the ordinance as an effort to prevent "ugliness, visual blight and clutter," because signs "tarnish the natural beauty of the landscape," and so forth.

The Court in *Gilleo* assumed that the ordinance was viewpoint and content-neutral and that the various exemptions in the ordinance reflected legitimate differences among the side of effects of various kinds of signs. The Court invalidated the law, not because of its various exemptions—that is, not because the law discriminated on the basis of the content of speech—but because the law simply prohibited too much speech. Even content-neutral restrictions are invalid if they unduly limit one's ability to engage in free expression.

Bans on Contraceptives Advertising. In *Carey v. Population Services International* (1977), the Court invalidated a prohibition of any advertisement or display of contraceptives, a product which was not only legal but constitutionally protected. The arguments that such a prohibition was necessary because advertisements would be offensive or embarrassing to some or would legitimize sexual activities were rejected as "classically not justifications. . . ."

(d) Problems Related to Lawyer Advertising

The *Bates* Case. In 1977, in *Bates v. State Bar* the Court struck down state limitations on attorney advertising. The majority noted that the case did not involve person-to-person solicitation nor advertising as to the quality of legal services, but only the question of whether lawyers may constitutionally advertise the prices of routine services, such as uncontested divorces, uncontested adoptions, simple personal bankruptcies, and changes of name. Such advertising is constitutionally protected.

The *R.M.J.* Case. *In re R.M.J.* (1982), applied *Bates* and invalidated various restrictions on lawyer advertising. Justice Powell spoke for a unanimous Supreme Court, The state supreme court had reprimanded R.M.J. because he had deviated from the precise listing of areas of practice included in the state's Rule 4 governing lawyer advertising; for example, his advertisement listed "real estate" instead of "property," and he listed "contracts," although Rule 4 did not list that latter term at all.

Because the state did not show that R.M.J.'s listing was deceptive and because the state could show no substantial interest which its restriction on advertising promoted, the Court invalidated it. Similarly the Court invalidated a part of Rule 4 prohibiting a lawyer from identifying the jurisdictions in which he is licensed to practice law. The Court also struck a prohibition against the lawyer widely mailing announcement cards to persons other than lawyers, former clients, personal friends, and relatives. These cards announced the opening of his law office. The state produced no evidence justifying such a restrictive prohibition.

Targeted Direct Mail–Advertising. *Shapero v. Kentucky Bar Association* (1988) invalidated, as a violation of free speech, state prohibitions against attorneys sending truthful, non-deceptive letters to potential clients known to face particular legal problems (i.e., targeted, direct-mail advertising). Mass mailing is a form of advertising and therefore also constitutionally protected. Given that attorneys may engage in mass mailing, it makes little sense for the state to prohibit targeted mailing, which is only a more efficient form of advertising than mass mailing. It is quite reasonable for an attorney to mail a letter only to those who are more likely to find it of interest.

Targeted Direct Mail Within 30 Days of an Accident. The ethics rules in Florida prohibited personal injury lawyers from sending targeted direct mail soliciting employment to victims and their relatives until 30 days have passed following an accident or disaster. This rule prevented the personal injury *plaintiff's* attorney from contacting the accident victim or a relative, but it imposed no restrictions on the *defense* attorney from contacting either the victim or the relative. In *Florida Bar v. Went for It, Inc.* (1995), the Court did not disturb *Shapero,* but held (5 to 4) that, even though targeted mailing is constitutionally protected, Florida may ban targeted mailing by plaintiffs' attorneys for 30 days after the cause of action has occurred. Justice O'Connor, who dissented in *Shapero,* wrote the majority opinion in *Went for It.*

Justice O'Connor, for the Court, applied the basic test advanced in *Central Hudson*, and ruled that the state had substantial interests to protect and that its restrictions were narrowly tailored to directly and substantially advance that interest.

By keeping people ignorant of the facts, the Florida rule takes away from clients the right to refuse to hire a lawyer who would send this type of targeted mailing. Meanwhile, under the Florida rule, clients are kept in the dark for 30 days while being fair game for defense lawyers, who can contact them.

The majority justified the Florida prohibition as a means to protect the public perception of lawyers. People might think better of lawyers if only they did not know the type of people that many of the lawyers are. As Justice Kennedy pointed out in his dissent, "for the first time since *Bates v. State Bar of Arizona*, the Court now orders a major retreat from the constitutional guarantees for commercial speech in order to shield its own profession from public criticism."

Advertising That a Lawyer Is a "Specialist" or "Certified." The Illinois Supreme Court promulgated ethical rules governing lawyers. These rules did not permit an attorney to hold himself out as "certified" or a "specialist" except for patent, trademark, and admiralty lawyers. Therefore the Illinois Supreme Court publicly censured Peel, an Illinois attorney, because his letterhead stated that he is certified as a civil trial specialist by the National Board of Trial Advocacy (NBTA), a bona fide private group that developed a set of objective and demanding standards and procedures for periodic certification of lawyers with experience and competence in trial work. In *Peel v. Attorney Registration and Disciplinary Commission of Illinois* the U.S. Supreme Court (five to four, with no majority opinion) reversed.

The facts on Peel's letterhead were both verifiable and true. Peel's statement of certification by a private group, the NBTA, has no more potential to mislead than an attorney advertising that he is admitted to practice before the U.S. Supreme Court, a statement the Supreme Court approved in, *In re R.M.J.* Thus, Peel's letterhead was neither actually nor inherently nor potentially misleading. If the state believes that statements of private certification might be potentially misleading, the state might be able to require a disclaimer about the certifying organization or the standards of a specialty. To require more disclosure is better than a total prohibition.

Lawyer's Designation as Certified Public Accountant and Certified Financial Planner. In *Ibanez v. Florida Department of Business and Professional Regulation, Board of Accountancy* (1994), Justice Ginsburg, for the Court, held that it violated free speech when the Florida Board of Accountancy reprimanded Silvia Ibanez, an attorney, because she truthfully stated in her advertising, that she was a Certified Public Accountant (CPA) and a Certified Financial Planner (CFP). The state Board of Accountancy licensed her as a CPA, and a bona fide private organization, not the state, licensed her as a CFP. Attorney Ibanez argued her own case.

Justice Ginsburg, for a unanimous Court, upheld Ibanez's right to use the CPA designation. "[W]e cannot imagine how consumers could be misled by her truthful representation" that she is a CPA.

The Court, seven to two, also rejected sanctions based on the fact that Ms. Ibanez had truthfully stated that she was a CFP. The Board relied on a Florida rule that prohibits the use of "specialist" unless accompanied by a disclaimer "in the immediate proximity of the statement that implies formal recognition as a specialist." It must also state that "the recognizing agency is not affiliated with or sanctioned by the state or federal government," and must set out the requirements for recognition, "including, but not limited to, education, experience[,] and testing." Justice Ginsburg, for the Court, remarked on the "failure of the Board to point to any harm that is potentially real, not purely hypothetical," and criticized the detail required on the disclaimer, which would effectively rule out use of the designation on a business card, letterhead, or yellow pages listing. She then concluded, "We have never sustained restrictions on constitutionally protected speech based on a record so bare as the one on which the Board relies here."

O'Connor, J., joined by Rehnquist, C.J., dissented on this point, arguing that the CFP designation is both inherently and potentially misleading because a private organization, not the state, confers the designation of Certified Financial Planner.

Disclosure Requirements. In *Zauderer v. Office of Disciplinary Counsel* (1985), Justice White for the Court held that the state may not discipline an attorney who solicits business by running newspaper advertisements containing nondeceptive illustrations and legal advice. The attorney in question placed an advertisement offering to represent women who had suffered injury from the Dalkon Shield Intrauterine Device. This advertisement included a drawing of the Shield and offered legal advice, such as the advice that claims may not yet be time barred. Though the legal advice regarded a specific legal problem, it was neither false not deceptive, and did not involve face-to-face solicitation.

However, the Court held that the state could discipline an attorney for failure to include in his advertisements some information reasonably necessary to make his advertisement not misleading. The lawyer advertised that he was available to represent clients on a contingent fee basis and that "if there is no recovery, no legal fees are owed by our clients." Thus, the advertisement failed to disclose that the clients might be liable for significant litigation costs even though their lawsuits were unsuccessful.

The Court first carefully distinguished between disclosure requirements and outright prohibitions of speech. A disclosure requirement prohibits no speech and the lawyer's "constitutionally protected interest in *not* providing any particular factual information in his advertising is minimal." As long as the disclosure requirements (1) are reasonably related to the state's interest in preventing deception of consumers, and, (2) there is no problem of vagueness, and, (3) they are not "unjustified or unduly burdensome," there is no First Amendment violation. This "unduly burdensome" caveat is an important one. The Supreme Court did not give regulatory authorities a blank check to make every advertisement look like a securities prospectus.

But if the disclosure requirements meet this three-part test, it is not necessary for the state to demonstrate that they are the least restrictive means to serve the state's purposes. Nor is a disclosure requirement invalid if it is underinclusive, i.e., if it does not get at all facets of the problem it is designed to ameliorate.

Solicitation of Legal Business and Face-to-Face Encounters. In the year following the *Bates* decision, the Court began to define the limits of state regulation of attorney solicitation of clients in two cases, decided the same day, in 1978, *Ohralik v. Ohio State Bar* and *In re Primus*. In so doing the majority, speaking through Justice Powell, appeared to resurrect some elements of the "commercial" speech distinction that had been discredited by the earlier cases. Justice Powell said in *Ohralik* that the distinction between other types of speech and commercial speech is a "commonsense" one, though later he stated in *Primus* that the line between commercial and noncommercial speech "will not always be easy to draw," an admission that suggests the distinction is not so commonsensical.

It is difficult to derive any specific principle of law from *Ohralik* and *Primus* because language in each case suggests both broad and narrow holdings. The decisions in the two cases, taken together, indicate that the state may regulate lawyer solicitation in order to protect the public from false or deceptive commercial practices, so long as the regulations are reasonable and are not applied to speech that does not clearly present such dangers to the public.

The *Ohralik* majority seemed careful to limit its holding to the facts before the Court. The opinion emphasized that the issue was whether the antisolicitation rule could constitutionally be applied to the appellant, and that "the appropriate focus is on appellant's conduct."

Justice Powell began the *Ohralik* opinion by summarizing in detail the appellant's outrageous in-person solicitation, and concluded by restating the factual context:

> [T]he disciplinary rules constitutionally could be applied to appellant. He approached two young accident victims at a time when they were especially incapable of making informed judgments or of assessing and protecting their own interests. He solicited Carol McClintock in a hospital room where she lay in traction and sought out Wanda Lou Holbert on the day she came home from the hospital, knowing from his prior inquiries that she had just been released. Appellant urged his services upon the young women and ... employed a concealed tape recorder, seemingly to insure that he would have evidence of Wanda's oral assent to the representation. He emphasized that his fee would come out of the recovery, thereby tempting the young women with what sounded like a cost-free and therefore irresistible offer. He refused to withdraw when Mrs. Holbert requested him to do so only a day after the initial meeting between appellant and Wanda Lou and continued to represent himself to the insurance company as Wanda Holbert's lawyer.

Justice Marshall's thoughtful concurring opinion specifically would allow "benign" commercial solicitation, that is "solicitation by advice and information that is truthful and that is presented in a noncoercive, nondeceitful and dignified manner to a potential client who is emotionally and physically capable of making a rational decision either to accept or reject the representation with respect to a legal claim or matter that is not frivolous." Nothing in the majority opinion rejects Justice Marshall's conclusions.

In the companion case, *In re Primus,* a lawyer whose firm was cooperating with the American Civil Liberties Union (ACLU) wrote to a woman who had been sterilized as a condition of receiving public medical assistance. The lawyer offered the ACLU's services to represent her. The state had disciplined the attorney for this action but the Supreme Court of the United States reversed that decision.

The Court distinguished *Ohralik* because of the nature of the interests involved. Solicitation for private gain under the circumstances of *Ohralik* could be proscribed without showing harm in a given case because the circumstances were likely to result in the misleading, deceptive, and overbearing conduct, but solicitation on behalf of nonprofit organizations which litigate as a form of political expression may be regulated only when actual harm is shown in the particular case. The Court reviewed the record in *Primus* and found nothing indicating fraud, overreaching or other behavior that the state could regulate. Consequently, it held the solicitation within the zone of political speech and association protected in *NAACP v. Button* (1963).

Justice Powell's opinion for the Court seems to emphasize two factors distinguishing *Primus* from *Ohralik:* the absence of misrepresentation and pressure tactics, and the lack of major pecuniary award. Yet a careful reading of the *Primus* opinion indicates a third, equally important factor: the form of the solicitation. In *Ohralik* the solicitation was "in-person," *face-to-face.* In *Primus,* the attorney first was invited to address a gathering of women and then sent a letter to one of them offering free representation after being advised that the woman wished to sue the doctor who had sterilized her. This "act of solicitation took the form of a letter. . . . This was not *in-person* solicitation for pecuniary gain."

Comparison of Lawyer Solicitation Cases With Accountant Solicitation Cases. The Court's deference to state regulation that limits the power of lawyers to engage in face to face, in-person solicitation of clients should be contrasted with the strict limits the Court has placed on the state powers to limit face to face, in person solicitation by accountants. In *Edenfield v. Fane* (1993), the Court invalidated a Florida ban on in-person, uninvited, direct *face-to-face* or telephone contact by Certified Public Accountants soliciting business in the business context. The Court held that, as applied, the Florida ban on CPA solicitation in the business context violated free speech. The CPA who is soliciting business intends to communicate truthful, nondeceptive information proposing a lawful commercial transaction.

Ohralik's "narrow" holding—said the Court in *Edenfield*—depended on "unique" features of in-person solicitation by lawyers.

The CPA, unlike a lawyer, is not trained in the art of persuasion. The CPA, in contrast to the lawyer, is trained in "independence and objectivity, not advocacy." In addition, the CPA's prospective clients, unlike the young accident victim in *Ohralik*, are sophisticated experienced business executives. The people whom the CPA wishes to solicit meet the CPA in their own offices, and there is no pressure to retain the CPA on the spot. *Ohralik*, in short, does not relieve the state of the obligation to prove that the preventative measures that it proposes will contribute "in a material way" to relieving a "serious" problem.

In *Friedman v. Rogers* (1979), the Court held that Texas constitutionally could prohibit the practice of optometry under a trade name, assumed name, or corporate name.

In upholding the ban on trade names the majority refrained from establishing rigid rules for the regulation of commercial speech.

Although the Court did not establish rigid categories of commercial speech, the *Friedman* majority indicated that there would be a distinction in the degree of permissible government regulation related to the types of commercial speech. For regulations of commercial speech that contain explicit product, price, or service information the state must demonstrate a clear relationship between the regulation and the avoidance of false, deceptive, or misleading practices. If it cannot do so, the state must demonstrate that the regulation of this commercial speech is a demonstrably reasonable restriction of the time, place, or physical manner of the commercial expression. However when the "commercial speech" conveys less substantive information the government has greater latitude in regulating the speech because, in the view of the majority, the state need not tolerate practices with little or no communicative content that might be used in a deceptive or misleading manner, even though the possible deception could also be cured by less drastic means, for example, if the state were to require the publication of additional information to clarify or offset the effects of the spurious communication.

News Racks on Sidewalks. In *City of Cincinnati v. Discovery Network, Inc.* (1993), the Court invalidated a Cincinnati ordinance that prohibited the distribution of commercial handbills on public property. The City applied this ordinance to require the removal of those news racks on the city sidewalks that contained so-called "commercial" publications (such as free magazines advertising real estate sales), but the city did not extend the ban to similar news racks containing newspapers.

Applying *Central Hudson*, the Court invalidated the city's ban. It concluded, first, that the city had the burden to establish a "reasonable fit" between its legitimate interests in safety and esthetics and its choice of a limited and selective prohibition of news racks as the means chosen to serve those legitimate interests. Second, Cincinnati did not meet its burden of establishing a "reasonable fit." Cincinnati's equivocal distinction that it attempted to draw between newspapers and commercial handbills "bears no relationship *whatsoever* to the particular interests that the city has asserted."

The city has a valid concern with the aggregate number of news racks on the streets, but not with their contents, because each news rack, whether it contains "newspapers" or "commercial handbills" is equally unattractive. Even if it were assumed that the city could ban all news racks on public property, that would not justify the discriminatory ban (based on the content of the news racks) that the city imposed.

§ 16.13　Group Libel Laws

Beauharnais v. Illinois (1952) upheld a state law making it a *crime* to libel a class of citizens on the basis of factors such as race or religion. Justice Frankfurter, for the Court, upheld the statute in a broad holding stating that libelous, insulting, or fighting words are not constitutionally protected speech. State statutes that curtail group libel do not raise a constitutional problem, he proclaimed, unless they are a "wilful and purposeless restriction unrelated to the peace and well being of the state."

The dissenting views in *Beauharnais* were a precursor to the future position of the Court concerning libel. Justice Douglas argued that the expansion of individual and criminal libel to include group libel constituted an invasion of free expression that should occur only in circumstances wherein the "peril of speech must be clear and present ... raising no doubts as to the necessity of curbing speech in order to prevent disaster." Free expression is more important than vindicating reputation, Justice Black argued, because of the "unequivocal First Amendment command that its defined freedoms shall not be abridged."

As we shall see in the next section, the views of Justices Black and Douglas, to a great extent, have prevailed in later cases. And while the Court has never explicitly overruled *Beauharnais*, it should be impossible to reach its results under the modern cases.

§ 16.14　*New York Times v. Sullivan* and Libel of a Public Official

(a) The Case

In *New York Times Co. v. Sullivan* (1964), the Court held that constitutional protections for speech and press limit state powers to award damages in libel actions brought by public officials against critics of official conduct.

Sullivan, one of three elected commissioners of Montgomery, Alabama, brought the action against four individuals and the *New York Times*, claiming he had been libeled in two paragraphs of a full page advertisement. Even though he was not mentioned by name in the advertisement, Sullivan recovered $500,000 damages against the *New York Times*, based on a state legal doctrine whereby criticism of the Montgomery Police Department was transmuted to criticism of him as the official in charge. The state court instructed the jury that such criticism was libel per se. Under such instruction Sullivan need only prove that the statement was false and that it referred to him.

The Supreme Court reversed in a holding broader than was strictly necessary given the facts of the case. The Court reasoned that a state must safeguard freedom of speech and press in its libel laws as required by the First Amendment as applied to the states through the Fourteenth Amendment.

The Test Under *New York Times*. The Court drew an analogy to the Sedition Act of 1798, an early attempt to prohibit criticism of the government. State statutes punishing libel of public officials must likewise be restricted by the First Amendment, for a broad libel law serving to protect public officials from criticism is closely analogous to the Sedition Laws. The Alabama statute did provide for a defense of truth, but given the importance of safeguarding the "breathing space" necessary so as not to discourage valid criticism of public officials, a "defense for erroneous statements honestly made" was essential.

Given this basic policy, the Court laid out the standard for recovery of any alleged defamatory falsehood relating to a public official's conduct. First, the defamatory statement would have to relate to the individual plaintiff-government official; no generalized criticism of government policy could be punished, for that would constitute a sedition action.

Second, plaintiff would also have the burden of proving that the statement was false.

Third, the plaintiff must allege and prove that the defendant had made the defamatory statements with "malice."

Fourth, the plaintiff must prove all elements of the case by clear and convincing evidence.

The Requirement of *New York Times* "Malice." The Court defined "actual malice" as "knowledge that [the defamation that was published] was false or with reckless disregard of whether it was false or not." While the Court used the word "malice," it was not referring to the old, common law libel meaning of "malice" as hatefulness or ill will; rather, from its definition, the Court meant "*scienter.*"

(b) *New York Times* Scienter

This scienter requirement was clearly applied in *Garrison v. Louisiana* (1964). There the Supreme Court struck down a Louisiana statute that permitted liability for true statements about public officials made negligently, "not made in the reasonable belief of its truth," or made with "actual malice" in the common law sense. The Court reiterated that only the knowing or reckless falsehood could be subject to civil or criminal sanction.

The standard is that the defendant must have known that the statement was false, or must have had serious doubts as to the statement's truth and have published it despite these doubts.

"Reckless disregard" means that the defendant has a "high degree of awareness" of probably falsity or has "entertained serious doubts" as to the truth of his or her publication. It is not enough for the plaintiff to show that the newspaper wished to promote the candidacy of someone opposed to plaintiff, or that the newspaper wished to increase its circulation, or that the newspaper engaged in an "extreme departure from professional standard", or that the newspaper bore ill-will towards the plaintiff.

(c) Burden of Proof

Convincing Clarity. According to *New York Times v. Sullivan*, plaintiff bears the burden of proving actual malice with "convincing clarity." This standard is somewhere between "preponderance of the evidence" and "beyond a reasonable doubt," because later the Court uses the term "clear and convincing," a standard of proof that historically has required plaintiff in a civil case to bear more of a burden than a bare "preponderance."

Appellate Review. Appellate courts must independently review a trial court finding of actual malice to determine whether the finding that the defendant acted with actual malice in publishing a knowing or reckless falsehood was established by clear and convincing evidence.

(d) Public Officials

A special reason for the constitutional restriction on libel laws is that they might deter criticism of official conduct. The Court later extended the *New York Times* privilege by expanding the definition of "public official" to include those who were candidates for public office and to statements that did not relate to official conduct but did relate to fitness for office. The Court also included certain non-elected officials in the expanded definition of "public official."

The breadth of the concept of "public official" is illustrated in *Rosenblatt v. Baer* (1966), where the Court applied the *New York Times* privilege to the discharged supervisor of a county-owned ski resort. The Court held that in order to encourage criticism of government, the "public official" designation must apply "at the very least to those among the hierarchy of government employees who have, or appear to the public to have, substantial responsibility for or control over the conduct of governmental affairs."

(e) Actual Damages, Punitive Damages, and a Right of Retraction

Punitive Damages. If the plaintiff in a libel action is a public official within the doctrine of *New York Times v. Sullivan*, or a public figure within the meaning of later case law that has extended *New York Times v. Sullivan* to those who assume "roles of especial prominence in the affairs of society"—then that plaintiff (suing on a matter of public concern) cannot collect actual damages (a monetary award based on injury proven at trial), punitive damages or damages not supported by the evidence (i.e., presumed damages) unless the plaintiff can prove *New York Times* "malice."

Rights of Reply & Retraction. The Supreme Court in *Miami Herald Publishing Co. v. Tornillo* (1974) held that it is unconstitutional for a state to force a newspaper to give a political candidate a right to equal space in order to reply to attacks on his record. But the Supreme Court has never ruled out the possibility that a court could order a retraction statement from a person who is found (under the proper standard for the case) to have defamed another.

In *Tornillo* Justices Brennan and Rehnquist have noted that the constitutional prohibition on "right of reply" statutes does not suggest that a right of retraction statute would be forbidden.

Prior Restraints and Injunctive Relief in Defamation Cases.

The California courts granted injunctive relief to the late attorney Johnny Cochran against an individual who attended public appearances of Mr. Cochran and held up signs, or distributed information, with false derogatory remarks about Mr. Cochran, whose defamation suit met the strict standards of *New York Times v. Sullivan*. He could have received a monetary award against the defendant, a former client. However, the defendant who issued the false defamatory statements was unlikely to be deterred by a monetary award, because he had very little financial resources. The California courts issued an injunction prohibiting the would-be speaker from engaging in speech activities that mirrored his prior defamatory statements.

While the case was pending in the U.S. Supreme Court, Mr. Cochran died; the Supreme Court remanded the case to the state courts for a determination of whether the issue had become moot or whether Mr. Cochran's family would be able to enjoin the individual from making any further statements that impugned Mr. Cochran's character). *Tory v. Cochran* (2005). If the injunction were to remain in effect, it would raise a very serious issue regarding the use of prior restraints in defamation cases.

§ 16.15   Libel of Public Figures

The *New York Times v. Sullivan* doctrine and its requirement of "actual malice," that is, scienter, applies to alleged defamations against people who do not fit into the definition of "public official" but who are nonetheless "public figures."

In *Gertz v. Robert Welch, Inc.* (1974), the Court has explained:

"For the most part [public figures are] those who attain this status [by assuming] roles of especial prominence in the affairs of society. Some occupy positions of such persuasive power and influence that they are deemed public figures for all purposes. More commonly, those classed as public figures have thrust themselves to the forefront of particular public controversies in order to influence the resolution of the issues involved."

Hustler Magazine v. Falwell (1988) held that the First and Fourteenth Amendments forbid a public figure from recovering damages for intentional infliction of emotional distress. The plaintiff, the Reverend Jerry Falwell, a nationally known televangelist, sued Hustler Magazine because it featured a parody of an advertisement that portrayed him and his mother as drunk and immoral. The parody was labeled as a parody, and the jury found that it could not be reasonably understood as describing any actual facts.

The Court held that public figures—and also public officials—cannot recover damages for intentional infliction of emotional distress without also showing that the publication contains a false statement "of fact" made with actual knowledge that the statement was false or with reckless disregard of whether or not it was true. In this case, the parody could not reasonably be understood by readers to be a factual statement about Reverend Falwell, so no damages could be awarded.

§ 16.16   Libel of Private Individuals

(a) *Time, Inc. v. Hill*

Because of their general fame and notoriety both Walker and Butts could be considered public figures for all purposes. In *Time, Inc. v. Hill* (1967) the Supreme Court faced the issue of a private individual being thrust into the limelight for the purpose of one particular event. In 1952, the Hill family had been the subject of national news coverage when three escaped convicts held them hostage in their home. The incident was fictionalized in a play, and in 1955 Life Magazine published a picture story that showed the play's cast re-enacting scenes from the play in the former Hill house.

The Hills sued on the basis of a New York state privacy statute that made truth a complete defense but allowed a privacy action to "newsworthy people" or "events" in case of "[m]aterial and substantial falsification." However, the Supreme Court applied the *New York Times* standard of "knowing or reckless falsity" to alleged defamations concerning false reports of matters of public interest. However, later cases allowed private persons to collect actual damages for false factual statements that were made negligently.

(b) *Gertz v. Robert Welch, Inc.*

In *Gertz v. Robert Welch, Inc.* (1974), the Court created a third category within which the *New York Times v. Sullivan* doctrine applied: private citizens who obviously are not public officials and who are not public enough to be public figures for all purposes, may be public figures with respect to a particular controversy.

A person is not to be considered a public figure for the purpose of libel actions absent clear evidence of general fame and notoriety in the community or the assumption of roles of special prominence in the affairs of society. But even though one is not a public figure for all purposes, one may be a public figure for a particular incident. The Court did not exclude the possibility that a private person, involuntarily, could be caught up in a public issue so as to be a public figure. But that is an unlikely scenario.

The Burden of Proof Standard Against Private Persons. Actual damages are those monetary awards that are based on proof of damage that was offered at trial. If the plaintiff is a truly private person in a libel action, the plaintiff can collect actual money damages on the basis of defendant's negligence, if state law so provides. *Gertz* provides that a state could not provide a more favorable standard for libel plaintiffs: strict liability for defamatory speech would not be tolerated.

The Burden of Proof on the Issue of Falsity. In a *Gertz* situation, the plaintiff must not only prove negligence; the plaintiff, in general, has the burden of proving falsity. There can be no common law presumption that defamatory speech is false. Because of the need to encourage debate on public issues, it is unconstitutional for the state to shift the burden of proving falsity to the defendant.

Although *Gertz* also held that a private individual must prove actual damages in order to recover under a standard requiring less than knowing or reckless falsity in a libel action, the Court defined actual damages quite broadly to include not only out-of-pocket loss but also "impairment of reputation and standing in the community, personal humiliation, and mental anguish and suffering."

In order for a private individual who has been libeled to collect punitive damages the Constitution requires that such a plaintiff prove that the defendant engaged in *New York Times* "malice." Under the First Amendment, states may not permit recovery of presumed or punitive damages, "at least when liability is not based on a showing of knowledge of falsity or reckless disregard for the truth."

(c) *Time, Inc. v. Firestone*

In *Time, Inc. v. Firestone* (1976), a libel action was brought after Time Magazine reported that plaintiff's husband divorced her "on grounds of extreme cruelty and adultery." The state court had actually granted the divorce on the grounds that "neither party is domesticated, within the meaning of that term as used by the Supreme Court of Florida."

The Court decided that the *Gertz* standards [rather than *New York Times* scienter] should be the standard of recovery in the case; plaintiff's role in Palm Beach society did not make her a "public figure" for the purpose of the libel action, nor did plaintiff "thrust herself to the forefront of any particular public controversy in order to influence the resolution of the issues involved in it." The Court said that a "public controversy" is not *any* controversy of interest to the public.

Significantly the Court also said that Ms. Firestone's several press conferences during divorce proceedings did not convert her into a "public figure." The press conferences were not an attempt to influence the outcome of the divorce proceedings nor were they an attempt to influence the outcome of some unrelated controversy, according to the Court.

(d) *Dun & Bradstreet, Inc. v. Greenmoss Builders, Inc.*

In *Dun & Bradstreet, Inc. v. Greenmoss Builders, Inc.* (1985) Justice Powell, joined by Justices Rehnquist and O'Connor, wrote a plurality opinion. Chief Justice Burger and Justice White each wrote separate opinions concurring in the judgment, and Justice Brennan, joined by Justices Blackmun, Marshall, and Stevens, dissented.

In this case plaintiff was a construction contractor who discovered that Dun & Bradstreet, a credit reporting agency, had, on July 26, 1976, sent a report to five of its subscribers. This report mistakenly indicated that the contractor had filed a petition for voluntary bankruptcy. The contractor learned of this error on the same day, when the president of the contracting company talked to its bank about financing. The contractor called Dun & Bradstreet's regional office, explained the error, asked for a correction, and asked for the names of the firms to whom Dun & Bradstreet sent the false credit report. Dun & Bradstreet promised to look into the matter but refused to divulge the names of the recipients of the credit report. About one week after Dun & Bradstreet released the incorrect credit report to the five subscribers, it issued a corrective notice on or about August 3, 1976. It reported that one of the contractor's former employees, not the contractor, had filed for bankruptcy, and that the contractor "continued in business as usual." The contractor again asked for the list of subscribers and Dun & Bradstreet refused.

The contractor then sued in Vermont state court for defamation. The trial established that Dun & Bradstreet's error occurred when one of its employees (a 17 year old high school student) inadvertently misattributed the bankruptcy filing of the contractor's former employee to the contractor. Dun & Bradstreet did not check the accuracy of this report, though it was routine to do so.

The trial judge gave the jury instructions that failed to define many of the crucial terms. The trial judge did tell the jury that the credit report was libelous per se and that the plaintiff was not required to prove actual damages "since damage and loss [are] conclusively presumed." The trial court also permitted the jury to award presumed and punitive damages without proof of scienter. The jury awarded $50,000 in so-called "compensatory" or presumed damages and $300,000 in punitive damages. The Supreme Court, with no majority opinion, affirmed this award.

The Powell Plurality: Speech Involving Matters of Public Concern. Justice Powell's opinion, joined only by Justices Rehnquist and O'Connor, concluded that in all of the previous cases where the Court found constitutional limits to state libel laws, the speech involved expression "on a matter of public concern," or *"public speech."* These Justices believed that because speech on matters of "purely private" concern is of less First Amendment concern, "the state's interest [in reputation] adequately supports awards of presumed and punitive damages—even absent a showing of 'actual malice.'" They reasoned the plaintiff could collect "presumed" damages because proof of actual damage is often impossible and yet plaintiffs reputation has been tarnished. So a jury should be allowed to presume damages.

Justices Powell, Rehnquist and O'Connor clearly concluded that plaintiffs could collect punitive and presumed damages without any showing of "actual malice" or *New York Times* scienter if the alleged defamation did not involve a matter of "public concern." They did not discuss whether a plaintiff in such circumstances could collect presumed or punitive damages in the absence of even negligence on the part of the defendant. *Gertz v. Robert Welch* had required proof of negligence before a private person could collect damages for defamation, but Justices Powell, Rehnquist, and O'Connor explicitly limited *Gertz* as a case that "involved expression on a matter of undoubted public concern." Thus, for these three Justices, it may well be the case that if the speech did not involve a matter of public concern, they would allow plaintiff to collect presumed or punitive damages without proof of any kind of fault on the part of the defendant. Justice White's separate opinion concurring in the judgment so concluded.

Public Officials and Matters Not of Public Concern. There is nothing in the Powell plurality that would limit its application to cases where the plaintiff is a private person. That is, for the three Justices who make up the Powell plurality, it may well be the case that a public official or public figure could also collect presumed or punitive damages without even showing any negligence on the part of the defendant if the alleged defamation does not involve a matter of "public concern."

Defining a Matter of Public Concern. The final question for the Powell plurality was whether the credit report involved a matter of public concern. The Powell plurality argued that it did not.

First, the Powell plurality announced that the credit report concerned "no public issue. It was speech solely in the individual interest of the speaker and its specific business audience." From this statement one might be tempted to conclude that all credit reports or all commercial speech are in the category of reduced free speech protection as involving matters not of "public concern." But the Powell plurality, without discussion, specifically rejected that conclusion. Some credit reports are of public concern; some are not. "The protection to be accorded a particular credit report depends on whether the report's 'content, form, and context' indicate that it concerns a public matter."

Secondly, the Powell plurality relied on the fact that the credit report was made available only to five subscribers who were under contract not to disseminate it further: the confidential nature of the communication is evidence that it does not involve a matter of public concern. The anomaly created by Justice Powell's argument is that to the extent that the defendant's alleged libel is not treated confidentially, it is more likely to be protected by *Gertz* and *New York Times v. Sullivan*; to the extent that the defendant takes care not to spread the alleged defamatory remarks, he is more likely subject to liability.

Finally, the Powell plurality believed that speech involving credit reporting is likely not to be chilled by libel laws because the free market already provides many incentives to be accurate "since false credit reporting is of no use to creditors." However, that free market check would seem to undercut the need for libel protection.

The Burger and White Opinions. Chief Justice Burger concurred in the judgment. He had dissented in *Gertz* and now would overrule it. He also argued that *New York Times* should be reexamined.

Justice White also concurred in the judgment. Like Burger, he had dissented in *Gertz* and still believed that decision was wrong. He had joined the Court in *New York Times v. Sullivan* but he "came to have increasing doubts about the soundness of the Court's approach and about some of the assumptions underlying it." He suggested "that the press would be no worse off financially if the common-law rules were to apply and if the judiciary was careful to insist that damage awards be kept within bounds."

The Dissent. Justice Brennan's dissent would have applied *Gertz* to the facts of this case. And he criticized the five members of the Court who, in three different opinions, affirmed the damage award but "have provided almost no guidance as to what constitutes a protected 'matter of public concern.' "

The Future of the "Public Concern" Doctrine. Nearly a decade and half before the Supreme Court plurality decision in *Dun & Bradstreet* another plurality of the Court in *Rosenbloom v. Metromedia, Inc.* (1971) tried to offer *New York Times* protection for defendants who made defamatory statements about private individuals when those statements were related to matters of "public concern." In that case Justices Marshall, Stewart and Harlan in dissent warned that courts are not equipped for such an ill-defined task inevitably involving ad hoc balancing. Courts "will be required to somehow pass on the legitimacy of interest in a particular event or subject; what information is relevant to self-government. The danger such a doctrine portends for freedom of the press seems apparent." Judges are not able to determine what is "public concern" without examining the contents of the speech and then applying their subjective judgments.

It may well be that the road the Powell plurality in *Dun & Bradstreet* seeks to travel will end in a dead end, as it did the last time the Court took that route.

(e) Libel for Assertions of Fact versus Statements of Opinion

A plaintiff should not be able to bring a libel action merely when he is complaining that someone defamed him by publicizing an unflattering opinion. Any defamation action, in order to meet any First Amendment standard, must be based on a false factual assertion.

In *Milkovich v. Lorain Journal Co.* (1990), the Court, speaking through Chief Justice Rehnquist, rejected any artificial dichotomy between "opinion" and "fact." There is no "wholesale defamation exemption for anything that might be labeled 'opinion.' "In this case a newspaper columnist wrote an article implying that a local high school wrestling coach lied under oath in a judicial proceeding about an altercation involving his team at a home wrestling match. The article, for example, said that "Anyone who attended the meet ... knows in his heart that Milkovich and Scott lied at the hearing after each having given his solemn oath to tell the truth."

§ 16.17   Rights of Privacy and Rights of Publicity

Publication of "Private" Truthful Details. May the state, to protect an individual's privacy, prohibit the publication of information that is true but that admittedly relates to and infringes on private matters? This general issue was raised in *Cox Broadcasting Corp. v. Cohn* (1975) but the Court decided the case on narrow grounds.

Cohn, father of a deceased rape victim, brought suit against an Atlanta, Georgia, television station after a news broadcast reported the name of his victim-daughter. The television station obtained the name from judicial records open to public inspection and maintained in connection with public prosecution.

The Supreme Court held that a state may not impose liability for public dissemination of true information derived from official court records open to public inspection. The Supreme Court confined its holding to the narrow facts of the case—accurate republication of information in court records lawfully available to the public.

Cox Broadcasting reserved the question whether truth must be recognized as a defense in a defamation action brought by a truly private person (as distinguished from a public official or public figure).

Landmark Communications, Inc. v. Virginia (1978) answered one of the questions reserved in *Cox Broadcasting Corp.* when the Court held that the First Amendment prohibits the criminal punishment of persons (including newspapers) who are not participants to a judicial disciplinary inquiry from divulging or publishing truthful information regarding confidential proceedings of the judicial inquiry board. The Court found it unnecessary to hold broadly that truthful reporting about public officials in connection with their official duties is always insulated from criminal punishment by the First Amendment, nor did the Court consider any special right of access to the press or the applicability of the state confidentiality statutes to one who secures the information by illegal means and thereafter divulges it.

The Right of Publicity. In *Zacchini v. Scripps–Howard Broadcasting Co.* (1977) the Court upheld, in a five to four decision, the power of the state to allow a damage action brought by a performer against the operator of a television broadcasting station when it telecast a videotape of the plaintiff's entire 15 second act. The majority stressed that it was the entire act that was telecast. Plaintiff was a "human cannonball" who was shot from a cannon into a net at a county fairgrounds. The videotaping was done after Zacchini had asked the freelance reporter not to do it.

The majority divided privacy into four branches. (1) *Time, Inc. v. Hill* was a "false-light" privacy case; (2) an appropriation of a name or likeness for the purposes of trade; or (3) publicizing private details about a non-newsworthy person or event; or (4) a performer with a name having commercial value with a claim to a "right of publicity."

The plaintiff, Zacchini, fell into the fourth category of a person with a right to publicity, and the majority found that the unauthorized telecast of his entire performance (even though accompanied by favorable commentary) injured his propriety interest. Without violating free speech guarantees, the state need not, but may, protect this interest, which the Court found analogous to the goals of the copyright and patent laws.

It is unclear, given the majority's emphasis on the telecast of the "entire" performance, whether *Zacchini* has any application to cases where the videotaping is less than the entire act. Even in Zacchini's case, Justice Powell's dissent noted that the plaintiff-Zacchini might not be able to bring himself within the Court's holding because it is unlikely that the "entire" act took only 15 seconds. Fanfare likely accompanied it.

Zacchini was also unclear about the measure of damages in the case. The majority simply said that Zacchini had to prove his damages. Monetary damages would not exist if the defendant's news broadcast increased the value of Zacchini's performance by stimulating the public's interest in seeing the live act.

Free Speech and Copyright Laws

There is an inevitable tension between copyright protection and free speech. One cannot consider in detail all of this tension, for that would require a careful analysis of the entire statutory law of copyright.

To some extent, of course, copyright protects free speech, because it protects the value in speech created by authors.

Harper & Row, Publishers, Inc. v. Nation Enterprises (1985), held that *The Nation* Magazine violated the copyright laws when it published, without permission, extensive quotations from a purloined copy of former President Ford's then unpublished memoirs, "A Time to Heal." The Court held that *The Nation*'s "generous verbatim excerpts" were, under the circumstances, a copyright infringement that was not sanctioned as a "fair use" under the Copyright Act. The Court rejected the argument that the First Amendment protected copyright law violations simply because the information conveyed is of high public concern.

In *San Francisco Arts & Athletics, Inc. v. United States Olympic Committee* (1987), a divided Court offered broad protection for the United States Olympic Committee (USOC) and the International Olympic Committee in their use of the word "Olympics." Section 110 of the Amateur Sports Act of 1978 grants to the USOC the right to prohibit (without its consent) any person from using the word "Olympic" for the "purpose of trade, to induce the sale of any goods or services, or to promote any theatrical exhibition, athletic performance, or competition." San Francisco Arts & Athletics, Inc. (SFAA), a nonprofit corporation, sought to promote the "Gay Olympic Games" in 1982 and every four years thereafter. The Gay Games were touted as opening with a ceremony that "will rival the traditional Olympic Games." The winners of the various contests would receive gold, silver, and bronze medals. The SFAA proposed to sell T-shirts, buttons and other items, all showing the title "Gay Olympic Games."

At the request of the USOC the district court enjoined the use of the word "Olympic" in the description of the planned games (which were then held under the name "Gay Games I," in 1982, and "Gay Games II" in 1986). The Supreme Court, in a divided opinion, affirmed.

Justice Powell, for the Court, concluded that Congress intended to provide the USOC with protection broader than normal trademark protection in that the USOC has "exclusive control of the use of the word 'Olympic' *without* regard to whether an unauthorized use of the word tends to cause confusion." In addition, an unauthorized user of "Olympic" would not have the normal statutory trademark defenses. Nonetheless, the Court noted, given that the SFAA sought to sell T-shirts, bumper stickers, etc., all emblazoned with "Gay Olympic Games," the "possibility of confusion as to sponsorship is obvious."

The Court said that section 110 "extends to promotional uses of 'Olympic' even if the promotion is not used to induce the sale of goods." The Court then added language that narrowed its holding: under section 110, "the USOC may prohibit purely promotional uses of the word *only* when the promotion relates to an athletic or theatrical event. The USOC created the value of the word by using it in connection with an athletic event."

The Court did not decide whether Congress could ever grant a private entity exclusive use of a generic word, because, the Court said, "Olympic" is not generic. The Court found that it was reasonable for Congress to conclude that the commercial and promotional value of the word "Olympic" was the product of the USOC's own talents and energy. The USOC and the International Olympic Committee have used the word "Olympic" since 1896, when the modern Olympic Games began. Congress could reasonably conclude that the word has acquired a special "secondary meaning." Thus, Congress could grant the USOC a "limited property right" in the word "Olympic."

In addition, the majority argued, Congress acted reasonably when it did not require the USOC to prove that an unauthorized use of "Olympic" is likely to confuse the public. The Congressional prohibition did not prevent the SFAA from holding its athletic event in its planned format. Section 110 may not even restrict purely expressive uses of the word "Olympic." The Congressional restrictions on the use of "Olympic" are incidental to the primary Congressional purpose of encouraging and rewarding the USCC's activities.

§ 16.18 Fighting Words and Hostile Audiences

(a) In General

The Court allows government regulation of speech when the purpose of the statute is to prohibit "fighting words." While the definition of this phrase is discussed below, it is important, in understanding this doctrine, to understand the rationale that supports it. The traditional hypothetical situation of the individual shouting "fire" in a crowded theater illustrates the dichotomy between action and speech.

In one sense, a "fighting words" conviction regulates speech because "fighting words" are still just words. Yet fighting words also can be an incitement to unthinking, immediate, violent *action*, just like falsely shouting fire in a crowded theater immediately incites action (that is, a riot). The immediate reaction means that there is no time to debate, to trust the free marketplace of ideas. The state's interest in order overshadows the minimal protection to be afforded the "slight social value as a step to truth" of the speech.

Chaplinsky v. New Hampshire (1942), unanimously upheld a statute previously construed by the state court to ban "face-to-face words plainly likely to cause a breach of the peace by the address-ee." Chaplinsky's conviction was based on his face-to-face encounter with the City Marshal of Rochester whom he described as a "God damned racketeer and a damned fascist" as a policeman was leading Chaplinsky away from a public sidewalk because of fear that his distribution of religious literature was causing a public disturbance. Justice Murphy, for the Court, stated in dictum that " 'fighting' words—those which by their very utterance inflict injury or *tend to incite* an *immediate* breach of the peace"—are not constitutionally protected because their slight social value as a step to truth is "clearly outweighed by the social interest in order and morality."

Chaplinsky's basic test was whether or not people of common intelligence would understand the words as likely to cause the average addressee to fight. The Court gave no real consideration whether fire marshals or policemen should be expected to resist epithets that would produce violent responses in the average citizen who has not been trained to prevent breaches of the peace. That would be left to later cases.

Later cases recognize the potential social value in statements that might come under the initial definition of "fighting words." The Court did not overrule *Chaplinsky*, but narrowed its scope.

Terminiello v. Chicago (1949) overturned a municipal ordinance prohibiting breaches of the peace. The trial court's instruction to the jury construed the statute as prohibiting conduct that "stirs the public to anger, invites dispute, brings about a condition of unrest or creates a disturbance." Terminiello's address was a denunciation of Jews and persons of color. Outside of the auditorium where he spoke, a "howling" crowd gathered in protest and he denounced them as well. The majority opinion by Justice Douglas invalidated the statute as vague and overbroad, which allowed the Court to avoid the more difficult question of whether the First Amendment protected the speech. The strong language of the majority opinion did, however, indicate a retreat from the *Chaplinsky* "uncontrollable impulse" test by recognizing that a certain amount of provocative and challenging speech is protected.

Feiner v. New York (1951) upheld the conviction of petitioner under a state disorderly conduct statute. *Feiner* directly raised the question of the hostile audience. Feiner's address included descriptions of President Truman as a "bum", the mayor of Syracuse as a "champagne sipping bum", and the American Legion as a "Nazi Gestapo." Some of the onlookers made remarks to the police about their inability to handle the crowd and at least one threatened violence if the police did not act. There were others who appeared to be favoring petitioner's arguments." The police asked Feiner to stop, but he refused. After their request, the officer arrested Feiner, who had been speaking for over a half hour. The Chief Justice Vinson's majority opinion stressed that the arrest was not an attempt to censor the content of the speech, but an effort to protect the peace before the threatened violent reaction took place.

In *Feiner,* Justices Douglas and Black dissented vigorously, arguing that the minimal threat of violence was insufficient to justify this suppression. Moreover, both Douglas and Black emphasized that the first duty of the police is to protect the speaker's rights by dissuading those threatening violence, an attempt not evidenced in this case.

Later cases adopted Justice Black's view that the government could only order persons to stop speaking if, with reasonable effort, the government could not prevent violence by the audience.

Edwards v. South Carolina (1963), for example, involved a civil rights demonstration on the grounds of the state legislature. Although the state officials and lower courts found that the crowd observing the demonstration was growing increasingly restive, and the demonstrators refused to leave when requested, the Court (in 1963) refused to consider the conduct of the demonstrators—the singing of religious and patriotic hymns and a "religious harangue" urging them to go to segregated lunch counters—to constitute "fighting words." Neither did the "hostile audience" doctrine apply.

Although the situation in *Edwards* might have been potentially more dangerous than that of *Feiner*, the Court appreciated the ability of an expansive *Feiner* doctrine to suppress civil rights demonstrations by persons falsely claiming that their emotions were uncontrollably aroused. As a factual matter the Court found the situation in *Edwards* a "far cry" from the hostile audience problem in *Feiner*. Recall that the Court had found that Mr. Feiner was seeking to incite a riot.

It is important to distinguish *Terminiello, Feiner,* and *Edwards* from *Chaplinsky,* which involved *face-to-face* confrontation where insults were delivered that were likely to provoke violence by the listeners. The harangues delivered in the other cases were not personally directed to particular members of the audience—"fighting words," a *face-to-face* confrontation with particular members of the audience.

Cohen v. California (1971), provides important support for this distinction and leaves the authority of *Feiner* in a questionable state. *Cohen* was convicted for breach of the peace based on his presence in a Los Angeles courthouse wearing a jacket bearing the clearly printed words "Fuck the Draft."

The Court recognized that people in public places must be subject to some objectionable speech, but they could simply avert their eyes and ears. The Court, in the majority opinion of Justice Harlan, stated that—

> [T]he ability of government, consonant with the Constitution, to shut off discourse solely to protect others from hearing it is ... dependent on a showing that substantial privacy interests are being invaded in an essentially intolerable manner.

The fact that an offensive expletive was utilized does not detract from the protection afforded the speech, because, in Justice Harlan's phrase, "one man's vulgarity is another's lyric." Moreover, the offensive words were not "a direct personal insult" specifically directed at the hearer; neither was the state exercising its police power (as in *Feiner*) "to prevent a speaker from intentionally provoking a given group to a hostile reaction."

The *Cohen* limitations weakened *Chaplinsky* substantially. *Cohen* requires a critical examination of the audience, the results of the speech, the length of the speech, the actual results of the speech, and the wording of the statute:

> [W]e do not think the fact that some unwilling "listeners" in a public building may have been briefly exposed to [the offensive speech] can serve to justify this breach of the peace conviction where, as here, there was no evidence that persons powerless to avoid appellant's conduct did in fact object to it, and where that portion of the statute upon which Cohen's conviction rests evinces no concern, either on its face or as construed ... with the special plight of the captive auditor....

The Court has not overruled the "fighting words" doctrine, but any conviction based on it faces careful judicial scrutiny.

(b) Content Based Fighting Words—the Problem of Hate Speech

R.A.V. v. City of St. Paul (1992), is a significant decision explaining and limiting the "fighting words" doctrine. The City of St. Paul enacted an ordinance that provided:

> "Whoever places on public or private property a symbol, object, appellation, characterization or graffiti, including, but not limited to, a burning cross or a Nazi swastika, which one knows or has reasonable grounds to know arouses anger, alarm

or resentment in others on the basis of race, color, creed, religion or gender commits disorderly conduct and shall be guilty of a misdemeanor.''

The City alleged that R.A.V. and several other teenagers burned a cross inside the privately owned, fenced yard of a black family, who lived across the street from where R.A.V. was staying. R.A.V., of course, intended to terrorize the black family. The only question was the constitutionality of this ordinance.

The state supreme court held that the ordinance only reached expressions that constituted "fighting words," within the meaning of *Chaplinsky,* and that it was a "narrowly tailored means toward accomplishing the compelling governmental interest in protecting the community against bias-motivated threats to public safety and order." The state court upheld the ordinance, but the U.S. Supreme Court disagreed.

Justice Scalia, for the majority, accepted the state court's interpretation, but ruled that the ordinance is unconstitutional on its face, because it "prohibits otherwise permitted speech solely on the basis of the subject [that] the speech addresses." It has long been the rule that content-based restrictions on speech are presumptively unconstitutional. *R.A.V.* applied this principle to the "fighting words" doctrine: the government may not regulate even fighting words "based on hostility—or favoritism—towards the underlying message expressed."

The Minnesota Supreme Court, in upholding the ordinance, emphasized that the ordinance was directed against "bias-motivated" hatred, and messages "based on virulent notions of racial supremacy." This content-based purpose was the fatal flaw of the statute.

For example, *R.A.V.* said that the state "may not prohibit only that commercial advertising that depicts men in a demeaning fashion."

The state can ban certain discriminatory *conduct,* and one cannot immunize one's self from that ban merely by accompanying it with speech. A murderer does not cloak himself with the First Amendment merely because he shouts, "Death to Tyrants," while pulling the trigger. Pursuant to Title VII, Congress has banned sexual discrimination in employment practices. Such conduct (e.g., a refusal to promote someone to a better job because of sexism, or creation of a hostile work environment) is not immune from prohibition.

Although in *Dawson v. Delaware* (1992) the Court ruled that a sentencing judge may not constitutionally take into account the defendant's *abstract* beliefs, the First Amendment does not prevent the court from looking at the defendant's motive committing a crime. The more purposeful the offense, the more severely it may be punished. Thus, it is proper, in a murder case, for the trial judge (in deciding to sentence the defendant to death) to take into account the racial hatred of the defendant towards the victim.

The unanimous Court in *Wisconsin v. Mitchell* (1993) upheld a Wisconsin statute that enhanced a defendant's sentence if he intentionally selected his victim based on the victim's race. The statute in *R.A.V.* was explicitly directed at speech; but the statute in *Mitchell* was aimed at *conduct* (aggravated battery by Mitchell, who selected and beat up his victim on the grounds of color). The First Amendment does not protect this conduct. The trial court only looked at the defendant's motives in determining what sentence to impose.

(c) Threats, Intimidation & Cross–Burning

The state may, consistent with the First Amendment, ban "true threats." Thus, the state may prosecute an individual for cross-burning, if the state can prove that he burned the cross with an intent to *intimidate* someone. As O'Connor explained, in *Virginia v. Black* (2003), in a portion of the opinion that was the opinion of the Court:

> Intimidation in the constitutionally proscribable sense of the word is a type of true threat, where a speaker directs a threat to a person or a group of persons with the intent of placing the victim in fear of bodily harm or death.

The Virginia state law in question made it a felony "for any person ..., with the intent of intimidating any person or group ..., to burn ... a cross on the property of another, a highway or other public place." The statute also specified that "[a]ny such burning ... shall be prima facie evidence of an intent to intimidate a person or group." The Virginia Supreme Court held that, based on *R.A.V. v. City of St. Paul,* the cross burning statute was facially unconstitutional under the First Amendment and also overbroad.

Justice O'Connor, for the Court, reversed. She held that Virginia's ban on cross burning with intent to intimidate did not violate the First Amendment. The Court concluded that this case was different than *R.A.V.*

> Virginia's statute does not run afoul of the First Amendment insofar as it bans cross burning with intent to intimidate. Unlike the statute at issue in *R.A.V.,* the Virginia statute does not single out for opprobrium only that speech directed toward "one of the specified disfavored topics." It does not matter whether an individual burns a cross with intent to intimidate because of the victim's race, gender, or religion, or because of

the victim's "political affiliation, union membership, or homo-sexuality."

In fact, the record showed that cross burners do not direct their intimidating conduct solely to racial or religious minorities, but also burn crosses to intimidate union members, or others.

The law at issue in *R.A.V.* was flawed because it allowed the city to impose special prohibitions on speakers who express views on disfavored subjects. But the Virginia law did not share that infirmity. The Virginia law did not single out for opprobrium only that speech directed at certain disfavored topics.

In short, Virginia, under the First Amendment, may outlaw cross burnings done with the intent to intimidate because burning a cross is a particularly virulent form of intimidation. Instead of prohibiting all intimidating messages, Virginia may choose to regulate this subset of intimidating messages in light of cross burning's long and pernicious history as a signal of impending violence.

A flaw in the Virginia cross burning statute was the state court's interpretation that allowed the state to secure a conviction merely by proving only that a cross was burning in public view. The Supreme Court reversed the state court, because the law as interpreted: "does not distinguish between a cross burning at a public rally or a cross burning on a neighbor's lawn. It does not treat the cross burning directed at an individual differently from the cross burning directed at a group of like-minded believers."

(d) Fighting Words, Hostile Audiences, and the Problem of Vagueness and Overbreadth

In addition to the explicit limitations that *Cohen* and *R.A.V.* placed on *Chaplinsky,* other cases also indicate that the Court does not look with favor on prosecutions for "fighting words." The Court has often employed the vagueness and overbreadth standards to avoid upholding convictions. In *Gooding v. Wilson* (1972), the defendant addressed a policeman, "you son of a bitch I'll choke you to death." Similarly, in *Lewis v. City of New Orleans* (1974), the defendant said "you goddamn motherfucking police." The Court overturned both convictions because the statutes were vague and overbroad.

Gooding stated that convictions may be upheld under the *Chaplinsky* standard, if the statute is narrowly drawn or construed. The Court then went on to conduct its own examination of state case law. The state decisions did not really limit the statute "to words that 'have a direct tendency to cause acts of violence by the person to whom individually, the remark is addressed.' " And, in *Lewis* the Court made clear that words conveying or intended to convey disgrace are not "fighting words."

While the Court has never overruled *Feiner,* it has repeatedly distinguished it. The Court has not allowed the state to prosecute speakers for breach of the peace simply because the speech was before a hostile audience. Words are "fighting words" when they are an offer to exchange fisticuffs. But the state should not punish a person simply because others (who don't like his mental attitude) engage in violence against him.

§ 16.19　The Freedom to Associate and Not to Associate—Introduction

The Right of Association as Derived From Freedom of Speech and Assembly. In *NAACP v. Alabama ex rel. Patterson,* a unanimous Court, speaking through Justice Harlan, enunciated a right of association. The Court held that Alabama could not compel the National Association for the Advancement of Colored People to reveal to the state's Attorney General the names and addresses of all of its Alabama members without regard to their positions and functions in the NAACP. The NAACP showed that compelled disclosure of its rank and file members on past occasions exposed them to economic reprisal, loss of employment, threat of physical coercion, and general public hostility. The NAACP was not an organization with illegal ends, and its nondisclosure interest directly related to the right of the members of pursue their lawful interests privately. If an association can demonstrate that disclosure of its membership would result in significant harm to the association, or its members, the government's request for information must be narrowly tailored to an overriding or compelling interest.

The Court has based the right to associate for expressive activity on the express guarantees found in the First Amendment. The government cannot limit this right to associate unless the limitation serves a compelling or overriding governmental interest unrelated to the suppression of ideas and this governmental interest cannot be furthered through means that are significantly less restrictive of the associational or expressive freedom. In other words, the regulation of association must be narrowly tailored to promote an end that is unrelated to suppressing the message that will be advanced by the association and is unrelated to suppressing the association because of government disapproval of its purposes.

The *Roberts* Decision. In some instances the precise type of associational right that is asserted in a case may not be easily categorized, but the Court must consider the nature of the right in order to determine the validity of governmental restrictions at issue. The Court's diagnosis of the type of associational freedom at issue will dictate the position it should take in determining how much, if any, deference it owes the legislative or executive branches of government in the particular case.

Consider, for example, *Roberts v. United States Jaycees* (1984). The Court reviewed a state law and state administrative action that prohibited a state branch of a national nonprofit corporation from refusing to grant full membership rights to women solely because of their sex. The seven Justices who voted in this case were unanimous in upholding the state's ability to restrict this right of association, but there was some difficulty in identifying the correct standard of review that should be employed in this case. Justice Brennan spoke for the majority. He explained that the cases protect "freedom of association" in two distinct senses.

FIRST, to secure individual liberty, the Bill of Rights "must afford the formation and preservation of certain kinds of highly personal relationships a substantial measure of sanctuary from unjustified interference by the State." This type of freedom of association is related to the fundamental right of privacy that protects family relationships and personal decisions regarding such matters as childbirth and abortion.

This type of association is relatively small, highly selective, and, in its nature, almost exclusive because they concern highly personal relationships. On the other extreme would be a large business enterprise, which seems remote from this constitutional protection of association. The Constitution "undoubtedly imposes constraints on the State's power to control the selection of one's spouse that would not apply to regulations affecting the choice of one's fellow employees." There is a range of relationships between the most intimate, which embrace the fundamental right to privacy, and the non-intimate, economic associations, for which there is very little constitutional protection. The Jaycees were "outside of the category of relationships worthy of this kind of constitutional protection" because the organization was a "large and basically unselective" organization designed to promote commercial activity, community programs, and award ceremonies.

SECOND, there is the freedom of the association to choose its membership. Limitations on the organization's ability to choose its members should be subjected to significant review under the First Amendment because the Jaycees were organized in part for the purpose of expressive activity. The courts could not vigorously protect an individual's freedom to speak, to worship, and to petition the Government for the redress of grievances unless there exists a correlative freedom to engage in group effort toward those ends. Thus, implicit in the right to engage in activities protected by the First Amendment is "a corresponding right to associate with others in pursuit of a wide variety of political, social, economic, educational, religious, and cultural ends."

The Court found that this right of association is not absolute and that infringements may be justified by regulations adopted to serve "compelling state interests, unrelated to the suppression of ideas, that cannot be achieved through means significantly less restrictive of associational freedoms."

The Court upheld the state law requiring the Jaycees to admit women to full membership because the state interest in guaranteeing equal access to publicly available goods and services without racial or sex discrimination was a compelling interest. In addition to advancing a compelling state interest, the state demonstrated that its regulation was the least restrictive means of achieving its end because it did not impose serious burdens on the male members' freedom of expressive association.

Justice O'Connor wrote a concurring opinion in *Roberts* stating that the Court must determine whether the organization was significantly dedicated to First Amendment activity or whether it was primarily a commercial organization that only incidentally exercised First Amendment rights. The Court, she noted, should establish a strong presumption of validity for regulations of commercial organizations even though the Court also should "give substance to the ideal of complete protection for purely expressive association, even while it readily permits state regulation of commercial affairs."

The *Roberts* Court made quite clear that application of the state law imposed no restrictions on the right of an organization to exclude members based on their ideology. The choice of a speaker to propound, or not to propound, a particular point of view is a choice that is beyond the power of government to control. Thus, in *Hurley v. Irish-American Gay, Lesbian and Bisexual Group of Boston* (1995) the Justices unanimously ruled that the government could not force private parade organizers to include a group whose message was opposed by the parade organizers.

Perhaps it is best to think of associational rights as proceeding on a continuum from the least protected form of association in commercial activities to the most protected forms of association to engage in political or religious speech or for highly personal reasons, such as family relationships.

A boycott for political purposes may receive significant First Amendment protection, although a similar boycott for the purposes of maintaining a preferred economic position for one's business or union may receive very little protection. A prohibition of race or sex discrimination in the employment practices of commercial enterprises or in the admissions practices of schools open to a wide segment of the public should not present significant freedom of association problems. A similar restriction on the membership practices of a religious organization that was highly selective in its membership and dedicated to goals totally inconsistent with the acceptance of members of a particular race or sex might present a more significant freedom of associational problem.

Group Activity to Obtain Counsel. The association of persons for law practice may be regulated to prohibit discrimination on the basis of sex or race. Regulations of law practice that relate to the ability of persons to associate for the advancement of social goals, however, may be protected to a greater extent from governmental regulation. Under the freedom of association the Court has struck down laws that prevented the NAACP from assisting individuals and that prevented a labor union from assisting its members in hiring lawyers to assert the legal rights of these individuals.

§ 16.20   The Freedom to Associate & Political Party Regulations

The freedom of association allows political parties, within certain bounds, to regulate their candidate even when such regulations are contrary to state law.

Tashjian v. Republican Party of Connecticut (1986) invalidated a state law to the extent that it conflicted with a Connecticut Republican Party rule that permitted *independent* voters to vote in Republican primaries for federal and state-wide offices. The state *law* provided for a closed primary; the Republican party *rules* provided for an open primary for federal and state-wide offices but a closed primary for other offices (e.g., state legislator, mayor). State law provided that any previously unaffiliated voter may become eligible to vote in the Party's primary simply by enrolling as a Party member as late as noon on the last business day preceding the primary. The Supreme Court specifically approved of an earlier decision upholding the closed primary, but Justice Marshall, speaking for the Court, found that the earlier case was distinguishable because it was brought by independent voters, not by the Republican Party itself.

The Court in *Tashjian* assumed that there was a significant burden on the associational rights of independent voters as well as members of the Republican party. *Tashjian* only ruled that a political party had a First Amendment right to open its primary to independent voters and persons who were registered in the political party.

Laws restricting the ability of a political party to allow non-party members to vote in the party's primary give rise to First Amendment freedom of association issues. If the Court finds that such a law imposes a severe burden on the ability of persons to associate, the Court will require the government to demonstrate that the law is narrowly tailored to a compelling interest. However, if the law imposes only a minor burden on the associational interests of members of the party, or would-be voters, the Court will uphold the law if it is justified by an important state interest.

The important state interest test appears to involve balancing the burden imposed on persons who wish to vote in a particular party's primary, or the burden on party members who wish to invite other persons to vote in their primary, against a variety of state interests that the Court considers to be important. The government apparently has an important interest in protecting political parties from inter-party raiding of voters in primary elections.

Clingman v. Beaver (2005) upheld a state's semi-closed primary law. The state law, as presented to the Supreme Court, allowed a political party to open its primary election to participation by voters who had previously registered in that party and voters who had not registered as members of any political party (independent voters). The state law prevented the party in this case (the Libertarian party) from opening its primary to voters who were already registered in another party (e.g., Republicans and Democrats); the law also prevented voters who were registered in one party from voting in the primary election of another party.

A majority in *Clingman* found that this law did not place a significant restriction on the associational rights of members of the Libertarian Party or persons who were registered in other parties and who wished to vote in the Libertarian Party primary. The Court found that any burden imposed on those associational interests was justified by several important interests, including preservation of political party integrity and the operation of political parties. *Clingman* did not consider whether the state's laws regarding party registration imposed significant burdens on the ability of persons to associate to advance their political goals, because that issue had not been adequately addressed in the lower courts.

Prohibition of Fusion Candidates and Protecting the Two Party System. "Fusion" is the nomination of two or more political parties of one candidate for the same office at the same general election.

Timmons v. Twin Cities Area New Party (1997) held that it was constitutional for Minnesota to prohibit candidates from appearing on the ballot of more than one political party, even though the candidate in that case agreed to be nominated by the Democratic–Farmer–Labor Party (a major party); in addition, the New Party (a third party) wanted to nominate the same candidate and the

Democratic–Farmer–Labor Party (which had already nominated him) did not object to this dual nomination. Chief Justice Rehnquist, for the Court, concluded that the burden on the New Party was not severe (the New Party could endorse the candidate even if it could not nominate him), and that therefore the state need not assert any compelling state interest and there was no need for the state to offer any elaborate empirical justification of the state's asserted justification. The state argued that it needed to restrict ballot access to make sure that the ballot was not too complicated, although a demonstrated-support requirement would also serve to meet this interest.

In addition, the Court relied on another justification: the need to protect the two-party system—to encourage political stability and help preserve the two-party system in order to "temper the destabilizing effects of party-shattering and excessive factionalism." States may not prevent third parties from forming, but they "need not remove all of the many hurdles third parties face in the American political arena today."

§ 16.21 The Right Not to Associate

Earlier, § 16.4, we examined the right not to speak. The right of association raises the issue of the right not to associate. If the state requires an individual to join an organization—for example a union, as a requirement to work, or a state bar, as a requirement in some states to practice law—may, that organization, consistent with the freedom of association, use the dues required of its members to advance causes not favored by all of the members?

Abood v. Detroit Board of Education (1977) held that the state may require a public worker to pay dues or a service fee equal to dues insofar as the money is used to finance expenditures by the union for the purposes of collective bargaining, contract administration, and grievance adjustment. But, under the First Amendment, the workers may not be compelled to contribute to political candidates, and the workers may constitutionally prevent the union's spending a part of its required fees to contribute to political candidates and to express political views unrelated to its duties as exclusive bargaining representative.

Similarly, *Keller v. State Bar of California* (1990) unanimously held that the State Bar of California may not constitutionally use *compulsory* dues to finance political and ideological causes that the petitioners oppose. The California Bar was an "integrated bar" or a "unified bar," that is, an association created by state law, to which lawyers must join and pay dues as a condition of practicing law.

The State Bar may only use compulsory due to finance regulation of the legal profession or improve the quality of legal services (for example, bar dues may be used to propose ethical codes or discipline Bar members), not to promote political or ideological activities (for example, to endorse gun control or nuclear freeze initiatives). While it is true that government officials are expected, as a part of the democratic process, to represent and to espouse the views of a majority of their constituents, the State Bar of California is not part of the general government of California, even though state law creates it, and requires lawyers to join it. The State Bar is more analogous to a labor union representing public and private employees, and therefore it should be subject to the same constitutional rule in order to protect free speech and free association interests.

In *Board of Regents of the University of Wisconsin System v. Southworth* (2000), the Court did not apply *Keller*, because the fact situation involved student speech at a university. Students sued the University claiming that the mandatory student activity fee violated their Constitutional rights of free speech, free association, and free exercise, unless the University would give them the choice *not to fund* organizations (such as, *e.g.*, the International Socialist Organization, the College Democrats and College Republicans) that engaged in political and ideological expression offensive to their personal beliefs. The Court, speaking through Justice Kennedy, disagreed and ruled that a public university, unlike the State Bar, may charge its students an activity fee to fund a program to facilitate extracurricular speech "if the program is viewpoint neutral."

The Court distinguished this case from situations where the government itself is the speaker and seeks to advance a particular message. In that case, it is accountable to the electorate and the political process for its advocacy. Here, the University is not responsible for the speech and its content. Instead, it merely distributes the money to facilitate the students' exchange of ideas, which is part of the University's function.

The Court rejected the "germaneness" test found in *Keller*, both as unworkable as applied to student speech at a university, and as giving "insufficient protection" to the objecting students and to the university. Instead the proper test is to require viewpoint neutrality in the allocation of funding support. The Court borrowed the "viewpoint neutrality" test from the public forum cases, although the student activities fund is not a public forum.

The Court remanded the issue dealing with the allocation by student referendum because it appeared to be inconsistent with the requirement of viewpoint neutrality.

§ 16.22   Loyalty Oaths

The Supreme Court, at first, dealt with loyalty qualifications primarily by the use of the vagueness and overbreadth doctrines. Thus, *Shelton v. Tucker* (1960), invalidated an Arkansas statute requiring teachers to file an affidavit listing all the organizations to which they had belonged or contributed within the past five years. The state's legitimate interest in investigating the loyalty of its teachers did not justify the "unlimited and indiscriminate sweep" of the statute when less restrictive alternatives, offering less impingement on the teachers' freedom of association, were available.

In *Cramp v. Board of Public Instruction* (1961), the Court unanimously invalidated a Florida statute requiring employees to swear, "I have not and will not lend my aid, support, advice, counsel or influence to the Communist Party." The consequences of such vague and ambiguous wording would not only inhibit legitimate activity by those whose "conscientious scruples were the most sensitive," but would increase the likelihood of prosecution for ideas antithetical to those held by the general community.

Employing a similar rationale in *Baggett v. Bullitt* (1964), the Court invalidated two Washington loyalty oath requirements. The first required the affiant to promote, by teaching and example, "respect for the flag and the institutions of the United States of America and the State of Washington" and the second, to swear that he or she was not a member of a "subversive organization." Once again, the language was susceptible of an interpretation applying to a broad spectrum of behavior with which the State could not interfere. The lack of any criminal sanction for its future violation did not prevent the oath from being stricken, because this oath would not avoid the prohibited deterrent effect on those who will only swear to that which they can obey.

Elfbrandt v. Russell (1966) involved a challenge to an Arizona statute imposing an oath on the prospective employee that he had not knowingly and willfully become or remained a member of an organization dedicated to the overthrow by force or violence of the government with knowledge of its illegal aims.

The majority opinion found this oath to prohibit "knowing, but guiltless" behavior because the oath did not require the individual to have participated in, or subscribed to the unlawful activities in order for employment to be terminated and prosecution for perjury to be instituted. The Court relied on previous decisions involving criminal prosecutions of speech and association, and ruled that "knowing membership" coupled with a specific intent to further the illegal aims of the organizations would be required because "quasi-political parties or other groups . . . may embrace both legal and illegal aims."

United States v. Robel (1967) held that § 5(a)(1)(D) of the Subversive Activities Control Act was unconstitutionally overbroad by denying to members of designated "communist-action" groups employment in any defense facility.

The statutory language made irrelevant the active or passive status of the individual's membership, his knowledge of the illegal aims of the organization or lack of it, the degree of his agreement or disagreement with those aims, and the sensitive nature of his position of employment as it affected national security.

An individual may not be punished or deprived of public employment for political association unless: (1) he is an active member of a subversive organization; (2) such membership is with knowledge of the illegal aims of the organization; *and* (3) the individual has a specific intent to further those illegal ends, as opposed to general support of the objectives of an organization.

Cole v. Richardson (1972) relied on a distinction between oaths that require individuals to swear to the appropriateness of their past conduct, so-called negative oaths, and oaths that merely require the individual to swear support in the future to the constitutional processes of government, so-called affirmative oaths.

Unlike negative oaths, affirmative oaths have traditionally been viewed as constitutionally permissible despite the inherent vagueness of the terms employed. Indeed, the body of the Constitution requires such oaths: both the presidential oath and the oath for federal and state officials are affirmative oaths. The purpose behind the enactment of such affirmative oaths is merely to assure that those in positions of public trust are willing to commit themselves to live by the constitutional processes.

The oath in *Cole*, which Massachusetts required of its state employees, read as follows:

> I do solemnly swear (or affirm) that I will uphold and defend the Constitution of the United States ... and the Constitution of the Commonwealth of Massachusetts and that I will oppose the overthrow of the government of the United States of America or of this Commonwealth by force, violence or by any illegal or unconstitutional method.

Chief Justice Burger, writing for a four to three majority in *Cole*, read the first portion of the oath, swearing to "uphold and defend", as a permissible "affirmative oath." This result allowed the Court to conclude that a literal reading of the second part, requiring opposition to attempted overthrow, was unnecessary.

Thus, the second part of this oath was not unduly vague; it did not raise the specter of some undefinable responsibility to actively combat a potential revolution. Rather, it should be read as merely a restatement of the affirmative oath.

Thus, it is now clear that oaths must be clear, concise, and narrow in scope. The Court accords a wider ranger of permissibility to affirmative oaths, relating only to allegiance to constitutional processes of government. However, negative oaths cannot require a disclaimer of past conduct or belief other than that for which the employee may be constitutionally denied employment.

§ 16.23 Patronage

The Court (with no majority opinion) in *Elrod v. Burns* (1976), invalidated political patronage dismissals by the Democratic Sheriff of Cook County. Respondents' discharge was unrelated to membership in any subversive organization. They were Republicans discharged or threatened with discharge because they were Republicans. Dismissal merely for membership in an opposing political party that poses no illegal threat violates the First Amendment.

In *Branti v. Finkel* (1980), a majority ruled that the proper test, to determine whether political affiliation is a legitimate factor to consider in government employment is not whether the label "policymakers" or "confidential" fits a particular position. *Instead, the question is whether the hiring authority can demonstrate that "party affiliation is an appropriate requirement for the effective performance of the public office involved."*

Rutan v. Republican Party of Illinois (1990), extended *Branti*. Justice Brennan, for the Court, held that not only the patronage practice of discharging public employees on the basis of their political affiliation violates the First Amendment, but related patronage practices involving low-level public employees—regarding hiring, promotion, transfer, and recall after layoff—also may not constitutionally be based on party affiliation and support. "Unless these patronage practices are narrowly tailored to further vital government interests, we must conclude that they impermissibly encroach on First Amendment freedoms."

In *O'Hare Truck Service, Inc. v. City of Northlake* (1996), the Court refused to draw any distinction between government employees and independent contractors for the Government. Once again, the case arose in Illinois. O'Hare Truck Service, on a rotation list of companies available to perform towing services at the request of the city, was removed from the list allegedly because its owner refused to contribute to the respondent mayor's reelection campaign. The Seventh Circuit dismissed the claim, arguing that *Branti* and *Elrod* do not apply to independent contractors. Justice Kennedy, for the Court, reversed. If the government retaliates against a contractor or regular provider of services because of its exercise of rights of political association or the expression of political allegiance, there is a violation of the guarantee of free speech.

Board of County Commissioners v. Umbehr (1996) involved a trash hauler and an outspoken critic of the Board of County Commissioners. That person alleged that the County Commissioners voted to terminate or prevent the automatic renewal of his at-will contract to haul trash because of his criticism of them. Justice O'Connor, for the Court, held that the First Amendment protects independent contractors from termination of at-will government contracts in retaliation for their exercise of free speech.

§ 16.24   Restrictions on Entry Into the Bar

States routinely require that applicants for membership to the bar possess certain attributes of character that are consistent with the practice of law.

The general rule to be gleaned from the cases may be that past membership in a subversive organization cannot create an irrebuttable presumption of unfitness for the bar. But, the First Amendment will not protect an active, knowing member of an organization that has an end that is made illegal by a constitutional law who has specific intent to aid in its illegal goals.

The Court has dealt with a series of cases in which there was no claim that past incidents in the applicant's life had revealed characteristics incompatible with the practice of law. Rather, the applicants had asserted a privilege to refuse to answer questions that they believed intruded unnecessarily into their First Amendment freedoms.

Konigsberg v. State Bar of California (1957) *(Konigsberg I),* dealt with the range of inferences that could properly be drawn from the applicant's refusal to answer questions relating to his past political affiliations. The California Bar had determined that petitioner's refusal to respond to inquiries into his membership in the Communist Party, coupled with other characteristics, required it to deny admission on the grounds that the petitioner had failed to establish his good moral character as well as his non-advocacy of illegal overthrow of the government. The Court found this conclusion unjustified. There must exist some authentic, affirmative evidence of disloyalty to deny admission to an applicant, not a conclusion of disloyalty based on suspicions deduced from a refusal to answer questions.

Konigsberg (I) expressed no opinion as to the propriety of denying admission to the bar solely on the basis of an applicant's refusal to answer, because it did not consider that issue before it. Four years later the same parties appeared before the Court to litigate that question. On re-hearing for Konigsberg's application for admission to the bar of California, the applicant introduced further evidence of his good character and reiterated that he did not believe in or advocate violent overthrow of the government. Nevertheless, he steadfastly refused to answer questions concerning possible membership in the Communist Party. Relying solely on this refusal as an obstruction to a legitimate investigation, the bar examiners again denied him certification to practice law in that State.

In *Konigsberg v. State Bar of California* (1961) (*Konigsberg II*) the majority opinion of Justice Harlan rejected the claim that the state had placed on Konigsberg the burden of establishing his loyalty. The denial had not been based on any inference as to Konigsberg's character, but simply on his obstruction of the investigation. Because the state had the burden of producing evidence as to disloyalty, an applicant could not be allowed to frustrate that burden by refusing to submit relevant information. The majority reasoned that the regulatory statute imposed only an incidental infringement on speech. The state's interest in this regulation is weighed against the appellant's interest in remaining silent, with the balance struck in favor of the state.

The validity of *Konigsberg (II)* was reemphasized by a trio of cases decided in 1971. The primary case, *Law Students Civil Rights Research Council, Inc. v. Wadmond*, involved an attack on the manner in which New York screened its applicants for the bar. The appellants had challenged that the appellees' use of a questionnaire, which had a bifurcated inquiry between knowing membership and membership with intent to further illegal goals. They argued that the questionnaire unnecessarily intruded into rights of association by requiring applicants to divulge knowing membership although there could be no inference of disloyalty based on such information. The Court, however, held that it was within reasonable legislative boundaries to inquire into knowing membership as a preliminary inquiry on which to base further investigation.

Thus, an applicant to the bar may be required to answer a question concerning his knowing membership on pain of denial of certification. If the applicant responds affirmatively, the examiners may probe more deeply into the nature of that association to determine if it is appropriate to deny admission. Judicial review is available to remedy any abuses resulting from solely an admission of knowing membership. Moreover, *Wadmond* found that there was no constitutional infirmity in inquiring into the applicant's ability to take the oath required of attorneys without any mental reservations, because such inquiry is incorporated into the federal oath for uniformed and civil service personnel.

In the two accompanying decisions also handed down in 1971, *Baird v. State Bar of Arizona* and *Application of Stolar*, the Court reaffirmed the rationale of *Wadmond* by invalidating denials of admission to the bar based on the petitioners' refusal to answer questions that were not limited to ascertaining "knowing" membership. Because the questions were overbroad and beyond the legitimate interest of the state in the affiliations of its attorneys, the denial of admission to the bar was improper.

The First Amendment does not provide an unlimited sanctuary for a bar applicant who does not desire to disclose his political affiliations. The state has an interest in informing itself about the applicant, particularly since it has the burden of establishing affirmative evidence of disloyalty. Frustration of a legitimate inquiry is subject to a denial of application for membership in the bar. However, the state's interest does not extend beyond interrogation concerning knowing membership, and a question beyond that permissible spectrum may be refused without penalty.

§ 16.25 Licensing Schemes Implemented by Administrators and Injunctions Issued by the Courts

Often the state seeks to exercise time, place, or manner restrictions on speech in public places by use of licensing or permit regulations.

A permit or license regulation, first, may not grant to the government administrator an amount of discretion that might be used to allocate permits based on content. And second, the administrator must not base the decision to grant or to deny the permit on the content of the message.

For example, in *Thomas v. Chicago Park District* (2002), a unanimous Supreme Court rejected a facial challenge to a Chicago Park District ordinance that required a permit in order to conduct a public assembly, parade, picnic, or other event involving more than 50 people, or to engage in any activity emitting any amplified sound. The law simply imposed content-neutral regulations governing the time, place, and manner restrictions designed to coordinate multiple uses of limited space.

In *Lovell v. Griffin* (1938), a member of the Jehovah's Witnesses was prosecuted for disobeying a city ordinance that forbade the distribution of circulars, advertising matter, and similar material unless one secured a permit from the city manager. The city argued that its sanitary and litter problems made "apparent" the reasons for the ordinance.

In *Lovell* the defendant was convicted for distributing religious tracts. Because she had not secured a license nor even applied for it, the city argued that she was not in the "position of having suffered from the exercise of the arbitrary and unlimited power of which she complains." If she had applied and then been denied, the city argued, then she would have suffered loss of constitutional right; in other words, only then would she have standing to complain.

The city's arguments failed to persuade a unanimous Supreme Court. This ordinance had an unusually broad sweep: it prohibited the distribution of literature of any kind under every sort of circulation, at any time, at any place, and in any manner, without a permit from the City Manager. Its literal language could have been applied to newspapers, although there was no evidence of that. This law "strikes at the very foundation of the freedom of the press by subjecting it to license and censorship." Hence, it was invalid on its face, a prior restraint of free speech. And, because it was void on its face, the defendant did not have to apply for a permit before she could contest ordinance.

Forsyth County v. The Nationalist Movement (1992) invalidated, on its face, an ordinance that, in effect, allowed the administrator to base the permit fee on the content of the demonstration or parade. The fee was not to exceed $1000 per day of the parade, open air meeting, or procession.

First, the ordinance granted the administrator too much discretion. Second, the ordinance, in effect, required that the fee must depend on the content of the demonstration, parade, or procession.

As we saw in in the section regarding prior restraints, one may not disregard a court injunction or temporary restraining order issued by a court with jurisdiction, even though the court order is equally void on its face. The proper procedure to attack the court order is to appeal it, and therefore the individual may be barred in a collateral proceeding from contesting the validity of the injunction, if he is prosecuted for violating it.

Walker v. Birmingham (1967) upheld the contempt of court convictions of Martin Luther King Jr. and other black ministers who participated in civil rights marches and parades in violation of an *ex parte* temporary injunction issued by a state circuit court.

The Supreme Court found that the state court had jurisdiction over the petitioners and over the subject matter of the controversy. Moreover the injunction was not "transparently invalid" nor did it have "only a frivolous pretense to validity." The majority did not define those terms, but it should be understood that it would be the most atypical injunctive order that could probably meet this test, for the *Walker* order, as the majority admitted, was written in terms of such "breadth and vagueness" as to "unquestionably" raise a "substantial constitutional question."

Two terms later, in *Shuttlesworth v. Birmingham* (1969), the Supreme Court held that marchers in the same events involved in *Walker* did not have to comply with the same Birmingham licensing ordinance, because it was invalid on its face and could not be saved even by judicial construction applied to the parties before the state court. Thus, an *ex parte* court order is not "transparently invalid" simply because it "recites the words of the invalid statute." In other words the marchers could ignore an ordinance that was invalid on its face (pursuant to the *Lovell* doctrine) but they had to obey a court order that merely repeated the words of the invalid ordinance. Courts are much more disturbed when litigants disobey a court injunction than they are when litigants disobey a statute.

Walker was concerned that the petitioners did not even attempt to appeal within the Alabama court system the lower court's order. The proper procedure was to apply to the Alabama courts to have the injunction modified or dissolved.

Several years later, in *Carroll v. President and Commissioners of Princess Anne* (1968) the Supreme Court held unconstitutional the *ex parte* procedure in free speech cases such as *Walker*, where officials obtain an *ex parte* court order restraining the holding of meetings or rallies. An order in such cases is defective if it is issued *ex parte*, without notice to the subjects of the order, and without any effort, even an informal one, to invite or permit their participation, unless a showing is made that it is impossible to serve or to notify the opposing parties and give them an opportunity to respond. In the case in which the Court announced this holding, the petitioners *obeyed* the order and then appealed it rather than disobeying it and attacking it collaterally.

§ 16.26   Time, Place, and Manner Restrictions on Speech

In general, the state may place time, place, or manner restrictions on speech, but these regulations must be implemented without regard to the content of the speech. Otherwise the state would be able to cloak restrictions on speech in the guise of regulations of the mode of speech or the place—the streets, the parks, public buildings—that is used for the speech. To prevent abuse of the power to make reasonable regulations, and to help assure that the regulations are in fact reasonable, the Court will independently determine if the regulation is a narrow means of protecting important interests unrelated to content.

The Court has phrased its test in two slightly different forms. First, as stated in *United States v. O'Brien* (1968), there is a general principle that government regulation is permissible: "if it is within the constitutional power of the Government; if it furthers an important or substantial governmental interest; if the governmental interest is unrelated to the suppression of free expression; and if the incidental restriction on alleged First Amendment freedoms is no greater than is essential to the furtherance of that interest." The second method of analysis elaborates on this general principle by restating it in terms of a three-part test. The Court will uphold time, place, or manner restrictions if they are content-neutral, narrowly tailored to serve a significant government interest, and leave open ample alternative channels of communication.

Whether the Court states its test in terms of a general principle or a three-part test, when the Court reviews time, place, or manner restrictions, it really is engaging in a two-step form of analysis. First, it determines whether the regulation is in fact an attempt to suppress speech because of its message. A content-based restriction of is valid only if it fits within a category of speech that the First Amendment does not protect, for example, obscenity. If the First Amendment protects the category of speech, then the state may enforce a content-based restriction on speech only if its regulation is necessary to serve a compelling state interest and is narrowly tailored to achieve that goal.

If the regulation is not an attempt to censor content, the Court will go on to determine whether the incidental restriction on speech is outweighed by the promotion of significant governmental interests. Although this method of analysis is sometimes stated as a least restrictive means test, the analysis also evaluates whether the regulation leaves open ample means for communication of the message and is not an unnecessary or gratuitous suppression of communication.

Saia v. New York (1948) invalidated a city ordinance that forbade the use of sound amplification devices such as loudspeakers on trucks, except with permission of the Chief of Police. The ordinance was unconstitutional on its face because the Chief of Police had uncontrolled discretion. The abuses of loudspeakers can be controlled, the majority agreed, if the control is pursuant to a narrowly-drawn statute.

Kovacs v. Cooper (1949) upheld a noise control statute, though the fragmented Court could not agree on the reasons. Justice Reed's plurality opinion found the city ordinance in *Kovacs* not overbroad nor vague. It prohibited sound trucks and similar devices from emitting "loud and raucous noises." These words were found not to be too vague. Moreover the New Jersey courts by construction had narrowed the ordinance's applicability only to vehicles containing a sound amplifier or any other instrument emitting loud and raucous noises, when operated or standing in the public streets, alleys or thoroughfares of the city. Justice Reed added that just as unrestrained use of all sound amplifying devices in a city would be intolerable, "[a]bsolute prohibition within municipal limits of all sound amplification, even though reasonably regulated in place, time and volume, is undesirable and probably unconstitutional as an unreasonable interference with normal activities."

Regulation of Content. *Police Department of Chicago v. Mosley* (1972) considered the constitutionality of a city ordinance that prohibited picketing on a public way within 150 feet of a grade or high school from one-half hour before the school was in session until one-half hour after the school session had been concluded. However, the ordinance exempted peaceful labor picketing. The ordinance was invalidated.

While the ordinance purported to regulate the time, place, and manner of speech activities in the public forum, it did so based on the content of the speech. A careful look at the restrictions of the ordinance and its exceptions demonstrated that the law regulated content. That content regulation was the fatal flaw in the ordinance. *Carey v. Brown* (1980) invalidated an Illinois statute that prohibited all picketing of residences or dwellings except for the peaceful picketing of a place of employment involved in a labor dispute. The majority relied on *Mosley*. Though the Supreme Court in *Mosley* and *Carey* relied on equal protection reasoning, their importance is the rejection of the government's claim that a content-based classification could be a valid time, place or manner regulation.

§ 16.27 The Three Categories of Public Forum

The Supreme Court made the first major effort to recognize and classify the types of public forums in *Perry Education Ass'n v. Perry Local Educators' Ass'n* (1983). In that case a teachers' union, the Perry Education Association (PEA), was the duly elected exclusive bargaining representative of the teachers in a certain school district. A collective bargaining agreement granted this union, and no other union, the right to access to the interschool mail system and teacher mailboxes in that school system. The rival union, the Perry Local Educators' Association (PLEA), sought similar access. In a five to four opinion the Supreme Court, in an opinion by Justice White, found that the school's denial of access to the rival union of the mailboxes and interschool mail system was no violation of free speech.

Of significance is the majority's reasoning. The Court recognized that there were degrees of public forums. Along the spectrum, three major distinctions exist:

> In places which by long tradition or by government fiat have been devoted to assembly and debate, the rights of the state to

limit expressive activity are sharply circumscribed. At one end of the spectrum are streets and parks which "have immemorially been held in trust for the use of the public, and, time out of mind, have been used for purposes of assembly, communicating thoughts between citizens, and discussing public questions." In these quintessential public forums, the government may not prohibit all communicative activity. For the state to enforce a content-based exclusion it must show that its regulation is necessary to serve a compelling state interest and that it is narrowly drawn to achieve that end. The state may also enforce regulations of the time, place, and manner of expression which are content-neutral, are narrowly tailored to serve a significant government interest, and leave open ample alternative channels of communication.

The Court then turned to the second category:

A second category consists of public property which the state has opened for use by the public as a place for expressive activity. The Constitution forbids a state to enforce certain exclusions from a forum generally open to the public even if it was not required to create the forum in the first place. Although a state is not required to indefinitely retain the open character of the facility, as long as it does so it is bound by the same standards as apply in a traditional public forum. Reasonable time, place and manner regulations are permissible, and a content-based prohibition must be narrowly drawn to effectuate a compelling state interest.

Finally the Court turned to the third category of public forum analysis:

Public property which is not by tradition or designation a forum for public communication is governed by different standards. We have recognized that the "First Amendment does not guarantee access to property simply because it is owned or controlled by the government." In addition to time, place, and manner regulations, the state *may reserve the forum for its intended purposes, communicative or otherwise, as long as the regulation on speech is reasonable* and *not an effort to suppress expression merely because public officials oppose the speaker's view.* As we have stated on several occasions, "the State, no less than a private owner of property, has power to preserve the property under its control for the use to which it is lawfully dedicated."

A few years earlier the Supreme Court had held that a U.S. mailbox was not a public forum, and that therefore it was constitutional to prohibit the deposit of unstamped, "mailable matter" in a mailbox approved by the U.S. Postal Service. Now the Court ruled that the school mail facilities also fell in this third class.

After *Perry* it is clear that it is very important to determine into which category the alleged public forum falls. *Perry* really offered no litmus test to distinguish between the second category (public property opened for use by the public as a place for expressive activity) and the third category (public property not by designation or tradition a forum for public communication). *Perry* merely announced that the school internal mail system is in the third category, even though the mail system was open to nonschool groups like the Cub Scouts.

In later cases, the Court said that *designated* public fora, in contrast to *traditional* public fora (like the streets and parks) are created by purposeful governmental action. The government must intentionally open a nontraditional public forum for public discourse, to make the property "generally available." A designated public forum is not created when the government allows *selective access* for individual speakers rather than general access for a class of speakers. For example, said the Court, if a university were to make its meeting facilities "generally open" to registered student groups, it would create a designated public forum. "General access" indicates that the property is a designated public forum, while "selective access" indicates the property is a nonpublic forum.

It appears that forum analysis applies only to a place or channel of communication that is owned by the government.

§ 16.28 Applying the *Perry* Forum Analysis

(a) Three Types of Government Owned Property or Channels of Communication

When the government regulates speech in a traditional public forum it may only base its restrictions on the content of the speech being regulated (1) if that content falls within a category of speech that the Supreme Court has held is not protected by the First Amendment (e.g., obscenity), or (2) if the government can demonstrate a compelling interest in suppressing the speech and the content-based restriction is narrowly drawn to achieve this interest.

The government may impose a time, place, or manner regulation of speech in a public forum, but the regulations must be *content neutral*; they must be *narrowly tailored* to serve a significant government interest; and they must *leave open ample alternative channels* of communication.

If the government opens public property to the public as a place for expressive activity, even though it is not a traditional public forum, the government is subject to the same restrictions of its actions in this forum as would be applicable to regulations of speech in a traditional public forum. The government will be able to employ only reasonable time, place, or manner regulations. Any content based prohibition of speech in this forum must relate to a compelling governmental interest. However, the government may choose to close the forum to the public and expressive activities. It does not have to keep this type of forum open indefinitely.

Perry's third category is public property not open to the public, either by designation or by tradition. The government may dedicate property to the promotion of a specific governmental purpose. Government may reserve this type of property for its intended purpose, and regulate expressive activity occurring on this type of property as long as the speech regulation is reasonable and not an effort to suppress expression merely because public officials oppose the speaker's view. Let us consider these general statements in light of the specific facts that follow.

(b) Content Neutral Regulations

United States v. Grace (1983) invalidated a portion of a federal statute prohibiting picketing on the public sidewalks surrounding the United States Supreme Court building. *Grace* summarized and restated the test for time, place, or manner regulations of speech in a public forum as follows: "[t]he government may enforce reasonable time, place, and manner regulations as long as the restrictions are content neutral, are narrowly tailored to serve a significant government interest, and leave open ample alternative channels of communication."

Clark v. Community for Creative Non–Violence (1984), upheld a regulation limiting the time when a public park could be used, even though the limitation restricted the ability of the would be demonstrators to bring their message to the attention of the public by sleeping in symbolic "tent cities" in the park. The refusal to allow a demonstration was a valid time, place, or manner regulation because it was a content neutral means of promoting the government interest in preserving parks and the regulation allowed adequate alternative channels of communication.

In *United States v. Kokinda* (1989), the Court, with no majority opinion, upheld the constitutionality of a federal law prohibiting solicitation on postal property. The respondents in this case were members of a political advocacy group who set up a table on a sidewalk near the entrance to a United States Post Office in order to solicit contributions, sell books and subscriptions, and distribute literature. The sidewalk, which lies entirely on Postal Service property, was the only way that customers could travel from the post office to the parking lot. The solicitors impeded the normal flow of traffic, and it is intrusive for the postal customers to confront people, face-to-face, soliciting contributions.

The City of Cincinnati banned the distribution of "commercial" publications (such as free magazines advertising real estate sales) through the use of free-standing news racks on public property, such as city sidewalks. However, the city did not extend the ban to similar news racks containing newspapers. The city argued that the purpose of its prohibition was to make the sidewalks more attractive and promote safer streets (e.g., people might trip over the news racks). However, while the city sought to remove the 62 news racks distributing these commercial publications, it did not apply its prohibition to news racks (numbering about 1,500 to 2,000) that sold regular *newspapers*. Because the city law was based on the content of each type of publication, it was not content neutral. The Court in *City of Cincinnati v. Discovery Network, Inc.* (1993), invalidated the ban.

In *Frisby v. Schultz* (1988) the Court, over several dissents, approved a residential picketing statute, but only after interpreting it in an unusually narrow fashion. The majority rejected a facial challenge to a statute that it interpreted to ban only "focused" picketing, that is, picketing that would take place solely in front of a particular residence. Such picketing is directed at the household, not the public at large. The statute did not preclude marching through residential neighborhoods or even walking in front of an entire block of houses.

(c) Some Nonpublic Forum Rulings

Recall that the third category of public forum analysis under *Perry* is public property not open to the public either by designation or by tradition. The government may operate property that is dedicated to the promotion of a specific governmental purpose. As stated in *Perry*, the government may reserve this type of property for its intended purpose, and regulate expressive activity therein, "as long as the regulation on speech is reasonable and not an effort to suppress expression merely because public officials oppose the speaker's view."

Members of the City Council of Los Angeles v. Taxpayers for Vincent (1984) upheld a city ordinance that prohibited posting of signs on public property and upheld the application of that ordinance to prohibit placing campaign signs on street light posts in the city. The majority opinion by Justice Stevens noted that light posts are not a type of government property traditionally designated for public communication and did not constitute a public forum. The prohibition of speech was permissible because it promoted important government interests in aesthetic values and the environment that were unrelated to the suppression of a particular viewpoint.

Minnesota State Board for Community Colleges v. Knight (1984) upheld a state law that required academic administrators to "meet and confer" with teachers regarding questions of policy and governance but limited these discussions to representatives of the teachers selected by a union that had been elected to be the exclusive bargaining representative of the teachers. Justice O'Connor, for the Court, found that the meet and confer sessions were not a forum of any type and could be reserved for discussions between administrators and representatives of the exclusive bargaining agent of the teachers even though the issues to be discussed at these meetings were outside of the scope of contract negotiations. The regulation did not significantly restrict the ability of nonunion employees to communicate their views on policy issues to college administrators. Because this meeting was not open to the public, it could be reserved for communication between the administration and union representatives.

The Court, in a four to three opinion, upheld an Executive Order limiting charitable solicitation of federal employees during working hours, in *Cornelius v. NAACP Legal Defense and Educational Fund, Inc.* (1985). The federal government participates in the Combined Federal Campaign (CFC), a charity drive directed at federal employees during working hours. An Executive Order limited participation to tax-exempt, nonprofit charitable agencies that provide direct health and welfare services to individuals or their families. The Order specifically excluded legal defense and political advocacy organizations. The Court, applying *Perry,* upheld the constitutionality of the Executive Order.

The Court concluded that the CFC is a nonpublic forum. Neither the Government's practice nor policy demonstrated that the government had convicted the CFC into a public forum open to all tax-exempt organizations. The Court concluded that control "over access to a nonpublic forum can be based on subject matter and speaker identity so long as the distinctions drawn are reasonable in light of the purpose served by the forum and are viewpoint neutral." The Court found that it was reasonable for the Government to conclude that money given directly for food and shelter to the needy is more beneficial than money given for litigation. The majority also believed that the restrictions on access avoided the appearance of government favoritism or entanglement with particular viewpoints.

The majority ruled that the First Amendment does not forbid a viewpoint neutral exclusion of speakers who would disrupt a nonpublic forum and hinder its effectiveness for its intended purpose.

Because this is a nonpublic forum, there is no requirement that the Government's restrictions on access be "narrowly tailored," or that its interests in exclusion be "compelling." The Court added: "Although the avoidance of controversy is not a valid ground for restricting speech in a public forum, a nonpublic forum by definition is not dedicated to general debate or the free exchange of ideas."

The Court then remanded to determine whether the Government had impermissibly excluded the respondents from the CFC because it disagreed with their viewpoints.

(d) Schools and Forum Analysis

School Assemblies. *Bethel School District No. 403 v. Fraser* (1986) upheld the power of school authorities to discipline a student for delivering, at a school assembly, a speech that promoted another student as a candidate for student government by the use of "persuasive sexual innuendo." A school assembly, much like a class session, is not a public forum. Schools may make content based decisions that are reasonable and are not attempts to suppress a viewpoint.

Chief Justice Burger's majority opinion said that the speech "was plainly offensive to both teachers and students," "was acutely insulting to teen-age girl students," and "could well be seriously damaging to its less mature audience, many of whom were only 14 years old and on the threshold of awareness of human sexuality." Burger asserted, "The determination of what manner of speech in the classroom or in school assembly is inappropriate properly rests with the school board."

Justice Brennan, normally a strong proponent of free speech, concurred in the result. He said that the speech was no more obscene or lewd "than the bulk of programs currently on prime-time television or in the local cinema." Nonetheless, he would uphold the school board action because this speech may be punished as "disruptive" in the school environment.

School Libraries. In *Board of Education, Island Trees Union Free School District No. 26 v. Pico* (1982) the Court reviewed the decision of a local school board to remove certain books from the libraries of a public high school and public junior high school. The school board had determined that the books were not obscene, in a legal sense, but the board also concluded that the books were "anti-American, anti-Christian, anti-Semitic, and just plain filthy." With no majority opinion, the Supreme Court sent the case back to the lower court for a trial that was to determine the motivation of the school board.

If the school board removed books from the school library for the purpose of suppressing a viewpoint, the action would have been ruled invalid. Justice Brennan's plurality opinion in *Pico* emphasized that the case did not involve text books or decisions regarding the acquisition of books for the library, although he did not clearly explain how he would have approached viewpoint suppression issues in litigation involving such subjects. Justice Brennan's plurality opinion, and a separate concurring opinion by Justice Blackmun, struggled with the problem of trying to define the role of courts in identifying governmental attempts to suppress viewpoints. However, neither Brennan nor Blackmun was very clear regarding how courts could, or should, identify a motive to suppress viewpoints in the operation of a school library.

Justice White, who concurred in the judgment in *Pico*, found no reason to address constitutional issues until after the trial court had the opportunity to determine whether the school board had removed the books from the library for the purpose of suppressing ideas or viewpoints. The dissenting Justices in *Pico* thought that the Court should defer to any arguably reasonable decisions of school authorities regarding material that would be kept in a library and available to the students.

School Newspapers. *Hazelwood School District v. Kuhlmeier* (1988) relying on *Bethel*, affirmed the broad power of a *high school* over expressive activities such as *school-sponsored* publications and school sponsored plays. The school and its newspaper were not traditional public forums, and the evidence indicated that the school did not intend to convert its newspaper to a public forum. The school newspaper was part of a Journalism course, for which the students received academic credit and grades. The Journalism teacher exercised a great deal of control over the newspaper by selecting its editors, setting publication dates, editing stories, etc. The school principal then reviewed every issue prior to publication. Because the high school sponsored this newspaper, it could properly exercise a great deal of control over it.

The high school did not offend the First Amendment by exercising editorial control over the style and content of student speech if its actions are reasonably related to "legitimate pedagogical concerns." Applying this test the Court upheld the high school principal's decision to excise two pages from the student newspaper because he reasonably concluded that the articles unfairly impinged on the privacy rights of pregnant students and others. The Court specifically noted that it need "not now decide whether the same degree of [judicial] deference is appropriate to school-sponsored expressive activities at the college and university level."

School Buildings, After Hours. In *Lamb's Chapel v. Center Moriches Union Free School District* (1993) and *Widmar v. Vincent*

(1981) the Court invalidated laws that allowed all public organizations, or all student organizations, to use school facilities (when classes were not in session) unless the group was religious in nature. The government had created a designated public forum. The content based regulation was not narrowly tailored to promote a compelling interest.

State University Funding of Student Organizations, Including Student Religious Groups. The University of Virginia, a state school, paid the printing costs of publications of student groups. These student groups were independent of the University and not controlled by it. The Student Activities Fund (SAF) would pay outside contractors for these printing costs. In administering SAF, the University engaged in viewpoint discrimination against a particular student newspaper; the school refused to pay the publication costs of a particular student group because it had a Christian perspective. University regulations gave funds to student groups *except* those that "promot[ed] or manifest[ed] a particular belie[f] in or about a deity or an ultimate reality." These regulations violated the First Amendment.

In *Rosenberger v. Rector and Visitors of the University of Virginia* (1995), the Court held that the SAF was a limited public forum, and—in light of *Lamb's Chapel*—the University was unconstitutionally discriminating against the viewpoint advocated by this particular student publication. Providing funds to student publications on a neutral basis is no different than providing access to facilities. Just as the school in *Lamb's Chapel* could not constitutionally deny access to a public forum on the basis of religious belief, so also the University of Virginia could not constitutionally refuse to provide funding for a particular student publication because of the religious advocacy of that publication. The University could not deny funding to the publications of a student group based on the secular views of the group; religious views are deserving of no lesser status under the First Amendment. There was no establishment clause violation because the government was neutral towards religion.

(e) Prisons

Turner v. Safley (1987) upheld prison regulations that, in effect, prohibited prison inmates from writing to non-family inmates. The Court rejected the argument that the ban on inmate-to-inmate correspondence violated the First Amendment. It also rejected a strict scrutiny test. The evidence showed that the prison adopted the correspondence rule primarily for security reasons. Inmate mail between prisons can compromise protective custody offered to inmates from other institutions; such correspondence facilitates communications between gang members who had been transferred to other prisons in an effort to break up the gang; and such correspondence helps communicate escape plans and assault efforts. The correspondence rule is content-neutral, logically advances the goals of institutional security and safety, and is not an exaggerated response to those objectives.

In *Overton v. Bazzetta* (2003), a unanimous Court emphasized that the test in these cases is whether the prison regulations are rationally related to legitimate penological objectives. Courts must grant "substantial deference" to the professional judgment of prison administrators, because they bear a significant responsibility for defining the legitimate goals of a corrections system and for determining the most appropriate means to accomplish them. In this case, the Court held that various restrictions on prison visitation did not violate any right of association or other constitutional rights.

(f) Airports

The Board of Airport Commissioners of Los Angeles International Airport adopted a Resolution that explicitly provided, in part, that "the Central Terminal Area at Los Angeles International Airport is not open for First Amendment activities by any individual and/or entity." Jews for Jesus, Inc., a nonprofit religious corporation, challenged the Resolution and a unanimous Court invalidated it in, *Board of Airport Commissioners of City of Los Angeles v. Jews for Jesus, Inc.* (1987). The Court ruled that, even if the airport were a nonpublic forum, the Resolution is still unconstitutionally overbroad.

Subsequently, *International Society for Krishna Consciousness, Inc. v. Lee* (1992) surprised many observers by holding that a government-owned airport open to the public is *not* a public forum. The International Society for Krishna Consciousness challenged the New York Port Authority's restrictions on the distribution of literature and the solicitation of contributions in airport terminals.

The majority emphasized that state-owned airports are like privately owned airports in that they are *commercial* establishments funded by user fees and designed to make a regulated profit. This purpose may be frustrated if airports are also required to provide for the free exchange of ideas.

Solicitation of Funds. *International Society for Krishna Consciousness, Inc. v. Lee* (1992) also held that prohibiting the solicitation of funds in an airport terminal (a nonpublic forum) is constitutional because it is *"reasonable."* Solicitors might slow down the pace of traffic, affecting passengers in a hurry to catch a flight. The solicitation of funds in an airport creates special risks of duress and fraud. For these reasons, the Port Authority limited solicitation to the sidewalk areas outside of the airport terminals. The Court upheld these anti-solicitation regulations, because it was not necessary for the Port Authority to demonstrate that they were the most reasonable, or only reasonable, way of dealing with the problem.

Distribution of Literature. In *Lee v. International Society for Krishna Consciousness, Inc.* (1992), a short per curiam opinion following *Lee,* a different majority of judges (unable to agree on a rationale) held that the First Amendment does *not* allow the Port Authority to ban the distribution of literature in the airport terminals. Justice O'Connor's separate opinion made clear that only the *free* distribution of literature or leafleting is protected because it does not present the same kinds of problems (other than litter) associated with face-to-face solicitation of funds. That opinion, together with the views of Chief Justice Rehnquist and Justices White, Scalia, and Thomas, added up to a five person majority that allowed the Port Authority to ban the face-to-face *sale* of literature. Justice O'Connor noted that the government could use content neutral regulations to limit the distribution of free material to only designated times or designated areas in the airport.

(g) Content-Based Restrictions Surrounding Polling Places

Burson v. Freeman (1992) is an atypical case. The Court, with no majority opinion, approved content-based restrictions in a public forum. The Court balanced two important rights: the right to engage in political speech, which is at the heart of the First Amendment, and the right to vote, the right that is preservative of all our rights and at the heart of democracy.

A Tennessee law (like the law of many other jurisdictions) prohibited the solicitation of votes and the display or distribution of campaign materials within 100 feet of the entrance to a polling place. The law was clearly content-based. It did not prohibit commercial solicitation in the area immediately surrounding the voting booth, but it banned public discussion of an entire topic within the "campaign free" zone. The Supreme Court, with no majority opinion, upheld the law.

Justice Blackmun's plurality found that the section survived an exacting scrutiny test. The law served a compelling state interest, to prevent voter intimidation and election fraud. "The only way to preserve the secrecy of the ballot is to limit access to the area around the voter." The next question is *"how large* a restricted zone is permissible or sufficiently tailored." The plurality rejected the argument that the 100 foot boundary was not narrowly tailored. The Tennessee Supreme Court had required that the boundary be reduced to 25 feet, but it takes only about 15 seconds to walk the 75 additional feet. Whatever the boundary is, the plurality concluded that a 100 foot boundary is on the constitutional side of the line. This is the "rare case" that "survives strict scrutiny."

Justice Scalia, concurring in the judgment, argued that the area around the polling booth, *"by long tradition,"* was not a public forum. He viewed the law as a reasonable, viewpoint-neutral regulation of a *non*public forum.

(h) Protests in the Public Forum: Abortion Clinics

Madsen v. Women's Health Center, Inc. (1994) considered the constitutionality of a state court injunction entered against protestors at a Florida abortion clinic. The original state court injunction prohibited petitioners from interfering with public access to the abortion clinic and from physically abusing persons entering or leaving the clinic. The injunction applied to protest activities in the traditional public forum, the streets and sidewalks. The state court broadened this injunction after it concluded that protestors were still interfering with clinic access. This broadened injunction applied to petitioners, Operation Rescue and various other named organizations, their agents, and "all persons acting in concert or participation with them, or on their behalf;" it prohibited them from engaging in various acts. Chief Justice Rehnquist, for a divided Court, invalidated parts of this injunction and upheld other parts.

Madsen concluded that, given the particular factual circumstances and the record before the Court, the state court's establishment of a 36 foot buffer zone on a public street from which demonstrators were excluded does not violate the First Amendment because it burdened no more speech than necessary to prevent unlawful conduct. But *Madsen* invalidated other parts of the injunction as violating the First Amendment because they were broader than necessary. The Court invalidated a 36 foot buffer zone applied to private property, a prohibition of "images observable" from the abortion clinic, and a 300 foot buffer zone around residences.

Although the amended injunction did not apply to prohibit demonstrations by people supporting abortions, that fact did not make it content based, said the majority, because there were no demonstrations by people favoring abortions and thus no request for relief from such demonstrations.

Madsen evaluated an injunction, not a statute. Though the Court concluded that the injunction was content neutral, it still limited protest activities in the traditional public forum. A statute or ordinance is generally applicable and represents a choice made by the legislative processes. In contrast, an injunction has a greater risk of censorship and discriminatory application because one judge imposes it on certain individuals, without any legislative debate. Unlike a law, an injunction can be specifically tailored.

In light of these considerations, there should be a "somewhat more stringent application of general First Amendment principles" than would be applied in traditional time, place, and manner analysis. The proper test is to determine whether the injunction burdens "no more speech than necessary" to accomplish its objective. The injunction must be narrowly drawn, "couched in the narrowest terms" necessary to accomplish its "pin-pointed objectives."

On the factual record of this case, *Madsen* found that the governmental interests that the Florida Supreme Court had identified were "quite sufficient" to justify an appropriately tailored injunction.

Statutory Restrictions on Abortion Protests. *Hill v. Colorado* (2000) upheld (five to four) the constitutionality of a 1993 Colorado statute that regulates speech-related conduct within 100 feet of the entrance to any health care facility. The specific section of the statute challenged, made it unlawful for any person within the regulated areas to "knowingly approach" within eight feet of another person, without that person's consent, "for the purpose of passing a leaflet or handbill to, displaying a sign to, or engaging in oral protest, education, or counseling with such other person...."

The majority concluded that the statute was (1) a narrowly-tailored content-neutral time, place and manner regulation; (2) was neither overbroad nor unconstitutionally vague; and (3) did not any impose unconstitutional prior restraint on speech.

The Court ruled that the statute was content-neutral for three reasons. First, the statute regulates the places where some speech may occur, rather than regulate speech itself. Second, the legislature did not adopt the law because of disagreement with the message of any speech, and the state court had held that the restrictions apply to all demonstrators, without regard to viewpoint. The statute, in short, made no reference to the content of speech. Third, the State's interests, said the Court, were unrelated to the content of the demonstrators' speech.

However, the statute applies to persons who "knowingly approach" within eight feet of another to engage in "oral protest, education, or counseling." Hence, the petitioners said that the law was "content-based" because it requires examination of the content of a speaker's comments. The Court, however, responded that state enforcement authorities may look at a statement's content in order to determine whether a rule of law applies to a course of conduct. "it is unlikely that there would often be any need to know exactly what words were spoken in order to determine whether 'sidewalk counselors' are engaging in 'oral protest, education, or counseling' rather than pure social or random conversation."

Thus, the majority said, the Colorado law is "easily distinguishable" from *Carey v. Brown* (1980), where the Court invalidated a law that prohibited all picketing except for picketing of a place of employment in a labor dispute, thereby preferring expression concerning one particular subject.

(i) Regulation to Prevent Fraud and Annoyance

Anonymity. An author is generally free to be anonymous. *The Federalist Papers* were published anonymously. Anonymity protects the author who may be motivated by fear of economic, official, or social reprisal, or merely has a desire to preserve her privacy. An author's decision to exclude her name is like other editorial decisions, an aspect of free speech.

Talley v. California (1960) invalidated, on its face, a state statute banning anonymous handbills. Throughout history, some persecuted groups have been able to criticize oppressive practices either anonymously or not at all. This right to anonymity is a function of the freedom of association, because identification and the subsequent fear of reprisal could effectively chill legitimate discussions of public interest. *Talley* specifically did not pass on the validity of a more narrowly tailored ordinance, limited to identifying those responsible for fraud, false advertising, or libel.

The Court dealt with that question in *McIntyre v. Ohio Elections Commission* (1995), which invalidated an Ohio statute that prohibited the distribution of anonymous campaign literature. Margaret McIntyre distributed leaflets objecting to a proposed school tax levy. Some of the handbills identified her as expressing the views of "concerned parents and taxpayers." The Ohio Election Commission imposed a $100 fine. The United States Supreme Court acknowledged that the State might be able to justify a limited identification requirement, but Ohio's restriction was too broad.

In *United States v. Harriss* (1954), the Court upheld limited disclosure requirements for lobbyists. Unlike the situation in *McIntyre,* lobbyists have direct access to elected officials, and the lack of any disclosure may cause the appearance of corruption and improper influence. Disclosure requirements related to campaign financing and elections are examined elsewhere in this chapter.

Watchtower Bible & Tract Society of New York, Inc. v. Village of Stratton (2002), invalidated a village ordinance that prohibited "canvassers" and others from "going in and upon" private residential property to promote any "cause" without first securing a

"Solicitation Permit" from the mayor. There was no charge for the permit, which was issued routinely after an applicant filled out a detailed "Solicitor's Registration Form." The canvasser could then visit premises listed on the registration form, but he must carry the permit and exhibit it if a police officer or resident requests it. The ordinance sets forth grounds for the denial or revocation of a permit (e.g., incomplete information or fraud by the applicants in filling out the form), but the record before the Court did not show that any application had been denied or that any permit had been revoked. Jehovah's Witnesses (who offered religious literature without cost, but did accept donations) objected to the permit requirement and did not apply for it.

The Court held that this municipal ordinance violated the First Amendment protection accorded to anonymous pamphleteering or discourse. The Court invalidated the ordinance as it applied to religious proselytizing, anonymous political speech, and the distribution of handbills. The ordinance necessarily resulted in surrender of anonymity of individuals supporting causes; it imposed an objective burden on some speech of citizens holding religious or patriotic views; it banned a significant amount of spontaneous speech. The Court ruled that the law was not narrowly tailored to protect the privacy of residents. The Court said that, had the ordinance applied only to commercial activities and the solicitation of funds, arguably the ordinance would have been tailored to the Village's interest in protecting the privacy of its residents and preventing fraud.

If a city seeks to regulate to prevent fraud, its law must be carefully tailored to achieve this purpose without unduly limiting speech. *Village of Schaumburg v. Citizens for a Better Environment* (1980) invalidated, as overbroad, a local ordinance that prohibited the solicitation of contributions by charitable organizations that do not use at least 75% of their receipts directly for "charitable purposes," which the law defined as excluding the expenses of solicitation, salaries, overhead, and other administrative expenses.

The Court ruled that the Village could protect its antifraud interests by more narrowly drawn regulations that would directly prohibit fraudulent misrepresentations, or require that charitable organizations inform the public how their moneys are spent.

The Court in *Secretary of State v. Joseph H. Munson Co., Inc.* (1984) examined a statute that placed a twenty-five percent limitation on charitable fund raising expenses. The statute was slightly different from that examined in *Citizens for a Better Environment* because the statute in *Joseph H. Munson* allowed for an administrative waiver of the limitation based on a demonstration of financial necessity by a charity. The Court still concluded that a waiver provision did not save the statute from being stricken as unconstitutionally overbroad.

Waiver of the limitation for a charity that faced economic hardship did not significantly decrease the restriction on protected First Amendment activity because the waiver did not exempt from the spending ceiling the money spent on the dissemination of information by the organization. Because this statute involved a direct restriction on speech and the means chosen to prevent the public from being defrauded were "imprecise," the Court found that the statute created an unnecessary risk of chilling free speech and should be validated on its face.

However, *Illinois ex rel. Madigan v. Telemarketing Associates Inc.* (2003) ruled that the First Amendment does not bar fraud claims asserted under Illinois law against professional fundraisers hired by charitable organization, if the claims are based on allegations that fundraisers made false or misleading representations designed to deceive donors about how their donations would be used. For example, it is misleading for a Telemarketer to affirmatively represent that a significant amount of each dollar donated would be paid over to a veterans' organization to be used for specific charitable purposes if in fact Telemarketers knew that only 15 cents or less of each dollar would be available for those purposes.

The Government may require labeling or disclosure requirements in order to protect (or disclose information) to recipients so long as these requirements do not unduly burden the free speech of the disseminators and are not based on content. Thus, *Rowan v. U.S. Post Office Department* (1970) ruled that it is constitutional for a statute to provide that the addressee of mail may instruct the post office not to deliver all future mailings from any given sender. The government, in such a case, itself places no restrictions on speech on the basis of content. The government merely respects the wishes of the intended recipient.

However *Lamont v. Postmaster General* (1965) ruled that a statute cannot authorize the Secretary of the Treasury to prohibit the post office from delivering mail to an address if the Secretary decides it is "communist political propaganda," unless the addressee returns a reply card certifying his desire to receive such mail. That law violates the First Amendment, because neither the Secretary nor the Post Office may regulate the flow of mail based on its content. The government's physical detention of the materials, not the fact that a government official labeled them as "communist political propaganda," offended the First Amendment.

This point is made clear in *Meese v. Keene* (1987). In that case the Court upheld certain provisions of the Foreign Agents Registration Act. That Act defines the term "political propaganda" to include any communication that is reasonably adapted to, or intended to, influence the recipient within the United States with reference to "the policies of a foreign country or foreign political party." When the agent of a foreign principal disseminates this "political propaganda" the law requires that he or she must make a disclosure statement to the recipients; this disclosure includes the agent's identity, the identity of the principle for whom the agent acts, a statement that a report describing the extent of the material is registered with the Department of Justice, and that such registration "does not indicate approval of the contents of this material by the United States Government."

The term "political propaganda" does *not* appear in the disclosure form that must be filed, but it is used in the Act. This registration requirement "is comprehensive, *applied equally* to agents of friendly, neutral, and unfriendly governments." The Act defines, "propaganda" as all advocacy materials, even those that are completely accurate. The purpose of the statute, was to inform recipients of the source of advocacy materials produced by or under the aegis of a foreign government. The statute did not prohibit, edit, or restrain the distribution of the foreign advocacy materials. Congress simply required disclosure—the labeling of information to disclose its foreign origin.

§ 16.29 Symbolic Speech

When courts, or professors, refer to a problem as being one that involves symbolic speech, they are only identifying a problem where the key issue is whether non-verbal activity should be treated as if it were speech. As we explained in the introduction to this section, if non-verbal activity is to be considered speech, then we would look at the restriction on the non-verbal activity in the same way as we would look at the restrictions on any other types of speech.

The Supreme Court has not identified any standard for determining whether non-verbal activity should be considered speech. In *United States v. O'Brien* (1968) the Court upheld a law banning the destruction of the selective service registration certificates (even when the destruction was part of a protest regarding governmental policies). The *O'Brien* Court assumed that the destruction of the draft card was speech. The majority opinion stated that the mere intent of the speaker could not be determinative as to whether the non-verbal activity should be considered speech.

The governmental action regarding the non-verbal activity, very often, will identify for the court or student the speech element that is involved in that activity. Thus, in *Stromberg v. California*

(1931), the Supreme Court invalidated a state statute prohibiting the displaying of a red flag because the statute prohibited the display of such a flag "as a sign, symbol or emblem of opposition to organized government." The law was clearly aimed at the content of the speech; the government admitted that the red flag constituted a non-verbal form of communication.

In *Tinker v. Des Moines Independent Community School District* (1969) the Court invalidated a public school authority's decision to ban students from wearing black armbands in the school. The school admitted that the reason for banning the armbands was the message of protest identified with the armband; and the school authority's fear that the message might disrupt the school. On that basis, the Court found that the armband constituted expression. The Court then ruled that the total suppression of the form of communication [the arm band] was not tailored to preventing actual disruption of school activities; and that the government regulation was a form of content regulation that violated the First Amendment.

In *Texas v. Johnson* (1989) the Court invalidated a state law that banned desecration of the United States flag. The Court invalidated a similar federal statute in *United States v. Eichman* (1990). In each case, there was no doubt that the banned action [desecration of the flag] constituted speech. The government law did not ban the burning of all red, white or blue material but, rather, banned only the burning of such material when it was a disrespectful treatment of the flag of the United States of America. The traditionally proper disposal of the flag requires burning or burial of the flag; these methods for flag disposal would not have been banned by these laws. Because each law was content-based, the Court had to determine whether the banned speech fit within a previously established category of punishable speech, which it did not, or whether the law was narrowly tailored to promote a compelling governmental interest. A majority of the Justices found that the government did not have a compelling interest in protecting the burning of privately owned flags from desecration. Perhaps the Court should have allowed the government to ban the expression of that viewpoint in this particularly offensive manner. Nevertheless, a majority of the Justices rejected the government's argument.

Perhaps the most difficult determination of whether non-verbal activity constituted speech involved the regulation of nudity. As we will see in the section on obscenity, which concludes this Chapter, the Court has upheld restrictions on human nudity even when the nudity was involved in dancing or other live artistic activity. The laws banning public nudity were upheld in two cases as applied to human activity, without the Court giving a clear rationale for its rulings. The bans on public nudity, and their application to dancers in private clubs, seem to have been upheld as content-neutral time, place or manner regulations, a subject which we examined previously in this Chapter.

The interesting question in the nude dancing or nude human art cases is: why did the Court have to address any First Amendment issue in these cases? Is it clear to you that someone dancing in the nude conveys a different idea or form of expression than someone doing the identical dance with a minimal amount of clothing? In the nude dancing cases, a majority of the Justices assumed that nude dancing constituted speech. However, in these cases, the Court did not enunciate a clear standard for determining the types of non-verbal conduct that should be treated as speech.

Under *O'Brien* the government can restrict the non-verbal speech if the government's action is (1) within the constitutional power of government; (2) related to an important or substantial government interest; (3) is unrelated to the suppression of expression; (4) no greater than essential to further that interest.

When stated as a general principle, the *O'Brien* standard requires courts to uphold the restriction of non-verbal speech so long as the speech regulation is narrowly tailored to promote an important or substantial governmental interest (within the constitutional power of government) that is unrelated to the suppression of expression.

When the Court apply this standard to a time, place or manner regulation [which is simply a government law dealing with the aspects of speech that are not content-related], the Court converts this principle into a three-part test, and requires that the regulation: (1) be content-neutral; (2) be narrowly tailored to an important or substantial government interest; (3) and, to leave open adequate alternative channels of communication. The bans on nudity met this standard. A majority of the Justices believed that the bans on nudity survived these tests for the regulation of the non-communicative [time, place or manner] aspects of speech.

§ 16.30   Regulating the Electoral Process: Election Promises

A political candidate promised the voters that he intended, if elected, to serve at a salary less than that "fixed by law." The state claimed that such statements violated a statute prohibiting candidates from offering material benefits to voters in consideration for their votes. One does not have to be cynical to realize that incumbents did not like it that a challenger promised to not accept a pay raise if elected. So, the state tried to prosecute the candidate for bribery of the voters.

Without a dissent, in *Brown v. Hartlage* (1982) the Court held that the statute could not constitutionally be applied in such circumstances; the promise hardly fitted into the category of a private, politically corrupt arrangement. The state can prohibit bribes, but it cannot constitutionally prohibit open promises made to voters generally. As a matter of free speech, the candidate has the right to make such promises. The state law, in effect, made it a crime for a politician to make and keep a campaign promise. Under the state's view, incumbents would be protected from challengers who tried to make an issue of salaries that the incumbents had voted themselves.

Regulating the Campaign Promises of Judicial Candidates. The Court has also upheld the political campaign speech of judges running for election, but, unlike *Hartlage*, the Court was not unanimous.

Minnesota, like 39 other states, chooses judges through popular elections. Rules of judicial conduct limit the candidates' speech. One rule (which *White* did not challenge) prohibits a judicial candidate or judge from making "pledges or promises" on how he will rule in a particular case. A second rule of judicial ethics prohibits a candidate for judicial office from "announcing" a view on any "disputed legal or political" issue if the issue might come before a court. This cause prohibits a candidate's "mere statement" even if he does not bind himself bind himself to maintain that position after election.

In *Republican Party of Minnesota v. White* (2002), the Court held that this second prohibition on judicial candidates violates the First Amendment. Citing *Brown v. Hartlage*, the Court said, in order for the announce clause to be narrowly tailored, it must not "unnecessarily circumscribe protected expression". The Minnesota rule did not meet this test. One common view of "impartiality" is no bias for or against any party to the proceeding. But the clause is not tailored to serve that interest because "it does not restrict speech for or against particular parties, but rather speech for or against particular issues." "Impartiality" in the sense of no preconception for or against a particular legal view, is not a compelling state interest, because it is "virtually impossible, and hardly desirable, to find a judge who does not have preconceptions about the law," particularly since the Minnesota Constitution requires judges to be "learned in the law."

Nor does the prohibition promote impartiality in the sense of "openmindedness" because the announce clause was in the majority's view "woefully underinclusive." For example, a judge could confront a legal issue on which he has expressed an opinion while on the bench. Judges often state their views on disputed legal issues outside the context of adjudication, if they teach classes or write books or give speeches.

Under the Minnesota rule, judges could criticize the opinions of other judges by writing dissents or dictum in their own decisions, but challengers to the sitting judge did not have this option. This restriction on campaign speech is like incumbent protection legislation, for it served to limit criticism of existing judges by the people most likely to engage in such criticism—the people running for office to unseat them.

§ 16.31   Regulation of Campaign Financing

(a) Introduction

Due to concern for the possible effects on democratic government of the spiraling costs of election campaigns, Congress enacted the Federal Election Campaign Act of 1971 and added more stringent Amendments with the Federal Election Campaign Act Amendments of 1974. These statutes involved the federal government in the regulation of much of the day-to-day operation of political campaigns for federal office. There are four primary regulations: (1) regulating the amounts contributed to or expended by the candidate or his campaign committee; (2) forbidding "dirty tricks" by creating penalties for the "fraudulent misrepresentation of campaign authority"; (3) requiring public disclosure of contributions to and expenditures by a candidate, his campaign committee or individual expenditures on behalf of a candidate; (4) providing for public financing of all phases of presidential elections.

The Supreme Court heard a comprehensive challenge to this statute in *Buckley v. Valeo* (1976), which raised significant First Amendment issues relating to central provisions of the Act. Distinguishing between the speech interest inherent in campaign contributions and campaign expenditures, the Court, per curiam, upheld the limitations imposed on contributions, but invalidated those related to expenditures. The disclosure and reporting requirements were sustained as necessary for the enforcement of the Act.

It is important to note the underlying rationale for the result in *Buckley*. Campaign contributions and expenditures are speech or are so intrinsically related to speech that any regulation of campaign funding must comply with the First Amendment. *Buckley* recognizes that, under the First Amendment, "money talks," not just figuratively, but literally.

(b) Campaign Contributions and Expenditures

The primary importance of *Buckley* lies in its distinction between campaign contributions and expenditures.

Buckley concluded that the speech interests in campaign contributions are marginal, because they convey only an undifferentiated expression of support rather than the specific values that motivate that support.

The Federal Election Campaign Act of 1971 limited contributions by individuals to any single candidate for federal office to $1,000 per election. The Court upheld these contributions limits, noting that they left persons "free to engage in independent political expression...." Years later the Court, in *Nixon v. Shrink Missouri Government* (2000) held that this $1000 did not have to be indexed for inflation.

Buckley v. Valeo made clear that Congress cannot impose limitations on expenditures by third parties ("independent political expression") by treating them as "contributions" to candidates. The government's interest in preventing corruption is inadequate to justify a ceiling on independent expenditures.

Buckley distinguished expenditures, because they are directly related to the expression of political views. They are on a higher plane of constitutional values, so the justification for such legislative intrusion into protected speech requires more exacting scrutiny. *Buckley* held that the amount of money an individual can spend to advocate either his own candidacy or that of another is a matter within his own discretion.

(c) The Political Speech of Corporations and Other Entities

First National Bank v. Bellotti (1978) held unconstitutional a Massachusetts law that prohibited corporate expenditures for the purpose of influencing the vote on any referendum submitted to the voters other than one materially affecting the property, business, or assets of the corporation. The statute was applied to corporations that had sought to spend money to publicize their view in opposition to a proposed progressive income tax on corporations.

Bellotti rejected the argument that corporate speech is protected only when it pertains directly to the corporation's business interests. No precedent supported this arbitrary distinction. Then *Bellotti* considered the question of whether the state statute, which restricted corporate speech, could "survive the exacting scrutiny necessitated by a state-imposed restriction on freedom of expression." Measured by this test, the state did not show that the law was narrowly tailored to promote a compelling interest.

The *Bellotti* majority opinion distinguished corporate contributions to referenda from corporate contributions to political candidates on the grounds that the latter raises more clearly problems of corruption through the creation of political debt. The government has an important interest in regulating such corruption.

In other cases the Court has distinguished between funds accumulated in the economic marketplace versus funds accumulated in the political marketplace. Congress may protect an individual (who invests in a commercial, corporate enterprise) so that the commercial enterprise does not use those funds (invested for economic gain) for political candidates that the investor does not support.

In *Federal Election Commission v. Massachusetts Citizens for Life, Inc.* (1986) a fragmented Court considered a different situation, the case of the Massachusetts Citizens for Life, Inc., a nonprofit corporation, that published a newsletter urging readers to vote "prolife" in an upcoming primary election. The Federal Election Commission ruled that the nonprofit corporation violated a section of the Federal Election Campaign Act prohibiting direct expenditures of corporate funds in connection with election to public office. The Supreme Court, speaking through Justice Brennan, held that the section violated the First Amendment, as applied.

The money that a commercial enterprise collects from investors does not reflect the investors' support for the political ideas favored by the corporation's management. "Direct corporate spending on political activity raises the prospect that resources amassed in the economic marketplace may be used to provide an unfair advantage in the political marketplace." Thus, it should be proper for Congress to require *commercial* corporations that make expenditures in connection with any election to any public office to finance those expenditures by "voluntary" contributions to a separate, segregated fund, although such a requirement would be unconstitutional as applied to voluntary political associations that happen to be incorporated but that cannot engage in business activities, have no shareholders or others who have a claim on its assets or earnings, and are not a conduit for a business corporation or a union.

Federal Election Commission v. Beaumont (2003) upheld the federal ban on direct corporate *contributions* to federal candidates as it is applied to nonprofit advocacy corporations. *Beaumont* distinguished *Massachusetts Citizens for Life*, which invalidated a parallel *expenditure* ban as applied to such entities, by concluding that such non-profit advocacy entities pose a potential for corruption if they are allowed to contribute anything without complying with PAC regulations. The Court rejected the argument that a non-profit corporation's supporters (unlike stockholders in a for-profit corporation) know that it exists in part to influence the political process and this purpose is not corrupt. The Court responded that non-profits may well be able to amass substantial political war chests and may be misused as conduits for circumventing the contribution limits imposed on individuals.

In *Austin v. Michigan Chamber of Commerce* (1990) the Court upheld provisions of the Michigan Campaign Finance Act that prohibits corporations—excluding media corporations—from using corporate treasury funds for independent expenditures in support of, or in opposition to, any candidate in elections for state office. The law, however, did allow corporations to make expenditures from segregated funds used solely for political purposes. The law in question did not regulate independent expenditures of unincorporated labor unions.

The Michigan State Chamber of Commerce challenged the law. The Chamber is a nonprofit corporation with both political and nonpolitical purposes, as its bylaws explain. It funds its activities through annual dues from its members, three-quarters of whom are for-profit corporations. The Chamber wanted to run an advertisement, in a local newspaper, in support of a particular candidate for state office. It sought to enjoin the Michigan statute as unconstitutional but the Court upheld the provision, reversing the Court of Appeals.

The Chamber, said the Court, is not a voluntary political association like *Massachusetts Citizens for Life (MCFL)*. MCFL's narrow focus on promoting particular political ideas assured that its resources reflected its political support. It was formed for an express political purpose and could not engage in any business activities. MCFL had no shareholders or other persons with a claim on its assets or earnings. If any of MCFL's members disagreed with its political activities, they could dissociate themselves without suffering any economic disincentive.

In contrast, many of the Chamber's activities are "politically neutral" and focus on economic and business issues; it provides its members with, for example, group insurance and educational seminars. While the Chamber also has no shareholders, its members have economic disincentives that discourage them from disassociating themselves with the Chamber; the members, for example, might wish to enjoy the Chamber's nonpolitical programs and the contacts with the other members of the business community acquired through membership in the Chamber.

MCFL took no contributions from business corporations, while the Chamber receives three-quarters of its contributions from for-profit corporations, who (by paying dues to the Chamber) would be able to circumvent the state restrictions on campaign contributions and expenditures. *Buckley v. Valeo* allows the state to regulate the campaign contributions and expenditures of these for-profit corporations. Thus for-profit business corporations should not use the Chamber as a conduit.

The Court concluded that the state's decision to regulate only corporations—not unincorporated labor unions, and not media corporations, such as broadcasting stations, newspapers, magazines, or other commentary in the "regular course of publication or broadcasting"—did not violate the equal protection clause of the Fourteenth Amendment. Michigan's decision to regulate only non-media corporations is "precisely tailored to serve the compelling state interest of eliminating from the political process the corrosive effect of political 'war chests' amassed with the aid of the legal advantages given to corporations."

California Medical Association. In *California Medical Association v. Federal Election Commission* (1981), a fragmented Court rejected new challenges to the Federal Election Campaign Act of 1971. The California Medical Association (CMA), an unincorporated association of doctors, formed a political committee, the California Medical Political Action Committee (CALPAC), which was registered with the Federal Election Commission. The Federal Election Commission charged CMA with making contributions in excess of $5000 to CALPAC and also charged CALPAC with knowingly accepting such contributions in violation of the Act, which prohibits individuals and unincorporated associations from contributing more than $5000 per year to any multicandidate political committee such as CALPAC. The Act similarly prohibits political committees such as CALPAC from knowingly accepting contributions in excess of this limit.

The Court ruled that, although a corporation or labor union's contributions to a segregated political fund are unlimited under the Act, the limitation on the unincorporated association's contributions did not violate the equal protection aspects of the Fifth Amendment. "Appellants' claim of unfair treatment ignores the plain fact that the statute as a whole imposes far *fewer* restrictions on individuals and unincorporated associations than it does on corporations and unions." For example, individuals and unincorporated associations may contribute to candidates, and their committees, and to all other political committees while corporations and unions are absolutely barred from making any such contributions.

Nor did the law violate the First Amendment. Justice Marshall's plurality opinion on this issue found that the statute did not limit the amount that CMA or its members may independently spend to advocate political views. Rather the law only limits the amount that CMA may contribute to CALPAC.

Independent Expenditures by Political Committees. *Federal Election Commission v. National Conservative Political Action*

Committee (1985) invalidated a section of the Presidential Election Campaign Fund Act that makes it a criminal offense for an *independent* political committee to spend more than $1,000 to further the election of a presidential candidate who elects public funding. In this case the National Conservative Political Action Committee (NCPAC) and the Fund for a Conservative Majority (FCM), two political action committees or PAC's, solicited funds in support of President Reagan's 1980 presidential campaign. They spent these funds on radio and television advertising. These expenditures were "independent"; that is, these political committees did not make any expenditures at the request of, or in coordination with, the Reagan Election Committee.

The Court—relying on *Buckley v. Valeo* and the distinction it drew between expenditures and contributions—held that the political committee's *independent* expenditures were constitutionally protected, for they "produce speech at the core of the First Amendment."

(d) Disclosure and Reporting Requirements

The statutes challenged in *Buckley*, also required the campaign committees to disclose a list of their contributors as well as requiring individual contributors to report contributions to a candidate or expenditures in support of a candidate. In the only previous case challenging the disclosure of campaign finances, decided in 1934, the Court had upheld the requirement over claims that such a disclosure impaired the individuals' right of association. Following that decision, the Court recognized that compelled disclosure of membership lists may constitute a restraint on the associational rights of the members, because there may exist an interest in maintaining the privacy of such associations.

NAACP v. Alabama (1958) had denied the State the right to compel the disclosure of the NAACP's members for the purpose of ferreting out subversives within the association. The state's interest was only tenuously related to the request and was outweighed by the legitimate fears of the members that they would be subject to harassment and intimidation if their associational ties were made public, regardless of the presence of any subversive connection.

The appellant in *Buckley* relied on this case to argue that disclosure in campaign financing would violate those interests in private political associations. *Buckley* Court distinguished *NAACP v. Alabama* because, unlike that case, the countervailing interests of the state, to be served by such disclosure—providing information in order to allow the voter a more informed judgment as to the candidates' future performance in office; deterring corruption by providing notice that contributions and expenditures would be exposed; and establishing machinery for the enforcement of the Act—were directly related to the purposes in requiring the disclosure.

The Court emphasized that there had been no showing in *Buckley* that potential contributors were deterred by fear of humiliation or public ridicule if their identities were linked to a particular candidate. Although such fears were not unreasonable when related to the funding of minority parties, there also existed no evidence that legitimate associational activity would necessarily be dampened in all minority parties by disclosure. Therefore, only if a party could show a reasonable probability that compelled disclosure of the list of its contributors—or the recipients of campaign disbursements—would subject those contributors or recipients to threats, harassment, or reprisals from either government officials or private parties, will an exemption from the disclosure provisions for that organization be granted. In *Brown v. Socialist Workers' 74 Campaign Committee* (1982) the Court ruled that a minority party had made a showing that justified its exemption. The creation of a blanket exemption, for all minority parties, irrespective of the inherent administrative difficulties, was simply not shown to be necessary to protect the individual member's rights of association.

(e) The Political Party Expenditure Provision of the Federal Election Act of 1971

The Federal Election Campaign Act of 1971 included a provision that imposed dollar limits on a political party's expenditures "in connection with the general election campaign of a [congressional] candidate." In *Colorado Republican Federal Campaign Committee v. Federal Election Commission* (*Colorado* I) (1996), the Colorado Republican Party (before it had selected its Senate candidate) bought radio advertisements attacking the Democratic Party's likely candidate for Senate. The Federal Election Commission claimed that this "expenditure" exceeded the dollar limits that the Federal Election Campaign Act imposed on a political party's expenditure in connection with the general election campaign. A fragmented Court, with no majority opinion, ruled that the First Amendment prohibited applying that limitation to expenditures that the political party made "independently," that is, without coordination with any candidate. The Court then remanded to consider the Party's broader claim that even coordinated limits on a party's congressional campaign expenditures are unconstitutional on their face. In *Colorado* II (2001), the Court (5 to 4) rejected the facial challenge and held that Congress can restrict a party's coordinated expenditures (unlike expenditures truly independent) to minimize circumvention of contribution limits.

(f) The 2002 Reform Act: *The McConnell Decision*

McConnell v. Federal Election Commission (2003), upheld (5 to 4) most of the constitutionality of The Bipartisan Campaign Reform Act of 2002 (BCRA), often called the McCain–Feingold campaign finance law, after its two main sponsors. This law amended the Federal Election Campaign Act of 1971 (FECA), the Communications Act of 1934, and various other portions of the United States Code, in a far-reaching and elaborate effort to purge national politics of what the sponsors believed to be the pernicious influence of very large campaign contributions. The opinion is both long and complex. The Court's syllabus alone is nearly twenty pages in length. The entire opinion in the U.S. Reports totals 298 pages. The Court itself split a variety of ways, with various justices writing parts of the majority opinion. It delivered its ruling in December, 2003, on an expedited basis after the justices returned early from their summer recess in September. It rejected most of the facial challenges to the law and found that no one had standing to raise certain issues.

BCRA dealt with three important developments in the years since *Buckley v. Valeo*.

First, the enactment of the FECA led to the increased importance of "soft money," The FECA imposed stringent disclosure and reporting requirements on so-called "hard money," that is, contributions made for the purpose of influencing an election for federal office. Political parties and candidates were able to circumvent FECA's limitations by contributing "soft money"—money unregulated under FECA—to be used for activities intended to influence state or local elections; for mixed-purpose activities such as get-out-the-vote drives (GOTV) and generic party advertising; and for legislative advocacy advertisements, even if they mentioned a federal candidate's name, so long as the advertisements did not expressly advocate the candidate's election or defeat.

Second, parties and candidates eluded FECA by using "issue ads," which were intended to affect election results, but did not contain explicit words, such as "Vote Against Jane Doe" that would have subjected these advertisements to FECA's restrictions.

Third, a Senate Committee, in 1998, investigated the 1996 Presidential Election and concluded that the "soft money loophole" had led to a "meltdown" of the campaign finance system that had been intended "to keep corporate, union and large individual contributions from influencing the electoral process."

Justices Stevens and O'Connor concluded their portion of the lengthy opinion with a caveat:

We abide by that conviction in considering Congress' most recent effort to confine the ill effects of aggregated wealth on our political system. We are under no illusion that BCRA will be the last congressional statement on the matter. Money, like water, will always find an outlet. What problems will arise, and how Congress will respond, are concerns for another day. In the main we uphold BCRA's two principal, complementary features: the control of soft money and the regulation of electioneering communications.

The Court, in brief, held: (1) BCRA may constitutionally ban political parties and candidates from using "soft money" for federal election activities; (2) BCRA's ban on party donations to tax-exempt entities tax-exempt political organizations that make expenditures in connection with federal elections did not violate free speech rights, at least in so far as it prohibited donation of unregulated "soft money"; (3) "soft money" could not be used for issue ads that clearly identified a candidate; (4) the restrictions on the disclosure of persons who fund "electioneering communications" and restrictions on the corporations' and labor unions' funding of electioneering communications are valid; (5) the cost of third-party issue advertisements that are coordinated with federal candidates' campaigns may validly be considered as contributions to those campaigns; (6) it is constitutional to require labor unions and corporations to pay for issue advertisements from separately segregated funds; (7) however, the statutory prohibition on political donations by minors was invalid; and (8) the requirement that broadcasters disclose records of requests for air time for political advertisements is valid.

§ 16.32   Regulating the Speech and Associational Activities of Government Employees

Government employees may have their speech and associational activities restricted with regulations that could not be applied to members of the public at large. However, the government does not have complete control over the speech or associational activities of its employees.

The phrase "political patronage" refers to government employment practices that are based on political party affiliation. The Court has ruled that basing government employment decisions on political party affiliation, in most circumstances, violates the First Amendment. The government can only make political party affiliation a job qualification when political party affiliation is a reasonable standard for determining whether an individual could perform a particular government job. For example, the President of the United States is free to make membership in the President's political party a qualification for high government offices such as cabinet members, including the Attorney General. The President, as our chief law enforcement officer, may only have faith that Presidential law enforcement policies will be fully carried out by a person who shares the President's political views. However, even if there were no civil service system, the President could not make being a member of the President's political party a qualification for a *clerical* position in the Justice Department. Political party membership is not a reasonable standard for determining whether a person can perform clerical functions. *Elrod v. Burns* (1976); *Branti v. Finkel* (1980).

The Supreme Court has made a distinction between speech and associational activities of government employees that are related to issues of public concern, and speech or associational activities only related to private issues. If the government seeks to base employment decisions on speech or associational activities of its employees that relate to matters of public concern, the governmental regulation must be narrowly drawn to promote overriding government interests, which include the interest in efficiently providing government services. The government has much greater latitude when it regulates the speech or associational activities of its employees that do not relate to issues of public concern.

If the government discharges an employee because of the employee's speech to other employees on a matter of purely private concern (she complained of office transfer policy, office morale, etc.), courts accord great deference to the government decision-maker and uphold the firing, so long as the government action is not totally irrational or a pretext for punishing someone's political views. *Connick v. Myers* (1983).

When a government employee is disciplined or discharged because of speech that relates to a matter of public concern, the Court will apply a balancing test that gives great weight to First Amendment interests. Such government actions must be narrowly drawn to serve objectives that outweigh the interest of the individual in commenting on issues of public concern. *Pickering v. Board of Education* (1968), *Givhan v. Western Line Consolidated School District* (1979).

Sometimes it is easy to determine that a government employee's speech relates only to a matter of private concern. For example, the Court had no difficulty in upholding the firing of a police officer who was selling videotapes of himself involved in sexually explicit activity. *San Diego v. Roe* (2004). Sometimes cases are more difficult.

The government, as an employer, has an interest in peaceful labor relations and orderly labor negotiations. Therefore, the government may choose to deal with its employees only through a recognized union. The government may make it a job requirement for an individual to join the union that represents a class of government employees or to pay some dues to the union. The government can require its employees to pay the portion of the union dues that relate to the union's employee representation activities. The employee does not have to pay the portion of the union dues used to fund ideological positions with which the government employee disagrees. *Abood v. Detroit Board of Education* (1977).

The government may choose to have meetings where only union representatives or members of a recognized union may participate. *Minnesota State Board for Community Colleges v. Knight* (1984). However, the government may not punish an individual for making statements about matters of public concern at government meetings that are open to the public. *Madison School District v. Wisconsin Employment Relations Committee* (1976).

The Court has upheld state and federal laws prohibiting government employees from taking an active part in political campaigns. The government has an overriding interest both in having employees who deliver their services in a nonpartisan manner, and in fostering public confidence in the nonpartisan nature of government services. *United States Civil Service Commission v. National Association of Letter Carriers* (1973); *United Public Workers v. Mitchell* (1947).

§ 16.33 Picketing Related to Social Issues vs. Labor Disputes

Liability of Member of an Association for the Torts of the Association. Even if violence is advocated, the First Amendment rights require that the state may not impose tort liability for business losses caused by violence or the threat of violence, if such conduct occurs in the context of constitutionally protected activity, unless there is "precision of regulation."

NAACP v. Claiborne Hardware Co. (1982), overturned a Mississippi state court judgment of over one and one quarter million dollars against the NAACP and certain individuals for business losses suffered by several white merchants because of an economic boycott against them. On October 31, 1969, after black citizens in Claiborne County failed to achieve their demands for racial equality and integration several hundred blacks at a local NAACP meeting voted to boycott white merchants. Although some boycott supporters engaged in acts of violence, most of the practices used to encourage support for the boycott were peaceful, orderly, and protected by the First Amendment. All of the marches were carefully controlled.

The state can constitutionally impose liability for "the consequences of violent conduct [but] it may not award compensation for the consequences of nonviolent, protected activity. Only those losses proximately caused by unlawful conduct may be recovered." A member of a group cannot be liable simply because another member of the same group proximately caused damage by violence:

> Civil liability may not be imposed merely because an individual belonged to a group, some members of which committed acts of violence. For liability to be imposed by reason of association alone, it is necessary to establish that the group itself possessed unlawful goals and that the individual held a specific intent to further those illegal goals.

Mere association cannot make one liable, but those persons who actually engaged in violence or other illegal activity can be held liable for the injuries that they caused.

Claiborne Hardware Co. ruled that the lower court findings were also not adequate to support the judgment against the NAACP. "To impose liability without a finding that the NAACP authorized—either actually or apparently—or ratified unlawful conduct would impermissibly burden the rights of political association that are protected by the First Amendment."

Assemblies Related to Labor Disputes. Sometimes people question whether the freedoms of speech and assembly apply with equal force to the activities of individuals who engage in picketing, in distributing leaflets, or in other public speech relating to labor organization and labor disputes. Although the Supreme Court has allowed both state and federal courts and legislatures to control such activities, the Court has attempted to fit its rulings within the previously described principles regarding these First Amendment freedoms. Of course, those who picket, distribute literature, or speak in public regarding labor issues are subject to content neutral time, place, and manner restrictions, as would be any other person in a public place.

If a group of workers engage in a strike that is illegal under state or federal law, and they form a picket line or distribute literature outside of an employer's premises with the intent to cause other workers to join in their illegal strike, their activities may be punished or enjoined. The theory in these cases is that such picketing is only a call to illegal action by encouraging others to help the picketers engage in applying coercive pressure on an employer in a manner that violates state or federal law. Therefore, the picketing is enjoinable as an invitation to engage in illegal activity.

In other contexts, the Court has upheld lower courts prohibitions of organizations from engaging in conspiracies and other speech/action that constitute a violation of antitrust laws. In earlier decades the Court was quite lenient in upholding laws or court actions that restrained labor organization activities, such as the distribution of literature or the picketing of businesses, whenever these activities could be said to transgress state or federal policies regarding the proper conduct of labor disputes. But the Court has attempted to define a principle that the government could not prohibit or enjoin labor picketing unless there was some valid government policy regarding the control of labor organizations or labor disputes that was jeopardized by such picketing.

Where a labor organization is engaging in a strike or organizational activities that are clearly illegal under valid state or federal statutes, then laws restricting picketing or the distribution of information regarding such strike, even though the activity is called only "informational," may be compatible with First Amendment theory. The rationale is that the government can force persons in a labor dispute to resolve their grievance through legally established channels rather than seeking to secure the support of others, through illegal strikes or other illegal activities.

Secondary Boycotts. The Supreme Court has upheld prohibitions of union activities that constitute "secondary boycotts" even though those activities might be seen as only the distribution of information. In a secondary boycott case, union members picket or distribute information outside of a business asking persons not to deal with that business because the business uses the products of or otherwise deals with a second business with which the union has a dispute. Federal labor laws, with exceptions, require the union to picket only the primary business with which it has a dispute and not seek to coerce the persons with whom that business deals to side with the union.

The Court has held that such activity may be prohibited or enjoined because it constitutes coercion of persons (the boycotted enterprise) to aid the union in its attempt to violate federal law. However, giving information to the public, whether through picketing or other means, regarding the nature of a labor organization's dispute with a business (business #1) at the site of a second business (business #2) that engages in trade with business #1 (with whom the organization has a dispute) may be considered only the peaceful conveyance of information and protected by the First Amendment. Although the Court has not defined the exact nature of the informational activity protected by the First Amendment, it appears to be attempting to make some accommodation between proscribable and nonproscribable labor organization speech through its interpretation of federal labor relations laws.

Initially it may appear easy for the Court to justify the punishment of labor picketing that only coerces or "signals" others to aid the union in engaging in activity that violates valid labor statutes. But it is difficult to distinguish the area of informational activity by labor organizations that could be made punishable (because it relates to a labor dispute) from the constitutionally protected activities of persons who organize boycotts of businesses for the purpose of coercing those businesses to help them influence government action.

Thus, there may be some type of speech by labor organizations or employers that cannot be prohibited because it relates to public issues or the need to influence government action. In general, however, the Supreme Court will allow the injunction or punishment of speech by employers or organizations when that speech would undercut the legitimate governmental regulation of the manner in which labor disputes must be resolved.

§ 16.34   Obscenity—The *Roth* Case

Roth v. United States, was handed down in 1957, and at its core it is still the law of obscenity under the Constitution. In *Roth,* two state criminal statutes were invoked against the publication and sale of obscene matter.

After stating in a footnote that "[n]o issue is presented [here] concerning the obscenity of the material involved," Justice Brennan, writing for the Court, stated: "The dispositive question is whether obscenity is utterance within the area of protected speech and press." On the basis of a series of earlier cases in which obscenity had been discussed in dictum, [and with an analysis of First Amendment history that has been attacked by many scholars] Justice Brennan concluded; "All ideas having even the slightest redeeming social importance—unorthodox ideas, controversial ideas, even ideas hateful to the prevailing climate of opinion—have the full protection of the guaranties [of the First Amendment], that "obscenity is not within the area of constitutionally protected speech or press."

The Court drew a distinction between sex and obscenity. "Obscene material," said the Court, "is material which deals with sex in a manner appealing to prurient interest," while the mere portrayal of sex in art, literature, scientific works, and similar forums "is not itself sufficient reason to deny material the constitutional protection of freedom of speech and press." In fleshing out this distinction, the Court adopted the standard of whether "to the average person, applying contemporary community standards, the dominant theme of the material taken as a whole appeals to prurient interest."

Perhaps because the *Roth* Court refused to determine whether the material in the case was obscene, the opinion was not clear regarding the standard to be used in the lower courts. When reduced to a formula, *Roth* provided that material may be deemed obscene, and therefore wholly without constitutional protection, if it (a) appeals to a prurient interest in sex, (b) has no redeeming literary, artistic, political, or scientific merit, and (c) is on the whole offensive to the average person under contemporary community standards.

There is the problem with the word "prurient." This single word was quite clearly the touchstone of Justice Brennan's analysis of the case. Its application spelled the difference between sex and obscenity, between applicable community standards and mere community prejudice, between material that is sanctioned by the Constitution and material that may be subject to criminal penalty. To the Court, prurient material was that which has "a tendency to excite lustful thoughts." This definition deserved some further explication, and the Court provided it with excerpts from Webster's Second New International Dictionary, i.e., that "prurient" is " . . . [i]tching; longing; uneasy with desire or longing; of persons, having itching, morbid, or lascivious longings; of desire, curiosity, or propensity, lewd. . . ."

In *Brockett v. Spokane Arcades, Inc.* (1985) the Court made the concept of "prurient interest" incomprehensible when it excluded material appealing to a "good, old fashioned, healthy" interest in sex.

§ 16.35   The Development of the Case Law Under *Roth*

(a) Scienter

Two years after *Roth* the Court held that the state could not eliminate the need to prove *scienter* in an obscenity prosecution, in a case where a bookseller was convicted under a statute that dispensed with the state proving any requirement of knowledge of the contents of the books on the part of the seller. See, *Smith v. California* (1959).

(b) Appellate Review

In *Jacobellis v. Ohio* (1964), the Court held, *inter alia*, "that, in 'obscenity' cases as in all others involving rights derived from the First Amendment guarantees of free expression, this Court cannot avoid making an independent constitutional judgment on the facts of the case as to whether the material involved is constitutionally protected." In short, a trial court's findings as to the obscenity of the material at issue is not binding on review—if the appellate court takes the case, it will have to watch the movie or read the book itself.

Thus, the import of *Roth* would unfold as the Supreme Court was forced to reconsider the implications of the *Roth* test in terms of the problems of specific areas. As one might expect, the applications of *Roth* eventually subverted some of the major analytical elements of the opinion itself; it also revealed the failure of the Supreme Court to agree on any real tests to apply in practice to allegedly obscene material.

Brennan argued that each of the three elements of the *Roth* test must be applied independently, and thus that material cannot be adjudged obscene if it passes muster under any of them. Brennan reasoned that *Fanny Hill*, which has long been a classic of ribald literature, could not properly be deemed to be *"utterly without redeeming social value,"* and thus is sheltered by the First Amendment. By applying the elements of the *Roth* test independently, Brennan stepped away from the strict definitional approach employed in *Roth*. *Fanny Hill* may or may not have appealed to prurient interests under any definition or under any set of community standards, but this was now irrelevant; the book contained at least a modicum of literary value, and that was enough to save it from suppression by the Attorney General of Massachusetts. Suddenly "pruriency" was no longer the pivotal element of obscenity under the First Amendment.

(c) Pandering

In *Ginzburg v. United States* (1966), the Court was faced with three professionally produced publications devoted to sex, including EROS, which the Court described as "a hard-cover magazine of expensive format." The Court found the publications to be obscene because they represented "commercial exploitation of erotica solely for the sake of their prurient appeal." In reaching this conclusion, the Court stated that the "leer of the sensualist" had "permeate[d]" the manner in which the publications had been distributed and advertised: mailing privileges had been sought from Intercourse and Blue Ball, Pennsylvania, and Middlesex, New Jersey; and the advertising circulars describing the publications "stressed the sexual candor of the respective publications, and openly boasted that the publishers would take full advantage of what they regarded as an unrestricted license allowed by law in the expression of sex and sexual matters."

The Court argued that the "brazenness" of the defendant's marketing tactics unveiled his intent in distributing the materials, and that this intent was the heart of the matter: "Where the purveyor's sole emphasis is on the sexually provocative aspects of his publications, that fact may be decisive in the determination of obscenity." If the defendant had earlier claimed, even boasted that his publication was obscene, that "testimony" can be used against him.

Though it is difficult to understand why advertising tactics can be relevant to an obscenity determination, the Court continues to follow *Ginzburg*. See, e.g., *Splawn v. California* (1977).

The 1960s Rulings. Throughout the 1960s the Supreme Court was unable to produce a majority opinion defining the nature of obscenity. There was no majority agreement concerning the "contemporary community standards" aspect of the *Memoirs* plurality, with some Justices favoring a national community standard; others favoring a national standard for federal prosecutions; still others favoring local community or flexibility for state standards.

§ 16.36   The *Miller* Decision

In *Miller v. California* (1973) for the first time since *Roth* a majority of the Justices agreed to the proper test for obscenity.

The actual test for obscenity set forth in *Miller* is as follows:

> The basic guidelines for the trier of fact must be: (a) whether "the average person, applying contemporary community standards" would find that the work, taken as a whole, appeals to the prurient interest, (b) whether the work depicts or describes, in a patently offensive way, sexual conduct specifically defined by the applicable state law, and (c) whether the work, taken as a whole, lacks serious literary, artistic, political, or scientific value.

For pedagogical reasons it makes sense to consider these three elements out of order. First, we shall look at the third element, then the second element, and then the first element of the *Miller* test.

The Third Element of the *Miller* Test. The third element of the *Miller* test—"whether the work, taken as a whole, lacks serious literary, artistic, political, or scientific value"—appears on its face less restrictive than the "utterly without redeeming social value" test in *Roth*. The shift from "utterly" to "serious" indicates that juries may be given greater leeway under this standard. In addition, the Court eliminated the concept of "social value" and replaced it with "literary, artistic, political, or scientific value"—a distinction without a difference, perhaps. However, to the extent that the Court requires judicial supervision of these issues and the directing of verdicts when the evidence shows the speech to be "serious" in nature, there may be little practical difference.

In deciding this "value" question, the third prong of the *Miller* test, is *not* to be determined by reference to community standards. The first two prongs of *Miller* (patent offensiveness and prurient appeal) are discussed in terms of "contemporary community standards" but the third element is not. See, e.g. *Pope v. Illinois* (1987).

The value of a work does not vary from community to community based on the degree of local acceptance it has won. The test is whether a reasonable person (not an ordinary member of any given community) would find value in the material taken as a whole. The fact that only a minority of people in the relevant community may believe that the work has serious value does not mean that the "reasonable person" standard is not met.

The Second Element of the *Miller* Test. With respect to the second part of the *Miller* test, the Court offered "a few plain examples of what a state statute could define for regulation under part (b) of the standard announced in this opinion...." These examples were:

(a) Patently offensive representations or descriptions of ultimate sexual acts, normal or perverted, actual or simulated.

(b) Patently offensive representations or descriptions of masturbation, excretory functions, and lewd exhibition of the genitals.

The Court explicitly acknowledged that under *Miller*, "no one [may] be subject to prosecution for the sale or exposure of obscene materials unless these materials depict or describe patently offensive 'hard core' sexual conduct specifically defined by the regulating state law, as written or construed."

This portion of the test might have served as a basis for improving the ability of individuals to engage in publishing or filmmaking by offering them clear notice of what is prohibited by statute. But the Court has allowed state courts to save their statutes by construction. See, e.g., *Ward v. Illinois* (1977).

The Court continues to follow its ruling in *Mishkin v. New York* (1966) which held that material could be obscene if it appeals to the prurient interests of persons who would not be considered "average," (such as sadomasochist publication). Sadomasochistic materials may be constitutionally prohibited even though not listed in *Miller*: the *Miller* specifics "were offered merely as 'examples' ..., they 'were not intended to be exhaustive.' "

The First Element of the *Miller* Test. The most controversial aspect of the *Miller* decision may be the first part of its test with its rejection of national standards. The national standards concept had never been adopted by a majority of the Court. It was only the most restrictive concept that could get a working majority of Justices to suppress an item as obscene. Now a majority finally agreed on the national standards test—and they rejected it.

In *Miller*, the Court decided to give the "community standards" aspect of the *Roth* test a more literal meaning, and it held that trial courts may draw on actual community standards in determining whether the material at issue is factually obscene. As *Miller* explicitly stated: "In resolving the inevitable sensitive questions of fact and law, we must continue to rely on the jury system, accompanied by the safeguards that judges, rules of evidence, presumption of innocence, and other protective features provide. . . ."

§ 16.37 Special Considerations in Light of the *Miller* Case

(a) Private Possession

Stanley v. Georgia (1969), relying on the First and Fourteenth Amendments, held that "mere private possession of obscene matter" is not a crime. *Stanley*, however, must be read quite narrowly. The crucial fifth vote in *Stanley* was Justice Harlan's; in spite of the broad language of the opinion, the *Stanley* Court's own summary of its decision emphasized that "the States retain broad power to regulate obscenity; that power simply does not extend to mere possession by the individual in the privacy of his own home."

In many cases, including *Paris Adult Theatre I v. Slaton* (1973) the Court has refused to expand *Stanley*. Under *Stanley* one may enjoy obscene material in one's own home, but the state may prohibit an individual from transporting the material for private use, and may also prohibit the individual from receiving the materials through the mails, or from importing them from foreign countries. The state may regulate obscene materials even if those using them voluntarily sought them out. Though the private possession of obscene materials in the home is protected activity, virtually any process that leads to such possession may be declared illegal.

Stanley does not protect the possession of "child pornography" in the home.

(b) Protection of Minors As Viewers of Obscenity

Ginsberg v. New York (1968), adopted the "variable obscenity" approach suggested by Professors Lockhart and McClure and held that a statute defining obscenity in terms of an appeal to the prurient interest of minors was constitutional. As such, *Ginsberg* represents a departure from a neutral concept of "pruriency" as explicated in *Roth*; it is also a departure from the "average" person standard. In light of the Court's revision of the *Roth* test in *Miller*, however, *Ginsberg* may be theoretically reconcilable within the "community standards" test currently in operation. If the government seeks to prohibit the distribution of material to everyone (e.g. to have a total ban) the community standard cannot include possible child readers or viewers.

Statutes for the protection of children must be narrowly drawn in two respects. First, the state cannot prevent the general public from reading or having access to materials on the grounds that the materials would be objectionable if read or seen by children. Second, the statute must not be vague.

Butler v. Michigan (1957) reversed a conviction under a statute that made it an offense to make available to the general public materials found to have a potentially deleterious influence on minors. The state argued that by "quarantining the general reading public against books not too rugged for grown men and women in order to shield juvenile innocence, it is exercising its power to promote the general welfare." The unanimous Court answered: "Surely, this is to burn the house to roast the pig." This law was overbroad.

Second, the statute in *Butler* was too vague. The problem of vagueness is not reduced simply because the regulation is one of classification rather than direct suppression. In addition, the fact that the legislature adopted the statute for the salutary purpose of protecting children does not reduce the fatal flaw of vagueness.

In *Sable Communications of California, Inc. v. F.C.C.* (1989), the Court held that Congress can constitutionally impose an outright ban of "obscene" interstate, pre-recorded commercial telephone messages ("Dial–A–Porn"), because obscenity is not protected speech. But Congress cannot impose a *total* ban on non-obscene, "indecent" dial-a-porn because such speech is not obscene as to adults. A total legislative ban is not narrowly tailored to serve the compelling interest in protecting minors. A narrowly tailored rule might require the use of credit cards, access codes, and scrambling devices.

Later, *United States v. Playboy Entertainment Group, Inc.* (2000) invalidated "signal bleed" provision of the Telecommunications Act. This section required cable television operators providing channels "primarily dedicated to sexually-oriented programming" to "fully scramble or otherwise fully block" those channels. Alternatively, they could limit their transmission to hours when children are unlikely to be viewing, set by administrative regulation as between 10 p.m. and 6 a.m.

Because scrambling can be imprecise (either or both audio and visual portions of the scrambled programs might still be heard or seen; this is called "signal bleed"), the majority of cable operators adopted the "time channeling" approach. So, for two-thirds of the day, no household in those service areas could receive the programming, whether or not the household or the viewer wanted to do so. The Court, citing *Butler*, invalidated this requirement because there was a less restrictive alternative: the cable operator could fully scramble any channel the subscriber does not wish to receive, on a household-by-household basis ("targeted blocking").

(c) Protection of Minors: Child Pornography

New York v. Ferber (1982), without a dissent, upheld a law that passed both the vagueness and overbreadth requirements. The legislature had designed this statute to prevent the abuse of children. New York made it a crime for a person knowingly to promote sexual performances by children under the age of 16 by distributing material that depicts such performances even though the materials themselves were not "obscene" in a constitutional sense.

Ferber articulated five basic premises. First, the state's interests in protecting the physical and psychological well being of minors is compelling. Second, prohibiting the distribution of films and photos depicting such activities are closely related to this compelling governmental interest in two ways: the permanent record of the child's activity and its circulation exacerbates the harm to the minor, and the distribution encourages the sexual exploitation of the children and the production of the material. Third, advertising and selling the material encourages the evil by supplying an economic motive for the production of such visual depictions of children. Fourth, the value of allowing live performances and photographic reproduction of children engaged in lewd sexual conduct is *de minimis*. After all, the person who put together the material depicting the sexual performance could always use a model over the statutory age who looked younger. And, fifth, the classification of child pornography as outside of First Amendment protection is consistent with earlier precedent and justified by the need to protect the welfare of the children.

Ferber cautioned that there were limits to the extent to which child pornography is unprotected speech. The statute prohibiting the conduct must adequately define and describe it. And, the circumstances of this case require that the crime "be limited to works that *visually* depict conduct by children below a specified age."

The Court then explained how the *Miller* test must be modified when dealing with child pornography:

> The *Miller* formulation is adjusted in the following respects: A trier of fact need not find that the material appeals to the prurient interest of the average person; it is not required that

sexual conduct portrayed be done so in a patently offensive manner; and the material at issue need not be considered as a whole. We note that the distribution of descriptions or other depictions of sexual conduct, not otherwise obscene, which do not involve live performance or photographic or other visual reproduction of live performances, retains First Amendment protection. As with obscenity laws, criminal responsibility may not be imposed without some element of scienter on the part of the defendant.

Ferber dealt with the New York law as if it were a type of obscenity legislation. However, it is easier to understand the case if one realizes that the *Ferber* statute was really quite different. The purpose of obscenity legislation is to protect the minds and well being of the consumers or viewers of obscenity, by preventing them from watching the obscene movie, or reading the obscene magazine, etc. The purpose of the New York law is *not* to protect the consumers who watch a child's sexual performance; it is *to protect the young children* from being used and abused as performers in a sexual performance. Because the New York law focuses on protecting the juvenile performers it should be easy to uphold.

Osborne v. Ohio (1990) held that the state may constitutionally prohibit the possession and viewing of child pornography at home. The distinction with *Stanley v. Georgia* the Court concluded was "obvious." Unlike *Stanley* the state here does not rely on a paternalistic interest in regulating Osborne's mind. Rather, the purpose of the law is to protect the children, victims of child pornography. The state hopes to destroy a market for the exploitative use of children.

Osborne went on to conclude that the statute was not overbroad. The law prohibited any person from possessing or viewing any material or performance showing a minor who is not his child or ward in a state of nudity unless (a), the material or performance is presented for a bona fide purpose by or to a person having a proper interest therein, or (b) the possessor knows that the minor's parents or guardian has consented in writing to such photographing or use of the minor. As construed by the Ohio Supreme Court the law requires proof of scienter and is limited to depictions of nudity that involve *lewd* exhibition or involve graphic focus of the minor's genitals.

In *Ashcroft v. Free Speech Coalition* (2002), the Court invalidated part of the Child Pornography Prevention Act of 1996 (CPPA), which expanded the federal prohibition of child pornography to include "virtual pornography," that is, sexually explicit images that appear to depict minors but are produced without using any real children. The images could be created by using adults who look like minors or by using computer imaging. The new technology makes it possible to create realistic images of children who do not exist. The CPPA is not directed at obscene speech, which a different statute prohibits. The Court found CPPA unconstitutional to the extent that it prohibited speech that is not obscene under *Miller* and also to the extent it prohibited virtual child pornography because, under *Ferber*, the materials were not produced by the exploitation of real children.

(d) Prior Restraint

The Court has upheld a license requirement that involved a prior restraint for possibly obscene movies, but not books.

The Court has imposed constitutional safeguards on the procedures employed in the prior restraint of allegedly-obscene films.

Freedman v. Maryland (1965) held that before a local censorship board had the power to deny a motion picture distributor's application to distribute a particular movie it must: (1) afford the accused party a prompt hearing; (2) assume the burden of showing that the material is, in fact, obscene; and (3) either refrain from making a finding of obscenity or, as a requirement of law under the board's enabling statute or clear judicial mandate, take action on its own behalf in a court of law to seek an affirmation of its initial finding of obscenity.

In the court proceeding, the distributor or retailer may contest the issue of obscenity even though the book or film has been found to be obscene in other cases to which he was not a party.

(e) Zoning Laws and Public Exhibition of "Adult" Non-Obscene Material

Paris Adult Theatre I v. Slaton (1973), decided on the same day as *Miller*, held that the state may prohibit public exhibitions or displays of obscenity even if access to the exhibitions is limited to consenting adults.

In *Young v. American Mini Theatres, Inc.* (1976), the Court, without a majority opinion, held that an appropriately definite zoning ordinance prohibiting the location of an "adult movie theatre" within 1000 feet of any two other "regulated uses," including 10 different kinds of establishments in addition to adult theatres, is constitutionally permissible *even* if the theatre is not displaying obscene material.

While the ordinance in question characterized an adult theatre as one presenting certain specified "sexual activities" or "anatomical areas," the Justice Stevens' plurality opinion reasoned that the ordinance did not constitute an exercise in prior restraint, but rather a valid use of the city's zoning power. The zoning of a reasonable amount of space between such theatres avoided the concentration of the physical and economic effect on a neighborhood. Nevertheless the regulation describes the theatres in terms of the content of their films.

Schad v. Borough of Mount Ephraim (1981) distinguished *American Mini Theatres* and invalidated a zoning ordinance that, as construed by the state courts, forbade *all* "live entertainment," including nonobscene nude dancing, in a commercial zone. "[N]o property in the Borough may be principally used for the commercial production of plays, concerts, musicals, dance, or any other form of live entertainment." An adult book store, operating in a commercial zone in the Borough of Mount Ephraim, introduced a coin operated device: a customer, after inserting a coin, would be able to watch a live dancer, usually nude, perform behind a glass panel. The store was therefore found guilty of violating the ordinance.

Assuming that live entertainment would create special problems not associated with other commercial uses, the Borough had not narrowly tailored a zoning law to address any unique problems. The Borough's claim that its zoning restriction was an attempt to create a commercial area catering only to the residents' "immediate needs" also did not survive scrutiny. The Borough introduced no evidence to support this assertion and the face of the ordinance contradicted it, for the ordinance permitted car showrooms, hardware stores, offices, etc.

The *American Mini Theatres* analysis did not support the constitutionality of the ordinance, for the restriction in *American Mini Theatres* did not ban all adult theatres or even affect the number of adult movie theatres in the city. It just dispersed them. And in *American Mini Theatres* the city had presented evidence that a concentration of adult theatres led to a deterioration of surrounding neighborhoods.

While *American Mini Theatres* allowed a city to disperse adult theatres, *City of Renton v. Playtime Theatres, Inc.* (1986) allowed a city to concentrate them. Justice Rehnquist for the Court (with only Brennan and Marshall dissenting) upheld a zoning ordinance that prohibited "adult" motion picture theatres from locating within 1,000 feet of any residential zone, single or multiple-family dwelling, church, park, or school. The district court found that the city council's "*predominate* concerns" were with the secondary effects of adult theatres—e.g., to prevent crime, protect the city's retail trade, maintain property values, and preserve the quality of life—and not with the content of adult films themselves. This finding was "more than adequate to establish that the city's pursuit of its zoning interests here was unrelated to the suppression of free expression." The ordinance was a "content-neutral" speech regulation because it was *"justified* without reference to the content of the regulated speech."

The Court then upheld the ordinance because it served a substantial governmental interest (preserving the quality of life), and allowed reasonable alternative avenues of communication, for more than five percent of the entire land area of Renton was allowed to be used by adult theatres. And unlike *Schad,* the Renton ordinance was "narrowly tailored" to those theatres producing the unwanted secondary effects.

Erznoznik v. Jacksonville (1975) invalidated an ordinance that prohibited drive-in movies from showing films with nudity. This ordinance was overbroad because not all nudity is obscene. The drive-in theaters could be regulated or eliminated with a content neutral regulation.

(f) Obscenity and the Twenty–First Amendment

For a time, the Court ruled that the state had special power, under the Twenty–First Amendment, to regulate "adult" speech in establishments licensed by the state to serve liquor. See, e.g. *New York State Liquor Authority v. Bellanca* (1981).

The argument that the Twenty–First Amendment modifies the First Amendment is, frankly, a little strange. The Twenty–First Amendment has long been used to grant the states extensive authority over liquor, and to some extent immunize state regulation from commerce clause challenge. However, the Twenty–First Amendment has never been read to immunize state regulation over liquor from the civil liberties guarantees of the Constitution.

In *44 Liquormart, Inc. v. Rhode Island* (1996) the Court invalidated a state law that banned accurate retail liquor advertisements except at the point of sale, and rejected the state's argument that it could limit truthful information in an effort to manipulate consumers and promote temperance. In a portion of the decision that was an opinion of the Court, the Court emphatically disavowed the reasoning of cases like *Bellanca.* Justice Stevens, for the Court, announced that the result in the earlier cases, such as *Bellanca,* would have been "precisely the same" even if there had been no reliance on the 21st Amendment. The Twenty-first Amendment "does not qualify the constitutional prohibition against laws abridging the freedom of speech embodied in the First Amendment."

(g) Non–pictorial Obscenity

On the same day that *Miller v. California* (1973) was decided, the Court ruled in *Kaplan v. California* (1973) that books alone, containing only words and no pictures, may be obscene. The Court recognized that books "have a different and preferred place in our hierarchy of values. . . ." But they nonetheless may be found to be obscene.

(h) National Versus Local Standards

Part of *Miller v. California* (1973) held that a state court may decide the obscenity question by applying contemporary community standards, not national standards. In that case, the state trial court instructed the jury to consider state community standards.

The following year the Court extended the *Miller* holding to apply to a federal prosecution. See, *Hamling v. U.S.* (1974).

The Court has since made clear that *Miller* did not mandate use of a statewide standard. The trial court may instruct the jury to apply "community standards" without instructing it what community was specified.

In *Smith v. United States* (1977) the Court placed some limits on the power of the state to attempt to define legislatively the contemporary community standard of appeal to prurient interest or patent offensiveness. In *state* obscenity proceedings:

> [The state could, if it wished] impose a geographic limit on the determination of community standards by defining the area from which the jury could be selected in an obscenity case, or by legislating with respect to the instructions that must be given to the jurors in such cases. [However] the question of the community standard to apply, when appeal to prurient interest and patent offensiveness are considered, is not one that can be defined legislatively.

No state law can regulate distribution of obscene materials and define contemporary standards in *federal* obscenity proceedings. In a federal prosecution for mailing allegedly obscene material, it is irrelevant that the state in which the mailings took place did not even regulate obscenity aimed at adults, and that the mailings were wholly intrastate. A state's laissez-faire attitude towards obscenity cannot nullify federal efforts to regulate it. In federal obscenity prosecutions the federal courts should give federal jury instructions (not state jury instructions) as to community standards.

In *Pinkus v. United States* (1978), the Court clarified several requirements concerning jury instructions in federal obscenity prosecutions governed by the standards of *Roth v. United States*. While *Pinkus* was decided under the *Roth* test of obscenity, the instructions approved of as to which people are in the community still should be law under *Miller v. California*. because—as to that issue—*Miller* only rejected a national standards test in favor of a smaller geographic area: the actual local community.

The Court overturned Pinkus' conviction for mailing obscene materials based on its statutory interpretation that the court should not include children in determining what are the community standards. *Pinkus* went on to state that under the Constitution, it was permissible to include "particularly sensitive persons" when considering community standards, because the "community includes all adults who comprise it." The jury may not be instructed to focus on the most susceptible and sensitive members of the community, but the jury need not exclude such people from the community as a whole for purposes of judging the material's obscenity. Finally, the Constitution allows an instruction on prurient appeal to deviant sexual groups as part of the instruction concerning the appeal of the materials to the average person when the evidence supports such a charge.

In *Pope v. Illinois* (1987), the Court made clear that the "value" of an allegedly obscene work (the third prong of the *Miller* test) is not to be determined by the jury applying local "contemporary community standards" but by the jury being instructed to decide whether a reasonable person would find serious literary, artistic, political, or scientific value in the material taken as a whole. The value of a work, unlike its prurient appeal or patent offensiveness (the first two elements of *Miller*) does not vary from community to community based on the degree of local acceptance it has won.

(i) Nude Dancing

Without a majority opinion, the Court, in *Barnes v. Glen Theatre, Inc.* (1991), upheld an Indiana law that prohibited "knowingly or intentionally" appearing nude in "a public place."

Chief Justice Rehnquist's plurality opinion accepted the notion that nonobscene nude dancing has some free speech protection, but he also acknowledged the substantial governmental interest in protecting societal order and morality. He treated the Indiana law as a question of symbolic speech and upheld the law because its restrictions were unrelated content and hence unrelated to the suppression of free speech. The law prohibited nudity, whether or not that nudity is combined with any expressive activity. The law does not single out and ban only nudity that conveys an erotic message. It bans all nudity. Nor does the law ban erotic dancing. Dancers can present erotic dances so long, as they are not nude. They must wear at least a scant amount of clothing.

Justice Scalia concurred in the judgment on the grounds that the statute was a general law regulating conduct and thus was entitled to no First Amendment scrutiny. It was not specifically directed against expression and did not target nude expression.

Instead, it targeted public nudity and would apply to nude beaches as well as nude dancing.

Justice Souter also concurred in the judgment, and would uphold the law because he claimed that it is similar to a zoning law intended to deal with harmful secondary effects and reduced property values associated with adult entertainment. He did not appear to be concerned that Indiana did not justify the law on those grounds and introduced no factual findings to support his hypothesis of reduced property values. No other Justice agreed with Souter's rationale.

Justice White, joined by Marshall, Blackmun, and Stevens, dissented. They argued that the Indiana law was not really a general prohibition of nudity because the law did not prohibit nudity in the home. (They also noted that Indiana could not constitutionally prohibit nudity in the home.) Hence, they would invalidate the law and could find no way that the legislature could write a statute that would be constitutional.

City of Erie v. Pap's A.M. (2000) upheld a city's public indecency law, which prohibited nudity in public places. Plaintiff operated "Kandyland," featuring totally nude erotic dancing by women. The law in question was an almost identical one to the statute in *Barnes*. Justice O'Connor delivered the Opinion of the Court as to Parts I and II, which concluded that the case was not moot. On no other issue did any opinion muster a majority although a majority of the Justices agreed that the law was constitutional.

In a plurality opinion for four Justices, Justice O'Connor concluded that "[being 'in a state of nudity' is not an inherently expressive condition," but "nude dancing of the type at issue here is expressive conduct that falls within the outer ambit of the First Amendment's protection." Justice O'Connor stated: "By its terms, the ordinance regulates conduct alone. It does not target nudity that contains an erotic message; rather it bans all public nudity, regardless of whether that nudity is accompanied by expressive activity." Her opinion asserted that the government's purpose in this case—preventing harmful secondary effects related to adult entertainment such as sexual harassment, prostitution, public intoxication—is "unrelated to suppression of expression." Hence, the law satisfied the "less stringent" symbolic speech test of *United States v. O'Brien* (1968), which is virtually identical to the test for time, place and manner regulations. The ordinance, in their view, was not related to the content of the expression.

Justice Scalia, joined by Justice Thomas, concurred in the judgment on the grounds that the ordinance was a general law regulating *conduct* and thus is not subject to First Amendment scrutiny at all. Erie's ordinance prohibits simply the act of public nudity, whether or not it is engaged in for expressive purposes.

Justice Souter filed an opinion concurring in part and dissenting in part. Although he agreed with Justice O'Connor's analysis he wanted to remand so the case for a greater evidentiary showing of the secondary effects associated with nude dancing.

Only Justice Stevens, joined by Justice Ginsburg, completely dissented in the *Pap's A.M.* case. Stevens argued that the law was unconstitutional because of its censorial purpose. Moreover, Justice Stevens believed that the "secondary effects" rationale should only be used to regulate the location of this adult entertainment, not to totally suppress what he called "indecent entertainment."

(j) Sexually Oriented Material on Broadcast or Cable Channels

If materials are found to be constitutionally "obscene," the Government can ban them from broadcast or cable channels, because the Government can ban completely any obscene materials. However, the Court has not always agreed on the power of the Government to ban or restrict materials that are not "obscene" in the constitutional sense but are sexually oriented—often called "adult material"—when that material is broadcast over the airwaves or by cable.

In *FCC v. Pacifica Foundation* (1978), a majority of the Court, but without a majority opinion, concluded that the FCC constitutionally could regulate "indecent" or "adult speech" that was broadcast over the radio air waves in the early afternoon, when the Court assumed that children were more likely to be in the listening audience. (Oddly enough, the Court did not weigh the possibility that children are more likely in school during the early afternoon.) The five Justices who upheld the power of the FCC to sanction the radio station emphasized that their rule was very narrow and did not involve other means of broadcast, such as two-way radio or closed circuit transmission. Nor did the ruling, the Justices emphasized, cover broadcasts that had only an occasional expletive.

Denver Area Educational Telecommunications Consortium, Inc. v. FCC (1996) considered challenges to three sections of the 1992 Cable Act designed to regulate cable television broadcasting of "patently offensive" sex-related material. The very fragmented Court invalidated two provisions of the Cable Television Consumer Protection and Competition Act of 1992 and upheld one provision.

A majority of the Justices decided that a provision of the Act that *permitted* the cable operator to prohibit patently offensive or indecent programming on public access channels violated the First Amendment. "PUBLIC ACCESS CHANNELS" are channel capacity that cable operators agreed to reserve for public, governmental, and educational access as part of the consideration that municipalities obtained in exchange for awarding a cable franchise.

On the other hand, a majority of the Justices concluded that a provision *permitting* the operator to prohibit patently offensive or indecent programming on leased access channels was found to be constitutional. A "LEASED CABLE CHANNEL" is a channel that the relevant federal law required a cable system operator to reserve for commercial lease by unaffiliated third parties. Finally, the fragmented Court invalidated a third provision, that *required* leased channel operators to segregate "patently offensive" programming on a single channel and to block that channel from viewer access, and then to un-block it (or re-block it) within 30 days of a subscriber's written request.

Justice Kennedy's separate opinion concurring in the judgment would have invalidated all of the provisions of the law. Kennedy criticized the narrowness of the Breyer plurality. "When confronted with a threat to free speech in the context of an emerging technology, we ought to have the discipline to analyze the case by reference to existing elaborations of constant First Amendment principles." Justice Breyer, in contrast, was unwilling to embrace any definite standard.

(k) Sexually Oriented Material on the Internet

Reno v. ACLU (1997) invalidated various provisions of the Communications Decency Act of 1996 ("CDC"), which were designed to protect minors from allegedly "indecent" and "patently offensive" material on the Internet. Cyberspace, like the physical world, is entitled to the protections of the First Amendment. The Court has granted the Government greater power to regulation the broadcast media on the grounds that there is a scarcity of broadcast channels and it is invasive in nature. These considerations simply do not apply to cyberspace.

First, the Court concluded that the provisions of the CDC prohibiting transmission of obscene or indecent communications by means of a telecommunications to persons under the age of 18, or sending patently offensive communications to persons under the age of 18, were content-based restrictions on speech, not time, place or manner regulations. Because they were content-based, there they were overbroad on their face in violation of the First Amendment.

The CDC's prohibition of indecent transmission and patently offensive" communications abridge freedom of speech. These terms are vague and ambiguous, and the statute does not require that the patently offensive material lack socially redeeming value. It does not allow parents to consent to their children's use of the restricted materials. The law suppresses materials that adults have a constitutional right to send and receive. The law does not allow less restrictive alternatives, such as currently available user-based software that parents can use to limit what their children can access.

Pursuant to the severability clause in the statute, the Court severed the word "indecent" from § 223(a) of the CDC, and allowed the Government to prohibit the transmission of material that is constitutionally "obscene." The Government can ban "obscene" speech in its entirety, so it can ban such speech from cyberspace as well.

Congress responded to *Reno v. ACLU* by enacting the Child Online Protection Act ("COPA"). Respondents promptly filed a facial challenge to COPA on First Amendment grounds, the Third Circuit affirmed a preliminary injunction, but the Supreme Court reversed, holding that COPA's reliance on community standards to identify material harmful to minors "does not by itself render the statute substantially overbroad for purposes of the First Amendment." The Court then remanded for further proceedings. *Ashcroft v. ACLU* (2002). After remand, the Third Circuit again affirmed the preliminary injunction, which barred enforcement of COPA pending trial and a final determination of its constitutionality. In *Ashcroft v. ACLU* (2004) the Supreme Court affirmed the lower court's preliminary injunction, without ruling on the constitutionality of COPA. Nevertheless, Justice Kennedy's majority opinion indicated that COPA might violate the First Amendment because it might prove to be an overbroad restriction on the transmission of nonobscene material that adults had a right to view. If so, COPA would be invalid, because it would not be narrowly tailored to the protection of children.

Chapter 17

FREEDOM OF RELIGION

Table of Sections

§ 17.1 Introduction—The Natural Antagonism Between the Two Clauses

The two clauses of the First Amendment deal with religion. The Amendment mandates that "Congress shall make no law respecting an establishment of religion, or prohibiting the free exercise thereof...." The first clause is called the establishment clause; the second is the free exercise clause. Both of these clauses are applicable to the states by the due process clause of the Fourteenth Amendment.

There can be a natural antagonism between a command not to establish religion and a command not to inhibit its practice. This tension between the clauses often leaves the Court with having to choose between competing values in religion cases. The general guide here is the concept of neutrality. The opposing values require that the government act to achieve only secular goals and that it achieve them in a religiously neutral manner. Unfortunately, situations arise where the government may have no choice but to incidentally help or hinder religious groups or practices. For example, Congress should not pay the salaries of ministers, priests, and rabbis, but if the military ships its soldiers to places with no easy access to churches, synagogues, or mosques, it may hire military chaplains (that looks like an "establishment of religion") who minister to the soldiers, so that the government will not to interfere with their free exercise of religion.

The Court has reviewed claims under the different clauses and has developed separate tests for determining whether a law violates either clause. While "neutrality" is still a central principle of both clauses, we have no single standard for determining what a religiously neutral act is. Instead, we must examine the neutrality or permissibility of a law in terms of the challenge to it.

Both clauses prevent the government from singling out specific religious sects for special benefits or burdens. If the government were to give benefits to a group of persons defined by their religious beliefs, it would create a sect preference that violates the establishment clause unless the law is somehow necessary to promote a compelling interest. Similarly, if the government were to impose burdens on a group of persons solely because of their religious beliefs, its action would violate the free exercise clause unless the action was necessary to promote a compelling interest.

The Court has decided some cases that involve a tension between the free exercise clause and establishment clause values without stating any specific standard, although it appears to use the principle of religious neutrality as its guide.

Locke v. Davey (2004) upheld a state law that gave scholarship aid to post-secondary school students based on a student's academic performance in secondary school, and the income level of the student's family. Nevertheless, the state law denied scholarship to an otherwise qualified student if the student was pursuing a degree in "devotional theology."

Writing for the majority in *Locke*, Chief Justice Rehnquist found that the state could have provided scholarship aid to all students (including students who pursued a degree in devotional theology) based on religiously neutral criteria. Nevertheless, *Locke* ruled that the state was not required to fund the students who pursued a degree in devotional theology. The Chief Justice said that there was "play in the joints" between the free exercise and establishment clause values. The state law was valid because the refusal to fund certain types of theological studies did not impose burdens on persons due to their religious beliefs, or disfavored them on the basis of their religious faith. Rehnquist's majority opinion seems to imply that a denial of basic state services (such as police or fire protection) to organizations or individuals based on the fact that the service would help the religious mission of the organization, or the religious practices of individuals, would violate the free exercise clause. Unfortunately, *Locke* did not set out the criteria for separating forms of aid whose denial to religious persons would violate the free exercise clause from forms of aid whose denial to religious persons would not violate the free exercise clause.

In *Cutter v. Wilkinson* (2005), the unanimous Court held that the establishment clause was not violated by a federal statute that required all state and local governments to accommodate requests based on religious beliefs and practices from persons institutionalized in facilities that received federal funds (e.g., prisoners in correctional facilities), unless the accommodation would interfere with a compelling interest of the government, such as maintaining order and safety in such institutions. This law was one that fit with the "play in the joints," or "corridor," between the free exercise clauses. Alleviating the burdens imposed on an individual's ability to follow his faith, when he was involuntarily institutionalized, did not grant special benefits to institutionalized persons based on religion.

There is no presumption of constitutionality that insulates a law alleged to violate the establishment clause. When examining a law that provides incidental aid to religion, the Supreme Court will question whether the law has a non-religious purpose, whether its primary effect is one that advances or inhibits religion, and whether the law creates an impermissible entanglement between government and religion. The Court will give great deference to religiously neutral government actions that litigants challenge under the free exercise clause. The free exercise clause does not give an individual a right to be exempted from a religiously neutral criminal law based solely on the fact that the individual cannot comply with both the law and her religious beliefs. For example, a person whose religion requires polygamy has no exemption to a law that prohibits polygamy.

§ 17.2   The Appeal to History

There is a seemingly irresistible impulse for all sides to appeal to history when analyzing issues under the religion clauses, although there is often no clear history. Many colonists fled religious persecution from their home countries, but in this country the experience differed widely throughout the colonies. It is common to refer to the Virginia experience when arguing for a complete separation of religious matters from secular government. In Virginia, Jefferson and Madison led a continuing battle for total religious freedom and an end of government aid to religion. Their position was most clearly stated by Madison in his "Memorial and Remonstrance" against an assessment bill to aid religion. The First Amendment was a product of Madison and the Virginia influence in the first Congress. However, this is not the only history that is relevant to these issues. The clauses were ratified as a part of the Bill of Rights, and the intention of those in the ratifying states should be as important as that of the Virginia representatives. Moreover, because the First Amendment was only a limitation on the actions of the federal government, one could read this history as affirming state sovereignty over this subject.

At the time, some states kept close ties existed between church and state, and some other states actually had established churches until well after the Revolution. For these states the First Amendment insured that the federal government could not interfere with their state preferences for certain religions. It also would forbid the federal government from benefiting one religion over another. The close ties between religion and state governments indicate that many states would not have opposed federal government aid to all religions on an equal basis. Indeed, Justice Story was certain that the federal government was barred only from punishing or benefiting specific religions. He thought the Amendment allowed for aid to all religions on an equal basis. Even after the established churches had ended in the states, they continued aid to religious entities. For example, religious teachers often made use of public schools, and states guaranteed tax exempt status to churches.

The religion clauses were among the first portions of the Bill of Rights that the Supreme Court incorporated into the Fourteenth Amendment and made applicable to the states. Although the original understanding of the drafters of the First and Fourteenth Amendments may be unclear, a majority of the Justices, since the last half of the Twentieth Century, consistently have held that the religion clauses protect fundamental aspects of liberty in our society and these values must be protected from both state and federal interference. Since almost all of the important Supreme Court decisions in this area have come after 1940, we have only the modern Court's view of history and the Justices' current tests to guide us.

§ 17.3 The Establishment Clause—Introduction

The Establishment Clause applies to both the federal and local governments. It prohibits government sponsorship of religion and requires that the government neither aid nor formally establish a religion. While at its inception the framers may have intended that the Establishment Clause does not prohibit governmental aid to *all* religions, the accepted view today is that it also prohibits the government from preferring religion over non-religion. However, the government simply cannot avoid aiding religion in some manner unless it actively opposes religion—something that it is forbidden to do by the free exercise clause. For example, if the city grants police or fire protection to churches, that clearly aids the practice of religion, but withholding the services would single out religious activities for a special burden. Thus it is clear that some test is required to determine when such incidental aid is permissible and when it is prohibited.

Since 1970, the Supreme Court has considered three factors when determining whether a government action that does not include a "sect preference" violates the establishment clause. When determining whether a law that is religiously neutral on its face violates the establishment clause, the Court will consider: (1) whether the law has a secular purpose; (2) whether the primary effect of the law advances or inhibits religion; (3) whether the law creates an excessive entanglement between government and religion.

From 1970 to 1997, the Supreme Court ruled that a three part test would be used in establishment clause cases. The three part test is often referred to as "the *Lemon* test," or "the *Lemon* tests," because the Court in *Lemon v. Kurtzman* (1971) ruled that a law would violate the establishment clause unless it [1] had a secular purpose, [2] had a primary effect that neither advanced nor inhibited religion, and [3] avoided creating an "excessive entanglement" between government and religion. *Lemon* also found that, when in determining whether a statute that provided financial aid to an institution involved an "excessive entanglement" between government and religion, the judiciary must consider the nature of the institution that received the benefit from the government, the nature of the aid that the government gave to the religiously affiliated institution, and the resulting relationship between the government and religious authorities.

Agostini v. Felton (1997) found that the judiciary must consider the purpose and effect of a law to determine whether a law that provides government aid to a religious institution violated the establishment clause. Justice O'Connor, speaking for majority in *Agostini*, described the inquiry into whether the government aid program gives rise to excessive entanglement between the government and religion as a part of the judicial inquiry into whether the challenged governmental program had the impermissible primary effect of aiding or inhibiting religion. *Agostini* repackaged the three part purpose-effect-entanglement test that it had used from 1971 to 1997. Nevertheless, *Agostini* indicated that the Court would continue to examine the purpose, effect, and entanglement factors when determining whether a facially neutral law provided aid to religious persons, or religious institutions, in a way that would violate the establishment clause.

The Court will not make an inquiry into the purpose or effect of a law that creates a denominational preference or a sect preference for religious entities. Any law that employs such preferences violates the establishment clause unless the government can demonstrate that the law is necessary to promote a compelling interest. However, it is difficult to imagine why the government would have a compelling need to prefer some religions over others.

Because of the stringency of the test used to examine denominational preferences, some cases involve disputes concerning whether law creates a denominational preference. For example, *Larson v. Valente* (1982) invalidated a state statute that regulated the solicitation of donations by charitable organizations if, but only if, the organization solicited more than 50% of its funds from nonmembers. This law created a denominational preference because the burdens of the regulation disproportionately burdened, and thus discriminated against, religious organizations that were significantly involved in fund raising activities aimed at nonmembers. Justice Brennan, for the majority, held that these restrictions were not "closely fitted" to any compelling interest. Therefore, the law violated the establishment clause, and it was unnecessary to engage in any further of the statute under other types of establishment clause tests.

Larson chose based its decision on the establishment clause. It could have invalidated the law under the free exercise clause, if the majority had categorizes the law as an attempt to suppress the activity of identifiable religious groups with a law that was not a religiously neutral law of general applicability.

More recently, the Court has slightly modified the three part purpose-effect-entanglement test. Nevertheless, the Justices remained committed to enforcing the concept of religious neutrality in establishment clause rulings; neither denominational preferences nor delegations of government authority to religious sects survive establishment clause review.

Taxes and the Religion Clauses. *Hernandez v. Commissioner of Internal Revenue* (1989), upheld the denial of a tax deduction to a taxpayer for a contribution to a church that was a "fixed donation" for services that the church provided. In *Hernandez*, a member of the Church of Scientology wanted to deduct from his gross income the amount of money he paid for "auditing" and "training" services provided by the Church. The Church had a system of mandatory fixed charges for these religious services; no member would receive the service without paying the fixed price. The Internal Revenue Service and the Supreme Court interpreted the Internal Revenue Code to preclude a deduction for a payment made to a charity that constituted an exchange for a product or service. For example, if you pay the church $1 for six donuts, and the local donut store charges $1 for six donuts, you cannot deduct $1 paid to the church as a donation.

Hernandez ruled that the Internal Revenue Code prohibition of a charitable deduction under such circumstances does not violate the establishment or free exercise clauses of the First Amendment. The tax classification is not subject to the compelling interest test because the Internal Revenue Code did not on its face create any distinction between different types of religious entities. It was a neutral law. Because the statute, and the interpretation of it by the Internal Revenue Service, contained no denominational preference, the tax code provision was subject only to the three part establishment clause test (the purpose-effect-entanglement test). Moreover, there was no evidence that the purpose of the law demonstrated any animus to any religion, or to religion in general. In addition, tax law encouraged general gifts to charitable entities that were not in exchange for goods or services, and this purpose neither advanced or inhibited religion. Finally, the Internal Revenue Code did not create any entanglement between the government and religion, because the minimal regulatory interaction between taxpayers, churches, and the Internal Revenue Service was not the kind of administrative entanglement that endangered religion clause values.

Hernandez also did not violate the free exercise clause for two reasons. First, the Internal Revenue Code did not place a substantial burden on any person who was carrying out a tenet of a religious belief. Second, the law served the public interest of maintaining a tax system free of exemptions tailored to accommodate a wide variety of religions, and this benefit outweighed any burden on persons who were denied deductions under these circumstances.

Later, *Jimmy Swaggart Ministries v. Board of Equalization* (1990) held that a religious organization, and the members of the organization, had no right to refuse to pay general sales and use taxes for the sales of religious goods and literature. Because the state did not design its sales and use taxes to tax solely religious activities, it did not have to justify them by a compelling state interest.

In contrast, if the state imposes a "flat tax," e.g., a license fee (a fixed fee) that restricts the ability of persons to engage in religious activities, that tax would be analogous to a prior restraint on speech activities. The Court would find that the flat-tax license fee, as applied to religious activity, violated the establishment and free exercise clauses. *Murdock v. Pennsylvania* (1943).

Direct Entanglement with Religion—Delegation of Legislative Power. In some instances it is relatively easy to determine that a governmental action violates the establishment clause because it either delegates governmental power to a religious group in a manner that allows for excessive entanglement between the government and religion or it constitutes a preference for certain religions. For example, *Larkin v. Grendel's Den, Inc.* (1982) held a zoning law violated the establishment clause by granting to all churches or schools a veto power over the issuance of a liquor license for any premises within a five hundred foot radius of the church or school.

The Use of Historical Evidence to Determine Establishment Clause Violations. In several instances the Court has based a finding that a governmental practice did not violate the establishment clause on a history of that practice which the Court believed showed that the governmental practice involved no significant danger of eroding governmental neutrality regarding religious matters.

Thus, *Marsh v. Chambers* (1983) upheld a legislature's practice of employing a religious chaplain whose primary duty was to open each legislative day with a prayer. The Court based its finding that there was no establishment clause violation on the "unambiguous and unbroken history of more than two hundred years" of legislative prayer, although the majority opinion also stated that history "could not justify contemporary violations" of the First Amendment. In the majority's view, legislative prayer merely recognized a belief widely held among the people of the country; its history demonstrated that such activity did not constitute the type of religious purpose, religious effect, or entanglement between government and religion that threatened the First Amendment value of religious neutrality on the part of government.

Religious Expression and the Free Speech Clause. In a series of cases, the Supreme Court has prohibited government entities from suppressing, or discriminating against, speech of religious organizations. In each of these cases, a government entity attempted to deny access to government property to a religious group on the basis that, in the view of the government, the religious group's use of the public property would constitute a violation of the establishment clause. However, the Supreme Court ruled that allowing a religious organization to use a public forum for religiously oriented speech activities did not constitute a violation of the establishment clause, so long as the religious group was not given preferential treatment. Not to allow the religion to use the public forum would constitute improper discrimination against religion.

In these cases, the Court did not identify a specific standard for determining if, or when, speech by private persons on government property would constitute a violation of the establishment clause. While the Court did not formally reject the three-part *Lemon* Test, several Justices believed that the Court should employ an "endorsement test" for determining when government aid to religious activities or government connection to religious speech violated the First Amendment.

Consider, e.g., *Lamb's Chapel v. Center Moriches Union Free School District* (1993), which held that a government school board violated the First Amendment freedom of speech when it denied a religious organization the right to conduct a meeting in a school building after school hours, at a time when the board allowed nonreligious groups to use the school premises for their meetings. Regardless of whether the school building was viewed as a "limited public forum" or a "nonpublic forum," the government's discrimination against religious speech constituted a form of viewpoint discrimination that violated the First Amendment.

§ 17.4 The Establishment Clause—Aid to Religious Institutions

(a) Primary and Secondary Schools

The fact that most of the Supreme Court's decisions concerning the meaning of the establishment clause in the second half of the twentieth century involved governmental aid to religiously affiliated primary and secondary schools may explain why the Supreme Court was not clear in describing establishment clause principles.

In establishment clause cases concerning aid to religious schools prior to 1970, the Supreme Court considered only whether the challenged government aid program evidenced a purpose on the part of government to aid religion and whether the challenged program had the primary effect of advancing or inhibiting religious activity. Between 1970 and 1997, the Supreme Court adopted a three part test for evaluating whether government programs that aided religious schools violated the establishment clause. During this time, the Court held that any program that provided direct aid to religiously affiliated schools, or their students, would be invalid unless the government program: (1) had a secular purpose; (2) did not have a primary effect of advancing or inhibiting religion; and

(3) avoided the creation of an "excessive entanglement" between government and religion. In the 1970's and early 1980's, very few government programs that provided aid to religious schools or religious school students survived the three part test.

In the late 1980's and early 1990's, the Court applied the establishment clause tests in a different way and slightly modified the tests that would be used to review aid to students at religiously affiliated schools. Finally, in 1997, *Agostini v. Felton* (1997) upheld a government program that provided remedial services, including remedial educational services, to students at both religious and nonreligious schools, after concluding that this government program had a secular purpose and did not have a primary effect that advanced religion. *Agostini*, however, did not reject the use of the three part test of the previous decades. Rather, it found that consideration of whether a government program created an excessive entanglement between government and religion was a part of the Court's consideration of whether the challenged government program had the impermissible effect of advancing or inhibiting religion.

Agostini held that a law providing aid to religious institutions is invalid if it: (1) was enacted for the purpose of advancing or inculcating religious beliefs; or (2) had a primary effect that advanced religion. In determining whether the law had an impermissible effect, the Court would look at three factors: (1) whether the governmental aid involved religious indoctrination of students (2) whether the aid program defined recipients in religious terms; (3) whether the aid program created an excessive entanglement between government and religion.

Unfortunately, these standards are easier to state than apply. A few years after *Agostini*, the Court seemed hopelessly fragmented concerning how these standards should be applied.

The fact that a government program involves only aid to students or their parents (which allows those persons to make a totally free choice as to whether to use the aid in secular or religiously related schools) is likely to influence the Justices to rule that the program has neither a religious purpose nor primary religious effect that would violate the establishment clause. In other words, the government gives food stamps to poor people, and they can use it to buy kosher food or non-kosher. We do not say that the food stamps aid religion. Or, the government gives money to a worker who pays no income taxes (what is often called a "negative income tax"). The worker may decide to donate part of the money to a local church. We do not say that the government aids the church. The government may give money for school books to school-age children, and the children can decide to buy the books and attend a religiously-affiliated school.

Zelman v. Simmons–Harris (2002) distinguished true private choice programs from aid that went directly to religiously affiliated institutions. The five Justices who voted to uphold the tuition voucher program at issue found that it had neither a primary purpose of advancing religion nor a primary effect that advanced religion in a manner inconsistent with establishment clause values. Justice O'Connor, concurring in *Zelman*, stated that the *Agostini* decision had merely made a formal change in the *Lemon* tests by including the entanglement factor as part of effect analysis. The *Zelman* majority noted that "while our jurisprudence with respect to the constitutionality of direct aid [to religious institution] programs has changed significantly over the past two decades, [citing *Agostini*], our jurisprudence with respect to true private choice programs has remained consistent and unbroken." The dissenting Justices believed that the majority had not correctly analyzed the way in which the tuition voucher program constituted a direct form of aid to religious activity and had disregarded the extent to which this type of entanglement between government and religion would give rise to social divisions based along religious lines that violated establishment clause values.

The cases in the area, and the history as well, are as complex as the modern income tax code. Let us examine the major cases and leave the complex history to Nowak & Rotunda's one volume treatise on Constitutional Law.

Student Transportation. *Everson v. Board of Education* (1947) (5 to 4) upheld a program which in effect paid the transportation costs of parochial school students. Pursuant to a state statute, a local school board established a program which reimbursed the parents of students at public and nonprofit private schools for the amounts they spent for bus transportation. The only private nonprofit school in the district was a Catholic school. On the other hand, other private schools (whether or not religiously based) might come into being if they knew that the state could pick up the transportation costs for their students.

The majority viewed the state's providing free bus transportation to all school children on an equal basis constituted only a general service to benefit and safeguard children rather than an aid to religion. Basic governmental services, such as fire and police protection, can be extended to religious institutions along with the rest of the public without aiding religion. The general provision of free transportation to be akin to such a service.

Everson remains the law today and the Court has shown no inclination to reverse its position on basic bus fare reimbursement programs, even though, as discussed later in this section, the state cannot pay for parochial school field trips.

If a law limited a similar aid program to public and parochial school students (rather than public and non-profit schools) the Court may come to a different conclusion because excluding children in private nonprofit schools undercuts the theory that the state is providing a neutral benefit. Such a statute would have the effect of preferring religious school students over students at other nonprofit schools and this preference is likely to violate the establishment clause.

By the time that the Court was next confronted with a program of aid to parochial school students, it was employing the "purpose and effect" test to resolve establishment clause claims. Under this test the purpose of a state program must be secular in nature. Additionally, the program may not have a primary effect of either advancing or inhibiting religion or religious practices to withstand review under this test.

Textbooks. *Board of Education v. Allen* (1968) upheld a program that provided textbooks to public and private school students under the purpose and effect test, even though the students attended parochial schools. The New York textbook law under review required school boards to loan textbooks to students in all public or private schools. This resulted in books being given to parochial school students for their studies in the religious schools. However, the law allowed only books for secular studies to be lent to students and the books had to be either ones used in public schools or ones that the school board approved as secular in nature. There was no religious purpose in this law because the program was designed to aid the secular education of students. The Court has accepted this secular purpose—the improvement of the educational opportunities for all children—in every case relating to aid for religious schools.

In contrast, a textbook program that aided schools that discriminated on the basis of race would be invalid. *Bob Jones University v. United States* (1983).

Tax Exempt Status for Religious Organizations. *Walz v. Tax Commission* (1970) upheld granting of exemptions from property taxes to churches as a part of a general exception for a wide variety of nonprofit institutions. Presumably this ruling validates the granting of tax exemptions to religious schools so long as the exemption is granted to all nonprofit schools.

The majority also found that taxing church property would cause at least as much administrative entanglement between government and religious authorities as did the exemption. The long history of such exemptions also persuaded the Court; there was more than 200 years of a virtually uniform practice in the states without evidence of any "establishment" effects. The exemption served separation of church and state: the state does not support the churches, and churches (by way of taxes) do not support the state.

Other Forms of Aid to Religiously Affiliated Schools or Their Students. The Court invalidated two state attempts to subsidize the costs of parochial school education in *Lemon v. Kurtzman* (1971). Rhode Island provided a fifteen percent salary supplement to teachers of secular subjects in private schools where the per-pupil expenditure was below that of the public schools. In the second program, Pennsylvania authorized the reimbursement of nonpublic schools for a fraction of teacher salaries and instructional materials in secular subjects. Under both state systems, Catholic schools were the main beneficiaries of the programs. Of course, that might change in the future; other private schools might come into being if the law existed for a while, but the majority was concerned that the main beneficiaries at the time the law was enacted were Catholic schools.

Once again, the Court accepted the legislatures' position that they were pursuing the secular end of promoting the nonreligious education of young children. The Court did not come to an exact ruling on whether the programs had a primary effect of advancing religion, but its discussion of the need to avoid administrative entanglement indicated that it thought such programs could have a prohibited result. The majority assumed that religious elementary and secondary schools were likely to advance religion even in their secular subjects. However, instead of basing the ruling on the effect of these programs, *Lemon* struck down these statutes because it found that they fostered an excessive entanglement between church and state. Chief Justice Burger held that, in assessing the degree of entanglement, three factors were to be considered: (1) the character and purpose of the institution benefited; (2) the nature of the aid; (3) the resulting relationship between government and religious authorities.

In applying this three part test, the majority first found that Catholic elementary and secondary schools were an integral part of the religious program of that church. The religious atmosphere and control of this type of school showed that religious teaching might be advanced, even inadvertently, in secular courses. Second, the aid subsidized teacher salaries. The Court noted that, unlike textbooks, teachers could not be checked in advance to insure that they would not teach religion. Though the teachers could in good faith promise to remain neutral, they might inadvertently advance religion in the classroom. Finally, the majority found that, in order to insure that religious activities or teaching were not aided by the program, the state would have to place a great number of restrictions on the schools and engage in a monitoring program that would be little short of ongoing surveillance. The Court concluded that these factors showed that the program would result in an excessive entanglement violative of the establishment clause.

The Chief Justice also stressed the fact that these types of programs were politically divisive. The provision of significant ongoing aid to parochial elementary and secondary schools injected an explosive political issue that caused division along religious lines. However, the Court was not clear as to whether this "divisiveness" was the reason for strict application of the purpose-effect-entanglement test, a branch of the entanglement test, or a fourth test. Nor did the Court explain why the fact that some people would oppose this aid meant that the Court must prevent the majority from allowing it. All laws, after all, have some people opposed to them and we do not use that simple fact as a reason to prevent the aid.

Following this case were a host of others, leaving the law as complex as many sections of the Internal Revenue Code. Years later the Court adopted new reasoning that allows aid that benefits students attending private schools, even if the schools are religiously affiliated. The first major decision in this new line of cases was *Mitchell v. Helms* (2000). By a 6 to 3 vote, but without a majority opinion, the Court ruled that local school districts could use federal funds for providing educational equipment and materials to both public and private schools, including non-religious schools. In the *Mitchell* case, the school board had used part of its federal funds to provide "library books, computers, and computer software, and also slide and movie projectors, overhead projectors, television sets, tape recorders, VCRs, projection screens, laboratory equipment, maps, globes, film strips, slides and cassette recordings" to public and private schools, including 41 religiously affiliated schools. The persons challenging the program had not alleged that the law had a religious purpose, so that the Court's focus was solely on whether the granting of this type of aid to religiously affiliated schools and their students had an impermissible effect under the establishment clause.

In *Mitchell*, both the plurality opinion, written by Justice Thomas for four Justices, and the concurring opinion, by Justices O'Connor and Breyer, agreed that the effect of the law should be analyzed in terms of whether it: (1) involved governmental indoctrination of students; (2) defined recipients with religious references; or (3) created an excessive entanglement between government and religion. The plurality and concurring opinions also agreed that the program at issue in *Mitchell* was valid, and that contrary decisions should be overruled.

However, the plurality and concurring opinions took very different approaches to this result. Justice Thomas' opinion concluded that religiously neutral aid could be given to schools consistently with the establishment clause even though the recipient schools were pervasively sectarian. Thomas explained that whether governmental aid to religious schools results in religious indoctrination ultimately depends on whether any indoctrination that occurs could reasonably be attributed to governmental action. The answer to the indoctrination question resolves the question whether an educational aid program "subsidizes" religion. In order to distinguish between indoctrination that is attributable to the State and indoctrination that is not, the Court will turn to the neutrality principle and uphold aid that is offered to a broad range of groups or persons without regard to their religion. As a way to assure neutrality, the Court considers whether any governmental aid to a religious institution results from the genuinely independent and private choices of individual parents. Thomas explained that the presence of private choice is easier to see when aid literally passes through individuals' hands; however, there is no reason why the Establishment Clause requires such a form. In this case, Thomas examined the facts and concluded that the aid came because of the parents' free and private choices.

Justice O'Connor, joined by Justice Breyer, concurred in the judgment of the Court, and believed that a program of religiously neutral aid should be upheld but they also believed that a particular grant to a school would be invalid if the persons challenging the grant could show that the particular religious school in fact had diverted the religiously neutral materials given to the school by the government into religious education and religious indoctrination. They found no problem with the aid offered in this case.

Three Justices dissented in *Mitchell*, because they believed that any form of aid to religious schools that had the theoretical potential for being misused and diverted to religious indoctrination or religious education ran afoul of establishment clause principles.

Tuition Voucher Programs. Recall that the plurality in *Mitchell* said the presence of private choice is easier to see when aid literally passes through individuals' hands. *Mitchell* set the stage for *Zelman v. Simmons–Harris* (2002). In that case, a majority of the Court agreed that an Ohio tuition voucher program was constitutional. Ohio designed its program to help students in the worst performing schools in that state. In the mid–1990's a federal court had placed the entire Cleveland School District under the control of the State of Ohio, rather than local control, because the Cleveland schools were among the worst academically performing schools in the United States.

The State of Ohio passed its Pilot Project Scholarship Program (the program) that took several paths in the road towards improving Cleveland's schools. The program provided tutorial aid for those students who chose to remain enrolled in their public schools. The program also provided tuition aid (tuition vouchers) for students in elementary school who chose to attend a public or private school that participated in the program. Parents could choose to send their children to religiously-affiliated schools.

In addition to tuition aid, Ohio also established community and magnet schools. A community school would be run by its own school board rather than a local school district. For each student attending a community school, that school would receive over $4,500 in state funding (more than twice for that of the voucher program students). The Ohio magnet schools were public schools operated by a local school board that would emphasize one aspect of teaching or learning. Students at magnet schools received over $4,000 of state aid and the school district would receive almost $8,000 of government money for each student at a magnet school.

The tuition aid portion of the Ohio program (the voucher program) provided families with vouchers that could be used at participating public and private schools. Religious and non-religious private schools could participate in the program and accept students, together with their vouchers, so long as the school was located within the district and met certain educational standards. To be part of the program, a private school receiving student tuition vouchers would be required to agree not to discriminate on the basis of race, religious or ethnic background. Also, a participating private school must agree that it would not advocate, promote or teach hatred of individuals on the basis of their race or religion.

The Ohio program provided tuition aid to students in kindergarten through third grade; the program would expand each year so that students through the eighth grade would eventually be able to participate in the program. The program provided aid to students, and the families of students, in all districts that had been subject to federal court control due to the poor academic performance of the school district. Realistically, only Cleveland students would be receiving benefits through the pilot program.

Ohio gave tuition assistance to families of students in the eligible districts based upon financial need. Families with incomes very significantly below a poverty line set forth in the statute would receive assistance with up to 90% of private school tuition. The maximum amount that could be paid to a private school through the voucher for the poorest families was $2,250.00. The law prohibited schools that participated in the program from charging the lowest income families more than $250 in excess of the state voucher amount. For all other students, and their families, the Ohio program would pay 75% of the cost of tuition at a participating private school, up to a limit of $1,875. For families that did not meet the statutory definition of low-income families, participating private schools were free to impose additional charges not subject to state limitation. The Ohio program gave vouchers (checks) payable to the parents who chose a private school for their child. The parents then would endorse the voucher over to the participating private school.

Zelman stated that the program would be invalid if it had the purpose or effect of advancing or inhibiting religion. There was no contention at any point in the litigation that the program had been enacted for a religious, rather than a secular, purpose. For that reason, the Court considered only whether the program had an impermissible effect of advancing or inhibiting religion in violation of the establishment clause.

Zelman explained that its previous decisions drew a "consistent distinction between programs that provide a direct aid to religious schools ... and programs of true private choice, in which government aid reaches religious schools only as a result of the genuine and independent choices of private individuals...." Hence, if "a government aid program is neutral with respect to religion, and provides assistance directly to a broad class of citizens, who, in turn, direct government aid to religious schools wholly as a result of their own genuine and independent private choice, the program is not readily subject to challenge under the establishment clause."

The program was religiously neutral because it did not provide any financial incentive to parents to choose religious, rather than non-religious, education. *Zelman* rejected the dissent's argument that the Ohio program should be invalidated because most of the participating private schools (at the time the Court heard the case) had religious affiliations. The majority noted that making a program invalid merely because many students chose to use their vouchers at religiously affiliated schools would lead to "the absurd result" that a school choice program that was religiously neutral would be valid in parts of a state that happen to have a lower percentage of religiously affiliated private schools than parts of a state where the percentage of religiously affiliated private schools was higher.

Zelman was distinguishable from earlier where the Court invalidated a New York program that gave benefits only to students attending private schools. In *Zelman*, the Ohio tuition voucher program was simply part of a package of alternatives presented to parents, and that the program was entirely neutral with respect to religion.

Justice O'Connor wrote a concurring opinion in *Zelman*, and also joined with the Chief Justice's majority opinion. She emphasized the importance of considering all of the choices that Ohio presented to parents in terms of receiving state aid for their children's education. Justice Thomas also wrote a concurring opinion explaining the importance of providing all children with a wide variety of educational choices and why the provision of free choice did not violate establishment clause values.

Justice Souter, joined by three other justices, wrote a dissent. He argued that the Ohio program should not be considered neutral because the aid went primarily to students attending religious schools. He also argued that there was excessive entanglement by making the religiously affiliated private schools conform to a wide variety of state regulations in a way that would undermine the religious schools' freedom of belief.

Justice Breyer wrote a separate dissent, joined by Justices Stevens and Souter, but not Justice Ginsburg. Justice Breyer's dissent focused almost exclusively on political divisiveness caused by government aid to religiously affiliated institutions.

Justice Stevens, joined by Ginsburg, also wrote a separate dissent opinion arguing that the Court should focus on the fact that the tuition voucher program only helped children attending private schools, and that almost all of these students were attending religiously affiliated schools.

Zelman reflects a general principle that law providing aid to parents and students on a religiously neutral basis should not constitute prohibited aid to religion so long as the amount of aid provided to a particular student who attends a religiously affiliated private school is not greater than the aid given to students at public schools and the aid program does not encourage students to attend religiously affiliated schools rather than public schools or nonsectarian private schools. In the 1920's the Court had ruled that parents have a right to send their children to private schools so long as those schools meet reasonable accreditation standards. For the parents of many children that choice exists only in theory, because the parents cannot afford to send their children to a private school. If the state provides aid only in the form of public school opportunities the state effectively keeps low-income parents from exercising their constitutional right to send their child to a private school. Under the modern cases, providing parents with a wide variety of choices as to how they will receive state aid for their children, including the choice of taking a cash benefit in the form of a voucher, should be permissible so long as it is not slanted towards encouraging students to attend religious schools. Hence, *Zelman* found that such a tuition voucher program does not impermissibly advance religion.

Educational Aid Payments to Handicapped Students.

Witters v. Washington Department of Services for the Blind (1986) unanimously upheld a state program providing physically handicapped students with "vocational rehabilitation assistance" payments that allowed those students to obtain "special education and/or training in the professions, businesses or trades." There is a logical similarity between cases like *Witters* and *Zelman*. The Court issued the *Witters* decision 16 years before *Zelman*. Note that *Witters* was unanimous, but *Zelman* was 5 to 4. Yet, in a real sense, *Witters* portended *Zelman*: the state can offer tuition aid to a student, who can decide to use that aid to attend a religiously affiliated school.

The state courts had ruled that payment of aid to a blind student attending a Christian college and preparing himself for a career as a religious pastor, missionary, or youth director violated the First Amendment establishment clause. Justice Marshall, for the Court, held that the aid program, including payment to the blind student engaged in religious studies at a religiously affiliated school, was valid; it had both a sufficient nonreligious purpose and nonreligious primary effect.

All the Justices in *Witters* agreed that the state had no purpose to endorse religion. Even those persons who attacked the law admitted that it had a nonreligious purpose. The aid program also had no impermissible primary religious effect because it was a payment made directly to visually handicapped students to provide them with sufficient financial resources for vocational training. Justice Marshall reasoned that a student's decision to use the money at a religious school or for religious vocational studies was "only as a result of the genuinely independent and private choices of the aid recipient." In this sense, the aid did not differ from generalized aid to segments of society or payments to government employees. Persons who receive any type of monetary payment from the government could always make an independent decision to donate some of their money to a religious organization or to attend a religious school. Interestingly, the majority opinion stated that "nothing in the record indicates that, if petitioner [the blind student and the state] succeeds, any significant portion of the aid expended under the Washington program as a whole will end up flowing to religious education." It is difficult to understand the significance of this statement, since Justice Marshall did not state that the program would become invalid if a higher percent of students receiving the aid attended religious schools.

Zobrest v. Catalina Foothills School District (1993), involved a high school instead of a college, relied heavily on *Witters* and ruled that the establishment clause did not prevent a public school district from providing a sign language interpreter to a deaf student who was attending a religiously affiliated school within the district's boundaries. While he was in the public schools, the district furnished him with a sign language interpreter. When he entered a Catholic high school he claimed that the federal Individuals with Disabilities Education Act required the school district to provide him with a sign language interpreter. The school district refused because it claimed that providing such aid to a student in a religious school would violate the establishment clause.

Of the seven Justices who reached the constitutional issue in *Zobrest* (two went off on statutory grounds), five rejected the school district's claim that the provision of a sign language interpreter for the religious school student would violate the establishment clause.

(b) Aid to Colleges and Universities

While aid to nonpublic institutions of higher education has been the subject of only a few Supreme Court decisions, it is clear that government programs aiding these schools must be tested under the same tests that have been employed in the primary school cases. The aid must have a secular purpose, its primary effect cannot advance or inhibit religion, and it must avoid creating an excessive entanglement between government and religion. However, the Court, in general, has been more likely to approve of such aid because the Justices tend to conclude that higher education is not as "pervasively sectarian" as the education provided in religiously affiliated grade schools and high schools.

In determining whether excessive entanglement exists, the Court examines three factors: (1) the character of the institutions benefited; (2) the nature of the aid provided; (3) the resulting relationship between government and church authorities. In addition, the program must not be of a type which will cause political division along religious lines. The Court will accept the legislative purpose of the aid programs as secular in nature—the purpose, as in the grade and school cases, is to improve education by providing students with more choices. Competition tends to make the competitors better. While the Court has sometimes approved of aid and sometimes disapproved of aid, while it had reversed some decisions and distinguished others, it has never challenged the secular purpose of the legislature's interest in assisting the secular portion of all students' education.

The Court has found that these programs do not have a primary effect of aiding religion where there is at least some formal guarantee by the college authorities that the funds will not be used for religious instruction or other sectarian activities. The Court has refused to assume that religious colleges are so permeated with religion that their secular functions cannot be separated from their religious mission. Thus, a program that is tied to only secular instruction will not have an effect of advancing religion.

However, if the institution is sectarian to the extent that the advancing of religious beliefs permeated its entire program then this analysis could not apply. Such an institution would be similar to the parochial elementary and secondary schools that the majority of Justices have deemed to have a primary function of propagating religious doctrine. In such a situation the secular teaching function could not be sufficiently separated from the religious mission of the school. Thus any significant aid to the school would have the prohibited effect of advancing religion.

Thus, there is a two part test to determine whether a specific aid program for religiously affiliated colleges and universities has a "primary effect" of advancing religion. To avoid such an effect: (1) the institution's secular function must not be permeated with a religious atmosphere, and (2) there must be assurances by the college and the government authority that the aid will not be used for religious teaching or other religious activities.

It is relatively easy for these programs aiding higher education to pass the three factor test for determining the presence of excessive entanglement. First, because the institutions are not "permeated" with religion, the Court has told us that there is little need for extensive controls to insure against advancing religion.

Second, the aid is usually granted for a specific secular purpose. If so, it is likely to be only a one-time grant which is easily monitored. However, the Court has also upheld annual general grants to colleges where the college and government authorities would give assurances of their use for secular purposes.

Third, the administrative contacts between government and religious authorities can easily be kept to a minimum in such programs. Because the nature of the institution and aid do not have a high potential for advancing religion, the state need not engage in a program of constant surveillance. As long as the Court concludes that the program invokes little more contact between the religious authorities and the state than the normal accreditation procedures, it finds no excessive administrative entanglement.

Finally, the Court has not found these programs to be "politically divisive." Assuming that "political divisiveness" is still a relevant test under the more recent cases, the Court has decided that one-time grants for specific purposes rarely stir emotion concerning government subsidies to religion. The Court even concluded that annual grant programs are not the subject of debate along religious lines. The largely secular atmosphere of these institutions, and the public evaluation of higher education, helps to keep debate on such subjects focused on educational and fiscal policy rather than religion. Additionally, there are a high percentage of nonsectarian private colleges, and that fact prevents these programs from becoming religious issues.

A leading case is *Tilton v. Richardson* (1971), which upheld (5 to 4) the Higher Education Facilities Act, a federal law that funded grants for the construction of college facilities for other than religious activities or religious instruction.

Tilton did invalidate one section of the federal law. Under the act the government gave up any ability to demand a return of funds after twenty years even if the buildings then were used for religious purposes. The Court concluded that the limitation of the government's enforcement powers after twenty years would be the equivalent of an unrestricted gift to the college after that time. Because this delayed grant could have the effect of advancing religion, the Court held that both the assurance of secular use and the government power to demand return of money used for religious purposes must continue so long as the facility was of any value.

Hunt v. McNair (1973) upheld a state program of issuing revenue bonds for the benefit of private colleges, including religiously affiliated schools. An "Educational Facilities Authority" issued bonds to finance construction of facilities that did not involve sectarian uses and the schools repaid these bonds from their own revenues. Although the state incurred no financial obligation under the program, the state authority issued the bonds, financed the construction with the bond revenues and leased the facilities to the institution. The use of the state bonding system allowed these schools to sell bonds at a reduced interest rate, which saved the schools significant interest payments. The law authorized the Authority to establish regulations and conduct inspections to assure secular use of the buildings which were conveyed to it.

Roemer v. Board of Public Works (1976), with no majority opinion, approved an annual grant program that benefited religious colleges. Maryland established a program of annual grants that provided for each full time student (excluding those enrolled in seminary or theological programs) a grant of 15% of the per-pupil amount that the state spent in the public college system. Originally law imposed virtually no restrictions on the use of the grant money. However, Maryland amended the act to provide that the Maryland Council of Higher Education would screen the institution application to assure that the institution was not pervasively religious and that the institution had given adequate assurance that the funds would be used for a secular purpose. The Court (5 to 4) upheld this amended program.

(c) Other Issues in Aid to Religious Institutions

(1) Payments Under Programs Later Held Invalid. Even though a court may invalidate a program of aid to religious schools under the establishment clause, the government may have made payments to schools prior to the law's invalidation. The question then arises as to whether the recipient institutions must return the funds. *Lemon v. Kurtzman (Lemon II)* (1973) said no, under the facts of that case. Prior to the Supreme Court's decision in *Lemon I* (1971), Pennsylvania had made substantial payments to parochial schools under the challenged act. *Lemon I* had invalidated that act. *Lemon II* held that two factors were relevant in determining whether to grant a retroactive remedy: (1) the reasonableness and degree of reliance by the institution on the payments, and (2) the necessity of refunds to protect the constitutional right involved.

Lemon II concluded that reimbursement was not required because the schools' reliance had been reasonable. Also, the return of funds was not necessary to guard against impermissibly aiding religion because the schools had spent the funds on secular purposes under the supervision of secular authorities.

Contrast *New York v. Cathedral Academy* (1977), where the Court invalidated a state statute that would have granted reimbursement to private schools for state mandated record keeping and testing services under a program that previously had been held to violate the First and Fourteenth Amendments. In 1973 federal district court had held that the original state act regarding payments for record keeping and testing was unconstitutional, and the Supreme Court affirmed. Then, the district court had enjoined the distribution of funds for this program including distribution of funds for the last half of the 1971–72 school year. In June 1972, the state legislature attempted to limit the impact of the district court injunction by passing a new state statute granting reimbursement for expenses incurred prior to July, 1972, by schools that had attempted to follow the previous record keeping and testing requirements.

Cathedral Academy held that this reimbursement act was invalid, and distinguished it from the situation in *Lemon II*. In *Lemon I* the state program violated the First Amendment because it created an excessive entanglement between government and religion. The lower court's refusal to grant retroactive injunctive relief in that case was justified because allowing payments for the prior period did not do any further damage to constitutional values; those payments involved no further entanglement between government and religion, and the payments did not serve a religious purpose. In *Cathedral Academy*, the district court had enjoined all payments in the original action; the state legislature could not modify the impact of this injunction.

The reimbursement statute failed the three part establishment test on two bases: (1) the reimbursement payments would have a religious effect because the grant program itself had been a prohibited form of aid to religion; (2) the procedures required by the Act to assure the secular nature of the reimbursement payments would involve an excessive entanglement between state and religious authorities. Thus, there could be no reimbursement payments under the statute even though some religious schools might have relied on the original statute, prior to the first federal court action, when they incurred these expenses. The differences in the original trial court actions in *Lemon I* as well as the nature of the aid programs, resulted in the different holdings in *Lemon II* and in *Cathedral Academy*.

(2) Aid to Schools That Discriminate on the Basis of Race. Although a program of state aid to a private school may not violate the establishment clause, it cannot aid a school that discriminates on the basis of race. *Norwood v. Harrison* (1973) held the state may not constitutionally give or lend textbooks to students who attend a school that discriminates on the basis of race.

However, the state may give or textbooks to students even if they attend religiously affiliated schools. *Board of Education v. Allen* (1968). A textbook program may aid religious schools but they represent a value in the free exercise of religion that offsets any slight aid to religion. In contrast, there is no countervailing constitutional value that could justify state aid to a racially discriminatory system. Thus, the aid to these students would violate the equal protection clause.

A related issue is the question of whether Congress, by statute, can prohibit a private school from discriminating on the basis of race because it is affiliated with a religion that requires segregation as a tenet of the religious belief. It may well be that the free exercise clause requires only that such religious-segregated schools be accommodated in that their existence is not made illegal. Indeed, it is not clear whether the Thirteenth Amendment or legislation passed to enforce it may prohibit racially discriminatory private schools. *Runyon v. McCrary* (1976) held that federal statute prohibited racial discrimination in private schools but reserved the question whether the statute could apply to prohibit racial discrimination in religiously affiliated schools where the particular denomination believed that its religious doctrine required racial discrimination.

At a minimum, the Thirteenth, Fourteenth, and Fifteenth Amendments represent values that should prevent the government from actively aiding these schools. Because those schools represent values opposed to the constitutional rights of racial minorities, only accommodation of their existence and the provision of such general governmental services as police and fire protection may be required.

Bob Jones University v. United States (1983) upheld the authority of the Internal Revenue Service to deny tax exempt status to private schools that practice racially discriminatory admissions standards on the basis of their religious doctrine. While the denial "of tax benefits will inevitably have a substantial impact on the operation of private religious schools," it "will not prevent those schools from observing their religious tenets." Moreover, "the Government has a fundamental, overriding interest in eradicating racial discrimination in education" and this interest "substantially outweighs whatever burden denial of tax benefits places on petitioners' exercise of their religious beliefs."

The Court found that the compelling governmental interest in avoiding aid to racially discriminatory schools could not be equally served by "less restrictive means," through an accommodation of an exemption for schools that practice such discrimination on the basis of religious doctrines. Thus there was no free exercise clause violation. The establishment clause was not violated even though the effect of the requirement that schools not discriminate on the basis of race was to allow some religious schools to receive tax exempt status while other religiously affiliated schools(those that could not comply with the requirement) would fail to receive the tax exemption. This rule did not prefer one religion over another but merely carried out of a policy founded on a "neutral, secular basis" that uniformly applied to all schools.

In addition to the nonreligious purpose and primary effect of the Internal Revenue Service position, the denial of exemptions to all schools that practice racial discrimination avoided a potential for excessive entanglement between government and religion by avoiding the necessity of inquiring into the sincerity of those asserting a religious basis for their discriminatory practices.

(3) State Constitutional Restrictions. A number of states have constitutional provisions that specifically protect the free exercise of religion, or restrict aid to religious institutions. Some state constitutions might prohibit aid such as bus fees, textbooks to religious institutions. Because the Supreme Court has only indicated that such forms of aid are permissible if the state desires to furnish them, there does not appear to be violation of the First Amendment if a state refuses to aid religious schools.

If a state went so far as to deny basic governmental services such as police and fire protection to religious institutions, there would be a significant issue as to whether the denial of services so inhibited the practice of religion as to amount to a violation of the free exercise clause. However, no state has gone this far.

(4) Government Payments of Money "Owned" by Private Individuals. The government may pay the tuition of students at religious schools if the tuition payment is made with money owned or earned by the students. *Reuben Quick Bear v. Leupp* (1908) upheld a federal government payment to religious organizations on Indian reservations because the Indian tribes owed the money and the federal government only held it in trust. A similar analysis should support the government paying tuition payments for veterans of the armed services who decide to attend religious colleges, or the government lending money at reduced interest rates to all students regardless of whether they attend religiously affiliated schools.

§ 17.5   The Establishment Clause—Religion and the Public Schools

(a) Introduction

Questions concerning the introduction of religion into the governmentally operated school system may arise in several ways. Many of the cases examining particular ways in which public schools had become involved with religious activities or beliefs were decided before the emergence of the three-part purpose-effect-entanglement test and the most recent manifestations of that test. We will divide this section into various subsections based on the problem areas—the particular types of involvement between religion and public schools—that have been the subject of Supreme Court opinions. The reader can then evaluate the Court's use of establishment clause tests in terms of specific problem areas.

The cases examined in this section involve issues concerning religious activities in government schools or other connections between government schools and religious beliefs. The situations in these cases differ from the situation confronted by the Court in *Board of Education of Kiryas Joel Village School District v. Grumet* (1994). That case invalidated a state law that was enacted for the purpose of creating a separate public school district for a Village composed entirely of members of one religion. The only public school in the new Village School District was operated in a completely nonreligious manner for handicapped children within the district. The government school had no involvement with religion that would have violated the establishment clause. However, majority of the Justices in *Grumet* found that the state law creating the

Village School District was intended to be and was a preference for members of one religious sect that violated the establishment clause's neutrality principle.

(b) Released or Shared Time

Some public school programs involve exempting of public school students from class so that they could receive religious instruction. The Court has held that the students could not be given religious instruction on the public school premises because such a program has the direct effect of aiding the establishment of religious beliefs. However, the state may release students from school so that they may attend religious instruction away from the public school. This early release of students is viewed as only an accommodation of individual religious preferences rather than an aid to the religions.

Illinois ex rel. McCollum v. Board of Education (1948) invalidated a program where religious teachers came into the public school to teach students who wished to receive religious instruction. The program allowed members of any religious organization to instruct those students who had requested the instruction. Students who did not request instruction remained in the school, because the programs took place during a time when the compulsory attendance laws required all students below the age of 17 to be in school. The religious teachers taught on school property during the school day.

The Court found a direct aid to religion because it used government facilities to propagate religious beliefs. The Court employed no formal test but noted that this school program removed any "wall" between church and state because it the government gave direct help to advancing religion. It was irrelevant that the program could help all religions because the First Amendment forbids both the advancement of religious beliefs over nonreligious ones as well as the advancement of a particular sect.

In contrast, four years later, *Zorach v. Clauson* (1952) upheld a program where the public school released students who chose to be in the program from public schools so that they could receive religious instruction at other locations. Although the truancy laws required all children to be either in school or at religious classes during this period, the program did not constitute government aid to religion. No government funds or other support went to the advancement of religious ends, and these programs were not held on school property. Hence, the law only accommodated the desires of individual students and their families to be free of the public school system so that they could receive their religious education elsewhere. There was no religious doctrine taught on public property, in the public schools.

The key concept here is the neutral principle of "accommodation." If the program *coerced* students into attending religious classes, or if the school invited the religious teachers to teach religion on school property during the regular school day, the state support would violate the free exercise and/or the establishment clauses.

(c) Prayers or Bible Reading

The establishment clause forbids the government from using officially authorized prayers or Bible readings for motivational, that is, prayerful, purposes. Even though the practice may not be coercive in the sense that no law forces the students to participate or that the law specifically allows students to excuse themselves, the state's active support of a particular belief raises the danger of eventual establishment of state approved religious views. Although a given prayer or practice may not favor any one sect, any program that places tacit government approval on "religious" views or practices violates the principle of neutrality in religious matters. Thus the Court has invalidated these prayer services even prior to the use of the additional entanglement test.

On the other hand, the state need not ban all religious references in the public schools. Religion and religious literature, including the Bible, may be studied as an academic subject. So long as the study in the public schools does not amount to prayer services or the religious references are not used to proselytize religious beliefs, a teacher may discuss such materials in the secular course of study.

Another way of looking at the issue is that, as a general rule the government may not sponsor religious services on government property. We say that this is the "general rule," because there are exceptions. Religious references in official ceremonies, including some school exercises, are allowed as a part of our secularized traditions and are not an advancement of religion similar to state approved prayer. For example, in *Marsh v. Chambers* (1983), the Court upheld the power of the state legislature to employ a chaplain and use an opening prayer. This case does not modify the long series of cases prohibiting school prayer because the Court, in the legislative prayer case, emphasized the long history supporting legislative prayer, dating back to the Congress that drafted the First Amendment.

However, the Court has been more concerned with prayer in public schools. For example, a student may silently pray before an examination—an old saw is that the government will never eliminate prayers from school as long as there are examinations. But the government may not provide for school teachers conducting prayer services on school property during the school day with participation by young and impressionable students.

Engel v. Vitale (1962) held that the use of a "nondenomination-al prayer" that government authorities had composed violated the establishment clause. The Court reached this decision easily because the government writing of a prayer was sponsorship of religious views similar to the official establishment of religion, which many of the framers of the First Amendment had fled from and feared. Moreover, like the program in *Illinois ex rel. McCollum v. Board of Education*, discussed above, the religious exercise was performed on school property.

In a second case, *School District of Abington Township v. Schempp* (1963) the Court invalidated a public school program that provided for voluntary Bible reading or the use of the "Lord's Prayer." Unlike *Engel*, it was not part of the job of any public official to compose a prayer: the prayer came from the Bible. Yet this difference did not save the program from constitutional attack. In *Schempp* the Court used the purpose and effect test to review the programs under the establishment clause. Although the program was voluntary and did not favor any sect, the effect was to aid the advancement of religion; it constituted a generalized religious ceremony. Thus, it violated the concepts of separation and neutrality between government and religion and there was but one dissent to the invalidation of these practices.

An important part of the *Schempp* decision was the majority's answer to the argument that elimination of voluntary prayers would amount to government sponsorship of an anti-religious position. The Court held that neutrality in religious matters does not constitute the implied teaching of a "religion of secularism." This viewpoint is important to the decisions involving aid to religious schools for it rejects the argument that providing publicly funded education only in secular schools inhibits the free exercise of religion by those who want their children trained in a religious manner. So long as the state does not legally prohibit private, religious schools, its decision to fund only public education does not violate the religion clauses.

The religious prayer cases are not limited to prayer that is vocalized in the public schools. *Stone v. Graham* (1980) invalidated, under the establishment clause, a Kentucky statute requiring the posting of the Ten Commandments on the wall of each public classroom in the state. Any use of prayers or Bible passages in school must be reviewed under the three part test for compatibility with the establishment clause. First, the statute must have a secular legislative purpose. Second, its primary effect must neither advance nor inhibit religion. Third, the statute must not create an excessive entanglement between government and religion. Any use of prayers or religious literature for inspirational purposes would violate the purpose and effect tests for validity.

The *Stone* Court concluded that the preeminent purpose of the Kentucky statute was "plainly religious in nature" and had no secular legislative purpose, even though the legislation included a statement of avowed secular purpose. The law required that at the bottom of each copy of the Ten Commandments a sign my state: "The secular application of the Ten Commandments is clearly seen in its adoption as the fundamental legal code of Western Civilization and the Common Law of the United States."

The fact that the Bible verses were to be posted rather than read aloud, and the fact that they were to be financed by voluntary private contributions, had no bearing on the validity of the statute because it had a plainly religious purpose, and "it is no defense to urge that the religious practices here may be relatively minor encroachments on the First Amendment."

Some state governments and school boards, following the school prayer decisions, passed statutes either requiring or allowing a period of silence in each public school day. During this "moment of silence," the teacher would conduct no prayer, but students would be free to think, meditate, or pray silently. In *Wallace v. Jaffree* (1985) the Court did not rule on a true moment of silence statute but everyone assumed it would be constitutional. Indeed, the Court noted in a footnote that the appellees had "abandoned any claim that [this one minute moment of silence] is unconstitutional." Another statute authorized a prayer, and settled case law invalidated that provision.

The third statute created the only significant issue facing *Wallace*—the constitutionality of the period of silence for "meditation or voluntary prayer" statute.

Wallace is one of the rare cases where the Court invalidated legislation because the legislature was motivated only by a religious purpose in enacting the statute. Six Justices found that the legislative history of the Alabama statute made it clear that the law at issue was passed only for a religious purpose and that this improper motivation required the Court to invalidate the law. Justice Stevens, for the majority, stated that the Court must invalidate legislation under the First Amendment if it was motivated entirely for the purpose of advancing religion. Statements of legislators inserted into the legislative record, and testimony of the bill's sponsor before the district court, made it clear that the persons who drafted and passed the Amendment had not attempted to justify the statute in terms of any nonreligious purpose. The majority opinion concluded:

"the legislative intent to return prayer to the public schools is, of course, quite different from merely protecting every student's right to engage in voluntary prayer during an appropriate moment of silence during the school day." Although the Court did not rule on a true moment of silence statute, it appears that such a statute may be upheld if it was not passed for entirely religious purposes and if it was not used as a means for governmental encouragement of religious beliefs or religious activities on public school property.

Even if the Court in the future abandons the "*Lemon* tests" (the formal three part tests: purpose-effect-entanglement), the Court is unlikely to overrule its decisions finding that officially authorized prayers, or readings from religious texts, in government grade schools and high schools violate the establishment clause. *Lee v. Weisman* (1992) made this clear, when the Court held that religious invocations at public school graduations violate the establishment clause.

Lee involved a school district policy that allowed high school and middle principals to choose members of the clergy to give invocations or benedictions at formal graduation ceremonies. Though guidelines for writing the invocations or benedictions were designed to avoid offending anyone, the practice still violated establishment clause analysis.

The four dissenting Justices would approve government involvement with religion that arguably is supported by historical practices in our country, at least so long as the government action at issue did not involve a preference for one religious sect over another. However, Justice Kennedy, who wrote the majority opinion in *Lee*, held that the government practice of religious prayers at school graduations violated basic establishment clause principles, even though he did not use the purpose, effect, or entanglement tests.

This majority opinion is a strong endorsement of the concept that government neutrality in religious matters is a touchstone of establishment clause analysis. Kennedy did not find that a finding of coercion of individuals to give up or modify their religious beliefs, or to act inconsistently with their religious beliefs is necessary for an establishment clause violation.

The Court reaffirmed the *Lee* analysis in *Santa Fe Independent School District v. Doe* (2000) holding that a public school district policy that permitted public high school students to select one of their fellow students to deliver a non-sectarian prayer at high school football games violated the establishment clause. The school district that adopted the football game prayer program attempted to distinguish *Lee*, and other public school prayer cases, on the basis that: (1) students voted both for the adoption of the rule and selection of the student; and (2) football games, unlike classes or graduation ceremonies, did not require student attendance.

Justice Stevens rejected these distinctions. The government created the forum for the prayer. He also argued that there would be an element of coercion in the program, even if the Court assumed that every student's decision to attend the football game was truly voluntary, because the prayer had "the improper effect of coercing those present to participate in an act of religious worship." However, he also pointed out that no Supreme Court ruling prohibited "any public school student from voluntarily praying at any time before, during, or after the school day."

Three dissenting Justices wanted to uphold the program on its face, although they admitted that the program could be implemented in an unconstitutional manner under certain circumstances.

The *Santa Fe* decision, like the *Lee* decision before it, did not establish any specific standard for determining the extent to which government involvement with religion would violate the establishment clause.

(d) Modification of the Curriculum for Religious Purposes

A state may not eliminate the teaching of certain ideas related to normal classroom subjects solely because they conflict with religious beliefs. *Epperson v. Arkansas* (1968) examined the legislative history and invalidated a state law that made it unlawful for teachers in state schools to teach a theory of human biological evolution. The Court held that the statute violated the establishment clause because it had a religious purpose—thus failing the secular purpose test. It was an impermissible breach of the principle of government neutrality for the state to eliminate a particular piece of information from a course merely because it conflicted with some religious beliefs.

This case does not, by itself, eliminate the ability of the state to adjust or eliminate the subjects that are taught in its school system. Justice Black, in a concurring opinion, noted that a state should be able to eliminate any given subject matter from its school system without raising a First Amendment issue. As a matter of logic, if the state is under no obligation to teach a specific subject there should be nothing wrong with eliminating a given course.

However, there are two bases for making an exception to this deference to state educational authority. First, where the state has eliminated only one element from a course of study solely for religious reasons it has attempted to help the religious point of view by eliminating ideas that would challenge that view. *Epperson* focused extensively on evidence that the state's improper motivation for excluding the teaching of evolution. Second, if the state offers no secular educational reason for altering the curriculum there is no reason to defer to the state's educational policy. *Epperson* presented to the Court an unusual case of an open attempt to aid certain religious views. This official attempt to aid a specific religious view breached the principle of neutrality, which is the core of the religion clauses.

Edwards v. Aguillard (1987) invalidated another legislative attempt to modify the curriculum of the public schools for religious purposes. Louisiana legislation required "balanced treatment for creation-science and evolution-science in public school instruction." The law required any public school that taught the theory of human biological evolution to give equal treatment to "creation science." *Aguillard* held that the legislative history of the statute and the language of the statute itself, demonstrated that the legislation was designed to promote religion and, therefore, that it violated the establishment clause.

The Court did not restrict the authority of legislatures or school boards to design a curriculum for non-religious reasons. There is no need to excise all references to religion from a public school curriculum. References to religion may be a part of public school instruction in history or literature, or any other subject, so long as the references to religion or a religious text do not have the purpose or effect of advancing religious goals. The public schools, in other words, may not proselytize, but they may teach about religion when it is appropriate to do so for secular reasons. For example, one cannot understand the history of the middle ages without knowing something about the teachings of the Catholic Church, just as one cannot understand ancient Greek history without knowing something about the ancient Greek gods.

(e) Equal Access to School Facilities

Widmar v. Vincent (1981) invalidated a state university regulation that denied access to school facilities to religious student organizations as a violation of the freedom of speech. In so doing the Court provided some insight into the related problem of defining the scope of university involvement with religious organizations.

In 1977 the University of Missouri at Kansas City began to enforce a policy prohibiting the use of university buildings or grounds "for purposes of religious worship or religious teaching." University officials informed a registered student religious group that the University was discontinuing what had been a four-year practice of permitting the group to conduct its meetings in university facilities. *Widmar* found that once it had opened its facilities for use by student groups the university had created a public forum. It was then required to justify any content-based exclusions under the applicable standard of review and the regulation would be upheld only if it was necessary to serve a compelling state interest and if it was narrowly drawn to achieve that end.

While the university's interest in maintaining a strict separation of church and state was compelling, applying the three pronged purpose-effect-entanglement test and allowing equal access to university facilities to religious groups would not violate the establishment clause.

Widmar only ruled that a state university could not engage in content-based discrimination against religious speech. If the university had not created the "public forum" it would not have been required to furnish facilities for use by religious groups.

Board of Education of Westside Community Schools v. Mergens (1990) upheld a federal statute that requires any secondary school receiving federal financial assistance to provide "equal access" to student groups. The statute prohibited a secondary school from denying equal access to student groups on the basis of the group's religious, political or philosophical beliefs (or the content of their speech) if (1) the school received federal financial assistance and (2) if the school had created a "limited open forum" by providing access to any "noncurriculum related student group." The *Mergens* case presented only the issue of whether the statutory access granted to religiously oriented student groups violated the establishment clause.

Justice O'Connor's opinion in *Mergens* was, in part, a majority opinion and, in part, a plurality opinion. In the majority portion, O'Connor concluded that the statutory term "limited open forum" was different from the Supreme Court's definition, in First Amendment cases, of a "limited public forum." The statute applied whenever a "noncurriculum related" student group was given access to school facilities. A "noncurriculum related" student group was any student group whose activities and purpose did not directly relate to courses offered by the school. Thus, both a chess club and a student organization that provided social services for needy persons in the community were not curriculum related groups, even though math professors and social science teachers might strongly encourage participation in those clubs. The equal access requirement of the statute only prohibited the denial of access to school premises at noninstructional times to a group, if the denial was based on the religious or political content of the group's speech or beliefs. The Act allowed a faculty member to monitor the student group's activities, but the Act limited participation by school officials at any meeting of religious groups. Persons who were not a part of the faculty, staff, or student body would not be able to direct or regularly attend the activities of student groups at the public school premises.

The Court upheld the constitutionality of the Equal Access Act eight to one vote, but there was no majority opinion.

Widmar and *Mergens* established that the government may not disfavor a speaker by punishing his speech, or denying him the ability to speak, based upon his or her religious viewpoint. The Court unanimously reaffirmed this principle in *Lamb's Chapel v. Center Moriches Union Free School District* (1993). At issue was the implementation of a New York law that allowed local school boards to adopt regulation for the use of school property, at times when schools were not in session, for specified purposes, including "social, civic, and recreational meetings and entertainments and other uses pertaining to the welfare of the community." The state law stated that the uses should be: "non-exclusive and open to the public" but it left the implementation of the law and the definition of permitted uses largely to the local school boards in the state. In *Lamb's Chapel*, the school board authorized the use of school property, when it was not otherwise being used for school purposes, for social, civic, or recreational uses and for uses by political organizations, but it denied a religious congregation the ability to use the school property at a time when classes were not in session and the school was not being used for previously scheduled activities.

Lamb's Chapel held, without dissent, that this school board regulation, as applied, violated the free speech clause of the First Amendment. Justice White, for the Court, held that the board engaged in viewpoint discrimination because it would have allowed groups to use the school property for discussions about childrearing and family values that were not connected to the views of a religious organization. Such viewpoint discrimination violates the First Amendment freedom of speech even when the government is regulating access to a nonpublic forum.

The school board in the *Lamb's Chapel* case attempted to justify its action by alleging that it had a compelling interest in denying access to the religious organization in order to avoid violating the establishment clause of the First Amendment. But Justice White held that granting equal access to government property would not constitute a violation of the establishment clause. The school board also claimed that the particular church that wanted access to the property would be engaging in such highly sectarian proselytizing that the church's use of public property would lead to "threats of public unrest and even violence." However, there was "nothing in the record to support such a justification, which in any event would be difficult to defend as a reason to deny the presentation of a religious point of view about a subject that the [school district board] otherwise makes open to discussion on [school district] property."

Similarly, *Good News Club v. Milford Central School* (2001) examined a public school's refusal to allow a religious organization for children between the ages of 6 and 12 to use the school facilities at times when the school was not in session. The public school district policy allowed local residents to use school facilities at times when school was not in session for virtually any type of educational, artistic, entertainment or community event.

Rosenberger v. Rector and Visitors of the University of Virginia (1995) held (5 to 4) that a university violated the free speech clause when it refused to pay for a religious student organization's publication costs under a program under which the university funded other student organization publications. Once again, the state university engaged in viewpoint discrimination.

University of Virginia regulations authorized student groups to request that the university pay their bills from outside contractors that printed their newsletters. A group of students formed an organization named "Wide Awake Productions," which became a registered a student organization that qualified as a "contracted independent organization" so it would be eligible for payment of its publication bills. However, the University refused its request to pay for the publication of its newsletter, titled "Wide Awake: a Christian Perspective at the University of Virginia." The University asserted that the publication constituted religious literature that it could not fund because of the religious nature of the organization's expression in their newsletter. The University argued that government funding for a religious publication would violate the establishment clause.

Rosenberger, relying on the principles established in the *Widmar, Mergens,* and *Lamb's Chapel,* held that the University's refusal to fund the student publication solely on the basis of the religious content of its speech constituted viewpoint discrimination that violated the free speech clause.

The University engaged in viewpoint discrimination when it refused to pay for the student organization's publication costs because of the religious nature of the organization's expression. The Court could uphold this viewpoint discrimination only if the University had a compelling interest in disfavoring the viewpoint. If University payment for the religious organization's publication costs would violate the establishment clause, then the University would have a compelling interest (the need to follow the Constitution) in refusing to subsidize the publication. Justice Kennedy, for the majority, held that University funding for the publication would not violate the establishment clause and its refusal to fund the publication violated the free speech guarantee.

The majority opinion did not specify a clear test to be used for determining whether a government action violated the establishment clause. It said that in establishment clause cases, the Court "must in each case inquire first into the purpose and object of the government action in question and then into the practical details of the program's operation ... [a] central lesson of our decisions is that significant factor in upholding government programs in the face of establishment clause attack is their neutrality towards religion." The University program for funding all registered student organizations was religiously neutral, and that "the neutrality of the program distinguishes the student fees from a tax levied for the direct support of a church or group of churches." Once the university decided to fund registered student groups, it could not discriminate against religiously-affiliated groups. If a state school will support a group of students who establish a hedonist society that publishes a newspaper advocating the pursuit of pleasure, the school may not discriminate against a group of students who form another group that publishes a newspaper advocating Trappist austerity and silence for religious reasons, because the state should not discriminate against religion.

Rosenberger ruled that the First Amendment free speech clause prohibited the University from examining the content of publications for the purpose of denying funding to, and discriminating against, religious viewpoints and that there would be "no establishment clause violation in the University's honoring its duties under the free speech clause."

A state's refusal to provide basic services, such as police or fire protection, to organizations or individuals due to their religious affiliation would violate the free exercise clause. Nevertheless, there are some cases where there is, in the words of, e.g., *Locke v. Davey* (2004) room for "play in the joints." *Locke*, without stating any free exercise clause standard, held that a state could refuse to grant aid to college students who had otherwise qualified for that aid, solely on the basis that the students were pursuing a degree in theology. *Locke* found that the state could have granted these scholarships without violating the establishment clause, but that the state was free to refuse to fund certain theological studies. "In other words, there are some state actions permitted by the Establishment Clause but not required by the Free Exercise Clause."

§ 17.6 The Free Exercise Clause—Introduction and Overview

The text of the original Constitution contains but one specific provision regarding religious freedom. Article VI prohibits the use of any religious test as a condition or qualification for holding any office or position in the federal government.

The First Amendment provides, in part, that Congress shall make no law "prohibiting the free exercise" of religion. The free exercise clause, like all of the guarantees of the First Amendment, applies to state and local governments through the Fourteenth Amendment.

The Supreme Court has invalidated very few government actions on the basis of the free exercise clause. The Court has consistently held that the government may not punish religious beliefs. The government may not impose burdens on, or give benefits to, people solely because of their religious beliefs. Because federal, state and local governmental entities have not engaged in many activities that could be described as the punishment of religious beliefs, there are very few Supreme Court decisions explaining the meaning of that constitutional restriction.

A law would be invalid if the legislature passed the law prohibiting some type of activity for the purpose of discriminating against religion or a particular religion. For example, the state may ban killing animals in a way that is unnecessarily cruel, even though a particular religious sect believed in killing animals cruelly. However, if the state allows the killing of animals, but then forbids killing animals for sacrifice, it would be discriminating against a religion because it is only banning the killing if done for religious purposes (sacrifice).

Consider *Church of the Lukumi Babalu Aye, Inc. v. Hialeah* (1993), which invalidated a city's ordinances prohibiting animal slaughter, insofar as they were applied to a particular religious sect, because the Justices unanimously found that these ordinances were passed for the sole purpose of excluding the religious sect from the city. The Court avoided ruling on the issue of whether members of a religious sect that used animal slaughter in their rituals would be entitled by the free exercise clause to an exemption from a law prohibiting the slaughter of animals that was a religiously neutral law of general applicability. Instead, the Justices found that the city's ordinances (when all of the classifications and exemptions in the ordinances were combined) prohibited only the type of animal slaughter that was used in the ritual of the Santeria religion; the timing of the ordinances, and other facts in the record, demonstrated that the city had adopted these ordinances only after learning that members of the Santeria religion were going to establish a place of worship in the city.

Justice Kennedy wrote the majority opinion in *Church of the Lukumi Babalu Aye*. He began the opinion by noting that the Court was using a well established constitutional principle.

"The principle that government may not enact laws that suppress religious belief or practice is so well understood that few violations are recorded in our opinions.... Our review confirms that the laws in question were enacted by officials who did not understand, failed to perceive, or chose to ignore the fact that their official actions violated the Nation's essential commitment to religious freedom. The challenged laws had an impermissible object; and in all events the principle of general applicability was violated because the secular ends asserted in defense of the law, were pursued only with respect to conduct motivated by religious beliefs."

Church of the Lukumi Babalu Aye held that a law that failed the neutrality or general applicability standards is subject to strict judicial scrutiny; it is doubtful that any such law would be truly necessary to a compelling government interest. Justice Kennedy's opinion summarized the Court's ruling as follows:

"[A] law that is neutral and of general applicability need not be justified by a compelling government interest even if the law has the incidental effect of burdening a particular religious practice.... A law failing to satisfy these requirements [the neutrality and general applicability requirements] must be justified by a compelling governmental interest and must be narrowly tailored to advance that interest."

Religious Beliefs. Just as the establishment clause prohibits the government from providing benefits to one religious sect or denomination, the free exercise clause prohibits the government from denying benefits to, or imposing burdens on, persons because of their religious beliefs. The use of religious beliefs as any type of standard for the granting of government benefits and burdens might violate both the establishment and free exercise clauses by violating a religious neutrality principle that is central to both. As a technical matter, it is not clear whether the free exercise clause involves a total prohibition of the government use of religious beliefs as a means of allocating burdens and benefits or whether a government regulation that used religious beliefs in that manner could be justified by a "compelling" government interest. That technical distinction is probably unimportant because the Court has given us no reason to believe that a government law or regulation that denied a benefit to persons *because of* their religious beliefs would be upheld by a compelling interest.

There are Supreme Court cases that have invalidated a law on its face because it punished religious beliefs. Just as the federal government is prohibited from using religion as a test for government office, the state and local governments are prohibited from using such tests by the free exercise clause. The Supreme Court, by a unanimous vote but without a majority opinion, invalidated a law that prohibited ministers or members of religious orders from being members of the state legislature. Several of the Justices believed that the exclusion of ministers and clerics from the legislature constituted the imposition of a special disability on someone because of the strength or nature of his religious views.

While the free exercise clause gives no one the right to disregard criminal laws of general applicability, the government may not create a criminal law that is based upon the falsity of a particular religious belief. Such a law would violate the free exercise clause.

Regulations of Actions—Exemptions for Religiously Motivated Actions? A person's religious beliefs may prohibit him from taking an action that is required by law (such as paying a certain type of tax) or his religious beliefs may require him to do something that is prohibited by the law (such as ingesting an illegal drug). These situations raise the question whether the free exercise clause requires the government to grant exemptions from a law of general applicability to persons who cannot comply with the law due to religious beliefs.

It is important to keep in mind the typical fact and legal situations in the cases regarding religiously motivated actions. The law at issue in such a case will not be a law that includes religious criteria for determining who is benefited or burdened by the law, because a law that made use of religious criteria as a standard for determining the legality of actions, or for the allocation of benefits or burdens from the government, would be invalid as the direct punishment of religious beliefs. Nor will the law at issue be a law that enacted only for the purpose of harming people of one religion (who could not comply with the law), because proof of such a purpose on the part of the legislative entity would make the law invalid.

The law at issue in a religiously motivated action case will be a law of general applicability that requires all persons (or a class of persons defined by criteria that do not include religious criteria) to take an action or refrain from taking an action. The claim of the individual in the case is that she cannot comply with the law and remain faithful to her religious beliefs. The person alleges that she must receive an exemption from the law because of the burden placed upon her religious beliefs by the need to conform her actions to a law that conflicts with her beliefs.

Some Supreme Court cases include dicta describing the burden placed upon the person who cannot comply with a law of general applicability as a "direct" or "indirect" burden. The problem is that the Court does not really give us a test to determine what is "direct." The labels seem conclusory. Despite dicta in some cases indicating that a law imposing an indirect burden might be easier to uphold than a law which directly burdens religious activities, it seems clear today that the distinction between direct and indirect burdens does not have any legal significance.

The general free exercise principle regarding requested exemptions from laws of general applicability is easy to state: the free exercise clause does not require that an exemption be created from laws of general applicability to protect persons with religiously motivated actions. However, the state often may grant the exemption without violating the establishment clause. There is, some cases tell us, room "for play in the joints." In 1990, a Supreme Court majority opinion stated: "We have never held that an individual's religious beliefs excuse him from compliance with an otherwise valid law prohibiting conduct that the state is free to regulate." *Church of the Lukumi Babalu Aye, Inc. v. Hialeah* (1993), which invalidated a city's statutes prohibiting animal slaughter insofar as those laws banned the ritual slaughter of animals by a specific religious sect. The Court did not reach the issue of whether a religiously neutral law that banned all animal slaughter would have to allow exemptions from the slaughter of animals in religious rituals. The Court found no reason to question the principle that a religiously neutral law of general applicability could be applied to persons whose religious beliefs prevented them from complying with the law.

Defining Religion—Testing Sincerity. Assume that the Supreme Court ruled that the free exercise clause required the government to create an exemption to a criminal law for persons whose sincerely held religious beliefs made it impossible for them to comply with the law. That ruling would require the judiciary to define "religion" or to test the sincerity of individuals who claimed that their religious beliefs allowed them to disregard the law. If the Court did not narrow the potential group of persons who could claim the exemption, a ruling that the government must create a religious exemption from the criminal law would make compliance with the law optional for every person.

For example, let us assume (contrary to the Court's rulings) that the Supreme Court ruled that the government could not penalize a person for using an illegal banned substance (e.g., peyote) if the user said that he was using that substance for religious reasons. Every person who was arrested for using the banned substance might claim that he was using the substance because he was commanded to do so by the tenants of his religion. If the Supreme Court did not define religion or allow lower courts to test the sincerity of a person seeking immunity from the drug law, it would allow the individual to grant himself a religious exemption.

Any attempt to define religion, or to test sincerity, raises concerns under both the establishment and free exercise clauses of the First Amendment. It is difficult to see how the Supreme Court could define "religion" in a manner that would not involve the government punishing beliefs or granting denominational preferences. The Supreme Court has not attempted to define religion although it has noted that any exemptions that the judiciary created under the free exercise clause would be limited to persons asserting a religious belief. The Court has never ruled on whether the beliefs must be theocratic (God-centered) or whether a system of belief could be religious even though it was did not involve belief in gods or a God. The determination that certain beliefs constituted religious beliefs would have to avoid any government declaration (by any of the branches of government) that some beliefs do not qualify as religious beliefs because they are so far-fetched that no reasonable person would accept them.

We do know from the case law that religious beliefs are not limited to people who join organized churches. *Frazee v. Illinois Department of Employment Security* (1989). After all, Judaism began with one person, Abraham, and Christianity began with only twelve apostles (later reduced to eleven, before things started to grow).

It is possible that the Supreme Court might adopt different definitions of religion under the establishment and free exercise clauses, even though the word "religion" is mentioned only once in the First Amendment. Perhaps the Court should use a very narrow definition of religion in establishment clause cases (where the government is doing something that a litigant claims is an "establishment") because no significant danger to religious freedom would arise from government aid to persons or institutions that promoted a philosophy that is not God-centered and not a part of an organized religion. The Supreme Court has held that a public school curriculum that could not include prayer or Bible reading does not mean that the government was establishing a "religion of secularism." In the free exercise clause cases, one could argue that the Supreme Court should be more lenient in defining religion if the exemption of persons from a law may not raise significant establishment clause concerns.

The Supreme Court has indicated that the mere testing of a person's sincerity is not a *per se* violation of the religion clauses. However, in testing the sincerity of an individual, a government agency or a court could not use a definition of religion or a test for sincerity that would be based upon religious principles. Courts are precluded from ruling on the truth of religious beliefs.

The difficulty of defining religion or testing sincerity may be a reason why the Supreme Court has not created free exercise clause exemptions from laws of general applicability. In other words, the Court might consider the danger to establishment clause and free exercise clause values that would be part of the process by which courts or government agencies would determine who was eligible for a free exercise clause exemption. When the Court held that there was no free exercise clause right to use peyote in violate of state law, it avoided the problems inherent in judicial definitions of religion or the testimony of sincerity.

Although the Supreme Court's free exercise standards do not require the government to grant exemptions from neutral laws of general applicability, those standards prohibit government actions designed to suppress or burden a group of persons because of their religious beliefs. A law that bans certain actions only because they are of religious significance, and only to suppress a particular religious group, will violate the free exercise clause. Cases wherein the Court invalidates a law because the legislature designed the law to suppress religious beliefs or a religious sect are not likely to raise problems regarding the definition of religion or testing of sincerity.

Legislative Accommodation of Religion. In several cases where the Court found that the Constitution did not require a religiously based exemption from laws of general applicability, it has indicated that the legislature could take steps to *accommodate* the views of persons whose religious beliefs would not allow them to comply with the law. For example, *Employment Division v. Smith (Smith II)* (1990) upheld a state criminal law that totally prohibited the use of peyote, even when applied to someone who used peyote because of a sincerely held religious belief that he had to use the drug in a religious ceremony. Justice Scalia's majority opinion in *Smith II* also indicated that a state or federal legislature might create an exemption to drug laws that would accommodate the religious need of some persons to use a banned substance. Justice Scalia said: "Values that are protected against government interference through enshrinement in the Bill of Rights are not thereby banished from the political process.... But to say that a nondiscriminatory religious-practice exemption is permitted, or even that it is desirable, is not to say that it is constitutionally required ... it may fairly be said that leaving accommodation to the political process will place at a relative disadvantage those religious practices that are not widely engaged in; but that unavoidable consequence of democratic government must be preferred to a system in which each conscience is a law unto itself or in which judges weigh the social importance of all laws against the centrality of religious beliefs."

The Supreme Court has never explained the precise limits that the establishment clause may place on the ability of government to accommodate religion. An exemption from a law of general applicability (such as a criminal law or a tax law) that only provided an exemption to members of a specific religion, or an exemption only for persons who held religious beliefs, would establish a denominational preference that would violate the establishment clause. For example, a legislature cannot create a tax exemption from the sales tax solely for sales of religious literature, because that preference for religious activity violates the establishment clause. *Texas Monthly, Inc. v. Bullock* (1989).

In response to the Supreme Court's decision in *Smith II*, Congress passed, and the President signed into law, the "Religious Freedom Restoration Act of 1993" (RFRA). That law, among other things, sought to overrule *Smith II*. The Court held (6 to 3) that RFRA contradicted principles necessary to maintain the separation of powers and federal-state balance. It addressed laws of general application that placed only incidental burdens on religion that were not based on animus or hostility, did not indicate any widespread pattern of religious discrimination, and were not designed to identify and counteract state laws likely to be unconstitutional. Hence, section five of the Fourteenth Amendment did not authorize RFRA. *City of Boerne v. Flores* (1997).

Cutter v. Wilkinson (2005) unanimously upheld a federal statute that required all state and local facilities that received federal funds and in which persons were involuntarily institutionalized in facilities (e.g., prisons) to accommodate an institutionalized person's desire to act on his or her religious beliefs, unless denial of the accommodation was necessary to promote a compelling government interest. Justice Ginsburg indicated that the government could test the sincerity of a person (such as a prisoner) who asserted that his religious beliefs required that he be given some type of treatment not commonly granted to other institutionalized persons. The Court added that federally funded institutions, such as prisons, could deny requests for accommodation whenever accommodating the institutionalized person's application for specialized treatment might interfere with the institution's interests in maintaining order and protecting safety. *Cutter* did not set forth any standard for determining when an accommodation of religion might turn into the type of aid to religion that would violate the establishment clause. This law fit within the "play in the joints," between the free exercise clause and establishment clauses.

§ 17.7　The Free Exercise Clause—The Early Decisions

The claims of religious minorities received little serious attention from the Supreme Court until the middle of the twentieth century.

Reynolds v. United States (1878) upheld the application of a federal law prohibiting polygamy to a Mormon whose religion required him to engage in that practice. The majority opinion indicated that Congress was free to prohibit any action regardless of its religious implications so long as it did not formally prohibit a belief. The Court upheld other laws that burdened the practice of the Mormon religion by imposing various penalties on polygamy.

Jacobson v. Massachusetts (1905) upheld a government system of compulsory vaccinations as applied to those who objected to vaccinations on a religious basis.

Prior to the application of the religion clauses to the states the Supreme Court decided two cases under the due process clause of the Fourteenth Amendment that have significant free exercise implications. *Hamilton v. Regents of the University of California* (1934) held that requiring male students at a state university to take courses in military training did not deny liberty or violate due process. This decision is suspect in light of the Court's later decisions regarding the conscientious objector laws but it serves to emphasize the absence of judicial protection for religious minorities during this period.

The second major due process case in this area was *Pierce v. Society of Sisters* (1925), which struck down a statute which required that children attend only public schools. Today *Pierce* stands for the right of children to attend private (including religious) schools so long as they meet basic educational standards. The state cannot control every subject taught in those schools (it could not forbid, for example, teaching a foreign language), but it can assure that the school, in order to be accredited, must offer the children competent instruction in specified secular subjects, in a safe and healthy environment. The state, in short, may impose restrictions on the educational process that are necessary to promote important secular interests.

The Flag Salute Cases. Some states require public school children to take part in a flag salute ceremony. If the children did not salute the flag and say the Pledge of Allegiance, the schools would expel the school children. Several Jehovah Witnesses, parents of school children who refused to recite the Pledge, sued to overturn these laws based their religious objections to the honoring of "idols" (the flag).

The Court held that the schools could offer the Pledge but could not require the students to recite the Pledge. The Court, in short, did not treat the Pledge as a prayer—if it were a prayer the public school could not constitutionally offer it, even if it were voluntary. But, the Court said it was a Pledge. Hence the Court invalidated the *required* Pledge on First Amendment-free speech grounds, not on First Amendment-establishment or free exercise grounds. The public school prayer violates the establishment clause even if the school allows children to opt-out; the public school Pledge is permissible on free speech grounds as long as the state allows students to opt-out. *West Virginia State Board of Education v. Barnette* (1943), overruling *Minersville School District v. Gobitis* (1940). The requirement of reciting the Pledge invaded the sphere of free intellect and belief that is one of the core values of the First Amendment guarantee of free speech.

Under *Barnette* anyone opposed to saluting the flag has a right to be excused from the requirement without regard to whether her refusal was based on religious or nonreligious grounds. Justice Jackson, for the Court, said:

> If there is any fixed star in our constitutional constellation, it is that no official, high or petty, can prescribe what shall be orthodox in politics, nationalism, religion, or other matters of opinion or force citizens to confess by word or act their faith therein. If there are any circumstances which permit an exception, they do not now occur to us.

The First Amendment, as a matter of free speech, allows public schools to offer a pledge of allegiance but does not allow them to require its school children to take the pledge, because that would interfere with freedom of conscience. Yet cases like *Barnette* did not signal a right of anyone to be excused from laws of general applicability that did not touch on such basic First Amendment rights. *Prince v. Massachusetts* (1944) upheld the application of a law prohibiting the sale of merchandise in public places by minors to a nine year old child who was distributing religious literature with her guardian. The state's interest in the health and well-being of young people was a significant secular end that justified the incidental burden on religion.

In *Elk Grove Unified School District v. Newdow* (2004), five justices ruled that the father of a child, who had divorced her mother and who was not the legal custodian of his daughter, did not have standing to challenge the use of the phrase "under God" in the Pledge of Allegiance recited in the public school his daughter attended. The state did not require any student to recite the pledge but it did offer the pledge, and neither the child nor her mother objected to the Pledge. Three justices dissented on the standing issue and ruled, on the merits, that a state law requires teachers to lead willing students in reciting the Pledge of Allegiance, which includes the words "under God," does not violate the Establishment Clause. The Pledge, in short, was a "pledge" and not a state-imposed "prayer." Justice Scalia did not participate.

§ 17.8 The Free Exercise Clause—The Modern Cases

Employment Division v. Smith (Smith II) (1990) summarized a century of the Court's rulings concerning the free exercise clause. *Smith II* involved two individuals who were disqualified from receiving unemployment compensation benefits under a state law that disqualified anyone who had been fired from his job for job related misconduct. A private drug clinic fired respondents as drug and alcohol abuse rehabilitation counselors when the clinic discovered that they had ingested peyote, which state law banned. The former drug counselors claimed that the free exercise clause protected their use of peyote in connection with a religious ceremony.

Earlier, *Employment Division v. Smith (Smith I)* (1988) had remanded the case to the state court to determine if state law allowed use of peyote in a religious ceremony. If the state law had provided an exemption for the sacramental use of peyote, the Supreme Court might have avoided the free exercise clause question. However, the state supreme court, on remand, held that state law prohibited any use of peyote, including any religiously motivated or sacramental use. The state court also held that the state's total prohibition of peyote use violated the free exercise clause of the First Amendment to the Constitution of the United States and, for that reason, the state court held that the state could not deny unemployment compensation to the former drug counselors.

Smith II reversed. It held: (1) the free exercise clause did not require an exemption from criminal laws banning the use of peyote; and (2) the state could deny unemployment compensation to persons fired because they violated a valid criminal statute. The free exercise clause did not require the government to justify its refusal to exempt religiously motivated drug use from its general, neutral prohibition of drug use. The First Amendment does not authorize the judiciary to balance the societal interest in the drug proscription against the degree to which compliance with the law burdened the sincerely held religious beliefs of the individuals in the case.

The Court recognized two basic free exercise clause principles. First, the free exercise clause prohibits the government from regulating religious beliefs. This principle prohibits the government from compelling one to affirm religious beliefs, punishing religious expression thought to be false, or using religious doctrine as a basis for judicial decisions.

Second, the free exercise clause would invalidate a law that appeared to be religiously neutral on its face, if the plaintiffs could show that the legislative purpose is to prohibit or regulate an act only because of its religious significance. As Justice Scalia noted: "It would be true, we think (though no case of ours has involved the point), that a state would be 'prohibiting the free exercise [of religion]' if it sought to ban such acts or abstentions only when they are engaged in for religious reasons, or only because of the religious belief that they display. It would doubtless be unconstitutional, for example, to ban the casting of 'statutes that are to be used for worship purposes,' or to prohibit bowing down before a golden calf."

The free exercise clause does not require exemptions from religiously neutral laws for religious persons who cannot comply with the law. As Justice Scalia stated in *Smith II*: "The only decisions in which we have held the First Amendment bars application of a neutral, generally applicable law to religiously motivated action have involved not the free exercise clause alone, but the free exercise clause in conjunction with other constitutional protections."

Smith II argued that the only cases inconsistent with the principle that religiously neutral, generally applicable laws do not have to provide a religious exemption were cases where the Court required the government to waive a condition for unemployment compensation benefits (for persons who could not meet the condition due to their sincerely held religious beliefs). In those unemployment compensation cases, the Court had used a two-step balancing test. First, the individual must show that complying with the eligibility condition (such as a condition that the individual be available for work on Saturday) imposed a substantial burden on the person's ability to carry out his religious beliefs. Second, the government, in the second part of the test, must demonstrate that granting an exemption from the law at issue would interfere with a compelling or overriding government interest. *Smith II* argued that the Court had never used a balancing test except to examine conditions for unemployment compensation that were unrelated to a general criminal law.

The *Smith II* decision was reminiscent of *Braunfeld v. Brown* (1961), which upheld the constitutionality of applying laws that required businesses to be closed on Sundays even as applied to persons whose religious beliefs also required them to observe another day as their day of rest or Sabbath. A majority of the Justices in *Braunfeld* (but without a majority opinion) concluded that the additional economic burdens placed on a Sabbatarian (who would be required to be closed more days a week than his competitors) did not violate the free exercise clause. Chief Justice Warren, writing for four members of the Court in *Braunfeld,* found that the law placed a real burden on Sabbatarian retailers. The plurality opinion by Chief Justice Warren found that the state had an overriding nonreligious interest in setting aside a single day for "rest, recreation, and tranquility." Some portions of Chief Justice Warren's plurality opinion appear to involve a balancing of the societal interest in the Sunday closing laws against the burdens placed on

Sabbatarians, but the plurality did not require any real justification for the refusal to grant an exemption from the Sunday closing laws to Sabbatarians.

Justices Frankfurter and Harlan, in a concurring opinion in *Braunfeld* balanced the societal interest in the preservation of the "traditional institution" of a day of rest against the economic disadvantage to the retailer who had to be closed an extra day due to his religious beliefs. Despite the language in the concurring opinion regarding the need to balance the individual retailer's interests against societal interests, Justices Frankfurter and Harlan appeared to uphold the law simply because it imposed only an incidental burden on religious practices. Justices Frankfurter and Harlan found that even if there were no Sunday closing laws, the Sabbatarian retailer would still lose a day of sales opportunities that was available to his nonreligious competitors, due to his religious need to refrain from working on a certain day of the week.

Unemployment Compensation. *Sherbert v. Verner* (1963) held that the state cannot deny unemployment benefits to a Seventh Day Adventist because she refused to work on Saturday due to her religious beliefs. For the denial of benefits to withstand scrutiny under the free exercise clause "it must be either because her disqualification as a beneficiary represents no infringement by the state of her constitutional right of free exercise, or because any incidental burden on the free exercise of appellant's religion may be justified by a compelling state interest in the regulation. ...."

The Court employed a two-part balancing test. First, plaintiff had to show a substantial burden on the exercise of her religion from the law under review. Second, the Court would uphold this burden only if it is necessary to further a "compelling state interest" that outweighed the degree of impairment of a right of free exercise. This majority opinion implied that it would balance the degree of burden on religious activity against the importance of the state interest and the degree to which it would be impaired by an accommodation for the religious practice. Relevant to such an inquiry is the importance of the state's interest [is it a "compelling" one?] and the degree to which there are alternative means to achieve it which do not burden religious practices [least restrictive means are required]. However, it is difficult to weigh these interests without knowing how much they count: it is similar to weighing apples and electric volts.

Sherbert held that the denial of unemployment benefits was invalid under its two part test. First, there was a significant coercive effect on the practice of religion because the Sabbatarian was forced to make a choice between receiving state benefits or following her beliefs. Second, state showed no compelling or overriding interest in the regulation. The state claimed only that this restriction avoided fraudulent claims, but the state allowed workers to take Sunday as a day of rest. Moreover, even if the avoidance of false claims is *arguendo* a compelling interest there was no demonstration that alternative means of avoiding fraud were not available.

The majority opinion noted that the case was not one where "an employee's religious connections made her a nonproductive member of society." This language indicates that the state would not have to give benefits to those who were permanently unemployable because of their religious beliefs (e.g., every day is the Sabbath) because that would interfere with the state's goal of providing benefits to those involuntarily unemployed but available for work. While the state might have to accommodate certain religious practices, it is not required to abandon the goal of its program in order to accommodate everyone who might be unemployed for religious reasons.

There is another way to look at this case as not involving a balance at all. The Court said: "Significantly South Carolina expressly saves the Sunday worshipper from having to make the kind of choice which we here hold infringes the Sabbatarian's religious liberty." Once South Carolina decided to excuse Sunday-worshippers, it could not discriminate against Saturday-worshipers. Once South Carolina decided that there was no significant fraud issue as to people who claim that they cannot work on Sunday for religious reasons, South Carolina cannot argue that there is a fraud issue for people who claim that they cannot work on Saturday for religious reasons. In other words, in spite of the Court's language in parts of this opinion, one can treat this case as not using any vague balancing test at all. Once the state decides to grant a religious exemption, it simply cannot discriminate against people because of their religious beliefs. If the state decided not to grant any free days—i.e., not to exempt Sunday-worshippers or Saturday-worshippers—the Court, consistent with *Sherbert v. Verner* can uphold that law, although it did not grant any exemptions for religious reasons.

Thomas v. Review Board (1981) required the Court to determine the validity of an individual's claim that he was acting on the basis of a religious belief when a state asserted that the motivation for his action was nonreligious. Thomas, a Jehovah's Witness, quit his job when his employer transferred him from a metal foundry to a factory department that produced parts for military tanks. The employer gave him no opportunity to transfer to another job. Thomas testified that he believed his religion prohibited him from working on war materials although other Jehovah's Witness believed that such work did not violate tenets of the Jehovah's Witness. The state denied Thomas unemployment compensation because he voluntarily terminated his employment for reasons other than "good cause [arising] in connection with [his] work." The unemployment compensation hearing officer and state review board found that Thomas had left his job for religious reasons but that he did not qualify for benefits under the statute.

The state supreme court found that the denial of benefits for voluntary termination of employment did not violate the free exercise clause for three reasons: (1) Thomas's belief was more a "personal philosophical choice" than a religious belief; (2) the burden on Thomas's religious belief was only "indirect"; and (3) granting benefits only to persons who voluntarily left employment for religious reasons would violate the establishment clause. The United States Supreme Court reversed.

The Court indicated that judges had to accept an individual's assertion that his belief or motivation for his actions was religious so long as the person asserts the claim in good faith and the belief could arguably be termed religious: "Courts are not arbiters of scriptural interpretation." Moreover, if the state grants an exception to the conditions for unemployment compensation based upon religious objectives, that does not promote the establishment of religion but only moved the government to a position of neutrality toward religious beliefs.

Compulsory Education—The *Yoder* Decision. In *Wisconsin v. Yoder* (1972) the Court held Wisconsin could not require members of the Amish Church to send their children to public school after the eighth grade. Nearly twenty years later, the Supreme Court described *Yoder* as a case that was not based upon the free exercise clause alone, but, rather, upon the free exercise clause and the constitutional "right of parents . . . to direct the education of their children." *Employment Division v. Smith (Smith II)* (1990).

Although Chief Justice Burger's majority opinion cited due process rulings concerning parental rights, he focused on the free exercise clause and a two-part balancing test. First, the parents must show a significant burden on the free exercise of religion. Second, the Court will balance this burden against the importance of the state's interest and the degree to which a religious exemption would impair it.

Military Regulations. *Goldman v. Weinberger* (1986) held that the free exercise clause did not require the Air Force to allow a serviceman, an orthodox Jew and ordained rabbi, to wear his yarmulke while on duty and in uniform. The Air Force had a regulation that prohibited on-duty and in-uniform personnel from wearing any non-regulation items of clothing. For some years, this officer had worn his yarmulke while on duty and in uniform, without objection from Air Force authorities. Eventually, the authorities objected. The majority opinion had language that appeared to employ a two-step balancing analysis, although it also included statements concerning the need for the judiciary to defer to military authorities concerning matters of military deportment.

The first step of the inquiry in *Goldman* was easy, because the regulation clearly imposed a burden on the officer's ability to conform his actions to his sincerely held religious belief. The second stage of the balancing test required a determination whether the government had a sufficiently important or compelling interest that justified denying the requested dress code exemption. Justice Rehnquist's majority opinion in part appeared to apply this test and to find the interest in military discipline is a sufficiently important reason to outweigh the incidental burden on an individual's religious belief. In part, Justice Rehnquist's opinion appeared to require such deference to military authorities that the dissent questioned whether there was any meaningful judicial review of the nature of the government interest in this case.

Another way of looking at the result is that the military imposed a generally applicable regulation and it could, but need not, grant a religious exemption.

Johnson v. Robison (1974) upheld a federal law that granted educational benefits to veterans who served active duty but denied them to conscientious objectors who performed alternate service. In finding that there was no violation of the free exercise clause, the Court said that the program imposed little, if any, real burden on religious practices, and that the government interest in raising and supporting armies was of a "kind and weight" sufficient to overcome the alleged burden on the free exercise right of those who did not receive the educational benefits.

Government Administrative Systems—Using Social Security Numbers. *Bowen v. Roy* (1986) held that an individual child and her parent did not have a free exercise right to preclude a state agency from using a Social Security number to identify the child. This case involved a challenge to the use of Social Security numbers in federal Food Stamp and Aid to Families with Dependent Children programs. Federal statutes require state agencies administering these programs to employ Social Security numbers in identifying the recipients of aid.

Initially, the parents of the child contended that obtaining a Social Security number violated their Native American religious beliefs. Because obtaining and submitting a Social Security number was a condition to the receipt of such benefits, the state refused to pay benefits on the child's behalf. The trial revealed that the child (whose name was Little Bird of the Snow) received a Social Security number very near the time of her birth. At that point in the litigation, the child's father sought an injunction to prohibit the government from making any use of her Social Security number. The Supreme Court rejected the father's attempt to prohibit the state agency from using the child's Social Security number in administering aid programs.

The Court concluded that the government's use of a Social Security number, or the assignment of some type of identifying number to an individual's case file in order to efficiently operate a government program, does not violate the free exercise clause. Government administrative practices do not impose a clear burden on an individual's religious belief if the government is not forcing the person to take an action contrary to her religious belief. In addition, the government's use of the number promotes operating a welfare program in an efficient and honest manner, an interest that outweighs any incidental burden on the objecting individual. Someone might have a religious objection to the government identifying people by number or to the government using grey file cabinets. That objection does not convert into a constitutional right to force the government to change the way it operates.

In cases like this one, it is easy to say that the government could grant an exemption to someone who did not want to have a social security number. However, there are several hundred people who have social security numbers, and any or all of them could seek an exemption by claiming a religious exemption if the government by statute (or the Court by case law) provided for a religious exemption. Anyone could claim an exemption because the Court does not conduct heresy trials to determine if the individual's belief is part of the beliefs of the religion. Moreover, one does not have to belong to an established religion. Anyone can establish a religion, and the First Amendment does not limit its protection to any list of recognized religions or religions that existed in 1791 (when the First Amendment became part of the Constitution). Without social security numbers it becomes much more difficult for the government to collect taxes, control illegal immigration (because one needs a social security number to work legally in this country), reduce welfare fraud, and so forth.

Government Administrative Systems—Governmental Use or Destruction of Government Property. The government does not have to justify its administrative practices under the free exercise clause, even if its actions are inconsistent with the sincerely held religious beliefs of persons in our society. Thus, in *Lyng v. Northwest Indian Cemetery Protective Association* (1988), the Supreme Court held that the free exercise clause does not restrict the federal government from allowing timber harvesting and road construction in an area of a federally owned national forest, even though some members of American Indian tribes considered this land to be sacred, and even the destruction of the forested area imposed a significant burden on the sincerely held religious beliefs of those persons. *Lyng* adopted the principle that any burden on persons' religious beliefs caused by the government's conduct of its own internal affairs is not subject to free exercise restrictions.

Aid to Racially Discriminatory Schools. *Bob Jones University v. United States* (1983) held that the government does not violate the free exercise clause when it denies tax exempt status under the Internal Revenue Code to all schools that discriminate on the basis of race, including religiously affiliated schools that discriminate because of sincerely held religious beliefs. The Court found that the schools that claimed the exemption on the basis of religious beliefs did so sincerely, and denying the exemption would substantially affect their operation.

Nonetheless, the governmental interest in ending racial discrimination in education is both a "compelling" and a "fundamental, overriding interest." This interest cannot be achieved through "less restrictive means" because the interest that the schools asserted "cannot be accommodated" with the compelling (and completely contrary) governmental interest in ending racial discrimination in education.

The Court did not rule on whether the government could outlaw religious schools that engage in racial discrimination in their admissions or educational policy. It ruled only that the governmental interest outweighed "whatever burden denial of tax benefits places on petitioners' exercise of their religious belief" and the denial "will not prevent those schools from observing their religious tenets."

§ 17.9   Recurrent Free Exercise Problems

(a) Exemptions From Military Service

The Supreme Court has never held that the religion clauses *require* the government to grant an exemption from military service to persons who object to such service on a religious basis. However, such an exemption may be required if the interests of those who object to military service are balanced against the government's need for universal conscription in the same manner as the Court sometimes balances other interests under the modern free exercise clause cases.

While there are early decisions that state that the war powers of the government should not be required to yield for the accommodation of individual beliefs, strong considerations weigh in favor of requiring such an exemption under modern free exercise clause analysis. Conscription imposed a serious burden on those whose religious beliefs prohibit the use of violence. Additionally, the government's interest in raising armies may be adequately met without the forced conscription of these persons. Those who sincerely reject force may well be unsuitable for armed combat on the part of these persons. Hence, the Court may conclude that drafting of these persons into the armed services serves no important government interest.

Yet the Court has historically deferred to the government in military matters, especially in time of war. Thus, the Court could find that it will not weigh these individual interests against the national interest in defense. Indeed, the Court in 1971 approved the government's refusal to exempt those who objected only to particular wars and indicated that it may be the case that the government need not provide any exemption. *Gillette v. United States* (1971). Unless Congress imposes a draft and allows not conscientious exemption, the question will remain unresolved.

The Supreme Court has refused to declare a First Amendment right to avoid military service. However, it has read the language of the *statutory* exemption from service to apply to all persons who are opposed to war in any form, on the basis of beliefs that are the functional equivalent of a theistic religious belief. *United States v. Seeger* (1965). Thus, any person who objects to all wars on the basis of sincerely held personal principles that occupied a place in their lives similar to religion merits a statutory exemption. The Court avoided problems under the religion clauses by interpreting the exemption to apply to all who objected to participation in all war. The only ones who fail to qualify for an exemption were those whose objections to all war are not sincere or whose objections are based "solely upon considerations of policy, pragmatism or expediency." *Welsh v. United States* (1970).

Gillette v. United States (1971) held that it was constitutional for the government to grant an exemption from compulsory military service only to those whose beliefs opposed *all* war. That restriction did not violate the establishment clause, even though some religions or denominations believe that only *unjust* wars are morally wrong. The Court found secular purposes in defining the exemption so as to exclude those persons least readily available or suitable for service due to their beliefs. The narrow definition also avoided further entanglement between government and religion because there was less need to examine the sincerity and character of individual beliefs.

(b) Health and Medical Regulations

Sometimes people claim that the free exercise clause entitles them to an exemption from a health or medical regulation. The Supreme Court uses a free exercise clause test that makes it difficult, if not impossible, for an individual to prevail in such a case. As the Court said in *Church of the Lukumi Babalu Aye, Inc. v. Hialeah* (1993):

> "[A] law that is neutral and of general applicability need not be justified by a compelling government interest even if the law has the incidental effect of burdening a particular religious practice.... A law failing to satisfy [the neutrality and general applicability] requirements must be justified by a compelling governmental interest and must be narrowly tailored to advance that interest."

So long as the health regulation at issue in a free exercise clause case is a generally applicable law that is religiously neutral, the Court will not require the government to grant religiously based exemptions for the law.

(1) **Vaccinations.** The Supreme Court very early in this century held that an individual could be required to receive a vaccination against disease, even though that might violate the individual's religious beliefs. The compulsory vaccination program is a direct method of effectuating the secular interest in public health, even if the chance of epidemics is small. *Jacobson v. Massachusetts* (1905).

(2) **Medical Treatment of Children.** American courts have upheld the right of the state to protect the health and safety of minor children over the religiously based objections of the child or his parent. Thus, courts have appointed guardians to consent to necessary medical treatment (such as blood transfusions) for children even though the treatment violates the child's or parent's religion. Similarly appropriate action may be taken against parents for the neglect of the health or safety of their children regardless of whether the parent acted on the basis of religious principles.

(3) **Blood Transfusions and the "Right to Die."** Current developments in medicine have permitted the continuation of a person's life for extended periods of time after it is apparent that the person will never recover from some eventually terminal illness or injury. This scientific advance has raised serious questions as to whether an individual can be required to undergo such treatment or whether that person at some point has a "right to die." The law in this area is still developing.

§ 17.10 Sunday Closing Laws

In four companion decisions the Supreme Court upheld "Sunday closing laws" over objections based on the establishment clause, the free exercise clause, and the due process and equal protection clauses. These laws prohibited most (but not all) forms of commercial activity on Sundays.

The question of whether these laws violated the establishment clause received the most comprehensive analysis in *McGowan v. Maryland* (1961). Chief Justice Warren, for the Court, held that the present "purpose and effect" of these laws was not religious, even though the laws originally had a religious character. The history of these laws showed that they had become non-religious over the years. Sunday closing laws now appear in some form in every state and these laws had the support of labor and trade associations as measures for the health and welfare of commercial workers. Modern statutory programs appeared to be designed to insure a uniform day of rest and noncommercial activity. See also, *Two Guys from Harrison–Allentown, Inc. v. McGinley* (1961); *Braunfeld v. Brown* (1961); *Gallagher v. Crown Kosher Super Market* (1961).

§ 17.11 Inquiries Into Religious Frauds

A question may arise in some cases as to whether an individual is seeking to perpetrate a fraud on others through the false representation of religious beliefs. The religion clauses forbid a government inquiry into the truth or falsity of asserted religious beliefs. However, it is not clear when an inquiry may be made as to whether an individual is sincerely advocating a religious doctrine (regardless of the truth or falsity of that doctrine) or falsely professing such a belief for fraudulent purposes.

In *United States v. Ballard* (1944) (*Ballard I*), the defendants were charged with fraudulently using the mail to obtain money. The two defendants, Edna and Donald Ballard, claimed that they had been made divine messengers by "Saint Germain" who was Gary Ballard when he (Gary Ballard) was alive. They represented themselves as the divine messengers and teachers of the "I am" movement with powers to heal many diseases, including some medically classified as incurable. The indictment charged that they "well knew" that these representations were false and that they made the representations to fraudulently collect donations from their followers for themselves. The district court had submitted to the jury the question of whether the defendants in good faith believed the representations. The trial judge, however, did not submit to the jury any issue as to the truth or falsity of the representations. The Court of Appeals reversed the defendants' convictions on the basis that it was necessary to prove that the representations were in fact false. The Supreme Court in turn reversed the Court of Appeals decision.

Justice Douglas, for the Court, held that the guarantees against the establishment of any creed and the assurance of the free exercise of any religion constituted a prohibition of inquiries into the truth or falsity of an asserted religious belief. To hold otherwise would allow a trial for heresy. Otherwise, one could subject the beliefs of any religion to a civil trial, but we are free to believe what we cannot prove. While holding that a court could never inquire into the falsity of a religious belief, the Supreme Court did not rule on whether a court could inquire into whether the defendant honestly held the belief.

Justice Jackson, dissenting, argued that the government could prosecute a purely secular fraud such as using, for private purposes, money solicited for building a church, because the prosecution would not involve the testing of beliefs. But to find that a would-be religious leader was getting money for his general even though he did not really believe what he preached could endanger, or "chill", every religious teacher of any faith. That people may give their money or, more importantly, their minds and hopes to religions of dubious merit preached by persons with questionable faith is the price we pay for religious freedom.

The Court never ruled on this broader fraud issue, and when the case came back to the Court, it overturned the indictment because of the trial court has excluded women from the jury. *United States v. Ballard* (1946) (*Ballard II*).

It is not at all clear whether a majority of the Justices would accept the Jackson position that the sincerity of one asserting a religious belief may not be put in issue in a prosecution for fraud. However, note two points. First, the inability to inquire into religious beliefs does not prevent the government from outlawing actions based on those beliefs. The issue of whether the government may ban taking money for curing cancer by any means other than accepted medical procedure has no relation to an inquiry into religious beliefs. If the government prohibits the act (regardless of whether it is done on a religious basis) it is not inquiring into the merit of any religious belief. The only issue is whether prohibiting this activity violates the free exercise rights of those who believe in faith healing.

Second, even if the Court were to adopt Jackson's view, the government might still be able to test the sincerity of one who requested a religious exemption from some general regulation. Justice Jackson only took the position that the government could not prosecute a person for his failure to truly believe in some religious principle. He did not examine the question of whether anyone who seeks a benefit from government because of his religious beliefs must be taken at his word. If someone claims that he will go to hell if he serves in the military, a draft board can judge the sincerity of that belief without deciding whether or not there is a hell. There would seem to be merit in allowing these tests of sincerity when the person seeks to use his religious beliefs in this manner—as a sword (to secure an exemption) rather than as a shield (to defend in a prosecution for fraudulently taking money).

Promoting the values of the free exercise clause is only applicable where the person in fact does want to practice a religion. There is little or no danger of persecuting unorthodox beliefs here as the individual has requested the exemption. Thus, it is possible that the Court might adopt the Jackson view and prohibit inquiries into the sincerity of one asserting a religious belief where the action is one relating to misrepresentation of religious teaching to others, while requiring those seeking a religious exemption from secular regulatory statutes to demonstrate their sincerity in the asserted religious belief. Of course, in neither case could the agency or the court inquire into the truth or falsity of the belief itself—that is clearly barred by the decision in *Ballard*.

§ 17.12 State Involvement in Ecclesiastical Disputes

When there is a dispute between factions of a religious organization, one or more of the parties may seek resolution of the dispute by a state court. Of course, the government cannot declare which party is correct in matters of religion, for that would violate the principles of both religion clauses. Our civil courts do not resolve heresy disputes. However, when the opposing groups both claim the church property the state will have to make some judgment as to who is entitled to possession while avoiding civil court rulings on matters of religious belief.

Where the disputed property is subject to some express condition in a deed, a court can rule on the condition if that does not involve a ruling on religious matters. Thus, if a building is deeded to a church for so long as it is used as a place of religious worship, a court can order the return of the property if it is used as a retail sales establishment. But if the condition in the deed is that the general church can keep the property so long as it is true to its doctrine, the court will not enforce that condition because it cannot decide religious beliefs.

Most disputes center around property that is not subject to such a specific condition. In these situations two or more groups present themselves to a court and claim the right to possess and control church property. The permissible basis for court rulings in these situations varies with the type of church involved in the dispute.

Where the church group is an independent congregation, not subject to a general or higher church authority, the will of a majority of the members controls the decision. Because this church group is a self-governing unit, the only secular basis for a ruling between competing groups is based on the preferences of a majority of the members. There might be a separate secular way to determine ownership if the deed or incorporation documents specified some other form of resolving disputes that did not require the court to review religious doctrine.

Most commonly, disputes arise between a local congregation and a general church with which it has been affiliated in the past. Where the dispute involves a hierarchical church, or organized body subject to a common ecclesiastical authority, different principles apply. Here there are only two questions for state court resolution: (1) whether this is a hierarchical church, (2) whether the local group in the past affiliated itself and its property with the hierarchical church. If either of these questions is no, then the local group is an independent congregation. If these questions are answered affirmatively, the courts must defer to the hierarchical authority. The civil courts will enforce the rulings of the highest ecclesiastical authority. Only in the case of clear fraud by persons in that authority may the court question the judgment of ecclesiastical authority—and even this possible exception is subject to dispute. The general rule is that the highest ecclesiastical authority—an assembly in some religions or a clerical superior in others—is the final arbiter of the church doctrine and authority.

The few decisions in this area deal with widely varying fact situations. Let us look at two of them.

Gonzalez v. Roman Catholic Archbishop of Manila (1929) refused to allow a civil court to determine the qualification of a chaplain of the Roman Catholic Church. A testatrix had given funds to the Church to establish a "chaplaincy" to which the Church was suppose to appoint her nearest male relative whenever possible. One of her descendants sought the post, and the income from the fund, but the Church refused to appoint him because he failed to qualify under ecclesiastical law.

The Court held that a civil court could not award the fund or the position to the heir because it could not disturb the judgment of the church authorities because the chaplaincy was a part of a hierarchical church. The civil courts should not disturb the Church's rulings on ecclesiastical matters. However, the Court noted that this conclusion was true in the absence of "fraud, collusion or arbitrariness." In later years this statement has been regarded as dicta. There is no clear ruling of the Supreme Court that would allow courts to review church decisions to determine if they are arbitrary.

Compare *Jones v. Wolf* (1979), which examined a dispute between members of the Vineville Presbyterian Church of Macon, Georgia and the Augusta–Macon Presbytery of the Presbyterian Church in the United States. Approximately 40 years earlier, a local group in Macon, Georgia had founded a congregation and acquired property in the name of the trustees of the Vineville Presbyterian Church. When it was organized, the Vineville Church group became a member church of the Presbyterian Church in the United States (PCUS). PCUS has a higher hierarchical form of government, as contrasted with a congregational form, but the local church property was never formally deeded over to the general church or subjected to the control of the general church according to any identifiable document.

In 1973, a congregational meeting of the local Vineville Church voted to separate from PCUS and to unite with another Presbyterian denomination, the Presbyterian Church in America (PCA). A minority of the local church wished to stay with PCUS and, in response to the schism in the local congregation, PCUS appointed a commission to resolve the dispute. It concluded that the minority faction was the "true congregation" of the Vineville Church. The issue in state court was whether the PCUS and the local minority controlled title to the property or whether the majority, which had disaffiliated itself from PCUS, controlled title.

The Court (5 to 4) held that the Georgia courts could apply neutral principles of property law to determine that title remained in the local congregation and a majority vote of that congregation was controlling. State courts may examine the language of real and personal property deeds, the terms of church charters or state statutes relating to the control of property, and documents affiliating the local group with the general church and the constitution of the general church in order to determine technically if the local group had become a member of an hierarchical church and subjected its property to control of that church.

The majority opinion refused to adopt a rule of compulsory deference to the higher church authority in all instances because the neutral principles approach would involve less entanglement with religious doctrine by requiring judges to abstain from a determination as to what authority is the highest in a church organization. The courts should simply examine the documents in a secular manner to determine where title to the property had been formally placed.

Applying this rule to the specific case before it, the Court held that the Georgia courts could have found that the deeds, contracts of conveyance and trust, and church charters left title to the property in the local church. However, the Georgia courts had not explained how they had determined that the local church was represented by the majority rather than the minority. In determining which group would control the use of property by the local congregation the state was still required to adopt rules that did not involve an examination of religious doctrine. The state could adopt a presumptive rule of majority representation, which could be changed by a showing that the local church group had chosen another means for property control through contract or deed terms. In fact the state could adopt any method of overcoming the majoritarian presumption so long as the civil courts did not entangle themselves in religious controversy or impair free exercise rights.

It was unclear whether the Georgia courts had applied a truly neutral rule of majority ownership or a neutral examination of property and contract terms to determine if majority rule controlled under the terms of the property contracts and deeds of the Vineville Church. Thus, the Court remanded the case to the state courts to determine if Georgia had a rule requiring deference to a majority of the local congregation or whether state law provided that the identity of the controlling local group was to be determined on the basis of religious principles. The latter position would require a granting of automatic deference to the general church (PCUS) because otherwise the civil court would be involved in questions of religious doctrine rather than the following of neutral principles of contract and property law.

The dissenting Justices would have required automatic deference to the general church councils (PCUS) because they believed that only such deference could avoid impermissible entanglement between the state and religious authorities. Whenever a local group affiliates technically with a hierarchical church, the dissent would subject the local group to the control of the higher church authorities with no recourse to civil courts. The dissent believed that it would be impossible to apply the Court's neutral principles approach without examining religious documents and effectively making decisions on questions of religious doctrine.

If the majority in *Jones* is correct, and the state courts can be kept to a purely secular examination of documents relating to formal control of property, then its neutral principles approach does not deviate from the analysis employed in earlier Court decisions. But if ruling on these property disputes involves government agents or judges in examining religious charters in a manner that calls for some evaluation of religious principles or doctrine, the neutral principles approach will lead to an unconstitutional entanglement between government and religion.

§ 17.13   Legislative Action to End Religious Discrimination in Private Employment

Although the governmental may attempt to prohibit discrimination against employees based upon a *private* employee's religious beliefs, the establishment clause places limitations on the extent to which the government may force a *private* employer to make accommodations for the religious views and practices of employees. *Estate of Thornton v. Caldor, Inc.* (1985) invalidated a state statute that required private employers to honor every employee's desire to refuse to work on "his Sabbath." Although the law was an attempt to accommodate the free exercise of religion, the law violated the establishment clause. The Court found that the law was invalid because it had a primary effect that advanced religion.

The law at issue in *Estate of Thornton* gave every employee an absolute right to refrain from work on her or his Sabbath. It thus subjected employers and other workers to significant costs in order to accommodate the desire of an employee to take actions based upon religious beliefs. The statute did not require the employer to grant only reasonable accommodation of an employee's religious activities, or a merely prohibit discrimination on the basis of religious beliefs; the statute did not provide any exception for employers who were subject to special circumstances or who were presented by employee's claims that would impose a significant shifting of costs and burdens to other employees. A "fundamental principle of the religion clauses" is that no individual, in pursuing his own interests, has the right to insist that others conform their conduct to his religion.

Trans World Airlines, Inc. v. Hardison (1977) interpreted a statute not to require employers to alter their Saturday work schedules in violation of a seniority system established by collective bargaining. The Court held that requiring the law did not require employer to bear more than *de minimis* cost, thus avoiding a constitutional issue.

§ 17.14 Regulation of the Employment Practices of Religious Organizations

When the members of a religious organization take any action in society, they may be subject to religiously neutral regulations. When they claim that religiously neutral regulations of their commercial or noncommercial activities impose a burden on their ability to carry out the religious beliefs, the claim for an exemption from those regulations will be tested under the free exercise clause principles we have examined earlier in this chapter. When a religious organization employs persons in commercial activities that duplicate and compete with nonreligious businesses, it should not be surprising if the organization is subjected to religiously neutral business, labor, and taxation statutes.

Tony and Susan Alamo Foundation v. Secretary of Labor (1985) unanimously upheld the application of the federal Fair Labor Standards Act minimum wage, overtime, and record-keeping requirements to commercial businesses operated by a nonprofit religious organization even though it was claimed that those businesses were "churches in disguise" that were means of "spreading the gospel" and used, in lieu of employees, only members of the religious group who did not want to receive cash wages or overtime payments. This case presented no significant free exercise clause problem because the "employees" suffered no burden whatsoever from having to receive the minimum wage. The Court found that the employees, under the federal statutes, were free to accept the minimum wage in living arrangements and services and that they could voluntarily return any payments that they received from the religious employer back to that employer.

In *United States v. Lee* (1982) the law required an Amish employer and his employees to pay social security taxes. Congress had granted a statutory exemption to self-employed individuals who objected on religious grounds to making payments for government-operated retirement and welfare systems. The requirement that the employer pay the social security tax on the work of the employees operated as a burden on the employer's Amish faith but that burden is outweighed by the government interest in the efficient operation of the Social Security system. The principle in *Lee* is likely to be a guide for the Court in many of the free exercise clause cases:

> Congress and the courts have been sensitive to the needs flowing from the free exercise clause, but every person cannot be shielded from all the burdens incident to exercising every aspect of the right to practice religious beliefs. When followers of a particular sect enter into commercial activity as a matter of choice, the limits they accept on their own conduct as a matter of conscience and faith are not to be superimposed on the statutory schemes which are binding on others in that activity.

When the government regulates the practices of a religious organization, including commercial practices, questions may arise as to whether the regulation violates the establishment clause of the First Amendment. Such a regulation must have a secular purpose and a primary effect that neither advances nor inhibits religion. In addition, the regulation must not create an excessive entanglement between government and religion. When a religious organization is engaging in a business activity that mirrors nonreligious commercial enterprises, one can expect that the three-part purpose-effect-entanglement test may be easily met and the government regulation upheld. Business regulations are virtually certain to have a secular purpose; it is difficult to imagine what types of general business regulatory actions would not have a primary effect that was religiously neutral. The excessive entanglement test also should not present a significant barrier to most types of regulations of commercial enterprises owned and operated by religious organizations. The involvement between the government and religiously operated business incident to the enforcement of religiously neutral commercial regulations should not endanger governmental neutrality or religious organizational autonomy.

Tony and Susan Alamo Foundation v. Secretary of Labor (1985) unanimously upheld the application of the Fair Labor Standards Act wage requirements to the commercial activities of a religious organization, which alleged that the seemingly commercial enterprises were an integral part of its religious mission and that the recordkeeping provisions of the Act led to an excessive entanglement between government and religion. Justice White explained that the regulations applied only to "commercial activities undertaken with a 'business purpose' and would therefore have no impact on [the religious organization's] own evangelical activities or on individuals engaged in volunteer work for other religious organizations." The establishment clause does not exempt religious organizations from such secular government activity as fire inspections and building and zoning regulations. The record-keeping requirements of the Fair Labor Standards Act involve more paperwork, but are not significantly more intrusive into religious affairs.

Table of Cases

Burns v. Richardson, 384 U.S. 73, 86
S.Ct. 1286, 16 L.Ed.2d 376 (1966)—
§ 14.30.
Burson v. Freeman, 504 U.S. 191, 112
S.Ct. 1846, 119 L.Ed.2d 5 (1992)—
§ 16.28.
Burton v. Wilmington Parking Authority, 365 U.S. 715, 81 S.Ct. 856, 6
L.Ed.2d 45 (1961)—§ 12.3; § 12.4.
Bush v. Gore (Bush III), 531 U.S. 98,
121 S.Ct. 525, 148 L.Ed.2d 388
(2000)—§ 14.25.
Bush v. Gore (Bush II), 531 U.S. 1046,
121 S.Ct. 512, 148 L.Ed.2d 553
(2000)—§ 14.25.
Bush v. Palm Beach County Canvassing
Bd. (Bush I), 531 U.S. 70, 121 S.Ct.
471, 148 L.Ed.2d 366 (2000)—
§ 14.25.
Bush v. Vera, 517 U.S. 952, 116 S.Ct.
1941, 135 L.Ed.2d 248 (1996)—
§ 14.9.
Butler v. Perry, 240 U.S. 328, 36 S.Ct.
258, 60 L.Ed. 672 (1916)—§ 15.2.
Butler v. State of Michigan, 352 U.S.
380, 77 S.Ct. 524, 1 L.Ed.2d 412
(1957)—§ 16.37.
Butler, United States v., 297 U.S. 1, 56
S.Ct. 312, 80 L.Ed. 477 (1936)—
§ 5.3.
Butterworth v. Smith, 494 U.S. 624, 110
S.Ct. 1376, 108 L.Ed.2d 572 (1990)—
§ 16.11.

C

Caban v. Mohammed, 441 U.S. 380, 99
S.Ct. 1760, 60 L.Ed.2d 297 (1979)—
§ 14.13; § 14.17.
Cabell v. Chavez–Salido, 454 U.S. 432,
102 S.Ct. 735, 70 L.Ed.2d 677
(1982)—§ 14.11.
C & A Carbone, Inc. v. Town of Clarks-
town, N.Y., 511 U.S. 383, 114 S.Ct.
1677, 128 L.Ed.2d 399 (1994)—§ 8.3.
Calder v. Bull, 3 U.S. 386, 3 Dall. 386, 1
L.Ed. 648 (1798)—§ 11.1; § 11.6;
§ 11.8.
Calero–Toledo v. Pearson Yacht Leasing
Co., 416 U.S. 663, 94 S.Ct. 2080, 40
L.Ed.2d 452 (1974)—§ 13.9.
Califano v. Aznavorian, 439 U.S. 170, 99
S.Ct. 471, 58 L.Ed.2d 435 (1978)—
§ 14.31.
Califano v. Boles, 443 U.S. 282, 99 S.Ct.
2767, 61 L.Ed.2d 541 (1979)—
§ 14.13.
Califano v. Goldfarb, 430 U.S. 199, 97
S.Ct. 1021, 51 L.Ed.2d 270 (1977)—
§ 14.17.

Califano v. Jobst, 434 U.S. 47, 98 S.Ct.
95, 54 L.Ed.2d 228 (1977)—§ 14.22.
Califano v. Webster, 430 U.S. 313, 97
S.Ct. 1192, 51 L.Ed.2d 360 (1977)—
§ 14.17.
Califano v. Westcott, 443 U.S. 76, 99
S.Ct. 2655, 61 L.Ed.2d 382 (1979)—
§ 14.17.
California Med. Ass'n v. Federal Elec.
Com'n, 453 U.S. 182, 101 S.Ct. 2712,
69 L.Ed.2d 567 (1981)—§ 16.31.
California Retail Liquor Dealers Ass'n v.
Midcal Aluminum, Inc., 445 U.S. 97,
100 S.Ct. 937, 63 L.Ed.2d 233
(1980)—§ 8.8.
Caltex, United States v., 344 U.S. 149,
73 S.Ct. 200, 97 L.Ed. 157 (1952)—
§ 11.11.
Carey v. Brown, 447 U.S. 455, 100 S.Ct.
2286, 65 L.Ed.2d 263 (1980)—
§ 16.26; § 16.28.
Carey v. Population Services, Intern.,
431 U.S. 678, 97 S.Ct. 2010, 52
L.Ed.2d 675 (1977)—§ 14.21;
§ 16.12.
Carlton, United States v., 512 U.S. 26,
114 S.Ct. 2018, 129 L.Ed.2d 22
(1994)—§ 11.8.
Carmell v. Texas, 529 U.S. 513, 120
S.Ct. 1620, 146 L.Ed.2d 577 (2000)—
§ 11.8.
Carolene Products Co., United States v.,
304 U.S. 144, 58 S.Ct. 778, 82 L.Ed.
1234 (1938)—§ 11.4; § 11.6.
Carrington v. Rash, 380 U.S. 89, 85
S.Ct. 775, 13 L.Ed.2d 675 (1965)—
§ 14.25.
Carroll v. President and Com'rs of
Princess Anne, 393 U.S. 175, 89 S.Ct.
347, 21 L.Ed.2d 325 (1968)—§ 16.25.
Carter v. Carter Coal Co., 298 U.S. 238,
56 S.Ct. 855, 80 L.Ed. 1160 (1936)—
§ 4.4.
Case of (see name of party)
Castle Rock v. Gonzales, ___ U.S. ___,
125 S.Ct. 2796, ___ L.Ed.2d ___
(2005)—§ 10.5.
Causby, United States v., 328 U.S. 256,
66 S.Ct. 1062, 90 L.Ed. 1206 (1946)—
§ 11.11.
CBS, Inc. v. F.C.C., 453 U.S. 367, 101
S.Ct. 2813, 69 L.Ed.2d 706 (1981)—
§ 16.8.
Central Eureka Mining Company, United States v., 357 U.S. 155, 78 S.Ct.
1097, 2 L.Ed.2d 1228 (1958)—
§ 11.11.
Central Hudson Gas & Elec. Corp. v.
Public Service Commission of New
York, 447 U.S. 557, 100 S.Ct. 2343,
65 L.Ed.2d 341 (1980)—§ 16.12.

G

H

I

S

T

Index

A

E

†